Fodor's 90 New York State

D1039413

Fodor's Travel Publications, Inc.
New York and London

Fodor's New York State

Editors: Kathleen McHugh
Editorial Contributors: Joseph Bookbinder, Teresa Buckley, Vinod Chhabra, Charles De Motte, Theodore Fischer, Diane Gallo, Diane Galusha, Marian Goldberg, Peter Grondahl, David Laskin, Peter Oliver, Roswell Park, John Preston, Patricia Tunison Preston, Michele Schachere, Deborah Williams
Art Director: Fabrizio La Rocca
Cartographer: David Lindroth
Illustrator: Karl Tanner
Cover Photograph: U. Sjostedt/FPG

Cover Design: Vignelli Associates

MANUFACTURED IN THE UNITED STATES OF AMERICA
10 9 8 7 6 5 4 3 2 1

Contents

Maps

Foreword

This is an exciting time for Fodor's, as we continue our ambitious program to rewrite, reformat, and redesign all 140 of our guides. Here are just a few of the new features:

★ Brand-new computer-generated maps locating all the top attractions, hotels, restaurants, and shops

★ A unique system of numbers and legends to help readers move effortlessly between text and maps

★ A new star rating system for hotels and restaurants

★ Stamped, self-addressed postcards, bound into every guide, give readers an opportunity to help evaluate hotels and restaurants

★ Complete page redesign for instant retrieval of information

★ FODOR'S CHOICE—Our favorite museums, beaches, cafes, romantic hideaways, festivals, and more

★ HIGHLIGHTS—An insider's look at the most important developments in tourism during the past year

★ TIME OUT—The best and most convenient lunch stops along the shopping and exploring routes

★ Exclusive background essays create a powerful portrait of each destination

★ A mini-journal for travelers to keep track of their own itineraries and addresses

While every care has been taken to assure the accuracy of the information in this guide, the passage of time will always bring change, and consequently, the publisher cannot accept responsibility for errors that may occur.

All prices and opening times quoted here are based on information available to us at press time. Hours and admission fees may change, however, and the prudent traveler will avoid inconvenience by calling ahead.

Fodor's wants to hear about your travel experiences, both pleasant and unpleasant. When a hotel or restaurant fails to live up to its billing, let us know and we will investigate the complaint and revise our entries where the facts warrant it.

Send your letters to the editors of Fodor's Travel Publications, 201 E. 50th Street, New York, NY 10022.

Highlights '90 and Fodor's Choice

Highlights '90

The big news statewide is recent legislation requiring that basic car rental rates include collision insurance for all but a $100 deductible.

New York City The ancestors of more than 40% of all living Americans were processed on Ellis Island, a federal immigration facility, between 1892 and 1954. The first phase of the $140 million restoration, the 200,000-square-foot brick-and-limestone **Ellis Island Immigration Museum,** will open in 1990. Exhibits will document both the island's history and the story of American immigration.

When the Henry R. Kravis Wing of the **Metropolitan Museum of Art** opens in late 1990 the museum will finally have a back door—on Central Park. First-floor galleries will feature a European decorative arts collection, a series of period rooms, and an arcaded courtyard displaying European sculpture. The expansion of the **Pierpont Morgan Library** will incorporate the adjacent 45-room brownstone, which once belonged to Morgan's son J. P. Morgan.

The **American Museum of Natural History**'s Hall of South American Peoples—where bird calls and monkey howls are the soundtrack for a replica of the Amazonian rain forest—debuted in 1989. The **Museum of American Folk Art** has found temporary quarters, at Columbus Avenue and 66th Street across from Lincoln Center; the site will become an annex when the museum's permanent headquarters on West 53rd Street are completed in 1992. The **Children's Museum of Manhattan,** with interactive exhibits designed for toddlers through age 7, has moved to roomier quarters on the Upper West Side at 212 West 83rd Street.

The new Shellens Gallery of Brooklyn History, at the **Brooklyn Historical Society,** features such Brooklyn memorabilia as Brooklyn Dodgers baseballs, Coney Island wax figures, and props used on the set of the "Honeymooners." Also in Brooklyn will be the joint productions of the **Brooklyn Academy of Music** and the **Metropolitan Opera,** emphasizing new and contemporary works. From its Lincoln Center home, the Met will present a complete cycle of Richard Wagner's *The Ring of the Nibelungen* in the spring of 1990. **Carnegie Hall**'s 100th birthday bash will feature star-studded concerts by Luciano Pavarotti, Kathleen Battle, Yo-Yo Ma, the New York and Leningrad philharmonics, and the farewell tour of Sir Georg Solti conducting the Chicago Philharmonic. The six-year Shakespeare marathon continues downtown at the **Public Theater.**

Donald Trump made two moves affecting visitors to New York City in 1989: He bought and renamed the Eastern Shuttle to, what else? the **Trump Shuttle;** and he built the

Gotham Miniature Golf Course in Central Park, next to the Wollman Memorial Rink, which he renovated for the city the previous year.

After major renovation, the **Central Park Zoo** reopened in 1989 in a dazzling space organized with separate exhibits for each of the Earth's major environments: the refrigerated Polar Circle, the open-air Temperate Territory, and the atrium-like Tropic Zone, all clustered around a delightful central Sea Lion Pool. Two other city zoos—**Queens Zoo** in Flushing Meadows Corona Park and the **Prospect Park Zoo** in Brooklyn's Prospect Park—are closed at press time for complete renovation.

The crossroads of West 34th Street, Broadway, and 6th Avenue known as **Herald Square,** is already a prime retail hub that includes Macy's and the luxury shops in Herald Center across the street. With the opening of the nine-story **A & S Plaza,** anchored by the Abraham and Straus department store, Herald Square gains an additional 120 shops and restaurants.

The Big Apple will be able to accommodate more visitors with 11 hotels adding 4,614 rooms to New York's capacity by 1992. Major midtown developments include the **Royal Concordia,** a 54-story, all-suite hotel on West 54th Street between Sixth and Seventh avenues; the 46-story **Holiday Inn Crown Plaza** on Broadway at 49th Street; **Embassy Suites-Times Square,** a 43-story hotel with 460 suites on Broadway between 46th and 47th streets; **Regent of New York,** a 51-story property on 57th Street between Madison and Park avenues; and the **Hotel Macklowe,** a 638-room hotel on 44th Street between Broadway and Sixth Avenue. Chinatown will have its first hotel in the **Golden Plaza** on Centre Street near Canal, and the **Journey's End Hotel** will be the first hotel to be built in the South Street Seaport (scheduled for completion in fall 1991).

Ground-breaking is a few years off for **Hudson River Center,** a $320 million hotel and marina complex on a 13-acre site west of the Jacob K. Javits Convention Center between 34th and 40th streets. The center will include a 1,560-room hotel.

Long Island   Beaches on Long Island were cleaner in 1989, thanks to stepped up enforcement of antidumping laws and environmental pressure. Multimillion-dollar fines now face those who dump sewage or medical waste. In 1992 a federal ban on ocean dumping takes effect. The $3 million **Sag Harbor Inn,** the first hotel to be built in Southampton in 20 years, should be completed in 1990.

Hudson Valley   More than 45,000 weapons, uniforms, maps, pictures, paintings, dioramas, and flags are on display at the remodeled **West Point Museum** at the United States Military Academy at West Point. More than $10 million was spent in renovating the Gothic-style Rosary Hall—now Olmsted Hall—and creating new space for the museum's galleries.

Albany The capital's 15,000-seat sports center, the **Knickerbocker Arena,** is being readied for an early 1990 debut.

Saratoga Springs The **Gideon Putnam Hotel** and **Roosevelt Bathhouse** are undergoing a $5.2 million, three-year refurbishment. Also in the Capital-Saratoga region, **RiverSpark** debuted in 1989. The urban cultural park is a 28-mile Heritage Trail along the upper Hudson and Mohawk rivers. The trail connects 50 natural, cultural, or historically significant attractions. Towns and cities along the trail include Waterford, Cohoes, Green Island, Tory and Watervliet.

Fodor's Choice

No two people will agree on what makes a perfect vacation, but it's fun and helpful to know what others think. We hope you'll have a chance to experience some of Fodor's Choices yourself while visiting New York State. For detailed information about each entry, refer to the appropriate chapter in this guidebook.

Sights

Niagara Falls seen from the *Maid of the Mist* tour boat

The Statue of Liberty from the ferry headed to Staten Island, and the New York City skyline on the way back (25¢ round-trip)

Boscobel Mansion and its breathtaking view of the Hudson River, Garrison

The art colony at Woodstock

People-watching at Washington Square Park, Greenwich Village, New York City

People-watching at Saratoga during the racing season

The Atlantic Ocean from the lighthouse at Montauk Point, Long Island

Cargo ships passing through the Eisenhower Lock of the St. Lawrence Seaway, Massena

Covered bridge over the East Branch of the Delaware River, Downesville

Beaches

Fire Island State Park

The Hamptons on Long Island

Jones Beach, Wantagh

Romantic Hideaways

Lily Pond Lane at dusk, East Hampton

Room in the Runaway Inn, Fleischmanns

The Eggery Inn for breakfast, Tannersville

A stroll along the Promenade, Brooklyn Heights

Museums

Baseball Hall of Fame, Cooperstown

Metropolitan Museum of Art, New York City

Museum of Cartoon Art, Rye

The Hyde Collection, Glens Falls

Shaker Museum, Chatham

Trotting Horse Museum, Monroe

Historic Sites

Ellis Island, New York City

Federal Hall, New York City

Franklin D. Roosevelt National Historic Site, Hyde Park

Fraunces Tavern, New York City

John Jay Homestead, Katonah

Lindenwald, retirement home of Martin Van Buren, Kinderhook

Schuler Mansion State Historic Site, Albany

Stony Point Battlefield Historic Site, Stony Point

Sunnyside, estate of Washington Irving, Tarrytown

Thomas Paine Cottage, New Rochelle

Sports

Canoeing in the St. Regis Canoe Area, Saranac Lake

Cross-country skiing through Saratoga State Park, Saratoga Springs

Hiking in the High Peaks region of the Adirondacks

Ice skating in Wollman Rink, New York City

Rafting down the Hudson River Gorge, Adirondacks

Downhill skiing at Hunter Mountain, the Catskills

Hotels

Geneva-on-the-Lake, Geneva (*Very Expensive*)

Hotel Athenaeum, Chautauqua Institution, Chautauqua (*Very Expensive*)

The Pierre, New York City (*Very Expensive*)

Algonquin, New York City (*Expensive*)

Nevele Hotel, Ellenville (*Moderate–Expensive*)

1770 House, East Hampton (*Moderate–Expensive*)

Hotel Thayer, West Point (*Moderate–Expensive*)

Auberge des 4 Saisons, Shandaken (*Moderate*)

Hotel Saranac of Paul Smith's College, Saranac Lake (*Moderate*)

Wyndham Hotel, New York City (*Moderate*)

Three Village Inn, Stony Brook, Long Island
(*Inexpensive–Moderate*)

Hotel Iroquois, New York City (*Inexpensive*)

Pickwick Arms Hotel, New York City (*Budget*)

Restaurants

Chapels, Rochester (*Very Expensive*)

L'Auberge Du Cuchon Rouge, Ithaca (*Very Expensive*)

Le Bernardin, New York City (*Very Expensive*)

Lutèce, New York City (*Very Expensive*)

Rue Franklin West, Buffalo (*Very Expensive*)

Auntie Yuan, New York City (*Expensive*)

Belhurst Castle, Geneva (*Expensive*)

Chez Sophie, Saratoga Springs (*Expensive*)

DuPuy Canal House, High Falls (*Expensive*)

The Escoffier at the Culinary Institute of America, Hyde
Park (*Expensive*)

La Capannina, Spring Valley (*Expensive*)

The Sagamore, Bolton Landing, Lake George
(*Expensive*)

The Brae Loch, Cazenovia (*Moderate–Expensive*)

Bukhara, New York City (*Moderate–Expensive*)

La Marmite, Williston Park (*Moderate–Expensive*)

Le Petit Bistro, Rhinebeck (*Moderate–Expensive*)

Eartha's Kitchen, Saratoga Springs (*Moderate*)

Hickory Grove Inn, Cooperstown (*Moderate*)

Redcoat's Return, Elka Park (*Moderate*)

Ye Hares 'N Hounds Inn, Bemus Point (*Moderate*)

Cucina Stagionale, New York City (*Inexpensive*)

Hattie's Chicken Shack, Saratoga Springs (*Inexpensive*)

New York

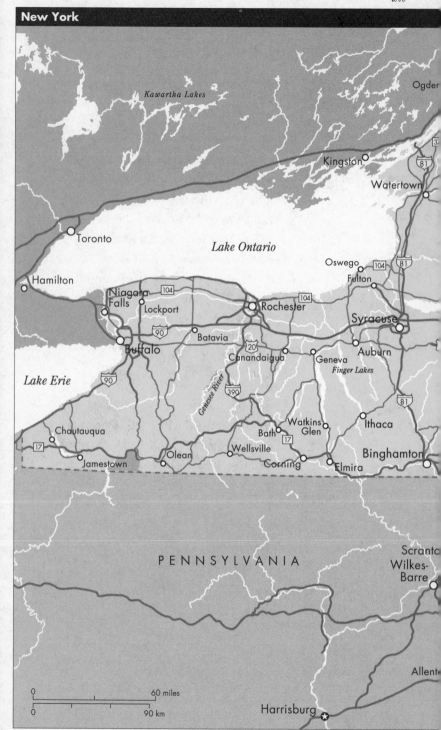

Ogder

Kawartha Lakes

Kingston

Watertown

81

32

Toronto

Lake Ontario

Hamilton

Oswego

Fulton

104

81

Niagara Falls

Lockport

104

Rochester

Syracuse

90

Batavia

20

Canandaigua

Geneva

Auburn

Lake Erie

90

390

Genesee River

Finger Lakes

81

Chautauqua

Watkins Glen

Ithaca

Bath

17

Wellsville

Jamestown

17

Olean

Corning

Elmira

Binghamton

Scranta

Wilkes-Barre

PENNSYLVANIA

Allente

0 ___ 60 miles
0 ___ 90 km

Harrisburg

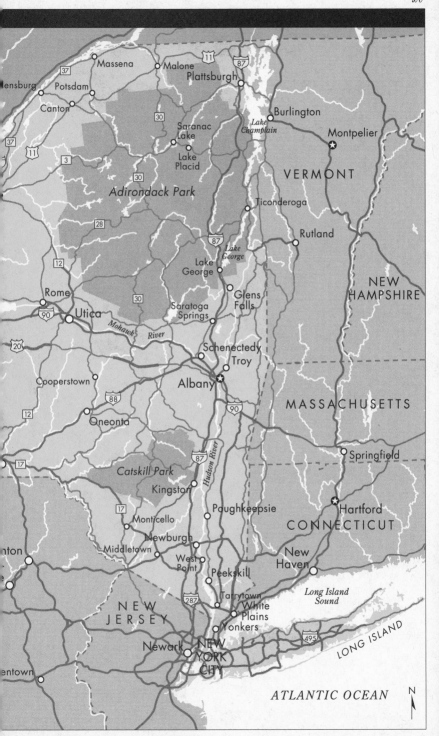

World Time Zones

MONDAY
SUNDAY

International Date Line

+12 +13

-9

-10

-7

-4

-3

25

-5 -4

-11

-10

-5 -4

-8

-6

-5

-4 -3

+11

+12

-3

Numbers below vertical bands relate each zone to Greenwich Mean Time (0 hrs.).
Local times may differ, as indicated by lightface numbers on the map.

| +11 | +12 - | -11 | -10 | -9 | -8 | -7 | -6 | -5 | -4 | -3 | -2 |

Algiers, **29**	Berlin, **34**	Delhi, **48**	Istanbul, **40**
Anchorage, **3**	Bogotá, **19**	Denver, **8**	Jerusalem, **42**
Athens, **41**	Budapest, **37**	Djakarta, **53**	Johannesburg, **44**
Auckland, **1**	Buenos Aires, **24**	Dublin, **26**	Lima, **20**
Baghdad, **46**	Caracas, **22**	Edmonton, **7**	Lisbon, **28**
Bangkok, **50**	Chicago, **9**	Hong Kong, **56**	London (Greenwich), **27**
Beijing, **54**	Copenhagen, **33**	Honolulu, **2**	Los Angeles, **6**
	Dallas, **10**		Madrid, **38**
			Manila, **57**

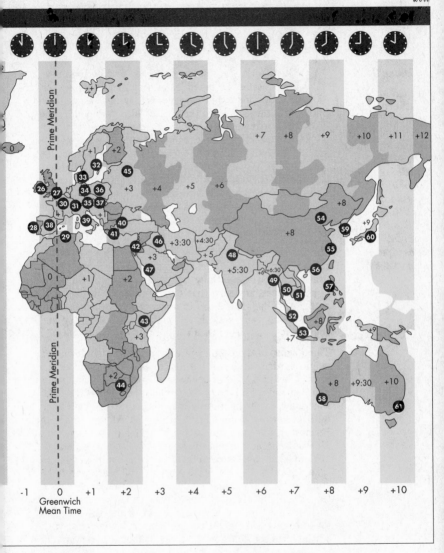

Introduction

by Diane Gallo

The editor of Southern Tier Images, *Diane Gallo has written extensively about New York's people, places, history, and events for a variety of national and regional newspapers and magazines.*

New York State has more to see and do than most countries. It has miles of oceanfront, rolling forests, mountain ranges, dizzying peaks, and plunging cataracts. More than 4,000 lakes and ponds, and 70,000 miles of rivers and streams course through its almost 50,000 square miles. For promotional purposes the state is subdivided into 11 regions, each with its own distinct flavor. (This regionalization makes for hot political battles.) The regions include New York City, Long Island, Hudson Valley, the Catskills, Capital-Saratoga, the Adirondacks, Thousand Islands-Seaway, Central-Leatherstocking, the Finger Lakes, Niagara Frontier (Niagara Falls-Buffalo area), and Chautauqua-Allegheny.

Despite these divisions, New York's 18 million people are rather cavalier about their geography. To the brash and brassy urbanites, anything not New York City is upstate. For upstaters, anything that's not New York City is downstate. And then there are those in the Adirondacks who think of themselves as living in the North Country and those who . . . you get the idea.

The essence of the Empire State can be distilled down to a single word: diversity. It has four distinct seasons of unsurpassed beauty. Winter snows range from the infamous whiteouts of Buffalo to the storybook snowfalls of the Hudson Valley. In spring, flower festivals herald the new season with azaleas on Long Island, tulips in Albany, lilacs in Rochester, and roses and apple blossoms from Niagara to Montauk. In the summer, playing fields and parks, and rivers and lakes come alive when more than 50 million visitors take advantage of the state's nearly 150 state parks, 35 state historic sites, and a variety of recreational, educational, and cultural facilities. In the fall, the forests and woods of New York match any autumn display the New England countryside might proffer when hillsides glow with scarlet, crimson, and gold, and weekly foliage updates alert the "leaf peepers" to the change in colors.

When Henry Hudson sailed into New York Harbor in 1609, Algonquian Indians came to offer greetings. Dressed in deerskins and ceremonial headfeathers, the Algonquians carried gifts of tobacco, sweet berries, and furs. Although the reception was apparently friendly, the crew's chief mate wrote in the log, "We durst not trust them." This set the tone for later generations of tourists to New York City.

A few years later in 1626, Peter Minuit, the first governor of New Netherland, arrived with orders from the Dutch West India Company to buy Manhattan Island from the Algonquians. With his famous $24 purchase, Minuit struck

New York's first marketing coup and became one of the few white men who ever paid the Indians for anything. The investment paid off. Today Manhattan is the national headquarters for communications and advertising, fashion and sports, banking and finance. The city is also a hub for publishing, shipping, and shopping. And it can rightly be called a world cultural capital: Artists, actors, musicians, writers, poets, conductors, magicians, and crafts-people, all work and play here.

New York City justifiably needs a list of superlatives to describe it. It has a reputation for being the best and the biggest. Despite residents' claims to be tops in everything, in recent years it has failed to make the FBI's list of the top ten most dangerous cities. (Do, however, be prudent and alert to realities. Sometimes crossing a street can mean moving from a safe harbor into a war zone.)

Viewed at night from the World Trade Center, the island of Manhattan spreads out in front of you, with equal parts glitter and greasepaint. From here you can make out Wall Street and the South Street Seaport, SoHo and the East and West villages, Rockefeller Center and Radio City Music Hall, Times Square and the convention center, and Central Park and Lincoln Center. Through the 12-mile length of the island runs the long ribbon of Broadway. Although you can't see them, down there are world-renowned museums of science, nature, film, and ethnic and creative arts; Broadway theaters and off-Broadway showcases; temples of haute cuisine and streets lined with ethnic eateries; and Art-Deco dance palaces and standing-room-only jazz clubs.

Some insist that Manhattan is the only *real* New York, but the purist will argue that the city is incomplete without the four other boroughs—Brooklyn, Queens, the Bronx, and Staten Island. And although many native New Yorkers rarely see more of the city than their own neighborhood, they take the attitude of one visitor who said, "Even if you can't do and see it all, it's nice to know it's all there."

Little has changed since 1644 when one cynical observer noted that 18 languages were spoken in Manhattan and that the city had acquired the "arrogance of Babel." During the late 1800s and early 1900s, Irish, Germans, Italians, Poles, Russians, Romanians, and Eastern European Jews emigrated to America through the Ellis Island processing facility in New York Harbor. Each group brought their varied customs, cultures, and religions, thereby enriching the melting pot of New York City and the nation.

New York City has one of the most diverse populations in the world. The ethnic composition changes so rapidly, it's tough to nail down exactly who is coming from where and when. (In how many places in the world could you find a Peruvian/Chinese bodega?) In addition to the enclaves of

Chinatown and Little Italy, there are large Indian and Latin American populations, as well as growing Russian, Korean, and West Indian communities. Dozens of languages rumble from throats like subways from tunnels.

Despite its slick urban reputation, New York State isn't all skyscrapers and city streets: It's farmlands and waterfalls, Long Island potatoes, Finger Lakes wine, and upstate fruit orchards. It's dairy farms (New York is the leading dairy state) and maple syrup (it outproduces Vermont), vineyards (on Long Island and in the Finger Lakes), strawberry fields, and pumpkin patches. The state's agricultural bounty surprises those who haven't ventured outside of New York City or explored beyond Niagara Falls.

Just a 45-minute drive on the Long Island Expressway (if it's not jammed up, as it's likely to be) takes you from Manhattan's crush to one of the world's premier playgrounds. A narrow spurt of land (23 miles at its widest) with 250 miles of accessible coastline, Long Island is the urban dweller's escape from New York. It has superb public parks including Jones Beach, the largest swimming facility in the world. On the island's smooth beaches, one may ignore the world and swim, jog, sunbathe, and clam.

Despite a housing explosion in the past 20 years, Long Island still has a strong appeal. The Hamptons, on its South Shore, offer summer ambience, accentuated by fashionable shopping streets, art galleries, theaters, and restaurants. At Montauk Point, the island's tip, the lighthouse built during Colonial times still flashes its warning beacon to signal home port to the Northeast's largest fleet of charter and party boats. On the North Shore are the beaches and harbors of Long Island Sound where Great Gatsby châteaux politely elbow for room on the Gold Coast.

If water is a region's lifeblood, then New York is blessed with a great circulatory system. In addition to the Atlantic surf, the state borders on two Great Lakes and has mountain streams and mighty rivers. Of New York's major waterways, the Hudson River is perhaps the most scenic and is often referred to as "America's Rhine."

On the west side of the Hudson are the Palisades and the Catskills; on the east are the Taconic Mountains. The heights of both sides offer splendid views. Seven scenic bridges cross the river allowing travelers to sample the best of both shores. Passengers aboard Metro-North's Hudson line train have an eye-level view as it wends its way upriver. Just south of dramatic Storm King Mountain is West Point, where young men (now also young women) have been molded into army officers since 1802.

The river towns cluster on the Hudson's banks harboring quaint restaurants, museums, art galleries, antique shops, marinas, amusement parks, county fairs, 19th-century mansions, and 17th-century manor houses. The landscape chronicles the names of those who contributed to a young nation's rise—Van Cortlandt, Livingston, Paine, Washington, Fulton, Carnegie, Vanderbilt, Harriman, Rockefeller. Although Dutch New Netherland lasted only 55 years, the Dutch legacy lives on in place names like Yonkers, Rensselaer, Tappan Zee, Kill Van Kull, and Peekskill.

History, innovative cuisine, and restored or original Victorian architecture are found north of Poughkeepsie, in the towns of Hyde Park and Rhinebeck. Springwood, the sprawling estate at Hyde Park, was built in 1867 by FDR's father and was not only the president's residence but his birthplace. Both FDR and Eleanor Roosevelt are buried on the grounds. The Italian Renaissance Vanderbilt Mansion, also in Hyde Park, has a magnificent view of the lower Hudson Valley from its backyard. The Culinary Institute of America (affectionately dubbed the CIA), is widely regarded as one of the country's best training grounds for up-and-coming restaurateurs. Students practice every aspect of running a restaurant from preparing the food to inventory at the three on-site restaurants. The small village of Rhinebeck, just north of Hyde Park, contains excellent examples of Victorian architecture. The Rhinebeck Arms, in operation since 1766, is one of the country's oldest inns, having once served George Washington himself.

Throughout the Hudson Valley are state historic sites that recall the courage of the rebel army. (Colonial New Yorkers bore the brunt of the Revolutionary War. About 45,000—or one-fourth of the state's population—took up arms. Nearly one-third of all Revolutionary War battles were fought in New York.) At each turn of the road, you'll follow Washington's trail as he battled, dined, and slept his way through historic moments of the war.

Northwest from the Hudson Valley is the Rip Van Winkle country of the Catskills. Deeply forested and beautiful, this area is where you are urged to slow down and enjoy the scenery. Pick any hill, climb it and savor the view. Skiing, camping, hiking, rock-climbing, and biking are challenges in this hilly country. But even with all that exercise, your waistline is in danger in a land where the rallying cry is, "Eat, eat."

The Catskills tradition of hospitality started during the 19th-century resort boom, when thousands of holiday travelers came to escape the city's swelter. Those traditions evolved into the posh resort hotels, inns, and guest farms like those in Monticello and Liberty and more modest inns and guest farms, and the area gained the nickname "borscht belt." (The recent film *Dirty Dancing* took place at such a Catskill resort set in the 1960s.) The borscht-belt quality has softened in recent years with the influx of young, upscale Manhattanites attracted by reasonably priced real estate within driving distance of the city. The old general stores are now gourmet delis that stock the *New York Times* and croissants for their well-heeled customers.

The once-quaint town of Woodstock, in the eastern Catskills, has cashed in on its association with the landmark rock concert of 1969, sharing the name but not the site: Its main drag is lined with T-shirt outlets and shops selling batik, tie-dye, and macrame. Bethel, some 50 miles southwest of Woodstock in Sullivan County, is where the Woodstock Music and Art Fair was moved after promoters had trouble getting permits for Woodstock.

To the north, the Catskills melt into the gentler terrain of the Capital-Saratoga district. Here, near the juncture of the Mohawk and Hudson rivers, lies Albany, the state capital and regional commercial center. The city's rich historic legacy is set within a bustling commercial framework. Despite startling differences in architectural eras, Albany's stylistic juxtaposition achieves a curious harmony. The modern space-age complex of the Empire State Plaza provides a spectacular introduction to the city's center. Against the backdrop of the futuristic government plaza with its landmark "egg" (the Performing Arts Center), stands the State Capitol, Albany's star attraction. This impressive example of Château architecture, boasts the "Million Dollar Staircase," a Romanesque version of the Paris Opera's elaborately curved staircase.

J ust about a 45-minute drive north is the smaller but no less sophisticated Saratoga Springs. At the turn of the century, Saratoga was *the* place to indulge oneself for the summer season. Saratoga casinos rivaled Las Vegas and Monaco for opulence. Whether visitors came to take the mineral waters or wager on their favorite racehorse, Saratoga offered hedonistic seduction. The town's main street is lined with boutiques, gallerias, hotels, and bistros; and visitors still come for the soothing mineral springs, and the world-class entertainment and cultural programs at the Saratoga Performing Arts Center.

To the north of the Capital-Saratoga district begins the slow rise of the Adirondack range. This vast wilderness area is rugged, timeless, and remote. The Adirondacks were the last region of New York to be explored and surveyed. Of the area's 11,000 square miles, nearly a third is reserved by the state to be held "forever wild."

With 6.2 million acres, the Adirondack State Park is the largest wilderness area west of the Mississippi. There are 42 peaks above 4,000 feet, among them the mile-high Mount Marcy and the east's highest ski slope, Whiteface Mountain. For those less physically inclined, Whiteface Mountain Memorial Highway leads visitors to one of the Adirondack's most spectacular views.

The region's magnificent upland lake district includes Lake Placid, Saranac Lake, Tupper Lake, and Lake George—Queen of the Lakes. Lake George has a "million dollar beach" and Lake Placid's ski lifts and elevators provide breathtaking excursions—winter and summer. Also prime among Adirondack attractions is the fully restored Fort Ticonderoga, the "Key to a Continent."

The Thousand Islands (the French call them Les Milles Isles) are actually 1,834 islands clustered in a 50-mile stretch of the St. Lawrence River. Curving northwest around the Adirondacks like a mother's protective arm, the Thousand Islands region still preserves vestiges of the romance of 19th-century grand hotels and mansions. Clayton and Alexandria Bay are headquarters for cruises in the area that often take in a tour of Boldt Castle, a 300-room replica of a Rhine castle on Heart Island.

The waters surrounding the Thousand Islands offer some of the best fishing in North America. By local custom, a shore dinner is freshly caught, then pan-fried by the guide on the nearest island. Every year anglers descend on Pulaski and Oswego for the towns' annual trout and salmon derbies. The St. Lawrence Seaway forms part of the world's longest unfortified international border. The Thousand Islands International Bridge at Alexandria Bay is a tribute to neighborly relations between the United States and Canada.

Surrounding the center of the state is the Leatherstocking region, so named for the leather breeches worn by its New England settlers. Leatherstocking Country's crown jewel is Cooperstown. Set at the foot of Lake Otsego, Cooperstown bills itself as the "village of museums." Most people know it as the home of the National Baseball Hall of Fame and Museum, but Cooperstown is more than a baseball fan's mecca. The Fenimore House, which has an extensive collection of American Folk Art is here, as is the Farmer's Museum and Village Crossroads, a re-creation of 19th-century life featuring craftspeople in authentic settings. The town is also the home of the Glimmerglass Opera.

Throughout the Mohawk Valley-Utica region you'll find Revolutionary War sites like Oriskany Battlefield where General Herkimer's men did battle with Chief Joseph Brant's in "the bloodiest battle of the Revolution." Erie Canal Village in Rome marks the spot where the first shovelful of dirt was turned for the 363-mile waterway between Albany and Buffalo. Built between 1817 and 1825, the artery —dubbed "Clinton's Ditch" after promoter De Witt Clinton—was a major pipeline for goods towed on barges by teams of mules. The many museums in the cities all along the canal route preserve the romance and excitement of the 19th-century days of growth and expansion.

Indian legend says that the Great Spirit put down his hand, and water sprang from where his fingers pressed the earth. It's not hard to imagine a master's hand at work in the Finger Lakes. The district has 11 bodies of water, including the five lakes of Cayuga, Owasco, Skaneateles, Otisco, and Seneca. Unimpeachable sources rumor that the trout in Seneca Lake weigh in at as much as 32 pounds. And when you reel in that big one, make sure you've got a bottle of Finger Lakes wine on hand. The region is famous for its wineries. Remember the rule for wine tasting: See, smell, swirl, and sip.

"Spectacular" is not too strong an adjective to describe Niagara Falls. Indians who witnessed the dramatic splitting of the Niagara River called it "thunder of the waters." In any given second, 200,000 cubic feet of water (weighing more than 62 pounds per foot) rush over the lip of the falls, providing the single greatest source of electric power in North America. Don a slicker and take a *Maid of the Mist* tour to the very foot of the cataracts. England's King Edward VII, India's Prime Minister Nehru, and America's own Marilyn Monroe are among the millions who have experienced the deafening roar of Niagara from these boats.

Tucked away in the state's southwest corner is the Chautauqua-Allegheny region. When pioneers and settlers headed west from the terminus of the Erie Canal, they largely ignored the southern region and left it relatively undeveloped and sparsely populated. Those who did settle here suffered the same lack of imagination as did the folks who brought us Main Street. The naming of things in this region is cause for some confusion. "Allegheny," "Cattaraugus," and "Chautauqua" crop up over and over as place names for lakes, rivers, and counties. Chautauqua is a county, a town, a lake, and an institute. Allegheny is a county, a river and a mountain range. Allegany, with a slightly different spelling, is a county and a state park. Cattaraugus is a county, a town, and a creek.

This westernmost region of New York is a land of small towns and lakes, one Great Lakes shore, and vast forests. Allegheny County alone has 23 almost untouched state forests and 50,000 acres of publicly owned wild woods. Farther west in Chautauqua County is Allegany State Park. With 94.5 square miles (65,000 acres), Allegany is New York's largest state park, as well as one of its most primitive. Wildlife is abundant (beaver, raccoon, deer, black bear, game birds) and the bird-watching, with more than 200 species, is superb. The park also has great fishing, hiking, and camping.

In the years since Henry Hudson first entered New York Harbor, a new world has flourished. Today New York City sets the pace for the nation in economy, cultural activities, and in urban living. From its urban centers to its rolling hillsides, New York is a microcosm of America.

1 Essential Information

Before You Go

Visitor Information

Contact the New York State Division of Tourism, (1 Commerce Plaza, Albany, NY 12245, tel. 518/474–4116 or 800/225–5697). Its *I Love NY* booklets are excellent resources on various areas of the state (including NYC). (*See* also Important Addresses and Numbers in each city/area section.)

In the United Kingdom, contact the New York State Tourist Office (25 Bedford Square, London WC1B 3HG, England, tel. 01/323–0648).

Tour Groups

Although you will have to march to the beat of a tour guide's drum rather than your own, a package tour is likely to save you money on airfare, hotels, and ground transportation while covering a lot of territory. For the more experienced or adventurous traveler, there is a variety of special-interest and independent packages available. Listed below is a sampling of options. Check with your travel agent or the New York State Division of Tourism (tel. 212/827–6250) for additional resources.

When considering a tour, be sure to find out (1) exactly what expenses are included (particularly tips, taxes, side trips, additional meals, and entertainment); (2) ratings of all hotels on the itinerary and the facilities they offer; (3) cancellation policies for both you and the tour operator; and (4) the single supplement should you be traveling alone. Most tour operators request that bookings be made through a travel agent—there is no additional charge for doing so.

General-Interest Tours "Autumn Highlights" from **Globus Gateway/Cosmos** (150 S. Los Robles Ave., Suite 860, Pasadena, CA 91101, tel. 818/449–0919 or 800/556–5454) takes you through some of the state's most scenic spots during the fall foliage season. "Historic East" tours New York; Washington, DC; Virginia; and Pennsylvania. Globus also has a 13-day tour that begins with the state and winds its way up through New England, Ontario, and Quebec.

American Express Vacations (Box 5014, Atlanta, GA 30302, tel. 800/241–1700 or in GA, 800/282–0800) has a similar tour called "Eastern Highlights."

Domenico Tours (751 Broadway, Bayonne, NJ 07002, tel. 800/554–TOUR) will take you to Niagara Falls and the Thousand Islands or from Niagara Falls through the state en route to Washington, DC.

Special-Interest Tours
Art **Esplanade Tours** (581 Boylston St., Boston, MA 02116, tel. 617/266–7465) offers a six-day "Art Treasures of New York" tour that shows off the riches of New York City's finest museums.

Music **Dailey-Thorp Travel** (315 W. 57th St., New York, NY 10019, tel. 212/307–1555) performs admirably with its deluxe New York City music and culture programs. Itineraries vary with available performances.

Nature **The Nature Conservancy** (1800 North Kent St., Suite 800, Arlington, VA 22209, tel. 703/841–5300) organizes nature tours of Adirondack Park.

Package Deals for Independent Travelers

American Fly AAway Vacations (tel. 817/355–1234 or 800/433–7300) offers New York City packages with discounts on hotels and car rentals. Its "Yankee Holiday" includes some New York City sightseeing and tickets to a Broadway show. **Firstours** (12755 State Highway 55, Minneapolis, MN 55441, tel. 612/540–5000 or 800/223–6493) has similar "Theater Weekends." **American Express** includes a half-day sightseeing tour in its city packages. Also check with **United Airlines** (tel. 312/952–4000 or 800/328–6877), **Continental Airlines** (tel. 713/821–2100), and **Eastern Airlines** (tel. 305/873–3000) for packages.

Tips for British Travelers

Passports and Visas You will need a valid 10-year passport (cost £15) to enter the U.S. You will not need a visa if you are staying for less than 90 days, have a return ticket, and are flying with a participating airline. There are some exceptions to this, so check with your travel agent or with the United States Embassy (Visa and Immigration Dept., 5 Upper Grosvenor St., London W1A 2JB, tel. 01/499–3443).

Customs Visitors 21 or over can bring in 200 cigarettes or 50 cigars or three pounds of tobacco; one U.S. quart of alcohol; duty-free gifts to a value of $100. Be careful not to bring in meat or meat products, seeds, plants, fruits, etc. Avoid illegal drugs of any kind.

Returning to Britain, you may take home (1) 200 cigarettes or 100 cigarillos or 50 cigars or 250 grams of tobacco; (2) two liters of table wine and, in addition (a) one liter of alcohol over 22% by volume (most spirits), (b) two liters of alcohol under 22% by volume (fortified or sparkling wine), or (c) two more liters of table wine; (3) 50 grams of perfume and ¼ liter of toilet water; and (4) other goods up to a value of £32.

Insurance We recommend that you insure yourself against health and motoring mishaps. **Europ Assistance** (252 High St., Croydon, Surrey CR0 1NF, tel. 01/680–1234) is a firm that offers this service.

It is also wise to take out insurance to cover loss of luggage if it isn't already covered by any existing home-owner's policies you may have. Trip cancellation coverage is another good buy. The **Association of British Insurers** (Aldermary House, Queen St., London EC4N 1TT, tel. 01/248–4477) will give comprehensive advice on all aspects of vacation insurance.

Tour Operators **American Airplan** (Marlborough House. Churchfield Rd., Walton-on-Thames, Surrey KT12 2TJ, tel. 0932/246166) has a seven-day "American Adventure" package that spends five jam-packed days in New York and two in the spectacular surroundings of Niagara Falls. Prices per person are from £565.

National (1A Martindale Rd., Hounslow West, Middlesex TW4 7EW, tel. 01/577–1786) offers excellent fly/drive vacations starting from New York that are ideal for exploring New York State on your own. The company suggests you plan your own itinerary, perhaps to Kingston, Albany, Saratoga Springs, Lake George, and Lake Placid, or east to Syracuse and Buffalo. Prices are from £299. Accommodation in New York City for seven nights is £300 to £330 per person per week.

Jetsave (Jetsave America, Sussex House, London Rd., East Grinstead, Sussex RH19 1LD, tel. 0342/312022) has seven-day vacations in New York, with a choice of hotels. Prices are from £499 per person.

Jetways USA (93 Newman St., London W1P 3LE, tel. 01/637–5444) offers a 15-day "Eastern Discovery" package. This escorted tour takes in New York City, Boston, Quebec, Niagara Falls, Buffalo, Pennsylvania, and Washington, DC. Prices on this motor coach tour start at £985 per person; round-trip airfare from the UK is included.

Poundstretcher (Airlink House, Hazelwick Ave., Three Bridges, Crawley, Sussex RH10 1YS, tel. 0293/548241) offers New York as part of a two-center vacation. Couple your stay in New York with a stay in Orlando, or extend your vacation further with a week in either St. Petersburg or Clearwater. Prices, per person, for nine nights in New York and Orlando are from £749, or New York, Orlando, and Clearwater/St. Petersburg for 16 nights from £889.

Airfares Independent travelers may want to take a cheap flight to any of the major cities in the state and explore from there. APEX round-trip fares from London at press time (mid-'89) to New York cost from £299; to Albany from £443; to Buffalo from £460; to Syracuse from £435. If you're flexible, look in the small ads of Sunday and daily newspapers for last-minute, low-cost tickets. Round-trip fares to New York can start as low as £199, but check if taxes are included in the price quoted.

Electricity 110 volts. You should take along an adaptor since American razor and hair-dryer sockets require flat two-pronged plugs.

When to Go

It's not being facetious to say that the tourist season for New York State runs from January through December. The best months for visiting, however, depend on which area of the state you plan to visit and what you wish to do. While some museums and historic sites in the Hudson Valley, the Catskills, and the Adirondacks may be closed for the winter, for instance, there are still enough places to visit, sights to see, and winter sports to enjoy (*see* Seasonal Events). Many hotels and resorts offer accommodations at lower off-season rates as well as attractive weekend packages. And while New York City can get very hot and humid in the summer, particularly in July and August, that's also the season when the city is most crowded—not only with tourists but with New Yorkers themselves enjoying hosts of street fairs, outdoor concerts, and other activities. For the rest of the state, the weather can be pleasantly warm during the summer. Fall months can be glorious throughout the state when the foliage is most colorful in the countryside and when cities regain their vitality. Reservations are a necessity at that time of the year for country inns and hotels and throughout the year for New York City.

Climate What follows are the average daily maximum and minimum temperatures for major cities in New York State.

Albany								
	Jan.	32F	0C	May	70F	21C	Sept.	74F	23C
		16	−9		49	9		54	12
	Feb.	32F	0C	June	79F	26C	Oct.	61F	16C
		16	−9		58	14		43	6
	Mar.	43F	6C	July	83F	28C	Nov.	47F	8C
		27	−3		63	17		32	0
	Apr.	56F	13C	Aug.	81F	27C	Dec.	36F	2C
		38	3		61	16		22	−6

Buffalo								
	Jan.	34F	1C	May	67F	19C	Sept.	72F	22C
		20	−7		47	8		54	12
	Feb.	34F	1C	June	77F	25C	Oct.	63F	17C
		20	−7		56	13		45	7
	Mar.	43F	6C	July	81F	27C	Nov.	49F	9C
		27	−3		61	16		34	1
	Apr.	56F	13C	Aug.	81F	27C	Dec.	36F	2C
		38	3		61	16		23	−5

New York City								
	Jan.	37F	3C	May	68F	20C	Sept.	79F	26C
		24	−4		53	12		60	16
	Feb.	38F	3C	June	77F	25C	Oct.	69F	21C
		24	−4		60	16		49	9
	Mar.	45F	7C	July	82F	28C	Nov.	51F	11C
		30	−1		66	19		37	3
	Apr.	57F	14C	Aug.	80F	27C	Dec.	41F	5C
		42	6		66	19		29	−2

Current weather information on 235 cities around the world—
180 of them in the United States—is only a phone call away. To
obtain the Weather Trak telephone number for your area, call
800/247–3282. A taped message will tell you to dial a three-digit
access code for the destination you are interested in. The code
is either the area code (in the United States) or the first three
letters of the foreign city. For a list of all access codes, send a
stamped, self-addressed envelope to Cities, Box 7000, Dallas,
TX 75209. For further information, phone 214/869–3035 or 800/
247–3282.

Festivals and Seasonal Events

Top seasonal events in New York State include the I Love New
York Winter Festival in Hamilton County (in the Adirondacks),
the I Love New York Fall Foliage Festival in the Catskills, the
New York City Marathon in November, Macy's Thanksgiving
Day Parade down Broadway, and the lighting of the Christmas
tree in Rockefeller Center. For a complete listing of New York
State events, request the "Major Events in New York State"
calendar from the **Division of Tourism** (1 Commerce Plaza, Albany, NY 12245, tel. 518/474–4116 or 800/823–4582).

Jan.–Feb.: I Love New York Winter Festival takes place throughout Hamilton County. Festivities include snowmobile races,
winter carnivals, and cross-country and downhill skiing. Tel.
518/548–7191.
Late Jan.–Feb.: Winter Carnival at Lake George includes four-
wheel drive races on ice, sky divers, and a golf tournament. Tel.
518/668–5755.

Jan.–Apr.: Competitive Events at Lake Placid include bobsled and luge competitions, ski jumping, and cross-country ski meets. Tel. 800/255–5515 and in NY, 800/462–6236.

Early Feb.: Winterfest in Syracuse includes parties, fishing derby, and fireworks. Tel. 315/470–1343.

Feb. 13–14: Westminster Kennel Club Show is a prestigious dogshow event held in Madison Square Garden. 4 Penn Plaza, New York, NY, tel. 212/563–1990.

Mid-Feb.: Winter Carnival at Saranac Lake is one of the oldest in the country. Tel. 518/891–1990.

Mid- to late Feb.: Ice Castle Spectacular in Mayville is centered around ice-harvesting from Chautauqua Lake. Tel. 716/754–4304.

Late Feb.–early Mar.: Empire State Winter Games are Olympic-style competitions held at Lake Placid. Tel. 518/474–8889.

Mid-Mar.: Big East Basketball Championship Tournament is held at Madison Square Garden in New York City. Tel. 212/563–8114.

Mid- to late Mar.: Northeastern Wildlife Expo in Albany includes a wildlife art show, crafts, wild-game cooking demonstrations at Empire State Plaza. Tel. 518/434–1217.

Apr.: Professional Baseball Season Opens. New York Mets are at Shea Stadium, the New York Yankees are at Yankee Stadium, and AAA (minor league) teams play in Buffalo, Rochester, and Syracuse.

Early May: Hudson River White Water Derby lures canoeists and kayakers to the upper Hudson River in North Creek. Tel. 518/761–6366.

May 20–21: Ninth Avenue International Festival is a huge outdoor festival, with one mile of ethnic foods from 37th to 57th streets in New York City. Ninth Avenue Association, 400 W. 50th St., New York, NY 10019, tel. 212/581–7029.

Late May: General Clinton Canoe Regatta is the longest flatwater race in the country, from Cooperstown to Bainbridge. Tel. 607/746–2281.

June and July: The Metropolitan Opera performs free starlit concerts in parks in all five New York City boroughs. Tel. 212/799–3100.

June–Aug.: The Season at Chautauqua Institution in Chautauqua includes workshops, classes, opera, and ballet. Tel. 716/357–6200.

Mid-June–Labor Day: The New York Shakespeare Festival brings the Bard to the Delacorte Theater in Central Park. Performances are free; tickets are necessary. Tel. 212/861–PAPP.

June 10: Belmont Stakes, thoroughbred racing's final Triple Crown event, takes place at Belmont Park in Elmont. Information from the New York Racing Association, Box 90, Jamaica, NY 11417, tel. 718/641–4700.

Mid-June: Allentown Art Festival in Buffalo includes 500 exhibitors outdoors. Tel. 518/849–6609.

June–Aug.: The New York Philharmonic's free summer concert series takes place in parks throughout New York City, and in Suffolk, Nassau, and Westchester counties. All begin at 8 PM. Tel. 212/580–8700.

Late June: Crafts Fair at Rhinebeck is a major show at Dutchess County Fairgrounds. Tel. 914/876–4001.

Early July: Harbor Festival means regattas, fireworks, and parades in New York City. Tel. 212/944–2990.

Mid-July: Empire State Summer Games take place in various locations. Tel. 518/474–8889.

July 23: National Baseball Hall of Fame Induction Ceremonies in Cooperstown. Tel. 607/547–9988.

Aug.–Sept.: New York Renaissance Festival in Tuxedo includes jousts, crafts, and Elizabethan theater. The festivities are on weekends only. Tel. 516/325–1331.

Early Aug.: Flight '90 Air Show in Schenectady features ground displays, aerial acts, and military team flights. Tel. 518/393–3606.

Mid-Aug.: Travers Stakes in Saratoga Springs is the oldest stakes race for three-year-olds at the nation's oldest racetrack. Tel. 718/641–4700.

Late Aug.–early Sept.: Great New York State Fair, in Syracuse, is the oldest state fair in the country. Tel. 315/487–7711.

Sept. and Oct.: I Love New York Catskills Fall Festival takes place during peak foliage season in Ulster, Greene, Sullivan, and Delaware counties. Tel. 800/343–INFO and in NY, 800/882–CATS.

Mid-Sept.: Canal Town Days in Palmyra consists of boat rides on the Erie Canal and a parade. Tel. 315/946–6191.

Mid- to late Sept.: Trout and Salmon Derby represents thousands of dollars in prizes for catches in Lake Ontario and the Niagara River. Tel. 716/439–6064.

Mid-Oct.: Craft Fair at Bear Mountain lures more than 100 exhibitors three weekends in a row. Tel. 914/786–2701.

Early Nov.: New York City Marathon, which winds through all of five boroughs, attracts 22,000 runners and 2 million spectators. Information from New York Roadrunners Club, 9 E. 89th St., New York, NY 10028, tel. 212/410–7770.

Nov. 23: Macy's Thanksgiving Day Parade is the world's largest, in New York City. Tel. 212/560–4670.

Late Nov.: Christmas Parade, in Schenectady the night after Thanksgiving, kicks off the holiday season. Tel. 518/372–5656.

Late Nov.–early Dec.: Festival of Lights in Niagara Falls is a bright and beautiful holiday celebration. Tel. 716/278–8010.

Early Dec.: Christmas Tree Lighting in Rockefeller Center, New York City, is a highlight of the city's holiday season.

Dec. 31: New Year's Eve celebration in Times Square is legendary. Fireworks go off in Central Park.

What to Pack

Pack light because porters and luggage trolleys are hard to find. Luggage allowances on domestic flights vary slightly from airline to airline. Most allow three checked pieces and one carry-on. Some give you the option of two checked and two carry-on bags. In all cases, check-in luggage cannot weigh more than 70 pounds each or be larger than 62 inches (length + width + height). Carry-on luggage cannot be larger than 45 inches (length + width + height) and must fit under the seat or in the overhead luggage compartment.

What you pack depends largely on where you're headed. New York City is basically informal but has many restaurants that require a jacket and tie. Theaters and nightclubs in New York City range from the slightly dressy on Broadway, to extremely casual Off-Broadway and in Greenwich Village. For sightseeing and casual dining, jeans and sneakers are acceptable just about anywhere in the state. Some country inns in the Hudson Valley request that men wear a jacket and tie for evening meals. Bed-and-breakfast establishments are totally informal. New

York City can be very cold in the winter, but there's not much snow. Upstate New York has lots of snow, so be prepared. Also be prepared for thunderstorms in the summer throughout the state. The humidity level tends to be high, so leave the plastic raincoats at home.

Cash Machines

Virtually all U.S. banks belong to a network of Automatic Teller Machines (ATMs), which gobble up bank cards and spit out cash 24 hours a day in cities throughout the country. There are some eight major networks in the USA, the largest of which are Cirrus, owned by MasterCard, and Plus, affiliated with Visa. Some banks belong to more than one network. These cards are not automatically issued; you have to ask for them. If your bank doesn't belong to at least one network you should consider moving funds, for ATMs are becoming as essential as check cashing. Cards issued by Visa and MasterCard may also be used in the ATMs, but the fees are usually higher than the fees on bank cards, and there is a daily interest charge on the "loan," even if monthly bills are paid on time. Each network has a toll-free number you can call to locate machines in a given city. The Cirrus number is 800/4–CIRRUS; the Plus number is 800/THE–PLUS. Check with your bank for fees and for the amount of cash you can withdraw on any given day.

Traveling with Film

If your camera is new, shoot and develop a few rolls of film before leaving home. Pack some lens tissue and an extra battery for your built-in light meter. Invest about $10 in a skylight filter and screw it onto the front of your lens. It will protect the lens and also reduce haze.

Film can be harmed in hot weather. If you're driving in summer, don't store film in the glove compartment or on the shelf under the rear window. Put it behind the front seat on the floor, on the side opposite the exhaust pipe.

On a plane trip, never pack unprocessed film in check-in luggage; if your bags get X-rayed, pictures can be ruined. Always carry undeveloped film with you through security and ask to have it inspected by hand. (It helps to isolate your film in a plastic bag, ready for quick inspection.) Inspectors at American airports are required by law to honor requests for hand inspection.

The newer scanning machines used in all U.S. airports are safe for anything from five to 500 scans, depending on the speed of your film. The effects are cumulative; you can put the same roll of film through several scans without worry. After five scans, though, you're asking for trouble.

If your film gets fogged and you want an explanation, send it to the National Association of Photographic Manufacturers, 600 Mamaroneck Ave., Harrison, NY 10528. Association experts will try to determine what went wrong. The service is free.

Car Rentals

Where to rent a car in New York State depends largely on your travel plans. A trip covering the Niagara frontier and a couple of upstate cities like Rochester and Syracuse should probably start in Buffalo, since the Greater Buffalo International Airport has the state's best connections outside of New York City. An Adirondack adventure could take advantage of Albany's rental rates, often the state's lowest. New York City has its own pros and cons as a rental location: You might find a better combination of budget rental companies, special deals, and low airfares, but it is also one of the worst places in the nation to drive a car—let alone a recreational vehicle. Almost all national companies have rental offices at the airports in Buffalo, Rochester, Syracuse, Albany, and Binghamton, plus downtown locations. Many also have offices in smaller cities like Jamestown, Elmira, Oneonta, Kingston, Lake Placid, Watertown, and Utica. Major companies with locations statewide include **Avis** (tel. 800/331–1212), **Budget** (tel. 800/527–0700), **Dollar** (tel. 800/421–6868), **Hertz** (tel. 800/654–3131), **National** (tel. 800/328–4567), and **Thrifty** (tel. 800/367–2727). **American International** (tel. 800/527–0202) and **Rent-A-Wreck** (tel. 800/221–8282) are budget firms with offices around the state, usually offering pickups and drop-offs at local airports.

New York City has the state's highest rates, ranging from $50 to $70 per day at major companies and bottoming out at $35 with local budget firms. Buffalo is about $10 cheaper than that, Syracuse slightly less, and Albany the best deal of all: Even leader Hertz charges less than $40 daily for a subcompact. New York State now requires that basic car rental rates include collision insurance for all but a deductible of $100. Find out if you must pay for a full tank of gas, whether you use it or not, and ask about promotional, weekend, and 14-day-advance-reservation rates.

Traveling with Children

Publications *Family Travel Times* is an 8- to 12-page newsletter published 10 times a year by Travel with Your Children (TWYCH), 80 Eighth Ave., New York, NY 10011, tel. 212/206–0688. Subscription includes access to back issues and twice-weekly opportunities to call in for specific advice.

Great Vacations with Your Kids: The Complete Guide to Family Vacations in the U.S. by Dorothy Ann Jordon and Marjorie Adoff Cohen (E.P. Dutton, 2 Park Ave., New York, NY 10016; $9.95) details everything from city and adventure vacations to child-care resources.

The Candy Apple: New York for Kids by Bubbles Fisher (Prentice Hall Press, New York; $12.50) profiles places and things especially suited to children.

ParentGuide (2 Park Ave., New York, NY 10016, tel. 212/213–8840) is a monthly newsstand publication with event and resource listings.

Hotels In New York City: **Hotel InterContinental** (111 E. 48th St., New York, NY 10017, tel. 212/755–5900, 800/327–0200) offers a gourmet-cooking class for children. The **Sheraton City Squire Hotel** (790 Seventh Ave., New York, NY 10019, tel. 212/681–3300, 800/325–3535) has a children's menu on room service.

The Catskills: **Mohonk Mountain House** (Lake Mohonk, New Paltz, NY 12561, tel. 914/255–1000) has scores of programs, facilities, and activities for children of all ages, as well as convenient two-rooms-connected-by-bath accommodations. **Pinegrove Resort Ranch** (Lower Cherrytown Rd., Kerhonkson, NY 12446, tel. 914/626–7345) has children's programs and activities. **Rocking Horse Ranch** (Highland, NY 12528, tel. 914/691–2927, 800/437–2624) welcomes families with organized activities, a day camp, and spacious accommodations.

The Adirondacks: **The Sagamore** (Bolton's Landing, NY 12814, tel. 518/644–9400) has children's programs and menus, plus family rates.

Home Exchange See *Home Exchanging: A Complete Sourcebook for Travelers at Home or Abroad* by James Dearing (Globe Pequot Press, Box Q, Chester, CT 06412, tel. 800/243–0495 or in CT, 800/962–0973).

Getting There On domestic flights, children under 2 not occupying a seat travel free. Various discounts apply to children 2–12. Reserve a seat behind the bulkhead of the plane, which offers more leg room and can usually fit a bassinet (supplied by the airline). At the same time, inquire about special children's meals or snacks, offered by most airlines. (See "TWYCH's Airline Guide" in the February 1988 issue of *Family Travel Times* for a rundown on the services offered by 46 airlines.) Ask the airline in advance if you can bring aboard your child's car seat. For the booklet "Child/Infant Safety Seats Acceptable for Use in Aircraft," contact the Community and Consumer Liaison Division, APA–400 Federal Aviation Administration, Washington, DC 20591, tel. 202/267–3479.

Baby-sitting Services Make child-care arrangements with the hotel concierge or housekeeper. New York City agencies: **Babysitter's Guild** (60 E. 42nd St., Suite 902, New York, NY 10017, tel. 212/682–0227), **Gilbert Child Care Agency** (115 W. 57th St., Suite 3–12, New York, NY 10019, tel. 212/757–7900), **Part Time Child Care** (19 E. 69th St., New York, NY 10021, tel. 212/879–4343).

Hints for Disabled Travelers

The Information Center for Individuals with Disabilities (2743 Wormwood St., Boston, MA 02210, tel. 617/727–5540) offers problem-solving assistance and information including lists of travel agents that specialize in tours for the disabled.

Moss Rehabilitation Hospital Travel Information Service (12th St. and Tabor Rd., Philadelphia, PA 19141, tel. 215/329–5715) provides information on tourist sights, transportation, and accommodations in destinations around the world. The fee is $5 for each destination. Allow one month for delivery.

Mobility International (Box 3551, Eugene, OR 97403, tel. 503/343–1284) has information on accommodations, organized study, etc. around the world.

The Society for the Advancement of Travel for the Handicapped (SATH) (26 Court St., Penthouse, Brooklyn, NY 11242, tel. 718/858–5483) offers access information. Annual membership costs $40, or $25 for senior travelers and students. Send a stamped, self-addressed envelope.

Greyhound (tel. 800/531–5332) will carry a disabled person and companion for the price of a single fare. **Amtrak** (tel. 800/USA–RAIL) requests 24-hour notice to provide redcap service, special seats, and a 25% discount.

Publications *The Itinerary* (Box 1084, Bayonne, NJ 07002, tel. 201/858–3400) is a bimonthly travel magazine for the disabled.

Access to the World: A Travel Guide for the Handicapped by Louise Weiss is useful but out of date. Available from Facts on File, 460 Park Ave. South, New York, NY 10016, tel. 212/683–2244.

Hints for Older Travelers

The **American Association of Retired Persons** (AARP, 1909 K St. NW, Washington, DC 20049, tel. 202/662–4850) has two programs for independent travelers: (1) The *Purchase Privilege Program,* which offers discounts on hotels, airfare, car rentals, and sightseeing; and (2) the *AARP Motoring Plan,* which offers emergency aid and trip-routing information for an annual fee of $29.95 per couple. The AARP also arranges group tours, including apartment living in Europe, through two companies: **Olson-Travelworld** (5855 Green Valley Circle, Culver City, CA 90230, tel. 800/227–7737) and **RFD, Inc.** (4401 West 110th St., Overland Park, KS 66211, tel. 800/448–7010). AARP members must be 50 or older. Annual dues are $5 per person or per couple.

When using an AARP or other identification card, ask for a reduced hotel rate at the time you make your reservation, not when you check out. At restaurants, show your card to the maître d' before you're seated, since discounts may be limited to certain menus, days, or hours. When renting a car, remember that economy cars, priced at promotional rates, may cost less than cars that are available with your ID card.

Elderhostel (80 Boylston St., Suite 400, Boston, MA 02116, tel. 617/426–7788) is an innovative 13-year-old program for people 60 and older. Participants stay in dorms on some 1,200 campuses around the world. Mornings are devoted to lectures and seminars; afternoons, to sightseeing and field trips. The all-inclusive fee for two- to three-week trips, including room, board, tuition, and round-trip transportation, is $1,700–$3,200.

Travel Industry and Disabled Exchange (TIDE, 5435 Donna Ave., Tarzana, CA 91356, tel. 818/343–6339) is an industry-based organization with an $18 per person annual membership fee. Members receive a quarterly newsletter and information on travel agencies and tours.

National Council of Senior Citizens (925 15th St. NW, Washington, DC 20005, tel. 202/347–8800) is a nonprofit advocacy group with some 4,000 local clubs across the country. Annual membership is $10 per person or $14 per couple. Members receive a monthly newspaper with travel information and an ID card for reduced-rate hotels and car rentals.

Mature Outlook (Box 1205, Glenview, IL 60025, tel. 800/336–6330), a subsidiary of Sears Roebuck & Co., is a travel club for people over 50, with hotel and motel discounts and a bimonthly newsletter. Annual membership is $7.50 per couple. Instant membership is available at participating Holiday Inns.

Travel Tips for Senior Citizens (U.S. Dept. of State Publication 8970, revised Sept. 1987) is available for $1 from the Superintendent of Documents, U.S. Government Printing Office, Washington, DC 20402.

Golden Age Passport is a free lifetime pass to all parks, monuments, and recreation areas run by the federal government. People over 62 should pick one up in person at any national park that charges admission. A driver's license or other proof of age is required.

Further Reading

For nonfiction about the area, look at Ted Aber's *Adirondack Folks; Niagara,* by Gordon Donaldson; Jack Hope's *A River for the Living: The Hudson and its People; The Catskills from Wilderness to Woodstock,* by Alf Evers; Edmund Wilson's *Upstate: Records and Recollections.*

Or pick up some historical fiction: Walter D. Edmonds's *Drums Along the Mohawk; Butt's Landing,* by Jean Rikhoff; Robert L. Taylor's *Niagara;* Jack Finney's *Time and Again.*

Suspense novels set in New York State include Bernard F. Conners's *Dancehall;* Donald E. Westlake's *Bank Shot;* and Joyce Carol Oates's *Mysteries of Winterthurn.*

Two family sagas set primarily in New York are Irwin Shaw's *Rich Man, Poor Man* and *Beggarman, Thief.*

Other novels set in the state include: *Ragtime,* by E. L. Doctorow; *Bullet Park,* by John Cheever; William Kennedy's Pulitzer Prize–winning *Ironweed;* Bernard Malamud's *Dubin's Lives;* and *A Bloodsmoor Romance,* by Joyce Carol Oates.

The Adirondacks has inspired many works of literature. Still foremost among these is William H.H. Murray's *Adventures in the Wilderness,* published in 1869. This century's books of note include William Chapman White's *Adirondack Country* and Lincoln Bennett's *Ancient Adirondacks.* For a compilation of short essays, there is Paul Jamieson's *Adirondack Reader* by various writers and Jamieson's own collection, *Adirondack Pilgrimage.*

Set in the Saratoga area are *Saga of an Impious Era,* by George Waller, and the lively novel *Saratoga Trunk,* by Edna Ferber.

Thousands of books have been written about or set in New York City, from Washington Irving's *Knickerbocker's History of New York* to the novel *The Bonfire of the Vanities* by Tom Wolfe, a harrowing look at the city today. The manners of early upper-crust New York society are dissected in Henry James's *Washington Square* and Edith Wharton's *House of Mirth.* New York and Long Island during the Roaring '20s are shown in F. Scott Fitzgerald's *The Great Gatsby.* Books describing the New York immigrant experience include *World of Our Fathers* by Irving Howe, *Call It Sleep* by Henry Roth, *The Invisible Man* by Ralph Ellison, and *Manchild in the Promised Land* by Claude Brown. For a behind-the-scenes look into politics and business, read *The Power Broker* by Robert A. Caro, *Mayor* by Mayor Edward I. Koch, and *Trump* by Donald H. Trump (with Tony Schwartz). For a building-by-building guide to the city's architecture, see *AIA Guide to New York City* by Norval White. Other useful guides are *A Guide to New York City Landmarks,* published by the Landmark Preservations Committee, *The Street Book* by Henry Moscow, and *The Movie Lover's Guide to New York* by Richard Alleman.

Getting to and around New York State

By Plane

Most major U.S. airlines schedule regular flights into New York. The major cities are serviced by **American** (tel. 800/433–7300), **Continental** (tel. 800/525–0280), **Delta** (tel. 800/872–7786), **Pan Am** (tel. 800/221–1111), **TWA** (tel. 800/221–2000), **United** (tel. 718/803–2030), and **USAir** (tel. 212/736–3200). Several of these airlines also have flights within the state. Many foreign airlines also fly into the three airports of New York City—LaGuardia, JFK, and Newark International.

Smoking If smoking bothers you, ask for a seat in the nonsmoking section. If the airline tells you there are no nonsmoking seats, insist on one: FAA regulations require U.S. airlines to find seats for all nonsmokers.

Carry-on Luggage New rules have been in effect since January 1, 1988 on U.S. airlines in regard to carry-on luggage. The model for these new rules was agreed to by the airlines in December 1987 and then circulated by the Air Transport Association with the understanding that each airline would present its own version.

Under the model, passengers are limited to two carry-on bags. For a bag you wish to store under the seat, the maximum dimensions are $9'' \times 14'' \times 22''$, a total of 45″. For bags that can be hung in a closet or on a luggage rack, the maximum dimensions are $4'' \times 23'' \times 45''$, a total of 72″. For bags you wish to store in an overhead bin, the maximum dimensions are $10'' \times 14'' \times 36''$, a total of 60″. Your two carryons must each fit one of these sets of dimensions, and any item that exceeds the specified dimensions will generally be rejected as a carryon, and handled as checked baggage. Keep in mind that an airline can adapt these rules to circumstances, so on an especially crowded flight don't be surprised if you are allowed only one carry-on bag.

In addition to the two carryons, the rules list eight items that may also be brought aboard: a handbag (pocketbook or purse), an overcoat or wrap, an umbrella, a camera, a reasonable amount of reading material, an infant bag, crutches, cane, braces, or other prosthetic device upon which the passenger is dependent, and an infant/child safety seat.

Note that these regulations are for U.S. airlines only. Foreign airlines generally allow one piece of carry-on luggage in tourist class, in addition to handbags and bags filled with duty-free goods. Passengers in first and business classes are also allowed to carry on one garment bag. It is best to check with your airline ahead of time to find out the exact rules regarding carry-on luggage.

Checked Luggage U.S. airlines allow passengers to check in two suitcases whose total dimensions (length + width + height) do not exceed 60″. There are no weight restrictions on these bags.

Rules governing foreign airlines vary from airline to airline, so check with your travel agent or the airline itself before you go. All the airlines allow passengers to check in two bags. In general, expect the weight restriction on the two bags to be a maximum of 70 pounds each, and the size restriction on the first bag to be 62″ total dimensions, and on the second bag, 55″ total dimensions.

Lost Luggage Airlines are responsible for lost or damaged property only up to $1,250 per passenger on domestic flights; $9.07 per pound (or $20 per kilo) for checked baggage on international flights; and up to $400 per passenger for unchecked baggage on international flights. If you're carrying valuables, either take them with you on the airplane or purchase additional insurance for lost luggage. Some airlines will issue additional luggage insurance when you check in, but many do not. One that does is American Airlines. Its additional insurance is only for domestic flights or flights to Canada. Rates are $1 for every $100 valuation, with a maximum of $400 valuation per passenger. Hand luggage is not included. Insurance for lost, damaged, or stolen luggage is available through travel agents or directly through various insurance companies. Two that issue luggage insurance are **Tele-Trip** (tel. 800/228–9792), a subsidiary of Mutual of Omaha, and **The Travelers Insurance Co.** (tel. 800/243–0191). Tele-Trip operates sales booths at airports, and also issues insurance through travel agents. It will insure checked luggage for up to 180 days and for $500 to $3,000 valuation. For 1–3 days, the rate for a $500 valuation is $8.25; for 180 days, $100. The Travelers Insurance Co. will insure checked or hand luggage for $500 to $2,000 valuation per person, and also for a maximum of 180 days. Rates for 1–5 days for $500 valuation are $10; for 180 days, $85. For more information, write The Travelers Insurance Co., Ticket and Travel Dept. (1 Tower Sq. Hartford, CT 06183). Both companies offer the same rates on domestic and international flights. Check the travel pages of your Sunday newspaper for the names of other companies that insure luggage. Before you go, itemize the contents of each bag in case you need to file an insurance claim. Be certain to put your home address on each piece of luggage, including carry-on bags. If your luggage is stolen and later recovered, the airline must deliver the luggage to your home free of charge.

By Bus

Greyhound offers frequent service throughout the state to and from major cities in the United States and Canada. Regional bus lines (Central New York Coach, Hudson Transit, etc.) offer service between points within the state.

Contact your local Greyhound office, or call toll-free, tel. 800/531–5332.

For information on specific bus stations, see the chapters on the individual regions.

By Train

Amtrak's Empire Corridor Service runs from New York's Grand Central Terminal to upstate New York with stops at Croton-Harmon, Poughkeepsie, Rhinecliff, Hudson, Albany-

Rensselaer, Schenectady, Amsterdam, Utica, Rome, Syracuse, Rochester, Buffalo, and Niagara Falls. The Adirondack runs from Grand Central (en route to Montreal) to Croton-Harmon, Poughkeepsie, Rhinecliff, Hudson, Albany-Rensselaer, Schenectady, Saratoga Springs, Fort Edward–Glens Falls, Whitehall, Fort Ticonderoga, Port Henry, Westport, Willsboro, Port Kent, Plattsburgh, and Rouses Point. The Lake Shore Limited, which runs between Grand Central and Chicago, makes stops at Croton-Harmon, Poughkeepsie, Rhinecliff, Hudson, Albany–Rensselaer, Schenectady, Utica, Syracuse, Rochester, and Buffalo.

For information on schedules and fares, tel. 800/USA–RAIL. For information on specific train stations, see the individual chapters.

Metro-North Commuter Railroad (tel. 800/223–6052) trains depart from Grand Central for points along the Hudson Valley into Connecticut on its Harlem, Hudson, New Haven, Port Jervis, and Pascack Valley lines.

By Car

The principal east–west highway in New York is the New York State Thruway from Buffalo and the Pennsylvania border on the west and New York City and the Connecticut border on the east. Several major highways, all accessible from the thruway, run in a north–south direction, including U.S. 87 from Albany to the Canadian border, U.S. 81 from Binghamton to the Thousand Islands, and I–390 from the Pennsylvania border to Rochester.

Wherever you drive in New York, remember to buckle up. It is against the law to drive anywhere in the state without the driver's and the front seat passenger's seat belts securely fastened.

The maximum speed limit on state highways is 55 miles per hour, with various lower limits within cities and residential areas. Be sure to watch road signs for these limits and any changes on major highways.

Unless otherwise stated, right turn on red is permitted almost everywhere except in New York City. Parking is an expensive proposition in the Big Apple—and there is very little street parking available. Parking in a "Tow Away Zone" will cost $100 in cash, plus the parking fine and a great deal of aggravation, to get your car back if it is towed.

In upstate regions, snow tires and/or chains may be required during the winter.

Staying in New York

Beaches

The best beaches in New York are found on Long Island's South Shore. Largest and best kept among these is Jones Beach State Park, Wantagh, with changing rooms, picnic grounds, boardwalk, restaurant, cafeterias, and food stands. The 2,400 acres of beaches and parkland also have facilities for outdoor theaters and concerts, miniature golf, and fishing.

Also on Long Island, Captree State Park, at the easternmost tip of Robert Moses State Park, features untamed grassy-duned beaches, with minimal facilities. Fire Island is perhaps the most popular beach area in New York for straight and gay singles. Despite its stunning beaches, however, you might find a day's visit arduous unless you are a guest of a summer resident. The Hamptons, from Westhampton east to Montauk Point, feature still more outstanding beaches with chic towns to explore.

The most famous beach in the outer boroughs of New York City is no doubt Coney Island in Brooklyn. Although the beach is a mere shadow of its former glory, the water is usually fine and there are changing rooms, restaurants, food stands, and other facilities. The other major beach within the city limits is in the Rockaways—a peninsula that juts out into the Atlantic. Jacob Riis Park in Queens, at the western end of the peninsula, is rated among the cleanest beaches in the city. Now part of the Gateway National Recreation Area, Riis has changing rooms, food stands, some shaded picnic areas, and numerous children's playgrounds and sports facilities. *Note:* Increased enforcement of antidumping laws and environmental pressure lead to cleaner Long Island beaches and very few closures in 1989.

Participant Sports

Biking Practically every city, state, and national park in New York has bicycle trails. In New York City, for instance, Central Park in Manhattan and Prospect Park in Brooklyn have roadways that are closed to cars and reserved for bikers (as well as joggers and walkers) during daylight hours on weekends and often during non-rush hours weekdays. You can find plenty of places to rent a bike on nearby streets—check the Yellow Pages—or you can rent in Central Park at the Loeb Boathouse near the 72nd Street lake. The New York State Tourism Division (1 Commerce Plaza, New York, NY 12425) publishes a brochure, *I Love NY Outdoors*, which has extensive information on biking and other sports in parks throughout the state.

Fishing The state's 70,000 miles of rivers and streams offer a wide range of fishing opportunities, with maps to each area available from Outdoor Publications (Box 355, Ithaca, NY 14850). The *I Love NY Outdoors* brochure also lists all the regional fishing offices and fishing hotlines throughout the state.

Everyone over age 16 needs a license, available at most sporting-goods stores, to fish in freshwater rivers, lakes, and ponds. No license is needed to fish in deep-sea or coastal waters. Best bet for deep-sea fishing boat excursions is at Sheepshead Bay, Brooklyn.

Hiking Part of the 2,000-mile Appalachian Trail winds through New York State. For hiking details consult Volume 4 of the *Appalachian Trail Guide Series* (Appalachian Trail Conference, Box 807, Harpers Ferry, WV 25425). Also useful is *Hiking Trails in the Northeast* by Thomas A. Henley and Neesa Sweet (Great Lakes Living Press). The *I Love NY Outdoors* brochure also includes some hiking information.

Winter Sports For skiers, the Catskills and the Adirondacks are favorites for downhill, with practically the rest of upstate New York for cross-country. The Catskills resorts also offer snowshoeing and tobogganing, while ice skating is available at rinks throughout the state—even at New York City's Rockefeller Center. Some of the rinks are in state parks and some are privately owned.

State and National Parks

State Parks An extensive state park system exists in New York, with many locations offering outstanding recreational features. An Empire State Pass, available at individual parks or by writing to State Parks (Albany, NY 12238) will take care of all day-use fees for the year from March 31 to April 30. The pass costs $25, with day-use fees at various parks running about $3.50 per automobile. Camping, boating, and other fees are extra.

National Park Gateway National Recreational Area extends through Brooklyn, Queens, Staten Island, and New Jersey. The area includes the Jamaica Bay Wildlife Sanctuary, Jacob Riis Park (*see* Beaches), and various facilities for outdoor and indoor festivals, beaches, and parkland.

Dining

In and around the major cities of New York State—especially the Big Apple—it is always best to have reservations at the most popular restaurants. These restaurants, particularly the most expensive ones, fill up rapidly. In New York City and the Hudson Valley, where the best food is to be found, tables may be at a premium during weekends. Prices will be about the same for comparable food and surroundings—$50 and up for first-class nouvelle American or French food.

At the less expensive options, reservations are well advised. We've singled out restaurants in all price ranges worth a special effort to visit, and provided guidelines for costs and what you might expect in the way of atmosphere and ambience as well as food. Inns and resorts offering accommodations as well as meals often represent excellent values. When dining out in New York City, expect to pay an additional 25%–40%.

Ratings

Category	Cost*: Major City	Cost*: Other Areas
Very Expensive	over $60	over $50
Expensive	$40–$60	$30–$50
Moderate	$20–$40	$15–$30
Inexpensive	under $20	under $15

per person, without tax, service, or drinks

Lodging

Wherever you decide to stay in New York, it's always best to reserve ahead. Booking may not be a problem in every corner of the state, but you don't want to be caught at dusk searching for a place to stay, particularly in New York City.

Hotels In addition to the major chains—Hilton, Holiday Inn, Hyatt, Marriott, Sheraton—the state has many independent luxury hotels and resorts, which offer just about the best of everything, from cuisine to recreation.

Motels All the motel chains are represented in the state, from strictly budget places to those with amenities equaling hotels. Rates may differ markedly from one area to another, even within the chains.

Lodges Popular around the ski areas, lodges offer a dormitorylike atmosphere, common meals (often buffet style), and relatively inexpensive accommodations.

Catskills Resorts Truly unique New York State, the Catskills resorts are cities unto themselves, where you probably won't need to leave the grounds: Meals are all-you-can-eat extravaganzas; sports range from golf to tobogganing; and singles weekends are regular attractions (some resorts even have resident matchmakers). Prices at the resorts reflect this all-inclusive nature, but for those who take advantage of the entertainment and activities available, they can be a bargain.

Ratings

Category	Cost*: Major City	Cost*: Other Areas
Very Expensive	over $125	over $100
Expensive	$100–$125	$80–$100
Moderate	$80–$100	$45–$80
Inexpensive	under $80	under $45

per room, double occupancy, without taxes

Bed-and-Breakfasts B&Bs offer room in the owner's home, with breakfast usually included. Each area of the state has its own bed-and-breakfast association, which can be contacted through the local chamber of commerce or the area telephone book.

Credit Cards The following credit card abbreviations are used in this book: AE, American Express; CB, Carte Blanche; DC, Diners Club; MC, MasterCard; V, Visa.

Camping and RV Facilities Most state parks have campsites as reflected in the *I Love NY Outdoors* brochure. Sites at state parks can be reserved ahead through Ticketron outlets or by mail to State Parks (Albany, NY 12238). However, only a small portion of campsites, as well as cabins, is available for reservation; most are first-come, first-served. There are numerous private campgrounds throughout the state, including some belonging to the KOA chain (Kampgrounds of America, Box 30558, Billings, MT 59114). The AAA also publishes annual camping directories for the state which are free to members. Be forewarned: There are neither campgrounds nor trailer parks near New York City. Bringing an RV to Manhattan is a mistake; few garages will accept them and street parking is hard to find.

2 Portraits of New York State

Tourists Who Stop at Nothing

by William E. Geist

Humorist William E. Geist writes for Esquire and Rolling Stone and does features and commentaries for CBS-TV network news programs. For four years he wrote the column "About New York" for the New York Times.

Leading his family on a forced march through Manhattan, Tom Sparacio of Snohomish, Washington, looked over his shoulder to announce that the next stop on their sightseeing tour was the New York Stock Exchange. His six-year-old son, Jeff, could not wait to see the cows and pigs.

This is tourist season in New York, a time when an inordinate number of pedestrians seem to be looking up and walking into things, when people with cameras around their necks can be seen greeting total strangers on the subways, when New Yorkers are asked to open their couches to visitors and when even hot-dog vendors and pigeons are expected to pose for family albums.

The first man in Budweiser logo shorts has been sighted in Times Square. "We're going to the Empire State Building," said the man, Earl Williams of Kansas City, Missouri, who also wore an Atlantic City T-shirt. "Then my wife wants to go to '21' for lunch." Mr. Williams said he had no reservation. "21" might.

With maps unfurled and two cameras at the ready, the Sparacio family scampered through New York, having allotted one day to see the city on their trip East. Mr. Sparacio, his wife, Rozaine, their sixteen-year-old daughter, Trish, and their two sons, Ted, fourteen, and Jeff, rose at 6 AM in Philadelphia and arrived in Pennsylvania Station on an early train. Mrs. Sparacio observed the hordes of commuters and uttered, "Oh, God."

"It's just so big and foreign to us," Mr. Sparacio said. "It's like if a New Yorker came out to climb Mount Pilchuck." The Sparacios were not about to travel by subway, not yet. They observed others catching yellow taxis, much as New Yorkers might watch Snohomish residents angling for brown trout, before hooking a taxi themselves to Battery Park to see Mr. Sparacio's top priority of the trip, the Statue of Liberty.

He bounded ashore on Liberty Island, climbing the steps of the statue's 142-foot pedestal, then the steep, narrow, 168-step steel staircase to the crown. Halfway up, Trish announced that the statue was not *her* first priority; Macy's was. Mr. Sparacio, who is in the sheet-metal business, marveled at the statue's construction. His wife said her legs hurt. Mr. Sparacio looked over at Ellis Island and said his grandfather had arrived there from Sicily in 1899.

Arriving at the World Trade Center, the Sparacios did what they were supposed to do: They stood outside and gawked for a few minutes, and after reaching the top, they remarked that the people 110 stories below looked "like ants."

Much to their mother's dismay, the children made a beeline for the souvenir shop, perusing everything from the phosphorescent NEW YORK CITY pillowcases that looked like they would make sleeping impossible, to T-shirts exclaiming I RODE ON A NEW YORK CITY SUBWAY . . . AND SURVIVED!

On their way to the stock exchange, they happened upon a convenient display of New York street life assembled in a tiny park. They saw street musicians and vendors selling tube socks and strawberry incense. They passed up an opportunity to get rich quick playing three-card monte.

From a large assortment of pushcart foods—from papaya drink to Tofu-zert—the Sparacios chose traditional hot dogs for lunch, devouring them while continuing their quick pace. "Alexander Hamilton is buried there," Mr. Sparacio shouted, never breaking stride while passing the Trinity Church cemetery.

The sidewalks of Wall Street were packed and nearly impassable. "Does everyone in New York just walk around all day?" asked Mrs. Sparacio. "Why aren't they working?"

Having seen a recent television show about the Brooklyn Bridge, Mrs. Sparacio was able to explain to Trish on their walk across it what exactly was "so hot about it, anyway," as Trish had wanted to know. But the children most appreciated the man roller-skating across while listening to a Walkman radio and juggling several balls.

"New York is expensive," another tourist, Dorothy Sholeen of Ithaca, New York, commented to them, "but the best part is looking at people and buildings." Indeed, Jeff's favorite sight was "that man with the neat Mohawk haircut." Trish liked "the strange clothes people wear and all the limousines." On a ten-day vacation, the family expected to spend about $3,500, but they would spend less than $50 in New York.

"This is where representatives of all nations come together to insure peace," Mrs. Sparacio told the children as their taxi sped past the United Nations. "It doesn't work."

Bloomingdale's was next, where they went up seven flights of escalators, back down and out the door. Trish checked the price tag on a blouse marked $178 and exclaimed, "Wait till I tell my friends." A woman tried to squirt "an exciting new fragrance" on Mrs. Sparacio, who recoiled in the nick of time.

"There's nothing where we live," said Trish. But her excitement at detecting the scent of horses as she neared Central Park betrayed her. She has a horse at home named Cinnamon. The children petted the carriage horses and tried to grab bullfrogs, which they were surprised to find in a pond one hundred yards from Fifth Avenue.

"Seen enough?" asked Mr. Sparacio, and they were off, swerving into Tiffany's to ogle a $21,000 diamond necklace.

Joining a group of jaywalkers, Mr. Sparacio said, "They arrest people for this in Seattle," and added with a touch of pride, "we're catching on fast."

He thought they were ready for the subway now, and Mrs. Sparacio nearly squeezed the blood from Jeff's hand as they descended into the strange and pungent world below. Asking directions, they caught an E train back to Penn Station.

"People are less rude and more helpful than I expected," said Mr. Sparacio. Samuel Silverman, a New Yorker, explained: "This is a big city. We're all tourists to some extent."

"This is New York, Jeff," said Mrs. Sparacio, riding the rush-hour subway train. "Squished." Noting an advertising message headlined IS RIDING THE SUBWAYS THE ONLY ADVENTURE IN YOUR LIFE? Mr. Sparacio, who was trying to keep his feet, commented, "This is adventure enough for us.

"It's regrettable," said Mr. Sparacio, arriving at Penn Station, "that we don't have more time."

"At least we can say we've been here," said Mrs. Sparacio, who had the Instamatic snapshots to prove it. All admitted to exhaustion after their sightseeing steeplechase, except Jeff. He announced that he might stay up until 3:00 AM, then fell over sideways in his Amtrak seat, to sleep, to dream, to wake up in Philadelphia.

The Heritage of the Hudson

by Carl Carmer

Hudson Valley historian Carl Carmer is the author of The Hudson *and* Songs of the Rivers of America.

Writing about the romantic Hudson River is a welcome task since it can begin at home. From the eight-sided, many-windowed cupola which surmounts my eight-sided house, I can behold not only the wide stream moving massively toward the sea but many a century-old dwelling which was planned long ago by people who thought it would be a credit to its neighborhood and a reminder of their period's dedication to beauty.

A little to the east I can see without the aid of binoculars the turrets of the Beltzhoover Castle (now known as the Halsey Castle) and I know that a rippling lake lies beside it—a lake that bears upon its surface the slow white swans that every visitor feels are essential to so beautiful a dwelling.

If I look south, I see the old home of Colonel James Hamilton, son of Alexander, and I must again wonder what motives led to the wild and untrue legend that the colonel built the house in which I stand as a convenient dwelling for his son's mistress.

As I look to the Hudson, I see projecting into its waters from the far side the long railroad pier which gave the little town of Piermont its name. History tells me that Daniel Webster once sat in a rocking chair on the floor of an open flatcar and was borne away by the first train of the just-completed New York and Erie Railroad toward a magnificent dinner in Fredonia, New York, on the banks of Lake Erie. The new railroad was not allowed to come farther than the middle of the river; hence the pier that would allow the new line to transfer all New York City–bound cargo to riverboats for the rest of the journey.

As for my northern view I can only say that, as soon as the War for Independence ended, building a house on the banks of the Hudson became an indication of status and many an ambitious and well-to-do citizen of New York City took advantage of the opportunity for becoming highly respected by his contemporaries.

If a good friend visited me on the east bank of the Hudson, I would take him first to look at the big yellow house called Nuit and tell him that its very name suggests the hours of evening when shadow supplants a western glory. I would make him aware that the cobbles which he treads toward the entrance had been shipped across an ocean from the streets of Marseilles and had a history of their own long before they had left the shores of France to glint under a stretch of American sunset.

From this home onward my guest and I would travel north to pass other homes or sites of vanished houses romantically named. Netherwood, Locust Grove, Windcliff, Ellerslie, Leacote, Tivoli, Rose Hill are only a few of the names that give evidence of the poetic fancies of their owners.

Broadway is the river road on the east side of the Hudson— the same Broadway that all America knows, it runs all the way from New York City to Albany. It passes the top of Main Street in Irvington and, as it does, the summer traveler may look down through a long, leafy tunnel to a splatter of shining Hudson water. Running parallel to that green-lined tube lies another, named Sunnyside Lane, which leads down to the charming and whimsical cottage that housed Washington Irving in his latter days. Restored to the exact image it presented when America's first world-famous author was its occupant, the house still looks as if it were wearing a cocked hat, as Irving said it did.

No restoration in the nation makes its guests feel more at home, perhaps because it continues to exist in the more august company of castles and mansions that grace the countryside. As it sits in delightful modesty beside the great river, I believe that it conveys more successfully than any other restored dwelling in America the character, the sly humor, the imaginative fancy of the man who chose to live in it. Somehow it creates a *neighborhood* in which at dusk the Hamiltons await, as they often did, the arrival at their home (now next door to my own) of the town's quite unpretentious author living a half mile away. Sometimes Irving would bring with him one of his own houseguests, such as the renowned Swedish spinster-writer Fredrika Bremer, who was so elated when her host did not fall asleep before the dessert, as he usually did, that she must record the fact in her diary.

The staff of the Sunnyside Restoration has been so successful in its researches that many of the homely day-by-day practices, routines, and habits which assume significance only when attributed to a great man are revealed. The sensitive visitor of today grieves with the long-dead Irving when he comes upon the gravestones of his dogs, or rejoices with him when he finds that shaving after midnight provides a temporary relief from the torture of sleeplessness. It is no wonder then that the writer's warm humanity seems to lie concentrated within the old Dutch house and the simple pattern of his living out his remaining years.

When Irving died in 1859, just after completing his biography of Columbus, ours was not the only nation that was in tears. England and Spain—particularly Spain—have mourned him until today. And many an American ignores the current revolt of the uncompromisingly literary against oversentimentality when he stands before the simple grave

at Sleepy Hollow Cemetery and reads the first lines of
Longfellow's tribute:

> *Here lies the gentle humorist, who died*
> *In the bright Indian Summer of his fame.*
> *A simple stone with but a date and name*
> *Marks his secluded resting place beside*
> *The river that he loved and glorified.*

Irving, one of the most famous men of letters, was also interested in art, for the river stirs every facet of the creative
instinct. Were he alive today, he would be rejoicing over the
current interest in the paintings of his contemporaries.
When he was young, he had considered becoming an artist
as a life-work, and his enthusiasm for art never left him.
The fact that he sometimes chose the pen name of Geoffrey
Crayon indicated his feeling for and knowledge of the products which he was given every opportunity to praise.

A new and spontaneous spirit rose among hills and
groves through which the Hudson passed. The
landscapes offered by the river were superior in
their beauty to any that might be admired in Europe, said
the sensitive Thomas Cole, and he set out to prove his statement. A believer in the close relationships of the arts, he
took his flute with him and sought rocky ravines, the channels whitened by splashing waters which inevitably ran
through steep tributaries to invade the level surface of the
three-mile-wide Tappan Zee. Having found a scene that
moved him, the young painter let his flute speak for him
and, once it had spoken, began to imitate with his brushes
and colors that part of the divine creator's universe he had
chosen for a painting.

The immeasurable expanses of an untamed land challenged
Thomas Cole and his artist colleagues, and they all were ac-
cepting the challenge. On enormous canvases for the most
part, they set about impressing potential patrons and pur-
chasers. They believed that their products were meticulously accurate as to subject matter. They also were encouraged by the fact that they *and* the possible purchaser
were convinced that a good picture cannot fail of having a
praiseworthy "moral effect." On a highly artistic plane they
were evangelists.

It has long been my contention that landscape has an espe-
cial influence on those who inhabit it—not merely in
economic ways, as the wheat or cotton spring from the
earth, not in geographic ways, as rivers and mountains become boundaries to be crossed, but in spiritual and psychic
ways. The look and feel of a land communicate not easily described messages to those who are sensitive enough to
receive them. Perhaps because rivers in their courses offer
poetic parallels to human life, people are inclined to attrib-
ute to them influences that strongly affect their lives.

In 1609 the Great River of the Mountains (as the Elizabethan explorer Captain Henry Hudson called it) had long awaited the inevitable dramas for which it would serve as a setting. Upon entering the wide stream, Hudson's crew were aware of the backdrop. Its banks, they said, "were so pleasant with grass and flowers—and goodly trees—as ever we had seen." They were more deeply concerned, however, as are most explorers, with their own roles on the great stage which encompassed them. The fortnight of sunlit September days during which the dusky natives sang choruses of welcome, and their ship drew near the blue mountains to the north, held no omen of the climatic day years later when the treacherous keeper of their log—old Robert Juet—would set their captain adrift in the arctic sea.

No change of backdrop would be necessary for ensuing acts. As might have been expected, then, characters and plot would supersede place. Early depictions of life along the river would therefore be more concerned with those stalwarts who lived it than with the river valley itself.

The Dutchmen who came from the Netherlands to the river were audacious adventurers, eager for profits in beaver and wildcat pelts obtainable in the valley woods. Their prosperity was immediate and the patterns of their living had little time to change from those they already knew. Portraits, showing the distinction of their wives and their own qualities as successful merchants and landholders, were symbols of high status. Painters were soon competing for commissions. Called "limners" by our frontier society, not many of the newly developed artists indulged in the subtleties of their professional European prototypes. They emphasized, rather, the obvious. The result was a group of boldly realistic portraits. The stamp of major characteristics was realized in them more directly than it would have been by more sophisticated painters. The carrying of this method further might have resulted (as it did in Washington Irving's amusing word portraits of Dutch dignitaries) in caricature. Hence the work of the "patroon painters" (so-called because their work was commissioned by the privileged Dutch patroons, or landowners, of the period) was not so important a contribution to American art as it was to American history. It might be noted in this connection that consciousness of place had already begun to grow, for Hudson River scenic backgrounds became both symbols and decorations in some of the limners' portraits.

Though, as always in time of war, the portraits of heroes assume authority, the fact that the Hudson River was of the greatest strategic importance and the realization that its beauty was overwhelming drew the attention of all who looked upon it. Even the British officer sent under a flag of truce by General John Burgoyne to offer surrender of his army at Saratoga discoursed for the first ten minutes of his visit on the colors of mid-October foliage in the Hudson Valley.

So compelling was the Hudson's beauty that it was regarded as a special gift of God. Painters, awed by the "divine architecture" they beheld in the mountains, hollows, and waters of its valley, chose to convey what God had said to them through these media of the "sublime subject" in terms of canvas and paint. They paid tribute to the blue stream and its bluer mountains with a conscientious and disciplined artistry which resulted in skills never before obtained by American artists. Not long after the mid-19th century they were designated as the "Hudson River School." Proud that they had won for themselves this unique distinction, they sought to express wild natural glories with ever larger canvases. On these they exulted in meticulous representations of foreground plants, of middle-ground waters, of distant peaks rising beyond both into mist-strewn heavens. Having nearly exhausted Hudson River scenes, they used their techniques on other subjects—the less dramatic, elm-punctuated slopes of the Genesee, the greater challenge of Niagara's plunging waters.

As art directions changed in the last quarter of the century, American landscape gave way to canvases depicting Americana—genre paintings, representations of life in the almost measureless gray city at the big stream's wide mouth. The river retired into its mists. Artists, stimulated by metropolitan vigor and excitement, began, to the stunned surprise of the public, to paint ashcans, dreary tenements, and drearier saloons.

As if fleeing from the cruel realism of these sights, other painters sought release in a dream world where juxtaposition of unrelated objects was a commonplace; but even there their surrealism produced little hope or joy. River water continued, however, to flow by their doors, and the incredible river itself offered so varied and glittering a pile of incongruous and challenging materials that an age of empirical and highly individualistic experiment began.

It still continues. Always, as in our past, the tidal waters of the river-that-flows-two-ways fill the brain with images so intimate that on occasion the artist must become interpreter as well as creator, and the viewer is often entranced by the strange language the paintbrushes speak. The lively minds that exist among the inhabitants of the river-girt City of Greater New York leave few avenues of artistic endeavor untraveled.

Adirondack Country

To Begin With

by William Chapman White

A former New York City newspaper columnist, William Chapman White summered in Saranac Lake, in the Adirondacks, for many years. He is the author of Adirondack Country.

It depends on what sort of day October 2, 1536, was. It may have been one of those high autumn days, so common in the northland, with infinite blue sky above, with clear air that brings distant horizons near. If so, the first white man ever to see the Adirondack Mountains of northern New York was the French explorer Jacques Cartier.

On that day, in the full flaming of autumn, he came to the Indian village that was to be the site of Montreal. The Indians led him up the high hills behind the mud flats. He saw the river below and the level woods that stretched away unbroken to the south. On the horizon, seventy miles off, were mountains, not one solid range but a broad sea of hills, intensely blue under the October sun. Cartier may have asked questions about them, for at some time he learned that to the south was "an unexplored region of lakes, of mountains, and delightful plains."

Three generations of Indians lived and died by the St. Lawrence before another white man looked on those hills. In July, 1609, Samuel de Champlain, who had been in Canada for a year trying to revive the French settlement, explored that land to the south. With a small group of Europeans and Indians he moved slowly down the Sorel River to the mouth of a lake and saw "a number of beautiful islands filled with fine woods and prairies." He named the lake after himself. As he continued down its west side he noticed high mountains on the east and to the south.

He saw no people, although his guides told him that the country was inhabited by Indians. Champlain found that out for himself a few days later as his group came near the head of the lake. Here they met a band of Iroquois; when Iroquois and Canadian Indians met a fight always followed. In this fight Champlain used his arquebus loaded with four balls. His one shot instantly killed two Iroquois. That shot, in the shadow of the Adirondacks, changed American history. The Iroquois never forgot it. Forever after, they hated the French with the special hatred usually reserved for the Canadian Indians.

By odd coincidence, less than two months after Champlain first saw the Adirondacks at close range, another European, Henry Hudson, came near them. In September, 1609, he sailed up the Hudson to stop above Albany where the rolling country hints at the blue hills to the north.

After Champlain's passage, the waters of Lake Champlain and Lake George just below it, which set the eastern boundary of the Adirondack country, were red with blood for the next 170 years. Blood of red men and white stained the pine duff on the forest floor by those lakes. A few Jesuit missionaries trod the Lake Champlain–Lake George route to constant torture from their Indian captors. Trappers from Montreal and from Fort Orange, later Albany, traveled the region. While a few men did settle on the fringes of the region in the middle of the 18th century, most of the history of that period is military history, of fighting between French and British and later British and American rebels for control of the lake route north and south.

Although the southern boundary of the Adirondack country is only 200 miles north of Manhattan and less than 50 north of Albany, it was not explored in any detail until the 1830s. Explorers had gone into the Northwest Territory as far as the Pacific before anyone even climbed Mount Marcy, the highest of the Adirondack peaks. The sources of the Columbia River were known 60 years before the northernmost source of the Hudson was finally located. The mountains were not named "the Adirondacks" until 1837. Less than 40 years later men were saying sadly that the Adirondack country, bristling with newly built summer hotels, was hunted out, timbered out, overrun with people, and ruined. When the country did develop, between 1840 and 1880, it developed fast.

Today almost every part has been trodden at one time or another by hikers, hunters, and visitors. Instead of being impassable no spot today is more than 10 miles from a road of some sort. The Adirondack country can be crossed by car, north to south or east to west, in three hours. Approximately a rectangle, it contains 5,000 square miles, which is roughly the size of Connecticut . . . .

Mountains, Lakes, Rivers

The Adirondack country is a varied land. Seen from the air, a series of high peaks at the center, most irregularly placed, run off almost to sea level on all sides. In 40 miles the land drops from 5,344 feet above sea level on Mount Marcy to 100 feet at the shores of Lake Champlain. Not all the region is mountain and lake. As the land slopes down from the higher altitudes in the northeast and the northwest, it levels off for a time into rolling country and broad plateaus.

To people who know the Alps or the Rockies the idea of calling the Adirondacks "mountains" may seem ridiculous; the city of Denver is higher than any Adirondack peak. They are not jagged brute rocks piercing the sky, with summits almost always cloud-wrapped. On clear days the round top of Marcy can be seen from 30 miles away. Almost all the Adirondack peaks have these rounded tops, worn by storm and time. . . .

While more than 100 peaks are higher than 3,500 feet above sea level, many seem only like giant bumps, for they take off from a plateau of 1,500 feet or more. The 46 that are more than 4,000 feet high represent the "high peaks." Almost all are crowded together in an area of 50 square miles, and topped by the summit of Marcy.

The many mountains have some things in common. Some have abrupt rocky slides, often rising out of lakes; these precipices may not be thousands of feet high, but even one 500 feet high, rising sheer, is quite a sight. As a group the mountains have little topsoil on them. Trees grow, but little farming has ever been done on their flanks. Another feature is the number of lakes found close to the mountains. The belief that between two mountains there must be a valley is not always true in the Adirondacks; likely as not, a lake is there instead. Finally, the interconnections of the various ranges are such that a man can climb up and down many peaks, one after the other, without coming down to the 2,500 foot level. . . .

The Adirondack people use their lakes, rivers, and woods, but, except for small boys on small peaks, they do not go in much for scaling the hills. No arrowheads or other relics have ever been found on mountaintops to show that the Indians climbed the peaks. Few pioneers did any mountain climbing; life was tough enough without that. Climbing as sport began after the announcement in 1837 that Marcy was the highest point in the state. Today it is the outsiders and the vacationists who do most of it. Thanks to the magnificent system of trails built by the Department of Conservation working with the Adirondack Mountain Club, climbing is more popular than ever today. Trails lead up most of the better-known peaks; along many of the paths are state-built lean-tos where hikers can spend the night. One favorite mountain hike is along the 135-mile trail from Lake Placid to Northville.

The existence of a marked trail does not mean therefore that the way is easy going. Climbing can be arduous, particularly on the more than 20 peaks over 4,000 feet that are still without trails. Those skilled enough to try unmarked ascents find exciting climbing on the many steep cliffs and precipices. The more daring, using regular Alpine equipment, try them each summer. In many places the rocks have been worn so smooth by slides that they offer few cracks for the pitons, the metal points which climbers use. In recent years winter climbing on snowshoes or skis has become popular. . . .

A view from any Adirondack height, even a lowly hill, or the view from an airplane over the region shows the second distinctive feature of the landscape, the tremendous number of lakes. The Adirondack country has more than 1,345 of them named, and more nameless. In the southwest quarter many are connected by inlets and outlets so that canoe trips of 100 miles can be made at will, broken only by a few portages of less than two miles each; at these carries today the

Conservation Department thoughtfully provides wheeled boat carriers. In the famous Fulton Chain, known to many children who have been summer campers and made a long canoe trip on these waters as the high spot of the summer, eight lakes are strung together like beads on a necklace.

Elsewhere the lakes are beside mountains, between mountains, and, in some cases, on mountains. The highest lake is Tear-of-the-Clouds, 4,400 feet high on the side of Marcy and the most northerly source of the Hudson. Many lakes are dotted with small tree-clad islands. Lake George has more than 200. Lower Saranac Lake has 50. Some few lakes have white sandy beaches but most are tree-girt to the waterline. . . .

. . . Lake Champlain is not usually counted as an Adirondack lake. If it were it would far surpass all of them in size and depth, for it is 107 miles long and 12 miles wide at its widest, with a depth of 400 feet at one place. The largest lake fully within the Blue Line is Lake George, 30 miles long. Next in order are Long Lake and Indian Lake.

The Adirondack lakes are of various sorts. Most have clear, clean water, spring-fed, with rocky shores. Because of their springs the water of the lakes is cold in summer although it may sometimes be 70° in a few places. In winter the lakes are covered with ice, sometimes 20 inches deep. At the bottom their winter temperature is a uniform 38°. Some of the smaller lakes are surrounded by swamp and mud and almost impossible to get at on foot in summer. Some were scooped out by glaciers and are small, neat ponds. Many, such as Long Lake, are the result of glacial widening of riverbeds, and are often long with narrow places; at some points Long Lake, in length 15 miles, is only 100 yards wide. Some of the lakes, like Cranberry and Flower in Saranac Lake village, are the result of damming a river or have been increased in size by such damming.

The naming of the lakes was as haphazard and unimaginative as the naming of the mountains. In a few cases Indian names were abandoned, as when some settler gave the name of Long Lake to what the Indians had called "Linden Sea." Early surveyors and settlers tagged on the first and handiest name which came to mind, with the result that there were many duplications, since so many of the lakes look round, muddy, or clear, and have duck and otter on them. The word "pond" is used quite as often as "lake." No one knows at what point of decreasing size a lake becomes a pond.

In the long list of Adirondack lakes, in addition to the well-known ones, are Single Shanty, Terror, Goose, Wild Goose, Whortleberry, Hog, Artist, Squaw, Poor, Big Slim, Little Slim, and three just plain Slim ponds. To confound visitors and natives, there are two Antediluvian ponds, 20 Long ponds, 10 East ponds, 16 Clear ponds, 20 Mud ponds, six

Mud lakes, seven Spring ponds, 10 Round ponds, 10 Duck ponds, 12 Otter ponds, along with one Pepper Box Pond and one Queer Lake. . . .

Seen casually, one Adirondack lake may look like another. No one man knows them all. To pick out the loveliest is impossible. From the highway on a hill at the south, Lake George is a magnificent sight. Blue Mountain Lake, with its many islands, the deep forest by its shore, its clear blue water reflecting the mountains nearby, is often called the loveliest lake of the lot—an opinion immediately challenged and hooted at by anyone who knows some other lake a little better.

Any Adirondack native will defend the right to call eminences of 5,400 feet "mountains," no matter what Colorado or Alpine people may say. He is not quite so sure that some of the streams deserve the name of "river." He has no doubt about the Hudson, rising on the side of Marcy, or the Raquette, the Saranac, the Oswegatchie, the Grass, and the Black, but he is uncertain about the other 20 and more "rivers," the Cold, the Bog, the Chazy, the Jordan, the Opalescent, the Chub, or the Cedar. At their mouths some of these streams may approach the common idea of river. Elsewhere they may often be only small mountain streams easily jumped by a deer and even by a hunter in pursuit.

These rivers carry much less water than in years past. Many a 19th-century story of adventure in the Adirondacks tells of pleasant boat trips down a number of the rivers; few people would try them today. The larger rivers and many of the small ones carried log runs in the spring that would be impossible on most of them today. That steadily decreasing volume of water has been noted in all Adirondack history. It is not a recent phenomenon but appeared after the first heavy lumbering.

The Hudson is the best known of the Adirondack rivers. Its northernmost source is more than 4,000 feet up on Marcy, in Lake Tear-of-the-Clouds. By the time the Hudson reaches Manhattan it is a sophisticated river, changing its mood many times. Below Luzerne, where the Adirondack foothills yield to rolling fields, it is broad and placid. At Glens Falls, out of the Adirondacks, it is a turbulent rapids and waterfall. At Troy it is dirty and bedraggled, showing no sign of the clear, green, mountain-water source whence it came. At Haverstraw it is a broad inland sea.

But up in the Adirondacks where it comes tumbling out of the mountains it is a gracious little stream that races over rounded pebbles and is all of ten feet wide. The children of the miners who work at Tahawus below Marcy cross back and forth, first carefully rolling up their jeans. The river that flows so majestically by the Palisades and on to its deep sea gorge may be the weary river of the poet at its mouth but it is fresh and young up where it begins. There it reflects the tamarack and the pine, and bears the little toy boats of the children. Far south it will reflect skyscrapers and carry ocean liners. It is still the same water, some of it, that has come gushing out of the ancient rocks of the Adirondacks.

More than any other stream, the Hudson helped to move the forest riches out to the mills. It carried lumber drives as early as 1813. During the mid-century most of the rivers of the Adirondacks were declared "public highways" for log driving by the state and log drivers were at work along them. Where rivers ran into lakes and then out into river again, the logs had to be floated through the lake in large booms to prevent them from piling up on shores. Today, shortage of water and scarcity of trained labor has made log driving forever a part of the Adirondack past. Trucks move the logs out of the woods faster, if less picturesquely.

The Adirondacks mark the water divide of the state. The same meadow on the shoulder of Marcy sends water south to the Hudson and north in the Ausable, which flows on to Lake Champlain and so to the St. Lawrence. This favorite two-pronged river of fishermen drops some 4,000 feet in covering its 50 miles. Near its mouth it runs through a chasm advertised 60 years ago as one of the natural wonders of the world, a miniature Grand Canyon, 150 feet high at some places and two miles long. Set conveniently by one of the main Adirondack highways, Ausable Chasm is still a tourist objective of the region. . . .

Each river has its own charms, although little traffic of any sort, even canoes, passes over them these days. The Raquette is the most meandering of rivers, coming out of Blue Mountain Lake through Long Lake. It flows 172 miles on to the St. Lawrence to cover a distance of perhaps 80 miles as the crow flies, and was once a favorite route for trips into the wilderness. Flowing south from Fulton Chain, the Moose connects more than 100 bodies of water, large and small. The Black River, flowing west out of the woods, has provided power and riches for the area around Watertown. The Oswegatchie, the Saint Regis, and the Schroon were all lumbermen's rivers in their day. Trout fishermen wade them in spring. The rest of the year the only sound along them is the rush of their own water, south to the Atlantic, north to the St. Lawrence. . . .

The Woods

Mountains and lakes may mark the region as unusual, but it is the woods, above all, that make the Adirondacks. They bring the summer people. They provide all or part of the income of many a family. For years it was believed that odors and chemicals borne on the air from the woods played an important part in curing the sick who came and found their health restored.

The Adirondack woods are not isolated patches but the ever present covering of the country. Now and then roads may run through a stretch of open country, but woods soon come to their sides, even on main roads. Driving them in spring and summer is like driving through green canyons. In many places, particularly on state land where the underbrush is never cleared, the woods seem impenetrable even a few feet back from the road. Woods frame almost every lakeshore. . . .

With a variation in altitude from almost sea level at Lake Champlain to more than five thousand feet on the high peaks, the Adirondack country has distinct forest zones. Red oak will grow in the lowland but not in the higher country. Balsam, tamarack, ash, cedar, and yellow birch are trees of the 1,500- to 2,000-foot plateau. Spruce and hemlock grow on the sides of the higher peaks where hardwoods disappear and the evergreens are eventually stunted. The top of Marcy is slightly above timberline; just below it dwarf balsams grow short and crooked but with as many as a hundred rings of growth, while on the peak is a genuine arctic or Alpine zone and many a rare plant. The southern border of the park also marks a dividing line in plant life. Poison ivy does not grow above it. The dogwood, so common to the south, dies in the Adirondack winter. The white pine does not do well below that line. . . .

Two characteristics mark the Adirondack woods. The first is the change in tree species. Because of changes in climate or for some other reason, in recent years the second growth has been largely hardwood, thus reducing the percentage of evergreens. After fires, inferior trees such as cherry and poplar are the first to come back and thrive; birches appear next, and beech, but other trees may not show for decades. While most of the woods seem thick and heavily grown, a large part, perhaps as much as 50%, has little or no timber worth the name. Except on the highest peaks, little is completely bare, but much is scrub growth, with many a meadow or sparsely grown clearing appearing in unexpected places. On the other hand, where lumbermen have worked on their own land or on leased land, fair second growth may show from "mamma trees," maples and spruces which have reseeded themselves. Parts of the Adirondacks that were cleared land 70 years ago are heavily and usefully wooded today. Such reforested farm land explains why, in places where trees are 60 years old and more, a hiker comes on a lone gnarly apple tree or even a lilac bush in the middle of deep woods. Nearby, usually, are the traces of the foundations of a house. But many parts of the woods still show in slash and vanished water resources where the 19th-century lumberman passed.

The second distinctive characteristic is the rich growth on the floor of the woods. Where no fires have destroyed the deposits of centuries, spring flowers are abundant, beginning with trilliums and lady's slippers. Ground pine is plentiful, along with partridge berry. Two years after storm damage or lumbering make a clearing, the open place can be a thick raspberry bramble. Ferns and mosses are abundant: 43 of the 60 varieties of ferns found in the state grow in the Adirondacks.

Of the various trees of the Adirondack woods, the tall white pine stands out as best loved and most prized. The Adirondack woods have other native pines, red and pitch, but the white pines tower over them as the symbol of the North Woods. Once they stood seven feet through at the base. Eight oxen had to be hitched up to budge one 13-foot log. A few old white pines still stand, either saved miraculously on state land or overlooked by the lumbermen.

The white pine often appears in early Adirondack history. In the 18th century the French cut suitable trees for ships' masts and spars. They were floated to Montreal, then shipped to France for the royal navy. The British were just as busy in the woods around Ticonderoga. Both the British and French ships that fought at Trafalgar may have had masts, spars, and planking from the Adirondack hills. The British continued to buy Adirondack pine after the Revolution and had it shipped to them down the Hudson, then by sailing vessel from New York. White-pine boards, sledded from the Lake George region to Albany and down the Hudson, were shipped to Europe and even to the West Indies in the early part of the 19th century. Adirondack white pine helped to build many an early American building in the seaboard cities.

By 1800 much of the great white pine along the shores of Lake Champlain was gone. By 1850 the great trees had been cut throughout the region and the amount of white pine taken from the woods fell off sharply. The thousands of feet timbered later came from second- and even third-growth trees. Today the state sets out millions of white-pine seedlings in an effort to return to the Adirondack country the glory of the dignified tree. Most of the seeds are handpicked from parent trees, but some are collected from hoards gathered by squirrels. Wherever the white pine grows in the woods, it is liable to a blight called Blister Rust. This mysterious spore disease, which must have wild currants or gooseberries nearby for part of its development, is kept under control. Many a taxpayer's dollar goes to pay for men to tramp the woods and weed out the wild currant.

As the white pine disappeared the red spruce took its place as the backbone of the woods and of the lumber industry. Some were giants in the early days. The average tree was 80 feet tall, with a diameter of eighteen inches and a ring count of 175 to 200 years. Sixty years ago one spruce was found near Lake Meacham in the northwest quarter that was 41 inches in diameter and overtowered the forest. It was later cut down for pulpwood.

The spruce entered into politics as the white pine never did. It was the decision of a pliant governor to let all spruce above a certain size on the forest preserve be lumbered that dramatized the need to protect the preserve, and brought about the "forever wild" amendment to the state constitution in 1894.

The most serious attack on the spruce was not the work of men who wanted it for lumber; it was, in fact, lightly timbered until the thick pine was gone, and even then only the largest trees were taken. The real attack came after 1867, when it was found that the long spruce fibers were by far the best raw material for paper pulp. Thereafter, the take was merciless and heavy. . . .

The spruces darken as winter comes and give the hills their black-green look, but two other trees add their coloring at other times. Maples fire the hills in autumn, birches set them shining in summer or winter. Of the four kinds of maples the hard maple is the most useful for lumber and sugar. The favorite birch of the woods is the canoe or paper birch, a dead-white chalky tree with black streaks on its bark which punctuates the lake shores and stands on the distant hills like an exclamation mark. The yellow birch, no less striking with its golden bark, is the favorite tree for furniture making and other commercial uses.

These and another score of species, from ash to ironwood and balsam, make up the Adirondack woods as they stretch from Poke O'Moonshine in the northeast to the shores of West Canada Creek in the southwest. They clothe the valleys, hills, and swamps. They give the land its color, through the greens of spring, the fire reds of autumn, and the blackness of winter.

3 New York City

Introduction

by Theodore Fischer

A freelance travel writer and editor, Theodore Fischer has worked on numerous publications and is the author of two books, Cheap/Smart Travel *and* Cheap/Smart Weekends. *He lives in New York City.*

Why does New York City attract more visitors—more than 17 million per year—than any city in the world? Consider its credentials:

In terms of background and education, New York is one of America's oldest cities, the first U.S. capital, and the nerve center of culture. New York has Broadway, the crème de la crème of American theater, and a vast supporting network of other theaters, repertory groups, playhouses, and workshops. In terms of serious music, New York is home to the nation's preeminent institutions: the Metropolitan Opera, the New York Philharmonic, the American Ballet Theatre, Carnegie Hall. New York also reigns as the capital of jazz. The Metropolitan Museum of Art and the Museum of Modern Art set national standards for the visual arts and no living artists can be considered truly first rate until they've had a New York gallery opening.

Regarding work experience, the New York City streets serve as a guide to provide emblems for half the industries in the world. "Wall Street" stands for the world of finance and banking. "Madison Avenue" means the advertising business—and thus the hub of graphic arts, photography, and modeling. "Seventh Avenue" means the garment industry, women's and children's fashions. New York is America's media capital: It has the headquarters of the three major television networks, national newspapers like the *Wall Street Journal* and the *New York Times,* the wire services, most book publishers, and almost every national magazine. Throw in the United Nations, three major airports, and one of the busiest seaports in the world and you get a city that obviously works as hard as it plays.

As far as visitors are concerned, this list of the biggest, best, and most important translates into a place where the energy overflows from museums, lofts, and office towers out into the street. First-time visitors are invariably astounded by New York's vibrant 24-hour street life—not only the rambunctious vehicles and breakneck pedestrians but all the commerce that transpires on the sidewalk. Food vendors (hot dogs and knishes are most common, but more exotic selections abound) operate on virtually every corner of the commercial districts. Traders of various goods (books, umbrellas, counterfeit designer watches are always in stock) turn the middle of a block into a bazaar. In residential neighborhoods, merchandise from vegetable markets (now mostly operated by recent immigrants from Korea) and newsstands spill across the sidewalk.

Beyond that, New York possesses an intangible aura that has something to do with the assumption that New York is the major league, big time, center stage—where everybody's watching and they really keep score. Some of that derives from the kinds of industries concentrated here. Financial news is New York news; so is news about the fashion industry, advertising, and publishing. And because of the concentration of media people and equipment, local New York stories can quickly escalate into national and international events.

Celebrities are omnipresent here; you can spot them doing mundane things like shopping, hailing taxis, or strolling down

Fifth Avenue. Witnessing a "shoot" location that you'll soon see in a feature film, TV show, or commercial is almost a common occurrence. To paraphrase the catchline of the Plaza Hotel, you get the feeling "nothing unimportant ever happens in New York," which makes everything that goes on here feel special.

For New Yorkers—roughly 8 million in the city proper and another 10 million in the metropolitan area—this sense of importance translates into a spirit of professionalism. New Yorkers take pride in being good—in their minds the best—at whatever it is they choose to do. It also begets an infuriating strain of provincialism that makes them infuriatingly incurious about the rest of the country, which they refer to as "the boonies" and loosely divide into New England, California, and the Middle West.

A word about New Yorkers: They're not as fierce as they look. Penetrate their defense system (a polite "Excuse me" usually works) and you'll probably encounter a person willing to provide assistance and information. New Yorkers are particularly empathetic to the needs of out-of-towners in distress: Almost all of them were out-of-towners themselves at some point and they never forget how it feels.

Certainly, New York's big-time mentality engenders some negative features. Since so many come here to live and to visit, prices for everything (particularly hotels and restaurants) are usually higher than elsewhere in the country. And while crime is hardly as inevitable as the cheap-shot comedians would have you believe, it's something to be aware of *at all times*. A real bottom-line New York–style point is that you can find high prices and crime in a lot of other places. But the volume and diversity of attractions, entertainment, the stores, the art, the music, and the intangible but very real sense of being in the place where it is and always has been happening—that you can get only in New York.

Arriving and Departing

By Plane
Airports and Airlines
Virtually every major U.S. and foreign airline serves New York's three airports: **LaGuardia Airport, John F. Kennedy International Airport,** and **Newark International Airport.** U.S. airlines serving the New York area include: America West, American, Braniff, Continental, Delta, Eastern, Midway, Northwest, Pan Am, TWA, United, and USAir.

Between the Airports and Midtown
LaGuardia Airport is located in the borough of Queens eight miles northeast of midtown Manhattan. **Taxis** cost $12–$18 plus toll (up to $2.50) and take 20–40 minutes. Group taxi rides to Manhattan are available at taxi dispatch areas just outside baggage claims during most travel hours (no service Saturdays or holidays). Group fares are $7–$9 per person (plus share of tolls) depending on destination. Call 718/784–4343 for more information.

Carey Express (tel. 718/632–0500) buses depart for Manhattan from LaGuardia every 20–30 minutes 6:45 AM–midnight; a 20- to 30-minute ride. They stop at 42nd Street and Park Avenue, directly opposite Grand Central Terminal. A **shuttle bus** serves the New York Hilton, Sheraton City Squire, and Marriott Marquis hotels; it's a short cab ride to other midtown hotels. Fare $7.50;

The Five Boroughs

40

WESTCHESTER

MT. VERNON

YONKERS

Long Island Sound

PORT WASHINGTON

Manhasset Bay

Pelham Bay Park

Hart I.

City I.

Eastchester Bay

KINGS POINT

GREAT NECK

GREAT NECK ESTATES

NASSAU

LITTLE NECK

Throgs Neck

Throgs Neck Bridge

Cross Island Pkwy.

Clearview Expwy.

BAYSIDE

Whitestone Bridge

East River

COLLEGE POINT

FLUSHING

Shea Stadium

USTA Nat'l Tennis Center

Flushing Meadow–Corona Park

Long Island Expwy.

Grand Central Pkwy.

ST. ALBANS

LITTLE NECK

FOREST HILLS

THE BRONX

I-95

Van Cortlandt Park

Fordham University

Bronx Park

Bronx Zoo

Crotona Park

Yankee Stadium

HUNTS POINT

Rikers I.

La Guardia Airport

Northern Blvd.

JACKSON HEIGHTS

QUEENS

ASTORIA

Triboro Bridge

Grand Central

LONG ISLAND CITY

Queensboro Bridge

Central Park

MANHATTAN

Harlem R.

RIVERDALE

Spuyten Duyvil

George Washington Bridge

FORT LEE

Hudson River

CLIFFSIDE PARK

WEST NEW YORK

NORTH BERGEN

Palisades Pkwy.

ENGLEWOOD CLIFFS

ENGLEWOOD

TENAFLY

BERGEN

PARAMUS

NEW JERSEY

4

I-95

I-80

EAST RUTHERFORD

Meadowlands Sports Complex

17

3

46

5 miles

5 km

0

N

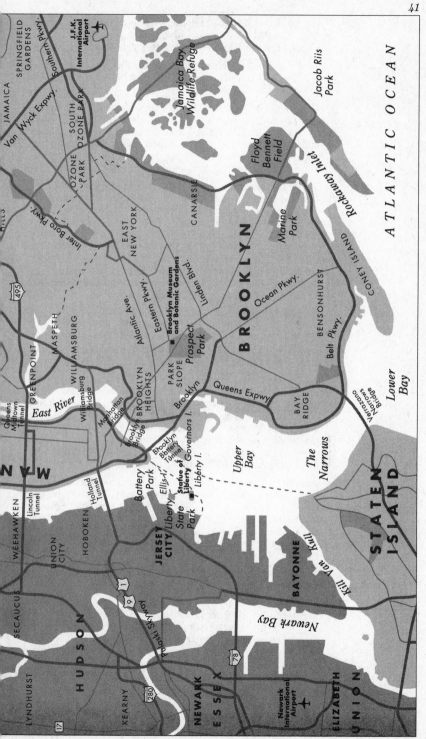

pay the driver. **Giraldo Limousine** serves major Manhattan hotels. Fare $9 per person; make arrangements at Ground Transportation Center or use courtesy phone.

John F. Kennedy International Airport (JFK), also in Queens, is 15 miles southeast of midtown. Taxis cost $24–$30 plus tolls (up to $2) and take 35–60 minutes.

Carey Express (tel. 718/632–0500) buses depart for Manhattan every 30 minutes from all JFK terminals. The ride takes about one hour to 42nd Street and Park Avenue (Grand Central Terminal), and the fare is 9.50. **Giraldo Limousine** also serves major Manhattan hotels, $11 per person. Make arrangements at Ground Transportation Counter or use courtesy phone.

The **JFK Express** (tel. 718/858–7272) is a special subway service from the Howard Beach station near JFK Airport to downtown Brooklyn, lower Manhattan, Greenwich Village, and midtown, terminating at 57th Street and Sixth Avenue. Shuttle buses from JFK terminals to the Howard Beach station depart every 20 minutes 6:03 AM–12:52 AM. The ride to 57th Street terminus takes 50 minutes. Trains have luggage space and plenty of transit police. Fare is $6.50 including connection to subway system; pay on train. (To reach JFK, you pay $1 to enter subway system and an additional $5.50 on board the train.)

Newark International Airport is located in Newark, NJ, 16 miles southwest of midtown. Taxis cost $28–$30 plus tolls ($3) and take 20–45 minutes. "Share and Save" group rates available for up to four passengers between 8 AM and midnight; make arrangements with taxi dispatcher.

NJ Transit Airport Express (tel. 800/247–7433) buses depart every 15–30 minutes for Port Authority Terminal, 42nd Street and Eighth Avenue. From there it's a short cab ride to midtown hotels. A 30- to 45-minute ride. Fare, $7; buy ticket inside terminal. The **Olympia Trails Express** (tel. 212/964–6233) buses to the World Trade Center and Grand Central Terminal depart every 20 minutes 5 AM–midnight. Travel time to WTC is 25 minutes, 45 minutes to GCT. Fare, $7; pay driver.

By Train **Amtrak** (tel. 800/872–7245) offers frequent service within the Northeast Corridor—Boston to Washington. Trains arrive and depart from Pennsylvania Station (31st to 33rd Sts., Seventh and Eighth Aves.). Amtrak trains also serve Penn Station from the Southeast, Midwest, and Far West. Purchase tickets from travel agent or in terminal; reservations required on some runs.

Amtrak service from upstate New York, Montreal, and the **Lake Shore Limited** from Chicago use Grand Central Terminal (42nd St. and Park Ave.).

Metro-North Commuter Lines (tel. 212/532–4900) serve Grand Central from the northern suburbs and from Connecticut as far east as New Haven. The **Long Island Railroad** (tel. 718/454–5477) has service from points around Long Island to Penn Station. Also at Penn Station, **New Jersey Transit** (tel. 201/460–8444) provides frequent service from the north and central parts of the state.

By Bus All long-haul and commuter bus lines feed into the **Port Authority Terminal,** a mammoth multilevel facility occupying a two-square-block area between 40th and 42nd streets and Eighth and Ninth avenues. Though modernized and reasonably clean, the terminal can be a harrowing place due to the large number of vagrants loitering there. Especially on night arrivals, plan to move swiftly through the terminal out to the Eighth Avenue taxi lines.

For information on service into or out of the Port Authority Terminal, tel. 212/564–8484. Some of the bus lines serving New York include **Greyhound** (consult local information for a number in your area), **Adirondack and Pine Hill Trailways** from upstate New York (tel. 914/339–4230); **Bonanza Bus Lines** from New England (tel. 401/331–7500); **Martz Trailways** from northeastern Pennsylvania (tel. 717/829–6911); **NJ Transit** from all over New Jersey (from northern NJ, tel. 800/772–2222; from southern NJ, tel. 800/582–5946; in the Northeast, 800/526–4514); **Peter Pan Bus Lines** from New England (tel. 413/781–2900); and **Vermont Transit** from New England (tel. 802/862–9671).

By Car The **Lincoln Tunnel** (I–495), **Holland Tunnel,** and **George Washington Bridge** (I–95) connect to the New Jersey Turnpike system and points west. The Lincoln Tunnel leads to midtown Manhattan, the Holland Tunnel to lower Manhattan, the George Washington Bridge to northern Manhattan. All arteries require a toll ($3 for cars) eastbound into New York; westbound is free.

From Long Island the **Midtown Tunnel** (I–495) and **Triborough Bridge** (I–278) are the most direct arteries to Manhattan. Both require tolls ($2.50 for cars) in both directions.

From upstate New York, the city is accessible via the **New York (Dewey) Thruway** (I–87) (toll) and **Major Deegan Expressway** (I–87) through the Bronx and across the **Triborough Bridge** (toll). From New England, the **Connecticut Turnpike** (I–95) connects to the **New England Thruway** (I–95) (toll), the **Bruckner Expressway** (I–278), and the **Triborough Bridge** (toll) to upper Manhattan.

Be aware that driving within Manhattan can be a nightmare of gridlocked streets and aggressive motorists. Street parking is almost nonexistent in the midtown area and parking lots are costly. If you do drive, plan to garage your car and use public transit and taxis within Manhattan.

Getting Around

New York is a city dense with major attractions and small finds best explored by foot. New York also covers a vast amount of territory and, since driving from place to place within Manhattan is impractical, you will need some form of motorized transit.

By Subway The 300-mile subway system is the fastest and cheapest way to get around the city. It operates 24 hours a day and serves most visitor attractions.

The subway costs $1, with reduced fares for disabled people and seniors. You must use a token to enter. They are sold at token booths that are *usually* open at each station. It's advisable to stock up on tokens since the token booth may not be open or, if open, may have long lines. Tokens can also be used on city buses. A token permits unlimited transfers within the system.

Manhattan Subways

Subway Lines

▬▬▬▬	BMT
─────	IND
▪▪▪▪▪▪	IRT

Free subway maps are available at token booths upon request. For route information, ask the token clerk, a transit policeman, or any knowledgeable-looking rider. Before embarking on a subway or bus trip, call 718/330–1234 (a local call, 25¢ from pay phones) for 24-hour information.

Although crowded cars, dirty stations, unreliable service, and lurking danger have given the New York subway system a deservedly negative image, the system is showing steady improvement. Don't write off the subway—it really is colorful and millions ride it every day without incident—but stay alert and avoid using it during rush hours. If you must ride late at night, stay in a car that has other riders.

By Taxi Taxis are usually easy to hail on the street or from a line in front of major hotels. Rates are posted on the door and inside the cab. At present, taxis cost $1.15 for the first ⅛ of a mile, 15¢ for each ⅛ of a mile thereafter, and 15¢ for each minute not in motion. A 50¢ surcharge is added to rides begun between 8 PM and 6 AM. There is no charge for extra passengers. Taxi drivers also expect a 15% tip. Barring performance above and beyond the call of duty, don't feel obliged to give them more.

By Horse-drawn Carriage Horse-drawn hansom cabs can usually be found along Central Park South (59th St. between Fifth and Eighth Aves.). Although most passengers use them for jaunts through Central Park or down Fifth Avenue, buggy rides can be tailored to your demands. Horse carriages operate in all but the most extreme hot and cold (blankets provided) weather. And the quality of the trip depends much on the disposition of the driver. Horse carriages have official rates of $17 for the first half hour and $5 for each additional 15 minutes. Drivers may ask for more and expect a tip: Settle upon a rate before setting forth.

By Bus Most buses follow easy-to-understand routes along the Manhattan grid. Routes go uptown or downtown on the north–south avenues, east and west on the major two-way crosstown streets. Most bus routes operate 24 hours, but service is very infrequent late at night. Buses are fine for seeing sights but traffic jams can make rides maddeningly slow.

Bus fare is $1 in change only (no pennies, no half dollars) or a subway token. You can request a free transfer good for one change to an intersecting route. Legal transfer points are listed on the back of the transfer. Transfers have time limits of at least two hours, often longer. Transfers cannot be used to enter the subway system.

Each of the five boroughs of New York has separate bus maps and they can be hard to find. They are occasionally available in subway token booths but never on buses themselves. Your best bets are the Convention and Visitors Bureau at Columbus Circle or the information kiosks in Grand Central Terminal and Penn Station.

Important Addresses and Numbers

Tourist Information The **New York Convention and Visitors Bureau** at Columbus Circle (58th St. and Eighth Ave.) provides a wealth of free information: brochures, subway and bus maps, listings of hotels and weekend hotel packages, free tickets for TV shows, and discount coupons for Broadway shows. Drop in or contact them before you arrive. *2 Columbus Circle, New York, NY 10019; tel. 212/397–8222. Open weekdays 9–6, closed weekends and holidays. Times Square (at 42nd St.) information booth open Wed.–Fri. 9–6, weekends 10–6. Closed holidays.*

Parks Department   Tel. 212/360–1333.

Consumer Affairs   Tel. 212/577–0111.

Travelers Aid   Tel. 212/944–0013.

Emergencies   For all police, fire, or medical emergencies, call 911.

Call **Doctors on Call, 24-hour housecall service** (tel. 212/737–2333). Near the midtown area, 24-hour emergency rooms are open at **St. Luke's-Roosevelt Hospital** (458 W. 59th St., tel. 212/523–4000) or **St. Vincent's Hospital** (Seventh Ave. and 11th St., tel. 212/790–7000). For a referral, call the **Dental Emergency Service** (tel. 212/679–3966; after 8 PM, 212/679–4172).

24-Hour Pharmacy   **Kaufman's Pharmacy** (Lexington Ave. and 50th St., tel. 212/755–2266).

Guided Tours

Orientation Tours   Take a crash course in Manhattan geography with a **Circle Line Cruise.** Once you've finished the three-hour, 35-mile circumnavigation of Manhattan you'll have a good idea of where things are and what you want to see next. *Pier 83, west end of 42nd St., tel. 212/563–3200. Fare: $15 adults, $7.50 children under 12. Operates daily early Mar.–Nov.*

At South Street Seaport's Pier 16 you can take two- or three-hour voyages aboard the iron cargo schooner *Pioneer* (tel. 212/669–9416). You can take 90-minute tours of New York Harbor aboard the sidewheeler *Andrew Fletcher* or re-created steamboat *DeWitt Clinton* (tel. 212/964–9082).

For a shorter excursion, the **TNT Express,** a new hydroliner, will show you the island of Manhattan in only an hour. *Pier 11, south of South Street Seaport, tel. 212/244–4770. Fare: $10 children under 12, $18 adults, $16 seniors. Boats depart weekdays 11 AM and 2 PM, weekends 10, 12, and 2.*

The Gray Line (tel. 212/397–2600) offers different city bus tours plus cruises and day trips to Brooklyn, West Point, and Atlantic City. Tours leave from Gray Line Terminal, 900 Eighth Ave. between 53rd and 54th streets. **Short Line Tours** (tel. 212/354–5122) offers a number of bus tour options out of a terminal at 166 W. 46th Street. **Manhattan Sightseeing Bus Tours** (tel. 212/869–5005) has 10 different tours from a terminal at 150 W. 49th Street. Reservations necessary.

Island Helicopter (Heliport at E. 34th St. and East River, tel. 212/683–4575) offers flyover options, from $30 for 16 miles to $139 for over 100 miles. From the west side, **Manhattan Helicopter Tours** (Heliport at W. 30th St. and Hudson River, tel. 212/247–8687) has tours $35–$144.

Special-Interest Tours   **Backstage on Broadway** (tel. 212/575–8065) takes you behind the scenes of a Broadway show and introduces you to show people. Reservations mandatory. **Gallery Passports** (tel. 212/686–2244) admits you to artists' studios and lofts and other art attractions in or near Manhattan. **Soho Art Experience** (tel. 212/219–0810) offers tours of Soho's architecture, galleries, shops, and artists' lofts. **Doorway to Design** (tel. 212/221–1111) tours fashion and interior design showrooms, as well as artists' studios. **Harlem Your Way!** (tel. 212/ 690–1687) has daily walking tours and Sunday gospel trips to one of the most vibrant areas of the city. **Lou Singer Tours** (tel. 718/875–9084, 7–11 PM) focuses on Brooklyn—"Beautiful Brownstone Brooklyn," "Brooklyn Roots" (with occasional inroads to Manhattan and the Bronx), "Noshing in New York," "Little Old New York."

Walking Tours   **Sidewalks of New York** (33 Alan Terrace, Suite #2, Jersey City, NJ 07306; tel. 201/517–0201) hits the streets from various thematic angles—"Ye Old Tavern Tour," "Celebrity Home Tour," "Final Resting Places of the Rich and Famous." Two-hour tours are offered weekend days and some evenings year-round. **Adventure on a Shoestring** (300 W. 53rd St., New York, NY 10019, tel. 212/265–2663) is a 27-year-old organization that explores unique New York neighborhoods. Tours are scheduled periodically. **New York Walk-About** (tel. 212/582–2015 or 914/834–5388) has two- to three-hour walking tours of Manhattan and outer borough neighborhoods each weekend.

The **Municipal Art Society** (tel. 212/935–3960) operates a series of bus and walking tours. The **Urban Park Rangers** (tel. 212/397–3080) offers weekend walks and workshops, most of them free, in city parks. The **92nd Street YMHA** (tel. 212/996–1105) always has something special going on weekends. Weekly expeditions of the **Shorewalkers of New York** (tel. 212/663–2167) explore various stretches of shoreline in the New York area. Joyce Gold's **Historywalks** (tel. 212/242–5762) focus on particular sections of mostly Lower (below 23rd St.) Manhattan. Each participant in a **New-York Historical Society New-York Walk** (tel. 212/873–3400) receives a map and reading list for areas covered in two-hour tours. Receptions follow walks.

The most comprehensive listing of tours offered during a particular week is published in the "Other Events" section of *New York* magazine.

Self-Guided   The **New York Convention and Visitors Bureau** provides three
Walking Tours   pamphlets that cover historical and cultural points of interest in Manhattan and Brooklyn: the *I Love NY Visitors Guide and Map, 42nd Street—River to River,* and *Brooklyn on Tour.* Pick up brochures from the bureau's information center *2 Columbus Circle, tel. 212/397–8222; open weekdays 9–6.*

The **Municipal Art Society of New York** has prepared a comprehensive *Juror's Guide to Lower Manhattan: Five Walking Tours* on behalf of those who must often kill a lot of time while serving in downtown courthouses. Pamphlet includes tours of Lower Manhattan and Wall Street; City Hall District; Chinatown and Little Italy; South Street Seaport; and TriBeCa. The pamphlet can be purchased at Urban Center Books (tel. 212/935–3595, 457 Madison Ave. at 51st St., New York, NY 10022).

Personal Guides   Contact **Around Town Inc.** (tel. 212/532–6877), **Guide Service of New York** (tel. 212/408–3332), or **Go Tours/Freedom Tours** (tel. 718/482–6600).

Manhattan Neighborhoods

UPPER WEST SIDE

W. 86th St.

Central Park West

Columbus Ave.

Central Park

W. 72nd St.

West End Ave.

Broadway

UPPER EAST SIDE

E. 86th St.

E. 79th St.

E. 72nd St.

Park Ave.

E. 65th St.

E. 59th St.

FDR Dr.

Roosevelt Island

Queensboro Bridge

W. 57th St.

E. 57th St.

11th Ave.

10th Ave.

9th Ave.

8th Ave.

5th Ave.

3rd Ave.

1st Ave.

Midtown Tunnel

W. 42nd St.

E. 42nd St.

Lincoln Tunnel

MIDTOWN

W. 34th St.

7th Ave.

Ave. of the Americas

Broadway

Madison Ave.

Lexington Ave.

2nd Ave.

QUEENS

W. 23rd St.

E. 23rd St.

East River

W. 14th St.

E. 14th St.

GREENWICH VILLAGE

EAST VILLAGE

W. Houston St.

E. Houston St.

Williamsburg Bridge

Holland Tunnel

SOHO

LITTLE ITALY

Canal St.

West St.

W. Broadway

CHINA-TOWN

Manhattan Bridge

Chambers St.

W.

Brooklyn Bridge

Hudson River

NEW JERSEY

LOWER MANHATTAN

BROOKLYN

0   440 yards

0   400 meters

Battery Park

Exploring New York City

Manhattan presents a split personality in finding your way around the city. North of 14th Street, the city is as rational as you could hope to find. Streets form a regular grid pattern. Avenues run north (uptown) and south (downtown). Crosstown streets run east and west. The sole exceptions are Broadway, a diagonal from 14th to 79th streets, and the thoroughfares along both rivers.

If you don't know the nearest cross street, you can calculate the location of an avenue address by using the formulas in the Manhattan Address Locator (*see* below).

Below 14th Street, all bets are off. Streets are either diagonals aligned with the existing or past shoreline, or the twisting descendants of ancient cow paths. Logic won't help you below 14th Street; only a good street map and good directions will.

Lower Manhattan

Numbers in the margin correspond with points of interest on the Lower Manhattan map.

Small in acreage, Lower Manhattan falls into three basic sightseeing categories: Historic—The Dutch established the New Amsterdam colony here in 1625 and the first capital of the United States was located in the area. Financial—Wall Street is here, which means the New York and American stock exchanges plus innumerable banks and other financial institutions. Waterfront—Boats depart for Staten Island, the Statue of Liberty, and various ferry and excursion routes. The waterfront also inspired the South Street Seaport Museum project.

❶ Begin at the **Staten Island Ferry Terminal** at the southernmost tip of Manhattan. For subway riders that's just outside the "South Ferry" station on the IRT No. 1 line.

The **Staten Island Ferry** is still the best deal in town. The 20- to 30-minute ride across New York Harbor provides scenic views of the Manhattan skyline, Statue of Liberty, **Verrazano Narrows Bridge** (world's longest suspension bridge), and the New Jersey coast—yet it costs only 25¢ *round-trip. Note:* Commuters love the ferry service's swift new boats, but they ride low in the water and have limited outside deck space. If one of the low-riders is next in line, you might want to bypass that one and wait for a more commodious and accommodating old-timer.

Directly north of South Ferry stands the **Shrine of St. Elizabeth Ann Seton** (7–8 State St.). The red-brick Federal-style town house was built in 1783 as the home of the wealthy Watson family. Mother Seton dwelled there and gave birth to her fifth child in what is now the rectory. Mother Seton went on to found the Sisters of Charity, the first American order of nuns, and in 1975 became the first native-born American saint. Masses are held daily.

❷ Detour a few blocks to the east for **Fraunces Tavern,** a combination restaurant/bar/museum that occupies a Colonial (brick exterior, cream-colored portico and balcony) tavern built in

Manhattan Address Locator

To locate avenue addresses, take the address, cancel the last figure, divide by 2, add or subtract the key number below. The answer is the nearest numbered cross street, approximately. To find addresses on numbered cross streets, remember that numbers increase east or west from 5th Ave., which runs north–south.

Ave. A... *add 3*

Ave. B...*add 3*

Ave. C...*add 3*

Ave. D...*add 3*

1st Ave....*add 3*

2nd Ave....*add 3*

3rd Ave.... *add 10*

4th Ave.... *add 8*

5th Ave.

Up to 200...*add 13*

Up to 400...*add 16*

Up to 600...*add 18*

Up to 775...*add 20*

From 775 to 1286... *cancel last figure and subt. 18*

Ave. of the Americas...*subt. 12*

7th Ave....*add 12*

Above 110th St... *add 20*

8th Ave....*add 9*

9th Ave....*add 13*

10th Ave....*add 14*

Amsterdam Ave. ...*add 59*

Audubon Ave. ...*add 165*

Broadway (23–192 Sts.)...*subt. 30*

Columbus Ave. ...*add 60*

Convent Ave....*add 127*

Central Park West... *divide house number by 10 and add 60*

Edgecombe Ave. ...*add 134*

Ft. Washington Ave. ...*add 158*

Lenox Ave......*add 110*

Lexington Ave....*add 22*

Madison Ave....*add 27*

Manhattan Ave. ...*add 100*

Park Ave....*add 34*

Park Ave. South ...*add 8*

Pleasant Ave....*add 101*

Riverside Drive... *divide house number by 10 and add 72 up to 165 Street*

St. Nicholas Ave. ...*add 110*

Wadsworth Ave. ...*add 173*

West End Ave. ...*add 59*

York Ave....*add 4*

1719 and restored in 1907. Best-remembered as the site of George Washington's farewell address to his officers celebrating the British evacuation of New York in 1783, Fraunces Tavern contains two fully furnished period rooms and other displays of 18th- and 19th-century American history. *Broad and Pearl Sts., tel. 212/425-1778. Closed weekends. Restaurant open for lunch and dinner weekdays. Museum open Oct.–May, weekdays 10–4, Sun. 12–5. Suggested contribution: $2.50 adults, $1 students, seniors, children; free Thurs.*

To the west of South Ferry lies **Battery Park,** a verdant landfill loaded with monuments and sculpture at Manhattan's green toe. The **East Coast Memorial** consists of a statue of a fierce eagle and eight granite slabs upon which are inscribed the names of U.S. casualties in the Western Atlantic during World War II. The steps of the memorial afford a fine view of all the salient features of **New York Harbor:** From left to right, **Governor's Island,** a Coast Guard installation; hilly **Staten Island** in the distance; the **Statue of Liberty** on Liberty Island; **Ellis Island,** New World gateway for generations of immigrants; the old railway terminal in **Liberty Park** in Jersey City, NJ.

❸ No New York public building has gone through more personality changes than **Castle Clinton.** It was built in 1811 as a defense for New York Harbor on what was then an island 200 feet from shore. In 1824 it became Castle Garden, an entertainment and concert facility that hit its high point in 1850 when more than 6,000 people attended the U.S. debut of the "Swedish Nightingale," Jenny Lind. After landfill connected it to the shore, Castle Clinton became, in succession, an immigrant processing center, aquarium, and, at present, a restored fort, museum, and ticket office for the Statue of Liberty ferry.

Castle Clinton will soon be the departure point for ferries to **Ellis Island,** reopening in 1990 after a $140-million restoration. Now a national monument, Ellis Island was a federal immigration facility between 1892 and 1954 that processed 17 million men, women, and children—the ancestors of more than 40% of the Americans living today. *Admission prices and times not available at press time. Tel. 212/883-1986.*

❹ A perennial major attraction, the popularity of the **Statue of Liberty** surged following its 100th birthday restoration in 1986. On Liberty Island you can visit the **Statue of Liberty Museum,** which exhibits a pictorial history of the statue and immigrants, then take an elevator 10 floors to the top of the pedestal. The strong of heart and limb can climb another 12 floors to the crown. However, you may have to wait in line for up to three hours for the "pleasure." *Tel. 212/363-3200. Round-trip fare, $3.25 adults, $1.50 children. Daily departures on the hour 9–5; extended hours in summer.*

At the end of a broad mall outside the landward entrance to Castle Clinton stands the **Netherlands Memorial,** a quaint flagpole depicting the bead exchange that established Fort Amsterdam in 1626. Inscriptions in English and Dutch describe the event which supposedly took place across State ❺ Street on the site of the imposing granite **U.S. Customs House.** Gaze up at the double row of statuary adorning the facade. The lower row depicts each of the continents; the higher row represents major trading cities of the world (for example, the lady to the left of the central shield is Lisbon).

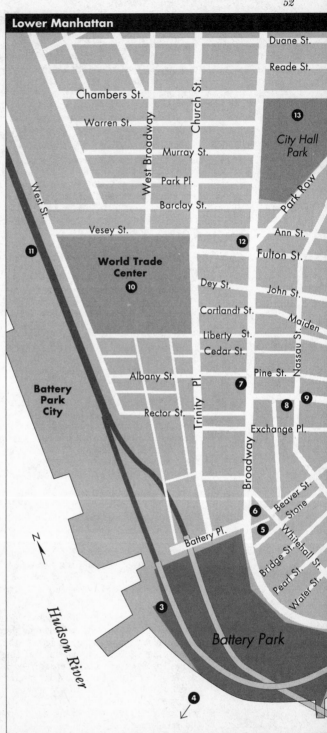

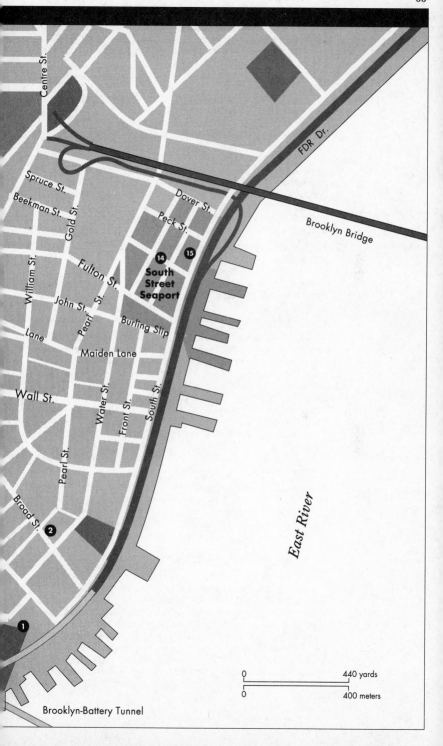

Centre St.

FDR Dr.

Spruce St.

Beekman St.

Gold St.

Dover St.

Peck St.

Brooklyn Bridge

William St.

Fulton St.

John St.

Pearl St.

14

15

South Street Seaport

Lane

Burling Slip

Maiden Lane

Wall St.

Water St.

Front St.

South St.

East River

Pearl St.

Broad St.

2

1

0 — 440 yards

0 — 400 meters

Brooklyn-Battery Tunnel

6 **Bowling Green** is an oval greensward that in 1733 became New York's first public park. On July 9, 1776, a few hours after citizens learned about the signing of the Declaration of Independence, rioters toppled the statue of King George III that had occupied the spot for years.

Time Out **Martins Pub** represents a genre of New York eating and drinking establishments: a no-frills bar that serves generous drinks and solid meals at reasonable prices. There's cafeteria-style service for hearty sandwiches (corned beef, pastrami, sliced steak) and down-to-earth steam-table specialties. *11 Broadway at Bowling Green.*

Broadway begins at Bowling Green, and **25 Broadway** used to be headquarters of the Cunard steamship line. The ground floor now houses a spectacular post office adorned with sea gods and mermaids romping across the vaulted ceiling and walls. Frescoes depict great vessels of yore and richly detailed wall maps of the seven seas.

7 Jet-black **Trinity Church** was New York's first Anglican Parish (1646). The present structure (built 1846) ranked as the city's tallest building for most of the last half of the 19th century. Alexander Hamilton is buried beneath a huge white pyramid in the southside graveyard; Robert Fulton, inventor of the steamboat, lies nearby. *Broadway and Wall St., tel. 212/602–0848. Tours weekdays at 2; free 30- to 40-min concerts Tues. 12:45.*

Probably the most famous one-third mile in the world, **Wall Street** was where stock traders congregated for business along the sidewalks or at tables beneath a sheltering buttonwood tree. The tree is gone and the august main entrance of Wall Street's focal point, the **New York Stock Exchange,** is around
8 the corner on Broad Street. Enter at 20 Broad Street and, after what can be a lengthy wait, take an elevator to a third-floor Visitor's Center. A self-guided tour, informative slide shows, video displays, and human guides may help you interpret the seeming chaos on the trading floor below. *20 Broad St., tel. 212/ 656–5167. Admission free. Open weekdays 9:20–4. Tickets available at 12 Broad St., 9:15–3:45.*

A regal statue of George Washington stands upon the spot where he was sworn in as first President in 1789. The building then located there, Federal Hall, was demolished when the cap-
9 ital moved to Philadelphia. The current **Federal Hall National Memorial** is a stately period structure containing museum exhibits on New York and Wall Street. *26 Wall St., tel. 212/264– 8711. Admission free. Open weekdays 9–5.*

Walk through Federal Hall, turn right onto Pine Street, and you quickly reach a plaza at the foot of the 65-story **Chase Manhattan Bank Building.** The perimeter of Chase Plaza has become an impromptu flea market—merchandise and fast-food—and the interior holds a striking potato-chiplike Dubuffet sculpture, *Trees.* Catercorner from the Chase Building, **Louise Nevelson Plaza** occupies the triangle formed by William Street, Liberty Street, and Maiden Lane. The Plaza contains benches and four abstract Nevelson sculptures of black welded steel, three midsize pieces, and one huge 70-footer.

Sit in the plaza and contemplate the wealth contained within the **Federal Reserve Bank** directly across the street. This bank looks like a bank ought to look: gray, solid, imposing, absolutely impregnable—which it better be since it holds a quarter of the world's gold reserves. Tours must be arranged at least one week in advance. *33 Liberty St., tel. 212/720–6130. Admission free. Open weekdays.*

⑩ Continue west on Maiden Lane to the **World Trade Center,** a 16-acre complex that contains New York's two tallest buildings, a modern hotel, a subterranean shopping center, and a huge main plaza. The Observation Deck is located on the 107th floor of 2 WTC, but the ride up takes only 58 seconds. The view is potentially 55 miles; signs posted at the ticket window disclose how far you can see that day and whether the outdoor deck is open. *2 World Trade Center, tel. 212/466–7377. Admission: $3.50 adults, $1.75 children. Open daily 9:30–9:30.*

You get the same view with a costly meal at **Windows on the World** atop 1 WTC; prices are somewhat less steep for breakfast or drinks and "grazing" at the **Hors d'Oeuvrerie at Windows on the World** (tel. 212/938–1111).

The **Commodities Exchange Center** affords a strategic overview of maneuvers in the silver, cotton, and cocoa markets. *4 WTC, 9th floor, tel. 212/938–2025. Admission free. Open weekdays 9:30–3.*

The rock and soil excavated for the World Trade Center became the land beneath **Battery Park City,** 100 new acres of Manhattan accessed by overpasses across West Street on the western border of WTC. Battery Park City is an instant neighborhood complete with office buildings, including the headquarters of *The Wall Street Journal* (no, it's not—and never was—on Wall Street), high-rise apartment houses, low-rise, old-looking town houses, and a modest selection of restaurants and shops. Gazing at the Hudson from the placid riverside promenade, you may find it hard to remember that the pandemonium of the New York Stock Exchange is less than a half-mile away.

⑪ Battery Park City is also home to the **World Financial Center,** a mammoth granite-and-glass commercial complex designed by arthitect Cesar Pelli. Inside the four-tower structure is a mélange of 30 upscale shops (including Ann Taylor, Barneys New York, Mark Cross, and Godiva Chocolatier) and a palatial public space called the Winter Garden. The room, adorned by a vaulted-glass roof, an immense stairway, and 16 palm trees (carefully transplanted from Borrigo Springs, California), hosts an array of performances through the center's Arts and Events program (tel. 212/945–2600).

⑫ Across Church Street from WTC stands **St. Paul's Chapel** (Broadway and Fulton St.), the second-oldest structure (1766) in Manhattan and the only survivor of the Colonial era. With George Washington's own pew on display, St. Paul's is open throughout the day for prayer, rest, and meditation.

Head north on Broadway to the so-called Cathedral of Commerce, the name bestowed upon the ornate 1913 **Woolworth Building** (Park Pl. and Broadway). At 60 stories, and at one time the world's tallest building, this agglomeration of architectural styles topped with Gothic spires still houses the Woolworth corporate offices. Notice the gargoyles set into arches in the lobby ceiling. They represent the founder, Frank W. Woolworth, pinching his pennies and the architect, Cass Gilbert, contemplating a model of his creation.

Park Row, the street across the City Hall Park from the Woolworth Building, was known as "Newspaper Row" from the mid-19th to early 20th centuries, when most of the city's 20 or so daily papers had offices there. In its day triangular **City Hall Park** has hosted hangings, riots, meetings, and demonstrations. Now it mostly welcomes brown baggers and pigeon fanciers.

❸ City Hall (built 1803–11) is unexpectedly sedate, graceful, small-scale, charming. Its exterior columns reflect the classical influence of Greece and Rome and the handsome cast-iron cupola is crowned with the statue of Lady Justice. The interior centers around a sweeping marble double staircase. The wood-paneled City Council Chamber in the east wing is small and clubby; the Board of Estimate Chamber to the west displays Colonial paintings; the Governor's Room contains a distinguished collection of historical portraits and furniture.

Behind City Hall stands the magnificently ornate **"Tweed Courthouse,"** actually an anonymous municipal office building nicknamed after the infamous Boss William Marcy Tweed, who allegedly absconded with more than $10 million of the $14 million budgeted for the project in 1872.

Directly east of City Hall is the **Brooklyn Bridge,** New York's oldest and best-known span. When built in 1883 it was the world's longest suspension bridge and the city's tallest structure. Walking across Brooklyn Bridge is an unforgettable experience. It's just over a mile long and thousands of commuters make the trip whenever the weather allows. Located in the center of the span, the walkway passes beneath the towers and through the filigreelike cables.

On the Brooklyn side the span bisects the expansive Watchtower complex operated by the Jehovah's Witnesses. Take the first exit to Brooklyn Heights, a charming brownstone neighborhood *(see* Outer Boroughs), or continue on to downtown Brooklyn. Catch a subway or taxi back to Manhattan.

❹ The **South Street Seaport** is an 11-block historic district that encompasses shopping centers, historic ships, cruise boats, a multimedia presentation, art galleries, and innumerable places to eat. Sure, it's "touristy"—it was developed by the Rouse Corporation, which similarly restored waterfronts in Boston and Baltimore—but it does have a New York flair.

Schermerhorn Row (2–18 Fulton St.), with early 1800s Georgian/Federal-style warehouses, comprises the Seaport's architectural centerpiece. Ground floors are occupied by shops and bars. The cobblestone street is closed to traffic and, on Friday evenings during summer, young professionals from Wall Street congregate for shoulder-to-shoulder cocktail hours. Markets have occupied the **Fulton Market Building** site across the way since 1822. The rebuilt structure now contains a variety of shops and stalls—even a fishmonger.

The 15 restored buildings in **Museum Block** across Front Street include Bowne & Co., a reconstructed working 19th-century print shop, and the museum shops along twisting Cannon Row. The **Trans-Lux Seaport Theater** presents the multiscreen "Seaport Experience" by day. At night it becomes an avant-garde cinema, showing foreign and American films. *210 Front St., tel. 212/608–7889. Seaport Experience admission: $4.75 adults, $3.25 children, $4 seniors. Hourly Mon.–Thurs. 10:30–3:30; Fri.–Sun. 10:30–6:30.*

Cross South Street to **Pier 16** to view the historic ships: the second-largest sailing ship in existence, *Peking;* the full-rigged *Wavertree;* and the lightship *Ambrose.* To visit the ships you have to buy a ticket to the South Street Seaport Museum; admission also accesses landward exhibit galleries, walking tours, Maritime Crafts Center, films, and other Seaport events. *Tickets available at the ticket booth on Pier 16 and Visitors Center at Fulton and Water Sts., tel. 212/669–9424. Admission: $5 adults, $4 seniors, $3 students, and $2 children. Open daily 10–5, longer in summer.*

Pier 16 is also the departure point for the 90-minute **Seaport Harbor Line Cruise** (tel. 212/385–0791; fare: $10 adults, $6 children). Notice how two large cargo containers used on modern-day freighters are transformed into a toy shop and a cafe.

Time Out Pier 17 is a massive shopping center built on a pier over the East River. Skip the overpriced seafood joints and head for the third-floor **Promenade Food Court.** Cuisine is shopping-mall eclectic: Third Avenue Deli, Pizza on the Pier, Wok & Roll, the Yorkville Packing House for meat, the Salad Bowl for greens, Bergen's Beer & Wine Garden among others. Better than the food are the views of the river, Brooklyn Bridge, and Brooklyn Heights from the tables in a glass-walled atrium or outdoors when weather permits.

As your nose may already have told you, the Seaport area still has a working fish market. Although the city has tried to relocate the hundreds of fishmongers of the **Fulton Fish Market** to the South Bronx, the area is still a beehive of delivering, buying, and selling. Get up early (or stay up late) if you want to see it. The action begins around midnight and ends by 8 AM. *Organized tours are offered Apr.–Oct. first and third Thurs., 6–7:45 AM. Tickets $12. Reservations required, tel. 212/669–9416.*

Lower East Side

"Waves of immigration" is the phrase usually used to describe the population of the Lower East Side. During the mid-19th century, Irish fleeing the potato famine took refuge here. Droves of Jews from Eastern Europe arrived between 1870 and 1920. More recently an influx of Hispanic and Chinese residents has superimposed its personality on the neighborhood. "Melting pot" is another term often heard, but it's hardly accurate. As long as the immigrants stayed on the Lower East Side (roughly the area bordered by Canal and Houston streets, the Bowery, and the East River—the northern sector of the old neighborhood has been upgraded into the East Village), they retained much of their Old Country culture and little "melting" took place.

The best reason for venturing into the Lower East Side these days is for the shopping, specifically bargains on clothing and ethnic foods. The legendary pushcarts may have disappeared but small shops spread in all directions from the unofficial hub of **Orchard and Delancey streets.** Count on bargains of at least 20%–30% off list—even more if you know how to haggle. Because many businesses are operated by religious Jews, most shops and stalls are closed on Saturday, but Sunday is the busiest day of the week.

The Lower East Side divides into a number of shopping districts. **Orchard Street** (plus Delancey and Rivington streets) is for clothing, sometimes quite fashionable attire meanly displayed on sidewalk racks and in disorganized heaps. Quality may be top-notch, but watch out for factory seconds. **Grand Street** between the Bowery and Chrystie Street is the "Street of Brides" and bridegrooms. It also has a lot of cut-rate linen and textile dealers. Notorious in legend and song, **the Bowery** is still a run-down strip of bars and flophouses. But it's also the city's Lighting District and a great place to find all sorts of electrical goods.

The indoor **Essex Street Markets** (Essex and Delancey Sts.) perhaps most closely approximate the spirit of the old Lower East Side. The cavernous buildings are crammed with privately owned stalls displaying an enormous array of clothing, textiles, hardware, and food delicacies. Choose a pickle right out of the pickle barrel or take home some ox feet. The market also has the city's smallest barber shop, a one-chair/one-barber unisex operation.

Time Out **Katz's** is one of the few delis that still hand-carves its corned beef and pastrami. Signs advise customers to "Send a salami to your boy in the Army" and sternly forbid tipping the countermen—but for you they'll make an exception. Cafeteria or table service. *205 E. Houston St. at Ludlow St.*

Chinatown

Numbers in the margin correspond with points of interest on the SoHo/Little Italy/Chinatown map.

Chinatown "officially" includes the area east of Broadway, north of the Civic Center, and south of Canal Street, a heavily traveled artery that links the Holland Tunnel (to New Jersey) and the Manhattan Bridge (to Brooklyn). In recent years, however, Chinatown has gained an influx of immigrants from the People's Republic of China, Taiwan, and especially Hong Kong. Real estate values have skyrocketed and Chinatown now spills north into Little Italy and east into the formerly Jewish Lower East Side.

Canal Street abounds with markets bursting onto the sidewalks with stacks of fresh seafood, odd-shaped vegetables in unearthly shades of green, and crisp roasted ducks hanging in the windows. Shop in slightly less frantic **Kam Man** (200 Canal St.), a bi-level supermarket that sells fresh and canned imported groceries, herbs, and the kind of cutlery and furniture familiar to patrons of Chinese restaurants.

Mott Street, Chinatown's main drag, is a picturesque narrow byway crammed with souvenir shops, food sellers and restaurants, and hordes of pedestrians all hours of the day or night. Within the few dense blocks of Chinatown, hundreds of restaurants serve every imaginable type of Chinese cuisine, from simple fast-food noodles or dumplings to sumptuous Hunan, Szechuan, Cantonese, Mandarin, and Shanghai feasts. How can you choose? Ask any New Yorker, each of whom is certain he or she has "discovered" the absolute best.

Amid the Mott Street hubbub stands the **Church of the Transfiguration** (Mott and Mosco Sts.). An imposing Georgian structure built in 1801 as the Zion Episcopal Church, it is now a Chinese Catholic church that delivers mass in Cantonese and Mandarin. Farther down Mott Street, the low-tech **Chinatown Museum** explains the symbolism of flowers, chopsticks, and incense. A quiz game tests your knowledge of matters Chinese. *8 Mott St., tel. 212/964–1542. Admission: $1 adults, 50¢ children. Open daily 10:30 AM–midnight.*

Double back to Pell Street, a narrow lane of wall-to-wall restaurants with bold neon signs. Turn onto **Doyers Street,** a twisting lane that houses an extraordinary density of barber shops. Duck into **Wing Fat,** a bizarre new multilevel shopping mall that snakes up and around and out to Chatham Square.

② **Chatham Square** is anything but square: It's more like a fun-house maze where 10 converging streets create pandemonium for motorists and nightmares for pedestrians. A Chinese arch honoring Chinese casualties in American wars occupies an island in the eye of the storm.

To examine remnants of Chinatown's pre-Sino past, walk down St. James Place to the **Shearith Israel** graveyard, the first Jewish cemetery in the United States. When consecrated in 1656, the area was considered outside the city. Walk a half-block farther, turn left on James Street, and you reach **St. James Church,** an 1837 Greek Revival edifice where Al Smith (former New York governor and Democratic presidential candidate) served as altar boy.

Return to Chatham Square and head up the Bowery to **Confucius Plaza.** The name applies both to the open area monitored by a statue of Confucius and the high-rise apartment complex at his back. At 18 Bowery (corner of Pell St.) stands one of Manhattan's oldest homes, a 1785 Federal/Georgian mélange built by meat wholesaler Edward Mooney.

Time Out The Chinatown equivalent of fast-food stores is noodle houses that serve Chinese noodles with meat, fish, shrimp, or vegetables. **Shanghai Snack Bar,** at the end of a shopping arcade that links the Bowery and Elizabeth Street, concocts 20 varieties of this filling low-priced dish as well as outstanding dumplings. *14 Elizabeth St.*

Head up the Bowery and you'll see the grand arch and horseshoe-shaped colonnade at the entrance to the Manhattan Bridge (built 1905). The corner of the Bowery and Canal Street used to be the hub of New York's Diamond District. Most of those jewelry dealers have moved uptown (to 47th St. between Fifth and Sixth Aves.), but a substantial number of jewelers occupy shops on the Bowery and the north side of Canal Street. All prices are negotiable.

Chatham Square, **2**
Chinatown Museum, **1**
420 West Broadway, **5**
Haughwout
Building, **6**
Museum of
Holography, **8**
New Museum, **7**
Old St. Patrick's
Church, **4**
Umberto's Clam
House, **3**

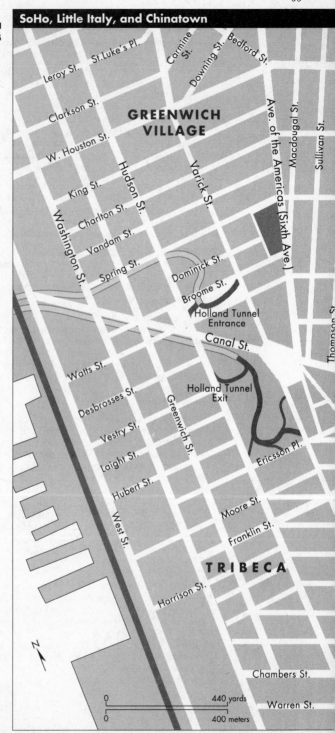

SoHo, Little Italy, and Chinatown

Carmine St.
Downing St.
Bedford St.
Leroy St.
St. Luke's Pl.
Clarkson St.
Ave. of the Americas (Sixth Ave.)
Macdougal St.
Sullivan St.
**GREENWICH
VILLAGE**
W. Houston St.
Hudson St.
Varick St.
King St.
Charlton St.
Washington St.
Vandam St.
Spring St.
Dominick St.
Broome St.
Holland Tunnel
Entrance
Canal St.
Thompson St.
Watts St.
Holland Tunnel
Exit
Desbrosses St.
Vestry St.
Greenwich St.
Laight St.
Ericsson Pl.
Hubert St.
Moore St.
West St.
Franklin St.
TRIBECA
Harrison St.
N
Chambers St.
0   440 yards
0   400 meters
Warren St.

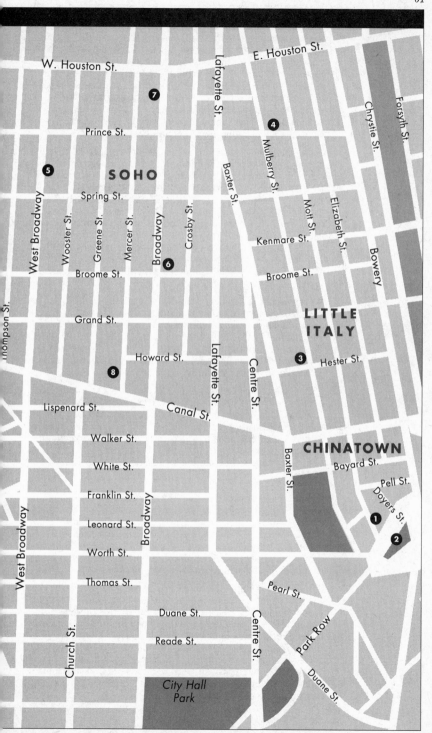

W. Houston St.

E. Houston St.

Lafayette St.

Chrystie St.

Forsyth St.

7

Prince St.

Mulberry St.

4

5

SOHO

Spring St.

Baxter St.

West Broadway

Wooster St.

Greene St.

Mercer St.

Broadway

Crosby St.

Kenmare St.

Mott St.

Elizabeth St.

Bowery

Broome St.

6

Broome St.

Thompson St.

Grand St.

LITTLE ITALY

Howard St.

8

Lafayette St.

Centre St.

3 Hester St.

Lispenard St.

Canal St.

Walker St.

White St.

CHINATOWN

Baxter St.

Bayard St.

Pell St.

Doyers St.

Franklin St.

Broadway

Leonard St.

1

Worth St.

2

Thomas St.

West Broadway

Pearl St.

Duane St.

Church St.

Centre St.

Reade St.

Park Row

Duane St.

City Hall Park

Little Italy

Begin a tour of Little Italy at Canal and Mulberry streets. Mulberry Street forms the heart of Little Italy; in fact at this point it's virtually the entire body. An estimated 98% of area inhabitants in 1932 were of Italian birth or heritage; in recent years, however, Chinatown has encroached upon the neighborhood. The spread of Chinatown became so threatening that merchants and community leaders of the Little Italy Restoration Association (LIRA) negotiated a truce in which the Chinese agreed to leave Mulberry Street an all-Italian street.

Today Mulberry Street between Broome and Canal streets consists entirely of restaurants, cafes, bakeries, imported food shops, and souvenir stores. Former residents keep coming back
③ to Little Italy's venerable institutions. At **Umberto's Clam House** (129 Mulberry St. at Hester St., tel. 212/431–7545), gangster Joey Gallo fell victim to mob justice in 1973. Peaceful now, Umberto's specializes in fresh shellfish in spicy tomato sauce. Another Little Italy institution, **Puglia** (189 Hester St., tel. 212/966–6006) seats guests at long communal tables for sing-alongs with house entertainers and moderately priced southern Italian specialties served with pitchers of homemade wine.

At the corner of Mulberry and Grand streets, **E. Rossi & Co.** (est. 1902) is an antiquated little shop that sells housewares, espresso makers, embroidered religious postcards, and "Kiss Me I'm Italian"–style buttons and T-shirts. Down the street is **Ferrara's** (195 Grand St., tel. 212/226–6150), a 97-year-old pastry shop that ships its creations—cannoli, peasant pie, Italian rum cake—all over the world.

④ Little Italy's oldest institution is **Old St. Patrick's Church** (Mulberry and Prince Sts.). Built in 1815 as New York's original Roman Catholic cathedral, it burned down in 1866, but part of the original facade was incorporated into the rebuilt church. In 1879 it was replaced by "new" St. Patrick's at Fifth Avenue and 50th Street.

SoHo

Twenty years ago SoHo—the area SOuth of HOuston ("Howston") Street bounded by Broadway, Canal Street, and Sixth Avenue—was just about left for dead. A 1962 City Club of New York study called this neighborhood of small 19th-century factories and warehouses "the wastelands of New York City" and "commercial slum number one." Numerous industrial fires earned it the nickname "Hell's Hundred Acres."

Two factors changed the image and fate of SoHo. One was the discovery that the area contained perhaps the world's greatest concentration of cast-iron buildings. An architectural rage between 1860 and 1890, cast-iron buildings required no massive walls to bear the weight of the upper stories. They were produced from standardized molds to mimic any architectural style—Italianate, Victorian Gothic, and neo-Greek, to name but a few styles visible in SoHo. Lighter and cheaper than stone, they eliminated load-bearing walls to gain interior space and to make possible larger windows.

The large, well-lighted spaces in those cast-iron buildings attracted many artists, a leading factor of the SoHo renaissance. Although at first it was illegal for artists to inhabit their lofts, a 1971 municipal zoning law was enacted to permit residence. Now artists certified by the city Department of Cultural Affairs may live in SoHo lofts but they had better be certified by bankers as well: The median 2,000-square-foot loft rents for $3,250 a month and sells for $535,000.

Today, SoHo offers architecture and art, stylish shops, and intriguing places to eat and drink. Action focuses on West Broadway, which on Saturday turns into a parade of high-style shoppers and gallery-hoppers. South on West Broadway from Houston Street, **Circle Gallery** (468 West Broadway) spotlights a number of artists at a time and sells posters and jewelry. **Suzanne Bartsch** (456A West Broadway) is a bizarre Far Eastern setting for British designed clothing. **Victoria Falls** (451 West Broadway) sells authentic antique and reproduced women's clothing including fine lingerie and hand-knit sweaters.

❺ Four hundred twenty **West Broadway** is one address with four separate galleries: **Leo Castelli Gallery** displays the big names of modern art; **Sonnabend Gallery** has important American and European artists; the **49th Parallel** features Canadian artists; **Charles Cowles Gallery** has fine painting, sculpture, and photography. The **Mary Boone Gallery** (417 West Broadway) displays what's hot in contemporary art. The **O.K. Harris Gallery** (383 West Broadway) has become known for exhibits of photo-realism and unusual sculpture.

The renovated interior of a landmark building dating back to the Civil War has been turned into the **SoHo Emporium** (375 West Broadway), a 35-shop mall for innovative designers and merchants. Wares include jewelry, leatherwear, furs, lamps, and handmade accessories, much of which is produced by young designers on hand to demonstrate their skills. The purple-hued space provides plenty of park benches for resting tired shoppers' feet.

Time Out The **Manhattan Brewing Company** is a boisterous converted factory setting for good food and great beer. Seven kinds of 100% natural beer are freshly brewed right on the premises (though not in the huge copper vats on view in the Tap Room). Reasonably priced menu selections include chili, burgers, Irish stew, and grazing fare like Buffalo wings, fried zucchini, and potato skins. *40–42 Thompson St. at Watts St.*

SoHo's most exemplary cast-iron architecture lies east of West Broadway. Head east on Broome Street and cross Wooster Street, which is paved with Belgian blocks, a somewhat smoother successor to cobblestones. The **Gunther Building**, with graceful curving window panes, stands at the southwest corner of Broome and Greene streets. Go north on Greene Street to No. 72–76, the so-called **King of Greene Street,** a five-story Renaissance-style cast-iron building with a projecting porch of Corinthian columns. Today the King (now clad in yellow) houses three art galleries—**Ariel, Condeso Lawler, M–13**—plus **The Second Coming,** a department store of "vintage"—too old for "second-hand," not old enough for "antique"—clothing and furniture.

Continue east on Broome Street to view a classic of the cast-iron genre, the 1857 **Haughwout Building** (488 Broadway at Broome St.). Inspired by a Venetian palace, this blackened five-story "Parthenon of Cast Iron" contained the world's first commercial passenger elevator, a steam-powered device invented by Elisha Graves Otis.

The Broome–Broadway intersection is a few blocks from SoHo's two unusual museums. The **New Museum** shows experimental, often radically innovative work by unrecognized artists. It will display nothing more than 10 years old. *583 Broadway between Houston and Prince Sts., tel. 212/219–1355. Suggested admission: $2.50 adults, $1.50 students, seniors, and artists. Open Wed.–Sun. noon–6, Fri. and Sat. to 8.*

The Museum of Holography has a permanent exhibit on the history of holograms, three-dimensional photographs created by laser beams. The science-show/art gallery also shows a film on holography and hosts three changing exhibits a year. The gift shop has a fine selection of 3-D art and souvenirs. *11 Mercer St. (near Canal St.), tel. 212/925–0581. Admission: $3 adults, $2.75 students, $1.75 children and seniors. Open Tues.–Sun. 11–6.*

Greenwich Village

Numbers in the margin correspond with points of interest on the Greenwich Village and the East Village map.

Considered by many as Manhattan's most livable neighborhood, Greenwich Village has undergone pronounced personality changes over the years. During the last half of the 19th century, the Village was one of New York's most fashionable addresses. Henry James's *Washington Square* depicted high-society Village people. In the 1920s it became a bawdy place where artists and writers could find inexpensive flats and everyone could find a speakeasy. Beatniks during the '50s and hippies in the '60s and '70s dominated the cultural image of the area. Now, as throughout Manhattan, high rents have priced out all but the most affluent writers and artists. Today the quiet streets and handsome town houses of Greenwich Village are inhabited by professionals, students, and other New Yorkers who want to spice up the flavor of small-town life with the bright lights of the big city.

Begin a tour of Greenwich Village at Washington Arch in **Washington Square,** at the foot of Fifth Avenue. Built in 1892 to commemorate the 100th anniversary of George Washington's presidential inauguration, the original arch stood a half-block north of its present site. The permanent arch was constructed in 1906; the statues—*Washington at War* (left) and *Washington at Peace* (right)—were added in 1913. Muscleman Charles Atlas posed for *Peace.*

Washington Square started out as a cemetery principally for yellow-fever victims; an estimated 10,000–22,000 bodies lie beneath the surface. In the early 1800s it became a parade ground and site of public executions, but by the end of the century it was the green centerpiece of a fashionable residential neighborhood. By the early 1980s, however, Washington Square had deteriorated into a tawdry place dominated by drug dealers and users. Lately, community pressure motivated a police crackdown that banished the druggies and made the square again safe for Frisbee players, street musicians, skateboarders, jugglers, sitters, strollers, and a twice-a-year (May and September) weekend art fair.

Turn north on MacDougal Street and walk a half-block to **MacDougal Alley,** a cobblestone private street (note the fence with locked gate) where 19th-century stables and carriage houses have been converted into charming homes adorned with gaslamps.

Eighth Street, the main commercial strip of Greenwich Village, is a charmless strip of fast-food purveyors, poster and record shops, and glitzy boutiques. For more authentic Village atmosphere, go north on Sixth Avenue to **Balducci's** (Sixth Ave. and Ninth St.), a full-service gourmet department store that evolved from Louis Balducci, Sr.'s vegetable stand. The family-owned establishment markets more than 80 Italian cheeses, 50 kinds of bread, foods, and a prodigious selection of fresh seafood.

The triangle formed by W. 10th Street, Sixth Avenue, and Greenwich Avenue originally held a greenmarket, jail, and the magnificent courthouse, now the **Jefferson Market Library.** Critics called the courthouse's hodgepodge of styles "Venetian," "Victorian," or "Italian"; Villagers, noting the alternating bands of red brick and granite, dubbed it "Lean Bacon Style." Over the years, the structure has housed a number of government agencies—public works, civil defense, census bureau, police academy. It was on the verge of demolition when public-spirited citizens turned it into a public library in 1967.

Take Christopher Street from the southern end of the library triangle a few steps east to **Gay Street.** During Prohibition these small old (circa 1810) row houses were a strip of speakeasies. Ruth McKinney lived and wrote *My Sister Eileen* in the basement of No. 14 and Howdy Doody was designed in the basement of No. 12.

At the end of Gay Street go west on Waverly Place to the midstreet island occupied by the **Northern Dispensary,** an institution that since 1831 has provided health care (first free, now inexpensive) for the needy. The **Lion's Head** (59 Christopher St.) is a renowned hangout for writers. At **Sheridan Square** Christopher Street becomes the heart of New York's gay community and the location of many intriguing boutiques.

West of Seventh Avenue the Village turns into a postcard-perfect town of twisting tree-lined streets and quaint homes. Follow Grove Street off Sheridan Square past the home of poet Hart Crane (No. 45) to the house at the corner of Grove and Bedford streets, one of the few clapboard structures in the Village—wood construction was banned as a fire hazard in 1822. Grove Street curves in front of an iron gate that accesses **Grove Court,** an enclave of brick-fronted mid-1800s town houses. Built originally as apartments for employees of neighborhood hotels, Grove Court now shelters a somewhat more affluent crowd: A town house there recently sold for $3 million.

Time Out A totally unmarked doorway on the west side of Bedford Street between Grove and Barrow streets leads to **Chumley's,** a place that has changed little since its origin as a 1920s speakeasy and

Greenwich Village and the East Village

Cherry Lane
Theater, **4**
Father Demo
Square, **5**
Jefferson Market
Library, **2**

Public Theater, **6**
St. Mark's Church-in-
the-Bouwerie, **7**
St. Marks Place, **8**
Sheridan Square, **3**
Tompkins Square, **9**
Washington Square, **1**

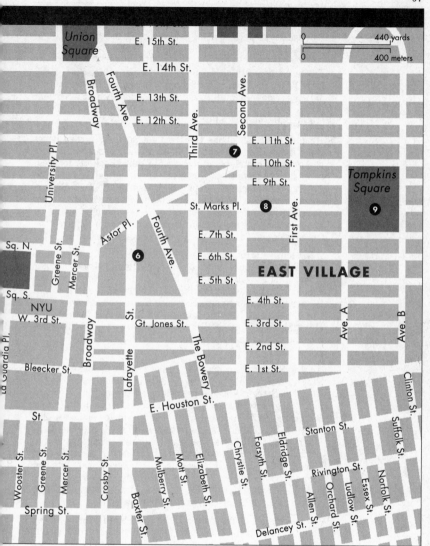

hangout for writers like John Steinbeck, John Dos Passos, Ring Lardner, and James Joyce. Menu features burgers, English-style specials, and a weekend brunch. *86 Bedford St. at Barrow St.*

The building at 77 Bedford Street is the oldest house in the Village (1799). The house next door at 75½ Bedford Street was not only the residence (at different times) of poet Edna St. Vincent Millay and John Barrymore but is also New York's narrowest house—only 9½ feet wide.

4 Heading west on Commerce Street you soon reach the **Cherry Lane Theater,** one of the first Off-Broadway houses and the site of American premieres of works of O'Neill, Beckett, Ionesco, and Albee. Across the street stand two identical brick houses separated by a garden. Popularly known as the **Twin Sisters,** legend has it that the houses were built by a sea captain for two daughters who loathed one another. Less dramatic historical record insists they were built by a milkman who required the two houses and an open courtyard to facilitate his work.

Head south on Hudson Street to **St. Luke's Place,** a row of classic 1860s town houses shaded by graceful ginkgo trees. Former Mayor Jimmy Walker lived at No. 6 and those lampposts are "Mayor's Lamps" sometimes placed in front of the residences of former New York mayors. Theodore Dreiser wrote *An American Tragedy* at No. 16, and No. 12 is the residence of the Huxtable family of the "Bill Cosby Show." At least that's the house depicted in the credits: the Huxtables "really" live in Brooklyn.

Across Seventh Avenue, St. Luke's Place becomes Leroy Street, which terminates in an old Italian neighborhood at Bleecker Street. Amazingly unchanged throughout the various Village alterations, Bleecker Street, between Sixth and Seventh avenues, is filled with old-style bakeries (**Zitos,** 259 Bleecker St.), butcher shops (**Ottomanelli's,** 285 Bleecker St.), pastry shops, fish stores, vegetable markets, pizza stands, and **5** restaurants. Activity here focuses on **Father Demo Square** (Bleecker St. and Sixth Ave.), once a cluster of pushcarts and still the site of the **Church of Our Lady of Pompei** where Frances Xavier "Mother" Cabrini, the first American (though not native-born American) saint, often prayed.

Across Sixth Avenue you reach the stretch of Bleecker Street depicted in songs by Bob Dylan and other '60s-era folksingers. Standing in the shadow of New York University, the area around the intersection of Bleecker and MacDougal streets attracts a young crowd to its cafes, bars, jazz clubs, coffeehouses, Off-Broadway theaters (Provincetown Playhouse, Minetta Lane Theater), cabarets (Village Gate), fast-food stands, and unpretentious restaurants.

Time Out The area around Bleecker and MacDougal streets has to be the coffeehouse capital of America. These traditional Village mingling and people-watching "scenes" offer sidewalk seating whenever weather is even tolerable, coffee-based drinks, pastries, and sandwiches. Favorite haunts: **Caffe Dante** (79 MacDougal St.), **Caffe Reggio** (119 MacDougal St.), **Le Figaro Cafe** (186 Bleecker St.), and **Caffe Lucca** (228 Bleecker St. at Sixth Ave.).

East Village

Time and gentrification have transformed the area bounded by
14th Street on the north, Fourth Avenue/the Bowery on the
west, Houston Street on the south, and the East River from the
northern reaches of the immigrant-filled Lower East Side to
the East Village. Until recently the East Village was one of the
last places in Manhattan where artists, writers, actors, and
marginally employed others could live relatively inexpensively.
Although booming real-estate prices have made apartments
here as costly and scarce as apartments elsewhere in Manhattan, in a way the area has the best of both worlds. In the East
Village, the restaurants, shops, and galleries that have accompanied the influx of new residents are superimposed upon the
colorful trappings of both the old world and the counterculture.

To explore the East Village, begin at the intersection of Eighth
Street, Fourth Avenue, Astor Place, and St. Mark's Place.
Works of modern sculpture occupy traffic islands in the square.
One island contains a massive black cube sculpted by Bernard
Rosenthal inexplicably entitled *Alamo*. Another island bears
an ornate Beaux Arts uptown subway entrance to the IRT No.
6 line. Weather permitting, the sidewalks on the southern edge
of Astor Place turn into a makeshift flea market.

Heading south on Lafayette Street, you quickly encounter **Colonnade Row**. Fronted by marble Corinthian columns, these
run-down 1833 row houses were first inhabited by John Jacob
Astor and Cornelius Vanderbilt. In 1854 Astor opened the
city's first free library in the imposing structure directly across
❻ the street, a building which now houses Joseph Papp's **Public
Theater**. The Public's six playhouses and cinema present such
hits as *A Chorus Line* and the *Pirates of Penzance*, plus challenging avant-garde work. It is currently in the midst of a six-
year Shakespeare marathon that, for the first time in America,
will present all 37 plays consecutively. *425 Lafayette St., tel.
212/598–7150. Tickets cost $25 for regular performances, $30
for Shakespearean productions. Half price QuikTix are available at 6 PM (1 PM for matinees).*

Cooper Square is named after Peter Cooper, an industrialist
who in 1859 founded an institution to provide free technical education for the working class and to function as a forum for
public opinion. The brownstone **Cooper Union Foundation
Building** at Astor Place and Fourth Avenue was the first structure to be supported by steel railroad rails—rolled in Cooper's
own plant. Cooper Union still offers tuition-free education and
an active public affairs program; a basement art gallery presents changing exhibits on history and design.

Surma, The Ukrainian Shop (11 E. Seventh St.) reminds you
that the East Village is basically a Ukrainian neighborhood of
onion-domed churches, butcher shops, bakeries, and restaurants serving hearty middle-European fare. This small and
friendly place sells all things Ukrainian: books, magazines, and
cassette tapes; greeting cards; musical instruments; painted
eggs and Surma's own brand of egg coloring; and an exhaustive
array of peasant blouses.

Veering away from St. Marks Place and Third Avenue,
Stuyvesant Street crosses what had been Governor Peter
❼ Stuyvesant's "bouwerie" or farm. It ends at **St. Mark's Church-**

in-the-Bouwerie, a 1799 fieldstone country church appended with a Greek Revival steeple and cast-iron front porch. The city's oldest continually used church has over the years hosted much East Village countercultural activity. In the 1920s, an iconoclastic pastor injected the Episcopalian ritual with American Indian chants, Greek folk dancing, and Eastern mantras. During the hippie era, St. Mark's welcomed avant-garde poets and playwrights. Today, they've removed pews from the main sanctuary to accommodate dancers, poets, and performance artists.

In the early part of the 20th century, Second Avenue was known as the "Yiddish Rialto." Between Houston and 14th streets eight theaters presented way-Off-Broadway Yiddish-language musicals and heart-wrenching melodramas. The theaters are gone; all that remains are Hollywood-style stars (Stars of David) embedded in the sidewalk in front of the **Second Avenue Deli** (Second Ave. and 10th St.) to commemorate Yiddish stage luminaries.

Time Out **Veselka** is a popular neighborhood luncheonette that serves hearty soups, overstuffed sandwiches, and solid Ukrainian-Polish specialties like blintzes, pierogi, and boiled beef with horseradish. *144 Second Ave. at Ninth St.*

---

❽ The intersection of Second Avenue and **St. Marks Place** (the latter an East Village pseudonym for E. Eighth Street) is the main line of the hip East Village. During the '50s, beatnik poets like Allen Ginsberg and Jack Kerouac lived and wrote in the area. The '60s brought Bill Graham's Fillmore East, the Electric Circus, and "acid tests." Black-clad pink-haired punks followed—and remain. St. Marks Place between Second and Third avenues today is a counterculture bazaar of vegetarian restaurants, jewelry stalls, leather shops, haircutters, book shops, and stores selling the next wave in weird apparel.

East of Second Avenue the East Village becomes more arty. **P.S. 122** (150 First Ave. at Ninth St., tel. 212/477–5288) is a dilapidated former public school transformed into a complex of spaces for avant-garde entertainment. Shocking, frequently crude, and always unusual, P. S. 122 happenings translate the spirit of the streets into performance art. Ticket prices are low, seldom over $10.

❾ Far East Village activities focus on **Tompkins Square,** the park bordered by avenues A and B and Seventh and 10th streets. Although the square itself could use a face-lift, restored town houses along 10th Street indicate that the Tompkins Square neighborhood is well on its way to gentrification.

Not long ago, the outer limits of the East Village were a hotbed of avant-garde activity. More than two dozen art galleries, with names like **Gracie Mansion** and **P.P.O.W.**, featured work that was often startling, innovative, or political. The art dealers, however, have either gone out of business or moved to more mainstream (and spacious) locations in SoHo or other parts of the Village.

Chelsea

At different times in its colorful history, Chelsea has been New York's paramount shopping area and entertainment center.

Like almost all of Manhattan, Chelsea (loosely defined as the area from the Hudson River to Fifth Avenue between 14th and 34th streets) is enjoying an upsurge of new building and brownstone renovation accompanied by an influx of trendy restaurants and chic shops. But more than most areas of the city it remains a picturesque and cosmopolitan mixture of ethnicity and social class.

During the latter part of the 19th century, the city's top dry goods stores were located along **Ladies' Mile,** Sixth Avenue (Avenue of the Americas) south of 23rd Street. The big stores—Simpson Crawford's, O'Neill's, Altman's, Cammeyer's—are long gone but some of the imposing limestone and cast-iron structures they occupied remain. Most elaborate was the vast 1896 Siegel-Cooper store, an extravagant cast-iron wedding cake that occupies two-thirds of the block between 18th and 19th streets.

Chelsea's moment in the show business spotlight peaked around the turn of the century when the Grand Opera House stood at the corner of Eighth Avenue and 23rd Street. The **Hotel Chelsea** was built in 1882; it's a redbrick structure with New Orleans–style wrought-iron balconies that, in 1978, became the first hotel proclaimed a national landmark. Generations of geniuses and superstars have stayed within its soundproof (three-foot thick) walls, from Mark Twain, Thomas Wolfe, Dylan Thomas, and Arthur Miller to Lenny Bruce, Jane Fonda, and Andy Warhol. Exhibits of modern art—some offered in lieu of rent by long-term residents—adorn the small lobby.

Time Out   **Chelsea Foods,** a vest-pocket gourmet food shop with a handful of tables, is an informally stylish place for fancy sandwiches, fresh salads, rich pastries, and zesty coffee. *198 Eighth Ave. at 20th St.*

The **Chelsea Historic District,** between 20th and 22nd streets from Tenth Avenue to a point halfway between Eighth and Ninth avenues, is a tranquil enclave of late 19th-century Greek, Italian, and Gothic Revival town houses. Chelsea's oldest building (1785) is the brick house with the steep roof and dormer windows at 183 Ninth Avenue at 21st Street. Almost half of the historic district belongs to the **General Theological Seminary** (Ninth Ave. and 21st St.), an Episcopal institution opened in 1826 on land contributed by Clement Moore, author of the poem, "A Visit From St. Nicholas" ("'Twas the night before Christmas . . ."). The secluded ivy-covered quadrangle offers visitors a pleasant refuge from New York street life. Enter through a modern structure on Ninth Avenue.

Lower Midtown

Numbers in the margin correspond to points of interest on the Midtown Manhattan map.

❶ Pennsylvania Station is the gateway to New York for most Amtrak passengers and commuters from New Jersey (NJ Transit) and Long Island (Long Island Railroad). It's a good place to begin an exploration of lower midtown but not in and of itself a pleasant spot. Though recently remodeled, the underground facility is still charmless and heavily populated with unsavory types. It serves as an embarrassing reminder of the civic short-

Midtown Manhattan

W. 58th St.
W. 57th St.
W. 56th St.
W. 55th St.
W. 54th St.
W. 53rd St.
W. 52nd St.
W. 51st St.
W. 50th St.
W. 49th St.
W. 48th St.
W. 47th St.
W. 46th St.
W. 45th St.
W. 44th St.
W. 43rd St.
W. 42nd St.
W. 41st St.
W. 40th St.

Tenth Ave.
Ninth Ave.
Eighth Ave.

THEATER
DISTRICT

Port Authority
Bus Terminal

Lincoln Tunnel

Dyer Ave.

W. 39th St.
W. 38th St.
W. 37th St.
W. 36th St.
W. 35th St.

Javits
Convention
Center

Eleventh Ave.

W. 34th St.
W. 33rd St.
W. 32nd St.
W. 31st St.

Post Office

W. 30th St.
W. 29th St.
W. 28th St.
W. 27th St.
W. 26th St.
W. 25th St.
W. 24th St.
W. 23rd St.
W. 22nd St.
W. 21st St. CHELSEA
W. 20th St.
W. 19th St.
W. 18th St.
W. 17th St.
W. 16th St.
W. 15th St.

Twelfth Ave.

Eleventh Ave.

Hudson
River

N

E. 58th St.
E. 57th St.

Carnegie
Hall

E. 56th St.
E. 55th St.
E. 54th St.
E. 53rd St.
E. 52nd St.
E. 51st St.
E. 50th St.

Radio City
Music Hall

E. 49th St.
E. 48th St.
E. 47th St.
E. 46th St.
E. 45th St.
E. 44th St.
E. 43rd St.

E. 42nd St.

E. 41st St.
E. 40th St.
E. 39th St.
E. 38th St.

Times
Square

Bryant
Park

Queens
Midtown
Tunnel

Broadway

(Sixth Ave.)

Seventh Ave.

Madison Ave.

Park Ave.

Third Ave.

Vanderbilt Ave.

Tudor City Pl.

Sutton Pl.

East River

MURRAY HILL

E. 37th St.
E. 36th St.
E. 35th St.
E. 34th St.
E. 33rd St.
E. 32nd St.
E. 31st St.
E. 30th St.

Herald
Square

Fifth Ave.

Ave. of the Americas

E. 29th St.
E. 28th St.
E. 27th St.
E. 26th St.
E. 25th St.
E. 24th St.

Lexington Ave.

Second Ave.

First Ave.

Madison
Square

E. 23rd St.
E. 22nd St.

Park Ave. S.

Gramercy
Park

E. 21st St.
E. 20th St.
E. 19th St.
E. 18th St.
E. 17th St.
E. 16th St.
E. 15th St.

Irving Pl.

Union
Square

Stuyvesant
Square

0   880 yards
0   800 yards

sightedness that countenanced the demolition of the magnificent old Penn Station in 1963.

Located directly above Penn Station is **Madison Square Garden** (tel. 212/563–8300), actually the fourth incarnation thereof, but certainly not the last. (Construction of a new Madison Square Garden, a few blocks to the west, is under discussion.) Home of the New York Knickerbockers (pro basketball) and New York Rangers (pro hockey), the Garden also lights up almost nightly with horse, dog, and cat shows, college basketball games, wrestling matches, rock concerts, circuses, and other events and expositions; boxing takes place in the smaller Felt Forum adjoining it. The Garden also contains one of Manhattan's last remaining bowling alleys, the 48-lane Madison Square Garden Bowling Center.

Head north from Penn Station on Seventh Avenue and you enter the tumultuous **Garment District.** Street signs label the stretch of Seventh Avenue between 31st and 41st streets "Fashion Avenue." The Garment District teems with warehouses, workshops, and showrooms that manufacture and finish mostly women's and children's clothing. On weekdays trucks clog the streets, and sidewalks are aswarm with daredevils hauling garment racks between factories and specialty subcontractors.

❷ **Macy's,** the largest department store in the world under one roof, occupies the entire block bordered by Broadway, Seventh Avenue, and 34th and 35th streets. World-famous for *The Miracle on 34th Street* and the terminus of the Thanksgiving Day parade, Macy's has in recent years vanquished its rival Gimbel's across the street (the A & S Plaza shopping mall opened on the site in late 1989) and been made over into a stylish competitor to trendy Bloomingdale's.

❸ The **Empire State Building** may no longer be the world's tallest building (that distinction belongs to the Sears Tower—Chicago) or even New York's tallest (World Trade Center), but it is certainly the most famous and best loved. King Kong's Art Deco jungle gym opened in 1931 after only a year and a half of construction. More than 15,000 people work in the building and more than 1.5 million visit the 86th and 102nd floor observatories every year. At night the top 30 stories are illuminated with colors appropriate to season (red and green around Christmas; orange and brown for Halloween). Lights go out at midnight—but sometimes earlier during foggy spring and fall evenings, to protect the bird migration. *Fifth Ave. and 34th St., tel. 212/736–3100. Admission: $3.50 adults, $1.75 children under 12. Open daily 9:30 AM–midnight.*

❹ Continue south on Fifth Avenue to the **Marble Collegiate Church** (Fifth Ave. and 29th St.), a marble-fronted structure built in 1854 for a Reformed Protestant Dutch Congregation first organized in 1628 by Peter Minuit, the canny Dutchman who paid $24 for Manhattan. In modern times the church is best known as the pulpit for Dr. Norman Vincent Peale *(The Power of Positive Thinking)*, pastor from 1932 to 1984.

At the end of the last century most of the city's music publishers were concentrated in a stretch of low-rise office buildings on 28th Street between Broadway and Sixth Avenue. Working in cubbyholes with upright pianos pushed against the front windows, they created such a brassy din that one passing reporter nicknamed the area **"Tin Pan Alley."** The term stuck and subsequently became synonymous for the world of pop music. The publishers are all gone, replaced by the wholesale suppliers of the city's street merchants.

Time Out The **Beaubern Restaurant and Bar** is an atmospheric neighborhood joint festooned with Tin Pan Alley memorabilia. Menu features fish and sandwiches. *42 W. 28th St.*

5 Bordered by Fifth Avenue, Broadway, Madison Avenue, and 23rd and 26th streets, **Madison Square** was the site (circa 1845) of New York's first baseball games. Though recently rehabilitated with modern sculpture, new benches, and a playground, Madison Square's most interesting features are found along the perimeter.

The block at 26th Street and Madison Avenue now occupied by the ornate **New York Life Insurance Building** is the site of the second (1890–1925) Madison Square Garden. The old Garden was designed by architect/playboy Stanford White who was shot on its roof by Harry K. Thaw, the jealous husband of actress Evelyn Nesbit. The roof balustrade above the imposing white marble Corinthian columns of the **Appellate Division— State Supreme Court** (Madison Ave. and 25th St.) depicts great lawmakers of the past: Moses, Justinian, Confucius. The **Metropolitan Life Insurance Tower** (Madison Ave. between 23rd and 24th Sts.) is modeled after the campanile of St. Mark's in Venice.

The **Flatiron Building** occupies the triangular lot formed by Broadway, Fifth Avenue, and 23rd Street. When this 20-story flounder-shaped skyscraper was built in 1902, it became a symbol for high-rising New York. Now it lends its name to SoFi (South of the Flatiron Building), an area to the south housing photographers' studios, living lofts, and advertising agencies that have fled the high-rising rents of upper Madison Avenue.

6 Continue on Broadway and turn east on 20th Street to the **Theodore Roosevelt Birthplace,** a reconstructed Victorian brownstone where Teddy lived until age 15. The house contains Victorian period rooms and Teddy-abilia; a selection of videos about the namesake of the Teddy Bear are shown on request. *28 E. 20th St., tel. 212/260–1616. Admission: $1. Open Wed.–Sun. 9–5.*

7 Just east of Park Avenue South between 20th and 21st streets lies **Gramercy Park,** a London-style city park complete with flower beds, bird feeders, sundials, cozy benches, and a statue of the actor Edwin Booth portraying Hamlet. Laid out in 1831, it remains pristine because it's surrounded by a cast-iron fence and locked gate, to which only residents of the property around the park possess keys.

Mrs. Stuyvesant Fish, a society doyenne best remembered for boldly reducing the time of formal dinner parties from several hours to 50 minutes, resided at No. 19. Edwin Booth lived at No. 16, now an affiliation of show-biz types called The Players Club. The site of the National Arts Club (15 Gramercy Park S) was the home of Samuel Tilden, a governor of New York and the Democratic presidential candidate in 1876, who lost the election to Rutherford B. Hayes—even though he received more popular votes!

Time Out The space occupied by **Pete's Tavern** has been a saloon bar since 1864 when it opened as Healy's Bar. Tammany Hall, New York's Democratic political machine, mapped strategy here; O'Henry wrote "Gift of the Magi" in the booth by the door; Prohibition inhibited activity hardly at all. Now it's a friendly neighborhood spot with a Gay '90s motif and a medium-priced menu of burgers, pasta, and some more ambitious selections. *129 E. 18th St. and Irving Pl.*

❽ Return to Park Avenue South and continue south to **Union Square,** bordered by Park Avenue South, Broadway, and 14th and 17th streets. During the early part of the century, Union Square had been a popular patch of green and the site of political orations and demonstrations. It deteriorated into an impenetrable infestation of drug dealers and kindred undesirables until a massive renewal program transformed it into one of the city's most attractive miniparks. The park features a Beaux Arts subway entrance—similar to the one in Cooper Square—and, in its southwest corner, a statue of Mahatma Gandhi.

If possible visit Union Square early on a Wednesday, Friday, or Saturday when the Greenmarket takes place. Farmers from New York, New Jersey, and Pennsylvania bring their just-picked crops, homemade baked goods, New York State wines, cheeses, cider, fish, and meat to sell at less-than-grocery-store prices. For locations and days of one of the other 15 greenmarkets in the Bronx, Brooklyn, or Manhattan, call 212/566–0990.

42nd Street

❾ Despite the richly deserved bad press, **Times Square** remains one of New York's principal energy centers. The square itself (actually a triangle formed by Broadway, Seventh Avenue, and 42nd Street) is occupied by the former Times Tower, now simply **One Times Square Plaza.** From its roof, workmen lower the 200-pound New Year's Eve ball down the flagpole hand-by-hand—as they have since 1908.

Since 1895, when Oscar Hammerstein I opened the Olympia Theater at Broadway and 44th Street, Times Square became the show-biz capital of the world. Most Broadway theaters are located on the numbered cross streets running west of Broadway from 51st Street down to 44th Street. The **TKTS** booth **❿** sponsored by the Theater Development Fund sells half-price day-of-performance tickets to Broadway and Off-Broadway shows; it is located on Duffy Square, Broadway and 47th Street (*see* Arts). The headquarters of the **New York Times** (229 W. 43rd St.), the institution for which the area is named, occupies much of 43rd Street between Seventh and Eighth avenues.

The title of David Merrick's long-running musical portraying the glamour of the New York stage notwithstanding, **42nd Street** around Times Square has no live theater. Just west of Broadway it's a disreputable strip of porno shops, dirty movies, and kindred sleaze. The most prominent vestige of the 42nd Street of *42nd Street* is the **New Amsterdam** (214 W. 42nd St.), a designated landmark that opened in 1903. The New Amsterdam is "dark" now—lying fallow in anticipation of the long-promised Times Square redevelopment project—but in its prime the opulent facility with a second rooftop theater had showcased Eddie Cantor, Will Rogers, Fannie Brice, and the Ziegfeld Girls.

Bryant Park and the **Central Research Library** occupy the entire block bounded by 42nd Street, Fifth Avenue, 40th Street, and Sixth Avenue (which carries the dual name Avenue of the Americas on its street signs). Named after poet/orator/journalist William Cullen Bryant (1794–1878), Bryant Park was the site of America's first world's fair, the Crystal Palace Exhibition of 1853–54. (At publication time, Bryant Park was closed while city planners weighed various proposals regarding its future.) Alongside the park on 42nd Street, **Bryant Park Half-price Tickets** sells same-day tickets for music and dance performances all over the city (*see* Arts).

⑫ The **Central Research Library**—aka Main Branch—is the research hub of the 85-branch **New York Public Library** system and one of the largest research libraries in the world. You enter between two crouching Tennessee marble lions—dubbed "Patience" and "Fortitude" by former Mayor Fiorello LaGuardia who visited the facility to "read between the lions." Inside you find not only a great library but a distinguished achievement of Beaux-Arts design (note the triple bronze front doors), an art gallery, and a museum. Along with periodic exhibitions on matters literary, the Main Branch displays Gilbert Stuart's portrait of George Washington, Charles Dickens's desk, and Jefferson's own handwritten copy of the Declaration of Independence. *Fifth Ave. and 42nd St., tel. 212/930–0800. Open Mon.–Wed. 10–9, Thur.–Sat. 10–6. Free tours 11 and 2 Mon.–Sat.*

Time Out A branch of the **Whitney Museum of American Art** occupies the ground floor of the Philip Morris Building. Each year this free museum presents five changing exhibitions of 20th-century painting and sculpture. It also has an espresso bar with snacks and sandwiches with seating areas that comprise a more agreeable place for rest and reconnaissance than anything across the street in Grand Central Terminal. *120 Park Ave. at 42nd St.*

⑬ Continue east to **Grand Central Terminal** (Park Ave. and 42nd St.). The terminal—never "station" since all runs begin or end here—was constructed between 1903 and 1913 from a design developed by a Minnesota architectural firm and later gussied up with Beaux-Arts ornamentation. Take note of the three huge windows separated by columns above the 42nd Street facade and the clock and sculpture on the facade above 42nd Street. The bronze statue represents Commodore Cornelius Vanderbilt, founder of the New York Central and Hudson River Railroad, which built Grand Central. Inside the terminal, the 12-story ceiling of the cavernous Main Concourse displays the constellations of the zodiac, its 2,500 stars painted backward— "as God would see it," according to the painter Whitney Warren. You're not likely to overlook the world's largest photographic slide, its subject changed periodically by Kodak. Free tours of Grand Central begin under the slide every Wednesday at 12:30 PM. Tours are sponsored by the Municipal Art Society (tel. 212/935–3960) and last two hours.

⑭ Ask New Yorkers to name their favorite skyscraper and most choose the **Chrysler Building** (Lexington Ave. and 42nd St.).

Even though the Chrysler Corporation itself is long gone from the premises, the graceful shaft that culminates in a stainless steel point (which temporarily put it over the top as the world's tallest building) still captivates the eye and the imagination. Look for the car-ornament detailing outside. The elegant Art Deco lobby, originally an auto showroom, is faced with African marble and covered with a ceiling mural that honors transportation and human endeavor.

Time Out The **Horn & Hardart Automat,** one block east, is the last survivor of the original fast-food chain. Patrons use coins or tokens to extract dishes—baked beans and macaroni and cheese are standbys—from glass-fronted cubbyholes, and crank coffee out of fish-head spouts. Authentic automat facilities are confined to one wall (a cafeteria, sandwich bar, and bakery dominate the space) but sleek Art Deco styling prevails throughout. The automat can also be rented out for private parties in the evening. *Third Ave. and 42nd St.*

⑮ New York's biggest-selling newspaper is produced in the **Daily News Building** (220 E. 42nd St.), a 1930 Art Deco tower designed with brown-brick spandrels and extra-wide windows to make it appear taller than its 37 stories. The lobby features a 12-foot-diameter revolving illuminated globe. The floor is a huge compass on which bronze lines indicate air mileage between principal world cities and New York.

⑯ The **Ford Foundation Building** (320 E. 43rd St.) encloses a 12-story, one-third acre, glassed-in jungle. The terraced garden, graced with a still pool and a couple of dozen full-grown trees, is open to the public for doses of sylvan tranquillity—but not brown bagging—weekdays from 9 to 5.

Climb the steps along 42nd Street between First and Second avenues to enter **Tudor City,** a self-contained complex of a dozen Tudor Gothic buildings highlighted by half-timbering and an amplitude of stained glass. Constructed from 1925 to 1928, the apartments of this residential enclave originally had no east side windows so tenants didn't have to gaze upon the slaughterhouses, breweries, and glue factories then located along the East River.

⑰ **United Nations Headquarters** occupies a lushly landscaped riverside tract along First Avenue between 42nd and 48th streets. In an ambitious attempt at international harmony, the complex was designed by a committee of renowned architects including Oscar Niemeyer (Brazil), Charles Le Corbusier (France), Sven Markelius (Sweden), Wallace Harrison (United States), and about seven others. A line of flagpoles with banners representing the current roster of 159 member nations stands before the striking 550-foot slab of the Secretariat Building. Interior corridors overflow with imaginatively diverse sculpture, paintings, tapestries, and crafts donated by member nations. Free tickets to most sessions are available on a first-come, first-served basis 15 minutes before sessions begin; pick them up in the General Assembly lobby. Visitors can take early luncheon in the Delegates Dining Room (good food, great East River view) or eat anytime in a coffee shop. *Visitors' entrance First Ave. and 45th St., tel. 212/963-7539. One-hour tours leave General Assembly lobby about every 20 min, 9:15-4:45* *daily. Admission: $4.50 adults, $2.50 students. Children under 5 not permitted.*

Rockefeller Center

⑱ The 19 buildings of **Rockefeller Center** occupy nearly 22 acres of midtown Manhattan real estate bounded by Fifth and Seventh avenues, and 47th and 52nd streets. Built during the Great Depression (1932–1940) by John D. Rockefeller, Jr., this city-within-a-city is the hub of the communications industry with the headquarters for a TV network (NBC), several major publishing companies (Time-Life, McGraw-Hill, Simon & Schuster, Warner Brothers), and the world's largest news-gathering organization, the Associated Press. Internationally oriented, Rockefeller Center shelters consulates of numerous nations, the U.S. passport office, and airline ticket offices. In addition, most mundane human needs can be accommodated by the restaurants, shoe repair shops, doctors, barbers, banks, post office, bookstores, and clothing stores in the underground passages that interconnect the various elements of the center.

Begin your tour at the **RCA Building**, a 70-story tower that occupies the block bounded by Rockefeller Plaza and Sixth Avenue, and 49th and 50th streets. An information desk just inside the stunning black granite lobby at the Rockefeller Plaza entrance can provide an assortment of free publications from a walking tour to guides to a calendar of events. Before setting forth look up at the ceiling: The Jose Maria Sert mural entitled *Time* was created with a trompe l'oeil effect so that the central figure seems to be facing you wherever you stand.

"Thirty Rock" is headquarters for NBC, and studio tours depart regularly. You can buy T-shirts, ashtrays, Frisbees, and other promotional items bearing logos from your favorite NBC shows at a boutique beside the entrance to NBC. *Tel. 212/664-7174. NBC studio tours leave every 15 minutes 9:30–4:30 Mon.–Sat. (also Sun. during summer). Admission: $7; children under 6 not admitted.*

To access the heavens you can either dine and dance in the posh (and pricey) Art Deco surroundings of the **RainbowRoom** (tel. 212/632–5100) or have a drink and a "little meal" at the adjacent **Promenade,** both on the 65th floor. For no charge you can roam the miles of marble catacombs that interconnect Rockefeller Center. A lot goes on down under: restaurants in all price ranges from the chic American Festival Cafe to McDonald's; a small Rockefeller Center Museum; the New England tourism office; a post office; and even clean public washrooms.

Across 50th Street from the RCA Building is America's largest indoor theater, the landmark 6,000-seat **Radio City Music Hall.** Home of the fabulous Rockettes chorus line (which actually started out as the Missouri Rockets in St. Louis in 1925), Radio City opened in 1933 as a movie theater with live shows (first feature: Frank Capra's *The Bitter Tea of General Yen,* with Barbara Stanwyck). It now hosts concerts, Christmas and Easter extravaganzas, awards presentations, and other special events. If there's no show you can tour the premises for $6. *Tel. 212/632–4041.*

Across Sixth Avenue the Lower Plaza of the 51-story **McGraw-Hill Building** contains a 50-foot steel triangle that points to the seasonal positions of the sun at noon and a pool that demonstrates the relative size of the planets. On the west side of the building a walk-through waterfall links 48th and 49th streets.

Time Out The **food vendors** along Sixth Avenue around Rockefeller Center offer the best "a la cart" dining in the city. Along with such pedestrian selections as hot dogs and knishes, vendors sell tacos, falafel, souvlaki, tempura, Indian curry, Afghani kofta kebabs, Caribbean beef jerky, and dozens of other selections. Food carts are licensed and inspected by the Department of Health. Nothing costs more than $5 and most dishes are much less. Seating available on the benches and low walls in the plazas beside the Sixth Avenue office towers.

A little street called Rockefeller Plaza separates the RCA Building from the famous **ice rink** in the Lower Plaza. Crowned by a gold-leaf statue of Prometheus, the rink hosts skaters September through April and becomes an outdoor cafe the rest of the year. Surrounded by the flags of all the members of the United Nations, the skating rink is the site of a huge Christmas tree and caroling concerts during December. Incidentally, those little "Private Street, No Parking" signs on Rockefeller Plaza are for real. It is a private street that has to be closed off to cars and pedestrians one day a year to retain its privacy.

Just east of the Lower Plaza are the **Channel Gardens,** a promenade of six pools surrounded by flowerbeds filled with seasonal plantings conceived by artists, floral designers, and sculptors—ten consecutively running shows a season. They are called Channel Gardens because they separate the British building (to the north) and the French building (to the south).

Upper Midtown

⑲ Angular Gothic-style **St. Patrick's Cathedral** is the Roman Catholic Cathedral of New York. Dedicated to the patron saint of the Irish—then and now one of New York's principal ethnic groups—the white marble-and-stone structure was begun in 1858, opened in 1879, and completed in 1906. Alcoves around the nave contain statues of saints, including a striking modern rendering of the first American-born saint, Mother Seton. Don't overlook the charming Lady Chapel in the back of the cathedral. If you drop by on a Saturday, you're likely to catch a wedding in progress. *Fifth Ave. between 50th and 51st Sts.*

⑳ Fifty-third Street around Fifth Avenue is a mini–Museum Row. Just east of Fifth Avenue, the **Museum of Broadcasting** presents periodic special screenings, normally retrospectives of the work of a particular radio or TV star or of an era in broadcasting. Its collection of more than 30,000 TV and radio programs is available for private viewing. *1 E. 53rd St., tel. 212/752-7684. Suggested contribution: $4 adults, $3 students, $2 seniors and children under 13. Open Tues. noon–8; Wed.–Sat. noon–5.*

㉑ The bright and airy **Museum of Modern Art (MOMA)** is a suitably up-to-date four-story structure built around a secluded sculpture garden. All the important movements of modern art are represented here: cubism, surrealism, abstract impressionism, minimalism, and postmodernism. Some of the world's most famous modern paintings are displayed on the second floor—Van Gogh's *Starry Night,* Picasso's *Les Demoiselles d'Avignon,* Matisse's *Dance.* Superstars of American art—among them Andrew Wyeth, Andy Warhol, Jackson Pollock, Mark Rothko—fill the third-floor galleries. Afternoon and evening film shows, mostly foreign films and classics, are free with museum admission. Day-of-performance tickets are distributed in the lobby; call for a schedule. *11 W. 53rd St., tel. 212/ 708–9500. Admission: $6 adults, $3.50 students, $3 seniors. Open daily except Wed. 11–6; Thurs. to 9. Pay what you wish Thurs. 5–9.*

㉒ The **American Craft Museum** spotlights the work of contemporary American and foreign craftspersons working in clay, glass, fabric, wood, metal, and paper. *40 W. 53rd St., tel. 212/ 956–3535. Admission: $3.50 adults, $1.50 students and seniors; free Tues. 5–8. Open Tues. 10–8, Wed.–Sun. 10–5.*

The stretch of Fifth Avenue on the eastern edge of Rockefeller Center glitters with world-famous stores. The shopping list begins with no less than **Saks Fifth Avenue** (Fifth Ave. and 50th St.), flagship of the national chain. **Cartier,** the exclusive jeweler, occupies the Renaissance-style palazzo at the corner of Fifth Avenue and 52nd Street. Then there's **Gucci,** actually two Guccis on adjacent corners of Fifth Avenue and 54th Street. **Bijan** sells wildly extravagant men's Continental clothing—by appointment only (699 Fifth Ave., tel. 212/758–7500).

Health warnings and New York State no-smoking ordinances notwithstanding, **Nat Sherman** (711 Fifth Ave.) continues to market his own brands of pastel-colored cigarettes and cigars from his clubby shop. **Steuben Glass** has a gallery of glassmaking art and a showroom on the ground floor of a green-glass tower at Fifth Avenue and 56th Street. **Tiffany and Company** (727 Fifth Ave. at 57th St.) is less intimidating and may be somewhat less expensive than you fear.

㉓ A block east on Madison Avenue and 55th Street stands Ma Bell's post-deregulated home, **AT&T World Headquarters.** The rose granite columns, regilded statue of the winged "Golden Boy" in the lobby, and curious Chippendale roof have earned its sobriquet as the first postmodern skyscraper. An adjacent structure houses the **AT&T InfoQuest Center,** a postmodern museum of communications technology. Displays are neither very technical nor zealously self-serving. Some exhibits—like the ones where you program your own music video and rearrange a scrambled picture of your face—are downright entertaining. *Madison Ave. and 56th St., tel. 212/605–5555. Admission free. Open Tues. 10–9, Wed.–Sun. 10–6.*

Time Out   **IBM Garden Plaza** is a spectacular public space sculpted from the ground floors of the green-granite IBM building. Bamboo trees rise to the heavens and seasonal flowers perfume the air. Brown-bag or buy light lunches, sandwiches, and pastries from a charming kiosk. Seating at chairs and marble tables and on benches alongside plantings. Free concerts Wednesdays at 12:30. The New York Botanical Garden operates a gift shop here and the free IBM Gallery of Science and Art is off the main lobby. *Madison Ave. and 56th St.*

㉔ **Trump Tower** is an exclusive 68-story dark-glass apartment house. What's open to the public is a six-story shopping atrium paneled in pinkish-orange marble and trimmed with high-gloss brass. A fountain cascading against one atrium wall drowns out the clamor of the city. In further contrast to the outside world, every inch of Trump Tower is kept gleamingly shined, and dark-suited security men are discreetly omnipresent. Shops are chic and expensive—Cartier, Bucellati, Abercrombie & Fitch, to name a few of the 50 or so—and public rest rooms in the basement are downright opulent.

The Upper West Side

Numbers in the margin correspond with points of interest on the Upper West Side map.

① **Lincoln Center** is an architecturally unified development that encompasses New York's major-league performing arts institutions. It was built—amid no small controversy—during the 1960s to displace a rundown urban ghetto. Occupying an eight-block area west of Broadway between 62nd and 66th streets, the complex can at one time seat nearly 15,000 spectators for performances of classical music, opera, ballet, drama, and film.

Lincoln Center's eight distinct units surround attractive fountains, pools, and tree-filled plazas. The grand **Metropolitan Opera House** is the classically designed centerpiece. Home of the Metropolitan Opera and American Ballet Theatre, it has a magnificent red and gold auditorium and brightly colored Chagall murals in the lobby. **Avery Fisher Hall,** named after the founder of Fisher Radio, hosts the New York Philharmonic Orchestra. A four-story foyer with decorative metal balconies at every level welcomes audiences to the 2,800-seat **New York State Theater,** home of the New York City Ballet and the New York City Opera.

The **Guggenheim Bandshell** in Damrosch Park seats 8,500 for free outdoor concerts. A single structure devoted to the dramatic arts includes the **Vivian Beaumont** and **Mitzi E. Newhouse theaters.** Visitors to the **Library and Museum of the Performing Arts** can listen to a collection of 42,000 records and tapes or tour four galleries. Across 65th Street, the ground floor of the world-renowned **Juilliard School of Music** houses intimate **Alice Tully Hall,** home of the Chamber Music Society of Lincoln Center, the Film Society of Lincoln Center, and the New York Film Center.

Visitors can wander freely through the lobbies of all buildings and relax in Damrosch Park or beside Lincoln Center's fountains. An outdoor cafe operates throughout the summer. A one-hour guided "Take-the-Tour" covers all buildings, delves into Lincoln Center legend and lore, and drops by any rehearsals that happen to be in progress. *Ticket office in Metropolitan Opera House lower level, tel. 212/877–1800 ext. 512 for schedules. Admission: $6.25 adults, $5.25 students and seniors, $3.50 children.*

② Across the busy intersection from Lincoln Center, the long-orphaned **Museum of American Folk Art** has found a new home at Columbus Avenue and 66th Street. Its collection includes primitive paintings, quilts, carvings, dolls, trade signs, painted wooden carousel horses, and a giant Indian-chief copper weather vane. *2 Lincoln Square, tel. 212/977–7175. Admission free. Open daily 9–9.*

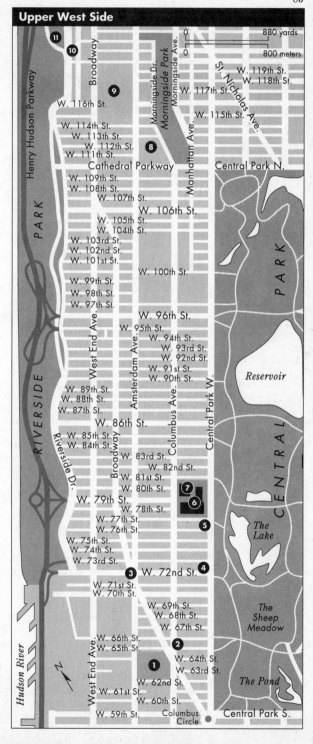

Time Out **Opera Espresso** offers a Lincoln Center–inspired backdrop of framed opera programs and ballet-star celebrity pix; anything from coffee to full meals. *1928 Broadway near 65th St.*

Until recently, the Upper West Side was a reasonably unfashionable district of intellectuals, striving young writers and artists, and marginal residents of SRO (single room occupancy) apartments. But now the neighborhood has come into its own. The SROs have gone co-op and high-living young professionals who can afford to live anywhere have moved here in droves. Though many of the old residents think their neighborhood—snidely redubbed the "Yupper West Side"—is no longer such a nice place to live, the area has certainly become a more entertaining place to visit.

The West Side story begins at the intersection of Broadway, Amsterdam Avenue, and 72nd Street. Officially, the triangle to the south is **Sherman Square** (for Union Civil War General William Tecumseh) and the triangle to the north is Verdi Square (for Italian opera composer Giuseppe).

Lush produce overflows bountifully from **Fairway Market** (2127 Broadway at 74th St.). Check out the handmade signs describing the produce and cheese: They can be as fresh and tart as the merchandise itself. When the **Ansonia Hotel** opened at 73rd Street and Broadway in 1904, its white facade, fairy-castle turrets, and new soundproof partitions began attracting show people, classical musicians, and writers to this hitherto unfashionable area. Never a transient hotel, the Ansonia's apartments have sheltered Florenz Ziegfeld, Enrico Caruso, Mischa Elman, Theodore Dreiser—and the great Babe Ruth.

Time Out For nearly 50 years, **Eclair** has been feeding neighborhood folks fine Viennese pastries, light sandwiches and quiches, and hearty Austro-Hungarian fare. Full soda fountain and bar. *141 W. 72nd St. between Columbus and Amsterdam Aves.*

For a dozen years **Columbus Avenue** in the West 70s was a workaday strip of nondescript tenements, laundromats, plumbing supply houses, and other marginal enterprises. Now it's one of the city's hottest strips of boutiques, bars, and restaurants. Although the boom has somewhat faded as many new businesses couldn't hack the skyrocketing rents, Columbus Avenue still attracts a mostly young upscale crowd of neighborhood residents and visitors.

Designed in 1884 by Henry J. Hardenbergh, the architect who built the Plaza Hotel, **The Dakota** apartments grandly preside over the corner of Central Park West and 72nd Street. Once it was famous only as one of the first fashionable apartment houses in the remote Upper West Side: It was named when someone quipped that "it might as well be in Dakota Territory." Through the years, it has always been a favored residence of stage and screen notables. Now the Dakota is better known as the place where John Lennon lived and was fatally shot. Directly across Central Park West, a knoll of Central Park has been designated as **Strawberry Fields** in Lennon's honor. A black-and-white-tile mosaic containing the word "Imagine," another Lennon song title, is embedded in the walkway.

❺ The city's oldest museum (founded 1804), **The New-York Histor-ical Society,** preserves what was unique about the city's past—including the quaint hyphen in "New-York." Along with chang-ing exhibits of American history and art, the museum displays original Audubon watercolors, rare maps, early-American toys, antique vehicles, and Hudson River School landscapes. *170 Central Park West, tel. 212/873-3400. Admission: $2 adults, $1.50 seniors, $1 children; Tues. pay as you wish. Open Tues.–Sat. 10–5.*

❻ The **American Museum of Natural History**, the attached **Hay-den Planetarium,** and surrounding grounds occupy a four-block tract bounded by Central Park West, Columbus Avenue, and 77th and 81st streets. With a collection of more than 36 million artifacts, the museum contains something for every taste, from the cross-section of a 1,300-year-old sequoia tree to the 563-car-at Star of India sapphire. Naturemax Theater projects true-life adventures on a four-story movie screen. *Main entrance on 79th St., tel. 212/769-5100. Suggested admission: $3.50 adults, $1.50 children; Fri. and Sat. free after 5. Open daily 10–5:45; Wed., Fri., Sat. until 9.*

❼ Two floors of astronomical exhibits at **Hayden Planetarium** re-veal your weight on Jupiter and why the sky is blue. Seasonal sky shows are projected on 22 wraparound screens. Teenagers gather on Friday and Saturday nights for a very popular rock-music laser show. *Central Park West and 81st St., tel. 212/769-5920. Admission and sky show: $3.75 adults, $2.75 students and seniors, $2 children under 12. Sky shows weekdays 1:30 and 3:30; Sat., 11 and hourly 1–5; Sun. hourly 1–5. Admission laser show: $6. Fri. and Sat. 7, 8:30, and 10 PM.*

Time Out Back to Broadway and 80th Street where another retail food landmark, **Zabar's,** sells exquisite delicatessen items, prepared foods, gourmet groceries, coffee, and cheeses. A mezzanine level features cookware, dishes, and small appliances. Try some of the delectables at a small snack bar or have a basket packed for a picnic in Central Park. *2245 Broadway, tel. 212/787-2000.*

Farther uptown you'll find **Pomander Walk,** a pleasing slice of England wedged between 94th and 95th streets between Broadway and West End Avenue. The mock Tudor homes were inspired by the sets of a 1911 British play, *Pomander Walk.*

❽ One block east of Broadway, the **Cathedral of St. John the Di-vine** is New York's major Episcopal church and the largest Gothic cathedral in the world—only St. Peter's Basilica of Rome is larger. The 600-foot nave can seat 5,000 worshipers. Small uniquely outfitted chapels border the nave, and a "Bibli-cal Garden" contains the herbs and flowers mentioned in the Bible. The cathedral is still only about two-thirds completed and master craftsmen are instructing neighborhood youth in traditional methods of stone cutting and carving. The cathedral operates community outreach programs and presents nonreli-gious (classical, folk, winter solstice) concerts. *Amsterdam Ave. and 112th St., tel. 212/316-7400. Sunday services at 8, 9, and 11 AM, and 7 PM. Tours Mon.–Sat. 11, Sun. 12:45.*

❾ **Columbia University** is a large, old (founded 1754), private in-stitution so effectively walled off from the city that it feels like one of the Ivy League's more rustic campuses. Central campus focuses on the rotunda-topped Low Memorial Library (named after Seth Low, former Columbia president and New York City mayor) to the north and massive Butler Library to the south. A cafe on the southwest corner of the quad has indoor and outdoor tables perfectly situated for student-watching. *Enter on 116th St. and Broadway or Amsterdam Ave.*

⓾ Nondenominational and multiracial **Riverside Church** is a highly political forum for community and global issues. It is also a uniquely striking structure with a 356-foot observation tower (admission $1) and a 74-bell carillon, the largest in the world. Political events, dance and theater programs, and concerts abound. *Riverside Dr. and 122nd St., tel. 212/222–5900. Carillon recitals before and after regular 10:45 Sunday services and Sun. at 3 PM.*

⓫ Adjacent to the church stands the **General Grant National Memorial Monument** popularly known as **Grant's Tomb.** The two-term president and Mrs. Grant lie in state in identical black marble sarcophagi surrounded by bronze busts of Grant cohorts. The tomb also contains photographs and other Grant memorabilia. *Riverside Dr. and 122nd St., tel. 212/666–1640. Admission free. Open Wed.–Sun. 9–4:30.*

Central Park and the Upper East Side

Numbers in the margin correspond with points of interest on the Upper East Side map.

Central Park The first city park created by a city, **Central Park** occupies an 843-acre tract that runs from 59th Street to 110th Street and from Fifth Avenue to Central Park West (Eighth Ave.). Spared from real-estate development by the efforts of a *New York Evening Post* campaign waged by William Cullen Bryant during the 1850s, Central Park was designed by Frederick Law Olmsted and Calvert Vaux and built by a crew of 3,000 Irish workers and 400 horses.

Surrounded by high-rise apartments and luxury hotels, Central Park has facilities for just about anything city dwellers like to do outside—from jogging, cycling, horseback riding, softball, and ice skating to croquet, tennis, bird-watching, boating, chess and checkers, theater, concerts, skateboarding, and break-dancing. Central Park is reasonably safe during the day and in populous areas at night. *For general information, tel. 212/397–3156; for a recorded message on city park events, tel. 212/360–1333; for information about weekend walks and talks led by Urban Park Rangers, tel. 212/397–3080.*

Begin a Central Park ramble at Grand Army Plaza (Fifth Ave.
❶ and 59th St.) and follow East Drive to the **Central Park Zoo.** Reopened in 1988 after a five-year renovation, this intimate 5.5-acre minizoo houses about 450 animals in three climate zones—tropical, temperate, and polar. The renovated zoo is much more animal-friendly, but unfortunately, for the first time since opening in 1864, it is no longer free. *Admission: $1 adults, 50¢ seniors, 25¢ children 3–12.*

❷ East Drive loops around **Wollman Memorial Rink,** a favorite place for ice skating during winter, to **The Mall,** a broad walkway lined with stately elms and statues of illustrious literary personages. Witness here any new craze—from the latest

Central Park Zoo, **1**

Cooper-Hewitt
Museum, **12**

El Museo del
Barrio, **16**

Frick Collection, **6**

Grand Army Plaza, **5**

Great Lawn, **4**

Guggenheim
Museum, **10**

International Center
of Photography, **14**

Jewish Museum, **13**

Loeb Boathouse, **3**

Metropolitan Museum
of Art, **9**

Museum of the City of
New York, **15**

National Academy of
Design, **11**

Ralph Lauren, **7**

Whitney Museum, **8**

Wollman Memorial
Rink, **2**

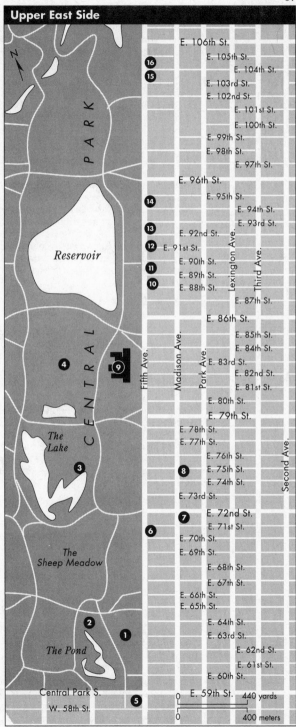

Upper East Side

E. 106th St.

E. 105th St.

E. 104th St.

E. 103rd St.

E. 102nd St.

E. 101st St.

E. 100th St.

E. 99th St.

E. 98th St.

E. 97th St.

E. 96th St.

E. 95th St.

E. 94th St.

E. 93rd St.

E. 92nd St.

E. 91st St.

E. 90th St.

E. 89th St.

E. 88th St.

E. 87th St.

E. 86th St.

E. 85th St.

E. 84th St.

E. 83rd St.

E. 82nd St.

E. 81st St.

E. 80th St.

E. 79th St.

E. 78th St.

E. 77th St.

E. 76th St.

E. 75th St.

E. 74th St.

E. 73rd St.

E. 72nd St.

E. 71st St.

E. 70th St.

E. 69th St.

E. 68th St.

E. 67th St.

E. 66th St.

E. 65th St.

E. 64th St.

E. 63rd St.

E. 62nd St.

E. 61st St.

E. 60th St.

Central Park S.

W. 58th St.

E. 59th St.

Reservoir

The Lake

The Sheep Meadow

The Pond

CENTRAL PARK

Fifth Ave.

Madison Ave.

Park Ave.

Lexington Ave.

Third Ave.

Second Ave.

0   440 yards

0   400 meters

dance to bizarre Oriental athletic discipline. The mall leads to **Naumberg Bandshell,** site of summer concerts, speeches, and performance art. Nearby, the renovated **Bethesda Fountain** and the graceful iron bridge often pose for pastoral "Sunday in New York" postcard shots.

❸ Continue east to **Loeb Boathouse** where you can rent a rowboat to cruise around **The Lake** or rent bikes to pedal around park roadways. Inside, you can get a fast-food snack or sit down for lunch. North of the boat house, **The Ramble** is a heavily wooded hill scored by twisting paths: It's great for birding but not too safe to wander alone.

❹ East Drive eventually leads to the **Great Lawn.** Carved into innumerable overlapping softball fields on most summer evenings, the Great Lawn was a Depression-era "Hooverville" tent city and more recently the site of free megaconcerts by Pavarotti, Diana Ross, and Simon and Garfunkel. If you see a seemingly unending line of picnickers around the edge of the Great Lawn it means the **New York Shakespeare Festival** performs that night. Shows are free and almost always filled to capacity. Lines begin to form before 4 PM to pick up tickets at 6 for the 8 PM performances. Call for information (tel. 212/598–7100).

The Great Lawn is adjacent to the Metropolitan Museum of Art and the onset of Museum Mile (*see* below).

The Upper East Side Encompassing the territory east of Central Park between 60th and 96th streets, the Upper East Side consists principally of stately apartment houses on grand avenues and smart town houses on dignified side streets. Not rich in sights, the area contains a wealth of museums, shops, and undiluted doses of sophisticated Manhattan style.

Begin an Upper East Side tour at "The Plaza." That means both **❺** **Grand Army Plaza,** the open space along Fifth Avenue between 58th and 60th streets, and the world-famous hotel along its western border. The **Plaza Hotel** is a registered historic landmark that has been in fashion for upper-crust transients, charity balls, coming-out parties, and romantic trysts since 1907.

Grand Army Plaza is flanked by an equestrian statue of William Tecumseh Sherman on the north and the Pulitzer (of Pulitzer Prize fame) Fountain to the south. Horsedrawn cabs await your custom (*see* Getting Around, above) and ambient food vendors cater fountainside snacks.

Fifth Avenue off Grand Army Plaza begins with a couple of **open-air bookstalls** that operate whenever the weather is passably clement. Stalls sell new and used books, New York maps and reference material, cassette tapes, and postcards. Best buys are half-price "reviewers copies" of hardcovers and trade paperbacks.

Upper Fifth Avenue was settled during the last decade of the 19th century by millionaire migrants from the 34th Street area—the Astors, Carnegies, Vanderbilts, Whitneys, and the like—who built palatial stone mansions overlooking newly fashionable Central Park. Today, most residential mansions are gone, supplanted by high-rise apartments or transformed into museums or foundation headquarters.

❻ **The Frick Collection** occupies the mansion built to display the private collection of Henry Clay Frick, the Pittsburgh coke and steel industrialist. Authentic masterpieces grace almost every room: El Greco's *St. Jerome*, Rembrandt's *SelfPortrait*, Fragonard's *The Progress of Love*, plus distinguished work by Bellini, Vermeer, Titian, Turner, Whistler, and Gainsborough. *1 E. 70th St., tel. 212/288–0700. Admission: $3 adults, $1.50 students and seniors. Open Tues.–Sat. 10–6, Sun. and holidays 1–6.*

The buzzword value of Madison Avenue, one block east of Fifth Avenue, has alternated in recent years. New Yorkers don't automatically associate it with the advertising business, much of which fled the avenue in the East '40s and '50s for less costly downtown quarters. Madison Avenue now equates to high chic, as the Madison Mile between 59th and 79th streets (20 uptown-downtown blocks equals one mile) has become an ultra-exclusive shopping area. The lower stories of Madison Avenue's brownstones house most of the major international fashion designers, patrician art galleries, and unique specialty stores. For the most part, these shops are small, intimate, expensive—and almost invariably closed on Sundays.

❼ If you have the time or inclination to visit only one Madison Mile store, choose **Ralph Lauren** (867 Madison Ave. at 72nd St.). Lauren has taken over the landmark Rhinelander Mansion, retained the walnut fittings, Oriental carpets, family portraits, and distributed his high-style preppy clothing inconspicuously about the house. Don't miss the fourth-floor home furnishings section where merchandise is arrayed in fantasy suites.

❽ Cross a drawbridge to reach the massive gray **Whitney Museum of American Art.** An outgrowth of a gallery founded in 1930 in the studio of sculptress/collector Gertrude Vanderbilt Whitney, the museum has a huge collection of 20th-century American art plus works in other media and alternative styles. *945 Madison Ave. at 75th St., tel. 212/570–3676. Admission: $4.50 adults, $2.50 seniors, students and children free; free Tues. 6–8. Open Tues. 1–8, Wed.–Sat. 11–5, Sun. noon–6.*

Museum Mile (actually, two miles) is a strip of solid cultural institutions located on or near Fifth Avenue between 82nd and 104th streets. Most of them are closed Mondays and (with the notable exception of the Metropolitan Museum) have free admission on Tuesday evenings.

❾ **The Metropolitan Museum of Art** is the largest art museum in the Western Hemisphere (1.6 million square feet) and its permanent collection of 3.3 million works contains art items from prehistory to modern times. Although its reputation rests solidly on a distinguished collection of pre-20th-century masterpieces, the museum in 1987 opened the Lila Acheson Wallace Wing devoted to its unsung 20th-century pieces.

Any of several walking tours and lectures is free with admission contribution. Tours begin about every 15 minutes on weekdays, less frequently on weekends. They depart from the Tour Board in the Great Hall (main entrance) but feel free to attach yourself to any you encounter along the way. Lectures, which are often connected with temporary exhibits, are given on Sundays, Tuesdays, and Fridays. *Fifth Ave. and 82nd St., tel. 212/535–7710. Suggested contribution: $5 adults, $2.50 seniors and stu-*

dents, children free. Open Tues. 9:30–8:45, Wed.–Sun. 9:30–5:15.

⑩ Frank Lloyd Wright's distinctive **Solomon R. Guggenheim Museum** is a six-story corkscrew through which visitors unwind past mobiles, stabiles, and other specimens of modern art. Displays alternate new artists and modern masters; permanent collection includes more than 20 Picassos. *1071 Fifth Ave. at 89th St., tel. 212/360–3500. Admission: $4.50 adults, $2.50 students and seniors; free Tues. 5–7:45. Open Tues. 11–7:45, Wed.–Sun. 11–4:45.*

⑪ Founded in 1825 and operated principally by artists, **The National Academy of Design** usually spotlights comparatively unsung artists of Europe and America. *1083 Fifth Ave. at 89th St., tel. 212/369–4880. Admission: $2.50 adults, $2 seniors and students; free Tues. 5–8. Open Tues. noon–8, Wed.–Sun. noon–5.*

⑫ A former residence of industrialist/philanthropist Andrew Carnegie now houses the **Cooper-Hewitt Museum,** officially the Smithsonian Institution's National Museum of Design. Exhibitions change regularly, each focusing on an aspect of contemporary or historical design. Major holdings include: drawings, prints, textiles, furniture, metalwork, ceramics, glass, woodwork, and wall coverings. *2 E. 91st St., tel. 212/860–6868. Admission: $3 adults, $1.50 seniors and students; free Tues. 5–9. Open Tues. 10–9, Wed.–Sat. 10–5, Sun. noon–5.*

Time Out **Jackson Hole** serves the great American hamburger plus other sandwiches, omelets, chicken, and salads amid the bracing ski-slope ambience of the eponymous Wyoming resort. Prices are reasonable; beer and wine available. *Madison Ave. and 91st St.*

⑬ The largest collector of Judaica in the Western hemisphere, the **Jewish Museum** features changing exhibits of modern art on Jewish traditions or various chapters of Jewish history. Gift shop offers wide selection of Jewish books and memorabilia. *1109 Fifth Ave. at 92nd St., tel. 212/860–1888. Admission: $4 adults, $2 seniors and students; free Tues. 5–8. Open Sun. 11–6, Mon., Wed., Thurs. noon–5, Tues. noon–8.*

⑭ A photography-only gallery housed in a Georgian mansion, the **International Center of Photography** (ICP) focuses on the work of a prominent photographer or one photographic genre (portraits, architecture, holography, etc.). The bookstore carries an array of photography-oriented books, prints, postcards; courses and special programs are offered throughout the year. *1130 Fifth Ave., tel. 212/860–1777. Admission: $3 adults, $1.50 students, $1 seniors and children under 12; free Tues. 5–8. Open Tues. noon–8, Wed.–Fri. noon–5, weekends 11–6.*

⑮ **The Museum of the City of New York** makes Big Apple history—from the Dutch settlers of Nieuw Amsterdam to recent headlines—come to life in period rooms, dioramas, slide shows, and clever displays of memorabilia. Weekend programs appeal especially to children. *Fifth Ave. at 103rd St., tel. 212/534–1672. Suggested contribution: $3 adults, $1.50 students and seniors, $1 children. Open Tues.–Sat. 10–5, Sun. and holidays 1–5.*

⑯ The final stop on Museum Mile, **El Museo del Barrio** concentrates on contemporary Latin culture with a particular emphasis on Puerto Rico. Permanent collection includes numerous pre-Columbian artifacts and hand-carved wooden saints. *1230 Fifth Ave. at 104th St., tel. 212/831–7272. Suggested contribution: $2. Open Wed.–Sun. 11–5.*

Harlem and Beyond

Encompassing the area of northern Manhattan from river to river between approximately 110th to 178th streets, Harlem began as a rural village founded by Dutch governor Peter Stuyvesant and during the second half of the 19th century became a fashionable suburb. After World War I, blacks moved into the area and Harlem became the center of the jazz and blues scene. While Harlem today is not an area for casual strolls, some of its attractions are well worth a special trip.

The **Schomburg Center for Research in Black Culture** (515 Malcolm X Blvd. at 135th St., tel. 212/862–4000) is an exhaustive reference library on black culture and a gallery for the work of black artists. New York's oldest black church, the **Abyssinian Baptist Church** (132 W. 138th St.), was the pulpit for the late U.S. Congressman Adam Clayton Powell, Jr., and contains a memorial room on his life.

Turn-of-the-century "Yuppies" moved to **"Strivers Row"** (W. 138th and 139th Sts. between Seventh and Eighth Aves.), four rows of distinguished Georgian town houses (Bob Dylan bought a town house here in 1988). Just up the hill is **Hamilton Grange** (287 Convent Ave. at 141st St.), the house where Alexander Hamilton lived the last years of his life. The neo-Gothic campus of **City College,** a branch of City University of New York, is located nearby (138th to 140th Sts. between Amsterdam Ave. and St. Nicholas Terr.).

Originally part of the estate of naturalist James J. Audubon, **Trinity Cemetery** (Riverside Dr. to Amsterdam Ave., 153rd to 155th Sts.) is the resting place of prominent New York families such as the Astors, Schermerhorns, Van Burens, and Bleeckers. Washington actually did sleep in the **Morris Jumel-Mansion** (Edgecombe Ave. and W. 160th St., tel. 212/923–8008), the oldest (1765) private residence remaining in Manhattan and Washington's headquarters during the Revolutionary War.

Perched atop a hill near Manhattan's northernmost tip is a medieval-style monastery, **The Cloisters Museum,** which houses part of the Metropolitan Museum of Art's medieval collection. Five cloisters connected by colonnaded walks transport you back 700 years. The view of the Hudson, Jersey Palisades (an undeveloped state park), and the towers of Manhattan far to the south are part of the experience. Catch the M4 "Cloisters-Fort Tryon Park" bus on Madison Avenue or ride the subway IND A line to 190th Street. *The Cloisters Museum, tel. 212/923–3700. Suggested contribution: $5 adults, $2.50 seniors and students, children free. Closed Mon., Jan. 1, Thanksgiving, and Dec. 25.*

Outer Boroughs

Although most visits duly focus on Manhattan (and only the southern half of Manhattan at that), the great majority of New Yorkers live in the four outer boroughs—the Bronx, Queens,

Brooklyn, and Staten Island (Richmond). Each borough is actually a separate county with its own borough president and county government. Each borough is also loaded with historic sights, restaurants, visitor attractions, and distinctive neighborhoods that can put a homey spin on the cosmopolitan New York experience.

To reach an outer borough from Manhattan, you must almost always travel over a bridge or through a tunnel, a routing that earns borough residents the not entirely flattering appellation of "bridge-and-tunnel people." Queens, Brooklyn, and Staten Island have a separate area code—718; however, there is no long-distance charge for calls between the 212 and 718 areas. All areas of New York City are accessible via subway, bus, or combinations of the two. For 24-hour subway and bus information, call 718/330–1234.

The Bronx The Bronx is New York's most northerly borough and the only part of the city on the American "mainland." The name—always *the* Bronx—derives from the estate of a 17th-century colonist named Jonas Bronck, or the Broncks. The Bronx name is attached to one of the world's greatest zoos, and the New York Yankees ("Bronx Bombers") play home games in the Bronx. Less favorably, the burned-out areas of the South Bronx have become synonymous with urban decline. The Bronx northern frontier is affluent Westchester County. In addition to New York City subways and buses, many Bronx attractions are accessible via the Metro-North Commuter Railroad; call 212/532–4900 for schedules and fares.

Bronx Zoo. Occupying 265 acres, the Bronx Zoo is one of the largest and most populous zoos—4,000 animals—in the world. Popular features include Wild Asia, a monorail ride over a 38-acre simulated natural environment; JungleWorld, an indoor Asian rain forest habitat; a Skyfari tram ride; and the new Himalayan Highland Habitat, a mountainous terrain for the endangered snow leopard. *Fordham Rd. and Bronx River Pkwy., tel. 212/367–1010. Take IRT no. 2 to "Pelham Parkway" and head west; or catch Liberty Lines Express bus (BxM 11) on Madison Ave., tel. 212/652–8400. Admission: Tues.–Thurs. donation; other days $3.75 adults, $1.50 children 2–12. Open Mon.–Sat. 10–5, Sun. and holidays to 5:30 (closes 4:30 during winter).*

New York Botanical Garden. Near the zoo, the Botanical Garden has 250 gorgeous acres of woods, waterways, and carefully tended gardens. The centerpiece is the Enid A. Haupt Conservatory within a magnificent crystal palace. *Southern Blvd. and E. 200th St., tel. 212/220–8700 or 212/220–8779. Take IRT no. 4 or IND D or C to "Bedford"; walk east to Southern Blvd. Admission: free to grounds; conservatory $3.50 adults, $1.25 children, students, seniors. Saturday morning free. Open Tues.–Sun. 10–5 (8 AM–7 PM Apr.–Oct.).*

Wave Hill. The former home of both Mark Twain and Arturo Toscanini, overlooking the Hudson River in the Riverdale section of the Bronx, is now a 28-acre public park with formal and wild gardens, nature trails, and two mansions. Indoor and outdoor concerts are scheduled frequently on weekends. *249th St. and Independence Ave., tel. 212/549–3200. Take IRT no. 1 to "231st St.," then Bx7 or Bx10 bus to 252nd St. Admission: weekdays free; weekends $2 adults, $1 students and seniors,* under 6 free. Concerts $7–$10. Open daily 10–4:30 (summer to 5:30, summer Sundays to 7).

Edgar Allan Poe Cottage. The well-preserved last home (1846–49) of the great American writer and the place where he penned "Chimes" and "Annabel Lee." *Grand Concourse and E. Kingsbridge Rd., tel. 212/881–8900. Take IND D or C to "Kingsbridge Rd." Admission: $1. Open Wed.–Fri. 9–5, Sat. 10–4, Sun. 1–5.*

Hall of Fame of Great Americans. One of New York's least-appreciated attractions, this 630-foot outdoor colonnade displays bronze portrait busts honoring outstanding Americans. Candidates are selected at least 25 years after their deaths by a committee of 100 representing every state. *Bronx Com unity College, University Ave. and 181st St., 212/220–6920. Take IRT no. 4 to "180th St." in Manhattan and Bx40 bus to Hall of Fame Terrace. Admission free. Open daily 10–5.*

Van Cortlandt Park. Nearly two square miles of swimming, horseback riding, golf, tennis—even a cricket "pitch." (**Van Cortlandt Mansion,** headquarters for both British and Colonial troops during the Revolutionary War, had just completed a renovation at press time. Tours are given on a limited basis. Call 212/543-3344 for hours.) *Take IRT no. 1 to "242nd St./Van Cortlandt Park." Enter at Broadway and 245th St.*

Belmont. Centered around Arthur Avenue and Fordham Road, the Bronx's Little Italy features turn-of-the-century apartment houses and an open-air market of Italian taste treats. *Take IND D or C to "Fordham Rd." and the Bx12 bus to Arthur Ave.*

City Island. An approximation of a New England fishing village just off the Bronx northeast coast. Go out to inhale the bracing Long Island Sound air, eat at a shoreside restaurant, rent a boat, and visit the **City Island Nautical Museum.** *190 Fordham St. Take IRT no. 6 to "Pelham Bay Park" and Bx12 bus to City Island.*

Queens The largest of the five boroughs, Queens occupies 121 square miles on the northwest tip of Long Island. Queens County is a mostly residential aggregation of erstwhile small towns to which residents still hold primary allegiance. Ask people from Queens where they live and they'll say Flushing, Jamaica, Forest Hills, Astoria, etc. Mail is addressed to individual localities, too.

There are plenty of reasons for visiting or at least passing through Queens. Both LaGuardia and Kennedy airports are located in Queens. So is Shea Stadium, home of the New York Mets. Louis Armstrong Stadium in Flushing Meadows is where the U.S. Open is played. Other attractions include:

Queens Museum. The museum is located within Flushing Meadow–Corona Park, site of the 1939 and 1964 world's fairs. The building itself was headquarters of the United Nations from 1946 to 1950. The main attraction here is the 9,000-square-foot model of New York City: The world's largest scale model, it depicts more than 865,000 buildings. *Flushing Meadow–Corona Park., tel. 718/592–2405. Take IRT no. 7 to "Willets Point/Shea Stadium." Admission: $2 adults, $1 seniors, students, children over 5. Open Tues.–Fri. 10–5, weekends noon–5:30.*

Flushing. Most Queens historic sights are located in Flushing, founded in 1643 as the Dutch settlement of Vlissingen and a major focus of Quaker (Society of Friends) activities. Built in 1694, the **Friends Meeting House** (Northern Blvd. and Linden Pl., tel. 718/358–9636) is one of the few still-active 17th-century places of worship in America. The **Kingsland House** (143–35 37th Ave., tel. 718/939–0647) is a three-story 1774 farm house that mingles English and Dutch architectural traditions. Built in 1661 by Quaker John Bowne, the **Bowne House** (37–01 Bowne St., 718/359–0528) is now a shrine to religious freedom. *Take IRT no. 7 to "Main St., Flushing."*

Jamaica Bay Wildlife Refuge. On this pleasant mile-long path through a section of the huge (9,152 acres) preserve, you may view up to 50 species of shorebirds, waterfowl, and small mammals on a given day. *Broad Channel between Howard Beach and the Rockaways, tel. 718/474–0613. Take IND A or C to "Broad Channel" and walk north to visitor center. Admission free. Open daily from 8:30–5.*

American Museum of the Moving Image. Located on the site of 1920s Astoria Studios complex, this new museum (opened 1988) is the first in the United States devoted exclusively to film, television, and video. Along with a 60,000-artifact collection of posters, costumes, film sets, and technical apparatus, the museum offers continuous video programming and screenings of full-length features. *35th Ave. at 36th St., Astoria, tel. 718/784–4520. Take N subway line to "Broadway" in Queens; walk east on Broadway to 36th St., turn right (south) to museum. Admission: $5 adults, $2.50 students and seniors, includes programs in main theater. Open Wed. and Thurs. 1–5, Fri. 1–6, weekends 11–6.*

Brooklyn Brooklyn begins across the East River opposite Lower Manhattan and extends across 70 square miles of the southwest corner of Long Island to the Atlantic coast. Brooklyn (Kings County) is the most populous New York City borough (2.23 million), and were it not for what many Brooklynites still insist upon calling "The Great Mistake," the 1898 incorporation of the independent municipality of Brooklyn into New York City, it would be the fourth-largest city in America.

Brooklyn today consists of many distinctive neighborhood communities. Hasidic Jews live in Williamsburg, Crown Heights, and Borough Park; Greenpoint is Polish; Flatbush is distinctively West Indian; young professionals of all persuasions inhabit Park Slope. Brooklyn is also a borough of handsome parks, long straight streets lined with fine 19th-century brownstone and limestone row houses, and some of the city's most important cultural institutions.

Brooklyn Heights. Brooklyn Heights lies at the foot of Brooklyn Bridge directly opposite the Financial District. The 50-block historical district preserves many original 18th- and 19th-century buildings. Palatial **Borough Hall** (209 Joralemon St.), an 1851 Greek Revival structure with an imposing cupola, was restored and reopened in 1989. The **Brooklyn Historical Society** (128 Pierrepont St., tel. 718/624–0890) displays memorabilia of all things Brooklyn, from bygone trolley lines to bygone baseball teams. Henry Ward Beecher preached fiery abolitionist sermons from the pulpit of the simple brick Plymouth Church, now the **Plymouth Church of the Pilgrims**

(Orange St. between Henry and Hicks Sts.). The 1829 structure at **24 Middaugh Street** (corner of Hicks St.) is one of the oldest remaining houses in the Heights. Cantilevered out from the Heights over the Brooklyn–Queens Expressway (BQE), **The Promenade** offers a spectacular view of New York Harbor and Lower Manhattan. *Take IRT no. 2, 3, 4, or 5 to "Boro Hall" or BMT N, R, or M to "Court St."*

Prospect Park. This vast 345-acre tract of meadows, woods, streams, and a large lake were left as unspoiled as possible by designers Frederick Law Olmsted and Calvert Vaux (who, according to Brooklynites, auditioned for this job by designing Manhattan's Central Park). Prospect Park also contains a Quaker cemetery, a zoo, a band shell, and the Dutch Colonial Lefferts Homestead. The park begins at **Grand Army Plaza** (Flatbush Ave., Union St., Prospect Park, and Eastern Pkwy.), a traffic circle surrounding a massive triumphal arch that occasionally serves as an art gallery and observation tower. *Take IRT no. 2 or 3 to "Grand Army Plaza."*

Brooklyn Botanic Garden. On the eastern fringe of Prospect Park, the 52-acre plot is noted for its trim Japanese garden, Shakespeare Garden (all plants here are mentioned in Shakespeare's writings), Children's Garden, Rose Garden, Herb Garden, and Garden of Fragrance maintained especially for the blind. The three-unit (tropical, desert, temperate) Steinhardt Conservatory, first expansion since 1910, opened in 1988. *1000 Washington Ave., tel. 718/622-4433. Take IRT no. 2 or 3 to "Eastern Parkway/Brooklyn Museum." Admission for conservatory: $2. Open Tues.–Fri. 8–6, weekends 10–6 (closes 4:30 March–Nov.).*

Brooklyn Museum. Situated at the northeast tip of Prospect Park, the Brooklyn Museum has a world-famous collection of Egyptian art, North and South American Indian handicrafts, and Oriental art. An outdoor sculpture garden displays detailing from demolished New York buildings. *200 Eastern Pkwy., tel. 718/638-5000. Take IRT no. 2 or 3 to "Eastern Pkwy./Brooklyn Museum." Suggested contribution: $3 adults, $1.50 students, $1 seniors, under 12 free. Open daily except Tues. 10–5.*

Coney Island. Though somewhat down-at-the-heels of late, Coney Island is still a rollicking beach and amusement park that attracts up to a million people on hot summer Sundays. Along with Astroland, Disco Scooter, and the original Nathan's Famous hot dogs, you can also tour the fascinating **New York Aquarium** (*see* What to See and Do with Children) or visit the Russian-Jewish émigré community at contiguous Brighton Beach. *Take B, F, D, or N to "Stillwell Ave./Coney Island."*

Staten Island Most visitors to Staten Island, New York's least populous borough, never get farther than the terminal for the ferry trip that has to be America's best cruise bargain. The Staten Island Ferry still costs only 25¢ *round-trip* for the 20- to 30-minute ride across New York Harbor. The rest of Staten Island extends 14 miles farther south, to where the Arthur Kill separates it from Perth Amboy, New Jersey. Although the topography is predominantly flat, the Island boasts the highest point on the Atlantic Seaboard, Todt Hill, 410 feet above sea level. It also has 5,000 acres set aside for parkland and vast stretches of underdeveloped territory where it's impossible to believe you're still within the boundaries of the nation's largest metropolis.

Verrazano Narrows Bridge. Connecting Staten Island to Brooklyn, the world's largest suspension bridge (total length 13,700 feet; main span 4,260 feet) is named after Giovanni da Verrazano, the Italian navigator who discovered New York Harbor in 1524. *For a scenic bus ride across the bridge into Brooklyn, take the S113 bus from Ferry Terminal to Clove Rd. and transfer to the S7 bus for bridge crossing. Ride R subway from "95th St./Ft. Hamilton" back into Manhattan.*

Snug Harbor Cultural Center. Overlooking Kill Van Kull, this 26-building National Historic Landmark District and former seamen's home encompasses a botanical garden, 80 acres of grounds, a children's museum, and a cultural arts complex. Concerts in Veterans Memorial Hall. *1000 Richmond Terr., tel. 718/448–2500. Take S40 bus or Snug Harbor Trolley ($1) from Ferry Terminal. Free tours weekends at 2 PM. Open daily 8 AM–midnight.*

Richmondtown Restoration. Ongoing restoration of 28 buildings in 17th-century town that became county seat of Richmond County. *441 Clarke Ave., tel. 718/351–1617. Take S113 bus from Ferry Terminal. Admission: $4 adults, $2.50 seniors, students, and children 6–18. Open weekdays 10–5; weekends 1–5.*

Jacques Marchais Center of Tibetan Art. Unexpectedly, two monastic-style stone buildings on Lighthouse Hill house one of the largest collections Tibetan art in the western hemisphere. *338 Lighthouse Ave., tel. 718/987–3478. Take S113 bus from Ferry Terminal to Lighthouse Ave. Admission: $2.50 adults, $2 seniors, $1 children. Open April–Nov., Wed.–Sun. 1–5.*

Conference House. This 1670 house close to New York City's southwesternmost point was the scene of the only British-American peace conference during the Revolutionary War. Overlooking Raritan Bay and the Jersey shore, the fieldstone manor has been restored with authentic working period pieces. *Foot of Hylan Blvd., Tottenville, tel. 718/984–2086. Take Staten Island Rapid Transit from Ferry Terminal to Tottenville, the last stop; walk south to Hylan Blvd. Admission: $1 adults, 50¢ children. Open Wed.–Sun. 1–4.*

New York for Free

Concerts. Much live music in New York is available to anyone willing to lend an ear. Free concerts, recitals, and dance presentations are presented in churches, college auditoriums, and public buildings all over town. During the summer, outdoor concerts are performed regularly at the band shell in Central Park and at the Guggenheim band shell at Lincoln Center. Free concerts are irregularly performed in other locations. The best sources of information on free concerts all over town are the weekly *New York* magazine and the *Village Voice*. The *Voice* "Cheap Thrills" section lists concerts, lectures, forums, street fairs, and sundry events that cost $2.50 or less.

Art Galleries. Whereas most museums charge admission or suggest a donation, private art galleries are absolutely free. And if you happen to stumble into a gallery during the opening of an exhibition, you'll even get free drinks and snacks. New

York's galleries are located in clusters: Madison Avenue in the 70s and 80s; 57th Street between Sixth and Park avenues; the East Village; SoHo; TriBeCa. To find out the location of the galleries and current exhibitions, consult *New York* magazine, *The New Yorker*, the *Village Voice*, and the Sunday *New York Times*.

Street Fairs. On weekend afternoons from mid-May through late September, street fairs turn New York's thoroughfares into carnival midways. While each fair has its own peculiar character, all offer at modest prices plenty of food, music, rides, local crafts, and flea-market merchandise. Action usually begins about noon and lasts until dusk. To find out the locations and times of street fairs, check out the "Other Events" section of *New York* magazine, the *Village Voice*, and Friday editions of the daily newspapers.

TV Shows. Tickets to tapings or live performances of the most popular TV shows ("Saturday Night Live," "Donahue," "David Letterman") are distributed by mail up to a year in advance. However, it is quite possible to get free tickets to less popular shows or pilots of next season's offerings—in fact, your reaction may help determine if a show ever hits the airwaves. The New York City Convention and Visitors Bureau (2 Columbus Circle) often distributes day-of-performance tickets. Also, personnel from the major networks station themselves in the Rockefeller Center area distributing passes to programs.

Con Edison Conservation Center. Located on the ground floor of the Chrysler Building, this facility has entertaining hands-on ways of raising energy-conservation consciousness. *405 Lexington Ave. at 42nd St., tel. 212/599–3435. Open Tues.–Sat. 9–5.*

Grand Central Terminal. Tours of one of the world's most famous transportation centers are offered Wednesdays at 12:30. *Park Ave. and 42nd St., tel. 212/935–3960.*

Mormon Visitor Center. Diorama, multimedia displays, and movies tell the story of Mormonism. *Broadway and 65th St., tel. 212/595–1825. Open daily 10–8.*

What to See and Do with Children

Zoos **Bronx Zoo.** The largest city zoo in the United States has more than 4,000 animals on 265 acres of woods, ponds, streams, and parkland. At Children's Zoo, kids can model a turtle's shell and climb through a prairie dog tunnel. *Fordham Rd. and Bronx River Pkwy., the Bronx, tel. 212/367–1010. Admission: Tues.–Thurs. (contribution days) free, Fri.–Mon. $3.75 adults, $1.50 children; Nov.–Mar. $1.75 adults, 75¢ children; over 65 and under 2 always free. Open Apr.–Oct., Mon.–Sat. 10–5, Sun. 10–5:30; Nov.–Mar. daily 10–4:30.*

Central Park Zoo. The newly remodeled zoo, just a few blocks from the Plaza Hotel, gives youngsters opportunities to get acquainted with animals. At the Lehman Children's Zoo, kids can pet farm animals and see pint-sized creatures from all over the world. *Fifth Ave. and E. 64th St., tel. 212/408–0271. Regular zoo admission: $1 adults, 50¢ seniors, 25¢ children. Children's Zoo admission: 10¢. Open daily 10–4:30.*

New York Aquarium. Just off the Coney Island Boardwalk, the aquarium has over 20,000 creatures on display and performing in periodic exhibitions. A new learning and exhibition center, Discovery Cove, opened in June 1989. *W. 8th St. and Surf Ave., Coney Island, Brooklyn, tel. 718/265–3474. Admission: $3.75 adults, $1.50 children. Open 10–4:45 (5:45 weekends between Memorial Day and Labor Day).*

Museums   **American Museum of Natural History/Hayden Planetarium.** This museum owns 36 million artifacts but most kids only remember the life-size dinosaur bones and moon rocks. Children can handle nature's wonders in the Discovery Room. The NatureMax Theater projects two or three different shows daily on a four-story-high screen. Hayden Planetarium shows augment star displays with laser beams and music (rock or classical). *Central Park West at 79th St.; Hayden Planetarium at CPW and 81st St., tel. 212/769–5100 for museum, 212/769–5900 for planetarium. Suggested contribution: $3.50 adults, $1.50 children, Fri. and Sat. 5–9 free. Admission NatureMax shows: $3.50 adults, $1.75 children. Planetarium admission and sky shows: $3.75 adults, $2 children under 12. Open weekdays 12:30–4:45, Sat. 10–5:45, Sun. 12–5:45.*

South Street Seaport Museum. Along with several old ships, galleries, restored port surroundings, and a new children's center, the Seaport Museum runs special afternoon tours of the area for kids. A multimedia "Seaport Experience" show is presented hourly in the Trans-Lux Seaport Theater. *Visitors Center, 207 Water St., tel. 212/669–9424. Admission: $5 adults, $4 seniors, $2 children. "Seaport Experience" showings: $4.75 adults, $3.50 children. Open daily 10–5.*

Museum of Broadcasting. Children can choose from the museum's collection of more than 30,000 taped TV and radio shows. *1 E. 53rd St., tel. 212/752–7684. Open Tues.–Sat. noon–5 (8 PM Tues.). Admission: $4 adults, $3 students, $2 seniors and children under 13.*

Intrepid Sea-Air-Space Museum. A decommissioned World War II aircraft carrier berthed in the Hudson River has displays on the history of naval aviation, today's navy, and man's conquest of space. Lots of films and hands-on exhibits. *Pier 86, Hudson River at 46th St., tel. 212/245–0072. Admission: $6 adults, $5 seniors, $3.25 children 6–11. Open Wed.–Sun. 10–5.*

Museum of Holography. Even kids are impressed with the strangely enchanting 3-D effects at this first museum of the holographic arts. *11 Mercer St., SoHo, tel. 212/925–0526. Admission: $3 adults, $2.75 students, $1.75 seniors and children under 12. Open Tues.–Sun. 11–6.*

Children's Museum of Manhattan. An all hands-on place with permanent exhibitions on nature, science, and art, plus major changing exhibits. *314 W. 54th St., tel. 212/765–5904. Admission: $1 adults, $2 children weekdays; $2 adults, $3 children weekends and holidays. Open Tues.–Fri. 1–5, weekends 10–5.*

Brooklyn Children's Museum. The world's first children's museum—founded 1899—invites participation on a steel mesh bridge, old trolley cars, a greenhouse, and a huge simulated river. The museum has more than 50,000 historic and technological artifacts and a collection of over 2,500 dolls. *145 Brooklyn Ave. at St. Mark's Ave., Brooklyn, tel. 718/735–4400. Suggested contribution: $2 adults. Open weekdays 2–5, weekends and holidays 10–5; closed Tues.*

Shows   For information on what's playing at particular theaters, check the Friday *New York Times*, the "Other Events" section of *New York Magazine*, and the *Village Voice*.

Mostly Magic. Magic shows combined with comedy and audience participation. *55 Carmine St., tel. 212/924–1472. Admission: $7.50. Sat. at 2.*

13th Street Repertory Company. Lots of audience participation in hour-long plays with music. *50 E. 13th St., tel. 212/675–6677. Admission: $4. Sat. and Sun. 1 and 3.*

Jan Hus Playhouse. Musical comedies suitable for 3 years and up. "Funzapoppin' Magic Show" from April through June. Reservations required. *351 E. 74th St., tel. 212/772–9180. Admission: $4.50. Sun. 1:30.*

Little People Theater Company. One of New York's longest-running children's theater groups presents audience-participation adaptations of "Red Riding Hood," "Three Little Pigs," "Cinderella," and other classics. Reservations advised. *Courtyard Playhouse, 39 Grove St., tel. 212/765–9540. Admission: $6. Labor Day through June, Sat. and Sun. 1:30 and 3.*

Off the Beaten Track

Roosevelt Island Aerial Tramway. Take a ride to Roosevelt Island, a modern residential complex in the East River. Running alongside the Queensboro (59th St.) Bridge, the tramway gives a thrilling high-wire ride and a great view of the Upper East Side. *Second Ave. at 60th St. One-way fare $1 (subway token).*

Playground, Sixth Avenue and Third Street. See urban street basketball at its free-swinging best on a patch of Greenwich Village asphalt. Contests all afternoon and evenings whenever weather permits.

Astor Place Hair Designers. A tonsorial supermarket where lines of men and women awaiting service by four levels of barbers spill out on the sidewalk. Choose a superhip cut from the Polaroid examples in the window—maybe the Village Cut, a Guido, or a Li'l Tony: It's only $10 for men and $12 for women. *2 Astor Pl., tel. 212/475–9854. Open daily.*

Carl Schurz Park. This delightful patch of green in the northeast corner of the Upper East Side overlooks Hell Gate, the confluence of the East River, Harlem River, and Long Island Sound. The park also encompasses **Gracie Mansion,** a 1799 country house that has served as the official residence of New York mayors since 1942. *East End Ave. at 88th St., tel. 212/570–4751. Tours Wed., Nov.–Apr. by appointment only; fee $3 adults, $1 seniors.*

Hanover Square. This island of relative tranquillity in the Financial District used to be on the East River waterfront. The pirate Captain Kidd lived in the neighborhood, and the adjacent 1837 **India House** used to be the New York Cotton Exchange. William, Pearl, and Stone Sts.

Gansevoort Market. Nondescript warehouse buildings in the northwest corner of Greenwich Village (around Greenwich and Gansevoort Sts.) each morning become the meat market for the city's butchers and restaurateurs. Check out **Restaurant Florent** (69 Gansevoort St., tel. 212/989–5779), a meat-and-potatoes diner by day and trendy French bistro by night.

Police Academy Museum. Here you can see displays of emergency procedures, bizarre weaponry, uniforms, and latest artillery in the war against crime. *235 E. 20th St., tel. 212/477–9753. Admission free. Open weekdays 9–3.*

Sutton Place Park. This vest-pocket park overlooking the Queensboro Bridge and East River is where Woody Allen and

Diane Keaton watched the sun come up in *Manhattan. East River and 58th St.*

Shopping

Like the city itself, New York stores are diverse, competitive, exciting, and challenging. Quality is high because merchandise must attain sufficient standards to please the world's fussiest shoppers. Competition is fierce, begetting closeouts, off-price dealers, outlet shops, and incessant sales in every area. Whatever you're looking for, you'll find it in New York—usually for less the next time you look.

Major department stores and other shops are usually open every day and keep late hours on Thursdays. Many of the upscale shops along Upper Fifth Avenue and the Madison Mile close on Sundays. Stores in nightlife centers such as SoHo and Columbus Avenue are usually open evenings.

Most department stores accept their own charge cards and American Express. Macy's, B. Altman's, and Alexander's also accept Visa and MasterCard. Smaller stores usually accept major credit cards. Paying by personal check is sometimes permitted but seldom encouraged. Sales tax in New York City is 8¼%.

Shopping Districts

Upper Fifth Avenue. Fifth Avenue from 49th Street to 59th Street and 57th Street between Third and Sixth avenues has Trump Tower and some of the most famous stores in the world, namely Saks Fifth Avenue, Bergdorf Goodman, Henri Bendel, Bonwit Teller, Steuben Glass, Tiffany, and Cartier.
Herald Square. The area extending from Herald Square (Sixth Ave. and 34th St.) along 34th Street and up Fifth Avenue to 40th Street encompasses several major department stores (Macy's, B. Altman's, Lord & Taylor) and a host of lower priced clothing and accessory shops.
Madison Mile. The low-rise brownstones on the 20-block span of Madison Avenue between 59th and 79th streets house the exclusive boutiques of American and overseas designers, elite galleries, and specialty shops.
SoHo. Along West Broadway between Houston and Canal streets you'll find art galleries, boutiques, crafts shops, and other enterprises that defy categorization.
Columbus Avenue. Shopping area between 66th and 86th streets mingles far-out Euro-styles with down-home preppy; there are also antique shops, vintage clothing stores, and outlets for adult toys.
Lower East Side. The intersection of Orchard and Delancey streets is a bargain-hunter's paradise of shops and stalls selling women's and men's fashions, children's clothing, shoes, accessories, linens. Closed Saturday; mobbed Sunday.

Department Stores

Alexander's. This is New York's least expensive, full-service department store. Men's department features moderately priced, high-quality imports; women's sections reward the sharp-eyed shopper. *Lexington Ave. and E. 58th St., tel. 212/593-0880.*

Henri Bendel. Prices in this agglomeration of stylish boutiques may not be as high as you fear and window displays are always worth a close look. *10 W. 57th St., tel. 212/247-1100.*

Bergdorf Goodman. A chic, very New York place for women's designer clothes, this store has an underrated men's department. *754 Fifth Ave. at 57th St., tel. 212/753-7300.*

Bloomingdale's. Occupying the entire block from 59th to 60th streets between Lexington and Third avenues, "Bloomie's" is the quintessence of New York style—busy, noisy, crowded, and thoroughly up-to-date. It's expensive but not punishingly so. *59th St. and Lexington Ave., tel. 212/705-2000.*

Bonwit Teller. This famous store is now smaller in square footage since the relocation to Trump Tower, but it's still a stylish venue for high-fashion design. *4 E. 57th St., tel. 212/593-3333.*

Lord & Taylor. This reasonably dignified establishment emphasizes well-made clothing by American designers. *424 Fifth Ave. at W. 38th St., tel. 212/391-3344.*

Macy's. Always comprehensive and competitive, the largest retail store in the United States has of late become quite stylish as well. *W. 34th St. and Broadway, tel. 212/695-4440.*

Saks Fifth Avenue. The flagship store of a nationwide chain, this emporium has an outstanding selection of women's and men's designer outfits. *611 Fifth Ave. at E. 50th St., tel. 212/753-4000.*

Flea Markets

Annex Antiques and Flea Market consists mostly of antiques dealers selling furniture, vintage clothing, books, and jewelry. *Sixth Ave. and W. 25th St., weekends 9–5. Free parking. Admission: $1.*

The **I.S. (Intermediate School) 44 Flea Market** earns money for an after-school program by selling used clothing, jewelry, and miscellaneous collectibles. "Greenflea" farmers' market, too. *Columbus Ave. and W. 77th St., Sun. 10–6.*

An empty lot at **335 Canal St.** becomes a beehive of treasures on weekends from March through December.

Auctions

Christie's. You can bid—if you dare—for fine art at suitably high-flying prices. *502 Park Ave. at E. 59th St., tel. 212/546-1000.*

Christie's East. This auction house has less expensive, more recent pieces than its Park Avenue parent. *219 E. 67th St., tel. 212/606-0400.*

Lubin Galleries. Here you can find reasonably priced furniture and antiques. *30 W. 26th St., tel. 212/924-3777.*

Manhattan Galleries. This place has an assortment of items from antiquity to the very recent past. *1415 Third Ave., tel. 212/744-2844.*

Sotheby's. Fine art, antiques, Americana, jewelry, and other high-toned merchandise are auctioned off feverishly at this noted house. *1334 York Ave. at 72nd St, tel. 212/606-7000.*

Sotheby's Arcade Auctions. This is the "budget" section of the exclusive auction gallery. *1334 York Ave. at 72nd St., tel. 212/606–7409.*

Tepper Galleries. Art and furniture can be bought here from $10 to $10,000. *110 E. 25th St., tel. 212/677–5300.*

Specialty Stores

Antiques **ABC Antiques.** This is virtually a department store of antiques (rugs and carpeting, too). *888 Broadway at W. 19th St., tel. 212/254–7171.*

Place des Antiquaires. Two brand-new subterranean levels of high-ticket antiques and art dealers have been added here. *125 E. 57th St., tel. 212/758–2900.*

Books **Barnes & Noble Sale Annex.** This two-story emporium of new books, used books, remainders, review copies, and "hurt" books features everything at discount. *105 Fifth Ave. at W. 18th St., tel. 212/807–0099.*

Gotham Book Mart. Here is a browser's paradise of books on every subject. *41 W. 47th St., tel. 212/719–4448.*

Strand Book Store. This Greenwich Village institution has a vast selection of used books and like-new review copies. *828 Broadway at W. 12th St., tel. 212/473–1452.*

Cameras, Electronics **47th Street Photo.** Climb a flight of stairs to a chaotic sales floor; no hand-holding but good discounts on everything. *Three locations: 67 W. 47th St., tel. 212/398–1410; 115 W. 45th St., tel. 212/398–1410; and 116 Nassau St., tel. 212/608–6934. Closed Sat.*

Crafts **Folklorica.** Ex–Peace Corps volunteers merchandise tasteful collectibles from Africa and other exotic locales. *89 Fifth Ave. at 17th St., tel. 212/255–2525.*

Museum of American Folk Art Shop. This Rockefeller shop features a charming array of Americana from the Lincoln Center–area museum. *62 W. 50th St., tel. 212/247–5611.*

Flowers and Plants The sidewalks are a jungle at the **Wholesale Flower District** along Sixth Avenue between 25th and 29th streets. They deal mostly with retail florists but happily sell to the public.

Housewares **Conran's.** This is the store, at three locations, that so cunningly furnishes those chic Manhattan apartments. *Citicorp Center, Third Ave. and E. 54th St., tel. 212/371–2225; 2248 Broadway at W. 81st St., tel. 212/873–9250; and 2 Astor Pl., tel. 212/505–1515.*

D. F. Sanders. There are SoHo and Upper East Side locations for the slick Euro-style products that almost make housework fun. *386 W. Broadway, tel. 212/925–9040, and 952 Madison Ave. at E. 75th St., tel. 212/879–6161.*

Jewelry Every store is a jewelry shop in the **Diamond District,** 47th Street between Fifth and Sixth avenues. Shop around—and don't pay the first price you hear. Most closed Sat.

Leather and Luggage **Mark Cross.** Featured here are fine traditional leather goods and pampered service. *645 Fifth Ave. at E. 51st St., tel. 212/421–3000.*

Fine & Klein. This is one of Orchard Street's illustrious discounters. *119 Orchard St., tel. 212/674–6720.*

Menswear **Barneys.** This Chelsea establishment claims to be the world's largest men's store. Fine quality at high prices is available in traditional and high-fashion tailoring. Women's clothes are now available, too. *106 Seventh Ave. at 17th St., tel. 212/929–9000.*

Pan Am Menswear. No gracious accoutrements are discernible at this Lower East Side spot but there are substantial discounts on brand names. *50 Orchard St., tel. 212/925–7032.*

Syms. Designer labels at bargain-basement prices are available here, one block from the World Trade Center. There is also women's clothing. *45 Park Pl., tel. 212/791–1199.*

Records and Tapes **Colony Records.** There are no discounts in this Theater District institution, which has a vast inventory. *1619 Broadway at 49th St., tel. 212/265–2050.*

Tower Records. Huge selections, reasonable prices, and late hours (both stores are open until midnight) attract a lively singles crowd. *692 Broadway at W. 4th St., tel. 212/505–1500, and 1965 Broadway at W. 67th St., tel. 212/799–2500.*

Sporting Goods **Paragon.** This three-level store near Union Square has reasonable prices on sporting goods, camping gear, running shoes, and clothing. *867 Broadway near 18th St., tel. 212/255–8036.*

Hudson's. You'll find this huge operation has low prices on outdoor clothing and camping equipment. *97 Third Ave. at E. 13th St., tel. 212/473–0981.*

Toys **F.A.O. Schwarz.** A cathedral of childhood delights—with similarly lofty prices—can be found in this famous store. *Fifth Ave. and 58th St., tel. 212/644–9400.*

Mythology. Outrageous toys and souvenirs for children and adults are available here, across the street from the American Museum of Natural History. *370 Columbus Ave. at W. 78th St., tel. 212/874–0774.*

Penny Whistle. Upper East Side, Upper West Side, and SoHo locations all feature high-toned selections of European and American novelties. *1283 Madison Ave. at E. 91st St., tel. 212/369–3868; 448 Columbus Ave. at W. 81st St., tel. 212/873–9090; and 132 Spring St., tel. 212/925–2088.*

Women's Clothing **Ms. Miss, or Mrs.** This division of Ben Farber Inc. is a Garment District standby with new designer fashions at 40%–60% off. *462 Seventh Ave. at W. 35th St., tel. 212/736–0557.*

Stanrose. This is a no-frills Garment District outlet for up-to-date designer outfits at big discounts. *141 W. 36th St. between Seventh Ave. and Broadway, tel. 212/736–3358.*

22 Steps. The name indicates how many steps you climb from the Madison Mile for low prices on designer outfits. *746 Madison Ave. at E. 65th St., tel. 212/288–2240.*

Opening and Closing Times

Banks. Open weekdays 9–3.

Museums. Most are open daily from 9:30 or 10 to 5 or 6, with evening hours until 8 or 9 on Tuesday. Many museums are closed Monday. Check individual listings.

Shops. Most shops and department stores are open daily from about 10 (noon on Sunday) to 6, with evening shopping hours on Thursday. Many shops on the Madison Mile and Upper Fifth Avenue are closed Sunday.

Bars. Many stay open until 4 AM Mon.–Sat., but must close at 3 AM Sun.

Participant Sports

Beaches and Water Sports

New York's most famous beach is **Coney Island,** a populous expanse of seashore on Brooklyn's southern coast. A boardwalk complete with carnival rides and sideshows borders the beach. Coney Island is at least an hour's ride on the subway from midtown; take the B, D, F, or N line from Manhattan to "Stillwell Ave./Coney Island." Just east of Coney Island, **Brighton Beach** is less populous and gets a distinctively European flavor from the Little Odessa neighborhood which it fronts. Take the D train to "Brighton Beach." Less well-known but perhaps the most scenic of Brooklyn's beaches is **Manhattan Beach.** It's a mile east of the "Brighton Beach" station on the D line; walk or take the B1 bus.

In Queens the major beach is **Jacob Riis Park,** on the Rockaway Peninsula. The beach is rated the city's cleanest and the park includes free tennis, handball, shuffleboard, and squash courts, plus an 18-hole pitch-and-putt course. Get there via the IRT no. 2 or 3 line to "Flatbush Ave./Brooklyn College" and take the Q35 bus the rest of the way.

Other popular New York City beaches include **Orchard Beach,** the so-called Riviera of the Bronx, and **Wolfe's Pond Park** on Staten Island.

Bicycling

Central Park roadways are closed to cars on weekends throughout the year and from early April to early November are closed weekdays 10 AM–3 PM and 7–10 PM. You can rent bicycles in Central Park from **Central Park Bicycle Rental** (beside the Loeb Boathouse parallel to 72nd St., tel. 212/861–4137). Outside but near the park, bicycles are available from **Metro Bicycles** (1311 Lexington Ave. at E. 88th St., tel. 212/427–4450), **Midtown Bicycles** (360 W. 47th St., tel. 212/581–4500), and **West Side Bicycle** (231 W. 96th St., tel. 212/663–7531).

Bowling

Among New York's few remaining bowling alleys are **Bowlmor Lanes** (110 University Pl. at W. 12th St., tel. 212/255–8188), a grungy bi-level facility in Greenwich Village, and **Madison Square Garden Bowling Center** (Seventh Ave. and W. 33rd St., tel. 212/563–8160), bright modern lanes inside Madison Square Garden.

Golf

Though far short of tournament quality, New York's golf courses are numerous and inexpensive—never over $15. In Brooklyn play at **Dyker Beach** (tel. 718/836–9722) or **Marine Park** (tel. 718/338–7113). Queens courses include **Clearview** (tel. 718/229–2570), **Douglaston Park** (tel. 718/224–6566), and **Forest Park** (tel. 718/296–0999). The Bronx has **Mosholu-Golf** (tel. 212/655–9164), **Pelham-Split Rock** (tel. 212/885–1258), New York's toughest, and **Van Cortlandt** (tel. 212/543–4595).

On Staten Island, tee off at **La Tourette** (tel. 718/351–1889), **South Shore Men's Club** (tel. 718/984–0108), or **Silver Lake** (tel. 718/447–5686).

Horseback Riding

To ride in style through Central Park, hire a mount from the **Claremont Riding Academy** (175 W. 89th St., tel. 212/724–5101). For equestrian experiences in Brooklyn's vast Prospect Park, there is **Prospect Park Riding Stables** (51 Caton Pl., tel. 718/438–8849). **Lynne's** (88-03 70th Rd., Forest Hills, Queens, tel. 718/261–7679) furnishes mounts for Forest Park along the Brooklyn–Queens border.

Ice Skating

Skate outdoors from November through early April in the shadow of the famous Prometheus statue in **Rockefeller Center** or in **Wollman Rink** (tel. 212/517-4800) near the southeast corner of Central Park. **Sky Rink** (450 W. 33rd St., tel. 212/695–6556) has rooftop indoor skating sessions for adults and children year-round.

Jogging

Central Park is the principal milieu for New York joggers, especially the 1.59-mile soft-surface track that encircles the Reservoir at Fifth Avenue and 90th Street. **Riverside Park,** along the Hudson River above W. 72nd Street, and **Washington Square Park** in Greenwich Village also attract devotees. For information on group runs contact **New York Road Runners Club** (tel. 212/860–4455).

Physical Fitness

Manhattan hotels with either in-house health clubs or arrangements with independent health clubs include the **Drake Swissotel** (440 Park Ave. at E. 56th St., tel. 212/421–0900), **Grand Bay Hotel at Equitable Center** (152 W. 51st St., tel. 212/765–1900), **Peninsula of New York** (700 Fifth Ave. at 55th St., tel. 212/247–2200), **Loew's Summit** (Lexington Ave. at E. 51st St., tel. 212/752–7000), **Parker Meridien** (118 W. 57th St., tel. 212/245–5000), **Sheraton City Squire** (790 Seventh Ave. at W. 51st St., tel. 212/581–3300), **United Nations Plaza** (First Ave. at E. 44th St., tel. 212/355–3400), and the **Vista International** (3 World Trade Center, tel. 212/938–9100).

Tennis

Outdoor tennis courts are maintained by the Parks Department. Residents purchase season (Apr.–Nov.) passes for $35, but visitors can obtain passes for $4, good for one hour of court time on any city court, from the **Central Park Courts** at W. 93rd Street near Central Park West. Even with passes, waiting time for courts can be considerable. Private indoor courts charge $16–$60 an hour depending on the court, time of day, day of week, and season (winter is much higher). Indoor tennis is available at the **Village Tennis Courts** (110 University Pl., tel. 212/989–2300), **Midtown Tennis Club** (341 Eighth Ave. at W.

27th St., tel. 212/989–8572), the **Tennis Club Grand Central Terminal** (15 Vanderbilt Ave., tel. 212/687–3841), **Manhattan Plaza Racquet Club** (450 W. 43rd St., tel. 212/594–0554), and **Sutton East Tennis Club** (488 E. 60th St., tel. 212/751–3452).

Spectator Sports

Baseball

New York's two major-league baseball teams, the Mets and the Yankees, play from early April through at least September. Since both teams have been successful in recent years, tickets for some games may be difficult to get.

The **New York Mets** play home games at **Shea Stadium** in Flushing, Queens. To get to Shea Stadium on the subway, take the IRT no. 7 line to "Willets Point/Shea Stadium." For information on schedules and tickets, tel. 718/507–TIXX. Mets tickets are available at the stadium box office, at Ticketron (tel. 212/399–4444) outlets, and by telephone charge (AE, MC, V) from Teletron (tel. 212/947–5850).

The **Yankees** play at **Yankee Stadium** in the Bronx, directly across the Harlem River from Manhattan. To get there from the East Side, take the IRT no. 4 to "161 St./Yankee Stadium"; from the West Side, take the IND D train to the same stop. For schedules and ticket information, tel. 212/293–6000. Yankee tickets are available at the stadium box office and by telephone charge (AE, MC, V) from Teletron (tel. 212/947–5850).

Basketball

The Greater New York area's two professional (National Basketball Association) teams, the **New York Knickerbockers** and **New Jersey Nets,** play a regular home season between November and April and may compete in postseason play through most of June. The Knicks play at Madison Square Garden, Seventh Avenue and 32nd Street; for schedule and ticket information, tel. 212/563–8300. The Nets play at the Brendan Byrne Arena at the Meadowlands Sports Complex in East Rutherford, NJ. For information on schedules and tickets, tel. 201/935–8888. For information about buses to the Meadowlands from the Port Authority Terminal, call 212/564–8484.

Madison Square Garden also hosts the final games of the pre- and postseason collegiate National Invitational Tournaments (N.I.T.) plus a regular-season slate of double-headers featuring local teams, particularly St. John's University. For information, tel. 212/563–8300.

Boxing

Madison Square Garden stages regular bouts year-round and the Golden Gloves amateur tournament in March in the smaller Felt Forum arena. Tel. 212/563–8300 for information. Check daily newspapers for locations of other boxing events.

Football

Although both area pro football teams play all home games at Giants Stadium in the Meadowlands Sports Complex in East Rutherford, NJ, the **Giants** and **Jets** retain their "New York" appellations. Season extends from September through December and, because of the large number of season ticket holders, tickets for both teams are scarce. Tel. 201/935–8222 (Giants tickets); 212/421–6600 (Jets tickets).

Hockey

The New York area's three National Hockey League teams—the **New York Rangers,** the **New York Islanders,** and the **New Jersey Devils**—play a regular season from October through April; postseason action may last until June. The Rangers play at Madison Square Garden, Seventh Avenue and 32nd Street; tel. 212/563–8300 for information. The Islanders inhabit Nassau Coliseum (Hempstead Turnpike, Uniondale) on Long Island. You can get there on the Long Island Railroad from Penn Station to Hempstead and take a bus or taxi the rest of the way; tel. 516/794–4100 for information. The New Jersey Devils play at the Brendan Byrne Arena at the Meadowlands Sports Complex in East Rutherford, NJ. For information on schedules and tickets, tel. 201/935–8888. For information about buses to the Meadowlands from the Port Authority Terminal (Eighth Ave. and 42nd St.), tel. 212/564–8484.

Horse Racing

New York is a handicapper's paradise with three flat and harness tracks operating year-round. **Aqueduct Racetrack** (tel. 718/641–4700) is the only track in New York City proper. Located at Rockaway Boulevard and 108th Street in Ozone Park, Queens, Aqueduct runs thoroughbreds from mid-October through May. Take the IND A train to "Aqueduct/North Conduit Ave."

The **Meadowlands Racetrack** in East Rutherford, NJ (tel. 201/460–4079) runs thoroughbreds from September through mid-December and trotters from January through August. Take a bus from the Port Authority Terminal. **Yonkers Raceway** (tel. 914/968–4200) in Yonkers just north of the New York City border in Westchester County runs trotters nightly throughout the year. Special bus service from the Port Authority Terminal is usually available to all area tracks; tel. 212/564–8484 for information.

Dining

Name any country, name any city or province in any country, and New York will probably have a *selection* of restaurants specializing in the cuisine of that area.

New York has more than 17,000 restaurants, from world-class temples of the culinary arts to humble cubbyholes serving pizza by the slice or hot dogs—New York–style, onions and sauerkraut optional. And though not even the most zealous New York food chauvinist would contend that every one of these places is fabulous, competitive pressures do effect a certain level of quality. No New York restaurant is likely to last long if its food doesn't taste good; few restaurants will survive if they don't serve reasonably large portions.

New York restaurants are expensive, yet savvy diners learn how to keep their costs within reason. Since most restaurants post menus in their front windows or lobbies, at least you will have a general idea of what you're getting into. But they don't post drink prices, and these can be high: $2.50 and up for a beer or a glass of wine; $3 and up for mixed drinks (some places charge *considerably* more). To run up your drink bill, many restaurants will ask you to wait in the bar until your table is ready. This occurs even when you have arrived on time and can see plenty of empty tables. While you may have to wait, you don't have to buy a drink.

One way to save money and still experience a top-echelon restaurant is to go there for lunch rather than dinner. It may also be easier to get lunch reservations on short notice.

Be sure to make a reservation when you intend to patronize a first-class restaurant. Be sure to make a reservation for *any* restaurant on a weekend, especially on Saturday night, when the only places that aren't filled up are the places you can live without. To limit no-show diners, many of the most popular restaurants insist that patrons reconfirm on the day of their reservation. Some restaurants will accept a reservation only if you supply a credit card number.

What follows is a selective list of New York restaurants serving a variety of cuisines in all price ranges in neighborhoods throughout Manhattan. As the list can by no means be comprehensive, some of the city's classic restaurants have not been included. In their place, however, you'll find some lesser-known eateries that are frequented by locals. Highly recommended restaurants in each price category are indicated by a star ★ .

Category	Cost*
Very Expensive	over $60
Expensive	$40–$60
Moderate	$20–$40
Inexpensive	under $20

per person without tax (8¼%), service, or drinks

American–Continental

★ **Four Seasons.** Menus and decor shift with the seasons in this class act. The bright and spacious Pool Room has a bubbly marble pool, changing floral displays, paintings by Picasso, Miró, and Rauschenberg. It's the rosewood Grill Room, however, where movers and shakers rendezvous for power lunches. Both settings have wide open spaces, impeccable service—and very high prices. An imaginative and unpredictable menu puts an Oriental spin on traditional American and French cuisine. Duck *au poivre* and tuna steak are reliable choices. The Spa Cuisine menu appeals to weight-watchers; lower priced pre- and post-theater menus (5–6:15 and 10–11:15) please wallet-watchers. *The Seagram Building, 99 E. 52nd St., tel. 212/754–*

9494. Jacket required. Reservations required, in advance for weekends. AE, CB, DC, MC, V. Closed Sun. Very Expensive.

Gotham Bar and Grill. A place with a name like Gotham better be huge, crowded, the quintessence of sophistication—and that's what this is. Owned by a former New York City commissioner, the Gotham Bar and Grill has a postmodern decor with tall columns, high ceilings decked with parachute shades, a pink-marble bar, and a striking pink-green-black color scheme. The menu is eclectic and surprising: Try duck roast carpaccio or roasted quail salad. *12 E. 12th St., tel. 212/620–4020. Dress: casual. Reservations advised. AE, CB, DC, MC, V. No lunch weekends. Expensive.*

Odeon. A converted Art Deco cafeteria in the TriBeCa neighborhood south of SoHo and north of the Financial District, this is a lively place where everyone can feel at home. The menu mingles French brasserie-style dishes with purely American fare. Steak and *frites* or fettuccine in shrimp are always good choices. *145 West Broadway at Thomas St., tel. 212/233–0507. Dress: casual. Reservations advised. AE, DC, MC, V. Expensive.*

One If by Land, Two If by Sea. As the name implies, this restaurant has a Colonial past. It occupies a converted coach house once owned, like much of the rest of Greenwich Village, by Aaron Burr. Located on an obscure back street with no exterior sign, it can be hard to find. Inside, the elegant two-floor setting divides into a number of warm Colonial rooms. The menu features Continental specialties like steak, veal, and rack of lamb. *17 Barrow St. between W. 4th St. and Seventh Ave., tel. 212/228–0822. Dress: casual. Reservations required. AE, DC, MC, V. Expensive.*

Greene Street Restaurant. At this bustling SoHo cabaret the quality of the food matches the high quality of the show. The vast bare-brick bi-level loft has dark romantic lighting and modern paintings all around. The menu features an eclectic selection of American, Italian, and French dishes—Dover sole and loin of lamb are recommended. Piano jazz accompanies nightly dinners; singers and comedians perform on Friday and Saturday nights. *101 Greene St. between Spring and Prince Sts., tel. 212/925–2415. Dress: casual. Reservations advised. AE, CB, DC, MC, V. Moderate–Expensive.*

★ **B. Smith's.** Owned by former model Barbara Smith, this spacious and airy West Side eatery is frequented by black professionals and a pretheater crowd. Walls are painted in pale earth tones, tables are draped with white cloths, and arrangements of exotic fresh flowers artfully grace the room. The innovative menu ranges from "light plates" (such as grilled duck sausage over charcoal with coarse mustard and warm potato salad) to pasta (Maine lobster raviolis with a tarragon shellfish bisque) to hefty salads (warm roast chicken breast with wild mushrooms, wilted Napa cabbage, and toasted sesame dressing). Fresh seafood dishes—especially salmon and scampi—are delightful. *771 Eighth Ave. at 47th St., tel. 212/247–2222. Dress: casual. Reservations accepted. AE, CB, DC, MC, V. Moderate.*

Amsterdam's Bar & Rotisserie. The name tells most of the story: It's basically a bar on the Upper West Side's Amsterdam Avenue where most of the food is prepared on an open rotisserie. Low prices for roasted poultry (chicken and duck are tops) and beef dishes, accompanied by a vegetable and an ambitious

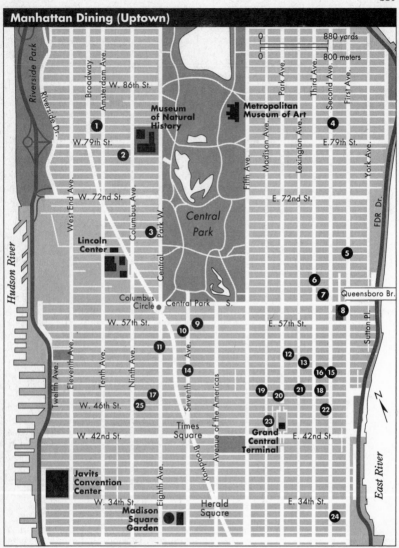

Manhattan Dining (Uptown)

Alo Alo, **6**	Café des Artistes, **3**	Greene Street Restaurant, **44**	Minetta Tavern, **41**
Amsterdam's, **1**	Carnegie Deli, **10**	Hatsuhana, **19, 20**	Mitali East, **36**
Arizona 206, **7**	Cent'Anni, **37**	HSF, **24, 47**	Mitali West, **39**
Auntie Yuan, **5**	Claire, **29**	Indochine, **35**	Montrachet, **45**
The Ballroom, **26**	Cucina Stagionale, **40**	Jane Street Seafood Cafe, **32**	Nice Restaurant, **50**
Bangkok Cuisine, **11**	El Quijote, **27**	Le Bernardin, **14**	Nippon, **13**
Blue Nile, **2**	Four Seasons, **12**	Lutèce, **16**	Odeon, **46**
B. Smith's, **17**	Gotham Bar & Grill, **33**	Mi Chinita, **30**	Omen, **43**
Bukhara, **21**	Grand Central Oyster Bar, **23**		One If By Land, **38**
Cafe de la Gare, **34**	Grand Ticino, **42**		Orso, **25**
			Peking Duck House Restaurant, **49**

Manhattan Dining (Downtown)

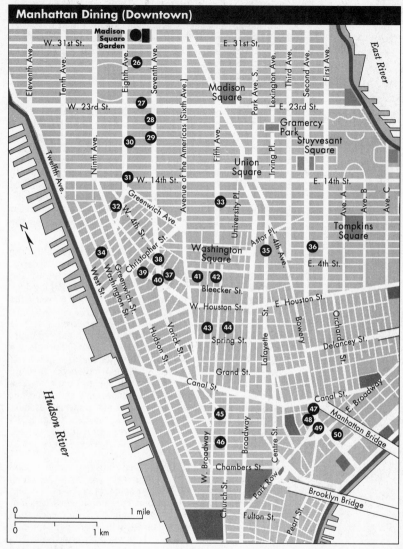

Pig Heaven, **4**

Quatorze, **31**

Rosa Mexicano, **8**

Russian Tea Room, **9**

Smith & Wollensky, **18**

Sparks Steak
House, **22**

Thai Taste, **28**

Viet-Nam
Restaurant, **48**

Zarela, **15**

house salad, elicit standing-room crowds late into the night. Fish dishes are also good and homemade ketchup graces every table. *428 Amsterdam Ave. between 80th and 81st Sts., tel. 212/ 874-1377. Dress: casual. No reservations. AE, CB, DC, MC, V. Inexpensive.*

Chinese

Note: Chinese food is a staple of the New York diet. Most restaurants serve interchangeable menus that combine dishes from various areas of China and use a star or red lettering to indicate spicy dishes. With few exceptions the food is good and truly inexpensive (less than $10 per person). Chinese restaurants typically offer low-priced lunch specials—soup, egg roll, main dish, tea—for between $3.50 and $5. Restaurants listed here offer something more than the typical neighborhood Chinese place. You can't go wrong, too, with any busy restaurant in Chinatown—the area bordered by Canal Street on the north, and the Bowery on the east.

★ **Auntie Yuan.** This Upper East Side spot breaks the mold of the standard Chinese restaurant. It has high-gloss, all-black decor; pin lights focusing on solitary flowers; and waiters ready and eager to explain any of the dishes. Orange beef and Peking duck are specialties; the tasting menu is costly but full of exotic flavors. *1191A First Ave. at 64th St., tel. 212/744-4040. Dress: casual. Reservations advised. AE, DC. Expensive.*

The Nice Restaurant. Bright and shiny, this Chinatown mainstay can serve Hong Kong–style dishes to over 400 people at a time on two floors. By day (8–4), the Nice features *dim sum*, bite-size dishes that you pick off circulating trays. Favorite choices include dumplings (filled with shrimp, pork, vegetables, or fish), pork wontons, beef balls, and small coconut cakes. The dinner menu contains photos of top specialties: minced squab in lettuce, deep-fried prawns, roast suckling pig. *35 East Broadway, tel. 212/406-9510. Dress: casual. Beer served; bring your own wine. Reservations advised for dinner. AE. Moderate.*

Pig Heaven. This popular Upper East Side restaurant is gimmicky to the max. A cut-out pig greets you with the menu; wallboards are painted a shocking pig pink; tea is served in pig-snout mugs. Yet the food is serious. Pork dominates the menu, with about 20 nightly specials available. Try Cantonese-style suckling pig or minced pork sauteed with corn, peppers, and pine nuts. Patience may be called for when big crowds slow up the mostly Occidental service staff. *1540 Second Ave. at 80th St., tel. 212/744-4333. Dress: casual. Reservations required. AE, DC. Moderate.*

HSF (for Hee Seung Fung). This Chinatown standby and its midtown spin-off are considered the best places in town for *dim sum* and other small delights which are rolled by on tray carts so you can have a look before selecting. Don't be too shy to ask what each dish is: Be daring and sample something unusual like chicken feet or squid. Large selections of Cantonese entrees are also available. Though the Chinatown restaurant is large (and noisy), you may have to share a table; try to pick one with a Chinese family. The midtown establishment is modern and more sedate. *Chinatown: 46 Bowery, tel. 212/374-1319. Dress: informal. No reservations. No credit cards. Midtown: 578 Second Ave. at 32nd St., tel. 212/689-6969. Jacket advised.*

Reservations advised weekends and holidays. AE, CB, DC, MC, V. Inexpensive–Moderate.

Peking Duck House Restaurant. You don't have to order the house specialty—Peking duck—24 hours in advance here as you do at most places. Furthermore, it is well prepared at this Chinatown favorite and compares favorably with the same dish at higher priced restaurants. *22 Mott St., tel. 212/962–8208. Dress: casual. Reservations suggested weekends. AE, DC. Inexpensive.*

Cuban-Chinese

Mi Chinita. This frenetic Chelsea spot exemplifies a unique and ubiquitous type of New York eatery: Cuban-Chinese restaurants. Operated by ethnic Chinese refugees from Cuba, these places do not allow the cuisines to mingle. Chinese dishes occupy one section of the menu, Latin specialties another. Mi Chinita is an informal stainless-steel diner with counter and table seating. Latin specials (here, as at most Cuban-Chinese places, the superior choice) involve permutations of shredded beef, pot roast, roast pork, fried plantain, yellow rice, black beans, and salad. Service is brisk, as lines frequently trail out to the street. *176 8th Ave. at 19th St., tel. 212/741–0240. Dress: casual. No reservations. Closed Sunday. No credit cards. Inexpensive.*

Deli

Carnegie Deli. This archetypal New York deli played a supporting role in Woody Allen's *Broadway Danny Rose.* Noisy and crowded, always in a frenzy, the Carnegie serves legendary corned beef hash and peppery pastrami, and merely great corned beef, chicken soup, bagels. Special sandwiches may be named after the joker sitting at the next table. Portions are gargantuan—be prepared to walk away with a doggie bag. And don't let the brusque waiters get you down; they're part of the show. *854 Seventh Ave. at 55th St., tel. 212/757–2245. Dress: casual. No reservations. No credit cards. Inexpensive.*

Ethiopian

Blue Nile. Dining in this bright and spacious basement on the Upper West Side near the Museum of Natural History is an experience. You sit on low, somewhat precarious three-legged stools, and a mushroom-shaped straw basket serves as your table. Folded sheets of soft Ethiopian bread *(injera)* play a crucial role. Dishes are served on it and you use other sheets in lieu of silverware, to scoop up your food. Most appetizers and entrees are easily scoopable pastes and stews; everyone shares everything. Try *afeza,* a spicy appetizer made with lentils and onions, a hot chicken dish called *doro wot,* and an Ethiopian rendition of steak tartare. *103 W. 77th St., off Columbus Ave., tel. 212/580–3232. Dress: casual. No reservations. AE. Inexpensive.*

French

★ **Lutèce.** There isn't anyone who doesn't adore Lutèce, a temple of largely Alsatian gastronomy for more than 25 years. The intimate and understated midtown town house has seating around an enclosed garden or in two more formal upstairs chambers. The regular menu is varied and specials vary daily; grilled trout and pheasant are always fine choices. The impeccable service is invariably attentive and helpful, to first-time and hundredth-time diners alike. *249 E. 50th St., tel. 212/752–2225. Jacket and tie required. Reservations required 2 weeks or more in advance. AE, CB, DC, MC, V. No lunch Sat.–Mon.; no dinner Sun.; closed in August. Very Expensive.*

Café des Artistes. A romantic and extremely popular Lincoln Center–area institution. Murals of nudes cavorting in a sylvan glade and sparkling mirrors transport you far from the madding Manhattan crowd. Food is country French with confit of duck and lamb with flageolet beans recommended specialties. The place crowds up with West Side locals and out-of-towners. *1 W. 67th St. at Central Park, tel. 212/877–3500. Jacket required. Weekend reservations required 2 wks or more in advance; weekday reservations required 2–3 days in advance. AE, CB, DC, MC, V. Expensive.*

Montrachet. This neighborhood French restaurant—the neighborhood is TriBeCa—evokes the flavor of back-street Paris. Inside the ambience is spare but attractive—wood tables with white cloths, dusty-rose banquettes, carpeting throughout— and the mood is chummy. The menu favors fresh full-flavored Provençale-style concoctions of seafood (black sea bass, lobster, red snapper) and fowl (pigeon wrapped in cabbage, duck with ginger). *239 West Broadway near White St., tel. 212/219–2777. Dress: casual. Reservations advised. AE. Closed Sun. and 1st week of July. Expensive.*

★ **Quatorze.** A Parisian bistro on 14th Street, at the border of Greenwich Village and Chelsea, Quatorze ("14") is fancy but congenial. It's basically a long and narrow neighborhood hangout with plush banquettes, soft lighting, colorful French posters. The menu is a brief and efficient card highlighted by *choucroute*, roast duck, and lamb medallions. The wine list is similarly brisk and fairly priced, the service helpful and friendly. *240 W. 14th St., tel. 212/206–7006. Dress: casual. Reservations advised. AE. No lunch weekends. Expensive.*

Café de la Gare. Enter an intimate storefront on one of Greenwich Village's quaintest streets. Both the atmosphere—a handful of romantic tables adorned with fresh flowers—and the menu are classic French. Cassoulet and seasonal preparations of veal, salmon, and game are specialties. Bring your own wine. *143 Perry St., tel. 212/242–3553. Dress: casual. BYOB. Reservations required. CB, DC, MC, V. Closed Mon. Moderate.*

Indian

★ **Bukhara.** This midtown spot features "frontier cuisine" from the northwest provinces bordering Pakistan. All entrees are either charcoal-grilled or roasted in *tandoors* (ancient clay ovens) and eaten without silverware (hot towels provided before and after). The menu provides vividly detailed descriptions of numerous chicken dishes, fish, prawns, beef. Hammered brass-and-copper trays and Bukhara rugs adorn rugged sand-colored walls. *148 E. 48th St., tel. 212/838–1811. Dress: casual. Reservations advised. AE, CB, DC, MC, V. Moderate–Expensive.*

Mitali. The original Mitali is one of several Indian places on and around 6th Street between First and Second avenues in the

East Village. Mitali West stands alone in the heart of Greenwich Village. Decor is somewhat elegant with red-jacketed waiters and walls faced with standard Indian prints. Menus feature Northern Indian specialties and bargain-price combination platters. Try Dopiaz curry or chicken tandoori. *Mitali East: 334 E. 6th St., tel. 212/533-2508; Mitali West: 296 Bleecker St. at 7th Ave., tel. 212/989-1367. Dress: casual. Reservations accepted. AE, MC, V. Inexpensive.*

Italian

Orso. A Theater District spot to meet before or after the show, Orso makes you feel you're in with the in crowd. It has an open steel-and-tile kitchen and walls adorned with celebrity photos. Theater folk congregate here for a brief menu highlighted by individual pizzas and pizza bread, tangy pastas, and hearty entrees like striped bass with fennel and grilled quail in brandy sauce. The all-Italian wine list has a number of fine moderately priced selections. *322 W. 46th St., tel. 212/489-7212. Dress: casual. Reservations required up to one week in advance. MC, V. Expensive.*

Cent'Anni. Situated in a Greenwich Village storefront, this downtown favorite serves authentic Italian dishes to a discriminating native crowd. The simple interior is tastefully decorated with wood furniture, fresh flowers, framed pencil drawings, and sketches of Italy. Featured menu items include rabbit with white wine, onions, carrots, and tomatoes; squid sautéed in oil, garlic, lemon, and spices; and linguine with tomato sauce, vodka, and red peppers. *50 Carmine St. at Bleecker, tel. 212/989-9494. Dress: casual. Reservations advised. AE. Moderate-Expensive.*

Alo Alo. People come to this sophisticated Upper East Side cafe for food and fun. Alo Alo is a glass-walled, high-ceilinged chamber with papier-mâché statues perched atop lofty ledges. Ambient conversation is multilingual, mostly European, and the music is loud. Menu selections are fresh, bold, and light. Unusual pasta creations are best; the *risotto* special of the day is a good choice; fresh fish and veal selections will delight. *1030 Third Ave. at 61st St., tel. 212/838-4343. Dress: casual. Reservations advised. AE, CB, DC, MC, V. Moderate.*

Grand Ticino. This casual 70-year-old Village favorite became an overnight success after inspiring the set for *Moonstruck*. (The movie was actually filmed elsewhere.) Located a few steps below street level, it is a simple and gracious setting for old standards like homemade *gnocchi al pesto* and *saltimbocca a la Romana. 228 Thompson St. between Bleecker and W. 3rd Sts., tel. 212/777-5922. Dress: casual. Reservations accepted. AE, CB, DC, MC, V. Closed Sun. Moderate.*

Minetta Tavern. Caricatures of local denizens—artists, poets, playwrights, entertainers, bootleggers—and murals of Village landmarks adorn the walls of this hospitable old Greenwich Village hangout. The food is Italian, tasty, and moderately priced; risotto with shrimp and breast of chicken Florentine are house specialties. But go there for the flavor of Village life, as it was and as it remains. *113 MacDougal St., tel. 212/475-3850. Dress: casual. Reservations accepted. AE, CB, DC, MC, V. Moderate.*

★ **Cucina Stagionale.** A truly good, inexpensive Italian restaurant in the heart of Greenwich Village, this is a white-tablecloth, storefront establishment with a selection of exotic pastas (spinach *penne* with seasonal vegetables, cold lasagne with goat cheese) and meat specialties. Main courses cost $6–$11 and you save even more by bringing your wine. Not surprisingly, a lot of people are on to this place, and lines can be daunting; lunch is much more accessible. *275 Bleecker St. between Jones and Cornelia Sts., tel. 212/924–2707. Dress: casual. No reservations. No credit cards. Inexpensive.*

Japanese

Hatsuhana. The authenticity of Hatsuhana's two bright and cheerful midtown locations is verified by conspicuous contingents of visiting Japanese businessmen. They come for ultrafresh sushi and sashimi, which are best enjoyed close up at the sushi bar. Other recommended items include bite-size Japanese fried crabs, nongreasy Japanese fried chicken, and any of the grilled fish teriyaki. *17 E. 48th St., tel. 212/355–3345; 237 Park Ave. at 46th St., tel. 212/661–3400. Dress: casual. Reservations required for dinner. AE, CB, DC, MC, V. No lunch weekends. Expensive.*

Nippon. Recently relocated to its present address, this 20-year-old midtown establishment serves traditional Japanese food in a traditional Japanese garden setting. Specialties include sautéed duck breast, tuna teriyaki, and softshell crab. Try a little bit of a lot of things by ordering one of the "tasting menus." Or be very daring and order something from the Special for Connoisseur items like salted sea cucumber or preserved herring roe. *155 E. 52nd St., tel. 212/758–0226. Jacket required. Reservations accepted. No lunch Sat., closed Sun. AE, CB, DC, MC, V. Expensive.*

Omen. Old brick, hardwood floors, timbered ceilings, and Oriental lanterns give this SoHo ex-store the relaxing ambience of a Japanese country inn. *Omen* is the name of an opening dish almost everybody orders. It's a dark hot broth served with lightly cooked exotic vegetables, sesame seeds, and noodles that you add to the soup. Other favorites include a boned chicken dish called *sansho*, scallops and blanched spinach, and avocado with shrimp in miso sauce. *113 Thompson St. between Spring and Prince Sts., tel. 212/925–8923. Dress: casual. Reservations advised. AE, DC. Closed Mon. Moderate.*

Mexican

★ **Arizona 206.** The ambience of the American Southwest is captured a block away from Bloomingdale's: stark white plaster walls, wood-burning fireplace, raw-timber trimming, and piped-in Willie Nelson songs. Spicy New-Wave Mexican cuisine stresses chili peppers, and the menu (by chef Marilyn Frobuchino) offers nothing ordinary, only the likes of green chili paella for two; grilled salmon steak with *poblano* corn pudding; and pistachio-crusted tenderloin of rabbit with *mole poblano* sauce. Desserts are just as unusual, and the service staff is downright perky. *206 E. 60th St., tel. 212/838–0440. Dress: casual. Reservations advised. AE, CB, DC, MC, V. Expensive.*

Zarela. Refined Mexican cuisine is served at this midtown spot. The menu features lightly seasoned *fajitas* (skirt steak), *salpicon* (red snapper), and grilled raw tuna. Diners occupy heavy wooden chairs and brightly cushioned benches which are positioned along a white brick wall. Pinatas, crepe paper streamers, and lively Mexican music add a festive touch. *953 Second Ave. at 51st St., tel. 212/644–6740. Dress: casual. Reservations advised. AE, DC. Expensive.*

★ **Rosa Mexicano.** This is a crowded midtown hangout for young professionals. Serious dining takes place amid subdued pink-stucco walls and lush horticulture. Two standard Mexican items are exceptional here: chunky guacamole prepared at your table and margaritas blended with pomegranate. Grilled versions of shell steak, chicken, and snapper; pork *carnitas;* and skinned breast of duck are other noncombustible house specialties. *1063 First Ave., tel. 212/753–7407. Dress: casual. Reservations advised. AE, CB, DC, MC, V. Moderate.*

Russian

Russian Tea Room. Russian food is probably the last reason to eat here. Located beside Carnegie Hall, the Russian Tea Room is a major New York scene loaded with media people, their agents, and kindred would-be deal cutters. (Dustin Hoffman lunched here with his agent in *Tootsie*.) It's also filled with local commoners and out-of-towners, some of whom get exiled to the celebrityless second floor—"Siberia." Best menu choices are hot or cold borscht, *karsky shashlik* (lamb with kidneys), and a selection of red and black caviars rolled into tender *blini* (pancakes). *150 W. 57th St., tel. 212/265–0947. Jacket required. Reservations advised. AE, CB, DC, MC, V. Expensive.*

Seafood

★ **Le Bernardin.** The New York branch of an illustrious Paris seafood establishment occupies the ground floor of the midtown Equitable Assurance Tower; the elegant decor was reportedly inspired by the Equitable boardroom. The all-seafood menu teems with rare treasures. For starters, try black bass flecked with coriander or sea urchins baked in their shell. Go on to lobster in pasta or any of the fresh, artfully arranged filets. *155 W. 51st St., tel. 212/489–1515. Jacket and tie required. Reservations required. AE, DC, MC, V. Closed Sun. and mid-Aug.– Labor Day. Very Expensive.*

Grand Central Oyster Bar. Down in the catacombs beneath Grand Central Terminal, the Oyster Bar has a reputation for serving ultrafresh seafood. The vast main room has a vaulted tile ceiling and lots of noise and tumult. Solos may prefer to sit at the wide, white counter. By contrast, the wood-paneled Saloon feels downright clubby. More than a dozen varieties of oysters may be on hand. Pan-roasted shellfish, a kind of stew, is a house specialty. Broiled filets change with the daily catch. *Lower level Grand Central Terminal, 42nd St. and Vanderbilt Ave., tel. 212/490–6650. Dress: casual. Reservations advised. AE, CB, DC, MC, V. Closed weekends. Moderate–Expensive.*

Claire. This lively Chelsea spot has a Key West theme: hanging plants, trelliswork panels, languid ceiling fans, skylights, a large airy dining area. Whether or not it originated in the Keys, all the seafood is fresh and tangy. Try anything involving oysters or mussels, blackened fish, Norwegian salmon. Naturally, the dessert menu includes Key lime pie. *156 Seventh Ave. near 19th St., tel. 212/255–1955. Dress: casual. Reservations advised. AE, DC, MC, V. Moderate.*

Jane Street Seafood Cafe. Old wood, brick walls, plank floors, bare wooden tables, and low ceilings import the cozy air of a

New England pub to Greenwich Village. The menu lists more than 50 seafood appetizers and entrees—we recommend mussels in broth and swordfish steak—all accompanied by hot crusty bread and big bowls of creamy cole slaw. Be prepared for a considerable wait at weekend dinner hour. *31 8th Ave. at Jane St., tel. 212/243–9237. Dress: casual. No reservations. AE, DC, MC, V. Moderate.*

Spanish

The Ballroom. Located in Chelsea a few blocks from Penn Station, this is the place to sample *tapas*, Spanish appetizers that quickly accumulate into a full meal. Some like their *tapas* hot—grilled eggplant, stuffed squid, baked fennel, sauteed shiitake mushrooms, baby lamb chops. Others prefer them cold—octopus in oil, bay scallops, *chorizo* (sausage) with peppers, chicken with tomato. The spacious, palmy setting focuses on a huge mural of local painters and art dealers. A popular cabaret theater occupies a separate room. *253 W. 28th St., tel. 212/244–3005. Dress: casual. Reservations advised. AE, CB, DC, MC, V. No lunch Sat.–Mon.; closed Sun. and Mon. Moderate-Expensive.*

El Quijote. A restaurant/bar on the ground floor of the Hotel Chelsea, El Quijote has been a haunt for generations of bohemians. The boisterous, popular neighborhood restaurant specializes in large portions and small prices. Lobster is the principal drawing card, with meaty 1½ pounders going for around $12.95. *Paella valenciana* is another specialty, as are shrimp, mussels, and oysters prepared in a variety of Spanish sauces. *226 W. 23rd St., tel. 212/929–1855. Dress: casual. Reservations advised. AE, CB, DC, MC, V. Lunch and dinner daily. Moderate.*

Steaks

Smith & Wollensky. This midtown steak house opened only in 1977, but plank floors, bentwood chairs, and walls decked with classic sporting prints make it look as if it's been here forever. Steak is the forte of this establishment, big blackened sirloins and filets mignon with a pepper sauce. Huge lobsters, veal chops, and terrific onion rings round out the menu. *201 E. 49th St., tel. 212/753–1530. Dress: casual. Reservations accepted. AE, CB, DC, MC, V. No lunch weekends. Expensive.*

Sparks Steak House. Steaks and male camaraderie are the specialties of this midtown restaurant. The tender prime sirloin is the most popular selection. Filets are unusually juicy and flavorful; lobsters cruise the three- to five-pound range. Although most of the former-jock clientele seem to go for beer or whiskey, Sparks boasts an award-winning wine list. *210 E. 46th St., tel. 212/687–4855. Jacket and tie required. Reservations required. AE, DC, MC, V. Closed Sun. Expensive.*

Thai

Bangkok Cuisine. New York's oldest Thai restaurant operates out of a remodeled storefront just north of the Theater District. Some of the spicy specialties include *tod mun pla* (deep-fried fish patties dipped in a sweet sauce), *pad thai* (an exciting noodle dish), and whole fish dinners. A small knife indicates superhot dishes on the menu—and here that warning means something. *885 8th Ave. at 53rd St., tel. 212/581–6370. Dress: casual. No reservations. AE, DC, MC, V. No lunch Sun. Inexpensive.*

Thai Taste. No big scene here, just a cozy Chelsea neighborhood restaurant with good prices and friendly service. The small dark room encourages subdued conversation over traditional, exotically spiced Thai dishes. Two of the best are mussels in a sauce made with lime and Thai-fried chicken. *208 W. 22nd St. at 7th Ave., tel. 212/807–9872. Dress: casual. Reservations accepted. AE, CB, MC, V. Inexpensive.*

Vietnamese

Indochine. On the ground floor of landmark East Village town houses, the scene here mingles downtown artists with displaced French colonialists. The space is large and airy, decorated with palm leaves and tropical murals. The menu offers spiced Vietnamese and Cambodian specialties. *Rouleau de printemps* (spring roll) is the standard appetizer; stuffed, boneless chicken wings or steamed fish in coconut milk make excellent entrees. *430 Lafayette St. between Astor Pl. and E. 4th St., tel. 212/505–5111. Dress: casual. Reservations advised. AE, CB, DC, MC, V. Expensive.*

Viet-Nam Restaurant. Down in a basement off one of Chinatown's most obscure streets, the Viet-Nam Restaurant is clean, friendly, and extremely inexpensive—most dishes go for less than $6. Many of the Vietnamese specialties involve clever preparations of seafood and fowl. Try the shrimp pâté on sugar cane for an appetizer. Follow it with chicken in lemon grass or stewed curried duck. *11 Doyers St., tel. 212/693–0725. Dress: casual. No reservations. AE. Inexpensive.*

Lodging

New York City hotels *are* expensive. Top hotels charge more than $200 a night for their humblest accommodations, double or triple that for deluxe rooms and suites. Added to that are combined state and city sales and hotel taxes of 13¼% *plus* a $2 per room per night occupancy tax.

However, given the high per night going rate, New York still has bargains. Obtaining a bargain usually involves sacrificing something in the way of decor, amenities, service, and, primarily, location. Many acceptable, lower priced properties are, for example, located around the Theater District, away from the most fashionable neighborhoods but safe and close to all the action.

Sometimes it can be difficult to find a room at any price. The average annual occupancy rate hovers around 80% and nears 100% during peak spring and fall seasons. Our listings include selected hotels in each price range but it is hardly exhaustive. To receive a more comprehensive free list of hotels (no descriptions—only addresses, local and toll-free phone numbers, and rates), contact the **New York Convention and Visitors Bureau** (2 Columbus Circle, 10019, tel. 212/397–8222). **Meegan Services,** a private company, can locate and reserve rooms in any New York hotel. The service is free and operates 24 hours (tel. 718/476–5587 in New York, 800/472–6699 elsewhere).

Weekend Packages Weekends are comparatively slow and virtually every New York hotel offers a bargain weekend package. Packages offer room rates of up to 50% below weekday prices and may also include meals, cocktails, free parking, upgraded rooms or suites, theater tickets, guided tours, cruises, or theme programs. Most weekend packages apply to Friday and Saturday nights; some also apply to Thursday and/or Sunday night. Some weekend deals require a two-day minimum stay. For information about weekend packages, request the free New York City Tour Package Directory from the New York Convention and Visitors Bureau. The Sunday *New York Times* travel section also carries numerous ads for weekend packages.

Highly recommended places in each price category are indicated by a star ★ .

Category	Cost*
Very Expensive	over $200
Expensive	$150–$200
Moderate	$100–$150
Inexpensive	$50–$100
Budget	under $50

double room; add 13¼% plus $2 per night for taxes

Chelsea

Hotel Chelsea. An 1882 structure that was the first hotel proclaimed a national historic landmark, this imposing red-brick building has sheltered generations of creative types, from Mark Twain, Thomas Wolfe, Dylan Thomas, and Arthur Miller to Lenny Bruce, Jane Fonda, William Burroughs, and Sid Vicious. Contemporary art brightens the tiny lobby. Rooms, though large, are furnished in "Fleabag Moderne," and you may not feel comfortable sharing the elevator with some fellow guests. Air-conditioned rooms cost more but are worth it in summer. *222 W. 23rd St., 10011, tel. 212/243–3700. 400 rooms. AE, MC, V. Inexpensive.*

Lower Manhattan

Vista International. Close to Wall Street, South Street Seaport, and the Statue of Liberty ferry (but miles from midtown) this lone hotel in Lower Manhattan tries a bit harder with a fully equipped fitness center and shuttle service to midtown. Weekend programs offer lower rates and an assortment of planned activities. *3 World Trade Center, 10048, tel. 212/938–9100. 829 rooms. AE, CB, DC, MC, V. Very Expensive.*

Midtown

Grand Bay Hotel at Equitable Center. The bygone Taft Hotel has been transformed into a new ultraluxurious hotel. Its Italian marble lobby features 19th-century period furn ture and bold floral displays. Extra-large rooms (average 450 square feet) have marble bathrooms equipped with tiny TVs. The hotel is close to the Theater District and Carnegie Hall. *152 W.*

Algonquin, **26**
Barbizon, **8**
Beekman Tower, **20**
Carlyle, **3**
Chatwal, **24**
Chelsea, **35**
Dumont Plaza, **31**
Eastgate Tower, **30**
Edison, **25**
Empire, **5**
Excelsior, **1**
Grand Bay, **13**
Grand Union, **32**
Inter-Continental, **19**
Iroquois, **27**
Lyden Gardens, **7**
Lyden House, **16**
Mayfair Regent, **6**
Morgans, **28**
New Carlton Arms, **36**
Novotel, **23**
Omni Berkshire
Place, **15**
Peninsula of New
York, **14**
Pickwick Arms, **17**
The Pierre, **9**
The Plaza, **10**
Plaza 50, **18**
Salisbury, **12**
Shelburne Murray
Hill, **29**
Sloane House
YMCA, **34**
Southgate Tower, **33**
Surrey, **2**
Vanderbilt YMCA, **21**
Vista International, **37**
Waldorf-Astoria, **22**
West Side YMCA, **4**
Wyndham, **11**

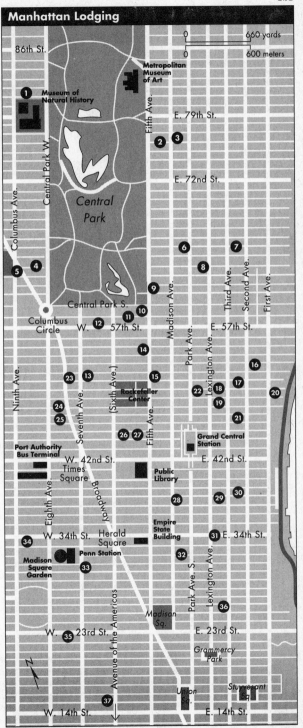

Manhattan Lodging

51st St., 10019, tel. 212/765–1900 or 800/237–0990. 178 rooms. AE, CB, DC, MC, V. Very Expensive.

Inter-Continental. The lobby of the former Barclay Hotel is an opulent beehive of inviting leather furniture, with a lovely Federal-style Tiffany skylight and the signature 14-foot-high brass bird cage. Rooms look classic but are functionally state-of-the-art: custom-designed cherry-wood armoires conceal remote-control cable TVs and minifridges. *111 E. 48th St., 10017, tel. 212/755–5900. 692 rooms. AE, CB, DC, MC, V. Very Expensive.*

Omni Berkshire Place. This is a luxurious but reasonably intimate 1926 hotel (restored) situated near Rockefeller Center. The atrium lobby resembles a private drawing room—complimentary coffee served each morning. Plant-filled guest rooms have plush and comfortable, soft-colored modern furniture. A reasonably priced theater package includes a three-course dinner at La Galerie restaurant, post-theater dessert and coffee. *21 E. 52nd St., 10022, tel. 212/753–5800. 415 rooms. AE, CB, DC, MC, V. Very Expensive.*

Peninsula of New York. The former Hotel Gotham is New York's newest superluxury hotel. Public areas express turn-of-the-century Beaux-Arts style with lavish marble paneling and flooring, an 11-foot crystal chandelier, towering palms, and a sweeping marble staircase. Large guest rooms in lush Art-Nouveau colors have fancy French furniture and marble trimming. *700 Fifth Ave. at 55th St., 10019, tel. 212/247–2200. 250 rooms. AE, CB, DC, MC, V. Very Expensive.*

Waldorf-Astoria. After a stem-to-stern renovation and restoration, the main lobby of this 47-story Art-Deco legend has retained its dark marble columns and centerpiece bronze clock. Rooms—nearly 100 fewer than before—are individually decorated in the Art Deco spirit, and the popular Peacock Alley bar still has Cole Porter's own piano. *301 Park Ave. at 50th St., 10022, tel. 212/355–3000. 1,692 rooms. AE, CB, DC, MC, V. Very Expensive.*

★ **Algonquin.** Opened in 1902, this is an up-to-date and extremely well-maintained hotel with a long literary history. The illustrious Round Table convened here in the 1920s, and *New Yorker* staff and contributors continue to frequent its bars and restaurants. The oak-paneled lobby projects the gracious atmosphere of an English club. Rooms are quiet and cozy, furnished in traditional English style with four-poster mahogany beds. *59 W. 44th St., 10036, tel. 212/840–6800 or 800/548–0345. 200 rooms. AE, CB, DC, MC, V. Expensive.*

Salisbury. This attractive and efficient hotel on the lower end of the moderate category is located across the street from Carnegie Hall. Rooms are reasonably large and furnished in Early-American decor with original paintings. All rooms contain safes and 95% have a refrigerator and pantry. *123 W. 57th St., 10019, tel. 212/246–1300 or 800/223–0680. 320 rooms. AE, CB, DC, MC, V. Moderate.*

★ **Hotel Iroquois.** This bargain property near the Theater District is fast becoming a small gem. The smallish lobby is a welcoming shade of pink. Renovated guest rooms have Early American decor; less expensive older rooms are decorated in "Early Goodwill." Enthusiastic and helpful staff members speak 14 languages. Some suites are available for under $100. *49 W. 44th St., 10036, tel. 212/840–3080 or 800/332–7220. 125 rooms. AE, CB, DC, MC, V. Inexpensive.*

Grand Union. This is a clean, safe, no-frills place about a block from the Empire State Building. Furnished in "Motel Moderne," rooms have window air conditioners and cable TV; some have refrigerators. A small lobby and coffee shop comprise the public space. Rooms with shared baths (two or three rooms per bath) cost $50 per night, single or double; those with private baths begin at $60. *34 E. 32nd St., 10016, tel. 212/683–5890. 95 rooms. AE, MC, V. Budget.*

New Carlton Arms. The management here has created an adventure in lodging by turning avant-garde artists loose on a once-decrepit, quasi flophouse. A room may resemble the inside of a submarine, the lost city of Atlantis, or a Hindu temple. Amenity-wise, rooms are small and Spartan—no TV or phone and subminimalist furnishing. But the hotel is clean, safe, and very cheap: Singles with shared bath cost $33, doubles are $44; private baths cost $6 more. Students (with ID) and foreign tourists (with passports) get about 20% off. *160 E. 25th St., 10010, tel. 212/679–0680. 54 rooms. MC, V. Budget.*

Pickwick Arms Hotel. The lobby of this East Side find has been recently redecorated and guests have access to a roof garden. Rooms are comfortably furnished in white bamboo. Standard renovated doubles cost $75 a night, but older singles with shared baths go for as little as $42. Families may wish to consider a studio for $85 and up. *230 E. 51st St., 10022, tel. 212/355–0300 or 800–PICKWIK. 400 rooms. AE, CB, DC, MC, V. Budget.*

Midtown–Central Park

★ **The Pierre.** The public areas of this 40-story tower suggest the subdued atmosphere of a French château. Rooms have a quiet dignity with Chippendale furniture; north, west, and south sides offer stunning views of Central Park. Amenities include attended elevators, twice-daily maid service, 24-hour room service, in-room safes, and packing/unpacking service upon request. *Fifth Ave. at 61st St., 10021, tel. 212/838–8000. 205 rooms. AE, CB, DC, MC, V. Very Expensive.*

The Plaza. Adjacent to the southeast corner of Central Park, this 1907 classic looks like a French château and its public areas contain the decor (crystal chandeliers, French Provincial furniture) to match. Don't worry about new owner Donald Trump making radical changes: He can't alter the exterior because it's a New York City and national landmark, and he's promised not to dramatically change the interior. *59th St., at Central Park, 10019, tel. 212/759–3000 or 800/228–3000. 807 rooms. AE, CB, DC, MC, V. Very Expensive.*

★ **Wyndham.** A cozy, friendly, impeccably maintained hotel at the low end of the moderate range, this hotel is just a half-block from the Plaza. Homey touches include buzz-in front door, attended elevators, and rooms individually decorated with bright floral wallpaper and comfy furniture. *42 W. 58th St., 10019, tel. 212/753–3500. 200 rooms. AE, CB, DC, MC, V. Moderate.*

Midtown–Murray Hill

Morgans. You'd never stumble over Morgans by accident. No sign identifies its exterior and nothing in the swanky ground-floor reception area suggests anything other than the entryway to an exclusive apartment building. Rooms, in black, white, and gray color schemes, are small but have high-tech trappings like VCRs and cassette decks. The brightest rooms and best views are on the east side. *237 Madison Ave. at 37th St., 10016, tel. 212/686–0300 or 800/334–3408. 154 rooms. AE, CB, DC, MC, V. Expensive.*

Midtown–Theater District

Chatwal Inn. The facade of the former Hotel President has been covered with new stone and augmented with a brass canopy. Lofty palms adorn the marble-paneled lobby. The rooms, though small, have pleasant pink wallpaper and sleek Art-Deco furnishings. This flagship of the growing Chatwal chain is popular with groups of overseas visitors. *234 W. 48th St., 10036, tel. 212/246–8800 or 800/262–4665. 400 rooms. AE, CB, DC, MC, V. Inexpensive.*

Hotel Edison. The Art Deco lobby of this huge, bustling hotel a half-block off Broadway offers comfy chairs strategically situated for people-watching. The Cafe Edison, aka "Polish Tea Room," serves hearty Eastern European dishes to deal-making show-biz types. Request a room in the renovated section. *228 W. 47th St., 10036, tel. 212/840–5000 or 800/637–7070. 1,000 rooms. AE, CB, DC, MC, V. Inexpensive.*

Midtown/Upper East Side

Manhattan East Suite Hotels. This alliance of comfortable midtown and Upper East Side hotels rents suites for what the competition charges for rooms. Each hotel is different but room formats are similar: Studio suites have oversize sleeping rooms and dining or sitting areas; junior suites have living rooms and separate sleeping areas; one-, two-, and three-bedroom suites have separate bedrooms. All accommodations have kitchens equipped with glassware, dishes, silverware, and cooking utensils. **Beekman Tower,** *3 Mitchell Pl. (near the U.N.), 10017, 160 rooms;* **Dumont Plaza,** *150 E. 34th St., 10016, 251 rooms;* **Eastgate Tower,** *222 E. 39th St., 10016, 191 rooms;* **Lyden Gardens,** *215 E. 64th St., 10021, 133 rooms;* **Lyden House,** *320 E. 53rd St., 10022, 81 rooms;* **Plaza 50,** *155 E. 50th St., 10022, 206 rooms;* **Shelburne Murray Hill,** *303 Lexington Ave. at 37th St., 10016, 248 rooms;* **Southgate Tower,** *371 Seventh Ave. at 31st St., 10001, 522 rooms;* **Surrey Hotel,** *20 E. 76th St., 10021, 117 rooms. Tel. 800/637–8483. AE, DC, MC, V. Expensive.*

Midtown–West Side

Novotel. This six-year-old European-owned hotel on the northern fringe of the Theater District has modern rooms decorated in muted pink. Choose a Broadway or Hudson River view. The Cafe Skylight Lounge and Terrace offer a variety of wines by the glass and occasional tastings. *226 W. 52nd St. at Broadway, 10019, tel. 212/315–0100 or 800/221–4542. 474 rooms. AE, CB, DC, MC, V. Expensive.*

Upper East Side

Carlyle. Located in one of New York's poshest residential areas, this luxury hotel is also handy to two of the city's best museums—the Metropolitan and the Whitney. Full-time residents occupy the best rooms, but transients need not fret—the rest of the rooms are elegant, with subdued decor and furnishings. Suites have a pantry and refrigerator and some have private terraces and/or wood-burning fireplaces. Vertès-decorated Cafe Carlyle, where Bobby Short's piano often echoes, has fine dining, and the Bemelman's Bar is decorated with whimsical murals by the artist himself. *35 E. 76th St., 10021, tel. 212/744–1600. 175 rooms. AE, CB, DC, MC, V. Very Expensive.*

Barbizon Hotel. Formerly a residence for "young ladies of good breeding" (Grace Kelly and Liza Minnelli among others), the Barbizon is now a privately run hotel. The atmosphere is elegantly homey, with smallish rooms made bright with soft colors, country French furnishings, and original posters. *140 E. 63rd St., 10021, tel. 212/838–5700. 368 rooms. AE, CB, DC, MC, V. Expensive.*

Mayfair Regent. Corporate chieftains and celebrities seeking to avoid public attention patronize this dignified European-style hotel on the Upper East Side, which was an apartment building until 1978. Its centerpiece Lobby Lounge is a refined setting for breakfast, light lunches, afternoon tea, and cocktails. Early American–style rooms have butler's pantries, humidifiers, and at least two phones. There are attendant-operated elevators at all times. *610 Park Ave. at 65th St., 10021, tel. 212/288–0800. 200 rooms. AE, CB, DC, MC, V. Expensive.*

Upper West Side

Excelsior. This is the best deal on the Upper West Side. Opposite the Museum of Natural History at the north end of the Columbus Avenue commercial strip, the Excelsior is heavily booked with Europeans and thrifty business travelers. Newly decorated guest rooms offer no-frills-but-nice decor. *45 W. 81st St., 10024, tel. 212/362–9200. 300 rooms. AE, MC, V. Inexpensive.*

West Side–Lincoln Center

Empire Hotel. The lobby of the drastically new and improved Empire now boasts marble pillars and high ceilings. Rooms were repainted in restful pastels and redecorated with dignified cherry-mahogany furniture. Even with a corporate program to entice a new clientele of business travelers, the relatively low rates and Lincoln Center location still attract musicians, music lovers, and tone-deaf bargain-hunters. *44 W. 63rd St. at Broadway, 10023, tel. 212/265–7400. 500 rooms. AE, CB, DC, MC, V. Moderate.*

YMCA Three Manhattan Ys, in unexpectedly convenient locations, offer men and women low-priced lodging plus exercise facilities, budget cafeterias, and plenty of opportunities to mingle with other guests. Rooms range between $30 and $40 for singles or doubles; most have shared baths. Ys are heavily booked in peak seasons and often require deposits or advance payment.

The 561-room **West Side Y** (5 W. 63rd St., 10023, tel. 212/787–4400) is a half-block from Central Park and around the corner from Lincoln Center. *MC, V.* The 438-room **Vanderbilt YMCA** (224 E. 47th St., 10017, tel. 212/755–2410) is situated on the

East Side not far from the United Nations. *MC*, *V*. The huge 1,490-room **Sloane House YMCA** (356 W. 34th St., 10001, tel. 212/760–5860) is near Penn Station and about a half-mile south of the Theater District. *No credit cards*.

Bed-and-Breakfast Hundreds of rooms are available on a bed-and-breakfast basis in Manhattan and the other boroughs, principally Brooklyn. B&Bs almost always cost below $100 a night; some singles are available for under $50. New York City B&Bs fall into two general categories: (1) *Hosted apartments* are bedrooms in an apartment where hosts are present; (2) *unhosted apartments* are temporarily vacant apartments. The unhosted option is scarcer and more expensive.

The following reservation agencies book B&B accommodations in and near Manhattan. There is no fee for the service, but they advise you to make reservations as far in advance as possible. They also suggest that you find out something about various areas of the city before you contact them and request accommodations in a specific neighborhood.

Bed and Breakfast Network of New York. 134 W. 32nd St., Suite 602, 10001, tel. 212/645–8134.
City Lights Bed and Breakfast, Ltd. Box 20355, Cherokee Station, 10028, tel. 212/737–7049.
New World Bed and Breakfast. 150 Fifth Ave., Suite 711, 10011, tel. 212/675–5600 or 800/443–3800.
Urban Ventures. 306 W. 38th St., 10018, tel. 212/594–5650.

The Arts

The most comprehensive and useful listings of weekly entertainment and cultural events appear in the weekly *New York* magazine. Listings include capsule summaries of all Broadway, Off-Broadway, and Off-Off-Broadway shows and concerts with performance times and ticket prices. The "Arts and Leisure Guide" in the Arts and Entertainment section of the Sunday *New York Times* lists events but lacks descriptions and service information. The "Theater Directory" in the daily *Times* includes ticket information on Broadway and Off-Broadway shows plus ads and reviews. Listings of events in the arts also appear in the weekly *New Yorker* and *Village Voice*.

It's easy to buy tickets for Broadway and Off-Broadway shows; you can even do it before you reach New York. All Broadway show tickets are available by phone from either Tele-Charge (tel. 212/239–6200) or Teletron (tel. 212/246–0102). You charge the price of the tickets plus a surcharge to a major credit card and pick up tickets at the box office before the show. Both of these services operate 24 hours a day, seven days a week. Similar arrangements are available for Off-Broadway through Hit-Tix (tel. 212/564–8038), Ticketmaster (tel. 212/307–7171), or at the theater.

In New York you can buy Broadway tickets at the box offices, which are open most of the day and all evening. Tickets for many Off-Broadway shows are available from *Ticket Central* (416 W. 42nd St., tel. 212/279–4200). Tickets for the hottest shows in town—of late *The Phantom of the Opera* and *Les Miserables*—may be available only through ticket brokers. Brokers in New York can sell the ticket for full price plus a *legal* surcharge of $2.50 per ticket; consequently, many operate out of New Jersey, where such limits don't apply. Look them up in the Manhattan Yellow Pages under "Ticket Sales—Entertainment & Sports."

For discounts of nearly 50% on Broadway and Off-Broadway shows, try your luck at **TKTS** (tel. 212/354–5800). This nonprofit service sells day-of-performance tickets for half the regular price plus a $1.50 per ticket service charge. Supply is erratic: Sometimes almost every show in town seems to be listed on the display boards just outside the ticket window. At other times only long-running hits and sleepers are available.

The main TKTS booth is located in the Theater District on Duffy Square, a triangle at the northern end of Times Square. It's open 3–8 daily for evening performances, 10–2 for Wednesday and Saturday matinees, noon–8 Sundays for matinee and evening performances. A TKTS booth at 2 World Trade Center opens earlier in the day and generally has shorter lines. Its hours are 11–5:30 weekdays; 11:30–3:30 Saturday; matinee and Sunday tickets are sold the day before the performance; Off-Broadway tickets are sold 11AM–1PM for evening performances only. Another TKTS booth in front of Borough Hall in Brooklyn (tel. 718/625–5015) operates Tuesday through Friday 11–5:30, Saturday 11–3:30 for evening performances only. Matinee and Sunday tickets are available the day before the performance; Off-Broadway tickets are sold only until 1 PM. TKTS accepts only cash or traveler's checks—no personal checks or credit cards.

A TKTS-like operation called **Bryant Park Half-Price Tickets** sells discount day-of-performance tickets for music and dance concerts all over the city—including Lincoln Center and Carnegie Hall. Tickets cost half the regular price plus a $1.50 service charge. *42nd St. just east of Sixth Ave., tel. 212/382–2323. Open Tues., Thurs., Fri. noon–2, 3–7; Wed. and Sat. 11–2, 3–7; Sun. noon–6. Cash or traveler's checks only.*

Theater

With nearly 40 Broadway theaters, three dozen Off-Broadway theaters, and 200 Off-Off-Broadway houses, the New York theater offers something for every taste. The principal differences between the three tiers of New York theater involve the location and size of the theater and the price of tickets.

Broadway theater is the top of the line. These theaters are located in the Theater District, most of which lies between Broadway and Eighth Avenue, and 43rd and 52nd streets. Some Broadway houses are small gems, comfortable and luxurious yet intimate enough to make the audience feel part of the production. The newer, larger theaters are no less luxurious but less intimate. Ticket prices range from $22.50 to $55 depending on the show, the time and day of performance, and the location of the seat. Generally, straight plays are less expensive than musicals; matinee (Wednesday, Saturday, and sometimes Sunday) and weeknight performances cost less than Friday and Saturday night. Most Broadway theaters are dark (closed) on Monday although some are dark on other days.

Off-Broadway theater has professional performers but generally less elaborate productions. Performers receive minimum salaries, but, since theaters are smaller and less luxurious, salaries and costs are considerably lower. Off-Broadway theaters are located all over town. Many can be found along a strip of 42nd Street between Ninth and Tenth avenues; others are in Greenwich Village, the Upper East Side, Chelsea, Harlem, and Brooklyn. Ticket prices range from $10 to $30 with most falling in the $20 to $25 range.

Some of the most consistently exciting Off-Broadway theater companies include the six stages (plus one cinema) of Joseph Papp's **Public Theater** (425 Lafayette St., tel. 212/598–7100). **Circle-in-the-Square (Downtown)** (159 Bleecker St., tel. 212/254–6330) manages to attract some top names (Al Pacino, George C. Scott) to its Greenwich Village quarters. The **Manhattan Theater Club** (131 W. 55th St., tel. 212/581–7907) premieres new plays by top authors. The **Ensemble Studio Theater** (549 W. 52nd St., tel. 212/247–3405) spotlights new playwrights and has a yearly mid-May–mid-June one-act play marathon.

Off-Off-Broadway theater is alternative theater. Performers and production staff may be professionals but when they work OOB they get little or no salary. Although you won't find lavish sets and plush seating, plays are smooth and well-rehearsed renditions of everything from Shakespeare to the first production of the next Samuel Beckett. Off-Off-Broadway houses are located in all kinds of spaces—lofts, church basements, converted storefronts—all over town. Tickets rarely exceed $10 and you can phone ahead for reservations. *New York* magazine contains the best information on Off-Off-Broadway shows.

Concerts

New York's serious music scene centers upon the concert halls and theaters of **Lincoln Center** (Broadway and 65th St., tel. 212/877–2011). **Avery Fisher Hall** (tel. 212/874–2424) is the home of the New York Philharmonic Orchestra, the Mostly Mozart festival, and visiting orchestras and soloists. The more intimate **Alice Tully Hall** (tel. 212/362–1911), in the Juilliard School of Music building, features chamber music and jazz performances. Although most tickets are sold on a subscription basis, individual seats may be available at the box office in advance or through Centercharge (tel. 212/874–6770).

Since it opened in 1891 (with Tchaikovsky conducting), playing **Carnegie Hall** (Seventh Ave. and 57th St., tel. 212/247–7800) has epitomized a musician's ascendancy to the big time. Now it presents visiting orchestras, recitals, chamber music, and pop concerts. The smaller **Weill Recital Hall** features lesser known artists at less-expensive prices. Student/senior rush tickets are available from 6 PM on performance nights. Public tours (admission $6 adults, $5 students, $3 children under 12) are given on Tuesday and Thursday at 11:30, 2, and 3.

Merkin Concert Hall (129 W. 67th St., tel. 212/362–8719) is a reasonably priced stop on the concert circuit. Though threatened with gentrification-motivated demolition, **Symphony Space** (2537 Broadway at 95th St., tel. 212/864–5400) continues to present an eclectic program of concerts, literary readings, dance, marathons (from James Joyce to Cole Porter), and drama at more or less painless (free–$20) prices. The **Metropolitan Museum of Art** (Fifth Ave. and 82nd St., tel. 212/570–3949) presents a popular concert series in its 708-seat auditorium. The **92nd Street Y** (YM-YWHA) on the Upper East Side (1395 Lexington Ave. at 92nd St., tel. 212/996–1100) offers chamber music, orchestral series, recitals by top-name musicians, and pop music programs.

Concerts are also performed regularly at churches, colleges, museums, recital halls, lofts, and other spaces throughout the city. To find out when and where, consult the "Music and Dance" section of *New York* magazine, the Sunday *New York Times* "Arts and Leisure Guide," or listings in *The New Yorker*.

Opera

The **Metropolitan Opera House** (Lincoln Center, Broadway and 65th St., tel. 212/362–6000) is a sublime setting for mostly classic operas performed by world-class stars. Tickets can be expensive—up to $90—and hard to get, but low-price standing-room may be available. Also at Lincoln Center is the **New York City Opera** (State Theater, tel. 212/870–5570), a first-class opera company with lower ticket prices than the Met—under $50—and an innovative and unpredictable schedule.

Other New York opera companies include the **Amato Opera Theater** (319 Bowery near 2nd St., tel. 212/228–8200), a downtown showcase for young performers, and the **Light Opera Company of Manhattan** (Playhouse 91, 316 E. 91st. St., tel. 212/831–2000), which presents energetic versions of Gilbert and Sullivan operettas throughout the year. Other companies produce operas on an irregular basis. Check *New York* magazine or *The New York Times* for current productions.

Dance

Under the direction of Mikhail Baryshnikov, the **American Ballet Theatre** (Broadway and 65th St., tel. 212/362–6000) is the resident company of the Metropolitan Opera House in Lincoln Center. ABT mingles classics with new ballets during the spring (May–June) season. Ticket prices start low, around $8 for standing room, and rise to more than $50.

The renowned **New York City Ballet** (State Theater, Lincoln Center, tel. 212/870–5570) attained universal prominence under the direction of George Balanchine. The largest dance organization in the West (107 dancers) performs a spring season in May and June, and a winter program from November through February. Tickets range from $6 to $45.

City Center Theater (131 W. 55th St., tel. 212/581–7907), a Moorish-style former Masonic temple, is home base for innovative modern dance companies like the Alvin Ailey troupe, the Paul Taylor Company, and the daring Joffrey Ballet. The **Joyce Theater** (175 Eighth Ave. at 19th St., tel. 212/242–0800), an Art Deco former movie house, is the setting for a contemporary fall and spring season and is the New York home of the Eliot Feld company. **Dance Theater Workshop** (219 W. 19th St., tel. 212/924–0077) is a second-floor performance loft that highlights the work of avant-garde dancers and choreographers. The 127-year-old **Brooklyn Academy of Music (BAM)** (30 Lafayette Ave., Brooklyn, tel. 718/636–4100) presents ballet, modern dance, and a futuristic Next Wave Festival each fall.

Weekly listings of other ballet, modern, and folk dance performances can be found in *New York* magazine and the "Arts and Leisure" section of the Sunday *New York Times*.

Half-price day-of-performance tickets are available at **Bryant Park Half-Price Tickets** (*see* The Arts, above).

Film

Few cities rival New York's selection of films. Along with all the first-run Hollywood features, an incomparable selection of foreign films, classics, documentaries, and experimental works are playing all over town. The daily *New York Daily News* and *New York Newsday*, the Friday *New York Times*, and the weekly *Village Voice* print schedules and show times for Manhattan movies. *New York* magazine and *The New Yorker* publish programs and capsule reviews but no schedules.

The vast majority of Manhattan theaters are first-run houses. Most charge $7 a ticket for adults at all times; some offer off-peak discounts for children and seniors. Even though New York has recently lost some venerable revival houses (Thalia, Regency), several cinemas still screen revivals, classics, foreign movies, and off-beat films—usually as double features:

Film Forum 1 & 2. 57 Watts St. near Sixth Ave., tel. 212/431–1590.
Thalia SoHo. 15 Vandam St. near Sixth Ave., tel. 212/675–0498.
Bleecker Street Cinemas. 144 Bleecker St., tel. 212/674–2560.
Cinema Village. 22 E. 12th St., tel. 212/924–3363.
Theatre 80. 80 St. Mark's Pl., tel. 212/254–7400.

Other institutions also present cinema programs. The **Public Theater** (425 Lafayette St., tel. 212/598–7171) concentrates on retrospectives and documentaries. The **Museum of Modern Art** (11 W. 53rd St., tel. 212/708–9490) shows film classics every day in two theaters; movies are free with museum admission. The **Whitney Museum** (945 Madison Ave. at 75th St., tel. 212/570–0537) showcases independent American films; free with museum admission. The **Collective for Living Cinema** (41 White St., tel. 212/925–2111) in TriBeCa has an ambitious, constantly changing program of experimental films.

Subtitled foreign-language films connected with the cultures of the particular institution are shown regularly at the **French Institute** (22 E. 60th St., tel. 212/355–6100), **Goethe House** (German) (1014 Fifth Ave. at 82nd St., tel. 212/972–3960), and **Japan House** (333 E. 47th St., tel. 212/832–1155).

Nightlife

For up-to-date information about what's going on after hours, check out the "Arts and Entertainment" section of the Sunday *New York Times* and the "Weekend" section of the Friday *Times*. Friday editions of *New York Newsday*, the *New York Daily News*, and the *New York Post* also detail nighttime happenings. The "Nightlife Directory" of the weekly *New York* magazine carries listings for live music and entertainment all over town. Check out the *Village Voice* for information on rock and jazz acts.

Cabaret

The Ballroom. This Chelsea *tapas* bar (Spanish appetizers) features top-name cabaret acts and outrageous revues. *253 W. 28th St., tel. 212/244–3005. AE, MC, V. Sets at 6:30, 9, and 11.*

Broadway Baby. At this piano bar, the waiters and waitresses are ready to perform for a song. *407 Amsterdam Ave. at 79th St., tel. 212/724–6868. AE. Open 8 PM–4 AM.*

Don't Tell Mama. There's a lively piano bar up front with no cover or minimum and risky "open mike" policy. Cabaret performers work the back room. *343 W. 46th St., tel. 212/757–0788. No credit cards. Shows 8 and 10.*

The Duplex. Torch singers and hot comics perform at this bi-level Village club. *55 Grove St., tel. 212/255–5438. No credit cards. Shows at 8, 10, and midnight Fri. and Sat.*

Greene Street. Posh bi-level SoHo restaurant, where a second-floor cabaret features singers or comics on Friday and Saturday night. *105 Greene St., tel. 212/925–2415. AE, CB, DC, MC, V. Cabaret Fri. and Sat. 8 PM–1:30 AM.*

Eleonora. An Italian restaurant with a variety of entertainers. *117 W. 58th St., tel. 212/765–1427. AE, CB, DC, MC, V. Closed Sun.*

Jan Wallman's. Hot restaurant/cabaret on ground floor of Hotel Iroquois features jazz-oriented singers and players. *49 W. 44th St., tel. 212/764–8930. AE, CB, DC, MC, V. Shows at 9 and 11. Closed Sun.*

Steve McGraw's (formerly Palsson's). This West Side showroom presents scathingly irreverent satirical revues and cabaret. *158 W. 72nd St., tel. 212/595–7400. AE, CB, DC, MC, V. Two shows nightly; call for times and reservations.*

Bars and Nightclubs

Cafe Carlyle. Master piano man Bobby Short or another sophisticated performer presides at this elegant club. *Hotel Carlyle, Madison Ave. at 76th St., tel. 212/744–1600. Shows 10 PM and midnight. AE, CB, DC, MC, V. Closed Sun. and Mon.*

California Club. This elegant nightclub and American-style restaurant hosts live Big Band and jazz music most evenings. *156 W. 43rd St., tel. 212/391–0001. AE, DC.*

5 & 10, No Exaggeration. At this fabulous '40s SoHo night spot, the music is live and the Art Deco furnishings are for sale. *77 Greene St. between Broome and Spring Sts., tel. 212/925–7414. AE, CB, DC, MC, V. Closed Mon.*

Nickels. Singer-pianists perform at this casual American-style restaurant. *227 E. 67th St., tel. 212/794–2331. AE, DC, MC, V. Nightly from 7:30.*

Notes. This is a late-night spot for piano music and dancing. *Omni Park Central Hotel, Seventh Ave. and 55th St., tel. 212/ 757–4441. AE, CB, DC, MC, V. Nightly 5 PM–2 AM.*

Jazz Clubs

Most jazz clubs have substantial cover charges and drink minimums for table service. You can usually save one or both of these charges by sitting at or standing around the bar.

Angry Squire. Contemporary sounds from small groups are featured at this Chelsea neighborhood pub. *216 Seventh Ave. near 23rd St., tel. 212/242–9066. AE, MC, V. Nightly from 9.*

Blue Note. Not the original, but nonetheless a swinging place to catch top names in jazz. *131 W. 3rd St., tel. 212/475-8592. AE, MC, V. Nightly from 9.*

Bradley's. Piano-and-bass combos are spotlighted at this smoky and crowded low-key spot. *70 University Pl., tel. 212/228-6440. AE, CB, DC, MC, V. Nightly from 9:45.*

Fat Tuesday's. Jazz superstars perform at this intimate downstairs stage. *190 Third Ave. at 17th St., tel. 212/533-7902. AE, CB, DC, MC, V. Nightly from 8.*

Knickerbocker Bar & Grill. Cool jazz circulates here in a clamorous Old New York setting. *33 University Pl., tel. 212/228-8490. AE, MC, V. Nightly from 9:30.*

The Knitting Factory. This hot new place on the Greenwich Village/SoHo frontier features avant-garde groups. *47 E. Houston St., tel. 212/219-3055. AE. Nightly from 9.*

Michael's Pub. Mainstream jazz, top vocalists, jazz-based revues are presented here, and Woody Allen's Dixieland band holds stage most Mondays. *211 E. 55th St., tel. 212/758-2272. AE, DC, MC, V. Nightly except Sun. from 9:30.*

Mikell's. This popular Upper West Side spot presents a variety of jazz-influenced sounds. *760 Columbus Ave. at 97th St., tel. 212/864-8832. AE, CB, DC, MC. Nightly from 9.*

Sweet Basil. A roomful of jazz memorabilia and top-name groups are featured here. *88 Seventh Ave. S near Bleecker St., tel. 212/242-1785. AE, CB, DC, MC, V. Nightly from 10.*

Village Vanguard. This basement standby has been riding the crest of every new wave for over 50 years. *178 Seventh Ave. S, tel. 212/255-4037. No credit cards. Nightly from 9:30.*

The Village Gate. Different acts and shows perform simultaneously in three places. No cover on the Village Gate Terrace. *160 Bleecker St., tel. 212/475-5120. AE, MC, V. Nightly from 9.*

Pop/Rock Clubs

The Bitter End. This Village institution has been giving breaks to folk, rock, jazz, comedy, and country acts for 25 years. *147 Bleecker St., tel. 212/673-7030. No credit cards. Nightly from 8.*

The Bottom Line. One of the city's best venues for rock, jazz, folk, and country/western is this institution near New York University. Limited menu of cheap, but greasy, food. *15 W. 4th St., tel. 212/228-6300. No credit cards. Nightly from 8.*

Cat Club. Go to the Cat for dancing, swing music (Sundays only) and good old rock-and-roll. *76 E. 13th St., tel. 212/505-0090. No credit cards. Nightly from 9.*

CBGB. This hard-core place still blasts eardrums with heavy metal plus the next hot sounds. *315 Bowery, tel. 212/982-4052. No credit cards. Nightly; call for set times.*

Island Club. This south-of-the-Village hideaway spotlights reggae, calypso, salsa, and other south-of-the-border sounds. *285 West Broadway at Canal St., tel. 212/226-4598. No credit cards.*

The Ritz. Though it's traded its Art Deco ballroom for a former disco palace (Studio 54), the acts are the same: newest New Wavers, bluesmen, and hard rockers, with a little reggae thrown in for good measure. *254 W. 54th St., tel. 212/541-8900. No credit cards. Nightly from 9.*

S.O.B.'s (Sounds of Brazil) This is a sophisticated and popular tropical setting for Latin music. *204 Varick St. at W. Houston*

St., tel. 212/243–4940. AE, DC, MC, V. 7 PM–4 AM. Closed Sun. and Mon.

Country/Western Clubs

Eagle Tavern. At this low-key Irish pub, there is traditional Irish music Monday and Friday, and comedy on Tuesday, Thursday, and Sunday. *355 W. 14th St., tel. 212/924–0275. No credit cards. Nightly after 9.*

Lone Star Roadhouse. A touch of down-home Texas is featured here, where big names in country swing and big-city blues play. *240 W. 52nd St., tel. 212/245–2950. AE, CB, DC, MC, V. Nightly from 9:15.*

O'Lunney's. This is a great place to dance to country music. *915 Second Ave. between 48th and 49th Sts., tel. 212/751–5470. AE, DC, MC, V. Closed Sun.*

Country acts also appear at the **Bottom Line** and **The Ritz** (*see* Rock Clubs).

Comedy Clubs

Caroline's at the Seaport. Big names perform here in stand-up comedy. National TV credit is a prerequisite for a headliner booking. *Pier 17, 89 South St., tel. 212/233–4900. AE, CB, DC, MC, V. Sun.–Tues. 8, Wed. and Thurs. 8 and 9:30, Fri. 8 and 10:30, Sat. 7, 9, and 11:30.*

Catch A Rising Star. Continuous comedy by performers on their way to the top? It's up to you. *1487 First Ave. near 78th St., tel. 212/794–1906. AE. Sun.–Thurs. 9, Fri. 8 and 11, Sat. 7:30, 10, and 12:30.*

Comic Strip. Like Catch A Rising Star, this is a showcase for tomorrow's great comics and singers. *1568 Second Ave. between 81st and 82nd Sts., tel. 212/861–9386. AE, MC, V. Nightly at 9 plus Fri. midnight and Sat. 11:30.*

Dangerfield's. The disrespected Rodney occasionally appears here but mostly up-and-comers are featured. *1118 First Ave. near 61st St., tel. 212/593–1650. AE, CB, DC, MC, V. Sun.–Thurs. 9:15, Fri. 9 and 11:30, Sat. 8, 10:30, and 12:30.*

The Original Improvisation. This is New York's original comedy showcase where the big-name yucksters (Rodney Dangerfield, Richard Pryor, Robert Klein) won their first giggles. *358 W. 44th St., tel. 212/765–8268. AE. Sun.–Thurs. 9, Fri. 9 and 11:30, Sat. 8, 10:30, and 12:40.*

Stand-Up New York. Sit down here and laugh at comics with TV and national club scene credits. *236 W. 78th St., tel. 212/595–0850. AE, MC, V. Sun.–Thurs. 9, Fri. 8:30 and 11:30, Sat. 8, 10:15, and 12:30.*

Discos/Dance Clubs

Adam's Apple. At this heavily foliated uptown spot, there is action on three separate dance floors. *1117 First Ave. at 61st St., tel. 212/371–8651. AE, CB, DC, MC, V. Nightly after 9.*

Chevy's. New York's hot new old time ('50s and '60s) hangout combines a rock-and-roll dance club with a diner. *27 W. 20th St., tel. 212/924–0205. AE, MC, V. Tues.–Fri. from 5 PM until late; Sat. from 9 PM.*

Hideaway. Dance cheek-to-cheek here in John Barrymore's former town house. *32 W. 37th St., tel. 212/947–8940. AE, CB,*

DC, MC, V. Mon.–Thurs. 7–midnight, Fri. 7:30–1, Sat. 8–1:30.

Palladium. This huge space is divided into a number of intriguing environments. *126 E. 14th St., tel. 212/473–7171. AE. Thurs.–Sat. after 10.*

Limelight. At this deconsecrated church there are enticing nooks and crannies, huge video screens, and a riotous dance floor. Amen. *660 Sixth Ave. at 20th St., tel. 212/807–7850. AE, MC, V. Nightly after 10.*

Pyramid. This *outre* East Village club has a variety of bizarre entertainments and very-late-night dancing. *101 Avenue A near St. Mark's Pl., tel. 212/420–1590. No credit cards. Nightly from 11.*

Rainbow Room. Dance yourself back to 1930s elegance on the 65th floor of the Art Deco RCA building. For dinner guests only. *30 Rockefeller Center, tel. 212/632–5100. AE. Tues.–Sat. 7:30 PM–1:30 AM., Sun. 6–11.*

Regine's. Buy dinner to gain access to the disco floor or eat elsewhere and pay the cover charge. *502 Park Ave. at 59th St., tel. 212/826–0990. AE, DC, MC, V. Mon.–Sat. 11–4.*

Roseland. You can still do "touch dancing" matinees and evenings to two orchestras at this New York institution. *239 W. 52nd St., tel. 212/247–0200. AE. Thurs.–Sun. from 2:30 PM.*

Tunnel. A cavernous riverside warehouse has been converted into a wild and funky disco/late-night club. *220 12th Ave. at 27th St., tel. 212/244–6444. MC, V. Wed.–Sat.*

For Singles (Under 30)

¡Caramba! Tropical concoctions, Mexican food, and a cocktail-hour crowd that won't stop. *Four locations: 684 Broadway at 3rd St., tel. 212/420–9817; 918 Eighth Ave. at 54th St., tel. 212/245–7910; 1576 Third Ave. at 88th St., tel. 212/876–8838; and 2567 Broadway near 96th St., tel. 212/749–5055. AE, CB, DC, MC, V.*

Ear Inn. This back-street hangout has a great jukebox and periodic poetry readings. *326 Spring St., tel. 212/226–9060. AE, DC.*

Hard Rock Cafe. Lines are omnipresent for this memorabilia-filled shrine to rock-and-roll. *221 W. 57th St., tel. 212/489–6565. AE, DC, MC, V.*

McSorley's Old Ale House. Young people throng for the house brands of ale at one of New York's oldest saloons. *15 E. 7th St., tel. 212/473–9148. No credit cards.*

Raccoon Lodge. The postcollege generation gathers for casual drinks and lively conversation at two Raccoon Lodges, named after the fraternal affiliation of Kramden and Norton in *The Honeymooners. 59 Warren St., tel. 212/766–9656; and 480 Amsterdam Ave. at 83rd St., tel. 212/874–9984. No credit cards.*

Shout! After five o'clock, this nifty bar and rock-and-roll dance club becomes a favorite spot for the workday crowd. *124 W. 43rd St., tel 212/869–2088. AE, MC, V. Wed.–Sat.*

T.G.I.Friday's. This is one of New York's oldest established singles meeting places. *1152 First Ave. at 63rd St., tel. 212/832–8512. AE, CB, DC, MC, V.*

For Singles (Over 30)

J. G. Melon's. These two casual neighborhood restaurant/bars swing in east and west side neighborhoods. *1291 Third Ave. at*

74th St., tel. 212/650–1310, no credit cards; 340 Amsterdam Ave. at 76th St., tel. 212/877–2220. AE, MC, V.

Lion's Head. This is a well-worn Greenwich Village basement hangout for writers and local politicians. *59 Christopher St. off Seventh Ave. S, tel. 212/929–0670. AE, DC, MC, V.*

P. J. Clarke's. You're liable to spot a movie or TV star at this welcoming old-style big-city bar in the heart of midtown. *915 Third Ave. at 55th St., tel. 212/759–1650. AE, DC.*

Runyon's. Named after Damon, this is New York's preeminent sports bar—now in two high-energy locations. *305 E. 50th St., tel. 212/223–9592; 932 Second Ave. near 49th St., tel. 212/759–7800. AE, CB, DC, MC, V.*

Stringfellows. This upscale bar/restaurant/dance club serves American cuisine and stays hopping with rock music until the wee, wee hours. *35 E. 21st St., tel. 212/254–2444. AE, CB, DC, MC, V. Closed Sun.*

Top of the Sixes. Go for a cocktail-hour scene 39 stories above the heart of midtown. *666 Fifth Ave. at 53rd St., tel. 212/757–6662. AE, CB, DC, MC, V.*

White Horse Tavern. This is the Greenwich Village drinking spot that figures prominently in the life and legend of Dylan Thomas. *567 Hudson St. at 11th St., tel. 212/243–9260. No credit cards.*

4 Long Island

Introduction

At 1,682 square miles, Long Island is not only the largest island on America's East Coast but the most varied. From west to east, Long Island shades from suburban sprawl to farm land and vineyards punctuated by historic seaside villages. It has what is arguably the nation's finest stretch of white-sand beach as well as one of our most congested highways, the notorious Long Island Expressway. There is the Long Island of the rich, who for generations have retreated to the princely estates of the North Shore's Gold Coast; the Long Island of the famous, who flock to the string of South Shore villages known collectively as the Hamptons; and the Long Island of hard-working commuters who journey each day from their "bedroom communities" to their Manhattan offices or to one of the many Long Island office parks. In addition to superb beaches, nature has given Long Island innumerable natural harbors, excellent soil, and a fascinating geology; man has given it a long and distinguished history, beautiful old homes, and, more recently, wonderful places to eat and to stay.

Although two of New York City's boroughs, Brooklyn and Queens, occupy Long Island's western section, the *real* Long Island—known to residents simply as the Island—begins only when one leaves the city behind and crosses into Nassau County (Brooklyn and Queens are described in the New York City chapter of this book). East of Nassau is the more rural Suffolk County, with its two "forks," north and south, extending far into the Atlantic Ocean. From the Nassau/Queens border to its eastern terminus at Montauk Point, Long Island is 103 miles long and from 12 to 20 miles wide. Together, Nassau and Suffolk counties have nearly three million residents, making Long Island more populous than 19 states.

On Long Island, the north/south distinction applies not only to the "forks" of the East End but to the North and South shores that run the length of the island. Jagged in its coastal outline and gentle in topography, the North Shore is lapped by Long Island Sound, which F. Scott Fitzgerald called "the most domesticated body of salt water in the Western hemisphere." The considerably less domesticated Atlantic Ocean sends its rollers onto the white-sand beaches that fringe the South Shore. Many of these beaches, including Jones Beach, Fire Island, and Westhampton Beach, are actually long, narrow barrier islands that wind and tide have thrown up as a kind of sandy protection to Long Island's South Shore. Noteworthy attractions of the North Shore include Teddy Roosevelt's summer home at Sagamore Hill, Walt Whitman's birthplace at Huntington Station, and a number of estates built by real-life Great Gatsbys. The Hamptons, the fascinating whaling village of Sag Harbor, the great oceanside park at Jones Beach, and the majesty of Montauk Point make the South Shore memorable.

Long Island was settled early and quickly, in part because two nations were planting colonies here simultaneously. While the Dutch were pushing eastward from their stronghold on New Amsterdam (today's Manhattan), the English were sailing down from newly settled Connecticut and Massachusetts to set up outposts at Hempstead, East Hampton, Southampton, Southold, and Brookhaven on central and eastern Long Island.

By 1650 the two nations brushed up against each other at Oyster Bay, and conflict ensued. Eventually, in 1674, the English took final possession of New Amsterdam, and all of Long Island came under the jurisdiction of the English crown.

Agriculture was the basis of Long Island's early economy, and later, in the 18th and early 19th centuries, whaling brought a brief period of wealth and prominence to places like Sag Harbor and Cold Spring Harbor. After the Civil War, when well-to-do Americans discovered the pleasures of saltwater bathing, the Hamptons were transformed from farming and fishing communities to fashionable summer resorts, and the North Shore became the playground of the Vanderbilts, Whitneys, and Roosevelts. It wasn't until after World War II, when highways were constructed and Americans began owning cars as a matter of course, that vast numbers of the middle class moved out to Long Island, transforming farm fields into new suburbs and shopping centers.

Today the suburbanization of Long Island continues at a dizzying pace as the population of Nassau and Suffolk booms. But amid the sprawl of new houses, old village centers remain intact. Historic sites and museums protect many of the oldest, finest, and most magnificent homes; and new farms growing wine grapes, herbs, sod, and nursery plants have been established on old potato and vegetable farms. Beyond the hubbub of development and traffic, the beaches and the waters of the sound and ocean beckon to swimmers, fishermen, yachtsmen, sunbathers, and beachcombers as they always have. Long Island today is, if anything, more varied, more richly diverse in vacationing possibilities, and more rewarding to the visitor than ever before.

Getting Around

By Plane In addition to John F. Kennedy International Airport and LaGuardia Airport in Queens, Long Island is served by Long Island MacArthur Airport in Ronkonkoma. For airline information at MacArthur Airport call 516/467-6161.

By Car The best and most convenient way to see Long Island is by car. There are four major east-west thoroughfares that stretch the length of the island. State Route 25A is on the North Shore, the Long Island Expressway passes through the middle of the island, and State Route 27 (Sunrise Highway) and State Route 27A (Merrick Road-Montauk Highway) are on the South Shore. Try to avoid the Long Island Expressway during rush hour, as its reputation as "the world's longest parking lot" is well justified.

Guided Tours

Harran Coachways run escorted day tours for groups and families to many Long Island points of interest. The tours cost about $32 with a restaurant lunch or $15 without lunch and include motor-coach transportation and sightseeing. *30 Mahan St., West Babylon. For registration and schedule information call 516/491-7100 or 718/343-6060.*

Hampton Express offers escorted day trips to eastern Long Island (the Hamptons, Shelter Island, etc.) from its office on the east side of Manhattan. The trips cost about $25 and include a box lunch, bus transportation, and sightseeing. *242 W. Montauk Hwy., Hampton Bays, tel. 516/728-4433; in New York City, 1429 Third Ave., tel. 212/233-4403.*

Long Island Railroad packages more than a dozen day tours to local attractions, including the Hamptons, the Bridgeport Ferry, a Long Island winery, and a number of spectacular mansions. The tours are offered between May and October with morning departures from the LIRR terminal at Penn Station in New York City, the Flatbush Avenue Station in Brooklyn, and the Jamaica Station in Queens, and returns to these stations in the evening. The price of each tour is approximately $35 and includes rail and tour-bus transportation, all admissions, and—as a rule—lunch. There is a reduced price for children 5–11. *Tel. 718/990–7498 or 718/454–LIRR.*

Cruises **Okenos Research Foundation** runs research cruises to view whales, dolphins, and sea birds in their natural environment. The six-hour cruise departs daily year-round from Montauk Viking Dock at 10 AM. From mid-July through Labor Day there are two sailings per day, 9 AM–1 PM and 1:30–5:30 PM. Admission is $25 adults, $15 children 13 and under, 10% discount for senior citizens. Group discounts are available. *Box 776, Hampton Bays, 11946, tel. 516/728–4522 or 4523, weekdays 9–5.*

Captree State Park Ferries runs 1½-hour cruises around the Great South Bay every Saturday, July 4–Labor Day. The price is $5 for adults, $4 for senior citizens, $3 for children 12 and under. *Captree Island, Babylon, tel. 516/661–5061.*

Fire Island Cruises runs a luncheon excursion to the Fire Island lighthouse every Friday July–Labor Day. It also has Sunday brunch cruises with special menus on Easter, Mother's Day, and Father's Day. Dinner cruises are available late June through New Year's Eve, every Thursday and some Tuesday evenings at 7:30, and on Mother's Day. Prices range from $20.45 to $38. *Maple Ave., Bayshore, tel. 516/666–3601.*

Port Jefferson Steamboat Co. offers evening Music Cruises July 4–Labor Day. The three-hour cruise leaves at 8 PM on Wednesday and Thursday, 9:30 on Saturday. The price is $10 per person. *102 W. Broadway, Port Jefferson, tel. 516/473–6282.*

Plane and Helicopter Tours **Barts Auto and Aviation Service** runs narrated "flightseeing" tours of Long Island. Cost is $1 per minute for the 10- to 30-minute flights, which run daily 8:30 AM–dusk. No reservations necessary. *Montauk Hwy., East Moriches, tel. 516/872–1125.*

Mid Island Aviation has one- to two-hour flights for up to three passengers at $99 per hour, year-round 8 AM–5 PM. *Tours leave from Brookhaven Airport, Grand Ave., Shirley and MacArthur Airport, Johnson Ave., Ronkonkoma, tel. 516/588–5400.*

American Helicopters sightseeing tours operate daily from MacArthur Airport. The per-hour price is $145 for one passenger, $250 for two passengers, and $595 for three passengers. *Two-day advance reservations required. Tel. 516/981–6555.*

Island Helicopter has charters available for four–five person tours of Long Island, daily 9–9, $600 per hour. *Reservations required, tel. 516/288–9355 or 212/925–8807.*

Important Addresses and Numbers

Tourist Information Long Island Tourism Association (tel. 516/794–4222). Visitor information centers are located at Eisenhower Park (parking field 6A, East Meadow, open Mon.–Fri. 9–5), Southern State Parkway (between Exits 13 and 14, Valley Stream, open daily 9–5, May–Oct.), and Long Island Expressway (Dix Hills–Deer Park, daily 9:30–4:30, May–Oct.). Most towns also have their own chamber of commerce offices that can supply information on the towns as well as scheduled local events.

Emergencies Dial 911 for **police** and **ambulance** assistance.

Hospitals The following hospitals have 24-hour emergency services: **Nassau:** *Long Island Jewish Hospital* (located on the Queens-Nassau border at Lakeville Rd., New Hyde Park, tel. 718/470–7500; physician referral, tel. 718/470–8690); *Huntington Hospital* (270 Park Ave., Huntington, tel. 516/351–1200); *Nassau County Medical Center* (2201 Hempstead Tpke., East Meadow, tel. 516/542–0123). **Suffolk:** *St. Charles Hospital* (200 Belleterre Rd., Port Jefferson, tel. 516/473–2800) and *Southampton Hospital* (240 Meeting House Ln., Southampton, tel. 516/283–2600).

24-hour Pharmacy **Stuart's Pharmacy and Surgical World,** 833 N. Broadway, North Massapequa (tel. 516/799–5858).

Exploring Long Island

Orientation

Long Island has plenty to see, but you'll only see traffic from the Long Island Expressway (LIE), which runs smack down the middle of the island from Long Island City in Queens to Riverhead in Suffolk. Largely contributing to that traffic is the fact that most visitors head straight for the Hamptons and points east to Montauk. But if you're more interested in museums, stately mansions, nature preserves, and other attractions the Island has to offer along its North and South shores, take the more leisurely roads that parallel the two coastlines. On the North Shore, your best bet is Route 25A; on the South Shore, follow Route 27 (Sunrise Highway).

A couple of days would be enough to explore all the way east to Orient Point at the tip of the North Fork, swing down to the South Fork, and return westward to New York City along the South Shore. But you can also go for the day or overnight to the Hampton area. There are many lateral roads that connect the North and South shores, so cutting back and forth is also easy. Travelers with less generous schedules can use the LIE to make better time between points of interest. By choosing the most direct route, it is possible to drive from Manhattan to Orient Point in less than four hours—although rush-hour and weekend traffic will slow the trip considerably.

When exploring the South Shore, switch from Route 27 (Sunrise Highway) to nearby Route 27A (Montauk Highway) in the vicinity of Bayshore in southwestern Suffolk County. This can be done by taking Exit 41 south off Route 27 on to the Robert Moses Causeway and then Exit C2 east off that to Route 27A. This route is more direct and avoids congestion.

Long Island Beaches

Numbers in the margin correspond with points of interest on the Long Island Beaches map.

Its beaches are what attract most visitors to Long Island. If you want to see gardens, historic houses, and historic towns, take the tours of the North and South shores that follow this tour.

Long Island's beaches will spoil you for beaches anywhere else. Although the beaches along the North Shore looking toward Connecticut are rocky, nearly the entire 103-mile length of the South Shore is fringed with wide bands of sand. These magnificent beaches are certainly no secret and they do tend to get crowded on summer weekends, but the crowds thin out as you move east and they vanish altogether in the off-season. Crowds also are much smaller at the North Shore beaches on Long Island Sound. Though they lack the drama of pounding surf and endless horizons, the North Shore beaches are ideal for young children because the Sound water is calmer and warmer than the ocean.

Long Island beach connoisseurs know that early autumn is the best time to come. The water stays warm into September and even early October. Recently, there has been some concern about organic and inorganic waste polluting beaches throughout the Northeast. For information on beach emergencies and closings in Nassau call County Executive Tom Gulotta's 24-hour hotline, 516/535–6000. In Suffolk, there is no 24-hour telephone service, but the Legislature's office will answer questions during business hours, 516/360–4070.

In terms of sheer magnitude and magnificence, no Long Island beach rivals Jones Beach. Yes, the crowds are notoriously large on hot summer weekends. The secret is to come early or late (bring a picnic supper in June or July and watch the moon rise out of the Atlantic as the people drain away) and to avoid the massive central parking lots. Fire Island, reached by causeway or ferry, has 32 miles of beach; you can simply walk away from the crowds, especially along the eight-mile stretch of wilderness at the island's eastern end. To avoid traffic completely, hop aboard the Long Island Railroad (tel. 718/454–LIRR), which beefs up its summer runs with trains to Freeport and Bayshore, that connect with shuttle buses to the beach or ferry. The East Hampton beaches offer some of the best people-watching, and there are unofficial nude beaches at the east end of Smith Point County Park and at Gibson Beach between Sagaponack and Wainscott (just west of East Hampton). The best-known gay beaches are on Fire Island (see below), and gays also congregate at East Hampton's Two Mile Hollow Beach.

Many beaches are restricted to Nassau and Suffolk County residents, and such restrictions are rigidly enforced. Luckily, some of the best beaches are open to the public as state parks. Here is the rundown, from west to east, first on the South Shore and then on the North Shore. If you are interested in camping at one of the park camping areas, you should get a camping permit from the park superintendent or camp supervisor. Lifeguards are on duty only from Memorial Day to Labor Day on South Shore beaches and from the end of June to Labor

Day on North Shore beaches; beach refreshment stands keep to the same schedule.

South Shore Beaches

❶ **Jones Beach State Park:** Five miles of ocean beach surrounded by 2,400 acres of parkland, Jones Beach has surf, bay, and saltwater-pool bathing; bathhouses; surf, bay, and pier fishing; boating, roller skating, pitch-and-putt golf courses, outdoor dancing, shuffleboard, paddle tennis, basketball, archery, exercise trails, picnic areas, refreshment stands and a terrific Boardwalk restaurant, extensive boardwalk, and the Jones Beach Marine Theater.

The parking fields situated right on the beach fill up by 10 AM on hot summer weekends, but spots will open up again by 2 or 3 PM. Field 6, at the very end of the beach, has the shortest walk to the ocean and may fill as early as 8 AM. Field 3 and the mammoth fields 4 and 5 are on the other side of the highway from the ocean and require a long, hot walk through cars and tunnel, and bring you to the most crowded part of the beach.

Jones Beach was established by Parks Commissioner Robert Moses in 1929 and has been New York's finest oceanside playground ever since. *Wantagh Pkwy., Wantagh, tel. 516/785-1600. Admission: $3.50 per car (Memorial Day–Labor Day). Open year-round sunrise–sunset; sunrise–midnight (late June–Labor Day) for special activities.*

❷ **Robert Moses State Park:** This 1,000-acre state park at the western tip of Fire Island is less than half the size of Jones Beach, but on a peak summer weekend it attracts only about one-fifth as many people, so there is really more beach per person. Though the beach itself is narrower than Jones Beach, you don't have to walk as far from your car to get to the sand. Perhaps because Robert Moses is farther away from the city, the water here is a shade closer to aquamarine than most area beaches.

Robert Moses has a number of parking fields. Field 3 is the smallest and will probably be full by 10 on a summer weekend. Field 5 is particularly nice because it has a boardwalk, and you can walk from there to the Fire Island lighthouse, which stands inside the adjacent National Seashore.

Facilities include boating, surf fishing, bathhouses, picnic grounds, and refreshment stand. *Babylon, Robert Moses Causeway, tel. 516/669-0449. Admission: $3.50 per car (Memorial Day–Labor Day). Open year-round sunrise–sunset.*

❸ **Fire Island National Seashore:** Fire Island, 32 miles of protected ocean beach punctuated by 17 summer resort communities, is like a never-never land for grown-ups. Little passenger ferries ply the shallow waters of Great South Bay with cargoes of vacationers. Since there are no cars or roads (except at the parks at the east and west ends—see above and below), everyone walks everywhere on boardwalks or sandy paths. But since the island is nowhere wider than half a mile, there isn't much of anyplace to walk except from the ocean to the bay and back, with perhaps a side trip to the tennis court or boat slip.

In 1964 the federal government declared Fire Island a National Seashore, thus protecting what open land had not yet fallen to development. The 17 resort communities, many dating from the turn of the century, were allowed to remain and continue to grow within designated confines. Fire Island has two gay communities—flamboyant Cherry Grove and the more discreet and expensive Fire Island Pines; the other communities reflect a wide range of tastes and lifestyles. Ocean Bay Park, Fair Harbor, and Kismet are party meccas for straight singles. Saltaire, Ocean Beach, and Seaview are fairly exclusive and extremely expensive retreats for families. Point O'Woods, Fire Island's oldest and stodgiest community, preserves its dignity behind a six-foot-high fence topped with barbed wire. **Ocean Bay Park** is one of the few communities where you can step off the ferry at **Bay Shore** without being bombarded by town rules and regulations and where you can wander down to the beach without feeling as if you're intruding on a private compound. It also has a decent no-frills hotel and restaurant, both rare on Fire Island. *The Ocean Bay Park and Saltaire ferries leave from Maple Ave., Bay Shore, tel. 516/665–2115, May–Nov.*

If you're coming to Fire Island to enjoy the beaches *and* observe the barrier island in its natural state, your best bet is to visit one of the National Seashore areas. From **Sayville,** you can get the ferry to **Sailor's Haven,** where there is not only a superb stretch of beach (with lifeguard protection during the summer) but a network of boardwalks through the Sunken Forest, a primeval maritime hardwood forest hidden behind the dunes. On the bay side of Sailor's Haven, there is a marina, a visitor's center, and a snack bar. *Ferry leaves from River Rd., Sayville, tel. 516/589–8980, May–Nov. For more information, contact the Fire Island National Seashore headquarters in Patchogue, tel. 516/289–4810.*

Farther east down the island at **Watch Hill,** there is another National Seashore visitor's center with the same facilities as at Sailor's Haven, as well as camping. To experience the beach in its primitive state, hike east from Watch Hill into the eight-mile wilderness area that extends to Smith Point West. This is New York State's only federally designated wilderness area. *Ferry leaves from West and Division Sts., Patchogue, tel. 516/475–1665, May–Nov.*

You can also approach the wilderness area from the east by driving to the end of the William Floyd Parkway and parking your car in **Mastic** at the **Smith Point County Park.** Technically, this 2,300-acre park belongs to Suffolk County, and the National Seashore (one-quarter mile west) belongs to the federal government—but it's all the same fabulous barrier beach. Smith Point County Park has a food stand open in the summer and a first-come first-served camping area. The National Seashore beach, known as Smith Point West, has parking only for the disabled, but it's a short walk from the county lot and the beach is much less crowded. There is also a visitor's center open 9–5:30, and a short boardwalk that serves as a self-guided nature trail through the fringe of the wilderness. After that you're on your own. *Smith Point County Park, end of William Floyd Pkwy., Mastic, tel. 516/281–6555. Admission: $3.50 per car Memorial Day–Labor Day. Open year-round sunrise–sunset. Smith Point West, end of William Floyd Pkwy., Mastic Beach, tel. 516/281–3010. Admission free. Open year-round.*

Heckscher State Park: This is a 1,500-acre park on Great South Bay, the shallow body of water that separates Fire Island from the "mainland" of Long Island. The protected bay waters are calmer and warmer than the ocean—and thus safer for young

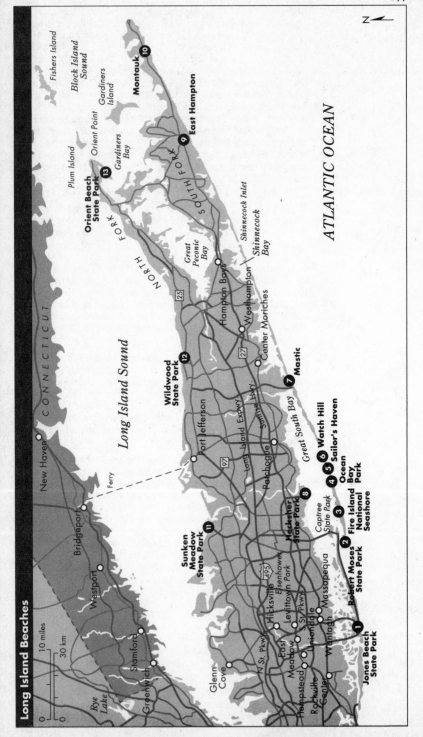

children. This is a popular park for families, who come to picnic, barbecue, and swim. There are three bay beaches, a pool, boat ramp, nature trails, a bathhouse, camping area, picnic grounds, refreshment stand, cross-country skiing, and hiking trails. *Heckscher State Pkwy., East Islip, tel. 516/581–2100. Admission: $2.50 per car Memorial Day–June, $3.50 per car July–Labor Day. Open year-round, sunrise–sunset.*

❾ East Hampton Village and Town Beaches: East Hampton has lovely white-sand beaches overlooked by beautiful, large summer homes, but only *Main Beach* at the end of Ocean Avenue is open to the general public without a permit. Consequently, the beaches attract different types of people here as opposed to, say, Jones Beach. Parking costs $10 per day. In order to park at the other East Hampton village beaches—*Georgica Beach* at the end of Apaquogue Road (family-oriented), *Wiborg Beach* on Highway Behind the Ponid, *Egypt* at the end of Old Beach Lane, and *Two Mile Hollow* at the end of Two Mile Hollow Road (popular with gays)—nonresidents must get a season permit from the East Hampton Village Hall at 27 Main St. (tel. 516/324–4150, open weekdays 9–4) or at Main Beach. The cost is $75 for the season, mid-May through September. Out of season, no permit is necessary to park at the village beaches.

There are also eight restricted beaches controlled by the Town of East Hampton. The ocean beaches are *Indian Wells* and *Atlantic Avenue* in Amagansett (east of East Hampton), and *Kirk Park* and *Ditch Plains* in Montauk; the bay beaches are *Maidstone Park* in East Hampton, *East Lake Drive* and *South Lake Drive* in Montauk, and *Albert's Landing* in Amagansett. Nonresidents can get a season sticker to park at these beaches for $20 at the East Hampton Town Hall, which is at 159 Pantigo Rd.—on Montauk Highway—between East Hampton and Amagansett (tel. 516/324–4143, open weekdays 9–4). Before June 25 and after Labor Day, town beaches are open and free to everyone.

❿ Hither Hills State Park: An oceanfront park at **Montauk** with beaches, bathhouse, surf fishing, oceanfront camping, picnic area, refreshment stand, hiking, central shower building, playground, and store (open in summer only). Hither Hills is the only official public beach in Montauk where you can park without a town permit. (There is an unofficial beach just over the dunes from the IGA supermarket at the west end of Montauk village.) *Rte. 217, Montauk, tel. 516/668–2493. Admission: $3.50 per car. Open daily sunrise–sunset, first week of Apr.–mid-Oct. Camping during July and Aug. is by lottery only. For camping information, tel. 516/668–2554.*

North Shore Beaches ⓫ **Sunken Meadow State Park:** One of the most popular North Shore public beaches, this 1,230-acre state park attracts as many as 40,000 people on peak summer weekends. On Sunday the four parking lots may fill up in the morning, so if the weather is hot, try to come on Saturday instead. This is a park for families, who come for the 5,000-foot sound beaches and the lovely wooded picnic and barbecue areas.

Other facilities include a boardwalk, bathhouses, two golf courses, hiking trails, and refreshment stands. *Kings Park, Rte. 25A, north end of Sagtikos Pkwy., tel. 516/269–4333. Admission: $3.50 per car Memorial Day–Labor Day. Open weekends 6–sunset, weekdays 7–sunset.*

12 Wildwood State Park: The big attractions at this lovely 737-acre park are the 1⅝ miles of beach on the sound and the 10 miles of hiking trails through the woods (good for cross-country skiing in the winter). There is also a woodland campground with 320 campsites. The younger, wilder crowd tends to congregate in the most remote section of the campground, and families in the areas nearer the parking lots. Wildwood is most crowded on summer Sundays, when the 500-car lot may fill up by 1 or 2 PM; on Saturdays parking spots are available all day. Other facilities include bathhouse, central shower building, picnic area, two refreshment stands, baseball field, and basketball courts. *Hulse Landing Rd., Wading River, Rte. 25A, tel. 516/929–4314. Admission: $2.50 per car Memorial Day–third week of June, $3.50 per car third week of June–Labor Day. Open year-round, sunrise–sunset.*

13 Orient Beach State Park: This 357-acre park has magnificent views in protected Gardiner's Bay at the eastern tip of the North Fork. Orient Beach is a favorite with bird-watchers and nature lovers who come to observe the osprey and wander in and out of the coves that comprise 10 miles of natural beach or collect shells. On weekends the parking lot can fill up, particularly on beautiful Sundays. Facilities include a bathhouse, fishing, hiking, picnic area, refreshment stand, and horseshoe court. *Rte. 25, Orient, tel. 516/323–2440. Admission: $2.50 per car Memorial Day–June, $3.50 per car July–Labor Day. Open sunrise–sunset; closed Tues. and Wed. in winter.*

The North Shore

Numbers in the margin correspond with points of interest on the Long Island map.

As you enter Nassau County on Route 25A, you'll cut across the bases of two large peninsulas, Great Neck and Port Washington, the West Egg and East Egg of Fitzgerald's *Great Gatsby*.

1 Slightly east is **Roslyn,** home to Long Island's largest art museum, the **Nassau County Museum of Fine Arts,** located on 145 acres of grass, wild berries, trees, and ponds. Formerly the Frick country home, the building was donated to Childs Frick by his father as a wedding present. With two floors, including 10 galleries and a gift shop, the museum displays a variety of changing exhibitions; the grounds include public sculptures. Grounds and museum are both open year-round and admission is free, but a donation is suggested. Call before planning a trip to make sure they are not between exhibitions. *Tel. 516/484–9333. Grounds open weekdays 9–5, weekends noon–5; museum open Tues.–Fri. 10–4:30, weekends 1–4:30.*

Farther east, 25A opens out into the horse country of Old Brookville and Upper Brookville. A short drive north from **2** there on winding country roads will bring you to **Oyster Bay** and the **Planting Fields Arboretum,** 150 acres of immaculately landscaped grounds that have the grace, style, and sense of permanence of an English country estate. At the center of an immense expanse of flawless greensward stands **Coe Hall,** a beautiful Tudor-style manor with imported antique furnishings. Botanical highlights include stands of rhododendrons and azaleas, greenhouses with stunning flowering plants from tropical and desert climes, and the five-acre synoptic garden (arranged alphabetically by scientific name). Guided tours of

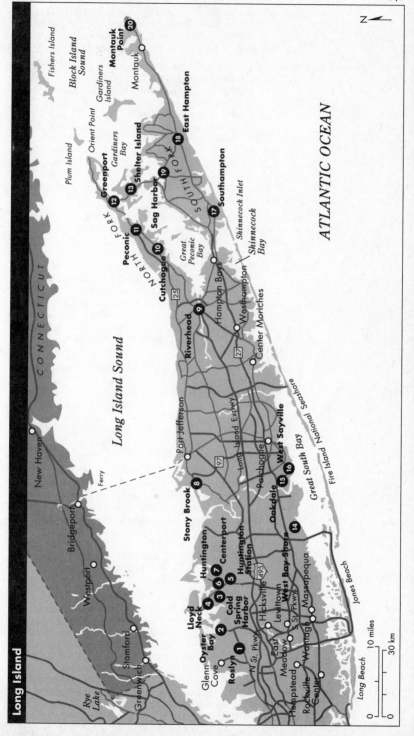

Long Island

Coe Hall are available May–September, Tuesday–Thursday 1–4 PM and year-round by appointment. *Planting Fields Rd., Oyster Bay, 2 mi. north of Rte. 25A, tel. 516/922–9200. Admission: $4 adults, children under 12 free. Open daily 9–4:30.*

East of the very posh town of Oyster Bay, a small peninsula called Cove Neck juts into Long Island Sound, and in the center of this peninsula stands **Sagamore Hill,** the summer White House of President Theodore Roosevelt and his permanent residence from 1887 to his death in 1919. The rambling, 23-room Victorian mansion contains many original furnishings, including T.R.'s big-game hunting trophies and gifts from rulers all over the world. The grounds comprise 88 acres of woodlands and manicured grass, and there is an apple orchard and pet cemetery. *Cove Neck Rd., Oyster Bay, 1 mi north of Rte. 25A, tel. 516/922–4447. Admission: 50¢ adults, children under 16 free. Open daily 9:30–5.*

From the grounds of Sagamore Hill you can take a guided nature walk through the woods to the beach at Cold Spring Harbor; then get back in your car and follow 25A to the Main Street of this historic village. During its heyday in the mid-
❸ 1800s, **Cold Spring Harbor** was home port to a fleet of whaling vessels, and today the **Cold Spring Harbor Whaling Museum** offers a fascinating glimpse into this exciting era. The museum contains four rooms of whaling memorabilia, including a fully rigged whaling boat. *Rte. 25A opposite the Turkey La. intersection, Cold Spring Harbor, tel. 516/367–3418. Admission: $1 adults, 50¢ children 6–14, 75¢ senior citizens. Open daily 11–5; closed Mon. Sept.–May.*

If you're interested in what fish look like before they're served at one of Long Island's restaurants, stop at the **Cold Spring Harbor Fish Hatchery and Aquarium.** Since it was established in 1881, more than 15 billion fish have been raised here. Children will enjoy viewing and feeding the numerous species of fish and turtles on display here. *Rte. 25A, Cold Spring Harbor, tel. 516/692–6768. Admission: $1.50 adults, 75¢ children 5–12 and adults over 65. Children under 5 free. Open daily 10–5.*

Caumsett State Park, one of Long Island's finest natural areas,
❹ occupies the bulk of the broad peninsula known as **Lloyd Neck.** Originally the estate of Marshall Field III, Caumsett, the Indian name for the area, is 1,500 unspoiled acres of cliffs, meadows, and woodlands; a two-mile hiking trail emerges on a long stretch of primeval beach on Long Island Sound, one of the very few wild beaches open to the public on the North Shore. The park permits surf fishing and cross-country skiing and offers guided nature walks by reservation. *West Neck Rd., Lloyd Neck, 2 mi north of Rte. 25A, tel. 516/423–1770. Admission: $2.50 per car May–Sept., free Oct.–Apr. Open daily 8–4:30.*

From Lloyd Neck, return to 25A, proceed a very short way east, and then head south on Route 110 through Huntington
❺ and **Huntington Station** to the **Walt Whitman House.** Huntington Station has changed beyond recognition since Whitman was born here in 1819, but the farmhouse where the poet spent his early childhood has been preserved in all its humble, homespun glory. Built by Whitman's father in 1810, the house contains a good collection of 19th-century furnishings as well as some fascinating Whitman memorabilia. *246 Old Walt Whitman Rd., Huntington Station, tel. 516/427–5240. Admission free. Open*

Wed.–Fri. 1–4, weekends 10–4. Closed New Year's Day, Easter, Thanksgiving, Christmas.

Continue south along Route 110, crossing over the Northern State Parkway. At Old Country Road head west to Round Swamp Road. Follow signs south to the **Old Bethpage Village Restoration.** On its 200 acres are a blacksmith, a general store, and a country inn with barrels of spices, and sarsaparilla (root beer) on tap. Tour the historic homes. *Round Swamp Road, Bethpage, tel. 516/420–5280 or 5281. Admission: $4 adults, $2 children, $1 discount for residents of Nassau County. Open daily 10–4 in winter, 10–5 spring–fall.*

6 Return north back up to 25A and **Huntington** to reach another important Long Island cultural landmark, the **Heckscher Museum,** which has a particularly rich collection of 19th-century landscape paintings. There are changing exhibits relevant to Long Island, and the museum staff offers guided tours. The museum's grounds include picnic areas. *Rte. 25A and Prime Ave., Huntington, tel. 516/351–3250. Admission free. Open Tues.–Fri. 10–5, weekends 1–5.*

Time Out After visiting the Heckscher Museum, stop off at the **Mediterranean Snackbar** for large portions of tasty seafood, souvlaki, and green salads. *360 New York Ave., Huntington, tel. 516/423–8982.*

Long Island has been a playground and retreat for the rich for well over 100 years, and there is no better place to see just how **7** different the rich really are than the **Vanderbilt Mansion** in **Centerport,** just a few miles east of the Heckscher Museum on 25A. The 24-room mansion is built in an ornate, Spanish-revival style, and its three impeccably manicured formal gardens. The Vanderbilt Museum houses 17,000 marine and wildlife specimens, and the nearby Vanderbilt Planetarium puts on a fantastic show of more than 11,000 stars in its modern sky theater. The planetarium's 16-inch telescope is available to the public for sky viewings on clear evenings. Call 516/757-7500 for planetarium information, charges, and show times. *Little Neck Rd., Centerport, 1 mi north of Rte. 25A, tel. 516/261-5656. Admission: $2.50 adults, $2 children. Open Tues.–Sat. 10–4, Sun. and holidays 12–5. Closed Thanksgiving, Christmas, New Year's Day.*

From Centerport, follow Route 25A east as it parallels the contours of Smithtown Bay. A few minutes' drive will take you to **8** **the Museums at Stony Brook,** a fascinating group of buildings and exhibits that focus on 19th-century America, which give an excellent portrait of the history and art of this epoch. Of particular interest are the Carriage Museum, which displays more than 100 horse-drawn vehicles, and the History Museum, famous for its collections of decoys, its exhibits of period clothing, and its display of period rooms in miniature. The complex also features an art museum, a blacksmith shop, and a restored 19th-century schoolhouse. *1208 Rte. 25A, Stony Brook, tel. 516/751–0066. Admission: $4 adults, $3 senior citizens, $2.75 students, $2 children 6–12, children under 6 free. Open Wed.–Sat. 10–5, Sun. 12–5. Closed Thanksgiving, Christmas Eve and Day, New Year's Day.*

Continue east along Route 25A, a hilly, winding, tree-lined road that opens into **Port Jefferson** harbor. Leave your car in

the parking lot behind Main Street to explore the waterfront
and its many unique craft and antiques shops. Walk to Prospect
Street and visit the **Mather House Museum** with its collection of
19th-century costumes, shell crafts, Indian art, model boats,
and antique furnishings. *Tel. 516/473–2665. Open late May–
Oct., weekends, 1–4; July and Aug., Wed. 1–4. Donation.*

To complete your tour of the North Shore, continue east on
Route 25A until it turns into the rural Sound Avenue just past
Wading River Station. Sound Avenue in turn becomes State
Route 48, the main road through the North Fork, which
branches off from the main body of Long Island east of **River-
head.** This is beautiful farm country, with fields stretching off
to the horizon, well-kept, picturesque farmhouses, and many
roadside farm stands open during the summer and early au-
tumn. Briermere Farm has homemade fruit and berry pies,
Berezny's Farm Stand has superior vegetables and flowers, and
Young's Orchard is the place to stop for apples. All are on Sound
Avenue, just east of Roanoke Avenue. In the past 15 years, the
North Fork has emerged as an exciting new wine district; there
are now 12 wineries and 30 commercial vineyards scattered
around **Cutchogue** and **Peconic.** The area is one of New York
State's sunniest spots, and the climate is very similar to the
Bordeaux wine-producing region of France. Among the most
popular vineyards are **Pindar** and **Hargrave.** While Hargrave is
the oldest, in operation since 1973, Pindar, in existence since
1979, has turned nearly 200 acres of former potato farms into a
thriving vineyard. Tours are offered daily every half hour year-
round, 11–6, concluding with a wine tasting. Long Island wineries produce a variety of wines, but their specialties tend to be
cabernet sauvignon and Chardonnay. In addition, in the fall of
1987, Pindar produced the first Long Island champagne.
*Hargrave is located on Rte. 48 in Cutchogue, tel. 516/734–5111.
Pindar is on Rte. 25 in Peconic, just south of Rte. 48, tel. 516/
734–6200.* For further information about other Long Island
vineyards and wineries, call the Long Island Grape Growers
Association at 516/734–6200.

After touring the Hargrave Vineyard, cut south to State Route
25 and drive east through the historic towns of Cutchogue and
Southold, through the old fishing village of **Greenport,** which
has a pretty Main Street with quaint shops and a picturesque
harbor, and finally east to Orient Beach State Park at the
tip of the North Fork. *(See* Exploring North Shore Beaches
above.)

While in Greenport, you might want to take the 10-minute car
and passenger ferry over to **Shelter Island,** a beautiful and historic island nestled between the North and South forks. Now
primarily a summer resort and boating center, Shelter Island
was among the first sections of Long Island to be settled by
the English. Points of interest include the **Havens House** on
Route 114, built in 1743; the **Victorian-era cottages** and **Union
Chapel** on Shelter Island Heights near the North Ferry
dock; the Manhanset Chapel on Route 114, built in 1890;
and the mansions along Shore Drive in Dering Harbor.
The entire southeast section of the island is the 2,000-acre
Mashomack Nature Preserve, with 12 miles of wild shoreline. There is also a ferry to Shelter Island from the town
of North Haven on the South Fork, and you can use the island as a scenic stepping stone to pass from one fork to the

other. North Ferry leaves from Route 114 off Route 25 in Greenport. Call 516/749–0139 for fares and schedule. South Ferry leaves from Route 114 in North Haven, three miles north of Sag Harbor *(see* below). Call 516/749–0007 for fares and schedule.

Although it is possible to tour the North Shore in one day, you may want to take refuge for the night in Greenport. Or you can stretch out the tour a day or two longer, stopping off at one of the hotels in Cold Spring Harbor, Huntington, or Stony Brook. *(See* Lodging below for each of these towns.)

The South Shore

Begin your tour of the South Shore 50 miles from Manhattan to visit the **West Bay Shore** and **Sagtikos Manor,** one of the finest Colonial homes in America. The British used it as a headquarters during the Revolutionary War; in 1790, after the defeated British cleared out, George Washington slept here during his tour of Long Island. The nearly 300-year-old house contains original furniture, family memorabilia, and Native-American artifacts. *Rte. 27A, West Bay Shore, tel. 516/665–0093. Admission: $1.50 adults, 50¢ children. Open Wed., Thurs., Sun. 1–4 July–Aug., Sun. only 1–4 June and Sept.*

A short drive east of West Bay Shore on Route 27A takes you to **Oakdale** and one of the great estates of the South Shore, the 690-acre **Bayard-Cutting Arboretum.** The noble Tudor-style mansion, the former residence of the Cutting family, serves as a natural history museum featuring an extensive collection of mounted birds and Native-American artifacts, but it is the grounds that lures most visitors. There are five self-guided nature walks you can take to see a wide variety of trees, shrubs, and flowers. *466 Montauk Hwy. (Rte. 27A), Oakdale, tel. 516/ 581–1002. Admission: $1.50 adults 12 and over May–Oct., free Nov.–April. Open Wed.–Sun. 10–5:30 May–Oct., 10–4:30 Nov.–April.*

West Sayville, a few miles east of Oakdale, is the site of the wonderful **Suffolk Marine Museum,** fittingly situated overlooking Great South Bay. The small-craft collection includes oyster vessels, South Bay sailboats, and ice scooters. Also noteworthy is the exhibit on the U.S. Life Saving Service, forerunner of the Coast Guard. *Rte. 27A, West Sayville, tel. 516/ 567–1733. Admission free (there is a charge for special exhibits). Open Mon.–Sat. 10–3, Sun. 12–4; closed Mon. Oct.– May.*

Proceeding east from West Sayville, you'll reach **Southampton** where the **Parrish Art Museum** features 19th- and 20th-century American paintings and prints and a superbly chosen collection of Renaissance works. Rare trees imported from all over the world offset the many fine works of art in the well-tended sculpture garden. A one-hour guided tour is available. *25 Jobs La., Southampton, tel. 516/283–2118. Admission free. Open Mon., Wed.–Sat. 10–5 Apr.–Oct.; closed Wed. Nov.–Mar. and most holidays.*

Southampton is in the heart of the Hamptons, a string of seaside villages that the East Coast upper crust "discovered" in the late 19th century and transformed into elegant summer resorts. At the pinnacle of fashion and fame is **East Hampton,** which, despite the hordes of celebrities and tourists who descend each summer, retains the grace and dignity of its Colonial heritage. If you are driving east along the Montauk Highway, you'll enter East Hampton on its elm-shaded Main Street, where the town's classic white Presbyterian Church (built in 1860), and stately old homes and inns *(see* Lodging) stand shoulder to shoulder with trendy shops and galleries. Main Street also has the **Guild Hall,** the town's center of culture, with changing art exhibits and a year-round program of community theater.

East Hampton is not a drive-through town; to really see it, leave your car at the large parking lot behind the school (turn left from Main Street onto Newtown Lane, left again on Race Lane and right on Gingerbread Lane). This is the only place in town where you can park free all day (village streets have one- or two-hour parking limits). The most beautiful walk in the village is around the Town Pond between Main Street and James Lane, where in the space of a few blocks you'll pass **Home Sweet Home,** the 1650 saltbox gem commemorated in John Howard Payne's song and now a museum; the **Mulford Farm** (built in 1680 and now a house museum with period furniture); the Hedges Inn at 74 James Lane (the oldest part was built in 1774); and one of the town's much-photographed and much-painted windmills (the other is at the north end of Main Street at the edge of the North End Burying Ground). *Home Sweet Home, 14 James La., tel. 516/324–0713. Admission: $1.50 adults, $1 children. Open Mon.–Sat. 10–4 and Sun. 2–4 July and Aug.; Mon., Thurs., Fri. 10–4 Sept.–June. The Mulford Farm, 10 James La., tel. 516/324–6869. Admission: $2 adults, $1.50 senior citizens, $1 children under 12. Open Tues.–Sun. 1–5 July–Labor Day; Sat. and Sun 1–5 Sept., by appointment only at other times.*

Follow James Lane until it runs into Ocean Avenue, and then go right onto Lily Pond Lane. The rambling, shingle-style houses on Lily Pond Lane, which parallels the ocean just a block away, may look like large, elegant, well-tended inns, but in fact they are private mansions, most of them dating from the turn of the century. Ocean Avenue, Lily Pond Lane, Egypt Lane, and Two Mile Hollow Road all dead-end at the ocean, but you need stickers to park your car at the lots *(see* Exploring Beaches above). Newtown Lane will take you back to your car at the school. Before you leave, you may want to browse in the shops and boutiques along Main Street and Newton Lane.

⑲ **Sag Harbor,** which is on the north shore of the South Fork, is a quick drive from East Hampton through some of the finest, richest farm country on the island. This quaint and quiet waterside village was an important whaling center from 1775 to 1871. The town today looks much as it did in the 1870s, with the stately homes of whaling merchants lining Main Street. Leave your car in the lot between Main Street and Meadow Street and stroll down the back lanes. Main Street terminates in the 1,000-foot Long Wharf (circa 1820), where there's a nice harbor view. Return to Main Street and walk past the American Hotel (built in 1825, it is an excessively expensive and snooty restaurant and inn); then head left down Washington Street to Division Street, where you'll find the Old Umbrella House, a hip-roofed home built before 1790 and the Georgian-style

Sleight houses. A right turn onto Union Street brings you
to the Whaler's Church, built in 1844 in the style of an Egyptian temple.

Union Street takes you back to Main Street and the **Sag Harbor
Whaling Museum,** the town's best-known attraction and one of
the most interesting museums on the island. You enter the collections, appropriately enough, through the jawbones of a
right whale. Featured attractions include logbooks, harpoons,
and scrimshaw. *Garden and Main Sts., Sag Harbor, tel. 516/
725–0770. Admission: $2 adults, $1.50 senior citizens, 75¢
children 6–12. Open daily mid-May–Sept., Mon.–Sat. 10–5,
Sun. 1–5.*

Across the street is the Italianate Hannibal French mansion,
built in the 1860s. Right next door on Garden Street is New
York State's first **Custom House** which dates from 1789. The
building, which also served as a post office into the 19th century, has been restored and contains some lovely antique
furnishings. *Garden St., Sag Harbor, tel. 516/941–9444. Admission: $1.50 adults, $1 children, 75¢ senior citizens. Open
Tues.–Sun. 10–5 June–Sept., Fri.–Sun 10–5 May and Oct.*

㉒ Return to State Route 27 and proceed through the village of
Montauk to Long Island's eastern extremity at **Montauk Point.**
The 109-foot **Lighthouse** at Montauk Point State Park was built
in 1797 by order of President George Washington. There is a
small museum housed in the old keeper's quarters, and you can
now climb up to the top of the light for a fantastic view of the
East End, the distant shore of Connecticut, and Block Island
off the coast of Rhode Island. *Rte. 27, Montauk, tel. 516/668–
2544. Admission: $2 adults, 75¢ children 6–12, children under
6 free. Open daily 11–6 May–Columbus Day, Sat. and Sun.
10–4:30 Columbus Day–Nov.*

What to See and Do with Children

New York State Fish Hatchery and Aquarium (*see* Exploring).

Lewin Farms, on Route 48 in Wading River (tel. 516/929–4327),
is one of the largest u-pick farms on Long Island. From June
through December you can pick strawberries, melons, nectar-
ines, peaches, corn, cucumbers, peas, peppers, squash,
tomatoes, and apples, among other fruits and vegetables.
Strawberry season is extremely popular. Generally you pay
only 50¢–$1 per quart, and there is no charge for strawberries
you eat while you pick. The New York State Department of
Agriculture's free "Guide to Farm Fresh Food" lists all farms
that allow you to pick your own with the dates and fruits and
vegetables available (tel. 516/727–3580). Additional information can also be obtained from the Riverhead Chamber of
Commerce (tel. 516/727–7600).

Long Island Game Farm. Children of all ages can cuddle and
bottle-feed baby animals and hand-feed deer. There is a 20-
minute wild-tiger show, a 10-minute elephant show, and an authentic 1860s train which takes you around the farm to see
zebras, llamas, monkeys, camels, bears, buffalos, peacocks,
and many other animals. There are also amusement rides, picnic areas, and snack bars. *Exit 70 of the Long Island Expressway to Chapman Blvd., Manorville, tel. 516/878–6644.*

Admission: $8.45 adults, $5.95 children 2–11 and senior citizens, children under 2 free. Open daily mid-April–mid-Oct. 9–6.

Animal Farm. Similar to the game farm, this facility has hundreds of animals to pet and feed, as well as an antique auto museum, a puppet theater, kiddie rides, and a picnic area. *184A Wading River Rd. (Exit 69 on the Long Island Expressway), Manorville, tel. 516/878–1785. Admission: $6 adults, $4 children 2–12 and senior citizens, children under 2 free. Open daily Apr.–Oct. 10–5.*

Off the Beaten Track

For a unique view of Long Island, you can learn to parachute and make your first jump on the same day. Call **Skydive Long Island** (tel. 516/878–1186) Thurs.–Mon., April-Nov. Rates are from $175 to $200, and you must be 18 or over.

Shopping

Long Island offers a rich variety of shopping opportunities. The island is known for its shopping malls, the largest of which is the **Roosevelt Field Mall** (tel. 516/742–8000) in Garden City, with 185 stores. Branches of many New York City department stores, including Bloomingdale's, Saks Fifth Avenue, and Lord & Taylor are also located in Garden City (on Franklin Avenue). Manhasset's "Miracle Mile" along Route 25A has such fashionable stores as Bonwit Teller, Brooks Brothers, Lord & Taylor, and Polo/Ralph Lauren.

If you're looking for bargains, visit the **Flea Market at Roosevelt Raceway** (tel. 516/222–1530) on Old Country Road, Westbury, which claims to be the largest flea market in the country (2,000-plus vendors). It is open on Sundays all year 9–5. ($1.50 per car, $1 per walk-in) and on Wednesdays from April to December 9–4 ($1 per car, 50¢ per walk-in).

The Hamptons are the place for shoppers looking for the most stylish, trendy (and expensive) clothing, artwork, leather goods, rugs, and antiques. Many shops and boutiques can be found along East Hampton's Main Street. (*See* Exploring South Shore.)

Participant Sports

Surf fishing, golf, hiking, horseback riding, roller skating, and cross-country skiing are popular activities at many of the state parks on Long Island. Call the Long Island Tourism Association (tel. 516/794–4222) or the individual state parks (*see* Beaches) for more information.

Boating The sailing, yachting, and deep-sea fishing possibilities on Long Island's waters are nearly limitless. For information about boat rentals, contact one of the organizations below.

Captree Boatmen's Association. The association has a combined fleet of 34 open- and charter-fishing boats with courteous crews. *Robert Moses State Park, Box 5372, Babylon 11707, tel. 516/669–6464.*

Great South Bay Charters, Ltd. Sailboat and windsurfer rentals, and yacht charters are available on a daily or weekly basis.

The company also offers private and group sailing and wind-surfing lessons by certified instructors. *5510 Merrick Rd. (Rte. 27A), Massapequa 11758, tel. 516/799–5968.*

Long Island Sportfishing Network. This is a booking and information service for all of Long Island. *Box 2008, Calverton 11933, tel. 516/369–0879 (after 3 PM).*

Spectator Sports

Car Racing   General stock car racing from late April–mid-September. *Riverhead Raceway, Riverhead, tel. 516/727–0010.*

Hockey   The New York Islanders of the NHL play at the Nassau Veterans Memorial Coliseum on Hempstead Turnpike in Uniondale. For ticket information call 516/794–4100, but keep in mind that Islander tickets may be difficult to obtain.

Horse Racing   Roosevelt Raceway, Monday–Saturday, post time 8 PM. *Old Country Rd., Westbury, tel. 516/222–2000.*

Dining and Lodging

Dining   When you mention Long Island food, most people tend to think of duckling, clams, and potatoes—but nowadays Long Island restaurants run the gamut from fast-food chains through pizzerias and family-style eateries to ethnic restaurants and elegant country inns.

Not surprisingly, Long Island draws on the bounty of its surrounding waters, especially on the East End, where commercial fishing remains a vital industry. The catch of the day at Montauk or Greenport may feature swordfish, halibut, flounder, bluefish, or shrimp. Many island restaurants reflect the area's large Italian-American population, either in their menus, their ownership, or both. The East End has long historic ties to New England, so don't be surprised to find such typically New England specialties as clam and corn chowder, clam pie, turkey, and lobster on the menus of restaurants out here. If the idea of dining near the water appeals to you, Long Island will reward you with many memorable meals with a view.

Category	Cost*
Very Expensive	over $60
Expensive	$40–$60
Moderate	$20–$40
Inexpensive	under $20

per person without tax, service, or drinks

Lodging   Not long ago, lodging on Long Island meant dreary guest houses, cozy bungalow colonies, or a few long-established and rather stodgy hotels—but recent years have brought all of the major motel chains to Long Island, as well as a resurgence in hotel construction. If you're spending the night on the island now, you should have little trouble finding accommodations to suit your itinerary and your budget. One of the more outstanding island lodgings, the Garden City Hotel opposite the Long

Island Railroad station in Garden City, sets the standard for luxury on Long Island. A landmark for over 100 years, the hotel was razed a decade ago and replaced by an even posher, more stylish incarnation.

Category	Cost*
Very Expensive	over $120
Expensive	$90–$120
Moderate	$50–$90
Inexpensive	under $50

The price categories reflect prices during the "season" (Memorial Day–Labor Day). Off-season prices are considerably lower. These prices are for a double room and do not include tax or gratuities.

Highly recommended restaurants and accommodations are indicated by a star ★.

Amagansett

Dining **Gordon's.** This airy, modern, and welcoming restaurant is a long-time favorite with the locals and popular with summer people. The best entrees are veal chops with brown sauce and mushrooms, Long Island duckling with apricot brandy sauce and wild rice, and scampi. This is not a flashy, ostentatious restaurant, but rather a simple and comfortable place to relax over very good food. *Main St., tel. 516/267–3010. Jacket required for dinner. Reservations essential for summer weeken s. AE, DC, MC, V. Closed for lunch July and Aug. Closed Mon.; Sun. and Mon. after Columbus Day; and Jan. and Feb. Expensive.*
Inn at Napeague. Nautical is the decor at this restaurant to match the fresh seafood served, including mako shark caught off the shores of Long Island. Besides the seafood specialties— bouillabaise, broiled swordfish, lobster fradiavolo—the inn serves Continental meat dishes such as beef Wellington. Special attention is given families; children's portions are available. *Montauk Hwy., tel. 516/267–3332. Dress: casual. Reservations advised. AE. Closed early Nov.–end of Apr. Moderate.*

Lodging **Sea Crest.** These full efficiency apartments are located on 500
★ feet of oceanfront, putting them several notches above the ordinary motel fare. The rooms are air-conditioned and have private balconies/patios. You have your choice of poolside or more expensive oceanside rooms. *Drawer X, 11930, tel. 516/267–3159 or 800/SEA–DAYS. 74 rooms with bath. Facilities: barbecue grills, heated pool, tennis. MC, V. Open Apr.–Nov. Very Expensive.*
★ **Windward Shores.** If you're looking for elegance with an oceanside setting, you'll find it in one of the modern suites of this five-and-a-half-year-old hotel. The suites have sun decks or patios, ceiling fans, skylights, and spiral staircases, and the tan and beige color scheme make the rooms look like an extension of the sand dunes right outside the picture windows. The 400 feet of ocean beach is private. *Box L, 11930, tel. 516/267–8600. 45 rooms with bath. Facilities: heated freshwater pool, tennis. No credit cards. Very Expensive.*

The Hermitage. Accommodations at the Hermitage include 56 two-bedroom, two-bathroom efficiency apartments. Prices are highest from Memorial Day through September 15. *Box 1127, 11930, tel. 516/267–6151. Facilities: cable TV, telephone, swimming pool, tennis, beach. Open mid-March–Jan. Moderate–Very Expensive.*

Ocean Dunes. A co-op of one- and two-bedroom suites, all with private deck/patios. Individual owners rent out the units through the central office. Ocean Dunes has a secluded, private beach; it's the only Amagansett oceanfront accommodation within walking distance to town. *Bluff Rd., 11930, tel. 516/267–8121. 50 suites with bath. Facilities: barbecue grills, surf fishing, golf privileges, heated pool, tennis privileges. No credit cards. Open Apr.–Nov. Moderate–Very Expensive.*

Sun Haven Motel. The rooms are clean and modern, with kitchenettes and ceiling fans, and the ocean is right at your doorstep. *Box BE, Montauk Hwy., 11930, tel. 516/267–3448. 48 rooms with bath. Facilities: heated pool, Chinese restaurant, sauna, tennis. AE, MC, V. Open late May–mid-Oct. Moderate–Very Expensive.*

East Hampton

Dining   **The Palm at the Huntting Inn.** The Palm (with two branches in New York City and another East Hampton location at the Hedges Inn) is a power restaurant. It attracts a powerful crowd of high-profile New York Upper East Siders who come here on weekends to see and be seen and to treat themselves to the lavish portions of steak and lobster for which the Palm has become famous. The New York–cut sirloins, 16-ounce filet mignons, and three-pound (and up) lobsters may not be the most delicate fare, but they are prepared carefully and served sumptuously. If you're not in the mood for beefsteak, you can choose a fish steak such as tuna, swordfish, or salmon; among the better pasta offerings are linguine with red or white clam sauce. What the Palm lacks in imagination, it more than makes up for in the generosity of the portions. Dessert may be unthinkable after three pounds of lobster or a pound of beef, but if you can contemplate a sweet, try the Key lime pie or pecan pie. The room is done in dark wood and brass fixtures, and there is a screened-in porch with ceiling fans. The lively lounge area features a guitar player on weekends. The Hedges location is quieter, more intimate, and less flashy, but the food is the same. *94 Main St., tel. 516/324–0410. Reservations for parties of four or more only. Dinner. AE, DC, MC, V. Expensive.*

The Laundry. Formerly a commercial laundry, this place is now one of the most chi-chi restaurants in an increasingly chi-chi town. It is also one of the few East End restaurants that stays open year-round. If you're looking for East Hampton celebrities, you'll find them here (one of the restaurant's owners is Hollywood super-agent Sam Cohen). American grill food is served in a simple, no-frills dining room that retains the brick wall and high-pitched ceiling from the old wash-and-fold days. Grilled seafood is the specialty of the house, and seafood entrees vary with the season. The smash-hit dessert is black and white chocolate mousse for two. There is a lively bar scene after midnight, and the lounge has a pit area with a fireplace roaring in the cooler months. *31 Race La., tel. 516/324–3199. No reservations. No lunch. AE, DC, MC, V. Moderate.*

Little Rock Lobster. Located right on the waterfront, this restaurant has huge glass windows so that guests can watch sailboats go by as they dine on their stuffed lobster, lobster fra diavolo, lobster thermador, or lobster stew. Of course, there are other seafood dishes of fish caught only hours before off the South Shore. Choose from an extensive wine list to complement your meal. *423 Three-Mile Hwy., tel. 516/324–7040. Dress: casual. Reservations necessary for dinner. AE, MC, V. Closed Sept.–Apr. Moderate.*

Little Rock Rodeo. A sister restaurant to Little Rock Lobster, this in-town place features a Southwestern theme, complete with mesquite grill to barbecue your beef, chicken, or ribs. Fresh, local seafood dishes are also available. L. B. Burrow, owner, suggests starting off with the Rodeo's special margarita. A young, attentive staff serves you in the plain-but-active 200-seat dining room, which is decorated in desert colors. Or, in pleasant weather, you can dine outdoors on the tree-shaded patio. *Montauk Hwy., tel. 516/324–7777. Dress: very casual. No reservations. AE, MC, V. Closed Nov.–Mar.*

Lodging   **Huntting Inn.** Each room at the Huntting, built in 1699 and run as an inn since 1751, is different, but all are furnished with floral chintz wall coverings, chaise-longue sofas, fluffy comforters, brass and wrought-iron beds, and fresh flowers; all are air-conditioned. The highly regarded Palm Restaurant is on its premises (*see* Dining). *94 Main St., 11937, tel. 516/324–0410. 26 rooms with bath. Facilities: bar, fishing, horseback riding, restaurant, tennis privileges. AE, DC, MC, V. Open late Mar.–Dec. Expensive–Very Expensive.*

Bassett House Inn. This 12-unit inn is noted for its friendly, home-style feel. Fireplaces and whirlpool tubs are available in some rooms, and there is a common living room/dining area where a full breakfast, included with reservations, is served. *128 Montauk Hwy., Box 1426, 11937, tel. 516/324–6127. Facilities: backyard with barbecue, beach. AE, MC, V. Moderate–Very Expensive.*

East Hampton Inn. This 52-unit inn located on six acres has deluxe, studio, and two-bedroom suites. Within walking distance of the beach, it includes a cafe that serves breakfast in season. *226 Montauk Hwy., 11937, tel. 516/324–4300. Facilities: efficiency kitchens, deck or patio, outdoor heated pool, 2 tennis courts. MC, V. Moderate–Very Expensive.*

★ **1770 House.** This Early American village house has been tastefully converted to a gem of a small hotel. Rooms are furnished with antiques from the owner's collection, which includes a number of superb old grandfather clocks and mantel clocks. There is a pretty little garden right outside the front door and a fine restaurant known for its Continental cuisine and candlelight dinners. *143 Main St., 11937, tel. 516/324-1770. 12 rooms with bath. Facilities: golf and tennis nearby. CB, DC, MC, V. Moderate–Very Expensive.*

★ **Maidstone Arms.** This historic inn, founded in 1850, is the coziest and most comfortable in town. It also has one of the best locations—right across from the town pond, a pristine park surrounded by East Hampton's oldest streets and most beautiful homes. The guest rooms are furnished with frilly curtains, claw-foot Victorian chests and tables, handmade patchwork quilts, china wash basins, and 19th-century prints. The rooms are air-conditioned and Continental breakfast is included. The inn's dining room features French country cooking. *207 Main St., 11937, tel. 516/324–5006. 16 rooms and 3 cottages with bath. Facilities: bar, restaurant. AE, MC, V. Moderate–Expensive.*

Freeport

Dining **Trudy B.** Situated right on the Hudson Canal, this Continental restaurant features fresh fish and lobster, as well as hefty meat dishes. The dining room is modern and stylish with lots of cedar wood, glass, and brass, and there is a stone fireplace. You can also dine overlooking the canal in a glassed-in greenhouse. If you're really hungry try the "Hudson Canal"—half a lobster, clams, scallops, squid, and shrimp in marinara sauce, served over linguine. The best dessert is homemade puff pastry filled with ice cream and covered with chocolate sauce and whipped cream. Friday and Saturday 9 PM–1 AM, enjoy live '50s & '60s music; there is a $5 cover without dinner. *255 Hudson Ave., tel. 516/546–5555. Reservations advised for Fri. or Sat. night. AE, CB, DC, MC, V. Moderate.*

Garden City

Lodging **Garden City Hotel.** Until it was razed a decade ago, this hotel
★ was a landmark of tradition and impeccable standards for more than a century. The all new Garden City Hotel is more luxurious, more sophisticated, and even more expensive than the original. This is a world-class hotel, the most opulent on Long Island, the rival of the finest Manhattan has to offer. Air-conditioned rooms are furnished with fine furniture and oversize beds and there is 24-hour room service. Special rates for senior citizens and facilities for the disabled are available. *45 Seventh St., 11530, tel. 516/747–3000 or 800/547–0400 outside New York. 280 rooms with bath. Facilities: shopping arcade, bar, health club, nightclub, golf nearby, indoor pool, beauty salon, lounge, and 2 restaurants. AE, CB, MC, V. Expensive.*

Glen Head

Dining **Pappagallos.** The Northern Italian cooking here makes this one
★ of the best restaurants on the North Shore. Under the striking modern chandeliers that hang from the high ceiling, you can feast on seafood, the pasta of the day prepared at your table, or dishes such as steak Rossini, filet mignon on toast served with truffles and topped with a rich wine sauce flavored with imported mushrooms. The dessert cart is also a knockout. *716 Glen Cove Ave., tel. 516/676–3400. Jacket and tie required. Reservations advised for dinner. AE, CB, DC, MC, V. Closed Sat., Sun. lunch, Mon. Moderate.*

Greenport

Dining **Claudio's.** A Greenport landmark for well over 100 years, Claudio's is the oldest family-owned restaurant in the United States. This is the place where waterside dining began. The two large dining rooms, decorated with artifacts from the J-boats that raced in the America's Cup during the 1930s, face the harbor through large picture windows. Local seafood is the specialty. The one fancy touch here is the 35-foot-long marble and mahogany bar with huge mirrors behind it. Claudio's, which also has a marina, is popular with yachtsmen in the summer. If you're coming from Shelter Island, you can walk here from the north ferry. *Foot of Main St. on the harbor, tel. 516/ 477–0627. Dress: informal. Reservations accepted. Lunch, dinner. MC, V. Closed mid-Nov.–mid-April; closed Tues. mid-April–May, Sept.–mid-Nov. Moderate.*

Lodging **Silver Sands Motel.** At this motel, you have Greenport at your backyard and 1,000 feet of private Peconic Bay beach in your front yard. There are a variety of rooms and cottages (some with kitchenettes); refrigerators, complimentary Continental breakfasts and, except for the cottages, daily maid service. *Box 285, Silvermere Rd., 11944, tel. 516/477–0011. 40 rooms with bath. Facilities: fishing, sailing, swimming pool, waterskiing. Special rates during the off-season. AE, CB, DC, MC, V. Moderate–Expensive.*

Townsend Manor Inn. This charming, historic inn, built in 1835, combines the best of country style with the convenience of a waterside location just one-half mile beyond downtown Greenport. There are single rooms, suites, and apartments, all air-conditioned. The decor is Colonial, but each room is furnished differently. An inviting family-type hotel, especially popular with yachtsmen because it has its own full-service transient marina. Wineries, beaches, and Greenport shops are nearby. *714 Main St., 11944, tel. 516/477–2000. 23 rooms with bath. Facilities: bar, marina, restaurant, swimming pool, with golf, fishing, and tennis nearby. AE, CB, DC, MC, V. Moderate–Expensive.*

Greenvale

Dining **Dar Tiffany.** Appearances notwithstanding—the gray-stone building looks more like a space-age fortress than a restaurant, and the inside is heavy on chrome, mirrors, and neon—this is a traditional steak and seafood house. The crowd is stylish. The extensive wine list features more than 140 varieties, and don't leave without sampling the homemade ice cream. *44 Glen Cove Rd., just north of Rte. 25A, tel. 516/625–0444. Dress: informal. Reservations advised. Lunch weekdays, dinner daily. AE, CB, DC, MC, V. Expensive.*

Hampton Bay

Lodging **Hampton Maid Motel.** Though it calls itself a motel, the Hampton Maid is a decided cut above the standard American roadside offering. Air-conditioned rooms are furnished with brass and antiques, and their private patios/balconies overlook Shinnecock Bay. Two units are located in a reproduction of an old windmill. The five acres of grounds are meticulously landscaped. Rooms have refrigerators. *Box 713, 11946, tel. 516/ 728–4166. 30 rooms with bath. Facilities: antiques shop, meeting rooms, playground, picnic tables, pool. AE, MC, V. Closed Nov.–Mar. Expensive.*

Huntington

Dining **Fabio's.** This intimate, romantic restaurant offers cuisines of both Brazil and northern Italy. A highly recommended Brazilian dish is Peixada, a fish soup brimming with lobster, shrimp, scallops, and clams. Italian cooking is deliciously represented by the black and white ravioli filled with lobster and served with a lobster tail. A piano bar and weekend samba player enhance the appeal of this popular, sophisticated place. *62 Stewart Ave., tel. 516/549–7074. Dress: informal. Reservations advised for weekend dinners. AE, MC, V. Closed Sat. and Sun. lunch. Moderate.*

Jericho

Dining **Milleridge Inn.** Basic, old-fashioned American food is served here in a historic, Colonial mansion, complete with fireplaces and antiques. Specialties include prime rib of beef and jumbo mushrooms stuffed with shrimp and crabmeat. Milleridge features a couple of low-calorie entrees for either lunch or dinner. Children will enjoy a visit to the replica of a Colonial village just outside; it has eight shops, including a bakery where the inn's bread is baked. The inn is appropriately decorated for every holiday, and carolers are a highlight of the Christmas season. *Hicksville Rd., tel. 516/931–2201. Jacket required. Reservations advised. Lunch, dinner and Sun. brunch, 11:30–2:30. AE, CB, DC, MC, V. Closed Christmas. Inexpensive.*

Melville

Lodging **Royce Carlin Hotel.** This midisland hotel, a blend of casual elegance and lush decor, has 305 spacious guest rooms and suites. *598 Broadhollow Rd., 11747, tel. 516/845–1000. Facilities: 2 restaurants, piano lounge; disco, indoor pool with waterfall, fitness center, health spa, outdoor pool, lighted tennis courts, game room. AM, MC, V. Very Expensive.*

Merrick

Dining **The Chinatown Seafood Restaurant.** Szechuan and Cantonese
★ dishes presented with style and priced reasonably make this a truly superior Chinese restaurant. A host of attentive waiters are ready to bring you such specialties as the Seafood Basket, a deliciously crunchy, deep-fried Taro basket filled with lobster, crabmeat, scallops, and Chinese vegetables. *2222 Merrick Rd. (Rte. 27A), tel. 516/546–0671. Dress: informal. Reservations advised for large groups on weekends. Lunch, dinner. AE, CB, DC, MC, V. Inexpensive.*

Montauk

Dining **Gosman's.** This classy fish restaurant has a spectacular location at the entrance to Montauk harbor, indoor and outdoor dining, and the freshest possible fish (Gosman's is also a wholesale and retail fish supplier). It's also huge—it seats 400 between its indoor dining room, done in a low-key nautical style, two deck dining areas, and patio on the water—and hugely popular. Since reservations aren't taken, you may have to wait some time to be seated and served in peak season. Spend the time browsing through the numerous art, gift, and clothing shops, located in the Gosman's Dock complex. Try the broiled fluke, which is not available at many places outside Montauk, or the broiled tuna. Good choices for dessert are chocolate torte, pecan chocolate pie, and lime pie. *West Lake Dr., tel. 516/668–5330. Dress: casual but proper (no jogging shorts). No reserva-*

*tions. No credit cards. Open noon–10 PM. Closed mid-Oct.–
Mar. Moderate.*

Lodging　**Gurney's Inn Resort and Spa.** Long popular for its fabulous loca-
★　　tion high on a bluff overlooking 1,000 feet of private ocean
beach, Gurney's has become even more famous in recent years
for its health and beauty spa, which features the use of seawa-
ter and sea plants. The large, luxurious rooms all have ocean
views. The indoor pool is nearly Olympic-size and has heated
salt water. Guests have the choice of a modified or full American meal plan; the ocean-view restaurant features spa and
French cuisines. *Old Montauk Hwy., 11954, tel. 516/668–2345.
125 rooms with bath. Facilities: Roman bath, bar, health club,
barber, drugstore, beauty shop, meeting rooms, recreation
room, indoor pool, restaurant, golf and tennis privileges, and
five extensive spa facilities. AE, DC, MC, V. Very Expensive.*

Driftwood. These deluxe studio or junior one-bedroom apartments or 2½-room suites feature daily maid and baby-sitting
services. The executive studios have private patios overlooking
the water. All 52 units have refrigerators. *Box S, Montauk
11954, tel. 516/668–5744. Facilities: pool, beach, tennis, playground, shuffleboard, ping-pong, volleyball. No credit cards.
Open May–Sept. Moderate–Very Expensive.*

★　**Shepherds Neck Inn.** This country inn gives you a real feel
for the simple, unpretentious seagoing style that sets Montauk apart from the trendier Hamptons to the west. Located
right in the village, it has five acres of quiet grounds and
spacious rooms. All rooms have color TV and cable, and all
are air-conditioned. Guests choose between two meal plans:
Bed & Breakfast or Modified American (breakfast and dinner).
The kitchen features seafood and locally grown vegetables.
Golf, beaches, and boats are nearby. *Second House Rd., Box
639, 11954, tel. 516/668–2105. 70 rooms with bath. Facilities: 2
conference rooms available with AV and VCR equipment, movie room with nightly features, horseback riding and fishing
nearby, restaurant, bar, heated pool, tennis. MC, V. Moderate–
Expensive.*

Northport

Dining　**Australian Country Inn and Gardens.** The owners of this restaurant have tried hard to re-create a little bit of "Down Under" in the midst of Northport. Waiters and waitresses wear
bush clothing, and the Australian beer comes in whopping
25-ounce cans. The downstairs dining rooms feature an
adventurous menu, and the bar area is casual and relaxing.
Specialties include Golden Mountain Lambatty (loin lamb
chops with peaches and brandy cream sauce) and Sydney
Steamboat (lobster tails with shrimps, clams, crab legs,
and Pacific Pearl mussels brewed in butter, garlic, scallions,
parsley and pimentos). *1036 Salonga Rd. (Rte. 25A), tel.
516/754–4400. Dress: informal. Reservations advised for
weekend dinners. AE, DC, MC, V. Closed Sat. lunch. Inexpensive.*

Oyster Bay

Dining　**Canterbury Ales.** Although you can still order such traditional
fare as shepherd's pie or brown stew, the kitchen of this publike

establishment has of late moved away from the English theme and turned to seafood. The oyster bar, one of the most extensive on Long Island, features oysters from Oyster Bay. (No relation to the Canterbury Ales at 314 New York Ave. in Huntington, tel. 516/549–4404.) *46 Audrey Ave., tel. 516/922–3614. Dress: informal. AE, CB, DC, MC, V. Inexpensive.*

Port Jefferson

Dining and Lodging
★

Danfords Inn at Bayles Dock. This exquisite English-style country inn, directly overlooking Long Island Sound, has all the amenities of a well-run modern hotel. The rooms are tastefully furnished with antiques or reproductions and first-class paintings from the owner's collection. Tennis courts and swimming are within walking distance. The inn's restaurant serves gourmet cooking in a dining room with a spectacular view of Port Jefferson Harbor. The sautéed filet of sole in pecan butter sauce and the jumbo shrimp wrapped in bacon and Swiss cheese are excellent. *25 East Broadway, 11777, tel. 516/928–5200. 80 rooms and suites with bath. Facilities: 75-slip transient marina, exercise room, conference rooms, FAX machine. Restaurant: reservations advised; dress: informal. AE, CB, DC, MC, V. Expensive–Very Expensive.*

Dining

Savories. Delicate French lace window curtains are a clue to the cuisine of this Northern Italian/French restaurant in the heart of Port Jefferson Village. House specialties include shrimp cognac and beef chanterelle. The Theatre III dinner/theater package ($31.95 per person) includes theater ticket, appetizer, soup or salad, main course, dessert, coffee or tea. Call in advance as tickets sell out quickly. *318 Wynne La., tel. 516/331–4747. Jackets recommended for dinner. Reservations recommended. AE, DC, MC, V. Expensive.*

Deep Sea Dive. This newly expanded 80-seat restaurant features fine seafood prepared with a fashionable Creole and Cajun twist. Two of the most popular dishes are blackened bluefish and award-winning monkfish with sauerkraut and caraway. The vegetable side dishes and desserts are also excellent. *181 Main St., tel. 516/883–0744. Dress: informal. Reservations advised. No lunch. AE, MC, V. Closed Mon. Inexpensive.*

Quogue

Lodging

The Inn at Quogue. This is a quaint 200-year-old inn with 15 rooms, 12 with private bath, TV, and telephone. Two cottages are also available. *Quogue St., 11959, tel. 516/653–6560. Facilities: restaurant, piano bar, and access to beach, golf, and shops. Open May–Oct. Expensive–Very Expensive.*

Roslyn

Dining

Il Villagio. This restaurant offers a touch of Continental sophistication in the heart of picturesque Old Roslyn village. Specialties include *Dentice Al Rosmarinio* (red snapper with white wine sauce), *Crevettes aux Roquefort* (large shrimp and Roquefort cheese), and *osso buco* (braised veal shanks). Valet parking is available. *1446 Old Northern Blvd., tel. 516/484–9550. Jacket required. Reservations advised for weekends. AE, MC, V. Moderate.*

George Washington Manor. Though George Washington did not sleep here, he did have breakfast in this 1740 Colonial mansion, now an elegant restaurant. The spacious, antiques-filled interior is divided into nine dining rooms. The kitchen does quite well with Yankee pot roast served with potato pancakes, Norwegian salmon, fried scallops, and prime ribs on Saturday nights. Black forest layer cake heads the dessert list. *1305 Old Northern Blvd., tel. 516/621-1200. Jacket and tie recommended. Reservations advised for weekend dinners and Sunday brunch. AE, CB, DC, MC, V. Inexpensive–Moderate.*

Sag Harbor

Lodging **Baron's Cove Inn.** This newly renovated motel has its own marina. The air-conditioned rooms have kitchenettes and color TVs and some have private patios/balconies with water views. *West Water St., 11963, tel. 516/725-2100. 66 rooms with bath. Facilities: fishing, golf, horseback riding, nearby marina, pool, room service, tennis, restaurant, meeting rooms. AE, MC, V. Open year-round. Moderate–Very Expensive.*

St. James

Dining **Mirabelle.** As soon as you're seated, complimentary pâté or
★ salmon-mousse tidbits are brought to the table. This is the first of the many fine touches that make a meal at this sophisticated but unpretentious French chef–owned restaurant so special. Among the entrees, rack of lamb and boned duck with glazed sauce show off the chef's strengths. And don't leave without sampling the ginger-almond tart. The elegant French-country atmosphere perfectly complements the food. *404 N. Country Rd. (Rte. 25A), tel. 516/584-5999. Dress: informal. Reservations advised. AE, CB, DC, MC, V. Closed Mon. Dinner only weekends. Moderate.*

Shelter Island

Lodging **Ram's Head Inn.** The Ram's Head has the most picturesque location on Shelter Island and makes the most of it. An attractive, shingle-style building, it sits atop a gentle hill with acres of lawn sloping down to the calm waters of Coecles Harbor. The rooms are small but comfortable with flowery wallpaper and maple furniture. The inn also has a fine restaurant featuring Continental cuisine, with such offerings as Long Island duckling, rack of lamb, and saffron shrimp. *Shelter Island Heights, 11965, tel. 516/749-0811. 18 rooms, 4 with private bath. Facilities: swimming, boating, tennis, restaurant. MC, V. Open May–Oct. Expensive.*

★ **Shelter Island Resort.** This is a friendly, family-run resort on a gentle bluff overlooking Shelter Island Sound. The resort's 750 feet of private beachfront is ideal for swimming: The water is warm and gentle, the sand soft and white. The comfortable air-conditioned rooms have large private sun decks with chaise longues and umbrellas. The charming Victorian district known as Shelter Island Heights is a short walk away. A modified American meal plan (breakfast, dinner) is available. *Box AO, Shore Rd., 11965, tel. 516/749-2001. 20 rooms with bath. Facilities: bicycles, barbecue grill, paddleboats, fishing, meeting room, restaurant, golf and tennis privileges. AE, DC, MC, V. Moderate–Very Expensive.*

Southampton

Dining **Lobster Inn.** As you might suspect from the name, this is a seafood restaurant specializing in lobster—steamed and simply served with fresh lemon and melted butter. Fresh fish of the day and the bizarrely named Splat (Steamed Shellfish Platter for Two) also are available. *162 Inlet Rd., eastern end of Rte. 27, tel. 516/283–9828. Dress: informal. No reservations. AE, MC, V. Expensive.*

Barrister's. If you come to Long Island for its famous duckling, this may be the place for you. Roast duckling is served in the crispness you desire with a variety of sauces, including the favored orange sauce. Other Continental and American dishes include roast baby lamb with mint sauce and prime rib and steaks done to your choice of rareness. Located in the center of Southampton, this publike 56-seat restaurant is decorated with antiques, Americana, and plants. *36 Main St., tel. 516/283–6206. Dress: casual. Reservations accepted for dinner. AE, CB, DC, MC, V. Moderate.*

Driver's Seat. Manhattan yuppies love this warm and rustic restaurant and others find it appealing, too. Winter guests like its fireplace-heated, 100-seat dining room, and summer visitors prefer its cheerful, umbrella-shaded patio. The cuisine is basic American (steaks, burgers, and chops), with the emphasis on local fishes (tuna, mako shark, and weakfish) caught in season. There are two bars for the thirsty. *62 Jobs La., tel. 516/283–6606. Dress: casual. No reservations. AE, DC, MC, V. Inexpensive.*

Lodging **Southampton Inn.** This is not a country inn but a deluxe miniresort with comfortable accommodations, tennis courts, a pool, and a health spa. The shops of Southampton are a short walk away, and the beach is just a mile and a half down the road. There is a good restaurant featuring standard American fare, live entertainment and dancing on weekends, and room service. Special rates for senior citizens and facilities for the handicapped are available. *Hill St. at First Neck La., 11968, tel. 516/283–6500. 90 rooms with bath. Facilities: bar, health club, fishing, golf privileges, game room, meeting rooms, recreation room, pool, restaurant, tennis, catering services. AE, CB, DC, MC, V. Very Expensive.*

South Hampton Resorts at Watch Hill. This family-style motel offers large suites that include living room, kitchen, and bedroom with two double beds. The rooms are clean and modern and each has a patio or terrace overlooking Peconic Bay. Continental breakfasts are included on Sundays during the summer season. *County Rd. 39, 11968, tel. 516/283–6100. 38 rooms with bath. Facilities: fishing, golf privileges, horseback riding, meeting rooms, pool, tennis. AE, MC, V. Moderate–Very Expensive.*

Stony Brook

Dining **Three Village Inn.** This is the perfect setting for traditional
★ American fare: a lovely old Colonial homestead set back on attractive grounds overlooking Stony Brook Harbor. Recommended entrees include Long Island duck with Grand Marnier (orange-flavored liqueur) sauce, New England lobster pie, and filet mignon stuffed with oysters. *150 Main St., tel. 516/751–*

0555. *Jacket required. Reservations strongly advised. Break-fast, lunch, dinner. AE, DC, MC, V. Inexpensive–Moderate.*

Westbury

Lodging **Island Inn.** This is a large, modern, well-run motel with many of the amenities of a hotel, including a beauty salon and drug-store. Located near some of the major shopping centers, the Island Inn offers a wide selection of rooms, all air-conditioned and newly renovated. As motel rooms go, these are fairly plush. Special touches include free newspaper, color TV with in-room movies, and valet service. There is also a restaurant, live entertainment, and dancing. Pets are permitted. Senior-citizen and some weekend rates are available. *Old Country Rd., 11590, tel. 516/228–9500. 204 rooms with bath. Facilities: bar, barber, beauty shop, drugstore, convention and meeting rooms, banquet rooms, pool, restaurant. AE, CB, DC, MC, V. Very Expensive.*

Williston Park

Dining **La Marmite.** Casually elegant, this French and Northern-
★ Italian restaurant in an old farmhouse is one of the best on the island. The four dining rooms, seating a total of 200 people, are decorated in a pleasing country-style, and the service is impec-cable. Some of the more memorable dishes include rack of lamb, lobster fricassee, and beef Wellington with spinach and mush-rooms. For dessert, there's *gateau St. Honore*, cheesecake, or delicate fruit tarts. *234 Hillside Ave., tel. 516/746–1243. Jack-ets required. Reservations strongly advised. AE, CB, DC, MC, V. Closed Sun., lunch Sat. Moderate–Expensive.*

The Arts

Culturally, New York City casts a long shadow over Long Is-land. Nonetheless, the island has a wide variety of its own cultural offerings, including professional theater, music con-certs, dance programs, and appearances by big-name enter-tainers. In addition to the places listed below, check the Friday edition of *Newsday*, the Long Island newspaper, which has a weekend supplement containing an abundance of information about Long Island arts, and the new magazine *Long Island Monthly*.

Theater

Airport Playhouse. This is a small, local playhouse not too far from MacArthur Airport. Tickets are $9–12. *Niverbocker Ave., Bohemia, tel. 516/589–7588.*
Arena Players Repertory Company of Long Island. This is the island's oldest professional repertory company; plays are pre-sented throughout the year. *296 Rte. 109, East Farmingdale, tel. 516/293–0674.*
Broadhollow Theatre. Broadway hits are the specialty of this professional cast and staff. *229 Rte. 110, Farmingdale, tel. 516/752–1400.*
John Drew Theatre. This is part of **Guild Hall** in East Hampton (tel. 516/324–1850).
Long Island Stage. As the island's only professional resident

theater, this company presents major plays year-round. *Hays Theatre, Rockville Centre, tel. 516/546–4600.*

Studio Theatre. The professional cast and staff here also mounts Broadway hits. *141 S. Wellwood Ave., Lindenhurst, tel. 516/226–1833.*

Theatre Three Productions. This nonprofit professional company offers productions throughout the year. *412 Main St., Port Jefferson, tel. 516/928–9202.*

Music

Jones Beach Marine Theatre. Major contemporary pop artists are booked for live concerts here during summer months. *Jones Beach, Wantagh, tel. 516/221–1000.*

Long Island Philharmonic. This orchestra performs classical contemporary music at the Tilles Center at C. W. Post College and Hauppauge High School, and gives free outdoor concerts in the summer. *For schedule and ticket information, tel. 516/293–2222.*

Nassau Coliseum. Major rock and pop concerts are scheduled here periodically throughout the year. *Hempstead Tpke., Uniondale, tel. 516/796–9300.*

Nassau Symphony Orchestra. Performances are given at the Hofstra University playhouse throughout the year. *For schedule and ticket information, tel. 516/877–2718.*

Westbury Music Fair. Live concerts and shows here feature major names in entertainment. *Brush Hollow Rd., Westbury, tel. 516/333–0533.*

Dance **North Shore Dance Theater.** Free performances of contemporary dance programs are scheduled in summer. *Heckscher Park, Prime Ave. and Rte. 25A, Huntington, tel. 516/271–8442.*

Cinema **New Community Cinema.** This filmtheater, specializing in superior American and international cinema, brings the best of New York City film culture to Long Island. Silent film series are often accompanied by live piano music, and film directors and producers are frequently on hand to discuss their films. New Community Cinema is a nonprofit educational organization housed in a converted elementary school. *423 Park Ave., just south of Rte. 25A, Huntington, tel. 516/423–7610 weekdays 10–6; 516/423–7653 after 7 weeknights and all day weekends. Admission: $5 for nonmembers, $3 for members and senior citizens Sun.–Thurs., $2.50 for children.*

Visual Art In addition to the art museums mentioned earlier the following are worth noting:

East End Arts Council. Exhibits include works by East End artists. *133 E. Main St., Riverhead, tel. 516/727–0900. Open weekdays 10–5.*

East Hampton Center for Contemporary Art. Exhibits by contemporary artists from Long Island and New York City fill 850 square feet of gallery space. *16R Newton La, East Hampton, tel. 516/324–8939. Open mid-April–Christmas, daily except Tues. and Wed., 11–7. Open Sat. during Feb. for children's programs.*

Emily Lowe Art Gallery. Exhibits at this Hofstra University gallery include a variety of art from different periods. *Hempstead Tpke., Hempstead, tel. 516/560–5672. Open Tues. 10–9, Wed.–Fri. 10–5, weekends 1–5. Admission free.*

Fine Arts Museum of Long Island. Work by Long Island and New York area artists is on display. *295 Fulton Ave., Hempstead, tel. 516/481–5700. Open Wed.–Sat. 10–4:30, Sun. noon–4:30.*

Firehouse Gallery. Month-long exhibits in a variety of media are featured at this Nassau Community College Campus gallery. *Stuart Ave., Garden City, tel. 516/222–7165. Admission free. Open Mon.–Thurs. 11:30–4 and Tues. 7–10 PM. Closed July and Aug.*

Staller Center for the Arts. Located on the campus of SUNY-Stony Brook, this fine arts center has performances of music and theater as well as an expansive gallery exhibiting first-rate contemporary art. *Nicholls Rd., Stony Brook, tel. 516/632–7240. For performances call 516/632–7230. Admission free. Gallery hours are Tues.–Sat. noon–4; also open evenings before some performances.*

Nightlife

Long Island is a hot place for singles and young couples. Clubs feature the loudest in music and the fanciest in video display, and there are big glitzy discos. For current club information, call 516/540–NITE; about $2 per call. Intimate jazz joints attract an older, mellower clientele. In recent years, comedy clubs have joined the other forms of nighttime entertainment on Long Island. The humor tends to be what they call adult, and the crowds are diverse in age. Check *Newsday* for information.

Discos

Bay Street. Popular with young crowds, this is one of the few East End clubs that stays open year-round. There's live music on Saturdays. *Long Wharf, Sag Harbor, tel. 516/725–2297. Open from 9, music at 11.*

Chevy's Bel Air Cafe. This swinging nostalgia club features danceable hits from the '50s through the '80s. *135 Sunrise Hwy., West Islip, tel. 516/422–5278.*

Decisions. Open seven days, serving lunch as well as great evening dance entertainment. Weekly music theme nights include Wednesday Sing-A-Long, Thursday New Wave, Friday House Music, Saturday Classic, and Sunday Light Rock. *170 Old Country Rd., Carle Pl., tel. 516/248–5130.*

Long Island Exchange. From happy hour on, this is one of the hottest clubs on the Island. *598 Broad Hollow Rd., Melville, tel. 516/845–1000.*

Malibu Night Club. This big dance club draws a young energetic crowd with New Wave and Top-40 hits. The room is big and classy, with multiple video displays. *Lido Blvd., Lido Beach, tel. 516/432–1600. Open 9:30 PM–3 AM Tues., Fri., Sat.*

Oak Beach Inn. There's jazz upstairs, disco down, deli-style food, and live bands play Top-40 dance music on weekends. The crowd ranges from 21 to 60. *Ocean Pkwy., Oak Beach, tel. 516/587–0097. Open 7 days midnight–4 AM.*

Park Bench. In addition to lunch and dinner Tuesday–Sunday, there's dancing 9 PM–4 AM. *Rte. 25A, Stony Brook, across from LIRR station, tel. 516/751–9734. No lunch on Mon.*

Stephen Talkhouse. Rock, blues, and folk music is performed in an intimate coffeehouse atmosphere. There is a full bar, and sandwiches are available. *Main St., Amagansett, tel. 516/267–*

3117. *Open from 5 PM with music most days during the summer, Thurs.–Sat. in the winter.*

Jazz

Sonny's. There's jazz seven nights a week at this intimate club, where the walls are covered with photographs of performers. There's no food; drinks only. *3603 Merrick Rd., Seaford, tel. 516/826–0973. Open from 2 PM; music 9 PM–1 Sun.–Thurs. and 9:30 PM–2 AM Fri. and Sat.*

Comedy Clubs

Brokerage Comedy. This small homey club features comedy shows on weekends, and rock, funk, and blues bands during the week. There's a full bar and pub food. *2797 Merrick Rd. and Bellmore Ave., Bellmore, tel. 516/785–8655. Open Mon.–Sat. 8 PM–2 AM.*

Chuckles. The fanciest comedy club on the island, this place has a nightclub atmosphere and features a full restaurant. *159 Jericho Tpke., Mineola, tel. 516/746–2770. Open Wed.–Sat. with shows at 9 Wed.–Thurs., 9 and 11:30 Fri., and 8, 10, and 12:30 Sat.*

East Side Comedy. The atmosphere is warm and cozy, and there's a full restaurant and bar. *326 West Jericho Tpke., Huntington, tel. 516/271–6061. Open Tues.–Sun. with shows at 9 Tues.–Thurs. and Sun., 9 and 11:30 Fri., and 7, 9:30, and midnight Sat.*

Governor's Comedy Shops. This casual place attracts a crowd ranging in age from 18 to 70. There's a pub-style menu and full bar. *90A Division Ave., Levittown, tel. 516/731–3358. Open Thurs.–Sun. with shows at 9 Thurs. and Sun., 9 and midnight Fri. and Sat.*

Laff's Comedy Club. Live stand-up comics entertain enthusiastic South Fork crowds here. *Montauk Hwy., Hampton Bays, tel. 516/728–LAFF. Shows 9:30 Sat.*

5 Hudson Valley

Introduction

The Hudson River, the estuary that links the fresh waters of
Troy, Schenectady, and Albany to the salt waters of the Atlantic, is one of the busiest and most beautiful waterways in
America. Beginning just above New York City and stretching
140 miles north to the state capital in Albany, the surrounding
lands—lush and rich on both sides of the river—comprise the
Hudson Valley.

If the number of Revolutionary War battle sites in the valley
are testimony to the strategic importance of the river, the dozens of stately mansions on magnificent estates affirm the scenic
attraction of the region. Indeed, the landscape's natural
beauty—dramatic palisades, pine-scented forests, cool mountain lakes and streams—inspired an entire art movement, the
Hudson River School, in the 19th century.

This is also a rich agricultural region, where visitors can visit
scores of orchards, vineyards, and farm markets along country
roads.

The Hudson Valley's proximity to Manhattan makes it a viable
destination for day trips, but the numerous country inns, bed-
and-breakfast places, and resorts make longer, more leisurely
journeys especially attractive.

Among the region's most important attractions are magnifi-
cently restored mansions such as Boscobel in Garrison,
Washington Irving's home near Tarrytown, and Franklin
Delano Roosevelt's home at Hyde Park; the U.S. Military
Academy at West Point; Bear Mountain State Park; and the
state capital in Albany.

The Hudson Valley tour begins just over the New York City line
at Yonkers in Westchester County.

Getting Around

By Plane Hudson Valley can be reached conveniently by major airlines
with flights into LaGuardia, John F. Kennedy, Albany, and
Newark (NJ) airports, or with local service to Dutchess County
Airport at Poughkeepsie and Westchester County Airport at
White Plains.

By Train **Amtrak** (tel. 800/872–7245) provides rail service from New
York City to Hudson, Rhinecliff, Rensselaer (Albany), and
points west and north of Poughkeepsie.
Metro-North Commuter Railroad (tel. 212/532–4900 or 800/
522–5624) trains leave Grand Central Terminal at Park Ave.
and 42nd St. in Manhattan for Poughkeepsie, Brewster, Dover
Plains, and other upstate points.
New Jersey Transit (tel. 800/522–5624 or 800/772–2222) trains
leave from Hoboken, NJ, for points in Rockland and Orange
counties.

By Bus **Adirondack and Pine Hill Trailways** (tel. 914/339–4230) has daily service between Port Authority Bus Terminal, 41st Street
and Eighth Avenue, New York City, and New Paltz, Kingston,
Albany, and other Hudson Valley towns. Charter and package
tours are available.

Leprechaun Lines & Tours (tel. 914/565–7900 or 914/896–4600) offers daily service to New York City and Atlantic City. Charter and package tours available.

Flight Catcher (tel. 800/533–3298) has daily van service between the Hudson Valley and New York area airports.

Shortline Bus (tel. 212/736–4700 or 800/631–8405) also has daily service between Port Authority Bus Terminal, area airports, and Hudson Valley communities. Charter and package tours available.

Important Addresses and Numbers

Tourist Information
All of the following tourist information offices are open weekdays 9–5:

Albany County Convention & Visitors Bureau, Inc., 52 South Pearl St., Albany 12207, tel. 518/434–1217 or 800/622–8464.

Columbia County Chamber of Commerce, 414 Union St., Hudson 12534, tel. 518/828–3375 or 800/777–9247.

Dutchess County Tourism Promotion Agency, 46 Albany Post Rd., Box 2025, Hyde Park 12538, tel. 914/229–0033 or 800/445–3131 (in N.Y.S.) and 800/343–7007.

Greene County Promotion Department, Exit 21, N.Y.S. Thruway, Box 467, Catskill 12414, tel. 518/943–3223 or 800/542–2414.

Hudson River Valley Association, 76 Main St., Cold Spring-on-Hudson 10516, tel. 914/265–3066 or 800/232–4782.

Office of General Services, Empire State Plaza, Visitor Assistance, Concourse Room 106, Empire State Plaza, Albany 12242, tel. 518/474–2418.

Orange County Tourism, 124 Main St., Goshen 10924, tel. 914/294–5151, ext. 1770 or 800/7C–TOUR.

Putnam County Tourism, 76 Main St., Cold Spring-on-Hudson 10516, tel. 914/265–3066.

Rockland County Tourism Board, One Blue Hill Plaza, Pearl River 10965, tel. 914/735–7040.

Ulster County Public Information, County Office Bldg., Box 1800, Kingston 12401, tel. 914/331–9300 or 800/DIAL–UCO.

Westchester Tourism Council, 148 Martine Ave., White Plains 10610, tel. 914/285–2941.

State Police Departments
Columbia: tel. 518/851–3111
Dutchess: tel. 914/876–4033
Greene: tel. 518/622–8600
Orange: tel. 914/562–1133
Putnam: tel. 914/279–6161
Rockland: tel. 914/353–1100
Ulster: tel. 914/338–1702

Emergencies County Fire Control and Ambulance
Columbia: tel. 518/828–4114
Dutchess: tel. 914/471–1427
Greene: tel. 518/943–2424
Orange: tel. 914/294–6106
Putnam: tel. 914/225–4300
Rockland: tel. 914/354–8300
Ulster: tel. 914/338–1440
Westchester: tel. 914/225–4300

Hospitals
Dutchess: *Northern Dutchess Hospital,* Rhinebeck (tel. 914/867–3001); *St. Francis Hospital,* Poughkeepsie (tel. 914/471–2000); *Vassar Hospital,* Poughkeepsie (tel. 914/454–8500).

Greene: *Albany Medical Center*, Albany (tel. 518/445–3125).
Orange: *Arden Hill Hospital*, Goshen (tel. 914/294–5441).
Putnam: *Putnam Hospital Center*, Carmel (tel. 914/279–5711).
Rockland: *Nyack Hospital*, Nyack (tel. 914/358–6200); *Good Samaritan Hospital*, Suffern (tel. 914/357–3300).
Ulster: *Kingston Hospital*, Kingston (tel. 914/331–3131); *Benedictine Hospital*, Kingston (tel. 914/338–5590); *Ellenville Hospital*, Ellenville (tel. 914/647–6400).
Westchester: *White Plains Hospital*, White Plains (tel. 914/681–0600); *Westchester Medical Center*, Valhalla (tel. 914/285–7000).

Guided Tours

Special-Interest Tours

Annandale Tours (Box 32, Annandale-on-Hudson 12504, tel. 914/758–0313) specializes in themed tours for individuals or groups showcasing the history of Hudson Valley.

Aristocrat Tours, Inc. (Box 3038, Poughkeepsie 12603, tel. 914/452–2130) provides complete tour packages for groups of 30 or more.

Grayline Transportation (900 Eighth Ave., New York 10019, tel. 212/397–2600) has summer tours to West Point, Wed. and Sat., July–Oct.

Hudson Valley Tours (8 Raymond Ave., Box 3513, Poughkeepsie 12603, tel. 914/452–5840) offers escorted tours for individuals and groups.

West Point Tours (Box 268, Highland Falls 10928, tel. 914/446–4724) offers guided tours of the U.S. Military Academy for groups and individuals.

Hudson River Cruises

Dutch Apple Cruises, Inc. (1668 Julianne Dr., Castleton 12033, tel. 518/463–0220), offers daily trips from Albany, with or without meals and entertainment. Moonlight cruising and private charters also available. Apr.–Oct.

Hudson Highland Cruises & Tours, Inc. (Box 265, Highland Falls 10928, tel. 914/446–7171). *M/V Commander* sails from West Point, West Haverstraw, and Peekskill. Daytime sightseeing cruises with historic narrations; private charters available. May–Oct.

Hudson River Cruises (Box 333, Rifton 12471, tel. 914/255–6515). Narrated cruises from Kingston and West Point aboard *M/V Rip Van Winkle*. Mini- and evening cruises and private charters. May–Oct.

Hudson River Day Line (Pier 81, west end of 42nd St., New York 10036, tel. 212/279-5151). Monthly mini-cruises to Bear Mountain and West Point from Manhattan.

Hudson Rondout Cruises (11 East Chestnut St., Kingston 12401, tel. 914/338-6280). Lighthouse cruises, charters, and dinner cruises from Kingston's Rondout waterfront. May–Oct.

Riverboat Tours (310 Mill St., Poughkeepsie 12601, tel. 914/473–5211). Sightseeing, dinner, brunch cruises, and private charters from Poughkeepsie. May–October.

Shearwater Cruises and Sailing School (RD 2, Box 329, Rhinebeck 12572, tel. 914/876–7350). Self-captained charters, two-hour sailing tours, and sailing lessons from Norrie Point Marina.

Exploring the Hudson Valley

Numbers in the margin correspond with points of interest on the Hudson Valley map.

Westchester and Rockland Counties

Located in the magnificent 1876 Trevor Mansion overlooking the Hudson in **Yonkers,** the collections of the **Hudson River Museum** include impressive paintings from the Hudson River School of artists, such as Jasper Cropsey and Albert Bierstadt. Many of the art, history, and science exhibits focus on the work of local artists. Furnishings of the Victorian era and personal objects of the Trevor family, including huge Persian carpets, are shown in the main building where the family lived. Also part of the museum is the Andrus Space Transit Planetarium, which offers simulated space travel as well as an awesome look at the stars. The museum hosts a series of chamber music concerts Oct.–Apr. *511 Warburton Ave. (off Rte. 9), Yonkers, tel. 914/963–4550. Admission: $2 adults, $1 children under 12 and seniors. Admission to the planetarium: $3 adults, $1.50 children under 12 and seniors. Open Wed.-Sat. 10–5, Sun. noon–5 (later hours on Thurs. in summer).*

Less than a mile south on Warburton Avenue is the **Philipse Manor Hall State Historic Site,** a history and art museum in a mansion once owned by the wealthy proprietors of the manor of Philipsburg. The loyalist Philipse family lost its mansion and vast landholdings during the American Revolution. The house, a fine example of 18th-century Georgian architecture, has ornate interiors including a rare rococo-style ceiling and contains an extraordinary collection of portraits of American presidents. *Warburton Ave. and Dock St., Yonkers, tel. 914/965–4027. Usually open in summer Wed.–Sun.; phone in advance for exact times.*

Head north on Route 9 several miles to **Tarrytown** and follow signs to **Sunnyside.** The romantic estate on the banks of the Hudson belonged to Washington Irving. The author of *The Legend of Sleepy Hollow* and *Rip Van Winkle* purchased the home in 1835. The 17 rooms, including Irving's library, contain many of his original furnishings. A stream flows through the landscape from a pond Irving called his "little Mediterranean." Sunnyside is a Registered National Historic Landmark and one of several Historic Hudson Valley Restorations. Tours and special events are organized, and picnicking is encouraged. *Rte. 9, Tarrytown, tel. 914/631–8200. Admission: $5 adults, $4.50 seniors, $3 students. Open Apr.–Oct., daily 10–5; Mar. and Nov.–Dec., Wed.–Mon. 10–4; and Jan.–Feb., weekends 10–4.*

Farther north on Route 9 is another Historic Hudson Valley Restoration, the **Philipsburg Manor Upper Mills,** an 18th-century Dutch-Colonial site that served as a trading center and the country home of the wealthy merchant Frederik Philipse. This 90,000-acre estate was the center of a bustling commercial empire, which included milling and trading operations. Tours visit the stone manor house, a gristmill still run by water power (you can purchase the flour which is ground here at the gift

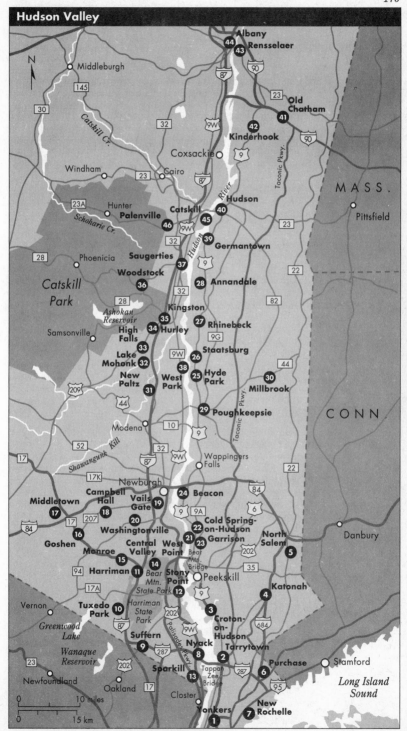

Hudson Valley

shop), and the farm's animals and gardens. *Rte. 9, North Tarrytown, tel. 914/631–8200. Admission: $5 adults, $4.50 seniors, $3 students. Open April–Oct., Wed.–Mon. 10–5; Nov.–Dec. and March, Wed.–Mon. 10–4; and Jan.–Feb., weekends 10–4.*

❸ Continue north on Route 9 to **Croton-on-Hudson** for yet another of the Historic Hudson Valley Restorations, **Van Cortlandt Manor.** This estate, home of a wealthy and prominent family that supported the American Revolution, shows life along the Hudson when the nation was young. Generals Lafayette and Washington were guests in this house, which is known today for its elegant antique furnishings and well-kept 18th-century gardens and orchards. *Rte. 9, Croton-on-Hudson, tel. 914/631–8200. Admission: $5 adults, $4.50 seniors, $3 students. Open April–Oct., Wed.–Mon. 10–5; Nov.–Dec. and March, Wed.–Mon. 10–4; and Jan.–Feb., weekends 10–4.*

Take Route 35 east 10 miles to the intersection at Route 22, in ❹ **Katonah,** to visit the **John Jay Homestead.** Jay was appointed by George Washington as the first chief justice of the United States and was co-author with John Adams of the "Federalist Papers." Jay also co-authored, with Benjamin Franklin and John Adams, the Treaty of Paris, which ended the Revolution. He was elected to two terms as governor of New York. He retired to this Westchester farmhouse in 1801 after three decades of public service and lived here until his death in 1829. The homestead remained in the Jay family until 1953, when the property was sold to the state. It is well stocked with furnishings and antiques. Sixty acres of the original 900-acre farm are part of this State Historic Site encompassing the homestead, gardens, and meadows. *Rte. 22, Katonah, tel. 914/232–5651. Admission free. Tours every half-hour; last tour begins at 4. Open May–Oct., Wed.–Sat. noon–4; Nov.–mid-Dec. by appointment; closed Jan.–Apr.*

Take Route 22 north for three miles to Girdle Ridge Road and the **Caramoor Center for Music & The Arts,** set on 117 acres of the estate built in the 1930s by Walter Tower Rosen to house his collection of fine art from Europe and the Orient. Caramoor is the setting for an acclaimed summer music festival. Operas and concerts are presented in the Venetian Theater, an outdoor showcase built around 15th-century Venetian columns, while smaller chamber concerts take place in the Spanish Courtyard. The House Museum displays period rooms from European palaces and hundreds of pieces of Oriental fine and decorative art. *Girdle Ridge Rd., Katonah, tel. 914/232–5035. Admission: $4 adults, $2 children under 12. Open May–Nov., Thurs. and Sat., 11–4 and Sun. 1–4; Nov.–May by appointment only.*

Leave Route 22 at Route 121 to connect with Route 116, which takes you east into **North Salem. The Hammond Museum and Oriental Stroll Gardens,** off Route 116, was created by Natalie Hammond and contains 15 small garden landscapes and a waterfall. The museum and the art collection represent a devotion to humanity, justice, and wisdom. *Deveau Rd., North Salem, tel. 914/669–5033. Admission: $3 adults, $2 seniors, $1 children under 12. Open Wed.–Sun., 11–5; museum, May–Dec., and gardens, May–Oct.*

❺ Westchester's only winery, **North Salem Vineyard,** can be reached from exit 8 off I-684. Follow Hardscrabble Road for

2½ miles until you see signs for the vineyard, a small private winery that produces three wines and opens its facilities for tours, wine tasting, and picnicking. A basket lunch and wine can be purchased here. *R.R. #2, Hardscrabble Rd., North Salem, tel. 914/669–5518. Admission free. Open daily June–Oct., weekends Nov.–May.*

6 Return to I–684 and head south taking the exit for the State University at **Purchase.** The **Neuberger Museum** on this campus has a fine collection of 20th-century American and European art as well as African art and Greek pottery. Outdoor sculpture is displayed throughout the 500-acre campus. *Anderson Hill Rd., Purchase, tel. 914/253–5134. Suggested donation: $2 adults. Open Tues.–Fri. 10–4, Sat. and Sun. 11–5.*

7 On Route 1, head south to the city of **New Rochelle** and the **Thomas Paine Cottage.** In 1784, one year after the end of the American Revolution, New York State granted Thomas Paine 300 acres of land as a reward for his vigorous written campaign during the Revolutionary War to incite Americans to defeat the British. The patriot, famous for his statement, "These are the times that try men's souls," lived in this little house until his death in 1809. The Thomas Paine Cottage was built in 1793 and originally stood atop a hill, but it was relocated to its current site. The author of *Common Sense* had lived frugally, leaving behind few possessions relating to his personal life. However, the artifacts that are shown in the cottage are typical of the Colonial period of New Rochelle and its Huguenot settlers. There are several authentic Franklin stoves, presented to Paine by Ben Franklin himself, and handmade quilts, including a Star of Bethlehem quilt. *983 North Ave., New Rochelle, tel. 914/632–5376. Suggested donation: $3 adults, $1 seniors and children under 12. Open 2–5 Fri.–Sun. or by appointment. Closed Nov.–Apr.*

Head back to I–287 and go west straight onto the Tappan Zee Bridge. Get on the New York State Thruway and take the **Nyack** exit, for that quaint village in Rockland County. The Dutch originally farmed this region but when the steamboats arrived, Nyack became a shipping and boat-building center. The town is now an antiques and arts center, and the village sponsors many special events and street fairs. Take a walking tour to see Nyack's architectural history in its public library, the Couch Court, the Presbyterian Church, the Tappan Zee Theatre, the Reformed Church, and the Congregation of the Sons of Israel; along with numerous shops, galleries, and antique shops. *Information booth on Main Street, or call the Art, Craft and Antique Dealers Association, tel. 914/358–8443. Most stores closed Mondays.*

8 While in **Nyack,** be sure to visit the **Edward Hopper House,** also known as the Hopper House Art Center. This was the birthplace and home of the American realist painter from 1882 until his death in 1967. Several of his paintings, featuring local landmarks, are on display. Hopper posters, books, and postcards are available for purchase. Exhibits by outstanding local artists are held year-round. Concerts and special events are held in the gardens. *82 North Broadway, tel. 914/358–0774. Suggested contribution: $1. Open Sat. and Sun. 1–5.*

9 Take Route 17 west to **Suffern.** The **Rhinebeck Crafts Fair** held at the Rockland Community College Fieldhouse each June is one of the premier craft shows in the Northeast. More than 200 craftspeople and artists sell and display their work. *145 College Rd., Suffern, tel. 914/356–4650. Admission: $5 adults, $2 children under 12; free parking.*

⑩ Continue west on Route 17 to **Tuxedo** and into Sterling Forest, located just off Route 17 on Route 17A. **Sterling Forest** is beautiful to visit anytime of the year, but it is especially enjoyable during the summer months when the **New York Renaissance Festival** is held on weekends. There are productions of Shakespearean plays by Equity actors, as well as jugglers, mimes, musicians, jousts on horseback, and plenty of food and drink. *Rte. 17A, Tuxedo, tel. 914/351–5171. Admission: $12 adults, $5 children under 12. Open weekends, Aug.–mid-Sept. 11–6.*

Take Route 17A north back onto Route 17 and follow signs for Route 202 onto the Palisades Interstate Parkway until you **⑪** reach the entrances for **Harriman** and **Bear Mountain State Parks,** the most famous parks of the vast Palisades Interstate system. The two parks share 54,000 acres and both offer plenty of outdoor activity year-round. Facilities exist for boating, roller skating, picnicking, swimming, hiking, and fishing, and there are rest rooms, a bookshop, and a restaurant. At the Trailside Museum in Bear Mountain Park, exhibits and programs describe native-American history as well as the natural history of the area. Children can enjoy the zoo and beaver lodge and reptile house. A drive, bike ride, or even a hike along the Seven Lakes Drive, and especially Lake Welch Drive, can be breathtaking in the fall and winter. Paddleboats and rowboats can be rented on the lakes. In January and February professional ski-jumping competitions are held in the park, and in the fall a country music festival and Oktoberfest are scheduled. *Entrance off the Palisades Interstate Parkway, tel. 914/786–2701. Admission free; parking $3 in summer. Open daily dawn to dusk.*

⑫ Route 9W south will take you to the **Stony Point Battlefield Historic Site** where George Washington demonstrated that American troops could stand up to superior British forces in the Hudson Highlands. In July 1779 General "Mad" Anthony Wayne led the elite Corps of Light Infantry in a daring midnight raid against the British. The British fortifications in the battlefield still stand. At the museum, a slide show depicts the events that led up to the battle, and there is memorabilia explaining the tactics and strategies which led to the American victory. *Park Rd., off Rte. 9W, Stony Point, tel. 914/786–2521. Admission free. Open late-Apr.–mid-Nov., Wed.–Sat. 8:30–5 and Sun. 9–4:30.*

⑬ Head back on Route 9W south to **Sparkill** and the **Piermont Marsh and Tallman State Park,** a nature preserve covering more than 1,000 acres of tidal marsh, mountains, and rivers, considered to be some of the most important fish-breeding areas along the Hudson. Wildflowers abound and bird-watching is a year-round possibility throughout portions of the marsh. There are manmade ponds, home to many varieties of reptiles and amphibians. *Rte. 9W, north of Palisades Interstate Parkway, exit 4, Sparkill, tel. 914/359–0544. Tallman Park cost: $3 per vehicle; Piermont Marsh, free. Open 8 AM–dusk summer, 8 AM–4:30 weekdays, 8AM–7:30 holidays and weekends remainder of year.*

Orange and Putnam Counties

Take the New York State Thruway north to Harriman Exit 16 and proceed to the junction of Route 17 for the town of **Central Valley. Woodbury Commons,** a group of world-famous factory outlets set in a charming Colonial shopping village here offers good values on clothing, shoes, jewelry, gifts, and household items. There is also a racetrack in the area. *Information booth in the Restaurant Court, tel. 914/928-6840. Open Mon.-Wed. and Sat. 10-6, Thurs. and Fri. 10-9, Sun. 11-5.*

⑮ Three miles west on Route 17 is the town of **Monroe** and **Museum Village,** where the daily life of preindustrial America has been re-created. There are more than 35 buildings on the site including a blacksmith's shop where artisans hammer and pound hot metal into door latches and horseshoes. Visit the potter's workshop and see butter churned and mugs shaped on the wheel. *Museum Village Rd., Monroe, tel. 914/782-8247. Admission: $5 adults, $4 seniors, $3 children under 15. Open Wed.-Fri. 10-5, Sat. and Sun. noon-5 May-Dec., shorter weekday hours after Labor Day.*

⑯ Back on Route 17, head west to its intersection with Route 17M, which leads to the village of **Goshen.** Noah Webster of dictionary fame was born in this 275-year-old rural town, as was Ulysses S. Grant. In the center of town is the **Trotting Horse Museum,** or Hall of Fame of the Trotter. Housed in a former stable are more than 100 Early American oil paintings and lithographs depicting the sport of harness racing. The museum contains a huge collection of Currier and Ives prints and famous racing silks, and a Hall of Immortals where dozens of small, lifelike statues recall great trotters. Restored stalls have full-size replicas of horses and their equipment. *240 Main St., Goshen, tel. 914/294-6330. Admission: $1.50 adults, 50¢ children. Open Mon.-Sat. 10-5, Sun. noon-5.*

⑰ Continue west on Route 17 a few miles and you will reach the junction with Routes 84 and 6 and the town of **Middletown.** This is the locale for the **Orange County Fair,** one of the oldest county fairs in New York State, in July or August. Started as a small-time agricultural display in 1818, the fair has expanded immensely since then. It is now an extravaganza featuring farm animals, exhibits, races, and top-name entertainment, lots of food booths, and thrilling rides. There are also Native-American shows, stock-car races, and petting zoos. *County Fairgrounds, Middletown, tel. 914/343-4826. Admission: $6 adults, $2.50 children under 12.*

⑱ You can also take Route 207 north from Goshen to **Campbell Hall** to visit a 1769 family farm and stone farmhouse, the **Hill-Hold Historic Farm Museum.** The land of this 300,000-acre estate was once owned by William Bull, an English stonemason. His son, Thomas, built Hill-Hold. This large, Georgian-style mansion, still owned by the Bull family, has elegant wood- and stonework, barrel-backed cupboards, paneling, and deep-silled windows. Rooms have original fu nishings in the Chippendale style. On the working farm, sheep, cows, chickens, and geese are raised. Guided tours are available. *Rte. 416, Campbell Hall, tel. 914/294-7661. Admission: $2.50 adults, $1.50 children. Open mid-Apr.-mid-Oct., Wed.-Sun. 10-4:30.*

⑲ Return to Route 207 and head east to **Vails Gate.** In this village stands **Knox's Headquarters State Historic Site.** The stone house, built in 1754, was owned by John Ellison. But during the American Revolution it was occupied by Continental officers including Major-General Henry Knox, chief of the artillery. The house served as headquarters for other Colonial heroes as well, such as Generals Horatio Gates and Nathanael Greene. It has been restored with camp beds and folding desks of the period. *Forge Hill Rd. and Rte. 94, Vails Gate, tel. 914/561–5498. Admission free. Open Apr.–Dec., Wed.–Sat. 10–5 and Sun. 1–5; Jan.–Mar., Sat. 10–5 and Sun. 1–5.*

Where Route 207 intersects with Route 32 in Vail's Gate is the **New Windsor Cantonment State Historic Site,** the last camp of Washington's army. Featured are exhibits, artillery displays, a blacksmith's shop, and military demonstrations. More than 10,000 soldiers, cooks, blacksmiths, and other camp followers constructed the log cabins, outbuildings, and the meeting hall where Washington quelled a mutiny by his troops who resented slow payment of wages and pensions. At the orientation center, a slide show illustrates the history of the area and the difficulties faced by the leaders and the troops. *Rtes. 300 and 32, Temple Hill Rd., Vails Gate, tel. 914/561–1765. Admission free. Open Apr.–Oct., Wed.–Sat. 10–5, Sun. 1–5.*

⑳ Take Route 207 east to Route 208 and then south to **Washingtonville.** Continue, following the signs for America's oldest winery, **Brotherhood.** More than 150 years old, the winery offers guided tours of its cavernous underground cellars. Tours end in a wine-tasting where hors d'oeuvres and a selection of pastries, cheeses, strudels, and quiches are also served. *Rte. 208, 35 North St., Washingtonville, tel. 914/496–9101. Admission: $3 adults, children under 21 free. Winery outlet open daily 11–6, year-round. Tours May–Oct., daily 11–6; Jan.–Apr. and Nov.–Dec., weekends noon–5.*

㉑ You can visit America's most distinguished and oldest military academy, **West Point,** by taking Route 94 west to Route 9W and then south. Situated on the bluffs overlooking the Hudson River, the Point has been the training ground for U.S. Army officers since 1802. Distinguished graduates include Robert E. Lee, Ulysses S. Grant, and Douglas MacArthur. There is a visitor center that shows an orientation movie. A museum at Thayer Hall houses one of the world's foremost collections of military memorabilia and equipment. Uniforms, weapons, field equipment, flags, and American military art are on display. On the grounds are memorials, cannons, and restored forts, such as Fort Putnam. *Rte. 9W, West Point, tel. 914/938–2638 or 5261. Admission free, but tours cost $3 adults, $2 children under 12. Open daily except major holidays 9–4:45.*

Constitution Island, a small island off the east shore of the Hudson, is separated from the mainland by marshes and can only be reached via a boat ride that leaves from West Point. The island played a critical role in General George Washington's strategy to keep the British naval traffic out of the Hudson River. During the Revolutionary War, the island had switched hands from American to British and then back to American. The British ships were stopped by an enormous iron chain that was stretched across the river from West Point to the island.

When the war ended in 1783, the barracks were decommissioned and the island returned to civilian control. However, the fort structure remains intact. Part of the present tour of the island includes a visit to the home of Susan and Anna Warner, sisters who were prolific writers under pseudonyms. The house has 15 rooms, all furnished in Victorian style. *Boats leave West Point's South Dock, Peekskill, tel. 914/446–8676. Cost: $5 adults, $4 senior citizens and students, $2 children under 5. Advance reservations required. Tours depart Wed. and Thurs. 1 and 2 PM.*

㉒ Cold Spring-on-Hudson, across from West Point, on the east side of the Hudson River, is a small 19th-century village in the heart of the Hudson Highlands. You can stroll in its quiet streets and antiques and crafts shops on your own, or join a guided walking tour of the historic district. *76 Main St. or write Box 71, Cold Spring-on-Hudson 10516, tel. 914/265–9060 or 800/232–4782. Donations accepted. Tours May–Nov., Sun. 2 PM.*

The **Hudson Valley Information Center & Gift Gallery** features gifts, mementos, hiking maps, postcards, travel guides and brochures, books, and even paintings—all dedicated to the Hudson Valley region. It's a good place to get oriented. *76 Main St., tel. 914/265–3060. Open Wed.–Mon. 9–5.*

Take Route 9D south to Garrison to visit **Boscobel,** an early 19th-century mansion that has been fully restored and furnished with the decorative arts of the Federal period (1800–1820), including elegant carpets, fine porcelains, and hand-carved furniture. Standing on a bluff surrounded by beautiful gardens with thousands of flowers that bloom in the spring, Boscobel affords a breathtaking view of the Hudson River. Concerts are held on the lawn throughout the summer. In the fall, apples from the Boscobel's orchards go on sale. *Rte. 9D, Garrison, tel. 914/265–3638. Admission: $5 adults, $4 seniors, $2.50 children under 14. Open Apr.–Oct. 9:30–5; Mar., Nov., and Dec. 9:30–4. Closed Tues.*

㉓ The **Garrison Art Center** is housed in a turn-of-the-century building facing the Hudson River, opposite the Garrison train station. The center's programs include an annual arts and crafts fair in August, as well as changing exhibits. Spring and fall auctions are held on the premises. *Garrison's Landing, Garrison, tel. 914/424–3960. Admission to the center is free, but $2 donations are usually requested for the annual fair. Open Mon.–Fri. 10–5; Sat. and Sun. noon–5; closed mid-Dec.–Mar.*

㉔ About 12 miles north on Route 9D in the town of **Beacon,** is the **Madam Brett Homestead,** a Dutch dwelling built in 1709 and visited by Washington, Lafayette, and Baron von Steuben. The furnishings reflect the lifestyles of the seven generations of the Brett family through 1954, when the Daughters of the American Revolution purchased the house. The 28,000-acre estate and gristmill were used to store military supplies during the Revolutionary War. There is original period furniture, Canton china, paintings, and a formal garden. The homestead is on the National Register of Historic Places. *50 Van Nydeck Ave., Beacon, tel. 914/831–6533. Admission: $2 adults, $1 children 13–18, 50¢ children under 12. Open May–Oct. weekends 1–4.*

A short distance away, **Howland Center,** a community arts center, is housed in an 1872 building designed by American architect Richard Morris Hunt. The center has a gallery for exhibits on art and history, a performance hall for concerts, dramatic productions, and dance, and a lecture hall. *477 Main St., Beacon, tel. 914/831-4988. Donations accepted. Gallery hours: Wed. and Sun. 1-5 and by appointment. Call for performance schedule.*

Ulster and Dutchess Counties

An appropriate place to begin touring the great estates of these two counties is **Hyde Park** and the **Franklin Delano Roosevelt National Historic Site.** The library and museum contain collections of manuscripts and personal documents displaying FDR's extensive career. Family photographs, gifts he received as president of the United States, his desk from the Oval Office, items dating from the period of his service in the U.S. Navy, letters, speeches, state documents, and official correspondence are on display. The large Roosevelt family house contains original furnishings. Tapes that feature the voice of Eleanor Roosevelt giving a tour of the home can be rented for $1.50. The rose gardens surrounding the gravesites of both Franklin and Eleanor Roosevelt are serene. The library is open only for research. *Rte. 9, Hyde Park, tel. 914/229-9115. Admission: $3.50 adults, senior citizens over 62, school groups, and children under 12 free. Open Apr.-Oct., daily 9-5; Nov.-Mar., Thurs.-Mon. 9-5, except major holidays.*

The only historic site in the nation devoted to a first lady is the **Eleanor Roosevelt National Historic Site** at nearby Val-Kill. Amid 172 acres of woods, the restored home of Eleanor Roosevelt is open for guided tours. Begin your visit by viewing the film biography, "First Lady of the World," followed by a tour of the Val-Kill cottage where Eleanor Roosevelt lived from 1945 to 1962. *249 Albany Post Rd. (RR. 9), Hyde Park, tel. 914/229-9115. Admission free. Open May-Oct., daily 9-5; Nov.-Dec., Mar.-Apr., weekends 10-4; closed Jan.-Feb.*

A short distance away on Route 9 in Hyde Park is the most respected cooking school in the United States, **The Culinary Institute of America (CIA),** founded in 1946. Located on a 75-acre campus overlooking the Hudson River, the institute is home to 1,850 students who are enrolled in a 21-month culinary arts program and more than 300 faculty and staff members. More than 90 chefs and instructors from 18 countries conduct courses in the fundamentals of cooking, charcuterie, American, Oriental, and international cuisines, with related courses in wines, table service, purchasing, stewarding, beverage control, and food service science.

The facilities include 18 commercially equipped production kitchens, five bakeshops, two food-preparation and demonstration auditoriums, a food and sanitation laboratory, meat room, 26,000-volume library, four residence halls, and eight instructional dining rooms including four student-staffed restaurants that are open to the public by reservation (*see* Dining).

Tours of the campus, designed primarily for prospective students, are conducted by appointment only, on Wednesdays when the school is in session, at 9:15 and 2:30. Tours are also available, by appointment, to small groups who have made reservations to dine at one of the school's restaurants; the fee for group tours is $2 per person.

After dining or taking a tour, visitors are free to visit the Culinary Institute's bookstore, and browse through the hundreds of titles of interest both to amateur and professional cooks. The shop is also a good source for kitchen accessories and baking aids. *For more information, contact The CIA, Rte. 9, Hyde Park 12538, tel. 914/471–6608. Bookstore open weekdays 10–7:45, Sat. 11:30–3:45.*

Northern Tour Head north on Route 9 for five miles to the town of **Staatsburg**
26 and follow signs for **The Mills Mansion,** the opulent country estate of Ogden and Ruth Livingston Mills. Original furnishings of the Louis XV and Louis XVI periods. Flemish tapestries, and Oriental porcelains embellish the oversized rooms of this mansion, which has panoramic views of the Hudson River Valley and the vast manicured acreage bordering the shoreline. Guided tours are available and hiking, picnicking, and cross-country skiing are encouraged. Special lawn concerts and workshops are held during the summer. *Old Post Rd., Staatsburg, tel. 914/889–4100. Admission free. Open May–Labor Day, Wed.–Sat. 10–5 and Sun. 1–5; Labor Day–Oct., Wed.–Sat. noon–5 and Sun. 1–5. Also special tours at Christmas time; call for schedule.*

Continue north on Route 9 for three miles and enter one of the
27 oldest villages in the country, **Rhinebeck. The Beekman Arms**
914 (1766), located here is purported to be the oldest inn in America
876– and was a meeting place for such famous people as George
1077 Washington and Franklin Roosevelt. Founded in 1688 and incorporated as a village in 1834, Rhinebeck contains a state historic district called White's Corner that has the town's second-oldest church, the Dutch Reformed built in 1802. Also in the area is the town post office, a Roosevelt-era WPA project that looks like a Dutch farmhouse. The district's Victorian-style buildings are charming, as are the antique shops, boutiques, and galleries that line the streets of the village center.

On Route 9 continue north for one mile and you will encounter the **Dutchess County Fairgrounds.** If you are lucky or smart enough to plan to be in the area during the second week of August, you can experience the Dutchess County Fair—the biggest and best in New York State—which has operated at the site every year since 1845 except during World War II. The event, created to promote agriculture in the area, lives up to its goals, exhibiting hundreds of different animals in the livestock shows, various kinds of food, an outdoor horse-racing track, plus an "old-fashioned" village. The Rhinebeck Crafts Fair is held at the fairgrounds in the month of June and two large antique fairs, one on Memorial Day weekend and one during the Columbus Day weekend, draw dealers and buyers from all over the county. *Rte. 9, Rhinebeck, tel. 914/876–4001. Admission: $5 adults, children under 12 free. Parking: $1. Open May–Oct.*

The **Old Rhinebeck Aerodrome** is three miles outside Rhinebeck Village—just follow the signs on Route 9. This museum has one of the largest collections of antique airplanes dating from 1900 through 1937. Many of these historic wonders are still flown in weekend air shows. Adventurous visitors can experience barnstorming rides in open-cockpit biplanes, such as a 1929 New Standard D-25, which carries up to four passengers. These 15-minute flights cost $20 per person. Rides book up early so call first thing in the morning. *42 Stone Church Rd., Rhinebeck, tel. 914/758–8610. Admission weekdays: $3 adults, $1 children under 10; weekends (includes an airshow): $7 adults, $3 children under 10. Open daily, mid-May–mid-Oct. 10–5, air shows at 2:30 weekends.*

Continue north on Route 9 to **Red Hook,** a village with many Federal- and Victorian-style homes and a number of fine antiques shops. In the center of the village, turn left onto Route **28** 9G. Turn right (north) and go three miles to **Annandale.** Take a left on Annandale Road and follow the signs to **Montgomery Place,** the Hudson Valley's newest great home to open its doors to the public. Situated on a 400-acre estate on the banks of the Hudson, Montgomery Place is a 23-room classical-revival mansion built in 1802–05 by Janet Livingston Montgomery, widow of the Revolutionary War hero, General Richard Montgomery. The interior, which is in the process of being restored, holds two centuries worth of family memorabilia as well as exquisite French china, chandeliers, leatherbound books, hand-carved furniture, ancestral portraits, and kitchen utensils. Tours are conducted regularly by uniformed docents. In addition, the sign-posted grounds offer views of the Hudson River and the Catskill Mountains, walking trails, gardens, woodlands, waterfalls, and an orchard of 5,000 fruit trees. (You can pick your own fruit in the autumn.) *Annandale-on-Hudson, tel. 914/758–5461. Admission: $5 adults, $4.50 seniors, $3 students under 18, children under 6 free. Open Apr.–Oct. daily 10–5 (except Tues.); Nov. and Dec., and Mar., weekends only 10–5; closed Jan. and Feb.*

Southern Tour **Poughkeepsie,** in the heart of Dutchess, New York's original **29** county, was founded in 1683. The Dutchess County Historical Society houses its collection in the **Clinton House** and the nearby **Glebe House,** two 18th-century buildings that served New York's fledgling government when it operated here in 1777. Three centuries of Hudson Valley history are documented by manuscripts, books, maps, photographs, art objects, and furnishings on display in these two historic houses. *Corner of Main and North White Sts., Poughkeepsie, tel. 914/471–1630. Admission free. Glebe House is open Wed.–Thurs. and Sun. 1–4; Clinton House, Mon.–Thurs. 9–3.*

Just down the road on Main Street in the Old City Hall is the **Mid Hudson Arts and Science Center (MASC),** a multi-arts service organization that organizes exhibitions and art shows throughout the year. The main floor contains two showcase galleries and the offices of the Summergroup Cooperative, a professional visual arts group that maintains a small gallery in the rear. The second floor is used by local theater and performing-art groups. *228 Main St., Poughkeepsie, tel. 914/471–1155. Donation: $1. Open Tues.–Sat. 11–3 and by appointment. Galleries closed Aug.*

Main Street intersects with Route 44/55 right off the Mid-Hudson Bridge. Head three miles west on Route 44 to Raymond Avenue and turn south to reach the **Vassar College Art Gallery.** Matthew Vassar not only broke new ground when he founded Vassar as a women's college in 1861, but he also was the first to include an art gallery and museum as part of an American college. The gallery owns 8,000 works of art, many of them Hudson River landscapes. There are also prints by Rembrandt and Whistler. After visiting the art museum, stop at the chapel to see the rare Tiffany glass windows. *Raymond Ave., Poughkeepsie, tel. 914/437–5235 or 914/437–5241. Admission free. Open Wed.–Sat. 10–5 and Sun. noon–5.*

Return to Route 44 and head east for 10 miles to the town of **Millbrook,** proceed 2½ miles past the town of South Millbrook and turn left on Tyrrel Road for **Innisfree Garden.** In this Oriental garden, designed in 1930 by Walter Beck, harmony and placement is valued more than color or species. Beck spent more than 22 years shaping the landscape to encompass streams, waterfalls, terraces, and rock walls. *Tyrrell Rd., Millbrook, tel. 914/677–8000. Admission: $2 weekends, free weekdays. Open May–Oct., Wed.–Fri. 10–4, weekends 11–5.*

Back in the town of Millbrook, turn left on Route 44A, the Sharon Turnpike. The **Mary Flagler Cary Arboretum** is headquartered in a red-brick building on the left, one mile north of Route 44. The Arboretum contains more than 1,900 acres of nature trails and plant collections, special horticultural displays, guided ecology walks, a greenhouse, and nursery. The **Institute of Ecosystem Studies,** which is a division of The New York Botanical Garden, is also located at the Arboretum. *Rte. 44, Millbrook, tel. 914/677–5359. Admission free; obtain an access permit at the Gifford House. Open year-round Mon.–Sat. 9–4, Sun. 1–4, with extended hours in summer. Closed major holidays.*

On Route 44, head east eight miles to Route 83, turn left and follow signs 5.5 miles to **Amenia** and the award-winning winery, **Cascade Mountain Vineyards.** There are daily tours of the winery and the vineyards, plus wine tastings. A restaurant on the grounds serves lunch (12–3) daily in summer, weekends during the rest of the year; and dinner by reservation on Saturday nights. *Flint Hill Rd., Amenia, 914/373–9021. Admission free. Open daily 10–6.*

Alternatively, from Route 44, proceed west to Taconic Parkway. Travel a mile north to Salt Point exit and follow the signs to **Clinton Vineyards** at **Clinton Corners.** Situated on a 100-acre farm, this winery produces the dry Seyval Blanc found in the top restaurants of the area, and Seyval Naturel, the Hudson Valley's first sparkling wine made in the French style of *méthode champenoise. Schultzville Rd., Clinton Corners, tel. 914/266–5372. Admission free. Tours and tastings, weekends 9–5 and by appointment.*

Take routes 22 and 55 back into Poughkeepsie and over the Mid-Hudson Bridge. Follow signs off the bridge for the New York State Thruway, the first right after the bridge. Stay on this road (Route 9W) until the intersection for Route 299 and follow Route 299 into **New Paltz.**

New Paltz offers a chance to see life as it was more than three centuries ago when the French Huguenots settled the area and founded the town in 1678. The **Huguenot Street Stone Houses** constitute some of the oldest streets in America with their original houses. A walking tour begins at an orientation center and visits six houses and a church where visitors can view a large collection of local artifacts, indigenous furniture, cos-

tumes, and portraits. The short tour takes 1½ hours, the long
tour is three hours. All the buildings are owned and maintained
by the Huguenot Historical Society. *18 Brodhead Ave., New
Paltz, tel. 914/255-1660. Admission: $5 adults, $1 children under 12. Open Memorial Day–late Sept., Wed.–Sun. 10–4.*

Take Route 299 six miles west of New Paltz over the Walkill
River into **Lake Mohonk** and then follow signs for the **Mohonk
Mountain House,** a resort located high above the Hudson River
Valley on several thousand unspoiled acres of the Shawangunk
Mountains. Built in 1869, Mohonk is furnished with Victorian
furniture and ornaments, and has oak paneling and floors. The
resort has a trout-stocked lake, and its gardens have won international awards. The mountains are ideal for hikers, bird-
watchers, golfers, ice-skaters, horseback riders, and cross-
country skiers. Day visitors are welcome for afternoon hikes or
a visit to the skytop observation tower. *Write Mohonk Mountain House, Lake Mohonk, New Paltz 12561, tel. 914/233-2244.
Admission to grounds: $6 weekends and $4 weekdays for
adults, $3 weekends and $2 weekdays for children under 12.
Open year-round, 7 AM–sunset.*

Five miles south of the turn for Mohonk Mountain House, via
Libertyville Road, is **Rivendell Vineyards** at **Chateau Georges
Winery,** one of the Hudson Valley's most acclaimed wineries.
The selection includes award-winning Chardonnays and blush
wines as well as cabernet sauvignon and unusual dessert
wines. Facilities include a tasting room with panoramic views
of the vineyards and farmlands, a gift shop, and picnic tables.
*714 Albay Post Rd., New Paltz, tel. 914/255-0892. Admission
free. Open for tours and tastings May–Sept., daily 10–6.*

In the middle of the village, take Route 32 to Route 213, and go
west into the town of **High Falls.** Turn right on Mohonk Road to
visit the **Delaware and Hudson Canal Museum.** The museum
commemorates the system of channels that was developed during the critical coal shortage brought on by the War of 1812.
Channels, locks, and structures that facilitated the transportation of coal on the Delaware River from the mountains of
Pennsylvania to New York City are displayed here. The D&H
Canal Historical Society has restored and preserved five locks
in the vicinity. They can be visited via a system of hiking trails.
At the museum ask for a copy of the self-guided 45-minute walk
and see the excellent collection of stonework, snubbing posts,
weirs, locks, and loading ships. *Mohonk Rd., High Falls, tel.
914/687-9311. Donation: $1. Open Memorial Day–Labor Day,
Mon., Wed.–Sat. 11–5, Sun. 1–5; May, Sept.–Oct., Sat. 11–5
and Sun. 1–5.*

Back on Route 213, head west to Route 209, then north for a
very scenic drive to **Hurley.** This village was established in 1651
by the Dutch and French Huguenot settlers who built wooden
homes along the Esopus Creek. After a short war with the
Esopus Indians that resulted in the burning of most of the
settlement, the homes were replaced with the **Hurley Stone
Houses,** of which 25 still stand. Hurley has the largest group of
stone houses remaining in the country. Hurley was also the
birthplace of the former-slave-turned-abolitionist Sojourner
Truth, the temporary seat of New York's capitol in 1777, and
the Jan Van Deusen House. A free brochure, available at the
library, banks, and most shops, describes the homes. Once a

year, on the second Saturday of July, the homes are open for tours. A festival is held in mid-August to celebrate the local sweet corn industry. *For more information, write Hurley Heritage Society, RR7, Box 100, Kingston 12401, tel. 914/338-7807. The annual house tours begin at 11 AM. Cost: $8.*

35 Route 209 north leads into **Kingston.** At the traffic circle take the second exit for Broadway. At the end of Broadway, make a right at the traffic light and follow the road to Clinton Avenue and the **Kingston Urban Cultural Park Visitors' Center.** Designated by New York State to preserve and develop urban settings with special historic and cultural interest, the center offers orientation displays on the entire Kingston area. Directions for self-guided walking tours are available, and guided tours can be arranged by appointment. *308 Clinton Ave., Kingston 12401, tel. 914/331-9506. Admission free. Open Mon. and Wed.-Sat. 11-5, Sun. 1-5, with shorter hours in off-season.*

From the center, you can walk to the **Senate House,** the meeting place of the first New York State Senate, in Kingston's historic stockade district. The state government had relocated upstate when it was forced to leave New York City during the Revolution. The house where the Senate meetings took place was built by a 17th-century Dutch settler, Wessel Ten Broeck. Tours of the historic house include an old kitchen with a huge stone fireplace, and the meeting room where the state constitution was created. There is also a museum building with 18th- and 19th-century paintings by Hudson Valley artists. One room of the museum contains works of Kingston native John Vanderlyn, considered o be one of the finest American painters of the 19th century. *312 Fair St., Kingston, tel. 914/338-2786. Admission free. Open Apr.-Dec., Wed.-Sat. 10-5 and Sun. 1-5; Jan.-Mar., Sat. 10-5 and Sun. 1-5.*

Take Broadway downtown to the **Hudson River Maritime Center** and **Rondout Landing** in the Rondout historic district. The port at the Rondout Landing was once a bustling area of boatyards and rigged lofts. The center opened in 1980 to preserve the heritage of the river. It comprises a visitor center, museum, several restored buildings, historic vessels, an exhibit hall displaying marine art, and a huge boat shop and rigging loft. Craftspeople restore boats at the river's banks. The 1898 steam tug, *Mathilda,* is docked here, and tours of the Kingston Lighthouse leave from the landing. Several special weekend festivals are held throughout the year, and there are art galleries and restaurants in the area. *1 Rondout Landing, Kingston, tel. 914/338-0071. Museum admission: $1 adults, 50¢ children. Open May-Oct., Tues.-Sun. noon-5.*

36 Back at the traffic circle, take Route 28 west 10 miles to the celebrated artist colony, **Woodstock.** Make a right turn off onto Route 375 and follow it a few miles until it ends, then make a left onto route 212 into the heart of the 200-year-old town. Woodstock has a long tradition of attracting creative people. In 1969, a music concert, actually held 50 miles away in Sullivan County, made Woodstock a rock-music legend. All the town's art galleries, theaters, unique shops, boutiques, and restaurants are easily reached by walking (*note:* parking is a problem on the main thoroughfare). The town has become somewhat commercial, but just the people-watching is interesting. *For more* *information, contact the Woodstock Chamber of Commerce, Box 36, Woodstock 12498, tel. 914/679–6234. In the summer months, an information booth is staffed on the main thoroughfare, Mill Hill Rd., at the intersection of Rtes. 212 and 375. Thurs.–Mon. 11:30–5, and on weekends during the rest of the year.*

37 Take Route 212 east 10 miles to a village that hangs a sign outside welcoming people: "Welcome to Friendly **Saugerties.**" This quaint village is much less expensive and crowded than Woodstock; it has a small but attractive town park by the water and good shops and restaurants.

38 Take Route 9W south from Saugerties a few miles to **West Park** where 170 acres of woodland, nature trails, and ponds comprise the **John Burroughs Nature Sanctuary.** The 19th-century nature observer and writer who led and influenced environmental conservation movements lived in a cabin known as Slabsides, creating some of his finest writing and illustrations. The grounds are open throughout the year. *Burroughs Dr., off Floyd Ackert Rd., West Park 12493, tel. 914/255–0108. Admission free. Open house for Slabsides is the third Sat. of May and first Sat. of Oct., 11–4; or by appointment, tel. 914/384–6813.*

Albany, Columbia, and Greene Counties

39 A good place to start exploring the upper region of the Hudson Valley is **Germantown** with a visit to **Clermont,** an estate that was home to seven generations of prominent Livingston families between 1728 and 1962. The historic house, gardens, and estate grounds have been restored to their 1930s appearance, and the setting offers magnificent views of the Hudson River. Special celebrations, including a sheep-shearing festival, a croquet day, a pumpkin festival, and a Hudson River steamboat festival, are held here throughout the year. *Off Rte. 9G, Germantown, tel. 518/537–4240. Admission free. The mansion is open May–Oct., Wed.–Sat. 10–5, Sun. 1–5, and on a reduced schedule at other times. The grounds are open all year, 8:30–sunset.*

40 Take Route 9G north on a scenic ride to **Hudson** to view the Persian-style castle created by artist Frederic Church, the foremost painter of the 19th-century Hudson River School. Church and his wife, Isabel, returned from Europe and the Middle East to build **Olana** or "our place on high." Picturesque grounds surrounding the villa offer panoramic vistas of the Hudson River Valley. The 37-room mansion features hand-painted tiles on the roof, turrets, and garden paths; rich Persian rugs; and hundreds of pieces of pottery and china as well as Egyptian wall paintings. *Rte. 9G, Hudson, tel. 518/828–0135. Admission: $1 adults, 50¢ children under 12. Reservations recommended. Open Memorial Day–Labor Day, Wed.–Sat. 10–4, Sun. 1–4, and Sept.–Oct., Wed.–Sat. 12–4, Sun. 1–4.*

41 Take Route 203 north to Chatham and then Route 66 northeast for a scenic drive to **Old Chatham.** Here, you'll find **The Shaker Museum,** dedicated to members of the sect of English men and women who immigrated to America in the late 18th century in order to practice their communal religion. Called "Shakers" because they danced and moved during worship services, the group established settlements throughout the new country.

The Shakers were known for being industrious, thrifty, and plain—attributes that are reflected in the artifacts and objects on display: chairs, seed packets, tin milk pails, brooms, clothing, cloaks, and another Shaker enterprise—pharmaceuticals. *Shaker Museum Rd., Old Chatham, tel. 518/794–9100. Admission: $5 adults, $4 seniors, $3 children 8–17, children under 8 free. Open May–Oct., daily 10–5.*

42 Take Route 398 heading west to **Kinderhook** for a visit to **Lindenwald,** the retirement home of Martin Van Buren, the eighth president of the United States. Van Buren was born in Kinderhook and returned here to purchase Lindenwald in 1839. The Federal-style house was built in 1797, and the mansion has been restored to reflect the original furnishings and architecture, complete with shutters, double chimneys, and arched windows. Today it is a National Historic Site. The house contains a fine collection of Van Buren memorabilia. *Rte. 9H, Kinderhook, tel. 518/758–9689. Admission: $1 adults, seniors over 62 and children under 12 free. Open May–Oct. daily 9–4:30; Nov., Tues.–Sun. hours vary.*

Also in Kinderhook is the **James Vanderpoel House,** an 1820 Federal-period house of the former prominent attorney, assemblyman, and judge. On display are early 19th-century furniture and decorative arts including a fine selection of paintings by local artists depicting Columbia County life. *16 Broad St., Kinderhook, tel. 518/758–1627. Admission: $2 adults, $1.25 seniors and children 12–18, children under 12 free. Open Memorial Day–Labor Day, Tues.–Sat. 11–5, Sun. 1–5.*

Columbia County Museum and Library is a complex established by the Columbia County Historical Society to interpret the 300-year history of the county. There is a gallery offering changing exhibits of paintings, costumes, photographs, and artifacts illuminating the county's cultural and historic heritage. *5 Albany Ave., Kinderhook, tel. 518/758–9265. Admission free. Open year-round, weekdays 10–4, weekends 1–5.*

Another beautiful drive is on Route 9J out of Kinderhook 15 **43** miles to **Rensselaer** to visit the **Crailo State Historic Site.** This museum, located in a house built by Hendrick Van Rensselaer in 1704, features the rich heritage of the Dutch in the upper Hudson River Valley. Exhibits detail such aspects of Dutch lifestyles as a cellar kitchen, herb garden, and riverside park. *9½ Riverside Ave., Rensselaer, tel. 518/463–8738. Admission free. Open Apr.–Nov., Wed.–Sat. 10–5 and Sun. 1–5, with shorter hours at other times.*

44 From Rensselaer, take Route 90 directly into **Albany.** Make your first stop the **Albany Visitors Center** at the Albany Urban Cultural Park. In addition to the information services available, there is a hands-on exhibit about the history of Albany, as well as walking and driving tours for adults and children. *Corner of Broadway and N. Pearl St., 25 Quakenbush Sq., Albany, tel. 518/434–6311. Hours change with the seasons; call for current hours.*

At the **Empire State Plaza** adjacent to the historic State Capitol, a half-mile concourse displays modern art and sculpture and an exciting architectural blend of government, business, and cultural buildings. There is an outdoor plaza, a skating rink, restaurants, and a 42nd-floor Observation Gallery. On site is the **New York State Museum** with life-size exhibits re-creating the natural and cultural history of New York. There are also changing fine-art exhibitions and special education and science exhibits for children. The **New York State Capitol** is one of the great examples of late 19th-century American public architecture. Built over a 33-year period, it combines the designs of five architects. The Capitol is currently being restored. *For information, contact Visitor Assistance NYSOGS, Concourse Level, Empire State Plaza, Albany 12242, tel. 518/474–2418. Admission free. Open daily 9–4.*

Centrally located in the city is the **Schuyler Mansion State Historic Site,** the 18th-century Georgian mansion of Philip Schuyler, a noted general of the American Revolution, who entertained George Washington and Benjamin Franklin at the estate. The elegant drawing room where his daughter Elizabeth married Alexander Hamilton is part of the guided tour. *32 Catherine St., Albany, tel. 518/434–0834. Admission free. Open Apr.–Dec., Wed.–Sat. 10–5, Sun. 1–5; days and times vary Jan.–Mar.; call to check.*

45 Take either the New York State Thruway south to Exit 21, or for a more scenic ride, take Route 9W south into the 150-year-old town of **Catskill,** which has long served as a stop for ships and sailors working on the Hudson River. There are walking tours offering interesting bits of history such as the Palmer-Willsey Ice House, one of the few surviving 19th-century commercial ice houses; the Catskill Inn, erected in 1797, and the Catskill Public Library, all combining 19th-century architectural styles. *For information, contact Greene County Promotion, NYS Thruway Exit 21, Catskill 12414, tel. 518/943–3223 or 800/542–2414. Open daily 9–5, with extended hours in summer.*

Right outside of Catskill in the small town of Lawrenceville is the **Catskill Game Farm,** one of the country's oldest and best-known game farms, which was built in 1933. Visitors can explore a zoological park housing rare and exotic animals such as lions, tigers, monkeys, elephants, and giant tortoises. There is a nursery for the baby animals and a petting zoo where you can feed tame deer and goats by hand. Trained bears, elephants, and dancing chickens also perform. *Located off Rte. 32 on Game Farm Rd., Catskill, tel. 518/678–9595. Admission: $9.50 adults, $5.50 children 4–12, children under 4 free. Open Apr. 15–Oct. 31, daily 9–6.*

46 Head south on Route 32, then west onto the Rip Van Winkle Trail, or Route 23A, to **Palenville.** The Interarts '89 Festival—World's Fair of the Arts, combining theater performances, dance, art classes, jazz, Dixieland shows, circus arts, magicians, and mimes—is scheduled throughout the summer months. *Woodstock Ave., off Rtes. 23A and 32A, Palenville, tel. 518/678–3332. Admission: $12 adults, $6 seniors and children under 12. Open July–Sept.*

Off the Beaten Track

Westchester County The **Museum of Cartoon Art,** about a mile northeast of Rye, was founded in 1974 by Mort Walker, the creator of Beetle Bailey. It is dedicated to the acquisition, preservation, and exhibition of all forms of cartoon art, including comic strips and comic books, book illustrations, caricatures, and animation. There are on-going and special exhibits and film and video programs. Visitors can buy original cartoon art from the museum's gallery, as well as less expensive items from the gift shop. *Comly Ave., Rye Brook, tel. 914/939-0234. Admission: $3 adults, $2 students and senior citizens, $1 children 5-12. Open Tues.-Fri. 10-4, Sun. 1-5.*

Near the Philipsburg Manor in North Tarrytown is the **Old Dutch Church of Sleepy Hollow,** one of the oldest churches in the Hudson Valley. Made famous in Washington Irving's *Legend of Sleepy Hollow,* the church is the only remaining example of 17th-century Dutch religious architecture in the United States. Stone walls surround furnishings typical of 17th- and 18th-century Netherlands. The grave of Washington Irving, a National Historic Landmark, is located on the grounds. *Rte. 9, North Tarrytown, tel. 914/631-1123 or write Friends of the Old Dutch Burying Ground, 35 South Broadway, Tarrytown 10591. Admission free.*

Rensselaer County The **Rensselaer County Junior Museum** offers everything from constellation shows in a Sky Dome Theater to reproductions of log cabins built in the 1800s. In addition, there are natural-science exhibits that include honeybees in a hive, live reptiles, and both salt- and freshwater aquariums. The main gallery of the museum features hands-on, interactive art, history, and science exhibits that change annually. *282 Fifth Ave., Troy, tel. 518/235-2120. Admission: $1.50, including shows. Open Sat.-Wed. 1-5.*

Ulster County Unusual, different, and unique are the words for **Opus 40,** "The Quarryman's Museum," described in its own pamphlet as a "monumental environmental sculpture rising out of an abandoned bluestone quarry." An artistic landscape, it is totally the work of sculptor Harvey Fite. The structure covers more than six acres and is made of more than 100 tons of finely fitted bluestone. Fite took more than 37 years to construct it. On the grounds is a museum built to house Fite's collection of quarryman tools and artifacts. Opus 40 is accessible by car from Exit 20, off the NYS Thruway, and Route 9W; follow signs to Opus 40. *7480 Fite Rd., Saugerties, tel. 914/246-3400. Admission: $3 adults, $2 for students and senior citizens. Open May-Oct., Mon., Wed.-Sat. 10-4, Sun. noon-5.*

In an area undergoing artistic resurgence, the town of Rosendale is home to several antiques shops and art galleries. Leader among these artistic adventurers is the **Women's Studio Workshop** which features photography, paintings, prints, woodwork, and sculpture shows by women artists. Head south on Route 32 from Kingston and turn right onto Route 213 in Rosendale. From there follow signs to the WSW at the Binnewater Arts Center. *Binnewater La., Rosendale, tel. 914/658-9133. Gallery open Tues.-Fri. 10-5, Sat. 12-4.*

Participant Sports

Fishing

The Hudson River Valley provides a wealth of fishing opportunities. The river is affected by the tides from the federal dam at

Troy, south to the Atlantic Ocean, providing an immense diversity of habitat and species.

Saltwater intrusion varies with the seasons; in the springtime, the saltwater line may be as far south as Yonkers, but in the fall and winter, saltwater has been found as far north as Hyde Park. Because of this, the Hudson River estuary contains a remarkable variety of fish, most notably American shad, fished at low slack tide from mid-April to early June, and striped bass, from June through November. Other species that are available, at various times, are black bass, small-mouth and large-mouth bass, and sturgeon. In addition, the lakes, ponds, and streams of the valley yield trout, pike, pickerel, and perch.

Almost everyone over 16 years old must have a license to fish in fresh waters, although no license is presently required for Hudson River fishing. For information on licenses, permits, or restrictions, as well as fishing hot spots and charts, contact the *New York State Department of Environmental Conservation (DEC), 21 S. Putt Corners Rd., New Paltz, NY 12561, tel. 914/ 255–5453; 50 Wolf Rd., Albany, NY 12233, tel. 518/457–3521; or Stony Kill Farm, Rte. 9D, Wappingers Falls, NY 12590, tel. 914/831–8780. Licenses can also be obtained at town and county clerks' offices, bait shops, and some sporting-goods stores.*

Golf

The fertile green hills and dales of the Hudson Valley make good golfing turf. In fact, this eight-county region has more than 50 golf courses that welcome visiting players. Lists and descriptions of the courses can be obtained by contacting the individual county tourist offices or area chambers of commerce.

Although many of the fairways are inland, there is one club that not only offers a golfing challenge, but also provides spectacular views of both the Hudson River and the distant Catskill Mountains—the 18-hole **Dinsmore Golf Course.** *Rte. 9, Staatsburg, tel. 914/889–4751. Open Apr.–Nov., daily.*

Two other outstanding, though not as scenic, courses are the 27-hole **Beekman Country Club** (Hopewell Junction, tel. 914/ 226–7700), open daily Apr.–Nov.; and the **James Baird State Park Golf Course** (Pleasant Valley, tel. 914/452–1489), an 18-hole championship course located off the Taconic State Parkway, open daily mid-Apr.–mid-Nov.

Winter Sports

Cross-country and downhill **skiing** are popular sports at a number of Hudson Valley locations, such as **Bear Mountain State Park** at Bear Mountain, **Rockefeller State Park Preserve** at North Tarrytown, the **Mills-Norrie State Park** at Staatsburg, the **Clermont State Historic Site** at Germantown, and **Olana State Historic Site** at Hudson.

In addition, **ice skating** is available at some park locations, as are **ice fishing, ice boat sailing,** and **snowmobiling.** For up-to-date information, contact the **Hudson River Valley Association** (76 Main St., Cold Spring-on-Hudson 10516, tel. 914/265–3066).

Two downhill skiing areas—the **Catskill Mountains** and the **Berkshires**—are also easily accessible from the Hudson Valley.

Dining

Highly recommended restaurants in each price category are indicated by a star ★.

Category	Cost*
Expensive	over $40
Moderate	$20–$40
Inexpensive	under $20

per person without tax (8¼%), service, or drinks

Westchester and Rockland Counties

Ardsley **Cantina.** Set in a beautiful, 100-year-old stone building overlooking Woodlands Lake, this restaurant's specialties are Mexican food and fresh fish; outdoor dining is featured in the summer months. *Saw Mill River Pkwy., tel. 914/693–6565. Dress: casual to neat. Reservations suggested. AE, MC, V. Moderate.*

Ship's Galley. This family-owned and -operated restaurant specializes in seafood dishes including trout, red snapper, salmon, bouillabaisse, and zuppa di pesce. The pasta is homemade and delicious. *5 Village Green, Rte. 9A, tel. 914/693–4878. Dress: casual. Reservations suggested. AE, DC, MC, V. Dinner only weekends and June–Aug. Inexpensive.*

Chappaqua **Crabtree's Kittle House.** A 200-year-old country house is the setting for this delightful restaurant, run by Dick and John Crabtree. The menu features American and Continental cuisine, with such dishes as shrimps Madagascar, roast duckling, rack of lamb, veal medallions, and daily seafood specials. *Kittle Rd. off Rte. 117, tel. 914/666–8044. Jacket or neat attire required. Reservations suggested. AE, CB, DC, MC, V. Dinner only Sat. Expensive.*

Congers **Bully Boy Chop House.** Specializing in steaks, chops, and seafood with an English touch, this restaurant is renowned for its prime ribs, rack of lamb, English pies, and Yorkshire pudding. There are seven dining rooms, some of which overlook a lovely pond with ducks. Other rooms are quite elegant with plush red carpeting. Homemade scones are served with butter and honey. *117 Rte. 303, tel. 914/268–6555. Dress: casual. Reservations suggested. AE, DC, MC, V. Dinner only weekends. Moderate.*

Romolo's. Veal dishes are the specialty here. Try the veal Verbena or scaloppine with white asparagus, prosciutto, and fresh mozzarella in wine sauce. If you prefer steak, order the filet mignon Zingara, sauteed in marsala wine with cream, ham, and mushrooms. The atmosphere is warm and friendly, a true Italian family restaurant. *Rte. 303 and Tremont Ave., tel. 914/268–3770/9855. Dress: casual. Reservations suggested. AE, CB, DC, MC, V. Closed Mon., dinner only weekends. Moderate.*

Dobbs Ferry **The Chart House.** This is a contemporary restaurant with magnificent views of the Palisades, the Tappan Zee Bridge, and the New York City skyline. The all-American specialties include prime ribs, thick steaks, and an enormous selection of seafood.

Mud pie is the preferred dessert. *High St., tel. 914/693–4131. Dress: casual chic. No reservations. AE, CB, DC, MC, V. Dinner and Sunday brunch only. Moderate.*

Hartsdale   **Auberge Arenteuil.** Set in a former 1920s speakeasy, this French restaurant is hidden high up in a wooded area overlooking Central Avenue. Specialties include lobster bisque, chicken with tarragon or raspberry vinegar, and veal with wild mushrooms. *42 Healy Ave., tel. 914/948–0597. Dress: casual. Reservations suggested. AE, MC, V. Dinner only weekends. Closed Mon. Expensive.*

Hawthorne   **Gasho of Japan.** Housed in a 400-year-old farmhouse, this Japanese restaurant is surrounded by three acres of lush Oriental gardens. The menu includes hibachi steak, chicken, and seafood prepared at individual tables. *2 Saw Mill River Rd., tel. 914/592–5900. Proper attire required. Reservations suggested. AE, CB, DC, MC, V. Moderate.*

Montrose   **India House Restaurant.** Lots of greenery surrounds this restaurant decorated to resemble a colorful tent. Dining rooms are covered with antique Indian tapestries. The specialties are Tandoori lamb, chicken, or shrimp. The vegetarian entrees are also excellent and can be prepared mild, spicy, or hot. *199 Albany Post Rd., tel. 914/736–0005. Dress: casual. Reservations accepted for parties of 6 or more. Dinner only; closed Tues. AE. Moderate.*

Mt. Kisco   **La Camelia.** Located in a 140-year-old restored clapboard house on the north side of town, this restaurant combines an old-world ambience with a mostly Spanish menu. Specialties include paella Valenciana with saffron rice, grilled shrimp in lobster sauce, and a variety of tempting tapas. *234 N. Bedford Rd., tel. 914/666–2466. Dress: neat attire. Reservations suggested, especially on weekends. AE, CB, DC, MC, V. Closed Mon. Dinner only weekends. Moderate.*

North Salem   **Auberge Maxime.** A restored country inn is the setting for this
★   classic French restaurant. There is a fixed price for five-course dinners. Specialties include duck prepared with various sauces and hot or cold soufflés. *Rte. 116, tel. 914/669–5450. Jackets required. Reservations suggested. AE, MC, V. Closed Wed., dinner only Sat. Expensive.*

Piermont   **The Turning Point.** This is a great place to relax and listen to live music, Wednesday–Sunday. Dinner specialties include poached salmon with tarragon and sautéed mushrooms, and there are always several vegetarian choices on the menu, along with 15 herbal teas and 20 types of beer. Sunday brunch features buttermilk pancakes, vegetarian omelets, or French toast. *468 Piermont Ave., tel. 914/359–1089. Dress: casual. Reservations suggested. AE, DC, MC, V. Brunch only Sun. Moderate.*

Pound Ridge   **The Inn at Pound Ridge.** Four American presidents have dined at this restaurant within the last 40 years. The original building dates back to 1883. Specialties include prime ribs, rack of lamb, roast duckling, and fresh seafood. *Rte. 137, tel. 914/764–5779. Jackets requested. Reservations suggested. AE, CB, DC, MC, V. Closed Tues., dinner only weekends. Moderate.*

Port Chester   **The Oasis.** International art fills the walls of this trendy enclave. The eclectic menu features "new American" versions of breast of duck, stuffed veal, grilled swordfish, and a variety of pastas. *23 N. Main St., tel. 914/939–7220. Dress: casual. Reservations suggested. AE, MC, V. Lunch weekdays, dinner Tues.–Sun. Moderate.*

Rye Brook **Mallard's at Arrowwood.** Reminiscent of a late 19th-century
★ gentlemen's club, this restaurant is rich with mahogany wainscoting, sterling-silver wall sconces, etched mirrors, and wildlife paintings. The American menu offers such choices as hickory-roasted duckling, blackened tenderloin of beef, poached striped bass, and lobster and scallop ravioli. *Anderson Hill Rd., tel. 914/939–5500. Jackets required. Reservations required. AE, CB, DC, MC, V. Closed Sun. and Mon., dinner only Sat. Expensive.*

Scarsdale **Il Cigno.** Owned and operated by the DePietro family for many years, this restaurant features grilled wild mushrooms, duck ravioli, fresh fennel, endive salad, and filet mignon with walnuts and gorgonzola. *1505 Weaver St., tel. 914/472–8484. Jackets preferred. Reservations suggested. AE, CB, DC, MC, V. Closed Mon. and 2 wks in July. Moderate.*

South Salem **Le Chateau.** Set on a 32-acre estate with a lake, gardens, and
★ woodlands, this elegant restaurant—in a Tudor mansion built by J. P. Morgan in 1907—has a turn-of-the-century ambience and a classic French menu. Entrees include rack of lamb, Muscovy duck in cherry port sauce, and venison with white raisins and green peppercorns. Cocktails are served on the terrace in the summer. *Rte. 35 at junction of Rte. 123, tel. 914/533–6631. Jacket required. Reservations required. AE, CB, DC, MC, V. Lunch Tues.–Fri., dinner Tues.–Sun. Expensive.*

Spring Valley **La Capannina.** The name of this restaurant means "little house
★ in the country" and gives a clue to its setting—an 18th-century Dutch home in the historic Haring Homestead. It is nestled amid seven acres of gardens with a duck pond and waterfall. The menu is mostly French and Italian, and daily blackboard specials often include rack of lamb, duckling, calves liver, or sweetbreads; for dessert, with a little advance notice, you can enjoy crepes Suzette, cherries jubilee, or sabayon. *606 S. Pascack Rd., tel. 914/735–7476. Jackets required. Reservations accepted. AE, CB, DC, MC, V. Closed Sun. Dinner only Sat., lunch only Mon. Expensive.*

Tappan **Giulio's.** Fine northern Italian cuisine is served in this 100-year-old Victorian house, which features romantic candlelight settings at dinner and a strolling vocalist or guitarist on Friday evenings. The *Valdostana Vitelle,* or veal stuffed with prosciutto and cheese in a champagne sauce, and the scampi Giulio, or jumbo shrimp sautéed with fresh mushrooms, are the house specialties. *154 Washington St., tel. 914/359–3657. Jackets preferred. Reservations recommended. AE, CB, DC, MC, V. No lunch weekends. Moderate.*

Tarrytown **Horsefeathers.** Dark-paneled walls and an antique bar distinguish this restaurant which features great hamburgers and steaks, barbecued baby-back ribs, overstuffed sandwiches, and rich New England clam chowder. The atmosphere is casual and comfortable. *94 N. Broadway, tel. 914/631–6606. Dress: casual. Reservations accepted for parties of 5 or more. No credit cards. Closed Sun. Moderate.*

Tuckahoe **Salerno's.** For more than 20 years, this family-run restaurant has been "the place" in lower Westchester for prime beef, lamb, and fresh seafood, as well as pastas and Italian specialties. *100 Main St., tel. 914/793–1557. Dress: casual. No reservations. MC, V. Dinner only. Closed Mon., 1 wk in Feb., and last 2 wks of Aug. Moderate–Expensive.*

Valley Cottage **Cottage Cafe.** This family-run seafood restaurant serves such dishes as seafood Fra Diavolo, which is a combination of mussels, clams, scallops, shrimp, and pasta. All desserts are made on the premises; try the chocolate cheesecake, peanut butter pie, or Swiss chocolate layer cake. *2 Lake Ridge Plaza, Rte. 303, tel. 914/268–3993. Dress: casual. Reservations suggested on weekends. AE, CB, DC, MC, V. Dinner only weekends. Moderate.*

White Plains **Quarropas.** The name means "white swamp," which is the original name for White Plains. The dining room contains a collection of antique American packing-crate labels and food ads. Specialties include ravioli filled with shrimp, crab, and escarole, and for dessert walnut strudel. *478 Mamaroneck Ave., tel. 914/684–0414. Dress: informal. Reservations required on weekends, appreciated on weekdays. AE, CB, DC, MC, V. Closed Mon. Dinner only Sat. Moderate.*

Orange and Putnam Counties

Cold Spring **Plumbush Inn.** Dating to 1867, this lovely inn is furnished in an
★ opulent Victorian style. It offers dining by candlelight amid a decor of rose-patterned wallpaper, dark oak paneling, paintings by local artists, and the warmth of wood-burning fireplaces. In summer there is also outdoor dining on a porch overlooking the gardens. The menu ranges from fresh seafood and veal to Swiss specialties, with both fixed-price and à la carte services. The inn also has three guest rooms with bath upstairs, if you want to plan an overnight. *Rte. 9D, tel. 914/265–3904. Jackets required in evening. Reservations suggested. AE, CB, DC, MC, V. Closed Mon. and Tues. Expensive.*

Breakneck Lodge. A restaurant for more than 50 years, this cozy old-world Swiss-Tudor lodge overlooks the Hudson River and Storm King Mountain. The menu features fresh seafood, beef, veal, and game, plus Austrian, Swiss, and German dishes. *Rte. 9D, Old River Rd., tel. 914/265–9669. Dress: neatly casual. Reservations suggested, especially on weekends. AE, DC, MC, V. Moderate.*

Dockside Harbor. Hard by the banks of the Hudson, this restaurant is at its best on the lazy, hazy days of summer. Depending on the weather, you can choose either indoor or outdoor dining, with varying riverside views. There is also music on the lawn each Sunday afternoon. The menu focuses primarily on seafood, steaks, and chops. *1 North St., tel. 914/265–3503. Dress: casual. Reservations suggested. AE, MC, V. Hours vary, check in advance. Moderate.*

Cornwall- **Painter's Tavern.** In the center of the village on the Square, this
on-Hudson Art Deco restaurant has a splendid display of paintings by local artists. The decor also features memorabilia and antiques from the area. The ever-changing chalkboard menu is equally eclectic, with a medley of regional and international selections, such as Cajun shrimp, chili and Mexican chicken, blackened steak, seafood diablo over pasta, surf and turf, scallops Dijonaise, as well as burgers, salads, and steaks. Most dishes owe their spe-

cial flavors to an herb garden behind the restaurant. *Rte. 218, tel. 914/534–2109. Dress: casual. Reservations suggested for weekends. AE, CB, DC, MC, V. Moderate.*

Garrison **The Bird and Bottle Inn.** Established in 1761, this spot was once
★ a major stagecoach stop along the route from New York to Albany. Today it has three dining rooms, all with wood-burning fireplaces. The Colonial ambience is enhanced by candlelit table settings, antiques, old prints, beamed ceilings, and wideplank floors. The menu choices include roast pheasant, rack of lamb, salmon Wellington, and fillet of sole poached in wine; and be sure to sample the special pumpkin bread. Desserts are also very tempting, from butter pecan soufflés to chocolate rum tortes. Open for dinner only and Sunday brunch, all meals are five courses and fixed price. *Old Albany Post Rd. (Rte. 9) at Nelson's Corners Rd., tel. 914/424–3000. Jacket required. Reservations advised. AE, DC, MC, V. Closed Mon., Tues. Expensive.*

★ **Xavier's at the Highland Country Club.** This elegant French restaurant sits in a country setting, surrounded by a golf course. Fresh flowers, crystal, and silver adorn each table, and on weekends there is background music by a harpist or pianist. In the summer, outdoor dining is also available on a covered terrace overlooking the putting greens. The menu changes often, but top entrees are grilled quail over pasta, medallions of rabbit with white grapes, and grilled Norwegian salmon basted with honey and Chinese mustard. *Rte. 9D, tel. 914/424–4228. Jackets required. Reservations required. No credit cards. Closed Mon. Dinner only Tues.–Sat. Expensive.*

New Windsor **Brewster House.** A registered landmark, this Colonial-era fieldstone inn dates back to 1762, and the decor features the original beams, floors, and doors. House specialties include lobster, barbecued shrimp, smoked fish, and pasta. There is also a raw bar, and piano entertainment on weekends. *Temple Hill Rd., tel. 914/561–1762 or 914/562–2018. Dress: casual. Reservations suggested. AE, CB, DC, MC, V. Closed Mon. Dinner only weekends. Moderate.*

Patterson **L'Auberge Bretonne.** This is a cozy French restaurant with a dining room enhanced by wood-beamed ceilings and large windows overlooking the foothills of the Berkshires. The menu changes constantly, but specialties often include breast of duck with a honey-mustard sauce, roast saddle of lamb in a puff pastry, and sea scallops Veronique. *Rte. 22, tel. 914/878–6782. Dress: neatly casual. Reservations required for weekends. AE, CB, DC, MC, V. Closed Wed. Expensive.*

Sugar Loaf **Barnsider Tavern.** This restaurant offers a choice of dining settings, including a rustic taproom with hand-wrought beams and country furnishings and a glass-enclosed patio that overlooks the Sugar Loaf crafts community. During the winter months, there is always a warming fire in the hearth. The menu is fairly simple, with steaks, burgers, quiches, chili, soups, and salads. *Kings Hwy., tel. 914/469–9810. Dress: casual. No credit cards. Moderate.*

Warwick **Warwick Inn.** Owned and operated by the Wilson family for a quarter of a century, this 165-year-old home contains original moldings, fireplaces, and furnishings. The menu offers a variety of seafood, from baked stuffed shrimp to broiled swordfish, as well as prime ribs and fresh turkey. *36 Oakland Ave., tel.*

914/986–3666. Dress: casual. Reservations suggested. AE, MC, V. Closed Mon. and Tues. Dinner only. Expensive.

Dutchess and Ulster Counties

High Falls   **DePuy Canal House.** Dating back to 1797 and originally a tav-
★ ern, this stone house is now the domain of John Novi, a chef ranked by a leading national magazine as "the father of American nouvelle cuisine." The menu, which offers fixed-price, three- or seven-course dinners, changes weekly; and features such dishes as rabbit pâté with pine nuts or poached sole with salmon and red-pepper mousse, as well as fresh fruits with goat cheese from nearby farms. An à la carte menu is also available. The wine cellar boasts more than 100 different wines from the Hudson Valley. *Rte. 213, tel. 914/687–7700. Dress: neatly casual. Reservations required. AE, MC, V. Closed Mon.–Wed. Dinner only Thurs.–Sun. Expensive.*

Highland   **Mariner's Harbor.** This restaurant overlooks the Hudson, with indoor and outdoor seating. It is popular with visiting celebrities such as Phil Rizzuto. Specialties are lobster, seafood combination platters, and steaks. *45 River Rd., tel. 914/691–6011. Dress: casual. No reservations. AE, CB, DC, MC, V. Moderate.*

Hopewell Junction   **Le Chambord.** You'll find this award-winning French restau-
★ rant northeast of Fishkill, in southern Dutchess County less than a mile east of the Taconic Parkway. It is housed in a restored 1863 Georgian-Colonial home that is furnished with fine paintings and antiques. The menu focuses on inventive dishes such as bay scallops with mushrooms and escargot, breast of chicken provençal, beef Stroganoff with fettuccine, salmon with truffles, chateaubriand with béarnaise, and seafood with fine herb sauces. There are nine rooms with bath upstairs for overnight guests. *Rte. 52 and Carpenter Rd., 12533, tel. 914/221–1941. Jackets recommended. Reservations recommended. AE, DC, MC, V. Dinner only weekends. Expensive.*

Hyde Park   **The Culinary Institute of America,** or CIA (*see* Exploring), located on Route 9, has four restaurants for public dining. *Tel. 914/471–6608 weekdays 9–5. Jackets and reservations are required for each venue. AE, DC, MC, and V. All are closed on school holidays and the first 3 wks of July.*

★ **The Escoffier.** This award-winning restaurant is the domain of students in their final semester at the school who practice the preparation and serving of classical haute cuisine. The menus are fixed-price or à la carte and the standards are impeccable— so much so, in fact, that the restaurant is often fully booked a month or more in advance, especially for weekends. *Closed Sun., Mon. Expensive.*

American Bounty. The focus here is on an à la carte service of American regional fare, including southern specialties like crawfish pie or shrimp etoufée and midwestern game dishes. *Closed Sun., Mon. Moderate–Expensive.*

Caterina de Medici. Regional Italian cuisine—both modern and traditional—is the focus here at the smallest of the CIA's four dining rooms, so space is very limited and the menu is fixed-price. *Lunch: one seating at 11:30, dinner: one seating at 6. Closed weekends. Moderate–Expensive.*

St. Andrew's Cafe. This is the most informal of the four CIA restaurants, offering à la carte service of well-balanced meals prepared according to sound nutritional guidelines. *Closed weekends. Moderate.*

Kingston   **Armadillo Bar and Grill.** Located in the historic Rondout district, this relaxed restaurant serves mostly southwestern and Mexican cuisine. Specialties include fresh grilled seafood, shrimp-stuffed jalapeños, *fajita* steaks, and frozen margaritas. There is both outdoor and indoor dining, depending on the season. *97 Abeel St., tel. 914/339–1550. Dress: casual. Reservations suggested for 6 or more (on weekends, smaller parties should phone 45 minutes in advance to check availability). AE, DC, MC, V. Closed Mon. Dinner only weekends. Moderate.*

City Hotel. Housed in a building dating back to 1905, this is one of Kingston's newest restaurants, in the heart of the business district. The decor of the dining room reflects the turn of the century, with deep-toned wood paneling, brass lamps, and stained glass. American regional cuisine is featured, with such entrees as steak au poivre, fettuccine carbonara, Yankee pot roast, roast pork stuffed with apples, barbecued baby-back ribs, and Louisiana blackened shrimp. *11 Main St., tel. 914/ 338–7070. Dress: casual. Reservations suggested. MC, V. Closed Sun. Dinner only Sat. Moderate.*

★ **Skytop Steak and Seafood House.** Panoramic views of the Hudson Valley are part of the attraction at this hilltop restaurant, located a quarter mile from Exit 19 of the New York State Thruway. The menu features steaks and meats grilled over a charcoal pit, fresh seafood including lobsters from a tank, and an all-you-can-eat salad bar. There is live entertainment Tuesday through Saturday. *Rte. 28, tel. 914/338–6161. Dress: casual. AE, CB, DC, MC, V. Dinner only. Moderate.*

Poughkeepsie   **Caesar's Ristorante.** As might be expected, the Caesar salads at this fine, northern Italian restaurant are exceptional, as is the antipasto. There are also many fine pasta, beef, chicken, and veal dishes on the menu. You'll find this restaurant in the heart of the historic district, directly under the Poughkeepsie Railroad Bridge. *2 Delafield St., tel. 914/471–4857. Dress: casual. Reservations not accepted. AE, CB, DC, MC, V. Dinner only. Moderate.*

John L's. Located in an early 1800s farmhouse about three miles east of the city, this restaurant has a warm and rustic atmosphere and a contemporary menu of mesquite-grilled fish, baby-back ribs, steak, prime ribs, and seafood. There is also a salad bar. *522 Dutchess Tpke. (Rte. 44), tel. 914/471–6660. Dress: casual. Reservations accepted except on Fri. and Sat. AE, DC, MC, V. Dinner only. Moderate.*

River Station. "Down by the riverside" dining is the theme of this informal restaurant overlooking the Hudson. You can enjoy river views either from the inside dining room or the outdoor deck. Specialties include seafood, veal, steak, and pasta. *25 Main St., tel. 914/452–9207. Dress: casual. Reservations not accepted on weekends. MC, V. Moderate.*

Red Hook   **Greene & Bresler Ltd.** This contemporary shopfront restaurant in the heart of town serves creative American and European cuisine, with such dishes as apple-smoked turkey and brie, smoked fish, charcoal-grilled filet of beef, Norwegian salmon, pastas, and a wide variety of colorful salads. In summer, tables are set up on an outside deck. *29 W. Market St., tel. 914/758– 5992. Dress: casual. Reservations suggested. AE, MC, V.*

Lunch and dinner daily in summer, with reduced schedule at other times. Moderate.

Duffy's Tavern. On the main floor of the Red Hook Inn (*see* Lodging), this old world restaurant has a decor with an Irish theme. You can dine beside the brick fireplace or by one of the windows overlooking the main thoroughfare of the village. The straightforward menu features steaks, ribs, honey-dipped chicken, corned beef, and seafood. *31 S. Broadway, tel. 914/ 758–8445. Dress: casual but neat. Reservations suggested. No credit cards. Closed Mon. Inexpensive–Moderate.*

Tivoli Garden. This bright, airy, plant-filled restaurant in the middle of the village has windows looking out onto the main thoroughfare (Rte. 9). Open for breakfast, lunch, and dinner, it's an ideal spot for a light meal, salad, quiche, casserole, sandwich, or just a cup of coffee. *10 S. Broadway, tel. 914/758–6902. Dress: casual. No reservations. AE, MC, V. Closed Tues., brunch only Sun. Inexpensive.*

Rhinebeck

★ **The Beekman Arms.** This historic spot, renowned as one of the nation's oldest hotels (*see* Lodging), presents a choice of four different dining rooms, starting with the **1776 Tap Room** which was the original bar and restaurant in Colonial days. It still has the 20-foot wooden benches from George Washington's day, as well as walls filled with old prints, deeds, maps, muskets, mugs, sabers, powder horns, and corncob pipes. At the south end of the Tap Room is the candlelit **Wine Cellar**, a cozy blend of old barrels, beams, and brick, with booth-style seating. The adjacent **Pewter Room** has a warm country-inn atmosphere, with a handsome corner cupboard, chiming clocks and prints on the walls. The fourth dining area is the conservatory-style **Greenhouse**, brimming with flower boxes and hanging plants. It faces the front lawn of the hotel and looks out onto Rhinebeck's main thoroughfare. No matter where you sit, however, the menu is the same, with emphasis on American regional fare. Entrees include pan roast of shrimp and scallops, blackened salmon filet, grilled apricot-ginger chicken, and pork medallions with Husdon Valley apples. *4 Mill St. (Rte. 9), tel. 914/876–7077. Dress: neatly casual. Reservations suggested. AE, DC, MC, V. Moderate–Expensive.*

★ **Le Petit Bistro.** Situated in the heart of Rhinebeck less than a block from the Beekman Arms, this is a small and intimate restaurant with a French ambience, artfully prepared food, and enthusiastic service. It is run by Yvonne and Jean-Paul Croizer, previously associated with the catering department of Air France and leading restaurants in New York City and the Hudson Valley. Featured dishes include duck with fruits, Dover sole, seafood crepes, coquilles St. Jacques, coq au vin, steak au poivre, and sautéed softshell crab in season. Desserts range from feather-light meringues to velvety fondues or *creme brulées.* The crusty breads and rich ice creams are made locally. *8 E. Market St., tel. 914/876–7400. Dress: neatly casual. Reservations suggested. AE, CB, DC, MC, V. Closed Tues. and Wed. Dinner only. Moderate–Expensive.*

Chez Marcel. Located less than two miles north of Rhinebeck, this French country inn is the domain of Renee and Marcel Disch (formerly of Chez Renee in Manhattan). Everything is cooked to order, and the menu includes such choices as sole *bonne femme,* chicken almondine, veal *cordon bleu,* and a delicately seasoned rack of lamb. *Rte. 9, tel. 914/876–8189. Dress:*

neatly casual. Reservations suggested. AE, DC. Closed Mon.
Dinner only. Moderate.

Mariko's. This is an authentic Japanese restaurant, specializing in "Tokyo nouvelle cuisine." The menu includes a full selection of sushi and sashimi, as well as yakitori, tempura, sukiyaki, and teriyaki entrees. Some unique dishes include softshell-crab tempura, vegetarian tofu delight, and "sushi 101," an introductory seven-piece assortment of sushi. There is Japanese flute on many Sunday evenings. Mariko's is located two miles north of Rhinebeck, one mile past the intersection of routes 9 and 9G. *Rte. 9, tel. 914/876–1234. Dress: neatly casual. Reservations suggested. MC, V. Closed Tues. Dinner only. Moderate.*

Fox Hollow Inn. Freshly made pasta and other Italian dishes are the specialties at this rustic restaurant, located in a converted country inn about two miles south of the village. Owned and operated by the LaRocca family for 35 years, this spot is also known for steaks and shellfish and thick cuts of prime ribs. *Rte. 9, tel. 914/876–4696. Dress: casual. Reservations usually not necessary, except weekends. MC, V. Closed Tues. Moderate–Inexpensive.*

Foster's Coach House. The site of this restaurant-pub was once the home of a Revolutionary War drillmaster who so loved his horse that he gave the animal a proper funeral when it died. You'll not only see hitching posts on the sidewalk outside and horse prints and racing scenes on the walls within, but you can also sit at a table in a horse stall or place a call from a phone booth fashioned from a horse-drawn carriage. The atmosphere is informal and the menu concentrates on burgers, steaks, and salads. It's in the heart of town, one block north of the Beekman Arms and adjacent to Upstate Films. *22 Montgomery St., tel. 914/876–8052. Dress: casual. No credit cards. Reservations not accepted. Closed Mon. Inexpensive.*

Schemmy's. For a light snack, lunch, or coffee, don't miss this old-fashioned ice cream parlor (with a wrought-iron ice cream cone hanging over the front door). Situated in the center of the village, it is a real Rhinebeck institution that used to be Schermerhorn's Drug Store. You'll see a wall lined with original medicine drawers, apothecary jars, and other local memorabilia. The menu features sandwiches, burgers, quiches, soups, salads, and homemade ice cream in assorted flavors. *19 E. Market St., tel. 914/876–6215. Dress: casual. No credit cards. Open daily 7 AM–5 PM. Inexpensive.*

Woodstock **Christy's.** Housed in an authentic gate house, this charming English-style restaurant has a two-sided fireplace, beamed ceilings and a cozy tap room. Fine artwork by local talent fills the walls. The house specialties include baked smoked chicken with a honey-mustard glaze, roast duck and orange sauce, and fresh local seafood. *85 Mill Hill Rd., tel. 914/679–5300. Dress: casual. Reservations not normally accepted. No credit cards. Closed Sun. and Mon. Dinner only. Moderate.*

Deming Street Trattoria. For a Northern Italian ambience and menu, this midtown restaurant is a good choice. Selections include veal scaloppine with lemon butter, salmon with artichoke and pine nuts, seafood primavera, and a variety of pastas. A guitarist plays on weekends. *4 Deming St., tel. 914/679–7858. Dress: casual. Reservations suggested. AE, CB, DC, MC, V. No dinner weekends. Moderate.*

Albany, Columbia, and Greene Counties

Albany **L'Auberge.** Situated in a historic building that once housed the
★ ticket office of the Hudson River Dayliner (circa 1907), the decor of this restaurant is a blend of rustic dark woods and
romantic pink fabrics and fixtures. Proprietor Nicole Plisson, a
native of the Loire Valley and a former cooking-school instruc-
tor, strives to maintain a distinctive menu, including such
specialties as Muscovy duck, goat-cheese ravioli, ragout of
snails, roast quail, scallop mousse, loin of veal, and French pastries. It is located just south of the state university at the foot of
State Street hill. *351 Broadway, tel. 518/465-1111. Jackets
preferred. Reservations suggested. AE, CB, DC, MC, V.
Closed Sun. Dinner only Sat. Expensive.*

Jack's Oyster House. Claiming to be Albany's oldest restaurant,
this revered spot has been in the same family for more than 75
years. The decor reflects the history of the capital, with old pictures, dark oak trim, and assorted memorabilia. The menu
beckons diners "with a hungry appetite," offering bountiful
dishes, with emphasis on seafood (from oyster stew to Boston
scrod), steaks, and chops. *42-44 State St., tel. 518/465-8854.
Dress: casual. Reservations suggested. AE, CB, DC, MC, V.
Moderate-Expensive.*

Coco's. This is a fun restaurant, known for its vast choice of giant drinks (often served with balloons attached) and for its four
carousel-style salad bars. The menu ranges from ribs and burgers to duck, veal, seafood, pastas, and steaks. *1470 Western
Ave., tel. 518/456-0297. Dress: casual. Reservations suggested
for 5 or more. AE, DC, MC, V. Moderate.*

Lombardo's. This restaurant has been an Albany institution for
more than 70 years. Known for its attractive wall murals, tile
floors, and well-prepared Italian dishes, its specialties include
all kinds of pastas, veal dishes, steaks, and seafood. *121 Madison Ave., tel. 518/462-9180. Dress: casual. Reservations not
accepted. AE, DC, MC, V. Closed Mon. and Tues. Moderate.*

★ **Ogden's.** Located on the ground floor of a 1903 brick and limestone building, this restaurant has a unique decor incor-
porating the original oak interior, tall arched windows, and lots
of leafy plants. In the summer, you can dine alfresco on an adjoining patio overlooking the Empire State Plaza. The menu
focuses on Continental cuisine, with such dishes as veal with
morels, roast duckling, tournedos Rossini, and Dover sole. *42
Howard St., tel. 518/463-6605. Dress: neatly casual. Reservations suggested. AE, CB, DC, MC, V. Closed Sun. Dinner only
Sat. Moderate.*

Quakenbush House. A few steps from the Palace Theater, this
restaurant is housed in one of Albany's oldest buildings, notable for its latticed windows and textured handmade brick.
The menu emphasizes veal, chicken, and seafood dishes. There
is classical guitar music Friday and Saturday nights. *Quakenbush Square at Clinton Ave. and Broadway, tel. 518/465-0909.
Dress: casual. Reservations suggested. AE, CB, DC, MC, V.
Closed Sun. Dinner only Sat. Moderate.*

Yono's. Located in historic Robinson Square, this restaurant
offers dining in a trilevel brownstone. The menu combines Continental and Indonesian cuisines, with noodle dishes, *satays*,
and eggrolls, as well as seafood and meats. *289 Hamilton St.,
tel. 518/436-7747. Dress: casual. Reservations required. AE,*

CB, DC, MC, V. Closed Sun. Dinner only Mon. and Sat. Moderate.

Catskill **La Rive.** An old farmhouse serves as the setting for this delightful country restaurant, off routes 23A and 47. You can feast on traditional French cuisine in the house or on an enclosed porch; the price of the entree includes a full five-course dinner (hors d'oeuvres, soup, main course, fruit and cheese, and dessert). Main courses include classics such as steak au poivre, fillet of beef bordelaise, sole almondine, salmon béarnaise, and roast duckling. *Old King's Rd., tel. 518/943–4888. Dress: casual. Reservations required. No credit cards. Closed Mon. Dinner only. Closed Thanksgiving–early May. Moderate–Expensive.*

Hillsdale **L'Hostellerie Bressane.** Transplanted from the Rhone Valley,
★ Jean and Madeleine Morel have graciously transformed an 18th-century Hudson Valley home into a French country inn. There are three cozy dining rooms, with brick walls, wood paneling, open fireplaces, and tables meticulously set with white linens, fine china and flatware, and fresh flowers and candles. The entrees, all artfully presented with colorful arrays of seasonal vegetables, include local trout, veal chop, roast duck, filet of beef, rack of lamb, braised chicken breast, and poached king salmon. For dessert, the hot soufflés are hard to resist. *Rtes. 23 and 22, 518/325–3412. Jackets suggested. Reservations suggested. No credit cards. Closed Mon. and Tues. Dinner only. Expensive.*

Kinderhook **Old Dutch Inn.** Set in the heart of the village and overlooking the green, this restaurant provides a look at Columbia County of yesteryear. The decor includes country-style furnishings, a brick hearth, and wood stove. Featured dishes include marinated lamb roast and grilled seafoods. *8 Broad St., tel. 518/ 758–1676. Dress: casual. Reservations suggested. DC, MC, V. Closed Mon. Moderate.*

Lodging

Highly recommended properties in each price category are indicated by a star ★.

Category	Cost*
Very Expensive	over $125
Expensive	$75–$125
Moderate	$50–$75
Inexpensive	under $50

per room, double occupancy, without tax

Westchester and Rockland Counties

Rye Brook **Arrowwood.** One of the area's foremost executive conference
★ centers, this hotel is situated in a country-club setting on 114 wooded acres, including a three-acre pond, across from the Pepsico Sculpture Gardens. *Anderson Hill Rd., 10573, tel. 914/ 939–5500 or 800/633–6569. 276 rooms with bath. Facilities: 3 restaurants, indoor and outdoor pools, 2 indoor and 2 outdoor tennis courts, racquetball, gym, squash, sauna, paddle ten-*

nis, jogging trails, 9-hole golf course, bicycling, cross-country skiing, and sledding. AE, CB, DC, MC, V. Very Expensive.

Rye Town Hilton. Nestled amid 50 wooded acres, this rambling contemporary inn provides deluxe lodgings in a relaxed setting less than 35 minutes from Manhattan. *699 Westchester Ave., 10573, tel. 914/939–6300 or 800/HILTONS. 440 rooms with bath. Facilities: restaurant, coffee shop, 2 lounges, indoor and outdoor pools, whirlpool, 3 lighted tennis courts, gym, sauna, game room, hair salon, florist. AE, CB, DC, MC, V. Expensive.*

Suffern **Holiday Inn and Holidome.** Situated just off the New York State Thruway at Airmont, Exit 14B, this modern hotel is close to Bear Mountain State Park as well as within 20 miles of West Point, shopping centers, and area wineries. *3 Executive Blvd., 10901, tel. 914/357–4800 or 800/HOLIDAY. 243 rooms with bath. Facilities: cable TV, 2 restaurants, lounge, indoor pool and recreation center/gym, 2 tennis courts, putting green, game room. AE, CB, DC, MC, V. Expensive.*

Wellesley Inn. Like most members of this chain, this property is conveniently situated and provides clean and comfortable accommodations with no frills. Free Continental breakfast. *17 N. Airmont Rd., Exit 14B, NYS Thruway, 10901, tel. 914/368–1900 or 800/441–4479. 97 rooms with bath. AE, DC, MC, V. Inexpensive–Moderate.*

Tarrytown **Tarrytown Hilton.** In a 10-acre garden setting, this multi-winged low-rise hotel makes an ideal base for exploring the Sleepy Hollow region. Although the architecture is modern, there are cozy touches in the public rooms such as beamed ceilings, wood-paneled walls, wood-burning fireplaces, Oriental rugs, antique furnishings, and crystal chandeliers, and most of the guest rooms have individual patios or terraces. *455 S. Broadway, 10591, tel. 914/631–5700 or 800/HILTONS. 249 rooms with bath. Facilities: restaurant, coffee shop, entertainment lounge, indoor and outdoor pools, 2 tennis courts, exercise room, jogging trail, airport shuttle, baby-sitter service. AE, CB, DC, MC, V. Expensive–Very Expensive.*

Westchester Marriott. This modern 11-story hotel is close to the NYS Thruway and other major thoroughfares and is a favorite with business travelers. *670 White Plains Rd., 10591, tel. 914/631–2200 or 800/228–9290. 444 rooms with bath. Facilities: 2 restaurants, 2 lounges, nightclub, indoor/outdoor pool, sauna, whirlpool, universal gym, gift shop; nearby are golf, tennis, jogging trails. AE, CB, DC, MC, V. Expensive.*

White Plains **Stouffer Westchester.** Although the furnishings are deluxe and
★ modern, the real charm of this hotel is its location—on a wooded 26-acre estate, originally known as Red Oaks and previously owned by noted architect John Carrere, codesigner of the New York Public Library. *80 W. Red Oak La., 10604, tel. 914/694–5400 or 800–HOTELS–1. 364 rooms with bath. Facilities: 2 restaurants, lounge, indoor pool, 2 tennis courts, whirlpool, exercise room, paddleball court, illuminated jogging trail. AE, DC, MC, V. Very Expensive.*

Holiday Inn Crowne Plaza. A modern 12-story complex, this hotel is in the heart of the city, within walking distance of major department stores. *66 Hale Ave., 10601, tel. 914/682–0050 or 800/2–CROWNE. 400 rooms. Facilities: 2 restaurants, lounge with nightly entertainment, indoor pool, whirlpool, sauna, ex-*

ercise room, free enclosed parking, airport and train shuttle, gift shop. AE, CB, DC, MC, V. Expensive.

Orange and Putnam Counties

Bear Mountain **Bear Mountain Inn.** For more than 50 years, this chalet-style resort has been known for both its bucolic location (in the Bear Mountain State Park on the shores of Hessian Lake) and its warm hospitality. There are rooms in the main inn and units in five different lodges on the opposite side of the lake. A two-night minimum is imposed on many weekends. *Rte. 9W, 10911, tel. 914/786–2731. 60 rooms with bath. Facilities: restaurant, lounge, outdoor pool, picnic grounds, hiking trails, and access to ice skating, ski jumping, sledding, cross-country skiing. AE, DC, MC, V. Moderate–Expensive.*

Cold Spring **Hudson House.** Formerly known as the Hudson View Inn, this
★ is a restored historic landmark (circa 1831), on the banks of the Hudson River. Several guest rooms have balconies with views of the Hudson, West Point, or the village. The furnishings include antiques and curios such as Shaker-style sconces, lamps made from French wine decanters, and wall decorations fashioned from cookie cutters. Continental breakfast is included. *2 Main St., 10516, tel. 914/265–9355. 13 rooms with bath, 2 with shared bath. Facilities: restaurant, lounge, bicycle rentals. AE, MC, V. Closed Jan. Expensive.*
Pig Hill Inn. This charming bed-and-breakfast home is located three blocks from the banks of the Hudson River. Innkeeper Wendy O'Brien has furnished most of the guest rooms with four-poster beds and antiques, some of which are for sale. Most rooms have either a fireplace or wood stove. *73 Main St., 10516, tel. 914/265–9247. 4 rooms with bath, 4 rooms with shared bath. Full breakfast included, picnic lunches available by request. AE, DC, MC, V. Closed 2 weeks in late Feb. or early Mar. Expensive.*
Olde Post Inn. This restored inn, dating from 1820, offers bed-and-breakfast in an old-world setting with such modern amenities as air-conditioning. The on-premises stone tavern features jazz entertainment on Friday and Saturday nights. Innkeepers are Carole Zeller and George Argila. *43 Main St., 10516, tel. 914/265–2510. 6 rooms with private bath. Facilities: tavern, patio, garden. MC, V. Moderate.*

Fishkill **The Residence Inn by Marriott.** Each guest unit in this all-suite property has a fully equipped kitchen, living room, one or two bedrooms, and a private entrance. Some suites have fireplaces. Continental breakfast is included. *Rte. 9 and I–84, 12524, tel. 914/896–5210 or 800/331–3131. 116 rooms with bath. Facilities: outdoor pool, hot tub, health club. AE, CB, DC, MC, V. Expensive.*

Garrison **The Bird and Bottle Inn.** Dating back to 1761, this one-time
★ stagecoach stop on the Albany Post Road is still primarily known for its award-winning restaurant (*see* Dining). Overnight accommodations with a Colonial ambience are available on the second floor of the inn and in an adjoining cottage. The guest rooms have four-poster or canopy beds, antique furnishings, and working fireplaces. Breakfast is included. *Old Albany Post Rd. (Rte. 9), Nelson's Corners, 10524, tel. 914/424–3000. 4 rooms with bath. AE, MC, V. Very Expensive.*

Golden Eagle Inn. Situated on the banks of the Hudson River, this bed-and-breakfast inn is listed on the National Register of Historic Places. Built circa 1848 and furnished with antiques, wicker furniture, and original art, it is a large semi-Federal mansion, with stately white columns and wide verandas overlooking the lawns and river. Not surprisingly, it is often fully booked months in advance; a two-night stay is required on weekends. *Garrison's Landing, 10524, tel. 914/424–3067. 2 rooms with bath. AE, MC, V. Closed Feb. and Mar. Expensive.*

Newburgh **Howard Johnson Lodge.** Convenient to major roadways (at the intersection of I–84 and Rtes. 17 and 211), this modern motor inn has recently been refurbished. *551 Rte. 211 East, 10940, tel. 914/342–5822. 74 rooms. Facilities: cable TV, restaurant, lounge, indoor pool, sauna, game room. AE, CB, DC, MC, V. Moderate–Expensive.*

West Point **Hotel Thayer.** On the grounds of the U.S. Military Academy,
★ this stately brick hotel steeped in history and tradition has been welcoming military and civilian guests for more than 60 years. The hotel's public rooms are highlighted by marble floors, iron chandeliers, military portraits, and leather furnishings. The guest rooms have standard appointments, but many have views of the river and the West Point grounds. *Rte. 9W, 10996, tel. 914/446–4731 or 800/247–5047. 197 rooms with bath. Facilities: restaurant, lounge, tennis court. AE, CB, DC, MC, V. Moderate–Expensive.*

Dutchess and Ulster Counties

Highland **Rocking Horse Ranch.** Now in its 32nd year, this lakeside resort is especially appealing to families because of its many outdoor activities. There is a variety of package rates, most of which include all meals and activities; inquire at the time of booking for the deal that most suits your requirements. *Rtes. 44/45, 12528, tel. 914/691–2927, 800/647–2624 in N.Y.S., or 800/437–2624. 120 rooms with bath. Facilities: restaurant, 3 lounges, evening entertainment, horseback riding, waterskiing, indoor and outdoor pools, sauna, 2 tennis courts, fitness room, mini-golf, volleyball, handball, softball, rowboats, paddleboats, shuffleboard, archery range, day camp. AE, CB, DC, MC, V. Moderate.*

Hyde Park **The Roosevelt Inn.** This relatively new Colonial-style motel is set back from the main road in a tree-shaded setting a few miles north of the Franklin D. Roosevelt National Historic Site. *38 Albany Post Rd. (Rte. 9), 12538, tel. 914/229–2443. 25 rooms with bath or shower. Facilities: coffee shop (breakfast only), nearby dining, tennis, golf, and cross-country skiing. AE, MC, V. Closed Jan. and Feb. Moderate.*

Dutch Patroon. This handy, well-kept motel is right on the main north-south route through Dutchess County. About one quarter of the units have kitchenettes. Complimentary Continental breakfast. *Rte. 9, 12538, tel. 914/229–7141. 33 rooms with bath. Facilities: outdoor pool. AE, MC, V. Inexpensive.*

Kingston **Holiday Inn.** Located at Exit 19 of the NYS Thruway, this modern two-story motor hotel is within a few minutes of Kingston's downtown attractions and less than 30 miles from the popular Hunter Mountain ski area. *503 Washington Ave., 12401, tel. 914/338–0400 or 800/HOLIDAY. 212 rooms with bath. Facili-*

ties: restaurant, lounge, indoor pool, whirlpool, sauna, putting green. AE, CB, DC, MC, V. Moderate–Expensive.

Sky Top. This resort off Exit 19 of the NYS Thruway is set on 11 acres high on a hillside, affording lovely views of the mountains and surrounding countryside. There is a Victorian-style lobby, but the guest rooms are furnished in contemporary style. Complimentary Continental breakfast is included. *Rte. 28, at Skytop Dr., 12401, tel. 914/331–2900. 72 rooms with bath. Facilities: cable TV, outdoor pool, gift shop. AE, CB, DC, MC, V. Moderate–Expensive.*

Howard Johnson Lodge. Located within a mile of the New York State Thruway (Exit 19) and two miles from downtown Kingston, this contemporary motel is newly refurbished. *Rte. 28, 12401, tel. 914/338–4200 or 800/654–2000. 118 rooms with bath. Facilities: cable TV, restaurant, lounge, indoor and outdoor pools, sauna. AE, CB, DC, MC, V. Moderate.*

Millerton
★
Simmon's Way Village Inn. Located near the Connecticut border in northeast Dutchess county, this inn is named in honor of E. W. Simmons, a local educator/statesman/lawyer who built the original house (in 1854) from which this inn has evolved. The current innkeepers, Richard and Nancy Carter, have decorated the guest rooms with antiques and furnishings that reflect the house's earlier days; some rooms have private porches, draped canopy beds, sitting areas, or fireplaces. Continental breakfast is included. Summer bookings require a two-night minimum on weekends. Closed Tuesdays. *33 Main St. (Rte. 44), 12546, tel. 518/789–6235. 11 rooms with bath. Facilities: restaurant and bar. AE, MC, V. Expensive.*

New Paltz
★
Mohonk Mountain House. Founded as a 10-room inn by Quakers in 1869, Mohonk Mountain House, situated on a lake amid 7,500 acres of land in the heart of the Shawangunk Mountains, has grown into one of the great resorts of the Hudson Valley. Declared a National Landmark in 1986, it is a mostly Victorian-style building, with various wings, turrets, cupolas, and spires. Run by the Smiley family, descendants of the original founders, it maintains some of the traditions (i.e., there is no bar or cocktail lounge, but drinks can be ordered with evening meals). The room prices include three meals and afternoon tea; there is also a variety of package plans ranging from mystery, musical, or cooking weekends to sporting, stargazing, or stress-management programs. The layout includes three verandas lined with rockers; 100 of the guest rooms have working fireplaces, and 200 have balconies. *Lake Mohonk, 12561, tel. 914/255–1000 or 212/233–2244. 300 rooms with private bath. Facilities: 3 dining rooms, 6 clay tennis courts, beach, basketball court, fitness center, aerobics classes, croquet, lawn bowling, shuffleboard, softball, volleyball, croquet, 9-hole golf course, horseback riding, 135 miles of hiking trails, nature preserve, cross-country skiing, ice skating, and more. AE, MC, V. Expensive–Very Expensive.*

Poughkeepsie
★
Inn at the Falls. Operating as a bed-and-breakfast, this relatively new inn combines the amenities of a modern hotel with the ambience and personal attention of a country home. Situated in a residential area beside a rushing waterfall about two miles southeast of the city, the inn has an arched courtyard that joins two wings of guest rooms. The public areas are bright and airy with pastel-toned furnishings, floor-to-ceiling paned windows, brass chandeliers, marble floors and an abundance of

leafy plants. The guest rooms, all accessible by computer card keys, vary in decor from English-mansion style to American country, Art Deco, or Oriental. Many bedrooms have four-poster, wrought-iron, or canopied beds, brass headboards, armoires, rolltop desks, crystal and china lamps. Continental breakfast, delivered to each guest room on a silver tray, is included. *50 Red Oaks Mill Rd., 12603, tel. 914/462–5770. 22 rooms and 14 suites, all with private bath. AE, CB, DC, MC. Expensive–Very Expensive.*

Radisson Poughkeepsie. Located in the heart of the city, this modern 10-story property is adjacent to the Mid-Hudson Convention Center. Relatively new (opened in 1987), it is the largest full-service hotel in the mid-Hudson Valley. The decor is bright and contemporary, enhanced by expansive views of the river from many of the guest rooms. *40 Civic Center Plaza, 12601, tel. 914/485–5300 or 800/333–3333. 225 rooms with bath. Facilities: cable TV, restaurant, lounge, nightclub, sauna, health club, gift shop, airport shuttle, valet parking and self-park garage. AE, CB, DC, MC, V.·Expensive.*

Courtyard by Marriott. Opened in June 1988, this contemporary inn has a homey, plant-filled atmosphere, with guest-room wings grouped around a central courtyard. It is located south of downtown, with easy access to Route 9. *408 South Rd., 12601, tel. 914/485–6336 or 800/321–2211. 149 rooms with bath. Facilities: cable TV, restaurant, lounge, indoor swimming pool, exercise room, whirlpool, game room, nonsmoking rooms. AE, CB, DC, MC, V. Moderate–Expensive.*

Edison Motor Inn. Situated east of the city, this dependable motel has equipped about one-third of its units with kitchenettes, ideal for family travelers. *313 Manchester Rd. (Rte. 55), 12603, tel. 914/454–3080. 138 rooms with bath. Facilities: restaurant, lounge, 2 tennis courts, outdoor pool, shuffleboard, playground. AE, DC, MC, V. Moderate.*

Red Hook ★ **Red Hook Inn.** In the heart of the village, this charming Colonial-style inn dates back to 1882, but it was restored, renovated, and reopened in 1986. The decor combines exposed brickwork, country furnishings, and area antiques. Full breakfast is included. *31 S. Broadway (Rte. 9), 12571, tel. 914/758–8445. 5 rooms with bath. Facilities: restaurant, lounge with music and dancing Fri. and Sat. nights, and limousine service to area attractions at supplementary charge. AE, MC, V. Moderate–Expensive.*

Gaslight Motel. Located three miles north of Red Hook and set back from the main road in a tree-shaded setting, Gaslight has a Colonial-style motif and country furnishings; about half of the units have kitchenettes. There are also views of the Catskill Mountains in the distance. *Rte. 9, 12571, tel. 914/758–1571. 12 rooms with bath. Facilities: private gardens, patio, barbecue. MC, V. Inexpensive.*

Hearthstone Motel. This is a basic one-story motel, situated on a hillside about three miles north of the village. The guest rooms have views of the Catskill Mountains to the west. *R.D. 3, Box 51, Rte. 9, 12571, tel. 914/758–1811. 8 rooms with bath. AE, MC, V. Inexpensive.*

Rhinebeck ★ **Beekman Arms.** One of America's oldest inns (dating back to 1766), this hotel has welcomed such historic guests as George Washington, Thomas Jefferson, and Franklin Roosevelt. A variety of accommodations are available, including 13 rooms in the original building (smallish units with authentic squeaky floorboards, braided rugs, and antique furnishings); and four motel-style rooms at the rear of the inn. About a block away, there are seven rooms in Delamater House (circa 1844), a delightful two-story, American-Gothic residence furnished with wicker furniture, huge armoires, and Victorian touches. There are also 24 new rooms located behind Delamater in a surrounding courtyard, carriage house, and restored town house; all have air-conditioning and some have working fireplaces. A room at the Delamater House comes with complimentary Continental breakfast. *4 Mill St. (Rte. 9) 12572, tel. 914/876–7077. 48 rooms with bath. Facilities: 4 dining rooms, tavern. AE, DC, MC, V. Expensive for the newer rooms, Moderate for the older sections.*

Village Victorian Inn. Located on a quiet residential street, this two-story Italianate home (circa 1860), is a quintessential bed-and-breakfast inn, with well-tended gardens, white picket fence, and front-porch rockers. The owners, Judy and Richard Kohler, have decorated the interior with area antiques, French Victorian fabrics, and Oriental rugs. Each guest room has a brass or canopy bed (king- or queen-size) adorned with a country quilt or comforter, a ceiling fan, books, and other homey touches. A gourmet breakfast (such as eggs Benedict, pecan French toast, or quiches) is included. *31 Center St., 12572, tel. 914/876–8345. 5 rooms with bath. AE, MC, V. Expensive.*

Rhinebeck Village Inn. Owned and operated by the Behrens family, this one-story motel, about a mile south of the village in a tree-shaded setting, has country-house charm. The spacious guest rooms are very homey, with hand-crafted local furnishings and wall hangings. Continental breakfast is included in the room charge. Weekend rates are slightly higher. *Rte. 9, Box 491, 12572, tel. 914/876–7000. 16 rooms with bath. Facilities: cable TV, refrigerators available on request. AE, CB, DC, MC, V. Moderate.*

Whistlewood Farm. For a more rural ambience, you can enjoy bed-and-breakfast at this 13-acre horse farm, located three miles east of Rhinebeck village, off Route 308. The grounds offer lovely gardens and views of the countryside, and the interior of the house is full of beamed ceilings and antique furnishings. Innkeeper Maggie Myer is well known for her hearty breakfasts (included in the rates) of fresh local fruits, cheese-filled omelets, sour cream coffee cake, blackberry or apple crumb pie, and blueberry-banana muffins. Rates are slightly higher on weekends. *11 Pells Rd., 12572, tel. 914/876–6838. 3 rooms with private bath, 2 rooms with shared bath. Facilities: pets can be accommodated in house or in adjacent kennels. No credit cards. Moderate.*

Albany, Columbia, and Greene Counties

Albany   **Albany Hilton.** Situated in the heart of the capital, this modern 15-story property is the leading full-service downtown hotel. It is within walking distance of the Empire State Plaza and the convention center as well as shops and other midcity attractions. *10 Eyck Plaza, State and Lodge Sts., 12207, tel. 518/462–6611. 387 rooms with bath. Facilities: 2 restaurants, 2 lounges, disco, indoor pool, Jacuzzi, valet service, shopping boutiques. AE, CB, DC, MC, V. Expensive.*

★ **Desmond Americana.** Located just outside Albany Airport, this hotel is laid out in a configuration reminiscent of a Colonial village, with various wings surrounding a central courtyard.

The decor also carries out an 18th-century theme, with Federal and Queen-Anne reproductions, vintage paintings, and wood paneling in the public rooms; and guest units have custom-made furnishings that feature Colonial-style fabrics and colors. *660 Albany-Shaker Rd., 12211, tel. 518/869–8100, 800/448–3500 in N.Y.S., or 800/235–1210. 324 rooms with bath. Facilities: cable TV, 2 restaurants, lounge, 2 indoor pools, health club, sauna, exercise room, billiards room, game room, gift shop. AE, CB, DC, MC, V. Expensive–Very Expensive.*

★ **Mansion Hill Inn.** Located around the corner from the Executive Mansion, this is Albany's only downtown bed-and-breakfast inn and a preservation award winner from the Historic Albany Foundation. Innkeepers Mary Ellen and Steve Stofelano, Jr. have decorated the rooms with antiques and vintage furnishings. Three of the guest units are suites, with bedroom, living room, study, and kitchenette; and two rooms have rear decks. Rates include a full breakfast. *115 Philip St., 12202, tel. 518/465–2038 or 465–2059. 7 rooms with private bath. Facilities: restaurant. AE, DC, MC, V. Moderate–Expensive.*

Canaan   **Queechy Lake Motel.** Nestled on Queechy Lake in a quiet tree-shaded setting, this contemporary two-story lodging in northeastern Columbia County is close to the Massachusetts border, less than 10 miles from Tanglewood and the Berkshire ski resorts. The guest units are furnished in a country style, but the biggest attraction is the sylvan lake view from each window. Continental breakfast included on weekdays; coffee shop operates on weekends. *Queechy Lake Dr. (Rte. 30), Box 106, 12029, tel. 518/781–4615. 18 rooms with bath. Facilities: outdoor heated pool, lake beach passes provided to guests. MC, V. Moderate.*

Palenville   **Hans' County Line Motel.** Situated on Route 32A, this comfortable lodging is in the heart of ski and festival country. Guest units feature all the standard amenities, including air-conditioning. *HCR #1, Box 52, 12463, tel. 518/678–3101. 42 rooms with bath, 5 cabins with bath. Facilities: restaurant, heated outdoor pool, game room, playground, complimentary shuttle service to ski slopes and summer festivals. AE, CB, DC, MC, V. Moderate–Expensive.*

Tannersville   **The Eggery Inn.** Nestled amid the ridges of the Catskill Mountains at an elevation of 2,200 feet, this rustic inn offers views of Hunter Mountain from every window and from a wraparound porch. Innkeepers Abe and Julie Abramczyk have added lots of country touches, such as a wood-burning Franklin stove, brick hearth, antique player piano, and a handcrafted oak bar. There is a two-night minimum stay on most weekends. *Rte. 16, 12485, tel. 518/589–5363. 13 rooms with bath. Facilities: cable TV, restaurant (dinner on Sat. only). AE, MC, V. Moderate–Expensive.*

Windham   **Albergo Allegria.** A real find in this area, this unusual inn is the
★ result of the joining together of two Victorian homes, replete with gingerbread trim, stained-glass windows, brass fixtures, dried floral arrangements, stenciled walls, and polished wood floors with braided rugs. There are two sitting rooms, both with fireplaces, and a small outdoor patio where breakfast is served in summer (full breakfast is included in the room rates). Innkeeper Lenore Radelich has recently launched a series of year-round seminars on northern Italian cooking for guests.

Rte. 296, 12496, tel. 518/734–5560. 24 rooms with bath (including 1 suite with a double Jacuzzi). MC, V. Moderate–Expensive.

The Arts

There are a number of excellent multipurpose performing arts centers throughout the Hudson Valley. Their schedules include a variety of shows from concerts by symphony orchestras to pop soloists to road-show theatricals. Here are the most important venues:

Eisenhower Hall Theater (U.S. Military Academy, tel. 914/938–4159). Although this West Point venue is best known for its military-band concerts, many other performances are also scheduled, ranging from full-scale musicals and appearances by pop artists to modern-dance ensembles and classical concerts. Normal starting time is 8, but afternoon performances are also often scheduled.

The Empire State Performing Arts Center (Madison Ave. and S. Swan St., Albany, tel. 518/443–5111). Drama, dance, and musical events are scheduled year-round in "The Egg," as this huge, curving concrete building in the Empire State Plaza is called. Home to the Empire State Institute for the Performing Arts, it has a 500-seat recital hall and an 886-seat main theater. The season is September to June, with most performances at 8.

Mid-Hudson Civic Center (Civic Center Plaza, Poughkeepsie, tel. 914/454–5800). In the heart of the city, this is a multipurpose recreation and entertainment center offering ever-changing programs, ranging from rock concerts and comedy shows to movies and country-western shows. Call for the latest schedule.

The Music Hall Theater (13 Main St., Tarrytown, tel. 914/631–3390) offers classical music, dance ensembles, and other musical works for both adult and student audiences. Adult programs are normally at 8, student shows at 2 PM and 3:30 PM.

Dance

Kleinert Gallery (34 Tinker St., Woodstock, tel. 914/679–2079). You can watch or participate in various types of folk dancing led by John Delson and Myra French. No experience or partners are necessary; regular sessions are held at 7:30 on most summer nights, but call for exact schedule.

Film

Upstate Films (26 Montgomery St., Rhinebeck, tel. 914/876–2515). Located less than two blocks from the landmark Beekman Arms, this repertory movie theater shows international and American classics, art films, and some new or experimental works. The schedule is usually Sunday through Thursday at 7 PM and 9 PM, Friday and Saturday at 7:30 PM and 9:30 PM, with variations possible. The shows are often augmented by comments from guest filmmakers.

Music

Caramoor Center for Music and the Arts (Rte. 22 and Girdle Ridge Rd., Katonah, tel. 914/232–5035). Chamber music recitals and brass concerts are among the many events scheduled during the annual summer-long music festival on this 117-acre estate. Call in advance for the program.

Emelin Theater (Library La., Mamaroneck, tel. 914/698–0098). An ever-changing program of solo instrumentalists, vocalists, and string quartets, as well as bluegrass bands and occasional foreign or classic films. Show time is usually 8:30.

The Music and Art Center of Greene County (Jewett Center, Rte. 23A, Jewett, tel. 518/989–6479). This is an ideal place to come during July and August for chamber music, recitals, and other serious music. Most performances are at 8.

Paramount Theater (19 South St., Middletown, tel. 914/342–6524). This theater showcases concerts and guest artists as well as the Hudson Valley Philharmonic. The curtain is normally at 8, but check for latest schedule.

Ulster Performing Arts Center (601 Broadway, Kingston, tel. 914/339–6088). A frequent showcase for the Hudson Valley Philharmonic on the west side of the river, this arts center also presents solo performances and orchestral concerts by visiting talent. Curtain is normally at 8; call for current schedule.

Theater

The Bardavon 1869 Opera House (35 Market St., Poughkeepsie, tel. 914/473–2072). The pride of the Hudson Valley, this is one of the oldest theaters in the country and is listed on the National Register. It is a year-round venue for all types of theatrical and variety productions, as well as concerts by the Hudson Valley Philharmonic. Curtain is normally at 8, Monday through Saturday.

Capital Repertory Company. Known locally as "Cap Rep," this Albany Equity company presents classic and contemporary drama productions at the 258-seat Market Theatre. *111 N. Pearl St., Box 399, 12201-0399, tel. 518/462–4534. Oct.–May, performances Tues.–Fri. at 8, Sat. at 4:30 and 9, Sun. at 2:30.*

An Evening Dinner Theater. Broadway musical productions are presented year-round at this suburban dinner-theater in Elmsford. *11 Clearbrook Rd., Elmsford, tel. 914/592–2222. Performances Wed.–Sun. at 6, matinees Wed. and Thurs. at 11 AM and Sun. at noon.*

MacHaydn Theater. For more than 20 years, this has been one of New York State's foremost summer-stock playhouses. The program usually features the best of Broadway's musicals. *Rte. 203, Chatham, tel. 518/392–9292. Open late May–end of Sept., Wed.–Fri. at 8, Sat. at 8:30, Sun. at 7; matinees Sat. at 5, Sun. at 2, and every other Wed. at 2.*

Nightlife

Bars and Clubs

Westchester/ Rockland Counties **Backstage Limited** (348 Huguenot St., New Rochelle, tel. 914/636–2111). This place offers a dance floor with live band music on Friday, plus comedy and cabaret acts on Saturday.

The Coven Cave (162 Main St., Nyack, tel. 914/358–9829). This spot is known for its live dance music Tuesday through Sunday nights.

Gambits (Rte. 119, Tarrytown, tel. 914/631–2200). There are two dance floors here and DJ music every night.

O'Donoghue's (66 Main St., Nyack, tel. 914/358–0180). Whether it's St. Pat's Day or not, this is a good place to hear folk and Irish music, with live guest performers on Monday.

Pars (189 E. Post Rd., White Plains, tel. 914/428–3377). A live band plays top-40 hits here Thursday, Friday, and Saturday nights.

Sneakers (173 Main St., Nyack, tel. 914/358–0802). There is live music here Thursday through Saturday, and a DJ at other times.

Orange/Putnam Counties

Gatsby's (Rte. 17M, Monroe, tel. 914/782–5152). For DJ music try this spot in the K-Mart Plaza, Thursday, Friday, and Saturday nights.

Memory Lane (Rte. 52, Walden, tel. 914/778–9913). Come here on Saturday night for live country-western music.

Rosebuds (Rte. 9W, New Windsor, tel. 914/565–6588). You'll find a bit of variety here—top-40 music on Friday and Saturday nights and comedy shows on Thursday nights.

Rusty Nail (50 Dunning Rd., Middletown, tel. 914/343–8242). There is usually live entertainment here on weekends.

Dutchess/ Ulster Counties

Bertie's. This is the place for continuous DJ music. *9-11 Liberty St., Poughkeepsie, tel. 914/452–2378. Open Wed.–Sat.*

La Fonda Del Sol (Rte. 9, Wappingers Falls, tel. 914/297–5044). This place offers a variety of music styles from blues and jazz to folk rock, often with live performers. There is also a dance floor.

Moogs Farm (Rte. 9 at I-84, Fishkill, tel. 914/896–9975). This is one of the valley's premier venues for country-western music, with live performances every Saturday.

The New Chateau (Rte. 9W, Port Ewen, tel. 914/338–5000). There is dancing to live bands and DJ music, Friday and Saturday nights, for a crowd that's mostly 25 and older.

P & G's (Main St., New Paltz, tel. 914/255–6161). Popular with college students, this spot offers live music Friday and Saturday nights.

Rhinebeck Tavern (19-21 W. Market St., Rhinebeck, tel. 914/876–3059). Located opposite the Beekman Arms, this informal spot often features live rock, country-western, and pop music, especially on weekends.

Skytop Lounge (Rte. 28, Kingston, tel. 914/338–6161). This is an ideal spot for panoramic night views and easy listening music, with dancing on weekends.

Town Crier Cafe. This suburban club offers well-known guest artists performing folk, traditional, contemporary, or classical music. *Rte. 22, Pawling, tel. 914/855–1300. Shows or concerts are usually on weekends, though times vary.*

Albany

Cahoots (State and Lodge Sts., tel. 518/462–6611, ext. 285). This classy downtown spot at the Albany Hilton has a DJ most nights.

Fenders. Here you will find live entertainment, Atlantic City cabaret-style. *Turf Inn, 205 Wolf Rd., tel. 518/458–7250. Live entertainment Mon–Sat., Sun. dance to "oldies."*

LP's Dance Club (Western Ave. and Quail St., tel. 518/436–7740). Dancing to the music of top-40 hits is featured here, as well as music videos on a large screen.

Van's Night Cap (177-179 Northern Blvd., tel. 518/463–1787). This club offers a potpourri of live jazz, reggae, Latin music, and disco.

6 The Catskills

Introduction

To early explorers, the Hudson was "the River of the Mountains." Sailing up the Hudson River today, one is struck by their grandeur. Possessing neither the jagged peaks nor the epic dimensions of other mountain ranges, the Catskills still have a magical presence that defines a vast region of the mid-Hudson valley and spreads westward across more than one million acres.

The highest peak in the Catskills is just 4,200 feet, so these are not the fierce guardians of the wilderness that challenge the mettle of mountaineers. Rather, the Catskills offer a quiet welcome and the promise of comfort and easy accessibility. Yet they have a beauty and variety disproportionate to their modest size.

"In no other American vacation land," writes T. Morris Longstreth in *The Catskills*, "can one find a more interesting alternation of forest tramping and village living, a richer background of subdued mountain and inviting valley. If the eternal isn't visible to you there it will never be in remoter lands."

One common theme of the Catskills is water. The name comes from the Dutch *Kaats Kill*, which means "wildcat stream." There is still something wild and untamed in the streams and rivers here as they tumble over rocky gorges and plunge from ledge to ledge. Some of the world's finest fly-fishing can be found in the Catskills' profusion of premier trout streams. Enthusiasts of all skill levels can enjoy just about any outdoor sport here, from camping to canoeing, hiking to bicycle touring, rock climbing to white-water kayaking. More leisurely pursuits beckon families with young children and those not athletically inclined.

Accommodations range from rustic inns to luxury hotels, offering peaceful surroundings, a refreshing dip in a pool, a good book, a cool drink, a fine meal, and a splendid view. Meandering country roads—there are no four-lane highways here—may lead motorists to the unexpected pleasures of a visit to an artisan's studio, a small museum, or a historic house.

The discoveries awaiting visitors are muted, delicate. The Catskills are the color of dusty blueberries just picked on a hazy morning, and their gentle hue and texture suggests undulating waves on a vast sea. A subtle romance lies waiting in their agreeable wilderness: the flash of a white-tailed deer bounding over a tangle of fallen birches, a pair of brook trout lying motionless as mossy stones in a limpid pool, a bald eagle perching on the highest branch of a pine upon a lofty limestone cliff.

This is the land of Rip Van Winkle, and it can still play tricks on one's sense of time and place. The mountains' enduring majesty continues to speak to scores of visitors each year in terms as poignant as those that inspired the landscape painter Thomas Cole, the naturalist John Burroughs, the writer Washington Irving, and countless other artists.

The Catskills are also full of paradoxes. They are settled but not overdeveloped, historic yet modern, used but not abused, and this careful balance of opposing forces gives the region its vitality. The Catskills, after all, are inextricably linked with

New York City: Reservoirs in the Catskills supply the metropolitan area with award-winning drinking water. And untold thousands of city swellers seek solace here at the end of a hectic work week, as their parents and grandparents did before them.

The throngs escaping New York City created a lucrative market for resort complexes, whose regimented leisure activities have been immortalized in movies such as *Dirty Dancing*. But that was another era, another sensibility. What's left of the famous "borscht belt" lives on mostly in the memories of senior citizens. Today the region is known more for its open spaces than for gaudy ballrooms, for its wilderness opportunities rather than cornball theme nights. And those lured from New York as permanent residents are likely to be dedicated to the arts, crafts, and nature. The Catskills have, once again, become a mecca for artisans whose exquisite quilts, ceramics, stained glass, furniture, and hand-woven cloth are sought by collectors around the world. In crafts, more than anything else, the Catskills reclaim their roots in an electronic age and offer a living testament to the belief that what's past is a prologue of what's to come.

The major transportation route to the Catskills is the New York State Thruway (I–87), which links New York City and Albany and runs parallel to the Hudson River. In the northern Catskills, the Hudson River towns of Catskill and Kingston (Thruway exists 19 and 20, respectively) are good entry points for New York Routes 23, 23A, and 28 covering Greene and Ulster counties. In Delaware County, the principal access routes are New York Routes 23, 28, and 30. Sullivan County and the Upper Delaware River area can be reached via Route 17. The Shawangunk Mountain section, which draws rock climbers from around the country, can be reached by U.S. 209. Because of the region's vastness, each area will be described separately in detail.

Getting Around

By Plane The Albany County Airport, a one-hour drive from the heart of the Catskills, is served by **American** (tel. 800/433–7300), **Bar Harbor** (tel. 518/482–4048), **Continental** (tel. 800/525–0280), **Delta** (tel. 800/221–1212), **Mall** (tel. 518/735–3383), **PanAm Express** (tel. 800/221–1111), **Precision** (tel. 800/451–4221), **United** (tel. 800/241–6522), and **USAir** (tel. 800/428–4322).

The Oneonta Municipal Airport, located off I–88 in the northwest corner of the Catskill region, is served by **Catskill Airways** (tel. 607/432–8222; 800/252–2144 in NY State; 800/833–0196 in the Northeast), which offers daily flights from New York–LaGuardia, Newark, and Boston.

Sullivan Aircraft Services (tel. 914/583–5830) offers charter service to Sullivan County International Airport in White Lake, six miles west of Monticello.

Sidney Aviation (tel. 607/563–9727) offers charter service to Sidney Airport in Delaware County.

By Limo **Empire State Shuttle Service** (tel. 800/367–4732) offers six trips on weekdays and four on weekends in each direction between JFK and LaGuardia airports in New York City and Albany, via New Paltz, Kingston, Catskill, and Hudson.

By Train The fastest and most memorable way from New York City and Albany to the Catskills is by **Amtrak** (tel. 800/872–7245). It operates eight modern express trains a day on the Grand Central Terminal to Albany-Rensselaer run, many of them stopping at Poughkeepsie, Rhinebeck, and Hudson. The trip from New York City to Hudson, 15 miles east of the town of Catskill, takes only two hours. The best views of the Hudson River are on the left, heading north. The $7.50 surcharge for a reserved seat in first class is money well spent. All trains have buffet cars, serving snacks and cocktails; the evening New York–Chicago *Lake Shore Limited* has a refurbished Art Deco full-service dining car, but the food and wine list are uninspired.

By Bus **Greyhound** (tel. 800/528–0447) offers regular service to several Catskills communities from New York City and Albany.

Shortline (tel. 212/736–4700 or 800/631–8405) serves a half-dozen Sullivan County communities from New York City.

By Car The region is quite spread out, so the best way to get around is by car. Bring a bicycle or rent one in any of several resort areas. (*See* Orientation for routes in and around the Catskills.)

Important Addresses and Numbers

Information Centers Each of the four counties in the Catskills region maintains separate information centers to distribute materials about their respective areas.

The **Delaware County Chamber of Commerce** (56 Main St., Delhi, 13753; tel. 607/746–2281, 800/356–5615 within New York State; 800/642–4443 in the Northeast) is open weekdays 9–5.

The **Greene County Promotion Department** (Box 527, Catskill, 12414; tel. 518/943–3223 or 800/542–2414) maintains an information center at New York State Thruway Exit 21, Catskill, open daily 8–6.

The **Sullivan County Office of Public Information** (Sullivan County Government Center, Monticello, 12701; tel. 914/794–3000, 800/882–CATS within New York State, 800/343–INFO elsewhere) maintains an information center at the Jamesway Mall, Route 42, Monticello. Open July and Aug., Mon.–Thurs. 10–6, Fri. 11–7, Sun. 10–4; May, June, and Sept.–Oct., weekends.

The **Ulster County Public Information Office** (Box 1800, Kingston, 12401; tel. 914/331–9300) operates tourism information counters located at New York State Thruway Exit 19, Kingston; on U.S. 9W, Highland; and on New York Route 28, Ellenville.

Contact the **Catskills Association for Tourism Services** (Box 449, Catskill, 12421; tel. 518/943–3223 or 800/542–2414).

Emergencies **Police and Ambulance** The New York State Police maintains several substations in the region. Many of the larger towns also support their own police departments, along with emergency squads and rescue vehicles. The State Police, sheriff, or hospitals can direct you to the nearest emergency unit.

Sheriff. Delaware County, 607/746–2336; Greene County, 518/943–3300; Sullivan County, 914/794–7100; Ulster County, 914/338–3645.

State Police. Catskill, 518/622–8600; Ellenville, 914/626–2800; Ferndale, 914/292–6600; Highland, 914/691–2922; Kingston, 914/338–1702; and Margaretville, 914/586–2681.

Hospitals **Callicoon.** Grover M. Herman Division of Community General Hospital of Sullivan County (Rte. 97, tel. 914/887–5530).
Catskill. Memorial Hospital of Greene County (Jefferson Heights, tel. 518/943–2000).
Delhi. O'Connor Hospital (Rte. 28, tel. 607/746–2371).
Harris. Community General Hospital of Sullivan County (Bushville Rd., tel. 914/794–3300).
Kingston. Benedictine Hospital (105 Mary's Ave., tel. 914/338–5590). Kingston Hospital (396 Broadway, tel. 914/331–3131). Medicenter (40 Hurley Ave., tel. 914/339–5285).
Margaretville. Community Memorial Hospital (Rte. 28, tel. 914/586–2631).
Stamford. Community Hospital (Rte. 23, tel. 607/652–7521).

Exploring the Catskills

Numbers in the margin correspond with points of interest on the Catskills map.

The High Peaks

From New York State Thruway (I–87) Exit 21, take Route 23A west from the Greene County village of Catskill (*see* Hudson Valley) toward **Palenville,** home of Washington Irving's legendary sleeper, Rip Van Winkle. It's still a pretty quiet community, although a lively summer arts scene and the week-long **Festival of Circus Theater** (tel. 518/678–3332), spanning the last week of June and the first few days of July, get things rolling nicely with circus theater performances, clowning, storytelling, and masked plays.

In between, performances of classical and modern music, dance and theater, children's programs and workshops take place at the **Bond Street Theater Coalition** (tel. 518/678–3332), site of the Circus Theater, a colony of professional artists.

Palenville marks the start of one of the most spectacular drives in the Catskills: an eight-mile stretch of Route 23A that climbs past the cliffs and cataracts of Kaaterskill Clove to ski centers at Haines Falls and Hunter. Precipitous drops and hairpin turns offer wonderful views and challenging driving. Bastion (or Sabastian) Falls along this route is a popular stop for picnickers, waders (caution is advised), and camera buffs.

❶ At **Haines Falls, North–South Lake State Park** offers swimming, fishing, boating, and camping from May through October. A short hike takes you to 180-foot **Kaaterskill Falls,** a favorite haunt for generations of artists (also accessible from the Bastion Falls trail). At the site of the famed Catskill Mountain House, you find the names of visitors carved in stone ledges a century ago. On clear days, the view encompasses much of the Hudson Valley and the Berkshire Mountains beyond, a vista that helped make this the preeminent vacation spot during the 19th and early 20th centuries. *Rte. 18, Haines Falls, tel. 518/589–5058 or 518/943–4030.*

❷ Continue west on Rte. 23A to **Hunter** and **Hunter Mountain,** a famous ski center which, thanks to its location and tremendous

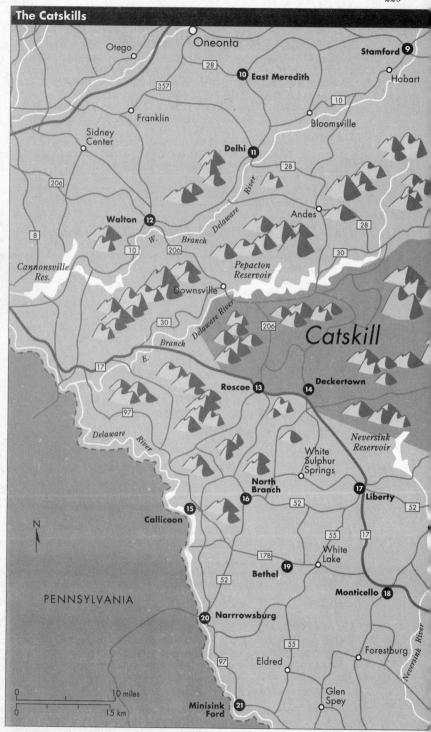

The Catskills

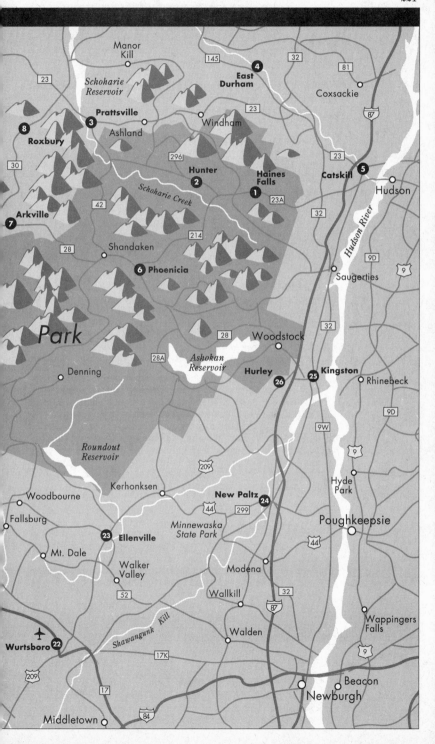

snowmaking capabilities, is open 160 days a year. Hunter is also known for its summer festivals, including the Italian Festival (June–July), the three-week German Alps Festival (July), a country music festival featuring Nashville stars (July and Aug.), the National Polka Festival where Bobby Vinton reigns (early Aug.), and celebrations devoted to "Golden Oldies" (late Aug.), Celtic heritage (mid-Aug.), and Native-American cultures (early Sept.). All festivals are held at the ski bowl. For schedule and ticket information contact *Exposition Planners, Bridge St., Hunter, 12422, tel. 518/263-3800.*

In summer, and particularly in fall when the mountains are ablaze with color, the **Hunter Mountain Sky Ride** (tel. 518/263–4223)—the longest and highest chair lift in the Catskills—offers breathtaking views of the region.

The Catskill slopes now enjoyed by skiers and hikers were once covered with thick stands of hemlock whose acidic bark generated a massive 19th-century tanning industry. Hunter, in fact, was once named "Edwardsville" after tanning mogul Colonel William Edwards, and the ski center is situated a short distance from Hunter Mountain on a peak known as Colonel's Chair.

❸ Once the biggest tannery in the world—500 feet long and two stories high—was owned by Zadock Pratt in **Prattsville**, the community that now bears his name. His 1828 homestead in the center of town, 12 miles west of Hunter, now houses the **Zadock Pratt Museum** of local history. *Rte. 23, Prattsville, tel. 518/229-3345. Admission: $1 adults, 50¢ children. Open Memorial Day–Columbus Day, Wed.–Sun. 1–5.*

Picnickers might want to stop at nearby **Pratt Rocks,** a wooded park with a steep trail to rock ledges carved in the 1860s with likenesses of Pratt, his horse, and the venerable hemlock. Take Route 23 back east to **Windham,** a lively ski town.

Time Out The drive from East Windham to Cairo is an eye-opening, ear-popping experience with Windham High Peak, Black Dome, and other mountains pushing in from the south, and expansive views of the valley below and New England beyond. Stop for a photo at the rest area halfway down the mountain.

❹ Back on the valley floor just before Cairo, take Route 145 northwest to **East Durham**. Irish immigrants visiting the Catskills from New York City early in the century established vacation resorts in this green, stream-crossed area that so resembled the Old Sod. Now, Irish pubs, hotels, and shops abound and an Irish-American heritage museum is being developed in this single-stoplight town. Summer is the busy season here, beginning with the Catskills Irish Festival (tel. 518/634–7100) that draws 20,000 people Memorial Day weekend, and concluding with the traditional Irish dance competition for children in late August.

Need to cool off after all that merrymaking? Try the **Zoom Flume Aquamusement Park.** Two 300-foot water slides, a 2,600-foot "river" for tube floating, bumper boats, and something called the Thrill Hill provide lots of wet fun. *Shady Glen Rd., off Rte. 145, East Durham, tel. 518/239-4559. Admission: $9.95, adults $7.95 children under 8. Open Memorial Day–Labor Day 10–7; June, weekends only.*

Also on Route 145 and housed in an 1837 schoolhouse, the **Durham Center Museum** is packed with genealogical records, pioneer tools, fossils, minerals, and Indian artifacts. *Rte. 145, East Durham, tel. 518/239-6461. Admission free. Open June–August, Sat., Sun., Wed., and Thurs. 1 to 4 PM.*

If speed on the tarmac is more to your liking, head to the nearby **Supersonic Speedway & Fun Park** with its twisting Go-Kart track. There's also a championship miniature golf course, batting cages and kiddie rides. *Rte. 145, East Durham, tel. 518/622-9531 or 518/634-7200. Open Memorial Day–Labor Day.*

❺ The shoot-outs and train robberies in **Catskill** at **Carson City** are a bit hokey, but children seem to love them. The set for several movies, Carson City has cancan dancers, prancing "Indians," and stagecoach holdups. *Rte. 32, Catskill, tel. 518/678-5518. Admission: $8.55 adults, $5.35 children 3–12, under 3 free. Open Memorial Day–June and Sept.–Nov., weekends; July and Aug., daily 9:30–6.*

The town of Catskill, eastern gateway to the Catskills, is the home of world heavyweight boxing champ Mike Tyson and the host of professional national bass fishing tournaments in summer. It also has its share of museums and quaint buildings.

The **Thomas Cole House** is a beautifully preserved home and studio of the founder of the Hudson River School of landscape painting. *218 Spring St., Catskill, tel. 518/943-6533. Free admission. Call for hours.*

Greene County Council on the Arts and the **GCCA Catskill Gallery** sponsor concerts, theater, literary readings, and shows by nationally known and local artists. *398 Main St., Catskill, tel. 518/943-3400. Open year-round.*

Also popular in town is the **Catskill Reptile Institute.** This unusual facility provides an up-close look at some of the world's most fascinating reptiles, from the playful garter snake to the exotic king cobra. *Rte. 32, Catskill, tel. 518/678-5590.*

Somewhere in the 417,900 acres of Greene County lies a stone marker with Rip Van Winkle's initials carved on it. It's here that he lost a precious ebony nine-pin he had spirited away from Hendrick Hudson's drunken crew of phantom revelers. A bit tipsy himself, Rip decided to take a nap in the woods, and when he awoke 20 years later, he couldn't remember where he had left it.

Today the nine-pin—studded with 68 diamonds, 21 moonstones, a 31-carat garnet and several ounces of pure gold, and insured for $100,000—is displayed in the Tanners branch of the Schenectady Trust Company on Main Street in Catskill. And it's yours—if you can find the stone marker. It's offered by The Kaaterskill Foundation, a group dedicated to preserving the natural beauty of Greene County. For clues and information about how to join this treasure hunt, send for a copy of *The Lost Treasures of Rip Van Winkle* ($5.95, plus $1.20 shipping), from the Kaaterskill Foundation (Box 551, Catskill, NY 12414).

Return to Route 23 and head south on Route 32 to the **Catskill Game Farm.** For more than 50 years the Lindemann family has operated this preserve, now home to 2,000 birds and animals including a large collection of rare hooved species. The petting zoo and playground are favorites with the kids. *Game Farm*

Rd., Catskill, tel. 518/678–9595. Admission: $8.75 adults, $5 children 4–12, under 4 free. Open mid-Apr.–Oct. daily 9–6.

Follow Route 32 south to Saugerties in Ulster County and take Route 212 west to **Woodstock,** home to artists, craftspeople, and musicians of all sorts (*see* Hudson Valley). Continue on through Bearsville, Lake Hill, and Willow to Mount Tremper; head north on Route 28 to **Phoenicia** on Esopus Creek. Long noted as an outstanding trout stream, the Esopus has in recent years developed a reputation for white-water kayaking in the spring and, in summer, the somewhat tamer sport of tubing— drifting along in inner tubes that can either be a relaxing pastime or a water-borne version of bumper cars. At least five outfitters rent tubes in Phoenicia and Mt. Pleasant.

Route 214 from Phoenicia north to Hunter winds through **Stoney Clove,** a spectacular mountain cleft that has inspired countless tales of witchcraft and the supernatural. Early entrepreneurs guided gullible tourists through rock formations they called the Devil's Kitchen, the Devil's Pulpit, and the Devil's Tombstone. The last—a six-by-seven-foot rounded sandstone slab—is the locale of Devil's Tombstone Public Campground. *Rte. 214, Hunter, tel. 914/688–7160 or 518/943– 4030. Open May 15–Labor Day.*

Back at Phoenicia, cross the Esopus and drive south up lovely **Woodland Valley** to the well-marked trail to **Slide Mountain.** At 4,204 feet, this is the highest peak in the Catskills, and those who make the moderately strenuous six-mile climb are amply rewarded with glorious views from the summit. Be prepared to encounter lots of weekend trail traffic in summer.

As you continue the westward climb on Route 28, it's easy to understand why the Ulster & Delaware Railroad was nicknamed the "Up and Down." For many decades the U&D carried tourists to hotels and boarding houses in Pine Hill, Fleischmanns, and other resort towns along this route, and took milk and farm products back down to Kingston for shipment to New York City. The milk trains and the Friday night "husband trains," filled with men rejoining vacationing families after a work week in the city are long gone. But you can still get the flavor of this important era in Catskill history with a 12-mile round-trip excursion between **Arkville** and **Halcottsville** aboard the **Delaware & Ulster Rail Ride.** There are four hour-long trips daily along the East Branch of the Delaware River, with a turnaround stop at Lake Wawaka in Halcottsville. *Rte. 28, Arkville, tel. 914/586–DURR. Fare: $6 adults, $5 seniors, $3 children 5–11. Open weekends June, Sept., and Oct.; Wed.– Sun. July–Labor Day.*

Another form of transport is spotlighted at the **Auto Memories Museum,** which displays 100 cars and trucks dating back to 1906. Volunteers staff the museum and proceeds go to community improvement projects. *Cut-off Rd., Arkville. No phone. Admission: $2 adults, children under 12 free. Open daily July 1–Labor Day; weekends Labor Day–Columbus Day, 10:30– 4:30.*

Delaware County

Newly discovered by big-city vacationers and second-home buyers, Delaware County is characterized by smaller peaks, shallower valleys called "hollows," and a generally gentler terrain than the abrupt "cloves" of the high peaks region. Traversed by the East and West branches of the Delaware River, the area is famous among anglers and hunters who annually take bountiful numbers of trout, deer, and wild turkey.

With more than 500 family farms, Delaware County is a land of roadside stands full of honey, eggs, apple cider, and maple syrup. Its rural heritage is celebrated throughout the summer at country fairs, farm days, lumberjack festivals, ox pulls, and Saturday-night auctions.

The county contains more than 11,000 acres of reservoirs and 750 miles of streams and rivers packed with small-mouth bass, walleye, and trout. The Beaver Kill, birthplace of dry fly fishing in America, has a solid reputation for the best fishing in the Northeast.

In spring, it's hunting country. In summer, hiking and horseback riding on marked trails, particularly in the 64,000 acres of state-owned "forever wild" land, are the major attractions. Fall spells spectacular foliage. And in winter, it's back to the outdoors on the runs of five major downhill ski centers and hundreds of miles of cross-country and snowshoeing trails.

8 **Roxbury**, on Route 30 in northeast Delaware County, has a Norman Rockwell-like, picture-perfect Main Street of tidy homes with century-old maples on wide front lawns. A Main Street landmark is the **Jay Gould Memorial Reformed Church**, a magnificent limestone, oak, and stained-glass edifice erected in 1892 by the children of the Roxbury-born railroad tycoon. Visitors are welcome at Sunday morning services (9:30 July 4– Labor Day, 10:30 during the rest of the year).

Another native son is recalled at the more humble **Burroughs Memorial** off Hardscrabble Road just north of Roxbury. He was John Burroughs, the naturalist and author whose summer retreat, Woodchuck Lodge, is located on the farm where he was born in 1837 and buried in 1922. Although most of his adult life was spent at West Park (*see* Hudson Valley), Burroughs wrote many of his 23 books and occasionally entertained influential friends like Henry Ford and Thomas Edison at his Roxbury cabin. *Burroughs Memorial Rd., Roxbury, tel. 518/299–3498. Donation. Open weekends July 4–Labor Day, 11–5.*

Go north from Roxbury on Route 30 to Grand Gorge, the headwaters of the East Branch of the Delaware, and take Route 23 **9** west to **Stamford**. During the fall, the **Log Cabin Cider Mill**, three miles east of Stamford, offers apple-pressing demonstrations, tours, and free samples of fresh cider. *Blackberry St., Stamford, tel. 607/652–3384. Open Sept.–Nov. 9–5. Closed Tues.*

On the outskirts of Stamford, turn south on Mountain Avenue, opposite the red information booth. This will take you to the top of **Utsayantha Mountain,** now a favorite launch site for hang gliders.

Stamford also claims renowned storyteller Ned Buntline, king of the 19th-century dime novels and the discoverer of Buffalo Bill. Buntline was born in Stamford and spent his last years at **Eagle's Nest.** The house still stands on South Delaware Street but is not open to the public.

Time Out   The unpretentious **Stamford Inn** (Main St., Stamford, tel. 607/ 652–4863) is famous for its stuffed "pizza." This inside-out pizza is deep-fried rather than baked and topped with a special sauce; you figure out how to eat it.

---

10   Continue west on Route 23 to Davenport Center and follow the sign to **East Meredith** and the **Hanford Mills Museum.** The sawmill, gristmill, and woodworking shop dating back to 1820 are powered by a 10-foot water wheel. The assemblage of wheels, belts, and pulleys churning along in continuous motion may resemble a Rube Goldberg arrangement but it undeniably works. The placid millpond is a lovely backdrop for a picnic. *Rtes. 10 and 12, East Meredith, tel. 607/278–5744. Admission: $2.50 adults, $1 children 6–12, under 6 free. Open daily May–Oct. 10–5.*

11   The nine-mile drive on Elk Creek Road south from east Meredith to **Delhi** is one of the least-known pleasures of Catskill touring. Lined with maples bearing sap buckets in the spring and blazing foliage in autumn, this classic country road winds past dairy farms and homesteads of amazing architectural variety.

Turn left (east) at Route 10 and travel a half-mile to the **Delaware County Historical Association.** The 1798 Gideon Frisbee house and tavern, an 1860s schoolhouse, and a 19th-century gun shop are open to visitors, as is a huge 200-year-old barn housing an extensive farming exhibit. A gift shop offers a good selection of books on local history. *Rte. 10, Delhi, tel. 607/746–3849. Admission: $1.50 adults, 75¢ children. Open Memorial Day–Oct., Tues.–Fri. 10–4:30, weekends 1–4:30.*

Route 10 west leads to Delhi, the county seat and home of the State University Agricultural and Technical College. Take Route 28 south for a scenic ride through Andes to Dunraven and the eastern end of the 22-mile Pepacton Reservoir, one of several regional sources of New York City water. The drive along the reservoir on Route 30 is beautiful, but be advised there are no services.

12   As an alternative, continue west on Route 10 from Delhi to **Walton.** This is dairy country and the boulder-strewn pastures show why longtime residents claim the Catskills are made of "two rocks for every dirt." Route 206 south over Bear Spring Mountain leads to Downsville, where a **covered bridge** built in 1874 still carries traffic over the East Branch of the Delaware. Route 30 south between Downsville and the community of East Branch hugs the river, passing through hamlets like Shinhopple, which hosts the Peaceful Valley Bluegrass Festival each July. Call for information (tel. 607/363–2211).

Sullivan County and the Upper Delaware

The four-lane divided Route 17 neatly bisects Sullivan County and accesses most of the major resorts. Pick up Route 17 in Delaware County at East Branch and head east to **Roscoe,** the self-styled "Trout Town, USA." In the mid-1800s, American fly-fishing was born east of Roscoe at Junction Pool, situated at the confluence of Willowemoc Creek and the Beaver Kill. On opening day of fishing season each year, it's lined shoulder-to-shoulder with hopeful anglers.

⑭ The **Catskill Flyfishing Center** at **Deckertown**, between Roscoe and Livingston Manor is a seven-acre pond, casting pool, and 2,000 feet of stream frontage on Willowemoc Creek. A museum displays exhibits on rods, flies, and other paraphernalia used by the greats of the sport. Guest flytiers demonstrate their skills each Saturday during July and August. *Old Rte. 17, Deckertown, tel. 914/439–4810 or 607/498–5500. Free. Open daily 10–5.*

Covered-bridge fanciers will find four such spans in this area: at Beaver Kill State Campground, in Hall's Mills over the Neversink River, and two over Willowemoc Creek, one near Livingston Manor, and another two miles west of the hamlet of Willowemoc.

⑮ Watch for the sign at the Roscoe exit of Route 17 for **Callicoon** and the **Apple Pond Farming Center.** Located about six miles south off Route 123, this organic, horse-powered farm offers two-hour tours and demonstrations of sheepherding, beekeeping, draft-horse driving, and other traditional rural skills. Along with lessons in local history and the environment, visitors get covered-wagon and sleigh rides. Breads, pies, meats, honey, and other homemade products are sold on the premises. *Hahn Rd., Callicoon Center, tel. 914/482–4764. Admission: $6. Reservations required. Open year-round.*

⑯ Just down the road, the Bernthal Brothers maintain another country tradition at the **North Branch Cider Mill.** Their turn-of-the-century press transforms apples into cider daily during spring and fall. Children can pet lambs, kids, ducks, and calves while adults sample a special hard cider. The adjacent Mill Store sells everything from pottery to pickles—cider, too. *Rte. 123, North Branch, tel. 914/482–4823. Free. Open daily Apr. 1–Dec. 24, 10–5:30.*

⑰ ⑱ **Liberty** and **Monticello** on Route 17 are jumping-off points for the legendary Catskill resorts. The cool, dry atmosphere of the region and its proximity to New York City attracted early sufferers of tuberculosis and other lung ailments. Later, Russian and Eastern European Jews, who were not always welcome at hotels and boarding houses in other areas of the Catskills, escaped the heat and disease of the immigrant ghettos here. Over time, this network of resorts and vacation spots became known as the "borscht belt," and served as boot camp for innumerable entertainers who later gained national prominence. Resorts like the 1,250-room Concord in Kiamesha Lake, Kutcher's Country Club in Monticello, and Brown's Hotel in Loch Sheldrake still offer guests three gargantuan meals a day including entertainment, and sports in self-contained communities.

Over the past decade, however, the trend has been away from such large resort hotels, and the region is rapidly reverting to its earlier state as a refuge for the backwoods adventurer and the New York City intelligentsia. Today, it's big on cabins, second homes, small hotels, and cozy, old-fashioned bed-and-breakfast places.

Time Out For 50 years, **Kaplan's,** the only authentic Kosher deli in the Catskills, has been serving overstuffed corned beef and pastrami sandwiches and stuffed cabbage. *319 Broadway, Monticello, tel. 914/794–6060.*

19 At Monticello, take Route 17B west nine miles to **Bethel,** site of the 1969 "Woodstock Music and Art Fair, an Aquarian Exposition," better known as **Woodstock.** When the fair's organizers were turned away from the original location in Woodstock, 50 miles northeast of Bethel, they used Max Yasgur's dairy farm for the gathering of a half-million folk and rock music fans. The event is commemorated by a monument located at the corner of Hurd and West Shore roads. (Take Hurd Road north from Route 17B.)

Stay on Route 17B until you reach Callicoon on the Delaware River. This is the midway point of the 73-mile National Park Service Upper Delaware Scenic and Recreational River.

20 Just north of **Narrowsburg** is **Fort Delaware**, a reconstruction of a stockade community inhabited by Connecticut Yankees from 1755 to 1785. Demonstrations of crafts like candlemaking and musket-firing are conducted by staff in period dress. *Rte. 97, Narrowsburg, tel. 914/252–6660. Admission: $3 adults, $1.50 children 6–16, $8.50 families. Open weekends in June, daily July–Labor Day, 10–5:30.*

The **National Park Service Information Center** in Narrowsburg offers advice on fishing (eel, trout, walleye, bass, American shad), boating (canoe liveries along the Delaware do a roaring business in the summertime), and other matters of interest to travelers along the Delaware, which forms the boundary between New York and Pennsylvania. *Main St., Narrowsburg, tel. 914/252–3947. Open Memorial Day–Labor Day daily 9–4:30.*

During the 1800s, the Upper Delaware River was a crucial route for gigantic rafts of Catskill Mountain logs bound for the shipyards and factories in Philadelphia and Trenton. In 1847, more than 30 years before he designed the Brooklyn Bridge, John A. Roebling built a span over the raft-crowded river. At **21** **Minisink Ford,** the one-lane **Roebling Suspension Bridge,** the oldest such structure in the United States, now carries pedestrians and vehicles between Lackawaxen, Pennsylvania and Minisink Ford, New York. Free tours are available from park-service interpreters stationed at the former tollhouse on the New York end of the bridge. *Rte. 97, Minisink Ford, tel. 914/557–6363. Tollhouse open Memorial Day–Labor Day, daily 9:30–6.*

Route 97 meanders along the New York side of the Delaware. From October to April, this area is home to dozens of wintering bald eagles. For a great view of the river and the Pennsylvania woods to the west, stop at Hawk's Nest, a cliffside parking area some 400 feet above the water near Cherry Island, the southern terminus of the Upper Delaware Scenic and Recreational River.

Make your way back to Monticello via Route 52 and Route 17B from Narrowsburg, or Route 55 and Route 17B from Barryville four miles south of Minisink Ford. Route 17 will take you east to Wurtsboro and the Shawangunks.

You hear a lot of talk about ridge lifts, thermals, and waves in the Shawangunk Mountains (more familiarly, the 'Gunks). Airplane gliders and hang gliders are often seen soaring above the whitish cliffs that rise from the flat valley floor. The family that **22** owns **Wurtsboro Airport** claims its facility is the oldest soaring site in the nation, going back to the 1920s. A glider ride costs $30. Pilot and passenger in an engineless sailplane are towed into the great beyond by a conventional craft and released to soar with the currents. *U.S. 209, Wurtsboro, tel. 914/888–2791. Airport open year-round daily 8:30–5, weather permitting.*

㉓ Between 40 and 60 hang gliders descend (or ascend) on **Ellenville** (Ulster County) in June and October for Fun Fly-Ins from launch sites atop 1,000-foot Ellenville Mountain. Three parking areas along scenic Route 52 are the best spots from which to watch the gliders soar overhead and land in a field alongside the Nevele Hotel. The U.S. record for time aloft is 11 hours and 20 minutes, set by a pilot who took off from Ellenville. Several flights have gone nearly 100 miles to points along the Connecticut and Rhode Island coasts. Aerobatic demonstrations are held each July 4 in Ellenville, when the World Champion Aerobatics Pilot is joined by 25 other pilots for airborne maneuvers.

Ice Caves Mountain is another reason for coming to Ellenville. A registered national landmark, the Ellenville Fault Ice Caves are part of a privately held attraction that includes a mountain-top drive around Lake Maratanza, a self-guided one-mile walk to caves where ice clings to the rocks all year, and a spectacular view from 2,255-foot Sam's Point. *Six miles east of Rte. 52, Ellenville, tel. 914/647–7989. Admission: $6 adults, $4 children, under 6 free. Open Apr.–Oct., daily.*

㉔ In **New Paltz**, the **Minnewaska State Park,** northeast of Ellenville on U.S. 44, is an 11,600-acre undeveloped day-use area famous for two glacial lakes and fabulous 360-degree views. More than 90 miles of hiking trails (with 40 miles groomed for cross-country skiing) follow carriage roads that once led to two bygone hotels. Hike or bicycle three-and-a-half miles to swim in Lake Awasting; or drive over to Lake Minnewaska and rent a boat. In early summer the park is filled with glorious displays of fragrant mountain laurel. *U.S. 44, New Paltz, tel. 914/255–0752. Admission: $3.50 per car, individual user fee pending for skiers. Open daily 9–6.*

㉕ Route 209 north to **Kingston** isn't especially noted for its natural scenery, but the proliferation of stone architecture en route is worthy of attention. The **Ulster County Historical Society Museum** in Stone Ridge is a particularly fine example. *Tel. 914/338–5614.*

㉖ **Hurley,** a postcard-pretty little town just west of Kingston boasts twenty-seven 200-year-old Dutch-built stone houses. Come on Stone House Day, the second Saturday in July, for guided tours of the privately owned homes. Follow the suggested walking tour. A map of the tour is mounted in a display case at the town offices on Main Street. Stroll down Main Street and through a grassy alley to a violet-strewn cemetery hidden among pines and birches. The stones, some inscribed in Dutch, date back to 1713. Visitors are welcome until dusk each day.

More stone houses are found in New Paltz (*see* Hudson Valley).

What to See and Do with Children

Kids should enjoy the many outdoor recreation opportunities in the Catskills, but when the younger set craves its own kind of entertainment, they can find it here as well. Of particular amusement to children are the **Zoom Flume Aquamusement Park**, the **Catskill Game Farm, Catskill Reptile Institute, Carson City, Delaware & Ulster Rail Ride, Supersonic Speedway & Fun Park, Festival of Circus Theater, Hanford Mills Museum, Fort Delaware, Apple Pond Farming Center** and the **Catskill Fish Hatchery**.

Off the Beaten Track

Catskill State Fish Hatchery. The New York State Department of Environmental Conservation Fish Hatchery in Debruce (Sullivan County) is home to 1.3 million trout (mostly German browns) in various stages of development. Kept in long concrete holding ponds, the fish are raised to stock lakes and streams in 11 surrounding counties. A separate set of runs contains the huge females (valued at $125 a piece) used as breeding stock. Feeding time is quite a spectacle. *Mongaup Rd., Debruce, tel. 914/439–4328. Open daily 8:30–4.*

Shopping

Shopping is a major diversion in the Catskills. Malls, factory outlets, and shopping villages abound in the Lower Catskills. Treasure-hunting at festivals, auctions, flea markets, crafts fairs, antiques shops, and galleries is an all-season pastime throughout the region. Here are a few of the most intriguing and unusual shops:

Ethnic Gifts The **German Alps Festival Store** (Main St., Hunter, tel. 518/263–4114). Hummel figurines, Bonn wood carvings, Christmas ornaments, cuckoo clocks, and other European items. Open daily.

Guaranteed Irish (Rte. 145, East Durham, tel. 518/634–7409). The nation's largest collection of Irish goods including glassware, knits and tweeds, art, music, and books. Closed January and February.

St. John the Baptist Ukrainian Catholic Church (Rte. 23A, Jewett Center, tel. 518/263–3862). Imported items including embroidered clothing, inlaid wooden boxes, and hand-painted Easter eggs.

Regional Crafts **Craftspeople** (Spillway Rd., Hurley, tel. 914/331–3859). Glass, pottery, jewelry, leather, and other handmade items produced by 200 regional artisans, as well as some locally produced food items.

Candyman Chocolates in Catskill (tel. 518/943–2122) features hand-dipped chocolates, fresh creamery fudge, and regional specialties. Watch your chocolates being made.

Four Corners Studio in Freehold (tel. 518/634–7386) is the studio and gallery of Stanley Maltzman, who paints regional scenes and landscapes. Visitors are welcome, by appointment only.

Outlet Stores **Apollo Plaza** (East Broadway, Monticello, tel. 914/794–2010). An enclosed mall with 30 manufacturers' outlet stores selling everything from toys to furniture at discounts of up to 70%.

Participant Sports

Canoeing

The 79-mile Upper Delaware Scenic and Recreational River is one of the finest streams for paddling in the region. For a list of trip planners and rental firms, contact the **Sullivan County Office of Public Information** (*see* Important Addresses and Numbers).

Fishing

Some of the best trout streams in the world lie within the Catskills: Esopus, Willowemoc, Schoharie, Catskill, East Kill, and West Kill creeks; the Delaware and Neversink rivers; Beaver Kill and the Batavia Kill. In addition, smallmouth bass, walleye, and pickerel can be found in many lakes and in six reservoirs. To obtain the brochure "Catskill Fishing," which contains a map and information about streams and rivers, contact the **Catskill Association for Tourism Services (C.A.T.S.)** (Box 449, Catskill, NY 12414, tel. 800/542–2414), or any county tourism bureau (*see* Important Addresses and Numbers).

Golf

The Catskill region has 43 golf courses. Many, including "The Monster" at the Concord Hotel, which ranks among the nation's top 100 golf challenges, are located at the big resorts. Most courses have resident pros, instruction, and tournaments. Many resorts offer golfing vacation packages. To receive the "Golf Catskills" brochure, which lists public and private courses, rates, and packages, contact **C.A.T.S.** (*see* Fishing, above, or any county tourism bureau).

Hiking

The New York State Department of Environmental Conservation maintains more than 200 miles of marked hiking trails through the Catskill Forest Preserve. Twenty of the 34 peaks above 3,500 feet have trails to their summits. To receive the booklet "Catskill Trails," contact the DEC, 50 Wolf Rd., Albany, NY 12233.

Horseback Riding

The best way to see the woodlands and meadows and rushing mountain streams is from atop an English or Western saddle. Riding opportunities for urban cowboys and cowgirls range from rental stables to formal academies to dude ranches, with lessons and terrains for all abilities. For a guided trail ride, there is the **K&K Equestrian Center** at Ravine Farm (Wright St. in East Durham, tel. 518/966–5752). For lessons and training, try **Bittersweet Knoll Stables** in Leeds (tel. 518/622–8799). And for short, by-the-hour rides, mosey down to **Silver Springs Ranch** on Route 16 in Tannersville (tel. 518/589–5559).

Hunting

Deer, bear, wild turkey, rabbit, pheasant, and grouse are among the game taken annually on public and private lands within the region. The Department of Environmental Conservation "Big and Small Game Season Guides," available at license-issuing offices, outline regulations and describe areas open for public hunting. Get more information in "Hunting the Northern Catskills" from the Greene County Promotion Department; "Ulster County Hunting" from the Ulster County Public Information Office; and "Hunting Bulletin 1989–90" from the Sullivan County Public Information Office (*see* Important Addresses and Numbers).

For inexperienced hunters who would like a shot at a pheasant dinner, there's the **JR Shooting Preserve** on Grove School Road in Catskill (tel. 518/943–2069). This licensed preserve is open to the public. Shotguns, hunting dogs, handlers, and instruction are provided.

Skiing

Downhill Area ski centers include Highmount (tel. 914/254–5265); Belleayre Mountain (the only state-run ski facility in the Catskills), Highmount (tel. 914/254–5600); Bobcat, Andes (tel. 607/832–4829); Cortina Valley, Haines Falls (tel. 518/589–6500); Deer Run, Stamford (tel. 607/652–7332); Holiday Mountain, Monticello (tel. 914/796–3161); Hunter Mountain, Hunter (tel. 518/263–4223); Plattekill, Roxbury (tel. 607/326–7547); Ski Windham, Windham (tel. 518/734–4300); Big Vanilla at Davos, Woodridge (tel. 914/434–1000). Details on most ski centers are included in the "Ski the Catskills" brochure available through county promotion departments (*see* Important Addresses and Numbers).

Ski Windham offers extensive ski programs for the blind, hearing impaired, developmentally disabled, amputees, and those with lower-body disabilities. There's also a wheelchair run. Lessons are by appointment.

Cross-country Some of the finest cross-country trails are found at Minnewaska State Park near New Paltz, where 40 miles of carriage roads are groomed in the winter (tel. 914/255–0752). Other Nordic ski facilities are White Birches Ski Touring Center, Windham (tel. 518/734–3266); Hyer Meadows, Tannersville (tel. 518/589–5361); Hanofee Park, Liberty (tel. 914/292–7690 or 9358); Town of Thompson Park, Monticello (tel. 914/796–3161); Frost Valley YMCA Camp, Oliverea (tel. 914/985–7400); North Lake Public Campground (tel. 518/589–5058); and Belleayre Mountain, Highmount (tel. 800/942–6904 in NY State or 800/431–6012 outside NY).

Tennis

Most courts are not located at the hotels and resorts, but at public parks, colleges, and schools scattered throughout the region. Many are free; others charge a nominal hourly fee.

Spectator Sports

Hang Gliding

The Southern New York Hang Glider Pilots' Association maintains launch sites at five Catskill locations. The highest is on 2,300-foot Overlook Mountain near Woodstock. Others are on High Point near Samsonville, Mount Utsayantha near Stamford, and Little Mountain near West Shokan. The most accessible site for both pilots and spectators is on Ellenville Mountain, where several events are slated each year (*see* Exploring). *For more information, contact Mountain Wings, 150 Canal St., Ellenville, 12428, tel. 914/647–3377.*

Horse Racing

Monticello Raceway is a half-mile harness track with racing dates in spring and fall. Club Escoffier, a glass-enclosed restaurant, overlooks all the action. *Rtes. 17 and 17B, Monticello, tel. 914/794–4100. Admission: $1.50. Post time Tues.–Sat. 7:30, Sun. 1:30.*

Rodeo

Staff members and those who board horses at Roundup Ranch Resort participate in weekly rodeos at the resort. *Rte. 206, Downsville, tel. 607/363–7300. Admission free. Mid-May–Labor Day, Sat. 7:30.*

Dining and Lodging

Lodging The Catskill area is noted for its mammoth resorts—the kind with hundreds of rooms, where amenities like pools, health clubs, child care, golf courses, and nightly entertainment are standard, and where watching the other guests is as much a part of the vacation as shuffleboard or tennis. These mega-resorts offer all-inclusive packages, but if you want to plan your own trip there are other options: personal-touch bed-and-breakfasts and country inns reminiscent of the era when Catskill boarding houses welcomed summer-long refugees from the city, ski-center condos for those who want to stay close to the action, and efficiency cabins in the woods for those who don't. Small hotels, inns, lodges, bungalows, dude ranches, "guest farms," and B&Bs are alternatives. County promotion offices (*see* Important Addresses and Numbers) are good sources of free information on them.

Some B&Bs and country inns are listed with **The American Country Collection of Bed & Breakfast Accommodations** (984 Gloucester Place, Schenectady, NY 12309, tel. 518/370–4948).

Of course, you could always pack the tent, sleeping bags, and Coleman stove and go camping. Area promotion offices (*see* Important Addresses and Numbers) can send you information on Catskill campgrounds.

Category	Cost*
Very Expensive	over $100
Expensive	$85–$100
Moderate	$45–$85
Inexpensive	under $45

Rates are per person per night, double occupancy. Some resorts rent only by the week or weekend with meals included. Unless otherwise indicated, all hotels are open year-round and all rooms have private bath. Room rates for hotels on the American Plan (AP) include three meals per day; Modified American Plan (MAP) includes breakfast and dinner.

Dining While there is some outstanding food in the region, the most inspiring aspect of Catskill restaurants is often their setting. Those restaurants that don't serve chops, steaks, chicken, and other standard American fare generally run along ethnic lines, principally German/Austrian, Italian, and French. Shellfish and seafood are surprisingly abundant in this land-locked region: Some restaurateurs travel frequently to Boston, New York, and Maine for the freshest catch—and a number serve Catskill Mountain trout. Some will even fix your own catch any way you like it.

Since most visitors are here for the outdoor life, casual dress is generally acceptable. Correspondingly, the price of dinner at most Catskill establishments falls into the inexpensive-to-moderate price ranges.

Many area restaurants close down or have abbreviated hours for at least part of the year. Some are open only during the summer months; others reopen for the ski season. It's best to phone ahead. While reservations are usually not required, they are advisable on holidays and on weekends in both summer and winter. Highly recommended places are indicated by a star ★.

Category	Cost*
Very Expensive	over $35
Expensive	$25–$35
Moderate	$15–$25
Inexpensive	under $15

per person, without tax, service, or drinks

Arkville (Delaware)

Dining **Patricia's.** Barnboard, country-print wallpaper, high-backed chairs, and marble-topped side tables give this 60-seat restaurant an air of casual elegance. The American-style menu features prime ribs on Saturday night. *Church St., tel. 914/ 586-2770. Dress: informal. Reservations appreciated. DC, MC, V. Closed Mon. Inexpensive–Moderate.*

Big Indian (Ulster)

Dining **Rudi's Big Indian.** Established in the 1960s by students of a
★ nearby Buddhist ashram as a vegetarian sandwich shop and antiques store, Rudi's has evolved into a popular spot for
sophisticated dining. Oriental rugs, antiques, and local artwork create the ambience. Entrees include medallions of pork
with pear butter and vegetable ricotta pie. Filled with greenery, the Conservatory dining room is a pleasant place for a full
meal or for a dessert stop—coffee-toffee pie is highly recommended. *Rte. 28, tel. 914/254-4005. Dress: informal. AE, DC,
MC, V. Closed Nov. Moderate.*

Bloomingburg (Sullivan)

Dining and **Eagle's Nest Hotel.** This is a Viennese-style establishment
Lodging where modest rooms come with three meals and afternoon coffee. Most rooms have twin beds, some have terraces. The
German chef prepares a Continental menu; *wienerschnitzel* is a
popular item. The view from the glass-walled dining room includes three states. *Mountain Rd., 12721, tel. 914/733-4561.
Motel: 67 rooms; AP. 3-night minimum stay. Restaurant:
Open to nonguests Wed.–Sun. in July and Aug., Fri.–Sun. in
spring and fall. No credit cards. Closed Dec.–Mar. Moderate.*

Bovina Center (Delaware)

Dining and **Suits-Us Farm.** The dining room is a former cow barn, guest
Lodging rooms are in the remodeled hayloft, and two-room family suites
now occupy the chicken house and the carriage house. This
family-oriented former dairy farm offers hayrides, square
dances, and bonfires during the summer, plus a few animals to
pet and milk. Rates include three hearty meals. *Off County
Rte. 5, 13740, tel. 607/832-4470 or 832-4369. 35 units; AP.
Facilities: Pool, tennis, fishing. MC, V. Open May–Dec.
Moderate.*
Mountainbrook Chalet. Ruffled curtains and bedspreads
brighten up two-room housekeeping apartments in this off-
the-beaten-track motel. The German restaurant, which specializes in 10-inch stuffed pancakes and is noted for its Saturday-
night German buffet, is open to the public six days a week in
summer, weekends the rest of the year. *County Rte. 6, 13740,
tel. 607/832-4424. 8 units. Restaurant: dress casual. MC, V.
Inexpensive.*

Callicoon (Sullivan)

Dining and **Villa Roma Resort & Country Club.** This Italian-American re-
Lodging sort has its own ski slopes, 18-hole golf course, and indoor
sports complex. The dining room is famous for its Caesar's
Night Dinner, an 11-course Roman feast held Friday evenings
in summer. *Beechwoods, 12723, tel. 914/887-4880, 800/553-
6767 in NY, 800/621-5656 outside NY. Hotel: 225 rooms; AP.
Facilities: indoor-outdoor pools, tennis, racquetball, health
club, golf, disco. Restaurant: dress informal. Reservations required for nonguests. AE, MC, V. Expensive.*

Debruce (Sullivan)

Dining and **Debruce Country Inn.** Individually designed rooms feature Ori-
Lodging ental rugs, silk drapes, and matching spreads. The restaurant
serves a variety of vegetable and pasta dishes along with fresh-
fish specialties like Willowemoc Swimming Trout, baked local
trout surrounded by rice and greens. *Debruce Rd., 12724, tel.
914/439–3900. Hotel: 15 rooms; bed-and-breakfast or MAP.
Facilities: outdoor pool, sauna, exercise room. Restaurant:
dress informal. MC, V. Moderate.*

Deposit (Broome)

Dining and **Scott's Oquaga Lake House.** A spring-fed lake is the focal point
Lodging of this resort, best-known for its family atmosphere and sing-
along cruises on a 60-passenger showboat. Seven buildings, including an 1869 farmhouse, accommodate guests in simple
surroundings. Rates include three home-cooked meals. *Oquaga Lake, 13754, tel. 607/467–3094. 140 rooms; AP. No credit
cards. Restaurant: dress casual. Closed Oct.–May. Moderate.*

Downsville (Delaware)

Dining and **Roundup Ranch Resort.** This is a place for horse lovers, with
Lodging trail rides, lessons, indoor arena, sleigh rides, even a rodeo ev-
★ ery Saturday night during summer. No two rooms are alike;
decor is contemporary. *Rte. 206, 13755, tel. 607/363–7300. 35
rooms (26 more under construction); AP. Facilities: 9-hole golf
course, stocked trout pond, gift shop. Restaurant: casual
dress. AE, MC, V. Open daily May–Oct., weekends rest of
year. Moderate.*

Dining **Old Schoolhouse Restaurant.** Steaks, chops, chicken, and veal
are now served where local kids learned the three Rs from 1905
to 1937. Hung with moose heads, deer racks, and mounted fish,
the Sportsmen's Bar used to be the first grade classroom. The
original tin ceiling, oak floors, and hemlock siding remain.
*Main St., tel. 607/363–7814. Dress: informal. No credit cards.
Inexpensive.*

East Branch (Delaware)

Dining and **Buck-Horn Lodge.** Period furnishings and family memorabilia
Lodging adorn the rooms in this Victorian-era guest house. Seven simply furnished housekeeping cottages are nearby. The dining
room features roast beef, fried chicken, fresh vegetables, and
other home-style fare. *Rte. 30, 13756, tel. 607/363–7120. Hotel:
7 rooms, 7 cottages. Restaurant: dress informal. Reservations
required. No credit cards. Closed Jan.–Apr. Inexpensive.*

East Durham (Greene)

Dining and **The Country Place.** Motel units, some with sitting rooms, take
Lodging a back seat to the main attraction here—the Zoom Flume
Aquamusement Park (*see* Exploring). *Shady Glen Rd., 12423,
tel. 518/239–4559. 20 rooms; MAP; 2-night minimum stay. Facilities: pool. MC, V. Open May–Oct. Moderate.*

Elka Park (Greene)

Dining and
Lodging
★
Redcoat's Return. The ambience of an English country inn is offered in beautiful Platte Clove. Guest rooms are individually decorated. Dinner, served in a room with a view of surrounding mountains or in the cozy library, might include Yorkshire pudding or steak and kidney pie. *Dale La., 12427, tel. 518/589–6379. Hotel: 14 rooms, 5 with private bath; breakfast included. Restaurant: dress informal. Reservations requested. AE, DC, MC, V. Open Memorial Day–Oct., Jan.–Mar. Moderate.*

Eldred (Sullivan)

Dining and
Lodging
Eldred Preserve. Hunting and fishing packages are offered on a 2,500-acre resort where deer, turkey, and trout flourish. Rooms are contemporary; many have recently been refurbished. Seven miles of nature trails are suitable for cross-country skiing. *Rte. 55, 12732, tel. 914/557–8316. 21 rooms. Facilities: pool, tennis, restaurant. AE, DC, MC, V. Moderate.*

Ellenville (Ulster)

Dining and
Lodging
★
Nevele Hotel. This is one of the most up-to-date of the legendary Catskill megaresorts. There are five buildings in this sprawling complex, ranging from two to six stories high. Most deluxe is the Empire Wing with suites containing two double beds as well as a dressing area. The Towers building offers the best views with vistas of the hotel's well-manicured grounds. The Art-Deco lobby was refurbished two years ago. *Nevele Rd., 12428, tel. 914/647–6000 or 800/647–6000. 400 rooms; MAP. Facilities: 18-hole golf course, 15 tennis courts, 5 pools, ice rink, horseback riding, skiing, private lake, boating, fishing, nightly entertainment. AE, MC, V. Moderate–Expensive.*

Fleischmanns (Delaware)

Lodging
The Runaway Inn. A bowl of fresh fruit awaits guests in Victorian rooms furnished with highboard beds, oil paintings, and period antiques. Breakfast may include raspberry French toast, eggs Benedict, or fresh muffins. *Main St., tel. 914/254–5660. 5 rooms, 3 with private bath; bed and breakfast. MC, V. No children. Moderate.*

Freehold (Greene)

Dining and
Lodging
Pleasant View Lodge and Golf Club. The rooms in the 12 buildings here are modern; some suites have fireplaces and balcony. There's also a dining room and cozy fireplace bar. *Gayhead Rd., 12431, tel. 518/634–2523. 120 rooms. Facilities: 9-hole golf course, indoor-outdoor pools, tennis, sauna, ballroom. Restaurant: dress informal. Reservations requested. AE, MC, V. Moderate.*

Grand Gorge (Delaware)

Lodging
The Colonial Motel. You may stay in standard motel units or in one of the antique-furnished rooms in the 1832 main house. All rooms feature 19th-century photographs of local people taken

by Anna Carroll. *Rtes. 23 and 30, 12434, tel. 607/588–6122 or 588–6495. 14 rooms. MC, V. Inexpensive.*

Greenville (Greene)

Dining and Lodging
Greenville Arms. Antiques decorate the rooms in the 1889 main house; contemporary furnishings outfit units in the former carriage house. *Rte. 32, 12083, tel. 518/966–5219. 19 rooms; meal plans available. Facilities: pool. AE, MC, V. Open May–Nov. Moderate.*

Pine Lake Manor. Landscaped lawns, putting greens, three well-stocked lakes, and a 19th-century main house complement this 150-acre resort. *Rte. 26, tel. 518/966–5745. 58 rooms. Facilities: handball/racquetball, tennis, pools. No credit cards. Open May–Oct. Moderate.*

Haines Falls (Greene)

Dining and Lodging
Hunter Mountain Resort Ranch. Bunk beds in some rooms indicate that this place caters to families. Wranglers lead rides on 20 acres of horse trails. Nightlife means square dances on Tuesdays and a country-western band on Thursdays. *Rte. 23A, 12436, tel. 518/589–6430. 24 rooms. Facilities: indoor-outdoor pools, tennis, volleyball, archery, shuffleboard, basketball, minigolf. No credit cards. Moderate.*

Villa Maria. This is a full-service resort during the summer and a bed-and-breakfast operation in the off-season and skiing months. Italian-American specialties are served at the adjacent Marianna Restaurant. *Rte. 23A, 12436, tel. 518/589–6200. 54 rooms. Facilities: indoor-outdoor minigolf. AE, MC, V. Moderate.*

Honsonville (Greene)

Dining
Vesuvio. The regional Italian menu here includes *ossobuco*, *pansotti* (homemade stuffed pasta with a walnut sauce), seafood specials, and desserts such as *zabaglione*, a hot custard prepared tableside and served over ice cream and fruit. A sophisticated wine list, candlelight, and fresh flowers contribute to an elegant atmosphere. *Goshen Rd., tel. 518/734–3663. Dress: casual (but no shorts). Reservations preferred. AE, DC, MC, V. Moderate.*

Seeley's. Seafood, steaks, and other American fare have been served here since 1911. The Friday night lobster and the Catskill Mountain Chicken (chicken breast on a bed of wild rice and spinach with a creamy cheese sauce) come highly recommended. *Rte. 296, tel. 518/734–9892. Dress: informal. AE, MC, V. Closed Tues. dinner. Inexpensive.*

Hunter (Greene)

Dining
Fireside. Chops, steaks, fish, and some Italian dishes are among the entrees at this no-frills eatery. A children's menu is available; a bar is not. *Main St., tel. 518/263–4216. Dress: informal. Reservations advised on weekends. AE, MC, V. Inexpensive–Moderate.*

Dining and Lodging
★
Scribner Hollow Motor Lodge. There are 16 fireplaces in this ultramodern lodge, plus theme rooms like Future World (sunken bath, waterfall, and an environmentally controlled bed cham-

ber) and Hunting Lodge (Remington prints and sporty decor).
The two-story Penthouse Suite (sunken living room, balcony,
king-size bed) costs $220 per night. The restaurant overlooks
the mountains. *Rte. 23A, 12442, tel. 518/263–4211. 38 rooms;*
MAP. Facilities: pool, Jacuzzi, sauna. AE, DC, MC, V.
Expensive–Very Expensive.

Sun-Land Farm Motel & Cabins. Motel, boarding house, and
housekeeping cabins make up this eclectic establishment. The
dining room has an American-Czechoslovakian menu that includes such entrees as roast pork with dumplings and sweet
and sour cabbage. *Rte. 23A, 12442, tel. 518/263–4811. 15*
rooms, 2 cabins. Facilities: pool. AE, DC, MC, V. Inexpen-
sive–Moderate.

Kerhonkson (Ulster)

Dining and
Lodging

Granit Hotel and Country Club. This is one of the big resorts,
and the rooms here come with three (American-style) meals.
Rooms range from "standard" to "ultra deluxe," but the differ-
ence is more in their size (and price) than amenities.
Kerhonkson, 12446, tel. 914/626–3141, 212/563–1881, or 800/
431–7681. Facilities: pools, tennis, ice rink, golf, health club,
nightclub. AE, MC, V. Moderate–Expensive.

Kiamesha Lake (Sullivan)

Dining and
Lodging
★

Concord Resort Hotel. This is one of the most enduring Catskill
resorts. The Concord's 3,000 acres encompass three golf
courses, 40 tennis courts, horseback-riding trails, an indoor-
outdoor skating rink, volleyball, basketball, shuffleboard, and
much more. The hotel annually serves more than 2.5 million
strictly kosher meals in dining rooms that can seat more than
3,000 people at a time. *Kiamesha Lake, 12751, tel. 914/794–*
4000 or 800/431–3850. 1,200 rooms; AP. Facilities: ski slope, 3
nightclubs, 2 pools, men's and women's health clubs, toboggan
run. AE, DC, MC, V. Moderate–Expensive.

Lexington (Greene)

Dining and
Lodging

Lexington Hotel. If you don't mind sharing a bath, this 103-
year-old hotel on the banks of Schoharie Creek is one of the best
bargains around. An unpretentious restaurant featuring a
Ukrainian buffet on Friday nights, and serving three meals
daily during July and August. *Rte. 42, 12452, tel. 518/989–*
9797. 24 rooms, no private baths. No credit cards. Inexpensive.

Liberty (Sullivan)

Dining

Pursuit of Happiness. Known for top-flight entertainment, this
nightclub also has a passable dinner menu. Entrees include
prime ribs and coq au vin; a cafe menu is available for light or
late-night diners. The homey Victorian structure is filled with
greenery, pottery, works by local artists, antique furniture,
and a custom-built oak bar. *117 S. Main St., tel. 914/292–6760.*
Dress: informal. Reservations suggested on show nights. Open
for dinner Tues.–Sat. in spring and summer; Sat. and show
nights the rest of the year. DC, MC, V. Inexpensive.

Dining and
Lodging

Days Inn of Liberty. The guest rooms are standard, but there's
a game room and bar where a DJ entertains a 30-ish crowd. The

Dynasty restaurant serves surf and turf and Oriental-style fare. *Sullivan Ave., 12754, tel. 914/292–7600. 120 rooms. Facilities: indoor-outdoor pools. AE, DC, MC, V. Inexpensive.*

Livingston Manor (Sullivan)

Dining and
Lodging

Menges' Lakeside. An informal family atmosphere, folk-dance weekends, and a beautiful location on Sand Lake distinguish this family-run resort. There's no air-conditioning and most baths are shared, but that doesn't deter the regular clientele from returning year after year. *Shandalee Rd., 12758, tel. 914/439–4569. 70 rooms, 40 with private bath; AP. Facilities: tennis, lake swimming, boating, fishing. No credit cards. Open daily July–Labor Day, weekends only May–June, Labor Day–mid-Oct. Moderate.*

Loch Sheldrake (Sullivan)

Dining and
Lodging

Brown's Resort Hotel. This family-oriented Catskill biggie comprises 17 buildings and a long list of resort amenities—two golf courses, minigolf, tennis, a health club, disco, horseback riding, two pools and an indoor roller rink, top-name entertainment, kosher food. *Loch Sheldrake, 12759, tel. 914/434–5151 or 800/3–BROWNS. 570 rooms; AP. AE, MC, V. Expensive.*

Maplecrest (Greene)

Dining and
Lodging

Sugar Maples. Taken over by a new owner in 1988, this traditional resort now has a Hellenic identity, with *moussaka* and lamb *kapama* in the dining room and Greek music in the nightclub. The rooms are modern, and rates include three meals. *Main St., 12454, tel. 518/734–4000. 150 rooms; AP. Facilities: pool, tennis, ice skating. MC, V. Moderate.*

Narrowsburg

Lodging

Wolfe's Pioneer Motel. Located within the New York State National Scenic and Recreation Area near Skinners Falls on the Delaware River, this motel caters to canoeists and fishermen. *Rte. 97, 12764, tel. 914/252–3385. Facilities: pool, picnic area. MC, V. Inexpensive.*

Dining and
Lodging

Narrowsburg Inn. Sullivan County's oldest inn (and the third-oldest in the state) was built in 1840 as a stopover for Delaware River loggers and raftsmen. Photos of old Narrowsburg and the rough-and-tumble tree cutters who once worked here hang on the walls. The restaurant serves homemade soups, steak, seafood, and veal dishes. *Rte. 52, 12764, tel. 914/252–3998. 7 rooms with shared bath. Restaurant: casual dress. Reservations recommended on weekends. Open daily Apr.–Oct. closed Wed. rest of year. Inexpensive.*

Margaretville (Delaware)

Dining and
Lodging

Kass Inn. About half of the summer guests here attend the Roland Stafford Golf School on the premises and practice at the nearby Hidden Waters Golf Course. Motel-type rooms come with two or three meals, served in the antiques-filled restaurant. Diners can choose from four or five daily specials in addition to regular offerings. Prime rib is a Saturday night tradition, as is the live music. *Rte. 30, 12455, tel. 914/586–9844. 68 rooms; MAP. Facilities: tennis, pool, fishing. Restaurant: casual dress. MC, V. Moderate.*

Lodging **Margaretville Mountain Inn.** Once an elaborate Victorian boarding house, this bed-and-breakfast establishment offers rooms decorated with antiques, quilts, and cheery curtains. The ivory-and-oak bridal suite comes with a split of champagne. A wide veranda overlooks a long, sloping lawn. *Margaretville Mountain Rd., 12455, tel. 914/586–3933. 5 rooms, 3 with private bath. AE, MC, V. Moderate.*

Dining **Binnekill Square.** Black Angus sirloin with blue-cheese butter and blackened breast of duckling with green peppercorns are among the entrees in this cozy eatery. If you prefer your duckling live, take a table on the deck overlooking Binnekill Creek and watch the mallards paddle under the building. *Main St., tel. 914/586–4884. Dress: casual. Reservations not accepted. No credit cards. Closed Mon. Moderate.*

Monticello (Sullivan)

Dining **Scalawags.** If this restaurant reminds you of Houlihans in New York City, it's because the same firm designed both. The menu ranges from hamburgers to lobster and duck. A DJ entertains most nights; live dance music is featured Saturdays starting at 11 PM. *358 Broadway, tel. 914/794–3131. Dress: casual. Reservations not accepted. AE, MC, V. Moderate.*

Lodging **Kutsher's Country Club.** A grand Catskill resort where golf, tennis, and swimming are summer pastimes, and cross-country skiing, snowmobiling, snowshoeing, and ice skating are winter pursuits. Children's and teens' programs are offered. *Anawana Lake Rd., 12701, tel. 914/794–6000, 212/243–3112, or 800/431–1273. 450 rooms; AP. Facilities: golf, tennis, racquetball, pool, health club. AE, DC, MC, V. Moderate–Expensive.*

Mount Tremper (Ulster)

Dining **Catskill Rose.** Imaginative entrees include curried mussels over pasta with peanut sauce and lamb chops with roasted red peppers. Art-Deco surroundings feature pink flamingos on the tables, an oak-and-mahogany bar with frosted-glass windows illuminated by colored lights, and a periwinkle and gray color scheme. Classical, jazz, or contemporary piano music is featured Saturday nights. *Rte. 212, tel. 914/688–7100. Dress: casual. Reservations appreciated. DC, MC, V. Closed Mon. in winter. Moderate.*

Lodging **Mount Tremper Inn.** This bed-and-breakfast inn has early-Victorian guest rooms and breakfasts featuring home-baked breads. The common room sports red velvet walls and a gold-leaf ceiling; shuffleboard and badminton are played on two acres of manicured lawn. One large suite contains two beds and two sitting rooms. *Rte. 212 and Wittenberg Rd., 12457, tel. 914/688–9938 or 688–5329. 12 rooms, 2 with private bath. MC, V. Moderate.*

Oliverea (Ulster)

Dining and **Slide Mountain Forest House.** This country inn in the woods ca-
Lodging ters to an outdoorsy crowd. With its mounted game, the sitting

room resembles a hunting lodge. The rooms have contemporary furnishings, and the restaurant serves German-American family-style food. *Oliverea Rd., 12462, tel. 914/254–5365. 24 rooms. Facilities: pool, tennis, handball. No credit cards. Open Memorial Day–Dec. 1. Inexpensive.*

Palenville (Greene)

Lodging   **Oak Lodge Cabins.** Each of four housekeeping cottages here accommodates from two to six people and contains a kitchen, bath, and bedroom with contemporary furnishings; five other cabins have only bedrooms. One housekeeping cottage is open year-round, the others from May to September. *Rte. 32A, 12463, tel. 518/678–9929. 9 cabins. No credit cards. Moderate.*

Dining and Lodging   **Friar Tuck Inn.** A big, contemporary resort near the base of Kaaterskill Clove, Friar Tuck features architecture and furnishings with a touch of Camelot, but the cuisine in the Sherwood Dining Room is Italian-American. There are boating and fishing on a man-made private lake, bikes for rent, and organized activities. *Rte. 32, 12463, tel. 518/678–2271. 550 rooms; MAP. Facilities: tennis, nightclub, sauna, gym. Restaurant: casual dress. AE, DC, MC, V. Moderate–Expensive.*

Phoenicia (Ulster)

Dining   **Margo's.** Sauerbraten with potato dumplings, veal goulash, and apple strudel are some of the Hungarian and German specialties here. There's a homey European atmosphere, with wood carvings of bears and birds throughout. *Rte. 28, tel. 914/688–7102. Dress: informal. MC, V. Open Fri.–Sun., mid-Apr.–Memorial Day; daily Memorial Day–mid-Nov. Inexpensive–Moderate.*

Yvonne's. Cassoulet and duck, especially smoked, and the confit are the specialties in this quaint eatery with a slight French accent. Yvonne's is best known for its unusual game–venison, antelope, moose and wild boar–all raised for the table at "game" farms. Quilts on the ceilings and mismatched chairs complete the country decor. *Rte. 28, tel. 914/688–7340. Dress: casual. Reservations suggested. No credit cards. Open weekends for dinner, Apr.–Oct., and also when the owner feels like it. Call ahead. Moderate–Expensive.*

Pine Hill (Ulster)

Dining and Lodging   **Pine Hill Arms Hotel.** At this country inn with a family air, you may have to step over the owner's cats, dogs, and kids to reach the front desk. Charcoal-broiled steaks and seafood are served in a greenhouse dining room. *Main St., 12465, tel. 914/254–9811. 30 rooms. Facilities: pool, game room, Jacuzzis. Restaurant: informal dress. Reservations recommended. MC, V. Moderate.*

Hideaway Hotel-Restaurant. There are motel units, cottages, and 14 rooms in the main inn situated on a quiet mountaintop. The German-American restaurant commands wide views from its picture windows. Room rates include two meals. *Huntersfield Rd., 12465, tel. 518/299–3616. 14 rooms; MAP. No credit cards. Moderate.*

Round Top (Greene)

Dining and Lodging **Winter Clove Inn.** Colonial architecture and decor (four-poster beds, wide-board pine floors, braided rugs) distinguish this 150-year-old inn. There are miles of foot trails on 400 acres adjoining the Catskill Forest Preserve. *Off Rte. 32, 12473, tel. 518/622–3267. 50 rooms. Facilities: pool, tennis, bowling, 9-hole golf course. DC, MC, V. Closed Dec. Moderate.*

Roxbury (Delaware)

Dining **Roxbury Run.** Lots of ornate woodwork and antiques highlight this rustic Swiss-style restaurant. Braised duckling, rack of lamb, veal cordon bleu, and chocolate fondue top the menu. *Denver Rd., tel. 607/326–7577. Dress: casual. Reservations required. Closed Mon.–Wed. MC, V. Moderate.*

Lodging **Scudder Hill House.** Home-grown, home-cooked food is the hallmark of this bed-and-breakfast inn located in a former farmhouse. Fresh eggs and bacon, pesto omelets, blueberry pancakes, and a variety of breads and cookies are served in the fireside dining room. Antiques, hand-stenciling, and attractive furnishings make it homey. *Rte. 30, 12474, tel. 607/326–4364. 5 rooms. MC, V. Moderate.*

Shandaken (Ulster)

Dining and Lodging ★ **Auberge des 4 Saisons.** The atmosphere of a European inn prevails here, with some of the rooms located in a chalet, others in the main house where baths are shared. The restaurant serves French country cuisine with specialties from different provinces featured on weekends. Goat cheeses and locally grown vegetables are featured. *Rte. 28, 12480, tel. 914/688–2223 or 5480. 36 rooms, 19 with private bath. Restaurant: casual dress. Reservations requested. AE, DC, MC, V. Open daily Memorial Day–Labor Day, weekends rest of year. Moderate.*
Copper Hood Inn. Colonial print bedspreads and Priscilla curtains give an Early-American look to the guest rooms here. It's quiet, too: no TVs or telephones and you can play tennis on a private island. The Continental restaurant serves hotel guests only. *Rte. 28, 12480, tel. 914/688–9962 or 212/261–2341. 20 rooms. Facilities: indoor pool, Jacuzzi, sauna. MC, V. Moderate.*

South Kortright (Delaware)

Dining **The Hidden Inn.** The Friday night surf-and-turf smorgasbord (prime ribs, shrimp, crab legs, clams) is a bargain here. Homemade rolls and desserts (cream puffs, chocolate mousse) are other favorites. Local artwork is exhibited in the Colonial dining room. *Main St., tel. 607/538–9359. Dress: casual. Reservations recommended. MC, V. Closed Mon. Inexpensive.*

Stamford (Delaware)

Dining and Lodging **Red Carpet Motor Inn.** Motel rooms, some with sitting areas, refrigerators, and small decks, surround the pool. Restaurant entrees include shellfish preparations, along with beef, chicken, and pork dishes. A pastry chef prepares mousses, tortes, and other specialties fresh daily. *Rtes. 10 and 23, 12167, tel.*

607/652–7394. 37 rooms. Facilities: pool, lounge. AE, DC, MC, V. Moderate.

Swan Lake (Sullivan)

Dining and Lodging   **Stevensville Country Club.** One of the major Sullivan County super-resorts. This place has 400 rooms, a kosher kitchen, and myriad activities for young and old. *Swan Lake, 12783, tel. 914/ 292–8000 or 800/431–3858. 400 rooms; AP. Facilities: pools, golf, tennis, racquetball, minigolf, health club, disco. AE, DC, MC, V. Moderate–Expensive.*

Tannersville (Greene)

Dining and Lodging   **Eggery Inn.** This picturesque bed-and-breakfast inn has a Franklin stove and player piano in the parlor lounge, a handcrafted oak bar in the dining room, and comforters on brass beds in individually appointed rooms. *County Rte. 16, 12485, tel. 518/589–5363. 13 rooms; breakfast included. Restaurant open for dinner summer and winter only. AE, MC, V. Moderate.*

Villa Vosilla Resort. A honeymoon suite with Jacuzzi and king-size bed, and a three-room family suite are among 100 motel and lodge units. The restaurant serves northern Italian fare. *Main St., 12485, tel. 518/589–5060 or 800/543–1450. 100 rooms. Facilities: pool, sauna/spa, exercise room, game room, nightly entertainment. AE, DC, MC, V. Moderate.*

Westkill (Greene)

Dining and Lodging   **Schwarzenegger's Sunshine Valley House.** The German owners call their location, in a wide valley surrounded by five mountains, "a small Bavaria." Rooms are available with breakfast only or with three German-American meals. *Spruceton Rd., 12492, tel. 518/989–9794. 18 rooms; bed-and-breakfast or AP. Facilities: pool. No credit cards. Inexpensive.*

White Lake (Sullivan)

Dining   **The Lighthouse.** The exterior doesn't look like a lighthouse, but there's a bit of a nautical theme in the dining room. Seafood, chops, steaks, and some Italian dishes are offered here, and the deck overlooks lovely White Lake. *Rte. 17B, tel. 914/583–9865. Dress: casual. MC, V. Inexpensive–Moderate.*

Windham (Greene)

Dining   **La Griglia.** Elegant and intimate, this fine northern Italian and ★ Yugoslavian restaurant specializes in items like scaloppini of pork, sautéed with tomato, garlic, and fruit juices and layered with grilled apples; desserts include chocolate Frangelica mousse torte and apricot *spuma*. It also may have the best wine list in upstate New York. A brunch-type menu, taken primarily from the appetizer list, is available at a cafe with outdoor seating overlooking the golf course. *Rte. 296, tel. 518/734–4499. Dress: casual (no jeans). Reservations required. AE, MC, V. Expensive.*

Chalet Fondue. As the name implies, fondues are the specialty here—beef, veal, cheese, chocolate. German, Swiss, and Austrian dishes, such as *jagerschnitzel*—fresh veal with a creamy mushroom sauce—are served in an Alpine atmosphere. Dine in the wicker-and-glass greenhouse or in the rathskeller, where wine barrels line the walls. *Rte. 296, tel. 518/734–4650. Dress: casual. Reservations required. AE, DC, MC, V. Open Thurs.– Mon. summer; daily except Tues. winter; other times call. Moderate.*

Dining and Lodging   **Christman's Windham House.** The main Gothic-revival building dates back to 1805, but most guest rooms are distributed among five other buildings. Rocking on the veranda, bingo, and walking along two miles of trails are popular with the older clientele. *Rte. 23, 12496, tel. 518/734–4230. 50 rooms. Facilities: pool, 9-hole golf course, recreation barn, entertainment 4 nights a week in summer. No credit cards. Inexpensive.*

★   **Thompson House.** Guests are remembered by their first names at this resort run for over a century by five generations of the same family. Guest rooms, including some Jacuzzi suites, are located in the 1860s-era main house, the Victorian Spruce Cottage, and several other buildings. *Rte. 296, 12496, tel. 518/734– 4510. 110 rooms. Facilities: pool, tennis, putting greens, recreation room. MC, V. Open May–Oct. and ski season. Inexpensive–Moderate.*

Wurtsboro (Sullivan)

Dining   **The Repast.** This is an elegant eatery in a country sort of way.
★   Entrees like salmon Dijon and *poulet portofino* (sautéed breast of chicken with a banana-liqueur sauce and almonds) are served with Caesar salad and homemade desserts. Come for lunch and follow it up with a visit to the adjacent Canal Towne Emporium, a restored 1845 country store. *Sullivan St., tel. 914/888–4448. Dress: casual. Reservations suggested. MC, V. Open daily for lunch; Thurs.–Sun. for dinner. Moderate.*

Yulan (Sullivan)

Dining   **YesterYears.** Try the blackened fish, jambalaya, or the duck l'orange at this rural restaurant that mingles French, New Orleans, and American cuisines. Red tablecloths covered with lace, red velvet drapes, and oak floors adorn the three dining rooms. Chocolate velvet cake is a favorite here. *Four Corners, tel. 914/557–6464. Dress: casual. Reservations suggested. MC, V. Open May–Oct. Moderate.*

The Arts and Nightlife

Arts

For centuries, artists have found their creative muse in the Catskills. The trend continues. Outstanding craftsmen are moving here from New York City and finding that, without the pressures of city life, they can make a living by their craft.

Several well-established regional art and cultural organizations offer a full menu of performing and decorative arts year-round, although in summer the cultural calendar is especially busy. The wide array of performances embraces music, theater, and dance, as well as film and literary series and changing art exhibits.

The Catskills arts scene is decentralized, with no major civic center or arts complex. Performances are held in historic buildings, barns, or former churches, at street fairs, under seasonal festival tents, and in college and school auditoriums. Several artists' leagues and cooperatives sponsor exhibits and offer the works of regional artists and craftspeople for sale in their galleries. Contact the following groups for schedules of events and exhibits:

Art Awareness, Inc. Sponsors exhibits, experimental theater, dance, and musical events in and around a former Victorian hotel on Schoharie Creek. *Rte. 42, Lexington, tel. 518/989–6433.*

Bond Street Theater Coalition. Offers music, theater, dance, children's programs, and workshops during August. *Palenville Interarts Colony, Woodstock Ave., Palenville, tel. 518/678–3332.*

Catskill Mountain Theatre. Summer performances by professional and local talent at various outdoor locations and at the Halcottsville Creamery. *Tel. 914/586–4894 or 212/884–4230.*

Catskills' Dance Theater. Dance company and schedule of guest artists. *Athens Community Center, Athens, tel. 518/734–3807.*

Delaware Valley Arts Alliance. Sponsors art events and maintains a gallery with rotating exhibits. *Main St., Narrowsburg, tel. 914/252–7576.*

Erpf Catskill Cultural Center. Named after the late Armund Erpf, art patron and philanthropist, the center sponsors summer readings, a winter concert series, and regular exhibits. It is reconstructing a round barn in Halcottsville for use as a regional museum and folk-arts center. *Arkville, tel. 914/586–3326.*

Green County Council on the Arts. Maintains galleries at 398 Main Street in Catskill, and on Main Street in Windham; also sponsors special arts events throughout the year. *Box 463, Catskill, tel. 518/943–3400.*

Handcrafts at Clearbrook. Works by local artists. *Rte. 32, Cairo, tel. 518/622–9083.*

Roxbury Arts Group. Programs year-round arts events for Delaware County including an annual Chamber Music Festival in July, an outdoor art show, a country fair, and changing gallery shows. *Main St., Roxbury, tel. 607/326–7908.*

Shadowland Theater. Professional stage company in residence year-round. *157 Canal St., Ellenville, tel. 914/647–5511.*

Silver Cloud Music Festivals. Wide-ranging musical offerings staged from June to September in a natural amphitheater at the Rondout Valley Country Club in Accord. *Box 346, High Falls, tel. 914/331–4183 or 914/687–9007.*

Stone House Gallery. Paintings, sculpture, furniture, jewelry. *Off Rte. 23A, 1 mi east of Lexington, tel. 518/989–6755.*

Sullivan County Museum, Art & Cultural Center. Shows, classes, lectures, and monthly exhibits at the headquarters of the Sullivan County Historical Society, the Catskill Art Society, and the Sullivan County Dramatic Workshop, all in Hurleyville. *Tel. 914/434–8044.*

Sullivan County Arts Council. Presents ballets, musicals, jazz, opera. *Sullivan County Community College, Loch Sheldrake, tel. 914/434–5750.*

Thornwood Center for the Performing Arts. Sponsors music and dance events and the annual Central New York Renaissance Fair in August. *Delhi, tel. 607/746–2910.*

West Kortright Centre. Storytelling, dance, community socials, and music held at an 1850s Greek Revival Church. *East Meredith, tel. 607/278–5454.*

Nightlife

It's not Manhattan north, but the Catskills offer a good variety of after-dark entertainment. Headlining musical acts and cabaret revues play the major "Lower" (southern) Catskills resorts nightly during summer. Although they aren't the kings of summer comedy that they once were, the big resorts continue to book some of the better-known names in the business. In winter the region's ski slopes bring in rock groups for those who like to pump up the volume after a day of skiing. Dancing, jazz, and folk venues are scattered throughout the region.

Some of the spots with regular live entertainment include the **Hunter Village Inn** (Main St., Hunter, tel. 518/263–4788), catering to the skiing-singles crowd; **Mount Pleasant Lodge** (Rte. 28, Phoenicia, tel. 914/688–2278), with weekend dance music primarily for the under-30 set; **Pursuit of Happiness** (117 S. Main St., Liberty, tel. 914/292–6760), where you'll hear local and nationally known performers of everything from bluegrass to jazz; **Railz** (Rte. 28, Arkville, tel. 914/586–2992), a pizzeria and Italian-food restaurant where New York metropolitan-area bands draw a 20- to 40-year-old crowd; **The Square Restaurant** (Binnekill Square, Main St., Margaretville, tel. 914/586–4884), with a piano bar popular with the over-40 crowd.

7 Leatherstocking Country

Introduction

"Off the Beaten Track," a subheading in most travel listings, sums up Leatherstocking Country. Encompassing nine counties and 7,000 square miles, the region is roughly defined by three rivers: the Susquehanna, Chenango, and Mohawk. These historic waterways, with their romantic Indian names, are now traced by the concrete infrastructure of Routes 88, 90, and 81. Travelers accustomed to exhaust-choked commutes at home will marvel as the panorama of pastoral central New York State swirls by on wide-open Route 88 between Schenectady and Binghamton, a 2½-hour drive.

Visit Bleinheim's historic covered bridge in Schoharie County. Take a side trip to Cooperstown, home of the Farmers' Museum, the Baseball Hall of Fame, and the lakeside Glimmerglass Opera. Divert the car to Route 7, which parallels both the river and Route 88, and be on the lookout for out-of-the-way antiques shops and canoeing and fishing spots.

Binghamton, at the junctions of Routes 88 and 81, is the largest city in the region, and has museums, theaters, a zoo, shopping, and a good variety of accommodations. State, municipal and county parks offer picnic spots, camping, and hiking. And, the Triple Cities—Binghamton, Johnson City, and Endicott—have five operating carousels.

Leatherstocking Country's diverse ethnic heritage is most evident in Binghamton. The early Yankees in their leather leggings gave the region its nickname, but the later waves of immigrants from Eastern Europe, attracted by the factory jobs in the "Parlor City" (so named for the Broome County cigar factories) have left a legacy of onion-domed churces, Lenten specialty feasts, and the Roberson-Kopernik Observatory, named for an early Polish astronomer.

Heading north, bypass I–81 for the slower pace of Route 12. The stately old villages along the way—Greene, Cazenovia, and Norwich among them—showcase small-town America. Take a walking tour down tree-lined avenues, past imposing, elegant houses and town halls; duck into an inn for lunch; then pause for a rest in the village square.

For a quintessential rural experience, check for signs announcing chicken barbecues. Firemen, both volunteer and paid squads, know the nuances of barbecueing chicken to perfection. And for the price of dessert at a big-city restaurant, you'll not only get a full dinner (perhaps with dessert), but an earful of suggestions from local residents sharing your table of things to see and do.

Where Route 12 meets the New York State Thruway (I–90), stands the city of Utica, at the far eastern edge of Oneida County. Take a brewery tour, visit the zoo or museums, or shop at Charlestown, the old munitions factory that's now a factory outlet center. Utica is rich with Italian restaurants. Just about anyone can direct you to the well-known ones, but save some time for the smaller, family operations in the city's Little Italy.

The Mohawk Valley's past as the site of Revolutionary War battles and, with the completion of the Erie Canal in 1825, the Industrial Revolution, is preserved in monuments, battlefields, and living museums such as Old Fort Johnson.

Follow Route 5, or drop down to Route 20, to explore the interior of Leatherstocking Country. Take the unmarked side roads and the county routes along the way. Asking directions could lead you to another find—a bookstore stacked with out-of-print treasures, an auction, a dairy bar with the cows dotting the hills in the background. Take along bicycles, hiking boots, or a canoe—or cross-country skis and snowshoes in winter—to explore the quietness of the gently rolling rural setting with only your exercise-labored breathing to disturb the sounds of nature.

Getting Around

By Plane Leatherstocking Country has three airports. Utica–Rome is served by **Catskill Airways** (tel. 800/252–2144), which also flies to Oneonta (Cooperstown). Binghamton's Link Field is served by **USAir** and **Allegheny Commuter** (both tel. 800/428–4253), **Continental Express** (tel. 800/525–0280), **Piedmont, Piedmont Commuter,** and **Brockway Commuter** (all tel. 800/438–7833), **TWA Express** and **Pocono Airways** (both 800/221–2000) and **United Express** (tel. 800/241–6522).

By Train **Amtrak** (tel. 800/872–7245) serves Amsterdam, Utica, and Rome.

By Bus **Greyhound** (tel. 800/528–0447) has regular service to several Leatherstocking communities from Buffalo, Scranton–Wilkes Barre, PA, Albany, and New York City.

By Car The region is 200–300 miles northeast of New York City via the New York State Thruway and Route 28 from Kingston. It can also be reached via I–81 from Scranton, about 70 miles south of Binghamton; I–90 from Boston to Buffalo, via Albany and Utica; and I–88 from Albany to Binghamton via Oneonta.

Guided Tours

Cooperstown Historic Tour (tel. 607/547–5134) is a 45-minute limousine tour that covers 200 years of local history and is available year-round. $8 per person, with a minimum of 4.

Important Addresses and Numbers

Tourist Information The Binghamton, Cooperstown, and Mohawk Valley–Utica tourist bureaus all publish a variety of free maps, booklets, and brochures with information about accommodations, restaurants, shopping, and entertainment. In areas without a tourist bureau, the local county or town chamber of commerce usually functions as the center for tourist information and referrals. Most offices are open weekdays 9–5.

Broome County Convention & Visitors Bureau, (Security Mutual Building, 80 Exchange St., Box 995, Binghamton 13902, tel. 607/772–8860).

Cooperstown Chamber of Commerce, (Chestnut Street, Box 46, Cooperstown 13326, tel. 607/547–9983).

Oneida County Convention & Visitors Bureau (Mohawk Valley–Utica, Box AA, Oriskany 13424, tel. toll-free in NY 800/237–0100).

Leatherstocking Country, NY (200 N. Prospect St., Herkimer 13350, tel. 315/866–1500).

Chenango County Chamber of Commerce (29 Lackawannna Ave., Box 249, Norwich 13815, tel. 607/334–3236).

Oneonta Chamber of Commerce (58 Market St., Oneonta 13820, tel. 607/432–4500).

Greater Utica Chamber of Commerce (258 Genesee St., Utica 13502, 315/724–3151).

Emergencies Dial "0" for police or ambulance assistance.

Hospitals Emergency rooms: **Binghamton General Hospital** (Mitchell Ave., tel. 607/770–6611), **The Mary Imogene Bassett Hospital** (Atwell Rd., Cooperstown, tel. 607/547–3355), **St. Elizabeth Hospital** (2209 Greene St., Utica, tel. 315/798–8111).

Exploring Leatherstocking Country

Numbers in the margin correspond with points of interest on the Leatherstocking Country map.

We'll start our tour at Cooperstown, then introduce you to the Mohawk Valley and Binghamton areas.

First made famous by James Fenimore Cooper's "Leather-
❶ stocking Tales," **Cooperstown** is now home to a number of museums and historic landmarks. Fans of the great American
pastime make pilgrimages to the **National Baseball Hall of
Fame** throughout the year, particularly in the summer. Even if
you're not a fan, you'll enjoy seeing this temple of baseball:
Babe Ruth dominates the entry area. Large displays, photographs, paintings, and audiovisual presentations trace the
origin of the game and the development of the museum from a
one-room exhibit to today's 50,000-square-foot display area.
Savor the nostalgia of Abbott and Costello's engaging "Who's
on First?" routine, as well as the radio broadcast from a 1950s
World Series game. Baseball movies are shown periodically
throughout the day in the National Baseball Library, and
there's a gift shop with all manner of baseball mementos. Just
down the street from the Hall of Fame is **Doubleday Field,**
where baseball began back in 1839 and where the annual Hall-
of-Fame Game takes place each summer when new members
are inducted. *Main St., tel. 607/547–9988. Admission: $5
adults, $2 children 7–15. Open daily except Thanksgiving,
Christmas, and New Year's. May 1–Oct. 31 open 9–9. Nov. 1–
Apr. 30, 9–5.*

Paramount among local landmarks is the **Farmers' Museum,** a
historic farm complex with permanent exhibits and daily demonstrations of blacksmithing, food preparations, spinning, and
weaving. Visitors can play 19th-century games, take a wagon
ride, or sample the food cooked in the fireplace of the Lippitt
Farmhouse. At the village crossroads, a group of 19th-century
buildings draws you back into history. The Main Barn, once a
working dairy, features an introductory exhibit, weaving loft,
and woodworking areas. *Route 80, 1 mile north of Cooperstown. Lake Rd., tel. 607/547–2593. Admission: $5 adults; $2
children 7–15. Open May–Oct., 9–6. Call for winter schedule.*

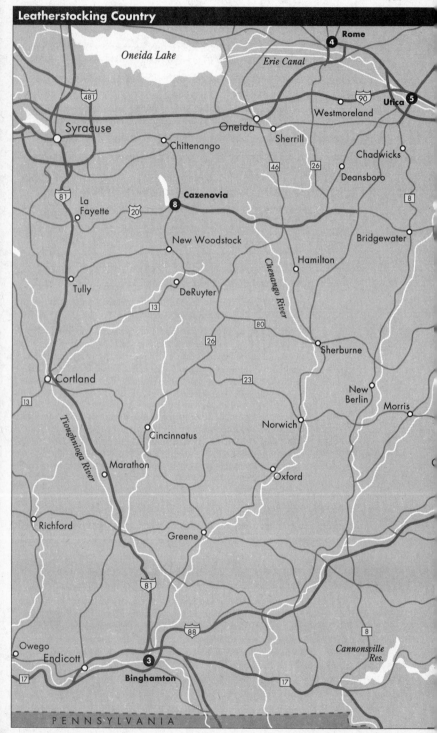

Leatherstocking Country

Oneida Lake

Erie Canal

Rome 4

5 **Utica**

I-90

Westmoreland

Syracuse

I-481

Chittenango

Oneida

Sherrill

Chadwicks

Deansboro

8

La Fayette

US-20

8 **Cazenovia**

New Woodstock

Chenango River

Hamilton

Bridgewater

Tully

DeRuyter

13

46

26

26

80

Sherburne

23

Cortland

13

Tioughnioga River

Cincinnatus

Marathon

New Berlin

Morris

Norwich

Oxford

Richford

Greene

I-81

I-88

3

Binghamton

Owego

Endicott

17

17

8

Cannonsville Res.

PENNSYLVANIA

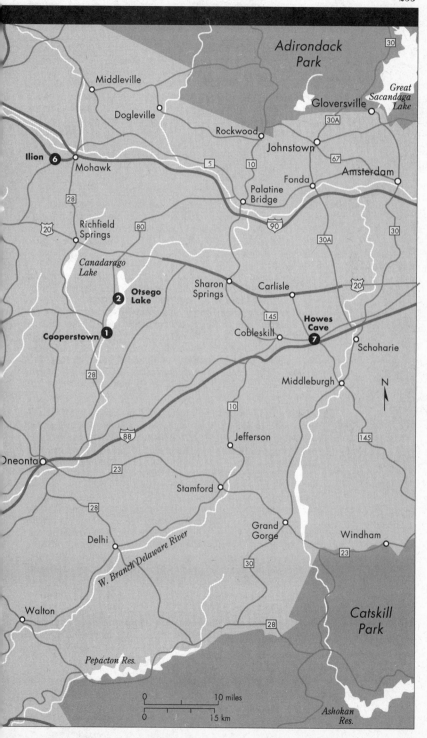

Down the road from the Farmers' Museum is **Fenimore House,** headquarters of the New York State Historical Association and a museum of James Fenimore Cooper memorabilia. It is home to a fine collection of American folk art—billed as the extraordinary creations of ordinary people. The collection includes 19th- and 20th-century paintings, sculptures, textiles, ceramics, decoys, weather vanes, and other decorative objects. *Admission: $4 adults, $1.50 children 7–15. Open daily May–Oct., 9–6. Call for winter schedule. Combination tickets are available with the Farmers' Museum and the Baseball Hall of Fame. All three attractions, $11.25 adults, $3.75 children. For more information about the Farmers' Museum and the Fenimore House, contact the New York State Historical Association, Lake Rd., Box 800, Cooperstown 13326, tel. 607/547–2533.*

Time Out   **Obie's Brot Und Bier** is a charming German-style restaurant that serves delicious sandwiches and cold beverages. In summer, there's alfresco dining on a flower-laden porch. *46 Pioneer Alley, Open May 1–Sept. 30, Mon.–Sat. 11–2:30 and 5–8; Sun. noon–6. No credit cards. Inexpensive.*

② For a relaxing prelude to dinner, take an hour-long cruise on **Lake Otsego**—James Fenimore Cooper's Glimmerglass. Excursions on the *Chief Uncas,* and the *Narra Mattah*—two classic wooden luxury launches built at the turn of the century and refurbished in the '50s—depart from the Lake Front Marina Lighthouse at the foot of Fair Street. Operated by Lake Otsego Boat Tours of Cooperstown, both hour-long cruises take in historic and scenic sights halfway up the nine-mile-long lake. *Tel. 607/547–5295; charter information, 607/547–6031. Fare: adults $7.50; children 3–12, $4.50. Departures daily on the hour 10–6, mid-May–mid-Oct.*

③ About a 1½-hour drive southwest of Cooperstown is **Binghamton,** a city of 64,000 whose civic pride centers on a bounty of attractions, including **The Roberson Center for the Arts and Sciences,** a complex of museums, galleries, ballet studios, a planetarium, and a 300-seat theater. The center's collections and exhibitions represent and interpret the region's history, art, and sciences. Exhibits range from ancient pottery to the paintings by American masters. Both the center's headquarters and the Broome County Historical Society's museum are located in the restored Roberson Mansion, a handsome Renaissance-Revival structure. Roberson offers classes in a variety of arts and crafts, sponsors an annual Holiday and Arts Festival in early September and a Christmas Forest each December, and publishes a monthly calendar of events. *30 Front St., Binghamton 13905, tel. 607/772–0660. Admission free. Some special activities or programs carry a nominal fee. Tues.–Thurs., Sat. 10–6, Fri. 10–9, Sun. noon–5.*

Ross Park Zoo opened in 1875, making it one of the country's oldest zoos. With its diverse terrain, rock hedges, and shale stratifications, the heavily wooded 25-acre compound displays animals in their natural habitat. The woodland waters exhibit provides a naturalistic setting for beaver, otter, native waterfowl, and fish. Recently completed was the cat-country exhibit, which has cougars, a white Bengal tiger, and an orange Siberian. The visitors' area is glassed, and the cats are free to prowl around among plants, rocks, and a pool. Special crowd-pleasers include the timberwolf pack, which thrives in the 2½-acre wolf compound, the children's petting zoo, and the free, recently restored carousel. There is also an education center, a waterfowl pond, a gift shop, an amphitheater, and picnic facilities. *185 Park Ave. and Morgan Rd., Binghamton 13903, tel. 607/724–5461. Admission: $2, 75¢ seniors, children under 2 free. Open Apr. 2–Nov. 15, 10–4:30.*

The $3 Ross Park Pass includes admission to the **Discovery Center,** a hands-on children's museum where the motto is "Nothing is ever complete." All exhibits are interactive, each spurring an idea that eventually turns into another exhibit. The Discovery Center was designed with kids in mind, but adults can't seem to stay away. Climb into a real jet cockpit or "drive" the fire truck. Bubble trays, light arcades, a zoo motel, and a dinosaur exhibit are a few of the attractions. *Tel. 607/773–8661. Admission: $2, children under 3 free. Open Tues.–Fri. 9–5, weekends noon–5.*

Time Out **Whole in the Wall** is a natural-food restaurant with the motto: "You are what you wheat." Try the locally famous cream of mushroom soup with some homemade whole grain bread and butter. Also featured are lovely fresh salads and chicken and seafood entrees. *435 Washington St. Open weekdays 11:30–2 and 5–9., Sat. 11:30–9. Inexpensive.*

Walter Edmonds made the Mohawk Valley famous in his Revolutionary War epic, *Drums along the Mohawk.* Here you'll find such historic monuments as Herkimer Home, Old Stone Fort, and Oriskany Battlefield, as well as at **Rome,** the **Fort Stanwix National Monument.** Originally a British post, Fort Stanwix was abandoned and later taken over by the Americans to defend the Mohawk Valley during the Revolutionary War. On Sunday, August 3, 1777, forces commanded by British General John Burgoyne and Colonel Barry St. Leger laid siege to the fort. Six days later, Colonel Peter Gansevoort wrote to St. Leger, "It is my Determined resolution with the Forces under my Command, to defend the Fort to the last Extremity. . . ." Fortunately, Gansevoort's "last extremity" was not required. After a 21-day siege, the British retreated in the face of the advancing relief troops of the Continental Army.

This Continental Army outpost is a faithful reconstruction of the original and includes barracks, storehouse, bastion, museum, indian trade center, and officers' quarters. Self-guided walking tour. *Located in downtown Rome off Exit 33 of the New York State Thruway, at the intersections of Rtes. 365, 49, and 69; 112 E. Park St., 13440, tel. 315/336–2090. Admission free. Open Apr. 1–Dec. 1, 9–5. Visitors may park at the city parking garage on N. James St.*

You can relive the days when the warning, "Low bridge—everybody down!" was commonplace at the **Erie Canal Village,** a circa-1840 village reconstructed near the spot where the first shovelful of dirt was turned for "Clinton's Folly," as the waterway was disparagingly known. Ride the 1840 horse-drawn passenger packet boat along a refurbished section of the original canal or take the narrow-gauge steam train ride and explore the village, a cluster of buildings typical of a 19th-century canal hamlet. These include Bennett's Tavern (still serving cold draft beer or root beer), a church meeting house, a blacksmith shop, a weaving and spinning house, a schoolhouse, and a settler's cabin. Seasonal events take place at the village amphitheater. There's the Visitors Reception Center, a gift shop, and a snack bar. *Rte. 49W, Rome 13440, tel. 315/336–6000 ext. 250 or 315/ 337–3999 (weekends). May–Sept. daily 9:30–5. Admission: $3 adults, $2 children 7–16, children under 7 free.*

Port Rickey Game Farm features exotic and native animals and a large petting and feeding area. There are pony rides, a gift shop, and a picnic area. *Rtes. 46/49W, 3 mi W., Rome, tel. 315/ 336–1930. Mid-May–Sept. 30, 10–6. Admission: $3.25 adults, $2.25 children 2–13.*

❺ **Utica** lies just east of Rome. Here you'll find the **Utica Zoo**, home to mammals, birds, reptiles, and a children's zoo with petting area and picnic facilities. Located in Roscoe Conkling Park—designed by Frederick Law Olmsted, who also planned Central Park in New York City—the zoo has more than 300 animals from polar bears and Siberian tigers to tropical birds and primates. In Zoolab, children can explore the contents of 10 self-discovery boxes dealing with such subjects as animal coverings, reptiles, and zoo-animal diets. The most popular exhibits are the big cats and the California sea lions. *Steel Hill Rd., Utica, tel. 315/738–0472. Open 10–5. Closed major holidays. Children's Zoo operates spring–fall. Admission: $2.50 adults, $1.25 children 2–12.*

The **Children's Museum of History, Natural History, and Science** is a handsomely restored building that houses what's billed as the finest children's museum between New York City and Toronto. It features hands-on exhibits, educational programs, and creative crafts. There is free parking in the lot diagonally across from the museum. *311 Main St., Utica, tel. 315/724–6128. Open July 5–Labor Day, Tues.–Fri. 10–5, Sat. and Sun. 1–5; Labor Day–July 5, Wed.–Sat. 1–5. Closed most major holidays. Admission: $1 adults, children under 3 free.*

For a refreshing change of pace, stop in for a tour of the **F. X. Matt Brewery**. The staff—some in period dress—greet visitors with a warm welcome; you can end the tour with beer (or root beer). The brewery tour, trolley shuttle, and a visit to the 1888 tavern takes about an hour. And it's all free. *Court and Varick Sts., 811 Edward St., Utica, tel. 315/732–0022. Open June–Aug., weekdays 10–5. Closed weekends and July 4th. Open Sept.–May, weekdays by reservation only.*

Annie Oakley wasn't called "Little Miss Sure Shot" for nothing; she hit the mark every time with a Remington 22 rifle. At the **❻** **Remington Firearms Museum,** in Ilion, you'll find a collection of handguns, rifles, and shotguns including flintlocks, percussion rifles, Civil War muzzle loaders, and "transition rifles" that led to modern repeaters. The gallery features guns belonging to the famous—and the infamous. *Catherine St. off Route 5S, Ilion, tel. 315/894–9961. Open year-round, Mon.–Sat. 8–5, May–Oct., Sun. 1–4:30. Admission free.*

If you're looking for a cool spot on a hot summer day, drop in at **❼** **Howes Cave** to check out **Howes Caverns,** Leatherstocking's underground natural wonder. Beneath the picturesque countryside is a prehistoric world. Guided tours through the underground caverns wind for nearly a mile and a half along paved walkways and over man-made and natural bridges. Knowledgeable guides explain uncommon rock formations such as the Titan's Temple with its Chinese Pagoda. The cavern tour includes a quarter-mile boat ride on an underground lake. *Rte. 7 between Central Bridge and Cobleskill, tel. 518/296–8990. Open year-round, 9–6. Admission: $7 adults, $3.50 children 7–12, $3.25 children 6 and under, free when accompanied by parents.*

8 **Cazenovia,** on scenic Route 20, is one of the region's prettiest towns. "Situation superb, fine land" were the words of John Lincklaen, agent for the Holland Land Company, when he first viewed the land at the foot of Cazenovia Lake, where he would build his home. Lincklaen's elegant Federal-style mansion, with 20 acres of lawns, formal gardens, and wooded groves, is known as **Lorenzo**. There's a collection of horse-drawn vehicles and a restored carriage house. Guided tours of the house are available, and picnicking and cross-country skiing are permitted on the grounds. Special events such as the Annual Driving Competition, Harvest Day, and Christmas Open House are held here. *Rte. 13 (¼ mile south of Rte. 20), tel. 315/655–3200. Admission free. Open May–Labor Day, Wed.–Sat. and Mon. holidays 10–5; Sun. 1–5. Grounds open year-round, 8–sunset.*

Time Out For a taste of the pioneering days and the true flavor of the backroads, head 25 miles south of Utica on Route 8 to the **Gates Hill Homestead** in Brookfield Valley. Donna Tunney wrote a children's book, *The Eternal Hills*, about the land her father settled and which she and her husband, Charles, turned into a rambling 1700s-style pioneering homestead from the fieldstone and logs they found on their 64 acres of land. Today, it's the Tunneys' restaurant and three-bedroom B&B. Guests are brought here—along the twisting road up the picturesque valley and over a covered bridge—by a four-horse stagecoach (sleigh ride in winter). Everyone feasts family-style, under candlelight chandeliers, on homemade buttermilk biscuits, chicken breast with cranberry-orange relish or smoked ham with cranberry-raisin sauce, various salads and home-baked desserts. Overnight guests don't soon forget the breakfast, either. *Gates Hill Homestead, Brookfield 13314, tel. 315/ 899–5837. Reservations required. MC, V. Dress: "respectably casual." Closed mid-March to end of April. Inexpensive– Moderate.*

What to See and Do with Children

Leatherstocking Country is family-oriented. Although some attractions might be a bit esoteric for very young children, most of them allow kids to participate. The **National Baseball Hall of Fame, Ross Park Zoo, The Discovery Center, Utica Zoo, Children's Museum of History, Erie Canal Village, Port Rickey Game Farm, Lake Otsego Cruise,** and **Howes Caverns** are all described in the Exploring section. Children will also enjoy the **Music Museum** (*see* Off the Beaten Track).

Rogers Environmental Center is a 571-acre preserve dedicated to teaching young people to appreciate and conserve natural resources. *Rte. 80, Box Q, Sherburne 13460, tel. 607/674–2861. Admission free. Open weekdays 8:30–4:50, weekends 1–5; grounds open during daylight hours.*

Off the Beaten Track

The "hands-on" policy of the **Musical Museum** in **Deansboro,** just south of Utica, invites you to crank, pump, and play restored music boxes, melodeons, nickelodeons, grind organs, and much more. Whether your musical tastes run to Paderewski playing Chopin's rousing "Polonaise in A" or Elvis singing "You Ain't Nothin' But a Hound Dog," this museum will strike just the right note with any music fancier. There are 17 rooms (don't miss the giant calliope), a shop that stocks parts, special fabrics, information on repairing various music antiques, and a picnic area. The Old Lamplighter shop specializes in antique lamps, lamp parts, repairs, and restorations and has an impressive variety of china shades. *Rte. 12B, Deansboro, tel. 314/841-8774. Open Apr. 1-Dec. 31, 10-4. Admission: $3.50 adults; $2.50 children 6-12, under 6 free; $3 senior citizens.*

Shopping

Auctions   A dollar can go a long, long way here, and given the quaint and the unusual items on the block, chances are you'll quickly become an auction junkie. It's fun and folksy, old-time Americana at its best, with a language all its own. Admission is free. A wealth of antiques—Civil War uniforms to toys, books to ornate furniture—are passed on in an amusing, mesmerizing blur. Snacks and homemade lunches can be hearty and downright cheap. Some autions are held at the "estates" themselves; but most are at auction barns. For locations, look for posters at the local general store, churches, in local newspapers.

Bazaars   Churches, schools, and community centers, particularly on weekends in summer and fall, are good places to sniff out excellent, true values in the otherwise forgotten American art of handicrafts.

For a break from the usual malls and shopping districts (which Leatherstocking Country has plenty of), visit **Charlestown Factory Outlet Center,** which features more than 40 name-brand stores. Though the prices are not particularly low, shopping in this converted munitions factory is fun. *311 Turner St., Utica, tel. 315/724-8175. Open Mon.-Wed. 10-5, Thurs. and Fri. 10-9, Sat. 10-6, Sun. noon-5.*

The region abounds in 19th-century Americana. Almost every town has its antiques dealers, so be alert for the signs. Saturdays are best; many dealers do not have set hours and are open by inspiration or by appointment. In Binghamton, don't miss **Clinton Street's** antiques row where deceptively derelict storefronts hide a multitude of treasures, including lots of oak furniture. There is also **General Clinton Antiques,** which offers period pieces and collectibles. *137 Clinton St., Binghamton, tel. 607/723-1596. Mon.-Sat. 10-5.*

A more upscale housewares outlet is the **Oneida Silversmith's Factory Store** in Sherrill, which features silver, stainless steel, pewter, silverplate, flatware, cutlery, hollowware, china, and glass. *Sherrill Rd. at Noyes Blvd., Sherrill, tel. 315/361-3661. Mon.-Sat. 9-4:30.*

Another good bet is the **China Factory Outlet** in Oneida, specializing in Noritake china and nationally advertised stoneware at discount prices. *30 Genesee St., Rte. 5, Oneida, tel. 315/363–4231. Weekdays 9:30–5:30, Sat. 9:30–5.*

Participant Sports

The Leatherstocking region lures a broad spectrum of sports lovers. Almost every town has swimming pools and tennis courts open to the public either free or for a modest fee. The fishing is excellent, with public access areas along rivers and streams.

Beaches   Although firmly landlocked, there are several large, beautiful lakes at state parks, with excellent beaches, boat rentals, concession stands, and hot showers. Except for weekends, they're uncrowded. Fees range from nothing to $3.50. Four-mile-long **Sylvan Beach** (tel. 315/762–9934) is one of the best known. Contact county tourist offices (*see* Important Addresses and Numbers, above).

Canoeing   **Canoes Along the Mohawk** rents canoes or kayaks for a nine-mile white- and still-water trip along the historic Mohawk River. Return transportation is provided to starting point. Call for season and rates. *Rte. 46N, Rome, tel. 315/337–5172.*

Horseback Riding   Hone your equestrian skills at **Thunderbolt Farm** (lessons, English-style) on Stokes Hill in Rome, tel. 315/339–0661, or **Fieldstone Farm** (lessons, western-style) in Richfield Springs, tel. 315/858–0295.

Golf   Leatherstocking has many courses; those listed here are 18-hole courses: **Afton Golf Club** (Afton, tel. 607/639–2454), **Seven Oaks Golf Club** (Hamilton, tel. 315/824–1432), **Maple Hill Golf Club,** Canasawacta Country Club (Norwich, tel. 607/336–2685), and **En-Joie Golf Club** (Endicott, tel. 607/785–1661). Golfers with short attention spans should try **Fort Putt Miniature Golf** (Rtes. 46/49, Rome, tel. 315/339–3333).

Skiing   Skiers can find downhill action at **Shu-maker Mountain** (Little Falls, tel. 315/823–1111), **Snow Ridge Ski Area** (Turin, tel. 315/348–8456 or 800/962–8419 in NY), or **Ironwood Ridge** (Cazenovia, tel. 315/655–9551).

Spectator Sports

Baseball   The **Oneonta Yankees** (a NY Yankees farm team) play Class-A ball at Damaschke Field in Oneonta, tel. 607/432–4500. Also, the National Baseball Hall of Fame's All-Star and Old Timers' games are played at Abner Doubleday Field in Cooperstown in August.

Hockey   The **Binghamton Whalers** promise hard and cold hockey action at the Broome County Veterans Memorial Arena (tel. 607/772–2611).

Horse Racing   Place your bets on spirited trotters and pacers competing for almost $5 million in purses at **Vernon Downs,** from mid-April through early November. Vernon (tel. 315/829–2201).

Motocross   In mid-July, the pace heats up with **U.S. Grand Prix Motocross** action at the Unadilla Valley Sports Center in New Berlin. For information, contact Ward Robinson, (Box 5119F, Edmeston 13335, tel. 607/965–8784 or 607/847–8186).

Polo Matches are played on Sundays at the **Village Farms Polo Club** (Gilbertsville, tel. 607/783–2764 or 607/783–2737). Season runs early June–early Sept. Starting time is 3 PM. *Admission: $3 adults, children under 12 free. Call for schedule.*

Dining and Lodging

Dining From price to cuisine, eating out in Leatherstocking Country exemplifies middle-American dining. The region's only culinary claim to fame is the *spiedie*, which hails from the Binghamton area. Spiedies (originally lamb, but now often beef, pork, or chicken) are lean chunks of marinated meat grilled on a skewer and served on Italian bread. Spiedies appear in many of the local restaurants, but most Binghamtonians maintain a loyalty to their favorite spiedie spot.

One of the pleasures of a summer evening is to drive into Endicott's Union District (near Binghamton) for a spiedie from Lupo's Deli and then backtrack to Pat Mitchell's on Main Street for a double dip of award-winning ice cream. To be really a part of the in crowd, you have to sit on the cemetery wall abutting Pat's store and eat a banana split while watching traffic pile up as half of Endicott stops in for its ice-cream fix.

Category	Cost*
Very Expensive	over $60
Expensive	$40–$60
Moderate	$20–$40
Inexpensive	under $20

per person without tax (6%–8%, depending on the county), service, or drinks.

Lodging "You get what you pay for" is a good rule in Leatherstocking. With few exceptions, most accommodations fall within the inexpensive-to-moderate range. Keep in mind that Cooperstown is a summer resort; reservations should be made at least six weeks in advance. The area has a lot of colleges and universities, which makes it a bit difficult to get a room if you're visiting Binghamton, Oneonta, Cobleskill, or Hamilton during late August—parents' weekend—or mid-May—graduation.

Bed-and-Breakfast Accommodations range from sharing the family homestead to cozy rooms in refurbished barns, furnished with antiques from the local auction; from Victorian cottages to luxurious Colonial mansions set in manicured, lakeside estates. For those who can't bear to be away from urban necessities, many B&Bs come with Jacuzzis and VCRs. Prices range from $35 to $75 for two persons, $10–$20 for an additional bed; big, back-to-the-farm breakfasts are included.

Some B&Bs don't list at all, they merely hang up a sign when they feel like it. If you don't like taking chances—and don't, especially in summer and fall—compare properties listed with B&B collectives. For details and reservations, two good bets are: **The American Country Collection** (984 Gloucester Pl.,

Schenectady 12309, tel. 518/370–4948) and **Bed & Breakfast Leatherstocking** (389 Brockway Rd., Frankfort 13340, tel. 315/733–0040).

Highly recommended dining and lodging places are indicated by a star ★.

Category	Cost*
Very Expensive	over $120
Expensive	$90–$120
Moderate	$50–$90
Inexpensive	under $50

double room without tax (4%–7%, depending on the county) or service

Binghamton

Dining ★ **Drovers Inn.** This lovely old mansion in Vestal (near Binghamton) has been converted into the most elegant inn in the area. A beautiful lounge has tables for two; even more intimate is the Rose Room (it seats a maximum of four diners). Try the chateaubriand for two; for dessert, nothing will do but Chocolate Decadence. *2 N. Main St., Vestal, tel. 607/785–4199. Dress: informal. Reservations strongly recommended. Rose Room must be booked in advance. AE, MC, V. Moderate–Expensive.*

Lodging **Best Western Hotel de Ville.** Located in the former City Hall in the heart of the downtown business district, this lovely hotel has 63 luxurious rooms. An outstanding example of French-Renaissance architecture in the late Beaux-Arts style, the building is listed on the National Register of Historic Places. *80 State St., 13901, tel. 607/722–0000. AE, MC, V. Expensive–Very Expensive.*

Holiday Inn Arena. This large hotel complex has 248 rooms done in comfortable, contemporary decor. After a walk along the Riverside Promenade, you might want to stop by for entertainment in the LeBar Lounge or browse in The Galleria—an attractive collection of clothing and specialty boutiques and service shops. The hotel offers indoor and outdoor pools, in-room movies, and free parking. The downtown location is convenient to shopping and entertainment. *2-8 Hawley St., 13901, tel. 607/722–1212. AE, MC, V. Expensive.*

Quality Inn. The 155 rooms in this centrally located motel are basic but pleasant. Some rooms have saunas, Jacuzzis, and waterbeds. There's an outdoor pool and a lounge with live music and a daily "happy hour" from 4–7 PM. *Upper Court St., 13904, tel. 607/775–3443. AE, DC, MC, V. Moderate.*

Cazenovia

Dining and Lodging ★ **The Brae Loch.** The staff wear kilts, and host Grey Barr sports full Highland regalia. The menu features Scotch steak (steak and kidney) pie, muckle sow (sugar-cured ham), cock o' the north (rock Cornish game hen), and Angus Dundee (beef filet with crab and mustard sauce). There's a Scots import shop on the premises. Guest rooms include four-poster beds, imported antiques, and complimentary Continental breakfast. *5 Albany*

*St., 13035, 315/655–3431. Dress informal. AE, DC, MC, V.
Moderate–Expensive.*

Cooperstown

Dining and Lodging   **Otesaga Hotel.** A grand hotel circa 1909 on a smaller scale—135 rooms and suites—with a manicured garden right on Otsego Lake, this property has tennis courts, a heated pool, and an adjoining 18 hole golf course. It wears the frown of age and is a bit set in its ways—no pets, men must wear jackets in public rooms, and so on. But it's an imposing presence and hard to ignore. So tourists come to walk the grounds, snap pictures, and have a spot of tea. The dining room is open to the public, but the food—'50s and '60 staples—isn't exactly its forte. However, all hotel guests are charged MAP—breakfast and dinner included in the rates. *Lake Rd., tel. 607/547–9931. AE, MC, V. Closed Nov.–mid-April. Expensive.*

Dining   **Hickory Grove Inn.** This renovated stagecoach stop has been serving travelers since 1804. The new management now offers Italian and Continental specialties. *Rte. 80, tel. 607/547–8100. Dress: informal. AE, DC, MC, V. Closed end of Oct.–early Mar. Moderate.*

Lodging   **Cooper Motor Inn.** This beautifully restored 1812 Federal mansion has 20 modern guest rooms. Guests are entitled to all privileges at the nearby Otesaga Hotel. Continental breakfast included in rates. *Main St., tel. 607/547–9931. Very Expensive.*

Hickory Grove Motor Inn. Situated six miles north of Cooperstown, this 12-unit, family-run motel offers a rare tranquility in manicured gardens reflecting the management's New Zealand hospitality. The rooms are comfortable and decorated with fresh flowers. *Rte. 80, 13326, tel. 607/547–9874. 12 rooms. Complimentary coffee. AE, MC. V. Open May through October. Moderate.*

Coventry

Dining and Lodging   **Silo Carriage House.** Built like a silo, in an old barn, this 166-acre landscaped estate has a winding staircase leading to a loft. There are spectacular views, especially at sunset, of Greene and the valley, six miles away. The food is straightforward American, with prime rib, big steaks and lamb chops, trout, lobster, and veal. *Moran Rd. off Rte. 206, tel. 607/656–4377. Reservations recommended. Dress: smart casual. AE, MC, V. Inexpensive–Moderate.*

Greene

Dining and Lodging
★   **Sherwood Hotel.** This refurbished 1838 hotel has a Victorian country flair. Its 34 beautifully appointed rooms and suites feature brass beds and modern conveniences. The cozy lounge has a fireplace and the cheery dining room (open to the public) seats 90. It serves country and continental fare—seafood, veal dishes, and steaks. *25 Genesee St., tel. 607/656–4196. Reservations recommended. Jacket for men. AE, MC, V. Moderate.*

Oneonta

Dining   **Brooks House of Barbecues.** This establishment, with its 30-foot-long pit, claims to be the world's largest barbecue, and the aroma of barbecued ribs, chicken, pork chops, and seafood can be sensed a mile away. The place seats 300, and serves up to 1,500 meals a day—in addition to a roaring take-out business. *Rte. 7, East End, tel. 607/432–1782. No reservations or alcohol. Dress: casual. No credit cards. Closed Mon. and last week Dec.–mid-Jan. Inexpensive.*

Rome

Dining and Lodging   **The Beeches-Paul Revere Lodge.** This 52-acre resort offers 75 rooms decorated in Early American style. The resort has a restaurant, breakfast room, pool, and miniature golf course. *Rte. 26, Turin Rd. 13440, tel. 315/336–1776. Moderate.*

Utica

Dining   **Grimaldi's.** Billed as one of Utica's oldest, largest, and finest restaurants and cocktail lounges, Grimaldi's serves a traditional Italian-American menu in a warm, friendly atmosphere. *418-428 Bleecker St., tel. 315/732–7011. Dress: informal. AE, MC, V. Open daily 11–11. Moderate.*

Lodging   **Sheraton Utica Hotel & Conference Center.** The 156 rooms here are attractive and comfortable, and the lobby was redone in black Italian marble. The skylit dining room has bamboo jungle decor. There's live entertainment in the lounge Tuesday–Saturday. Facilities include an indoor heated pool, whirlpool, and fitness center. Champagne brunch is served on Sunday. *200 Genesee St., 13502, 315/797–8010. AE, MC, V. Moderate.*

The Arts

Leatherstocking Country has a thriving arts community; its two major performance centers are the **Anderson Center for the Performing Arts** at the State University of New York (Binghamton 13901, tel. 607/777–ARTS) and the **Stanley Performing Arts Center** (259 Genesee St, Utica 13501, tel. 315/724–7196). These facilities present a full range of artistic performances including concerts, opera, and occasional ballets. Obtain tickets directly from the centers. For the most complete listing of regional arts events, check local newspapers.

Theater

Cider Mill Playhouse is the State University of New York's off-campus theater. Located at 2 S. Nanticoke Avenue in Binghamton, it's a 300-seat cabaret theater that presents a year-round bill of shows. Box office: weekdays noon–5:30, Room 133, Fine Arts Building, SUNY–Binghamton Campus (tel. 607/777–ARTS or 607/748–7363).

Binghamton's **Broadway Theater League** stages its performances at The Forum, 228 Washington St., but sells its tickets at the Arena Box Office (tel. 607/723–6626).

Broadway Theater League of Utica presents four performances a season at the Stanley Performing Arts Center (259 Genesee St., Utica 13501. Box Office, tel. 315/724–7196).

Beck's Grove Dinner Theater. (4286 Oswego Rd., Blossvale, tel. 315/336–7038). 12 miles south of downtown Rome, presents musical comedies and seasonal shows from mid-March through December, after an all-you-can-eat buffet.

Music

There's a wealth of concerts, operas, and other musical presentations at major centers. In outlying areas, performances of regional bluegrass, country-western, and other grassroots bands are listed in local newspapers.

The Forum (228 Washington St., Binghamton, tel. 607/722–0400) is the Center for the Broome County Performing Arts. A former vaudeville house, it is home to the B.C. Pops (country to classical), the Tri-Cities Opera, the Binghamton Symphony and Choral Society, and the Broadway Theater League.

Broome County Veterans Memorial Arena (Box 1146, Binghamton, 13902, tel. 607/772–6626) is the venue for a wide range of entertainment activities.

Opera

Glimmerglass Opera (Box 191, Cooperstown, 13326, tel. 607/547–2255). Summer festival performances are held at the Alice Busch Opera Theater on Route 80, eight miles north of Cooperstown and two miles south of the junction of Routes 20 and 80. This unusual, partially open-air theater features sidewall panels which dramatically roll back before performances and during intermissions to reveal the wooded landscape and to admit the fresh mountain air. Bring a sweater and a blanket. Evening performances and matinees.

Earlville Opera House (16 E. Main St., Earlville, 13332, tel. 315/691–3550). The summer season here comprises musical performances ranging from opera and string quartets to bluegrass and vaudeville variety shows. Call for schedule.

Film

Although the occasional art or foreign film shows up in college campus theaters and local arts centers, film is not especially distinguished in Leatherstocking Country. A notable exception is **The Art Theatre** (1204 Vestal Ave., Binghamton, tel. 607/724–7900). If you're looking for a movie, check the entertainment pages of local newspapers.

Nightlife

The great outdoors can be invigorating—and blissfully exhausting. Folks still gather around the family hearth, walk by the lake, or turn in early with a good book and a fire at their feet. The little nightlife that exists is in the cities. Check with local sources of tourist information (*see* Important Addresses and Numbers, above) and local periodicals. Here are some of the most popular gathering spots:

Dynasty. Comfortable for over-30 singles as well as for families and couples, this spot offers great Chinese food, as well as '50s and '60s music on Thursday nights. *3801 Vestal Pkwy. E, Vestal (near Binghamton), tel. 607/729–2904. AE, MC, V.*

Esprit. A major night spot with dancing for the young professional set. Proper attire means no shorts or midriffs for ladies, dress jeans for men, and shoes, not sneakers. Tuesday–Friday there's a shrimp buffet during happy hour. *Ramada Inn, 65 Front St., Binghamton, tel. 607/773–8390. AE, MC, V. Closed Mon. and Tues.*

Lily Langtry's. There is live entertainment Tuesday evening and happy hour 5–7 Wednesday. *700 Varick St., Utica, tel. 315/724–5219. AE, DC, MC, V. Open 3 PM–3 AM; no cover, no minimum.*

Number 5. Downstairs, have drinks in a trendy lounge reminiscent of television's *Cheers*, then retire upstairs to the supper club, where the menu offers satisfying Continental and American cuisine. *33 S. Washington St, Binghamton, tel. 607/723–0555. AE, DC, MC, V. Daily.*

Peper's Market Place. The restaurant (*see* Cooperstown Dining, above) features live jazz and big-band music Friday nights until 10. *93 Main St., Cooperstown, tel. 607/547–5468. No credit cards.*

8 Saratoga Springs and the North Country

Introduction

by Peter Oliver

A New York writer who covers sports, travel, and the outdoors, Peter Oliver's articles have appeared in Backpacker, Signature, Skiing, Travel-Holiday, and USA Today.

George Meegan, an Englishman who made a seven-year, 19,000-mile journey on foot through the Americas, wrote in his account, *The Longest Walk*, "Upstate New York may be America's best kept secret." The "secret" world of the North Country of New York includes everything from refined civility to absolute wilderness. You might cross paths with the rich and famous, or you might cross paths with deer and bear; it just depends on how and where you choose to spend your time in the North Country.

Saratoga Springs, in the southeast corner, is one of America's oldest summer playgrounds of high society. Northwest of Saratoga, and in stark contrast, is Adirondack Park. With six million acres, a million of which have been declared "forever wild" by New York State, it is the largest park expanse in the United States outside of Alaska. Girding the entire region are lakes and rivers, principally Lake George and Lake Champlain to the east, the St. Lawrence River to the north, and Lake Ontario to the west.

The secret character of the North Country came about both through disregard and design. Early American settlers didn't show much interest in the region. The rugged land, inhospitable soil, and often unmerciful winter conditions sent them elsewhere in search of good land to clear for farms. Only the east, from Saratoga north to Lake Champlain, saw any significant settlements in the 1700s.

In the 1800s, wilderness lovers as disparate as Ralph Waldo Emerson and Teddy Roosevelt discovered the Adirondack wilds and returned extolling their virtues. Wealthy families from New York City built what came to be known as the "great camps"—large lodges in remote areas. Meanwhile, doctors were recommending that their patients partake of the benefits of the clean Adirondack air, and sanitoriums, most notably the Trudeau Sanitorium in Saranac Lake, were built. Doctors also recommended that their patients go to Saratoga for the healthy spa waters, but Saratoga also attracted visitors with its gambling casinos and horse racing. In any event, the North Country became one of the first regions in America where tourism was a principal industry. Enormous hotels were built in Saratoga, and as the railroads reached as far north as the Thousand Islands area along the St. Lawrence River, enormous hotels were built there, too.

In the 1950s, the area declined as summer vacationers began to opt for seaside beach resorts rather than mountains and lakes. When gambling was outlawed about the same time, Saratoga lost much of its appeal.

Winter travelers seemed to prefer Vermont and the Rockies, where ski resorts were better developed. Farming, mining, and shipping kept economic life ambling along, but tourism played much less of a role.

In the last 10 years or so, however, interest in the North Country has regained momentum. The enduring attraction of horse racing, the growing appeal of the Saratoga Performing Arts Center, and the proximity for commuters to the capital area of Albany contributed significantly to Saratoga's comeback. The

1980 Winter Olympics in Lake Placid helped to renew interest in the Adirondacks in general and Lake Placid in particular as a winter and summer sports center.

Watertown, with a population of about 28,000, is the largest city in the North Country. The smaller cities of Massena and Odgensburg have grown modestly since 1959 and the opening of the St. Lawrence Seaway, connecting the Great Lakes and the Atlantic Ocean. Glens Falls and Plattsburgh were given a push with the opening of the Northway (I–87) in the 1960s. But none of these cities is a "big city" in any sense of the word. Except for Saratoga, North Country cities are not the attraction. The region is now, as it has been historically, a place of escape, a place to retreat to from the pressures of city life.

Even during the peak periods of summer, there is no bustle, no commotion, no crowds. To be sure, there are hives of tourist activity in Saratoga, Lake George, Lake Placid, and the Thousand Islands. But if you consider the size of the North Country—equal to the states of Massachusetts, Connecticut, and Rhode Island combined—that leaves plenty of quiet, uncrowded space.

And what visitors seem to enjoy most about the North Country is this lack of civilization. The vast, interconnected waterways and hiking trails of the Adirondacks cover one of the two areas of genuine wilderness left in the U.S. Northeast, the other being northern Maine. The abundance of lakes and rivers throughout the region offer plenty of opportunity to hop aboard a canoe or houseboat and explore, fish, or just separate yourself from land-locked civilization. In the fall, when the leaves change color, the great expanses of forested land make for one of nature's most dramatic and fleeting spectacles.

What the North Country lacks sometimes creates inconveniences. The region has no major airports. To reach the North Country generally means flying first into a peripheral city—Albany, Syracuse, Montreal, or New York City. From there, you can get a connecting flight to one of the smaller airports in the region, but there are relatively few scheduled flights.

There are also just two interstate highways in the North Country, I–81 and I–87, both running north-south. There are no major east-west highways, except for the New York State Thruway, which runs just south of the North Country's southern rim. Although most roads in the region are in very good condition, traveling on two-lane highways through small towns can be slow.

The operative words throughout most of the North Country are simple and rustic rather than elegant and refined. That is as it should be in a region that makes its statement as a world of retreat and escape. Lodging is generally simple and comfortable, and food is generally simple and good. Except for one or two places in Saratoga and Lake Placid, haute cuisine is an unknown concept in the North Country. And save for a few hot spots in Saratoga, Lake Placid, Lake George, and Alexandria Bay, nightlife tends to fade with nightfall.

The North Country is also very much a seasonal world. Tourism is in high gear in June, July, and August, downshifts in September and October, and slows considerably thereafter. Such areas as Lake Placid and North Creek continue through the winter as active skiing centers, and snowmobilers, cross-country skiers, and ice fishermen throughout the region make what they can of the cold winter months. With sizeable winter populations, such cities as Saratoga, Watertown, Glens Falls, and Plattsburgh remain reasonably active during the off-seasons. Generally speaking, though, the North Country itself goes into something of a retreat from November through April.

Getting Around

The principal international gateways are New York City to the south and Montreal to the north. The New York City airports are about a four-hour drive from Saratoga Springs; Montreal's Dorval Airport is about an hour-and-a-half drive from the city of Plattsburgh.

Some airlines serve the tri-city area of Albany–Troy–Schenectady, 25 miles south of Saratoga, and Syracuse, 65 miles south of Watertown. To fly into these cities, however, usually requires an indirect or connecting flight through a major Eastern seaboard airport.

By Plane The principal carrier throughout the North Country is **USAir** (tel. 800/251–5720), which has scheduled flights to and from Albany and Plattsburgh. Commuter airlines such as **Allegheny Commuter** (tel. 800/428–4253) also provide service throughout the region.

Charter air services make it possible to reach smaller airports or remote areas of the North Country. **Adirondack Flying Service** (tel. 518/523–2473) in Lake Placid and **Bird's Seaplane Service** (tel. 315/357–3631) in Inlet operate flightseeing trips into the Adirondack wilderness and are permitted to land on some lakes to provide access for fishermen or canoeists.

By Bus **Greyhound** (tel. 800/528–0447) and **Adirondack Trailways** (tel. 800/225–6815) provide bus service throughout the region. More than two dozen charter operators also offer sightseeing tours in the summer, foliage tours in the fall, and ski tours in the winter. Call *I Love New York* (tel. 800/225–5697) for information about operators and the tours they offer.

By Train **Amtrak's Adirondack** (tel. 800/872–7245), operates daily between New York and Montreal, with North Country stops in Saratoga Springs, Fort Edward–Glens Falls, Whitehall, Fort Ticonderoga, Port Henry, Westport, and Plattsburgh. The section of the route along Lake Champlain is particularly scenic.

By Car Most people drive to the North Country. The primary route through the region is the Northway (I–87), which links Albany and Montreal. The major north-south route in the west is I–81, which runs from Syracuse through Watertown and into Canada over the Thousand Islands International Bridge.

There is no major north-south highway through the central part of the North Country, nor is there any east-west highway. However, the main roads through the Adirondack region, including routes 3, 8, 28, and 9N, are all well maintained, with 55-mph speed limits for most sections. Keep in mind that considerable snow falls throughout the North Country in winter, so have your car ready for snow conditions.

The **Adirondack North Country Association** publishes a first-rate map of the region (although, curiously, mileages are not included). It is a big map, hard to open in the car, but it outlines several scenic and historic driving routes throughout the region, including the Seaway Trail along the St. Lawrence River, the Adirondack Trail, and the Underground Railroad Trail. The map is free from local tourism offices (*see* Important Addresses and Numbers).

Scenic Drives Route 28N between North Creek and Long Lake and Route 73 between Lake Placid and Keene offer some of the best views of the mountains, with numerous trailheads along the way, should you feel so inclined. For river scenery, routes 86 and 9N, from Lake Placid to Keeseville, and Route 9 toward Plattsburgh, follow the Ausable River and its West Branch much of the way.

Trips by Car, available from *I Love New York* as well as at many regional and local tourist information centers, outlines several scenic and historic car tours throughout New York State. The publication also lists hotels and inns offering special daily tour rates if you inquire ahead.

Car campers and recreational-vehicle travelers might enjoy touring the Seaway Trail along the St. Lawrence River. State campgrounds near the river's edge and along the Lake Ontario shore between Massena and Oswego are generally large and well maintained, but you must make reservations ahead of time if you expect to get a space on summer weekends.

By Boat A popular way to see the Thousand Islands and St. Lawrence Seaway area is by houseboat. **Remar Rentals** in Clayton (tel. 315/686–3597), can set you up, but remember to reserve at least six months ahead for peak season, July and August.

Power boats for cruising, fishing, or waterskiing can be rented on a daily or weekly basis at marinas at Lake George, Lake Champlain, Lake Saratoga, and at other lakes in the Adirondacks that permit power-boating. Summer boat traffic can be heavy, particularly on Lake George. It is less congested—and safer—at Bolton Landing or Dunham Bay, a few miles north of the town of Lake George.

On Foot The New York State **Department of Environmental Conservation** (DEC) maintains more than 1,000 miles of hiking trails throughout the Adirondack region. Free trail maps for nine different hiking regions in the Adirondacks are available from DEC Publications, 50 Wolf Rd., Albany 12233.

Guided Tours

Many charter-bus operators feature foliage tours in fall and ski tours in winter, leaving from a number of metropolitan areas in the northeast, including New York City, Philadelphia, and cities in western New York. *I Love New York* (tel. 800/225–5697) can provide a list of operators and the tours they offer. A more intimate, if more energetic, way to see the changing colors of fall is by bicycle. You can stick to the road with **Adirondack Bicycle Touring** (tel. 518/523–3764) in Lake Placid or go off-road with **Adirondack Wilderness Tours** (tel. 518/835–4193) at Caroga Lake. Operators of foliage tours tend to define the season as Labor Day through October, but the peak period—the time when you really want to be there—is considerably shorter, usually about a week and generally during the first two weeks of October. **Upstate Transit Tours** (tel. 518/584–5252) and the **Saratoga Circuit Tour** (tel. 518/587–3656) both feature tours of Saratoga Springs and its environs during the summer.

For a bird's-eye view of the North Country, **Adirondack Balloon Rides** (tel. 518/793–6342) offers flights of up to two hours long in the early morning and evening, when the winds are lightest. Flights are expensive—up to $150–$175 per person—and unpredictable, as they operate only when weather conditions are ideal. But champagne is a traditional perk on balloon flights. Sightseeing flights by airplane are offered by **Adirondack Flying Service** (tel. 518/523–2473) in Lake Placid, **Bird's Seaplane Service** (tel. 315/357–3631) in Inlet, and **Helms Aero Service** (tel. 518/624–3931) in Long Lake. The flights are the quickest way to get to see the deep wilderness areas of Adirondack Park.

If you are interested in the Adirondack backcountry, you can hire a canoe or fishing guide. For a list of licensed guides, contact the **New York State Guides Association,** (Box 4337, Albany 12204) or the New York State **Department of Environmental Conservation,** (50 Wolf Rd., Albany 12233). If you are interested in an extended hiking or backcountry-skiing tour of the region, the **Adirondack Mountain Club** (*see* Important Addresses and Numbers, below) offers many backcountry trips, some of which include wilderness-skills training and ecology study.

Important Addresses and Numbers

Information Centers

I Love New York, the public information wing of the New York State Division of Tourism, is the best general source for most tourism materials, including maps, visitor guides, tour and package information, and events listings. The regional *I Love New York* office in Lake Placid (90 Main St., tel. 518/523–2412) also has information on all North Country regions except the Saratoga. The best source for information on that city is the **Greater Saratoga Chamber of Commerce** (494 Broadway, Saratoga Springs 12886, tel. 518/584–3255).

For other specific North Country regions, the main contacts are: The **Thousand Islands International Council** (Box 400, Collins Landing, Alexandria Bay 13607, tel. 800/8–ISLAND or 800/5–ISLAND in New York), the **Central Adirondack Association** (Tourism Information Center, Old Forge 13420, tel. 315/369–6983), and the **Olympic Regional Development Authority** (Olympic Center, Lake Placid 12946, tel. 512/523–1655, 800/255–5515, or 800/462–6236 in New York).

Tourism information centers are located along the Northway (I–87) between exits 11 and 12 and between exits 17 and 18 northbound, and at Exit 32 and between exits 40 and 41 southbound. Information centers can be found for the Thousand Islands region off I–81 at Exit 45 at the Zayre Plaza booth in Watertown and at the Thousand Islands International Council office at the foot of International Bridge.

The **Adirondack Mountain Club** (174 Glen St., Glens Falls 12801, tel. 518/668–4447) is the best source of backcountry information throughout the region. The club is a good source for up-to-date information on trail conditions both for hiking as well as backcountry skiing in winter and for waterway conditions for canoeists. Alpine skiers can get current snow conditions by calling the toll-free *I Love New York* phone number: 800/225–5697.

Emergencies The emergency phone number throughout the North Country is 911.

Hospitals The major hospitals in the region are **Saratoga Hospital** (Church St., Saratoga Springs, tel. 518/584–6000), **Glens Falls Hospital** (Park St., Glens Falls, tel. 518/792–3151; 518/761–5261 for the emergency room), **Champlain Physicians Hospital** (in Plattsburgh, tel. 518/561–2000), and **Mercy Hospital** (in Watertown, tel. 315/782–7400).

Late-Night Pharmacies There are no 24-hour pharmacies in this region, but **Grant's Drugs**, at 101 Public Square, Watertown (tel. 315/788–1291) is open until 9:45 weeknights and Saturday. **Fay's** at Holbrook Plaza in Lake Placid (tel. 518/523–2011) is open until 9:30 weeknights and Saturday.

Exploring the North Country

Saratoga

Saratoga County stretches south to the Mohawk River and east to the Hudson, west to Great Sacandaga Lake and north to Glens Falls. But most people who visit the area come to spend most of their time in Saratoga Springs, a historic spa resort (also referred to simply as Saratoga). Beautiful Victorian homes, historic sites, horse racing, cultural events, and mineral waters—not necessarily in that order—are the town's primary attractions.

Saratoga in August, when the racing fraternity is in residence, is quintessential Saratoga. With owners, breeders, and trainers on hand for the races, the socializing, and the wheeling and dealing of the yearling auction during the second week of the race meet, the old town takes on a bit of the glamour it had in the days when wealthy families came to take the waters and high-stakes gamblers peopled its fancy casinos. A spin down Broadway will give you a glimpse of bygone days when members of the upper crust kept a little mansion in Saratoga as part of the roving social scene of summer.

The crush of visitors drawn by the thoroughbred-racing session provides many businesses in the community with the wherewithal to make it through the other 11 months of the year. The track itself is open for just 24 racing days, yet it manages to turn enough of a profit in that time to be able to maintain the rambling, big-roofed grandstand, the grounds, and the barns (all listed on the Register of Historic Places) in impeccable condition throughout the year.

Those who visit Saratoga in August should expect crowds and premium prices as well. Hotel-room rates typically double and triple for the month. Although restaurant prices remain about the same, extravagant specials such as Beluga caviar tend to show up on the menus of such Saratoga institutions as the Union Coach House. August visitors tend to be more indulgent than the year-round crowd. Dinner reservations must be made well in advance.

So, too, must lodging reservations. The Greater Saratoga Chamber of Commerce can scrounge up a room for you somewhere should you come into town unannounced on, say, a Saturday in August. Such lodging arrangements may fall below your normal standards and above your normal price range and will probably be several miles from the center of town. You should book accommodations for the peak season at least six months in advance.

After the racing meeting, Saratoga reverts to its true self—a compact city of historical, cultural, and architectural significance, a community experiencing something of a renaissance. The tri-city area (Albany–Schenectady–Troy) 25 miles to the south seems to have adopted Saratoga in the last decade as a distant suburb, and about half of Saratoga's population today is made up of commuters.

June and September are especially good months to visit. It's best to avoid the crowds of August and fall, when countless foliage tours roll through town.

Saratoga Springs

Numbers in the margin correspond with points of interest on the Saratoga Springs map.

Most people come into Saratoga from the Northway (I–87), taking exits 13, 14, or 15. Turning north on Route 9 from Exit 13, you pass on your left the 2,000-acre **Saratoga State Park** and its performing arts center, some monolithic spa buildings constructed under the Work Projects Administration of the 1930s, two golf courses, tennis courts, and other facilities. On your right is the back entrance to Saratoga's harness-racing track which, unlike its more renowned thoroughbred-racing cousin, is open for close to 11 months of the year. A bit farther along on your left is the **National Museum of Dance**, housed in a handsome, low-slung building that was once a public spa facility. A mile or so farther, Route 9 turns into Broadway, the main drag that runs through the center of the city.

1 If you take Exit 14, you enter town on Union Avenue. **Yaddo,** a highly regarded retreat for artists and writers is on your left; its 400-acre grounds and its rose garden are open to the public. Closer to town on the left is Saratoga Raceway, partially obscured by cultivated stands of shade trees.

2 A few blocks west on Union Avenue is the **National Museum of Racing,** just across Union Avenue from the race track. A $6-million upgrading of the museum was completed in June of 1988. A highlight of the museum is its Hall of Fame, with video clips of races of the horses and jockeys who have been enshrined. *Tel. 518/584–0400. Admission: $2.50 adults, $1.50 students and seniors, children under 5 free. Open Tues.–Sat. 10–4:30, Sun. 1–5 until mid-Dec., then closed Sun. and Mon.*

3 Union Avenue leads into Circular Street, which forms the back border of **Congress Park,** the small patch of greenery that marks the center of town. Turn left, and the street winds back to south Broadway. Turn right, and you will be heading north, passing on your left the narrow passageways of Spring, Phila, and Caroline streets, where several of the city's best restaurants are located. Phila and Caroline streets are one way, and you must turn left on Lake Avenue and left again on Broadway,

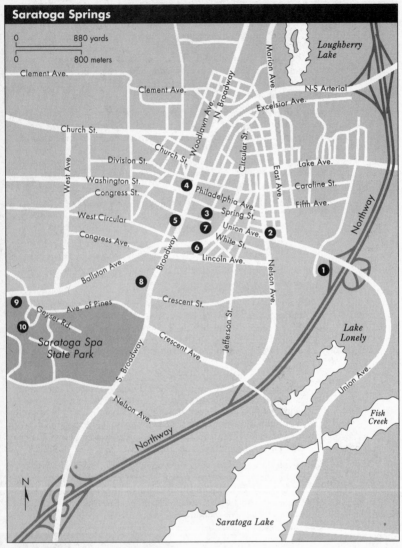

Saratoga Springs

Loughberry Lake

Clement Ave.
Clement Ave.
Marion Ave.
N-S Arterial
Excelsior Ave.
Church St.
Woodlawn Ave.
N. Broadway
Circular St.
Lake Ave.
West Ave.
Division St.
Church St.
Caroline St.
Washington St.
Philadelphia Ave.
East Ave.
Congress St.
4
Spring St.
Fifth Ave.
3
West Circular
5
Union Ave.
7
Congress Ave.
White St.
2
6
Broadway
Lincoln Ave.
1
Ballston Ave.
8
Nelson Ave.
Crescent St.
9
Ave. of Pines
Lake Lonely
10
Geyser Rd.
Jefferson St.
Saratoga Spa State Park
Crescent Ave.
S. Broadway
Union Ave.
Nelson Ave.
Fish Creek
Northway
N
Northway
Saratoga Lake

Adelphi Hotel, **4**
Batchellor Mansion, **6**
Canfield Casino, **7**
Congress Park, **3**
National Museum of Dance, **8**

National Museum of Racing, **2**
Roosevelt Bath House, **10**
Saratoga Performing Arts Center, **9**
Saratoga Springs Urban Cultural Visitor Center, **5**
Yaddo, **1**

heading south, if you intend to give these streets a look-see. The blocks of Broadway between Lake Avenue and Spring Street is where you will find many of Saratoga's better boutiques.

In the summer, especially during the racing session, people-watching in Saratoga is a finely honed art, and one of the best ❹ places to get started is on the balcony of the **Adelphi Hotel** (*see* Lodging), overlooking Broadway, at breakfast time.

The Adelphi is also an excellent introduction to Saratoga's Victorian past. Furnished with authentic period pieces—everything from swayback love seats to a century-old cash register in the lobby—the hotel is in the process of being restored, a few rooms a year, to its original grandeur. The small balcony opens off of a second-floor parlor, from which coffee and pastries are served in the morning. The Adelphi is a last vestige of great hotels of the 1800s, when such luminaries as Andrew Jackson and Washington Irving came to Saratoga and Ballston to partake of the spa waters.

In July and August, guided walking tours of the city are ❺ offered from the **Saratoga Springs Urban Cultural Visitor Center** (on Broadway across from Congress Park), but, armed with literature from the visitor center, you can get around on your own reasonably well. *Tel. 518/584–3913. Open weekdays 10–4; guided tours $2, leaves 10 AM for the east side of Saratoga, 1 PM for the west side.*

There are more than two dozen active springs in and around the city, and you can drink or fill containers free of charge. Each spring has water of varying mineral content and effervescence; taste carefully—the water from some springs, such as the notoriously noxious stuff that comes from Hathorn No. 1 off Spring Street, may take some getting used to.

More than 700 structures in Saratoga are listed on the National Register of Historic Places, and about 400 of them are ornate homes dating back to the Victorian era. Ten years ago, most of these homes were in disrepair and even decay, but private initiative, along with various forms of public support, has spearheaded a citywide restoration effort.

Many of the most impressive Victorian houses are behind Congress Park, along Union and Circular avenues. Especially ❻ noteworthy is the **Batchellor Mansion,** on Circular Avenue two blocks from Broadway, with its turrets and multiangled facade restored to mint condition. Unfortunately, like most of the Victorian structures, the Batchellor Mansion is a private home and is not open to the public for tours.

❼ **Canfield Casino,** the lone building in Congress Park, is now a museum devoted to Saratoga's colorful history as a gambling center, beginning in 1842. Gambling was a thriving enterprise in Saratoga for more than 100 years until the 1950s, when a U.S. Senate commission headed by Estes Kefauver cracked down on unlawful betting. In fact, until its demise, gambling was a bigger drawing card in Saratoga than horse racing or the spa waters. Bettors stayed at the gargantuan hotels of the time, such as the United States Hotel and the Grand Union, whose dining rooms could seat up to 1,000 people. Among the frequent visitors to Saratoga were such infamous gamesmen as Bet-A-Million Gates and Diamond Jim Brady. Brady, never

short on showmanship, arrived in Saratoga in 1896 with 27
houseboys and daily changes of jewelry. Lillian Russell,
Brady's companion, entertained herself about town on a gold-
plated bicycle.

After a few brushes with the law, the casinos finally closed for
good in the 1950s. It touched off an immediate and severe tourism decline in Saratoga, which had little other economic
activity to support itself. Yet Saratoga's gambling legacy was
kept alive with the Canfield Casino museum as well as two notable contributions to American culture. The Canfield Casino is
reputed to be where the card game was invented and the first
place where a club sandwich was served. *Tel. 518/584–6920.*
*Admission: $2 adults, $1.50 students and seniors, 25¢ children
under 7. Open 1–4 Wed.–Sun. Nov.–late May; 10–4 Mon.–Sat.
and 1–4 Sun. during June, Sept., and Oct.; 9:30–4:30 daily
July and Aug.*

On your way to the **Saratoga State Park,** make a point of stopping in at the **National Museum of Dance.** Opened in 1987, the
museum features rotating exhibits on the history and development of dance. The gallery that houses the dance hall of fame
honors dance luminaries such as Fred Astaire and Martha Graham. Small television monitors show five- to 10-minute video
vignettes of each inductee, and there are terrific photos of
dancers and choreographers in action. *Rte. 9S, tel. 518/548–
2552. Admission: $2.50 adults, $1 seniors and students, 50¢
children under 12. Open Thurs.–Sat. 10–5, Sun. noon–4.*

Saratoga State Park has more activities packed into one open
space during the summer than any place in New York north of
New York City's Central Park. From June to September, the
New York City Opera, the Philadelphia Orchestra, the New
York City Ballet, and acclaimed dance companies make the **Saratoga Performing Arts Center** (tel. 518/584–7100), in Saratoga
State Park, their home away from home. Of course, the events
that really pack the house—or the open-air amphitheater and
surrounding grounds—are pop performances by the likes of
the Grateful Dead and Linda Rondstadt. During the off-
season, local and regional performing groups keep the stage of
the park's Little Theater alive.

The park itself has two golf courses (18-hole and 9-hole), eight
tennis courts (free), two swimming pools, and cross-country
skiing and ice skating in winter. The mineral bath,
wrapped-towel rest, and massage special at the **Roosevelt Bath
House** is one of the best deals in town at $17. There are also sev-
eral picnic areas in the park, for which a small per-car fee is
charged during the summer months. *Tel. 518/584–2000. No admission charge. Park closes at dusk daily.*

Excursions from Saratoga Springs

*Numbers in the margin correspond with points of interest on
the North Country map.*

The requisite excursion from **Saratoga Springs** is to the **National Historic Park,** site of an important battlefield of the
American Revolution and nine miles from center city. Take
Route 9 south beyond I–87 to Route 9P east, to Route 423 east,
and Route 32 north. The way is well marked. A loop back to the
city can be made by heading north on Route 32 to Schuylerville

(the original Saratoga of the 1700s) and turning left on Route 29 west.

British general John Burgoyne had planned to move south from Canada with his troops, take command of the waterways between Montreal and New York, and eventually consolidate with the forces of William Howe in New York City. Instead, American generals Horatio Gates and Benedict Arnold engaged him in two fierce battles here in the fall of 1777 and eventually forced him to surrender.

The battlefield tour starts at the visitor center, which houses a few artifacts—small cannon, infantry gear, and other battle materials recovered at the site—as well as maps and history books. The most compelling reason to drop by the visitor center (other than paying the park fee) is to watch the 21-minute film about the two battles. It is a good primer since there is really not much to *see* at the battlefield, other than some fine views of the Hudson River farming country. Designated stopping points along the way are equipped with audio recordings to explain what you would be seeing if you were there in 1777. But there are few structures or archaeological remnants. *Rtes. 4 and 3 at Schuylerville, tel. 518/664–9821. Admission: $3 per vehicle or $1 per person. Open 9–5 daily; visitor center open year-round, battlefield closed to vehicles Dec.–Mar.*

On your way to or from the battlefield, you might want to make a stop at **Saratoga Village,** a few miles south on Route 9 past the turn-off for Route 9P. This mall, built like a neo–New England village, houses 60 stores, mostly factory outlets.

② Another worthwhile excursion is south on Route 50 to **Ballston Spa,** if for no other reason than to visit the **National Bottle Museum,** with its antique bottles, jars, stoneware, and related items. *Verbeeck House, 20 Church Ave., tel. 518/885–7589. Donations. Open daily 10–4, June–Labor Day.*

The Adirondacks

Adirondack Park is a place of big numbers. The official boundaries of the park encompass six million acres (9,375 square miles), almost three times the land area of Yellowstone National Park. There are 1,000 miles of rivers, 30,000 miles of brooks and streams, and more than 2,500 lakes and ponds. At an estimated 1.2 billion years old, its mountains are "the survivors of the most ancient geologic formation in North America," according to the Adirondack Park Association.

The numbers impress, but they are just by way of introduction to the Adirondacks. Understanding the Adirondacks is a matter of sensory perception rather than number crunching. It is a place not only to be seen but also to be heard and smelled and, during winters that are often harsh, felt as well.

From spring through fall, every lake view or mountain vista or walk in the woods comes with the fragrance of hemlock and spruce and musty soil and the sounds of songbirds, woodpeckers, loons, or any of the 220 species of birds in the region.

By and large, the Adirondacks were so ignored by early American settlers that it wasn't until 1837 that the first white man, Ebenezer Emmons, on assignment from the New York State
③ legislature to catalog the region, reached the top of **Mt. Marcy.**

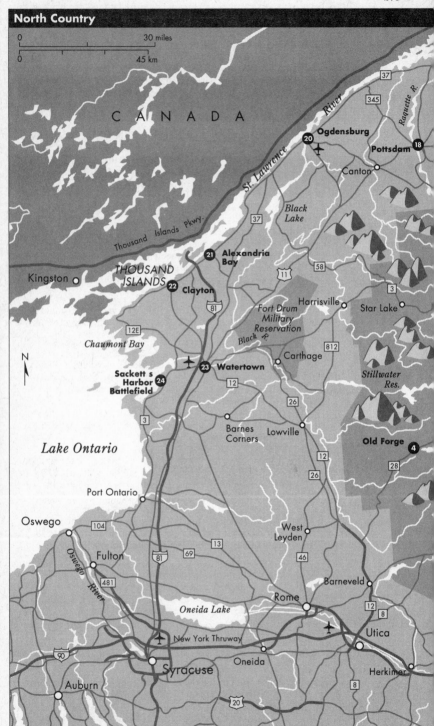

North Country

0   30 miles
0   45 km

C A N A D A

St. Lawrence River

Raquette R.

37

345

20 **Ogdensburg**

Pottsdam **18**

Canton

Black Lake

37

Thousand Islands Pkwy.

21 **Alexandria Bay**

11

58

3

Kingston

THOUSAND ISLANDS

22 **Clayton**

81

Harrisville

Star Lake

12E

Chaumont Bay

Fort Drum Military Reservation

Black R.

812

N

23 **Watertown**

Stillwater Res.

Sackett s Harbor Battlefield **24**

12

Carthage

3

26

Barnes Corners

Lowville

Old Forge **4**

Lake Ontario

28

12

26

Port Ontario

Oswego

104

West Leyden

Oswego River

Fulton

81

69

13

46

Barneveld

481

12 8

Rome

Oneida Lake

New York Thruway

Utica

90

Oneida

Herkimer

Syracuse

8

Auburn

20

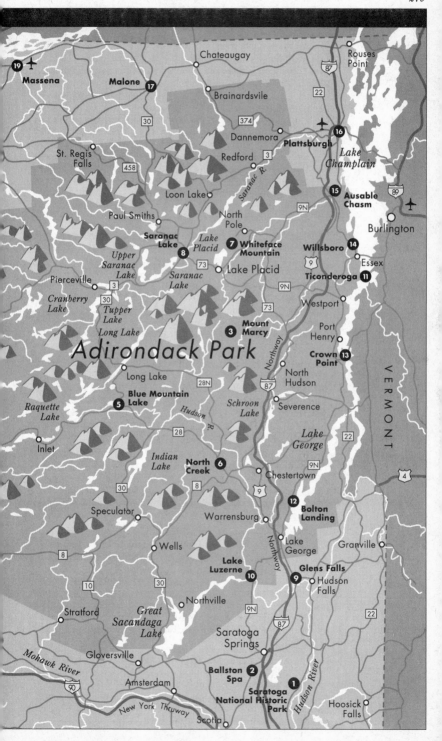

Mt. Washington in New Hampshire, by comparison, had been climbed almost 200 years earlier in 1642.

This extended disinterest in the Adirondacks proved, in the long run, a boon for wilderness lovers. By the 1800s, the idea that there was value in the wilderness itself began to gain popular support. Ralph Waldo Emerson became an Adirondacks admirer after his 1858 stay at "Philosophers' Camp" with a group of Boston intellectuals. (Originally named Camp Maple by James Lowell Russell, it was given the nickname, Philosophers' Camp, by guides for the group). After publication in 1869 of William H. H. Murray's classic *Adventures in the Wilderness*, extolling the freshness and purity of the Adirondack air, the region became recognized as a place of recuperation. The famous Trudeau Sanitorium in Saranac Lake was visited by many notables of the late 1800s, among them Robert Louis Stevenson, who apparently didn't care much for the cold winter air, no matter how pure it was.

Wealthy families discovered the Adirondacks toward the latter part of the 19th century, giving rise to a concept of rustic elegance that became known as the "great camps." These camps were generally built of native materials—wood and stone—and had a rough-hewn look to them, but were otherwise spacious and luxurious. **Camp Sagamore,** four miles south of Route 28 at Racquette Lake Village (tel. 315/354–5311), one of the great camps built in 1897 and now open to tours in the summer months, is a good example of what it means to rough it, upper-crust style.

The wilderness was also protected by law very early; Adirondack Park was created by the state in 1892, and two years later a large chunk of the land was designated as "forever wild," prohibiting future development; today, about one million acres in the park are so classified. However, the Adirondacks is not a complete wilderness area; almost two thirds of the land within the park boundaries is privately owned.

Trails for hiking, snowmobiling, or cross-country skiing are generally well cleared and well marked, as are water accesses. Campgrounds are well maintained. As a state-managed park, regulations are somewhat different from those at national parks; for example, fire regulations in the park are somewhat less restrictive.

Also, the checkerboard of public and private lands gives the Adirondacks a different character from most national parks. Motels, lodges, and restaurants can be found throughout the park region on private land and are privately owned and operated. Canoe rentals, seaplane (or lake plane) services, and guide services are all private enterprises, while most campgrounds, trails, and waterways are maintained on public land by the state, through the Department of Environmental Conservation (DEC).

For the most part, the public-private union has been harmonious, although environmentalists occasionally express concern about potential development of private lands within the park, and private landowners occasionally complain about trespassing. One area of dispute, for example, is the right of free passage through private waters—a right that canoeists and fishermen claim, but one that many landowners refuse to recognize.

Keep in mind the substantial distances between settlements with lodging and services when exploring the region. Stretches of 30 or more miles between settlements are common, especially in the central Adirondacks and the far north. Keep an eye on the gas gauge.

Life in much of the Adirondacks is seasonal. Lakeside lodges and motels tend to close between November and April. Although interest in winter activities such as backcountry skiing, snowshoeing, snowmobiling, and ice-fishing is on the rise, many places aren't properly winterized. If you are traveling through the Adirondacks in winter, you may have to travel a long way before finding a place to bed down, except in the Lake Placid area, with a rich and established winter tradition.

Southern and Central Adirondacks The two main roads—virtually the only roads at all—through the southern and central Adirondacks are routes 28 and 30. Route 28 forms an east-west crescent from Warrensburg through Old Forge to Woodgate. Route 30 reaches north from Gloversville to Tupper Lake. The two routes run together for about 10 miles between Indian Lake and Blue Mountain Lake, the approximate geographical center of the Adirondacks. Route 28N makes a northerly swing from Route 28 at North Creek before turning west and joining Route 30 at Long Lake, 11 miles north of Blue Mountain Lake. Route 8, which runs along West Canada Creek and Piseco Lake and Lake Pleasant, joins Route 30 in Speculator and is the major road in the southwestern part of the park. (The Lake George region, as well as the Lake Champlain region, is technically within the park boundaries. *See* Lake George and Lake Champlain.)

Even in the peak season of July and August, peace and tranquility are the underlying themes of the southern and central Adirondacks. This is early-to-bed, early-to-rise country. Lodges often serve dinner at 6 PM; dinner at 8 is considered late. Gigantic breakfasts tend to be the order of the morning: Oatmeal, eggs, bacon, pancakes, toast, juice, coffee, and morning indigestion are de rigueur. The big-breakfast tradition probably has its roots in the logging days, but a big-breakfast, light-lunch formula makes sense, since most people are on the go in the middle of the day, hiking, fishing, exploring, or touring by car.

Although most people associate "Adirondacks" with high mountains, the southern and central landscape is primarily one of lakes, rivers, and rolling hills. The notable exception is Blue Mountain, which stands 3,828 feet above everything that surrounds it. Its summit lookout tower affords a sweeping 360° view that includes the chain of lakes that reach toward Inlet, but the price of that view is a fairly steep scramble of about a mile.

❹ The center of tourist activity in the southern and central Adirondacks is **Old Forge,** but even its amusements and lakeside activities are low-key in comparison to Lake George. In fact, one of its most popular spots is the Old Forge Hardware store on the main drag, which sells exotic gifts, paintings, sculpture, pottery, and books, in addition to the usual camping equipment and tools.

❺ **Blue Mountain Lake,** the cultural center of the region, is home of the **Adirondack Museum,** the best museum about the Adirondacks. The museum covers the entire cultural and historical spectrum of the region. It is easily possible to spend two full days exploring the museum, but if you don't have that kind of time, the canoes and guideboats, Adirondack furniture, and outdoor sporting-paraphernalia displays are the most fascinating. *Rte. 28N, tel. 518/352–7311. Admission: $7.25 adults, $4.50 children. Open Memorial Day–mid-Oct. 9:30–5:30.*

Blue Mountain Lake is also home of the **Adirondack Lakes Center for the Arts,** (tel. 518/352–7715), a working retreat for artists, writers, and musicians. The center also stages musical performances, craft demonstrations, and other cultural activities open to the public during the summer. Crafts, incidentally, are a vital part of the central Adirondacks character, and many artists, furniture builders, weavers, and boat builders live in the area around Long Lake and Blue Mountain Lake. A few tend to be reclusive, but others welcome visitors interested in their craftsmanship. The **Adirondack North Country Association** (Box 148, Lake Placid 12946, tel. 518/523–2062) or the **Adirondack Lakes Center for the Arts** in Blue Mountain Lake can provide lists of local craftspeople and those who welcome visitors at their workplaces.

❻ Route 28 east from Blue Mountain Lake leads to **North Creek,** which could be considered the sporting capital of the central Adirondacks. Gore Mountain, with a 2,150-foot vertical rise, is the second-largest ski area in the state (after Whiteface), but is something of a secret among skiers in the know in New York. Gore doesn't have as severe a climate as Whiteface to the north, nor does it have near the crowds of Hunter Mountain in the Catskills. Nonskiers can get in on the view from the top of Gore in the summer and fall when the gondola operates for sightseers; there is also a road leading up the mountain. *Tel. 518/251–2411. Gondola ride is $4.*

Skiing isn't the only athletic activity in North Creek. The town is also the white-water hub of the Adirondacks and site of the annual **Whitewater Derby** in late May (*see* Spectator Sports). Spring is the time when the real white-water daredevils like to put their kayaks and canoes into the river because the water is highest after the run-off from the snow melt. The most popular runs are along the Indian River from Indian Lake and then on to the Hudson River leading to North Creek. If you want to give the river a go—by raft, innertube, or kayak—Hudson River Rafting Company (Main St., North Creek 12853, tel. 518/251–3275), a leading white-water outfitter, operates out of North Creek.

If you have the time, the drive between Long Lake and North Creek on Route 28N is one of the prettiest in the Adirondacks and less traveled than Route 28 to the south. While the trip along Route 28N is worthwhile for the mountain and lake views alone, there are also a few points of interest along the way. A historic marker between Minerva and Newcomb commemorates the estimated point where, in 1901, Teddy Roosevelt became President after the assassination of William McKinley. Roosevelt had been climbing in the High Peaks at the time, and it had taken considerable effort to get word to him of McKinley's death. A small road leading north from Route 28N between Newcomb and Minerva provides southern access for hikers going into the High Peaks region, and the road follows the Hudson River along its northernmost extreme. If the out-of-the-way world of Route 28N really captivates you, try the 90-site Lake Harris Campground, three miles north of Newcomb off Route 28N, on the shores of Lake Harris (tel. 518/582-2503).

For the most part, the tranquillity of the southern and central Adirondacks turns to dormancy in winter. However, because the terrain is gentler than the High Peaks region to the north—and nearer the population centers of the south—snowmobiling and cross-country skiing are popular winter activities. The substantial snowfall and the interconnected lake and trail systems form an extensive snowmobile network. Old Forge, Schroon Lake, and Speculator are towns where snowmobilers tend to congregate.

Lake Placid If there is an aortal link between the southern, central, and northern Adirondacks, it is the **Northville–Placid Trail.** The trail meanders along 130 miles of generally rolling terrain from Northville, past Great Sacandaga Lake, then on to Lake Placid. The full trip is made by serious backpackers in summer—and *very* serious backcountry skiers in winter—although the northern section of the trail, from Long Lake to Lake Placid through the High Peaks area, is the more traveled.

Lake Placid is unquestionably the hub of the northern Adirondacks. Most Lake Placid visitors come in from the east, off Exit 31 or Exit 34 on the Northway (I-87). From Exit 31, Route 9N leads through Elizabethtown before joining Route 73 in the Keene area. Route 73 climbs for seven, often-steep miles toward Lake Placid before topping out near Cascade Mountain. In summer, world-class cyclists can be seen making the climb as part of regular training rides; in winter, you might spot ice climbers on the cliffs above Cascade Pond. From here Route 73 descends six miles to Lake Placid.

From Exit 34, Route 9N follows the Ausable River to Jay; from there, Route 86 forks right and leads through Wilmington to Lake Placid. No matter which route you take into Lake Placid, there are early indications that you are coming into Olympic country. Along Route 73, you pass **Mt. Van Hoevenberg,** site of the luge and bobsled runs, as well as the cross-country ski tracks. Soon, the towers of the 70- and 90-meter ski jumps loom on your left. The jumps are stark and exposed and seem out of place, but the view from the top of the 90-meter jump is dramatic. You get a bird's-eye view of the entire lay of the land and the High Peaks around Lake Placid. You also get a stomach-gripping view of what the jumpers see while preparing to take flight.

7 If you come into Lake Placid on Route 86, **Whiteface Mountain,** New York's largest ski area, will be on your right. On spring and summer mornings, you are apt to see fly fishermen in hip boots casting their lines out onto the waters of the Ausable River.

Lake Placid's mile-long Main Street, from the intersection of routes 73 and 86 to the swing left onto Saranac Avenue, is a tight cluster of hotels, restaurants, and shops, not to mention the Olympic Ice Arena and the speed-skating oval. For that reason, traffic is often backed up in summer; the best way to enjoy Lake Placid is to park—if you can find a parking space—

and walk around. An alternate way to get around is via Holly the Trolley, a 75¢ bus ride making a 21-stop tour of Lake Placid from Memorial Day to Labor Day. Main Street is great for browsing; if you are looking for books about the life and history of the Adirondacks drop in at With Pipe and Book (91 Main St., tel. 518/523–9096).

Take one of the boat tours that leave from the marina at the end of Main Street; guides point out all the summer homes (or "camps") of the well-to-do along the lake shores. Unless you're well-acquainted with New York State's social register, though, the tour is most enjoyable as a nice easy spin around the lake on a hot summer day. You can also take a guided tour of Olympic sites, which includes a visit to the Olympic Winter Sports Museum, which opened in spring 1989. Contact the Olympic Regional Development Authority (tel. 518/523–1655).

Self-guided tours can be made of the **John Brown Farm** (tel. 518/523–3900), home and burial place of the famed abolitionist who operated the farm for runaway slaves. Located off Route 73 just past the Olympic ski jumps, the farm is open from early May to late October.

During the summer, you can reach the top of Whiteface either by chairlift or by car on Veterans Memorial Highway, and the short walk to the summit provides a superb view—Lake Placid in one direction, Lake Champlain in another, and the High Peaks to the south. Go on a clear day, if possible.

There isn't much to do at Mt. Van Hoevenberg in summer, except to ride to the top of the bobsled run, but in winter you can try bobsledding—as a passenger with an experienced driver—or luge. On the luge run you are on your own, although you only have to maneuver through the last few turns of the course. Still, it's not for the timid.

⑧ Ten miles west of Lake Placid is **Saranac Lake,** where, more than a century ago, the **Trudeau Sanitorium** opened, establishing forever the healthy-air reputation of the Adirondacks. In February, Saranac Lake hosts the most celebrated winter carnival in the Adirondacks. Revelers seem to enjoy wreaking havoc on the ice sculptures on Flower Lake as much as they do creating them; the storming of the Ice Palace, complete with fireworks, is the traditional carnival finale. (For information, tel. 518/891–1990).

From Saranac Lake, Route 3 leads west through Tupper Lake and Cranberry Lake on its way to Watertown. The mountains gradually give way to more rolling forest land as you make your way westward. You are entering prime canoe country, as the **St. Regis Canoe Area,** which includes much of Upper Saranac Lake, is off-limits to power boats. Tupper Lake and Raquette Pond are also great for exploring by canoe, and the reedy nooks of Raquette Pond provide some of the best black-bass fishing grounds in the North Country. The lakes and ponds of this area are part of a vast network of interconnected waterways, linked primarily by the Raquette, St. Regis, and Saranac rivers. You could hire a guide or spend months trying to cover just a fraction of the network by canoe.

Cranberry Lake is the largest body of water in the relatively unexplored northwestern corner of the park. Several long and gentle hiking trails wind through the area around the lake, and the quick and easy hike to a lookout from Bear Mountain provides a sweeping view of the lake and the unspoiled countryside beyond. The hike can be combined with a swim and picnic at the 173-site Cranberry Lake Campground, off Route 3, from which the trail up Bear Mountain leads (Cranberry Lake Village, tel. 315/848–2315).

Lake George and Lake Champlain

Just 40 miles north of Saratoga, the village of Lake George is altogether another world. If Saratoga is culture and sophistication, with a little snobbishness thrown in, Lake George is unabashed kitsch. That's what makes it fun, especially for families with young children; there are endless pop-culture activities to keep them amused. Saratoga and Lake George have one common denominator: large crowds in July and August. Even more than Saratoga, Lake George is a summer community. About 90% of the community shuts down after Labor Day and doesn't reopen until May.

You may feel as if you are entering a time warp as you drive north along Route 9 into the village of Lake George, at the southern end of the lake. The clusters of small motels, amusement parks, miniature golf courses, and stores selling ersatz Indian artifacts seem drawn from American Vacationland, circa 1958. You get the feeling that at any time, you might see Ricky, Lucy, little Ricky, and the Mertzes zip by in the old Rambler, on their way to some place like Magic Forest, a funland with a 30-foot statue of Uncle Sam out front. This kind of thing might be a bit dated, but it certainly isn't run-down. The continuing popularity of Lake George as a moderately priced weekend or summer-vacation resort ensures that the attractions are well maintained.

9 The road to Lake George really begins in **Glens Falls,** about halfway between Saratoga and Lake George. The city of 18,000 is home to a minor-league baseball team in summer and a minor-league hockey team in winter. It is where you'll find the **Adirondack Mountain Club** (*see* Important Addresses and Numbers), which can provide all sorts of valuable information if you are planning to continue north to the park. Another reason to visit Glens Falls is the **Hyde Collection.** Housed in the former residence of a prominent Glens Falls family, the collection features a broad and exemplary group of works by artists ranging from Rembrandt to Whistler. *161 Warren St., tel. 518/792–1761. Admission charge. Open Labor Day–Nov.*

Heading north on Route 9, you'll know you're entering Lake George country when you pass **Great Escape** (tel. 518/792–6508; open Memorial Day–Labor Day 9–6 PM), the North Country's largest amusement park, and the motels begin to appear fast and furiously. Just before the village of Lake George,
10 Route 9N branches left from Route 9 and leads to **Lake Luzerne,** a smaller and quieter vacation community 10 miles away. Lake Luzerne is known for its dude ranches and is sometimes called "Big Hat" country, as in ten-gallon hat. It is the southern Adirondack center for horseback riding, pony riding, or extended trail rides into the park. At Hadley, the little village neighboring Lake Luzerne, you can rent a houseboat and explore Great Sacandaga Lake, equal in size to Lake George but less trafficked.

Another road branching off of Route 9 just before you get to Lake George leads up **Prospect Mountain,** to its ballyhooed 100-mile view. You can drive it or hike it—the trip is fairly short either way—but there are other short climbs around that are more enjoyable and far less congested. The three-mile hike up Buck Mountain, beginning near Pilot Knob, offers a terrific view of the lake with the Adirondacks as a backdrop.

Route 9 through Lake George village is tightly packed with motels, moderately priced and inexpensive restaurants, and a few stores. The road that branches right around the southern extreme of the lake leads past the boat docks and the beach, with a small public park for walking, picknicking, and bicycling across the way.

Boat cruises from the town dock are extremely popular from May through October. The Lake George Steamboat Company operates three cruise ships for sightseeing tours on the lake to
11 **Ticonderoga,** as well as dinner cruises complete with Dixieland band. Boats can be rented at the dock, although congestion in the summer in recent years has raised increasing concerns about safety at the southern end of the lake. If you want to rent a boat, it is worth driving the few miles up the east side of the lake to Dunham Bay or 10 miles on Route 9N to Bolton Landing. *Tel. 518/668–5777. 1-, 2- or 4½-hour cruises from $5.95–$11.50 adults to $3–$4.50 children.*

12 **Bolton Landing** is best known as the home of **Sagamore,** a sprawling and luxurious year-round resort on its own small island. The centerpiece of the Sagamore is the old hotel, built in 1883 and recently restored. The resort features seven outlying lodges, several restaurants, myriad recreational facilities and a slate of activities that includes theater productions and "murder-mystery weekends" during the quiet winter months (*see* Lodging).

One worthwhile excursion from Lake George village is to **Warrensburg,** a low-key clapboard village eight miles north on Route 9. Several antique stores here can make for a pleasant day or afternoon of browsing.

The Champlain   In addition to the Northway, there are two ways to reach Ti-
Valley   conderoga from Glens Falls: Route 4 to Route 22 and Route 9 to 9N. Route 4, which can be reached from Glens Falls by taking 32 west, is worth following for two reasons. Between Fort Ann and Whitehall, it runs along the Champlain Canal, which connects Lake Champlain and the Hudson River. If your timing is good, a barge or boat will be passing through the lock five miles north of Fort Ann. Take the time to pull over and watch the intricate maneuvering. The other reason is to pass through Whitehall, which claims "the birthplace of the American Navy": There Benedict Arnold launched America's first fleet in 1776 to do battle with the British on Lake Champlain. The Skenesborough Museum in Whitehall commemorates this historic event.

Fort Ticonderoga (Rte. 74, tel. 518/558–2821) was built by the French in 1756 to take control of the southern extreme of Lake Champlain—and, in effect, the entire water route between Montreal and Albany. It was strategically important—a position that was fought for dearly. It was held by the French, captured by the British (during the French and Indian Wars), and later by the Americans during the Revolution. The fort has been beautifully restored, and its museum, with uniforms and weaponry, is an excellent primer in 18th-century military history. The Revolutionary hoopla that takes place in the summer months—dress parades, cannon firings, and the like—tends toward hokiness, but it is the sort of stuff that is close enough to living history to be of interest to children. The fort is open from Memorial Day to mid-October.

⑬ Farther north is a state historic site at **Crown Point** (Rtes. 9 and 22, tel. 518/597–3666), where another French fort was built in 1734, but it is an archaeological site, not a restored site like Fort Ticonderoga. Plan to spend a few hours at the lakeside village of Essex, which has several 18th- and 19th-century buildings in fine condition, good shops for browsing, and an active marina. There is also a ferry that runs during the summer months from Essex to Vermont, if you have time for a short excursion onto the lake.

Route 22 angles away from the lake after Essex, and the next
⑭ stop worth making is the **fish ladder in Willsboro,** especially in the fall when the land-locked salmon make their most concerted rush north; there's a viewing window here that lets you view the action.

⑮ Just after Keeseville is the **Ausable Chasm.** The Ausable River has carved a seemingly impossible path through deep layers of sandstone, leaving cliffs that reach well over 100 feet high in places. This geological spectacle is often overrun during summer months—it is a stop on every tour-bus romp through the region.

North of the chasm are some interesting wetlands—the **Ausable Marsh State Wildlife Management Area**—where birdwatchers might want to pull in, especially during the fall migration. There is a state campground just beyond the wildlife
⑯ management area. The small city of **Plattsburgh,** six miles to the north, is more likely to be a supply stop in your travels through the North Country rather than a destination. It was, however, a city of strategic importance during the War of 1812, when the U.S.-Canadian border was an issue of dispute. Stop at the Kent-Delord House (17 Cumberland Ave., tel. 518/561–1035), which was seized by the British in 1814 and affords a good capsule look at family life in the 19th-century. It has a fine collection of portrait paintings.

Two things to keep in mind as you tour through the Champlain Valley. Legend persists that a Loch Ness–like monster makes its home in the lake. Even Samuel Champlain claimed he saw some unusual creature during his original exploration of the lake in 1609. If you think you see something, report your sighting to a local town clerk or harbormaster. Your sighting will be laughed at and duly filed away as part of the legend.

More important, the Champlain Valley is a productive farming region in the North Country. If you are visiting the area during the late summer or early fall, be sure to sample the regional produce at farm stands, farmers' markets, or local restaurants. And if you are in the area in October, apple-picking is a popular activity. Many orchards allow visitors to pick their own. New York cheeses are famous and available any time of year.

The Thousand Islands—Seaway

The name "Thousand Islands" is less than accurate; there are, in fact, nearly twice that number, depending on who is doing the counting and what you consider an island. Any clump of land that could support two trees was the definition used by the National Geographic Society when it counted "1,800 or so islands" a few years ago. But that doesn't quite have the proper ring to it.

There is also much more to the region than the island-studded area of the St. Lawrence River called the Thousand Islands. The name usually refers to an area defined by the Adirondacks to the east, the St. Lawrence River to the north, and Lake Ontario to the west. Its largest city, Watertown, is more than 30 miles south of the Thousand Islands and is itself something of a misnomer, since it is not on any water at all.

Most of the region is flat or rolling farmland, but the economy is heavily dependent on the St. Lawrence Seaway. The river defines a coastline running for more than 100 miles southwest from Massena to Cape Vincent, where the river meets Lake Ontario. The St. Lawrence is the throat of a waterway that leads through the Great Lakes and which, with the completion of its lock system in 1959, formed the longest navigable inland passage—more than 2,300 miles—in the world.

The main roadways of the Thousand Islands area are I–81, which runs north from Syracuse through Watertown, and the Seaway Trail, a combination of Routes 37, 12, and 12E, which follows the river and the Lake Ontario shore. The two main roadways intersect at the Thousand Islands International Bridge, leading into Canada. The juncture of the two roads is the geographic nexus of the region, and the two riverside towns of Alexandria Bay and Clayton see a considerable amount of summer traffic. The small cities to the northeast, Odgdensburg and Massena, are more shipping towns than they are tourism towns, although they are not without their attractions. The locks at Massena, in fact, are the best place to see the shipping industry of the Seaway in action.

An inland road that parallels the Seaway Trail for much of the way is Route 11, which runs from Lake Champlain through the cities of Malone, Potsdam, and Canton to Watertown. There are a couple of points of interest along this route. Ballard Mill **17** (tel. 518/483–5190), a converted woolen mill in **Malone,** is an arts and crafts center with demonstrations and theater presentations in the summer. Route 11 is also the college route, to a branch of the State University of New York in Potsdam and St. Lawrence University in Canton. The Crane School of Music **18** (tel. 315/267–2000), affiliated with the university in **Potsdam,** stages excellent music-theater presentations in summer. Don't be surprised to see horse-drawn carriages along the route, as there are pockets of Amish settlement in this part of the region. Route 11 for the most part, however, is the east-west route of expedience through the north rim of the North Country. The more scenic route is the Seaway Trail following the river.

The Seaway Trail The thing to see in **Massena** is the **Eisenhower Lock,** through **19** which huge cargo vessels pass on their way to and from the Atlantic and the industrial heartland of America. To be sure you'll see the lock in action, call ahead (tel. 315/764–3232) to find out what time a ship is scheduled to pass through. During the nine months of the shipping season (the Seaway freezes in winter), traffic is fairly steady.

The procedure of getting a ship through the lock takes about 45 minutes, and the statistics are amazing: Raising or lowering a ship by more than 40 feet requires the displacement of 22 million gallons of water in the lock and that amount can be flooded or drained in just 10 minutes. The statistics at the nearby St. Lawrence–Franklin D. Roosevelt Project, one of the largest hydroelectric stations in the United States, are also awesome: 150 million gallons a minute pass through the dam, propelled by the force of all the water stored in the Great Lakes. The power project can be reached by continuing through the tunnel beneath the Eisenhower Lock for three miles.

From Massena, the Seaway Trail follows Route 37 southwest to **⓴ Ogdensburg,** the oldest settlement in the region. Its custom house, built in 1809, is the oldest active federal building in the United States. But the main reason to stop in Ogdensburg is the **Remington Museum** (303 Washington St., tel. 315/393–2425). Although Frederic Remington gained fame as a painter of the American West, he was born just to the south in Canton. The museum houses more than 200 of his works, the largest collection in the United States.

The Seaway Trail joins Route 12 in Ogdensburg, and state campgrounds begin to appear at regular intervals of 15 miles or so along the route. One bears the name of Jacques Cartier, the Frenchman who first explored the St. Lawrence in 1535 and who gave the river its name. Making nightly stopovers in the campgrounds is a popular way to tour the Seaway during the summer. The campgrounds are well maintained, with plenty of room for picnicking or recreational sports. For example, the state park at Wellesley Island, just below the International Bridge, has a golf course and a nature preserve in which to explore. But the real appeal of the campgrounds is the fascination of the Seaway traffic, from small sailboats to large tankers, passing before your campsite. For summer weekends, campsites must be booked well ahead of time, especially if you have a vehicle that requires hookups.

Alexandria Bay and Clayton are the focal points for summer visitors to the Thousand Islands. They are the ports from which most of the island owners make their way to their secluded summer homes. Both are good walking towns since they are well away from the highway traffic and are fairly compact. They are also the dining and lodging centers of the region. Lunching dockside or at one of the restaurants with outdoor patios is one of the great pleasures of the Thousand Islands on a summer day.

㉑ Alexandria Bay is the place from which tour boats leave to explore the Thousand Islands; unless you have your own boat, taking a cruise tour is one of the obligatory things to do in the Thousand Islands. The trip includes the option of stopping at **Boldt Castle,** the signature structure of the islands. The 120-room replica of a stone castle was built by George Boldt, developer of the Waldorf-Astoria Hotel in New York City. The castle was to be a gift from Boldt to his wife. In the spirit of romanticism, he even had the island reshaped in the configuration of a

heart, and hearts are integrated as design elements throughout the house. Boldt's wife died in 1904 before construction was
finished, and he never visited the island again. The castle has a
dark and ponderous character, but it is definitely worth a visit.
In summer, Uncle Sam Boat Tours (tel. 315/482–2611) and Empire Boat Tours (tel. 315/482–9511) offer guided cruises of one
to two hours from the dock at Alexandria Bay. Empire also features a "Late Night Love Boat" cruise, departing at 11 PM.

㉒ **Clayton** is a compact copy of Alexandria Bay in its shingled,
clapboard character. The **Thousand Islands Shipyard Museum**
houses everything from a small launch that is believed to have
belonged to Ulysses S. Grant to a collection of outboard motors
dating to the first one mass produced. *705 Mary St., tel. 315/*
686–4104. Open mid-May–mid-Oct. Admission: $4 adults, $3
seniors, $2 children 7–17.

The other point of note in Clayton is the children's playground,
a wonderful jumble of turrets and wood planks to climb and
crawl over. If you have children under 10, expect them to be entertained for hours at a time.

The Seaway Trail from Clayton then follows Route 12E to Cape
Vincent. As Route 12E hooks back to the southeast after Cape
Vincent, you enter the breadbasket of the Thousand Islands region. This is the world of silos and pastureland, with occasional
glimpses of Lake Ontario in the distance off to the right. This
㉓ interior nook of the North Country, bounded by **Watertown,**
Lake Ontario, and the St. Lawrence Seaway, is active farming
country, although the harsh winter conditions that charge off
of Lake Ontario make for a short growing season. If you are interested in the farming life of the region, you might want to
make a short detour to the **Agricultural Historical Museum** at
Stone Mills, in the middle of the Thousand Islands–Cape
Vincent–Watertown triangle. The museum, with its cheese
factory and farm kitchen and demonstrations of farming activities, provides a good feel for farming in the region a century
ago. *Box 108, Rte. 180, La Fargeville 13656, tel. 315/658–2353.*
Open May–Sept., 10–4.

The history of settlement in this part of the North Country
does not reach back much more than a century and a half. The
㉔ one historical site worth visiting is **Sackets Harbor Battlefield**
(tel. 315/646–3634), which you reach by following the curl of the
Seaway Trail along the lake on Route 180 and then Route 3.
Sackets Harbor was the headquarters of U.S. naval operations
in the St. Lawrence–Lake Ontario region for much of the 19th
century. During the War of 1812, when the border between the
United States and Canada was under dispute, Sackets Harbor
was the scene of heavy fighting between American and British
troops. The battlefield holds a position of prominence overlooking the harbor and Lake Ontario, and the breezes that come off
the lake make for welcome relief in the heat of summer; it is
open from mid-May through October. What is most interesting
about Sackets Harbor is its number of well-preserved 19th-
century structures. A particularly appealing stop is the quirky
Pickering-Beach Museum, a small house built in 1817 that hardly feels like a museum. Instead, with its furnishings and
trinkets from the 19th century, it gives more of a sense of stepping into someone's home of a previous era (tel. 315/646–2052;
open June–Labor Day, 11–5).

Keep in mind that following the Seaway Trail by car is not the only way to explore the Seaway. Many summer visitors enjoy meandering through the Thousand Islands and the lake by boat— some just poking around, others with rod and reel in hand. The St. Lawrence is known as one of the best bass and muskellunge rivers in North America, and you can hire a guide service in Alexandria Bay or Clayton to get to the best fishing spots. (Fishing is not just a summertime pursuit in the Thousand Islands. Ice fishing also has its adherents during the winter-weekend derbies.) For those who want to spend just a few days exploring the islands, houseboat rentals are available in Clayton in summer, and there are many campgrounds and marinas where boats are welcome to pull in for the night. During July and August, houseboats must be booked several months in advance.

What to See and Do with Children

The Adirondacks have long been summer-camp country, and the many activities that keep campers occupied in the summer are activities that families can enjoy together: camping, hiking, canoeing, fishing, white-water rafting, etc. Keep in mind, of course, the physical capabilities of your children. Many hikes, particularly in the High Peaks region, can be rugged, with long, steep sections, and might be difficult for smaller children. Both alpine and cross-country skiing, as well as skating, are popular activities in winter throughout the North Country (*see* Participant Sports).

Less strenuous access to the beauty of the Adirondack region is possible at **Ausable Chasm** on Route 9, just north of Keeseville; High Falls Gorge off of Route 86 near Wilmington; and **Natural Stone Bridge and Caves** near Potterville. The chasm, where the Ausable River, flowing down from the High Peaks, cuts through sandstone cliffs, is especially dramatic. Guided boat rides take visitors through parts of the chasm. The chasm is one of the oldest organized tourist attractions in the United States, dating back to 1870.

For a good look back at New York's farming past, the **Agricultural Museum at Stone Mills** (Box 108, LaFargeville 13656, tel. 315/658–2353) is open from mid-May to mid-September. Cheese-making demonstrations, craft fairs, and horse pulls are among the museum's demonstrations. Family farms and farm-product markets throughout the region, in cooperation with the **Adirondack North Country Association** (ANCA) offer tours and demonstrations of milking, wool-shearing, maple-syrup making, and other activities. Contact ANCA, Box 148, Lake Placid 12946, tel. 518/523–9820 for information.

The 12 county fairs scheduled throughout the region in late July and August feature various amusements and musical performances, in addition to the traditional livestock and produce competitions. The three-day Warren Youth Fair in Warrensburg in August is specifically geared toward the young farmers of the future. For fair dates, contact the **Agricultural Farm Liaison** (NYS Dept. of Agriculture and Markets, 1 Winners Circle, Albany 12235 ,tel. 518/457–3412).

Younger children will also enjoy the **Thousand Islands Zoo and Game Farm** in Redwood (tel. 315/628–5821), which includes a petting zoo, and the fish hatcheries at Saranac Inn (north of Saranac Lake), Cape Vincent, Crown Point, and Warrensburg.

To learn more about local ecology and wildlife, visit one of the **Adirondack Park Interpretive Centers** scheduled to open on Route 28N in Newcomb and on Route 30 in Paul Smiths in 1989. For information contact the Interpretive Center Information Office (Adirondack Park Agency, Box 99, Ray Brook 12977, tel. 518/891–4050).

Lake George has several amusement parks. **Great Escape,** with 100 rides, minishows (short performances by clowns and magicians) and activities, is about five miles south of Lake George on Route 9. **Gaslight Village,** in the village of Lake George, offers 45 rides, along with magic shows, musical jamborees, and so on. For information about both theme parks, tel. 518/668–5459 or 792–6568.

Other amusement/theme parks in the North Country include **Waterfun,** just off the International Bridge in the Thousand Islands area, **Enchanted Forest** in Old Forge, and **Santa's Workshop** in North Pole, off Veterans Memorial Highway leading up Whiteface Mountain.

For more cultural and educational activities, the **Adirondack Museum** in Blue Mountain Lake, the **National Museum of Racing** in Saratoga, the **Six Nations Indian Museum** in Onchionta north of Saranac Lake, and the **Thousand Islands Shipyard Museum** in Clayton hold the greatest appeal for children. **Fort Ticonderoga** and the battlefields at Saratoga and Sackets Harbor are the primary historic spots to hit (*see* Exploring).

Children-only backstage tours are available before and after each New York City Ballet matinee at the **Saratoga Performing Arts Center;** you must make arrangements in advance by contacting the National Museum of Dance (tel. 518/584–2225).

Puppet shows are part of the schedule of the **Adirondack Lakes Center for the Arts** (tel. 518/352–7715) in Blue Mountain Lake. The center also features craft demonstrations, and art classes for children 5 to 14.

Off the Beaten Track

Off-track diversions are the very essence of traveling through the North Country. With most of the driving in the region on two-lane roads rather than interstate highways, there is plenty of opportunity to pull over for a good view, an interesting shop, a yard sale, or a place for a picnic. Here are a few interesting alternatives:

The Mansion (tel. 518/885–1607) in Rocky City Falls about seven miles west of Saratoga Springs on Route 29, is a good place to be close to the action but away from all the commotion of the summer scene. The stately Victorian home, with its 14-foot ceilings and eight-foot windows, is now a bed-and-breakfast. It exudes a quality of time-honored civility: fresh flowers adorn the five bedrooms, and home-baked breads and fresh fruit are served at breakfast. The Mansion even has its own little barn stuffed with antiques, if you want to poke around in the morning before heading off to the horse races.

Heading into the Adirondacks, you may want to stop by the **Barton Mines** off Route 28 in North River. Producing 90% of the world's industrial garnet (a deep-red mineral), the mine is a last vestige of the previous, and relatively unproductive, era of mining in the Adirondacks. There are tours of the mines as well as a gift shop with garnet jewelry.

Visiting a garbage dump might not seem the sort of thing you would want to do on a vacation, but taking dinner leftovers to the town dump is something of an evening ritual in the central Adirondacks. Bears, relatively tame and very responsive to the idea of a free meal, also tend to make it their presunset ritual to visit the dumps for an evening snack. The town dump at **Long Lake** is especially well-known as a place for feeding the bears. Keep in mind that although most of the bears aren't aggressive, it is still a good idea to keep a reasonable distance.

In the Thousand Islands area, the **Muskellunge Hall of Fame** (282 Mindall Ave., Clayton, tel. 518/236–1823), in the Old Town Hall at Clayton, honors one of the world's most neolithic-looking species of fish and the anglers who have become legends in pursuing it. The hall of fame is worth visiting less for what is there than for the peculiar thing that it is.

Shopping

Gift Ideas

The North Country is generally not the place for a shopping binge, but there are a few local items, such as maple syrup and cheeses—pungent, sharp cheddar in particular—that are widely available and make good gifts. You'll get a better feel for the character of the region—and save a dollar or two—by buying directly from the producer. Farmers' markets in the North Country and especially in the Champlain Valley and Thousand Islands areas are held most regularly in the late summer and early fall. You may also notice roadside signs near farmhouses advertising maple syrup, usually the proprietor's own reserve. Don't hesitate to stop, as passersby are usually offered a sample. Both the syrup and the cheese (if it is tightly sealed in heavy black wax) keep well for shipping.

Crafts

Crafts are another integral part of North Country life, with pottery, furniture, woolen products, wood carvings, and quilts among the products that might catch your interest. "Craft Trails in the Adirondack North Country," published by the **Adirondack North Country Craft Center** (Box 148, Lake Placid 12946, tel. 518/523–2062), is an excellent guide to shops, galleries, dealers, and individual craftspeople in the North Country. Among the places to find good crafts are the **Adirondack Lakes Center for the Arts** and **Blue Mountain Designs,** both in Blue Mountain Lake; the **Arts & Crafts Loft** in Lake George; the **Adirondack North Country Crafts Center** in Lake Placid; and **Ballard Mill Center for the Arts** in Malone. Many craft shops and galleries keep irregular hours during the off-season, so you may have to call ahead for an appointment out of season.

Outlets

There are a number of factory outlets worth a visit. Most notable is **Saratoga Village,** a 58-shop complex in Malta about five miles south of Saratoga Springs on Route 9.

Sporting Goods

There are numerous places for sporting equipment—outfitters, tackle shops, bait shops, etc. A good place for fishing gear is **Francis Betters** on Route 86 in Wilmington; a good place for canoes and canoe gear is **Moose River Outfitters** (tel. 315/369–3682) in Old Forge.

Participant Sports

It is hard to imagine coming to the North Country and not getting involved in some kind of physical activity. Hiking, canoeing, fishing, climbing, and white-water rafting are popular spring through fall, as are golf and tennis. Hunting is the sport in fall, and winter is the time for skiing (alpine and cross-country), as well as skating and ice fishing.

A guide can make your trip far more enjoyable, especially if you are making your first trip to the Adirondacks. They not only know the best routes and are well versed in the proper safety precautions, but they can also make light work of the cumbersome preparations and logistics necessary for any outing.

Guides are licensed by New York State. A list can be obtained from the **New York State Guides Association** (Box 4337, Albany 12204), the **New York State Department of Environmental Conservation** (DEC) (50 Wolf Rd., Albany 12233), or DEC regional headquarters (Ray Brook 12977, tel. 518/891–1370), Warrensburg (12885, tel. 518/623–3671), or Watertown (13601, tel. 315/785–2261).

If you are interested in improving your wilderness skills, the **Adirondack Mountain Club** (174 Glen St., Glens Falls 12801, tel. 518/793–7737) runs regular training programs. Group outings are also open to members through the club, and the nominal cost of membership may be a worthwhile investment if you are planning an extended visit to the Adirondack backcountry areas. **Sagamore Lodge and Conference Center** (Raquette Lake 13436, tel. 315/354–5303) also offers seminars in wilderness-skills development.

Pesky black flies and mosquitoes take over later in the summer. An effective bug repellent is essential equipment if you are planning to spend time in the outdoors. Black bears have made a strong comeback in the Adirondacks in recent years, primarily as scavengers, so if you plan on camping out, be sure to have enough rope to suspend your food from a tree limb at least 12 feet above the ground. Even if you aren't deep in the wilderness, you might still be susceptible to the probing ways of the ever-resourceful, ever-hungry black bear. Roadside sightings are common. So you should stow your food in your car or out of reach even at roadside campsites.

Bicycling

There are several designated bicycling routes throughout the North Country that are marked by roadside signs. The marked bicycling route on Route 28 covers some pretty mountainous terrain, but the Seaway Trail between Alexandria Bay and Cape Vincent runs through generally flat or rolling farmland. The **Warren County Bikeway** meanders through wooded areas, with glimpses of the mountains, on its eight-mile trail between Lake George and Glens Falls. "North Country Bike Routes" details bike tours through the region and is available from **New York State Parks** (tel. 518/474–0456).

Canoeing

The vast network of rivers and lakes in the North Country makes canoeing one of the best ways to experience the outdoors. Trips of 100 miles or more are possible with little or no portage required: The 170-mile Raquette River is the second-longest river in New York State. One of the best areas for canoeing in the Adirondacks is the St. Regis Canoe Area, east of Saranac Lake, where power boats are prohibited in more than 100 miles of navigable waters.

Canoe rentals are available at most lakes in the Adirondack region, both on a daily and an extended basis. For extended trips, hiring a guide service is strongly recommended. You might also find it advisable or necessary to hire a lake-plane service for pickup at the end of your trip, to avoid backtracking or car shuttling. **Bird's Seaplane Service** in Inlet (tel. 315/357–3631) and **Helms Aero Service** in Long Lake (tel. 518/624–3931) offer pickup service for canoe trips or fishing trips.

Fishing

Fishing is a year-round sport in the North Country. The St. Lawrence River offers some of the best bass fishing in the country. Muskellunges ("muskies," for short), averaging about 17 pounds, are also a common catch between Ogdensburg and Cape Vincent. Ice-fishing tournaments give Thousand Islanders a little sport on weekends in January and February.

Many lakes, ponds, and streams in the Adirondack area are stocked with trout and salmon. Brook trout and lake trout traditionally do well in Adirondack waters, although in recent years fishermen report catching land-locked salmon with increasing regularity. The Raquette River and Lake Champlain are reputed to be excellent waters for catching walleyed pike.

Anglers over the age of 16 are required to get licenses, which can be obtained at regional DEC offices, at town or county clerk offices, and at many sporting-goods stores, bait shops, and outfitters. The DEC maintains fishing hotlines to help steer you toward the best fishing; the number for the southeastern areas of the North Country is tel. 518/623–3682 and for the northeastern areas, tel. 315/782–2663. Again, hiring a guide is highly recommended, especially if you are interested in an extended backcountry fishing trip. Contact the New York State Guides Association or the DEC (*see* Canoeing above).

Golf

There are 35 18-hole golf courses in the North Country open to the public and numerous other nine-hole courses. The courses at the **Lake Placid Club** (tel. 518/523–9000) and the **Whiteface Resort** (tel. 518/523–2551) in Lake Placid and the **Sagamore** (tel. 518/644–9400) course at Bolton Landing are especially challenging.

Hiking

Hiking is the simplest and one of the best ways to experience the North Country outdoors. Most trails are well maintained and marked by the DEC, and many trailheads are along the major routes through the Adirondack area. Look for wood signs with yellow lettering.

The most popular area for hiking is the High Peaks region, accessible from the Lake Placid area in the north, Keene in the east, and Newcomb in the south. Much ado is made of Adirondack "46ers"—the people who have ascended the 46 highest peaks in the region (most over 4,000 feet high). The **Adirondack Loj,** seven miles south of Lake Placid, off Route 73, is an excellent place to stay for climbers; it is right at the main trailhead to Mt. Marcy, Algonquin, and the rest of the High Peaks core. This lodge is accessible by car; the **John Brooks Lodge,** operated by ADK, is accessible only by a three-and-a-half-mile hike. For more information, contact **ADK Lodges,** Box 867, Lake Placid 12946, tel. 518/523–3441.

Although the High Peaks region tends to draw the most attention, it has the most rugged hiking. Many less strenuous climbs and hikes offer rewarding views and backwoods experiences, whether for half-day hikes, full-day outings, or multiday backpacking trips. There is good hiking with minimal climbing around Cranberry Lake and Schroon Lake.

Horseback Riding

There are a number of dude ranches in the Warrensburg–Lake Luzerne area. Their season generally runs from May to November. Among the best is the **Roaring Brook Ranch & Tennis Resort** (Box 671, Rte. 9 N.S., Lake George 12845, tel. 518/688–5767). For North Country bridle path and trail maps, contact the DEC.

Ice Skating

People who like their ice skating with a touch of history should enjoy the public skating sessions at the **Olympic Center Ice Arena** in Lake Placid (tel. 518/523–3325), where the U.S. hockey team pulled off the "Miracle on Ice" in 1980 against the Soviet Union. There are also ice rinks at Glens Falls, Plattsburgh, Saranac Lake, Potsdam, and Canton. Speed-skating enthusiasts can get in their workouts on the ovals in Lake Placid and at Saratoga State Park.

Rafting

June is usually the best month for white-water rafting and tubing, when the rivers swell with waters from the mountain snow run-off. However, damming along many rivers in the region, particularly the upper Hudson, maintains a fairly steady flow of water throughout the year. The Hudson River Gorge and the Moose River have rapids consistently rated up to Class V, which is pretty bracing stuff. The waters of the Sacandaga River, another favored rafting route, are generally less fierce. The top rafting companies in the region are **Adirondack River Outfitters** in Watertown (tel. 315/369–3536) and **Hudson River Rafting Co.**, with offices in North Creek (tel. 518/251–3251), in Lake Luzerne (tel. 518/696–2964), and in Watertown (tel. 315/782–7881).

Skiing

Alpine   The largest alpine skiing resort in the North Country is **Whiteface Mountain** in Wilmington, eight miles east of Lake Placid and site of the 1980 Winter Olympic alpine events. Four other North Country areas have vertical rises of more than 1,000 feet. They are (in descending order of size): **Gore Mountain** in North Creek, **Hickory Ski Center** in Warrensburg, **Big Tupper** in Tupper Lake, and **West Mountain** near Glens Falls. Smaller areas with good skiing are **Oak Mountain** near Speculator and **Snow Ridge** near Turin.

Back-country   Backcountry skiing has become increasingly popular in the North Country. There are several trails to ski up and down Mt. Marcy, with access from Keene and from the Adirondak Loj (tel. 518/523–3441). It is rugged work, and backcountry skiers, especially in the High Peaks area, should be well versed in the potential hazards of winters in the backcountry.

Cross-country   With 50 kilometers of groomed tracks, **Mt. Van Hoevenberg**, the site of the 1980 Winter Olympic cross-country events, seven miles south of Lake Placid on Route 73, has the most extensive track system in the North Country. The tracks are used often for races and training. There are several first-rate ski centers in the North Creek–Gore Mountain area. Most private ski centers charge a trail fee of between $4 and $7; tracks in state parks, such as at **Saratoga State Park** and **Wellesley Island State Park** near Alexandria Bay, are free.

Sledding

For those looking for a different sort of winter thrill, there are the bobsled and luge runs at **Mt. Van Hoevenberg**. If you give bobsledding a shot, it will be as a passenger with an experienced driver; on the luge, you are on your own the last few turns of the course.

Snowmobiling

Trails cover many of the summer hiking trails, especially in the southern and western reaches of the Adirondacks and throughout th Thousand Islands area. Trail maps are available from the Department of Environmental Conservation, 50 Wolf Rd., Albany 12233.

Spectator Sports

The Lake Placid area has been designated by the U.S. Olympic Committee as an official training site, so at any time of year you may see Olympic-caliber athletes in a variety of sports, either in training or in competition. Summer athletic competitions are held in boxing, cycling, figure skating, and ski jumping on plastic mats on the 70-meter jump just south of town. This is also where freestyle skiers practice and perform "aerials"—the twisting and somersaulting jumps that are part of the growing sport of freestyle skiing. Aerialists can be seen training at the site for much of July and August, and a major competition is held at the end of August. Lake Placid is also the site of the *I Love New York* Horse Show that is held in mid-July and features some of the top show jumpers in the country.

The athletic competition picks up in winter at Lake Placid, with national and international competitions in bobsledding and luge at Mt. Van Hoevenberg, alpine racing and freestyle competition at Whiteface, and speed skating at the Olympic oval in the center of town. Hockey and figure-skating competitions are held in the Olympic ice arena, right next-door to the speed-skating oval. For information on Lake Placid athletic events, contact the **Olympic Regional Development Authority** (tel. 800/255–5515 or 800/462–6236 in New York State).

Boating

Sailing regattas are held on summer weekends on Lake Champlain, Lake George, and in the Thousand Islands region. Yacht racing can be visually dramatic, but the competition (unless you are well versed in the subtleties of the sport) can be less than enthralling. A more thrill-packed combination of vessel and water are the kayak races during the **Hudson River Whitewater Derby** (tel. 518/251–3465) in North Creek at the end of May.

Horse Racing

The 24-day thoroughbred-racing session at **Saratoga Raceway** (tel. 518/584–6200) each August is a major social as well as sporting event. The highlight of the season is the Travers Stakes, but the 100-year-old flat track attracts high-quality thoroughbreds for all its races. Post time for the first race is 1:30 PM, but true racing fans come for breakfast, served between 7 and 9:30, and spend the morning soaking up all the atmosphere in the barn and paddock areas.

Saratoga Harness (tel. 518/584–2110), about a mile from the thoroughbred track, is open throughout the year except for periods in April and December. Post time for the first race is at 7:45 PM, and the glass-enclosed grandstand provides welcome comfort during the winter months. The trackside restaurant is excellent.

Dining

Saratoga is indisputably the culinary champion of the North Country in quantity, variety, and, generally speaking, quality. Saratoga has the advantage of having a sizeable, relatively affluent year-round population that restaurants can bank on for business. This is not to say that the North Country north of Saratoga is a dining wasteland; the Olympic region in particular has a number of fine places to eat, primarily in Lake Placid. Alexandria Bay and Clayton have the largest clusters of good restaurants in the Thousand Islands–Seaway area.

Restaurant dining, however, throughout much of the Adirondack region is a limited concept. Meals at traditional lodges tend to be tied to accommodations, although many establishments will accept nonguests for dinner. The emphasis tends to be on large portions and on home cooking, meaning that fresh-baked breads and rolls are a common treat. Surprisingly, with all the fishing in the North Country, truly fresh fish is not an easy find. New York food inspection regulations require fish, by and large, to go through a food inspection center before it is okayed for consumption. There are, however, restaurants that will cook up your fresh catch for you. Just be sure to call ahead before walking through the door with your stuffed creel.

Highly recommended restaurants in each price category are indicated by a star ★.

Category	Cost*
Expensive	over $25
Moderate	$15–$25
Inexpensive	under $15

*per person without sales tax (6%), service, or drinks

Central Adirondacks

Expensive **Big Moose Inn.** A lot of Adirondack flavor is found in this off-the-beaten track, chef-owned restaurant and cocktail lounge overlooking the lake. A fireplace warms things up if needed, and there is outdoor dining when weather permits. Homemade breads, soups, and desserts and the prime rib, veal, and lamb dishes are the draws at this inn. Daily specials attract the budget-conscious; those who want a special lunch or evening treat come for the vintage wines and ambience. *5 mi from Rte. 28 at Eagle Bay, tel. 315/357–2042. Dress: casual. AE, MC. Closed Columbus Day–Christmas and Apr. 1–Memorial Day. Expensive.*

Friends Lake Inn. This restored 1860s country inn emphasizes sophisticated dining, although rooms and cottages also are available. The "regional imaginative" label doesn't begin to describe the range of choices on the menu. From appetizers to dessert, everything is fresh and flavorful. The distinctive dining room features low tin ceilings, slender columns, and wainscoting of chestnut wood. The cocktail lounge in the front has the best lake view and a respectable wine list. In winter, a free skiing package is arranged at nearby Gore Mountain.

Friends Lake Rd., Chestertown, tel. 315/494-4141. Dress: casual. Reservations preferred. AE, MC, V.

Rene's. A remarkable place that proves distance should be no hindrance when it comes to finding first-rate dining. Rene's sits on a high ridge between the Northway and Route 9, not far from Lake George, with a view of the mountains that is forgotten once food appears. Continental cuisine and luscious French dessert concoctions make a meal here a feast to remember. The decor, kept deliberately low key, is enhanced by candlelight and elegant touches. The lounge area is limited and subdued. *White Schoolhouse Rd., Chestertown, tel. 518/494-2904. Dress: informal. Reservations suggested. MC, V. Closed Mon.*

Moderate   **Eckerson's.** Long lines in summer testify to the popularity of this roadside restaurant. The building has little to distinguish it, inside or out, which is not an uncommon trait in the Adirondacks. However, the evident pleasure of people enjoying good food, also made and served without frills, is unmistakable. *Rt. 28, Eagle Bay, tel. 518/357-4641. Dress: casual. MC, V. Closed Tues.*

Long View Lodge. Many generations of travelers have found good food and shelter at this roadside inn, which sits on a low bluff looking down Long Lake. Area residents drive miles for the bountiful meals (breakfast and dinner only). The accommodations are not fancy, but the care of the long-term owners makes up for any lacks. Three housekeeping cottages and a tennis court are located near the beachfront area. The food is bountiful and well-prepared, and the buffets are famous. *Rt. 28N, Long Lake, tel. 518/624-2862. Closed Dec. 2-Apr. 30.*

Old Mill Restaurant. A huge mill wheel, a remnant of this building's former function, decorates the front of this restaurant on Old Forge's main street. The interior may seem dark and gloomy, but no one cares once the food is served. It is substantial and thoroughly American: steaks, seafood, and homebaked bread. The bar is designed for no-nonsense drinking, not sitting about all evening: in summer, outdoor dining can be very relaxed. *Rt. 28, Old Forge, tel. 315/369-3661. Dress: casual. AE, MC. V.*

Van Auken's Inn. This inn, in a historic building fronted by large white columns and two levels of porches, is being restored gradually, although the original bar, left from the old lumbering days, will never lose its aura. A family dedicated to producing good food has made it a place much sought, especially since it serves throughout the day. *Off Rte. 28, Old Forge, tel. 315/369-3033. Dress: casual. No credit cards. Closed Wed. in summer; check hours off-season.*

Inexpensive   **Cobbletone.** This long-time restaurant has an Adirondack ambience: a big, airy room with carpeting, nice lighting, and service bar. The service is generally good and the menu can extend from chicken wings and pizza to standard steak and seafood dishes. *Rte. 30, Long Lake, tel. 518/624-6331. Dress: casual. AE.*

Farm Restaurant. The big, open interior decorated with antiques and old farm implements is popular with families who really pay more attention to the liberal helpings of food. Adirondack-style breakfasts have real lasting power. Burgers, good soups, sandwichs, and omelets make up the lunch menu. This is a good place to stock up for the outdoor activities prevalent in the area. *Rte. 28, Old Forge. No phone. Dress: come as you are. No credit cards.*

Lake George Area

Expensive **The Algonquin.** "One if by land and two if by sea" might be the watchword; those who live or vacation on the lake arrive at this Sagamore restaurant by boat as often as by car. Two generations and 30 years' tradition account for its steady expansion. The downstairs Pub Room is more casual and stresses a burger-sandwich menu and light meals. The upper level Topside offers gourmet entrees featuring veal and seafood. Dockside activity provides entertainment for bar guests and front tables. *Lake Shore Dr., Bolton Landing, tel. 518/644–9442 or 518/644–9440. Dress: informal. Reservations requested for Topside. AE, DC, MC, V. Closed Nov. and Mar.*

The Grist Mill. Trappings of the original mill that literally overhangs the bubbling waters of the Schroon River are part of the Grist Mill's decor. A split-level interior hugs the bank; timbered ceilings, interesting woodwork, and strategic window placement add to the visual enjoyment. The preparation and presentation of the food, labeled American regional, are equally attractive. *River St., Warrensburg, tel. 518/623–3949. Dress: casual. Reservations advised. AE, DC, MC, V.*

The Log Jam. A new greenhouse has expanded the luncheon crowds. Steak and ribs plus creative seafood selections keep up with changing American tastes. *Rtes. 9 and 149, Lake George, tel. 518/798–1455. Dress: informal. AE, CB, DC, MC, V.*

★ **The Sagamore.** The three dining rooms at this island resort each has its own atmosphere and cuisine. **Trillium** features formal gourmet dining with a hint of nouvelle; **Sagamore Dining Room** features Continental and American fare (grilled seafood and veal are specialties) and a great Sunday brunch buffet; **Club Grill** re-creates a Tudor atmosphere and serves up steaks, burgers, and other grilled items. *Bolton Landing, tel. 518/ 644–9400. Reservations required. AE, DC, MC, V. Lunch and dinner in all but Trillium, which has dinner only.*

Shoreline Restaurant and Marina. A large, canopied deck puts visitors right in the middle of the action surrounding the Lake George public docks. Cajun and mesquite-grilled dishes and fresh seafood in some tantalizing combinations are among the specialties. The menu is less extensive than imaginative—just reading it makes the mouth water. *4 James St., Lake George, tel. 518/668–2875. Dress: casual. Reservations advised. AE, MC, V.*

Moderate **Bavarian House.** The solid look of this big, square brown building that sits above the highway is lightened inside by plenty of wide windows and welcoming service at any time of day. In warm weather, the terrace is used. German specialties at very reasonable prices and standard American offerings are offered on the dinner menu. *Lake Shore Dr., Lake George, tel. 518/668–2476. Dress: casual. AE, MC, V.*

Garden in the Park. The Queensbury Hotel in Glens Falls faces a small, neat park, hence the name of its restaurant. American cuisine—steaks and seafood—is featured. The Sunday brunch attracts locals as well as hotel guests. *Queensbury Hotel, 99 Ridge St., Glens Falls, tel. 518/792–1121. Reservations advised. AE, MC, V. Lunch and dinner.*

Mario's. Many call this the best Italian restaurant between Albany and Montreal. This interior of this sizable, white-clapboard building of no particular distinction resembles an Italian villa with red velvet trim and all the appropriate aromas. Fresh seafood and veal sdishes are featured. *469 Canada St., Lake George, tel. 518/668–2665. Dress: casual. Reservations requested Sun., holidays. AE, DC, MC, V.*

Red Coach Grill. An imposing building constructed of huge logs, this restaurant has a reputation for fine food that is as solid·as its fieldstone foundation. Inside, the veneered logs, heavy beams, wrought-iron fixtures, judicious lighting, and fireplaces continue the rustic atmosphere. Traditional American fare is highlighted by prime rib and seafood specialties. A salad bar, tasty soup concoctions, and homemade bread and pastries can make a meal simple or lush. *Lake George Rd., Rte. 9, Glens Falls, tel. 518/793–4455. Dress: casual. Reservations advised. Valet parking evenings in summer. AE, DC, MC, V.*

Olympic Region

Expensive **Charcoal Pit.** The main dining room has high ceilings, a fireplace, hanging plants, paintings on the walls, and big windows on two sides. All entrees have a Continental touch by the chef-owner, with a combination of Greek, French and Italian specialties; veal and seafood are particularly well done, as are beef and chops. A small bar and cocktail lounge and other rooms of varying size accommodate overflow in busy times. The wine vault is visible at the entrance. *Rte. 86 near Cold Brook Plaza, Lake Placid, tel. 518/523–3050. Reservations accepted. AE, DC, V.*

Frederick's of Signal Hill. The building, once part of a massive hotel complex, nestles into the side of a hill overlooking Lake Placid. A cocktail lounge, at entrance level, has the most unrestricted view, particularly lovely on summer evenings; on the lower level, most of the tables have a partial view. The food is Continental, with strong French leanings. An early-bird special is served from 5 to 6 PM. *Signal Hill, off Saranac Ave., Lake Placed, tel. 518/523–2310. Reservations advised. AE, DC, MC.*

Lindsay's at the Woodshed. Upstairs at the rear of a more conventional, streetside restaurant is a candlelit setting that gives the feeling of having stepped momentarily onto a movie set. Gourmet entrees with primarily French antecedents, coddled with wines, herbs, and sauces are featured. There are simpler dishes, too, and at least a sampling of most meat and seafood choices. Espresso and cappuccino generally suffice for the finishing touch. *237 Main St., Lake Placid, tel. 518/523–9470. Reservations advised. DC, V.*

Steak and Stinger. Genuine Tiffany lamps and barnsiding interiors were installed here before the style was imitated. These touches, along with a collection of paintings of uneven quality, contribute to a country setting. Cocktails are served in the greenhouse, and in high season, summer and winter, munchies can be ordered there if the wait is long. Daily specials lean toward fresh seafood and several exceptional appetizers are offered. Beef and veal are the headliners; soups are prepared in-house. *Rte. 73, Cascade Rd., Lake Placid, tel. 518/523–9927. DC, MC, V.*

Moderate **Alpine Cellar.** A modest motel occupies the main level, but a large downstairs room with high windows facing the mountains is the real draw. A cocktail lounge on a small balcony overlooks the dining tables and sets the atmosphere with its big steins for beer. Traditional German food is served. *Rte. 86, Wilmington*

Rd., Lake Placid, tel. 518/523–2180. Reservations advised. No lunch. AE, MC, V.

Cascade Inn. A pleasant, homey atmosphere is presented with simple decor and low-ceilinged rooms. On one side, the bar and some tables share a fireside setting that encourages before and after dinner chatting, if traffic permits. A straightforward American style offers few frills, but high quality. Nightly specials are highlighted on Saturdays by prime rib. The inn is the kind of place travelers are delighted to find after a hard day of driving or outdoor activities. A motel is attached. *Rte. 73, Cascade Rd., Lake Placid, tel. 518/523–2130. Reservations advised. AE, V.*

Great Adirondack Steak and Seafood. "Sophisticated rustic" might describe this interior warmed by real wood and a judicious number of antiques. The street and sidewalk scene visible from the front windows may prove diverting. Imagination goes into the treatment given to a basically American menu, with some lively regional twists, such as Cajun cooking. A small room keeps the bar activity separate from the dining area. The movie theater is next door and the public park, with weekly summer concerts, across the street. *Main St., Lake Placid, tel. 518/523–629. AE, DC, MC, V.*

★ **Red Fox.** The setting of this restaurant is less important than a reputation which is built on consistently good food, prepared with care, and generous libations. The interior, divided into four long, narrow rooms that make it intimate, is made comfortable with carpeting (except for a small dance floor), wood paneling, and subdued lighting. The bar shares the space at one end of the building but is not obtrusive; a more cozy corner with fireplace is an alternative. The cuisine is basically American, with plenty of choice and good specials. It's one of the first places the locals will recommend. *Rte. 3, Tupper Lake Rd., Saranac Lake, tel. 518/891–2127. DC, V.*

Villa Vespa. An unpretentious atmosphere pervades this unare homemade and others imported. In addition to the expected offerings, there are several good meatless dishes and fresh-baked breads. Daily specials include fresh seafood, and everything comes in generous proportions. It's a place favored by athletes taking part in the year-round cross-country skiing and running events. There is outside service on the patio for summer. *Rte. 86, Saranac Ave., Lake Placid, tel. 518/523–9959. Reservations advised. No credit cards.*

Inexpensive   **Artist's Cafe.** This popular spot on Lake Placid's Main Street has an enclosed lakeside deck and a coziness to its dining room and bar. Hearty soup, omeletes, and imaginative sandwich combinations make up the lunch menu. Dinner entrees are known for quality rather than quantity and carry the label "new American." Seafood dishes are particularly good, but standard fare is given distinctive treatment. *Main St., Lake Placid, tel. 518/523–9493. AE, V.*

Casa del Sol. Travelers who know the Southwest will be surprised to find this Mexican outpost so far from its origins. The food's spiciness is restrained, but the authenticity should not be questioned. Casa del Sol's popularity can be measured by the size of the crowd in the tiny bar on Friday nights off-season and any time in summer. *Rte. 86, Lake Flower Ave., Saranac Lake, tel. 518/277–1498. AE, V.*

Saratoga Area

Expensive **Chez Sophie.** The French cuisine here has a touch of nouveau
★ and the elegant Victorian surroundings lend an air of formality
that borders on the stuffy, but the prix-fixe dining is the best in
town. The bar has attractive brick-and-wood furnishings. *69½
Caroline St., Saratoga Springs, tel. 518/587–0040. Reservations required for dinner. AE, MC, V. Lunch and dinner.*

Cock N' Bull. The smallest incorporated village in New York
State (Galway) is the site of this barn-cum-restaurant featuring
chalkboard specials of pheasant, quail, and game (in season);
otherwise a Continental menu—prime rib and seafood—
prevails. *Parkis Mills Rd., off Rte. 147, Galway, tel. 518/882–
6962. Reservations accepted. AE, DC, V. Lunch June–Aug.
only, dinner daily.*

The Elms. Homemade pastas—including such novelties as red-
pepper pasta—and veal scallopine are the specialties of this
house, operated by the Viggiani family with lots of Italian-style
warmth. *Rte. 9, Malta, tel. 518/587–2277. Reservations advised. DC, V. Dinner only.*

Union Coach House. Adirondack smoked pork chops, which are
done over applewood, head the Continental menu of this establishment. In the summer a jazz pianist is featured and there's a
great private dining room upstairs for groups of 12 or more. *139
Union Ave., Saratoga Springs, tel. 518/584–6440. Reservations accepted. AE, V. Lunch, except Saturdays; dinner daily.*

Moderate **Eartha's Kitchen.** This small country kitchen is a local favorite,
★ especially for the mesquite-grilled seafood dishes chosen from
an outstanding chalkboard menu. *47 Phila St., Saratoga
Springs, tel. 518/583–0602. Reservations are a must. AE, MC,
V. Dinner only.*

Gaffney's. Many miles from Buffalo, yet that city's culinary
claim to fame is featured on the menu: Buffalo wings. If that
doesn't satisfy you, there's ample selections of salads, burgers,
pasta, and veal. The garden bar out back helps take care of the
spillover. *16 Caroline St., Saratoga Springs, tel. 518/587–7359.
Reservations accepted. AE, MC. Lunch and dinner.*

Wheatfields. This recent addition to the Saratoga scene has locals lining up for the more than two dozen pasta dishes. All
pasta and breads are made on the premises, and that is fresh.
*440 Broadway, Saratoga Springs, tel. 518/587–0534. Reserva-
tions not accepted. DC, V. Lunch and dinner.*

Inexpensive **Bruno's.** A pizza parlor circa 1955 is the best way to describe
this eatery where the menus are printed on album jackets and
the pies come with such unlikely toppings as zucchini and barbecued chicken. Yes, you can order mushrooms and sausage if
you care to be so mundane. *237 Union Ave., Saratoga Springs,
tel. 518/583–3333. Reservations not accepted. No credit cards.*

★ **Hattie's Chicken Shack.** The house special, surprise surprise, is
fried chicken. But the rest of the Southern fare, as served up by
Hattie and husband Bill Austin, an older couple with ties to the
Deep South, is just as tempting. *45 Phila St., Saratoga
Springs, tel. 518/584–4790. Reservations a must in summer.
No credit cards. Lunch and dinner.*

Lodging

Luxurious accommodations are hard to come by in the North Country, although good, comfortable lodging is plentiful. A few of the places listed are technically bed-and-breakfasts but feature enough hotel or motel amenities—private bath or privacy in general—to be included. Quite a few lodges offer meal plans, which are a recommended option, especially in the Central Adirondacks, where there are relatively few restaurants.

Room price and availability vary with the season. The highest rates coincide with the tightest room squeeze during Saratoga's racing season (the month of August) when rates more than double. Make reservations at least six months ahead. Throughout the North Country expect to pay more during July and August, the fall foliage season, and during the Christmas holidays. Many places offer special rates for children (sharing a room with their parents) and senior citizens. Be sure to inquire. In areas of the Adirondacks you might find it harder to come up with a room in the winter than in the summer, since many places close between November and May. Those that are closed in the off-season are so noted in the listings.

Though bed-and-breakfasts are common in this region of New York State, their character and quality varies considerably. You can stay in a farmhouse for less than $15 a night or opt for suitelike accommodations in a Victorian mansion for close to $100 a night.

Meals vary as well since they are generally prepared by the proprietor rather than by a chef. Many B&Bs are open only during the peak summer season, especially in the Adirondacks. Shared baths are common, in-room television or phones are rare, and warm hospitality is the norm. One advantage of a B&B over a hotel: The proprietors are often more willing to provide useful inside information on the best places to fish, shop, and eat.

For further information contact **North Country B&B Reservations Service** (Box 238, Lake Placid 12946, tel. 518/523–9474). In the Lake George area, contact the **Warren County Tourism Office,** (Municipal Center, Lake George Village 12845, tel. 518/761–6366). In Saratoga, contact the **Saratoga Chamber of Commerce** (494 Broadway, Saratoga Springs 12866, tel. 518/584–3255). And in the Thousand Islands, contact the **1000 Islands International Council** (Box 400, Alexandria Bay 13607, tel. 315/482–2520 or 658–4721, collect).

Highly recommended hotels in each price category are indicated by a star ★.

Category	Cost*
Very Expensive	over $80
Expensive	$60–$80
Moderate	$40–$60
Inexpensive	under $40

**per double room without meals, tax (8%), or service*

Central Adirondacks

Expensive **Balsam House Inn and Restaurant.** This elegantly restored inn
    ★ located on a bluff overlooking Friends Lake dates to 1860. A
spiral staircase, lots of wicker, and charming bedrooms all help
to connote the past. Balsam House has a bar, cocktail lounge,
patio, and windows that look out upon the beachfront. The dining room is a regional favorite for the candlelight, classical
music ambience, and the exceptional country French cuisine.
Specialties include rack of lamb, sweetbreads, and Adirondack
trout. Sunset cocktail cruises on the lake can be arranged.
*Friends Lake, Atateka Dr., Box 365, Chestertown 12817, tel.
518/494–2828 or 518/494–4431. 20 rooms. Reservations preferred; recommended in high season. AE, CB, DC, MC, V.*

Elk Lake Lodge. This 12,000-acre private preserve at the
southern edge of the High Peaks has its own and public hiking
trails, trout and salmon fishing in the lake and surrounding
streams, and designated hunting areas. The spacious common
rooms in the main lodge have the ambience of an old Adirondack
camp, which it once was; the fare generally is hearty American.
Quiet places can be found along the shore to picnic, swim, or do
a little reading. *Blue Ridge Rd., North Hudson 12855, tel. 518/
532–7616. 6 rooms in main lodge, 7 sleeping cabins. No credit
cards. Closed Dec.–Apr.*

Hemlock Hall. The complex lies at the end of the only public
road that reaches the farther shores of Blue Mountain Lake,
which gives guests great privacy. The main lodge feels old
without looking old and has the more intimate rooms of a private home. Modern cottages are set about the woodsy shore.
The meals are the most favored in the area, but space for outside diners is limited. Tennis court, beach with boats and
canoes, and box lunches for day trips are alternatives to a good
workout in a front porch rocker. *Hemlock Hall Rd., Blue
Mountain Lake 12812, tel. 518/352–7706. 13 lodge rooms, 12
cottages. No credit cards. Closed Nov.–Apr.*

Wood's Lodge. The main street bustle is only a few blocks from
this lovely old inn with cottages overlooking Schroon Lake, one
of the few survivors of its kind in the region. Big maple trees
dominate the scene; boats are provided on the private beach.
Wood's Lodge is a change of pace from the usual frenetic activity evident elsewhere on the summer scene. *East St., Schroon
Lake 12870, tel. 518/532–7529. 20 rooms. Kitchen apartments
and cottages. No credit cards. Closed Oct.–Apr.*

Moderate **Cold River Ranch.** The ranch is well off the beaten path and little known, which adds to its appeal. You can gain access on
horseback or cross-country skis to the western side of the High
Peaks Wilderness area, and the major canoe route through the
region is also not far away. Ice fishing and snowshoeing in winter, and guides and instruction are available.
Fishermen and hunters find the ranch an ideal haven. *Corey's,
Rte. 3, Tupper Lake 12986, tel. 518/359–7559. 6 rooms; shared
baths. No credit cards.*

Country Club Motel. A perfectly standard motel operation that
might be found anywhere, but this location has the advantage
of space and snow in winter so snowmobilers can head off from
home base for their cross-country forays. Some connected
units, some refrigerators, and extended-stay discounts en-
courage family groups in summer and long-weekend visits in
winter. The motel is near the golf course and has a heated out-

door pool on its ample grounds for summer enjoyment. *Rte. 28, Box 643, Old Forge 13420, tel. 315/369–6340. 17 units. AE, V.*

Dun Roamin Cabins. Although this cabin/cottage complex may look from the outside like a relic of the '30s, pine paneling, carpeting, and up-to-date furnishings have an entirely different effect inside. This property is hooked into one of the region's snowmobiling networks, and public hiking and cross-country ski trails are literally next door. Ice fishing is another sport option. In summer, boats are maintained at a nearby marina, and an outdoor pool, a variety of lawn games, grills, and picnic tables are available on the grounds. *Rte. 9, Box 535, Schroon Lake 12870, tel. 518/532–7277. 9 rooms: 3 cabins, 6 cottages (efficiencies). No credit cards.*

Garnet Hill Lodge. The main lodge, a former private camp, has a big main common room replete with a striking fireplace made from stone quarried nearby. The kitchen, one of the best in the region, serves American cuisine and a magnificent Saturday night buffet. Dining is also available on the porch, with a wonderful view. Except for one vintage summer cottage, outlying buildings and the lodge sleeping rooms are done in modern style. Wilderness, including nearby Thirteenth Lake, and the most extensive private cross-country ski trails in the region, is very much part of the scheme. Garnet Hill Lodge also features tennis courts. *13th Lake Rd., North River 12856, tel. 518/251–2821. 25 rooms, 9 cottages. No credit cards.*

The Hedges. The main inn of this sprawling complex has a Victorian look and a dining room serving guests only, and the cottages might be found along almost any beachfront. The current owners are updating their property but retaining the Adirondack rustic touches. The docks and beach are replete with boats and canoes; tennis courts are closer to the highway, but everything is screened from traffic and noise by trees. Picnic lunches can be arranged. *Rte. 28, Blue Mountain Lake 12812, tel. 518/352–7325. 13 rooms, 13 cabins. No credit cards. Closed Dec.–Apr.*

Inexpensive **Blue Spruce Motel.** A compact, crisp facility, this small motel near the center of the village does indeed have big spruces standing guard over the outdoor heated pool. It also sits next door to one of the best restaurants in Old Forge. Some units are connected, and one is an efficiency. Additional parking for snowmobile and boat trailers is available. *Main St., Box 604, Old Forge 13420, tel. 315/369–3817. 13 rooms. AE, DC.*

Inn on Gore Mountain. This resort often is overlooked because it lies just beyond the ski center entrance. The main lodge has a rustic interior, big beams overhead, and stone fireplaces. The restaurant, which serves dinner only, has a loft overlooking the main floor and a cocktail lounge downstairs. Skiing, an outdoor pool for summer use, river-running, hunting, and fishing are all available. *Peaceful Valley Rd., North Creek 12853, tel. 518/251–2111. 16 rooms. AE, V. Restaurant closed Aug.–Oct.*

Red Top Inn. This bright, well-kept inn has a desirable lake view. Like other area inns, it shares the shoreline with the highway, but the beachfront is nevertheless enjoyable. In winter, it has the advantage of proximity to Big Tupper Ski Center, which also operates chairlift rides in summer. An outdoor pool sheltered by the buildings is an alternative in case lake water is cool or the breeze is strong. A picnic area with fireplaces is provided. *Moody Rd., Tupper Lake 12986, tel. 518/359–9209. 15 rooms, 4 cabins, 4 efficiencies. AE, DC, V.*

Sunset Park Motel. This motel provides idyllic settings—a broad expanse of lake with low mountains on the far horizon—and activity at the village outdoor recreation center next door—everything from ballgames to annual lumberjack contests. Boats, motors, and canoes can be rented. Some of the units have kitchenettes, but shopping and fast-food service are close by. *Demars Blvd., Rte. 3, Tupper Lake 12986, tel. 518/359-3995. 11 rooms. No credit cards.*

Valhaus Motel. Large rooms and comfortable furnishings can be found in this alpine-design motel with appropriate wood trim and diamond-paned windows. There is little in the way of extras except for complimentary coffee in the rooms, but the motel is located on the road to Gore Mt. Ski Center and not far from the Hudson River. *Peaceful Valley Rd., North Creek 12853, tel. 518/251-2700. 12 rooms. DC. V.*

Lake George Area

Expensive **Canoe Island Lodge.** The island facing the main lodge and cottages provides an escape for shoreside activities. It also lends privacy and intimacy to one of the widest spots in 30-mile-long Lake George. This lodge is a carefully preserved former private retreat with an air of understated elegance. A leisurely attitude overtakes even the pursuit of water sports and tennis. A restaurant, coffee shop, and cocktail lounge cover all needs. Box lunches are provided for excursions. Guests may bring their own boats. *Lake Shore Dr., Box 144, Diamond Point 12824, tel. 518/668-5592. 72 rooms. No credit cards. Closed mid-Oct.-mid-May.*

Dunham's Bay Lodge. This resort motel is located on the quieter side of Lake George, the main lodge has a rustic old-inn feeling, with a large, inviting fireplace and spacious grounds. The indoor/outdoor pool and beach are the focal points, as viewed from sun terraces around the pool. A heated indoor pool, tennis courts, playground, and picnic area round out the recreation facilities. A coffee shop, snack bar, and cocktail lounge are also available. *Rte. 9L, RR 1, Box 1179, Lake George 12845, tel. 518/656-9242. 55 rooms, 10 cottages. AE, MC, V.*

Georgian Motel. Part of Lake George's largest and glitziest motel stretches alongside the village's main street and the remainder reaches to the waterside. Its elegant restaurant features French-American cuisine and a view of the lake. The night scene at the Terrace Lounge is about the liveliest in town, featuring entertainment and music for dancing. Leisure time can be divided between the 75-foot heated outdoor pool with patio and the lakefront. *384 Canada Street, Lake George 12845, tel. 518/668-5401. 167 rooms. AE, MC, V.*

Hidden Valley Mountainside Resort. Gem-like Lake Vanare and wooded hills give this complete resort a hidden air. It features tennis and other racquet games, archery, horseback riding, plus indoor and outdoor heated pools and a beach. Excellent food is served in several settings with separate spaces for cocktail lounges, entertainment, and dancing. Special theme weekends, including mystery-solving, go on throughout the year. In winter, on-premises skiing with chairlift and instruction, snowmobiling and sleigh rides are offered. *Hidden Valley Rd., RR 2, Box 228, Lake Luzerne 12846, tel. 518/696-2431 or NYS 800-HIDDENV. 105 rooms. AE, DC, V.*

Melody Manor Resort Motel. Spaciousness distinguishes this lakeside resort. Motel units are on broad lawns that slope gently to the private beach. Small boats are available, plus tennis, lawn games, outdoor pool, a playground, and a picnic area. In the highly recommended Manor Inn Restaurant, which serves breakfast and dinner, pine paneling and a large fireplace impart a welcoming atmosphere; there also is a cocktail lounge with entertainment. *Lake Shore Dr. Box 366, Bolton Landing 12814, tel. 518/644-9750. 40 rooms. No credit cards. Closed Nov.-Apr.*

Merrill Magee House. A narrow lane leads from the street to the rear of this restored 19th-century house, which has wide lawns, gardens, and big maple trees. Antiques are perfectly at home in the small, low-ceilinged rooms. A remodeled former carriage house attached at the rear has a cathedral ceiling and high windows that add charm to the main dining room. The Continental cuisine, with many choices in each course, has a well-deserved reputation for excellence; reservations are preferred. *Hudson St., Warrensburg 12885, tel. 518/623-2449. 13 rooms. AE, DC.*

Roaring Brook Ranch and Tennis Resort. This is a superb resort only a short drive into the mountains west of Lake George. The main building houses a rustic pub, coffee shop, sitting and game room with fireplace, and a spacious dining room with wide windows that face Prospect Mountain. Large, strategically placed motel units vary in style but blend well because of exterior woodwork. Three pools, one indoors, five lighted tennis courts, and horseback riding fill the day. Entertainment, dancing, and summer cookouts provide evening diversion. *Luzern Rd., Lake George 12845, tel. 518/668-5767. 141 rooms. MC, V.*

Tahoe Beach Club and Resort. Multilevel, deluxe motel units with private balconies or terraces extend down the steep slope between highway and the lakefront. The Tahoe Beach Club has a restaurant, bar, and cafe for breakfast and lunch. Service is available at the heated outdoor pool. The waterfront has a beach, boats, and dock space for rent. *Lake Shore Dr., Lake George 12845, tel. 518/668-5711. 73 rooms. AE, DC, V. Closed Nov.-Apr.*

Moderate **Colonial Manor Inn.** The trim and tended appearance of the buildings plus the convenient location make the Colonial Manor appealing. It features both cottages and motel units, where kids under age 12 stay free. The pool faces the street, but pleasant lawns, trees, and a playground offer alternative space at the rear. *Canada St., Box 528, Lake George 12845, tel. 518/668-4884. 35 motel rooms, 20 cottages. AE, V.*

Juliana Motel. Seclusion is provided by big trees that screens out both highway and neighbors. But the sloped setting allows for a clear view of the lake. The motel is set between the outdoor pool with a sun deck and the beachfront with its boats and aquabikes. Cottages, efficiencies, and connected units in the motel make for flexible arrangements. There also are a playground and picnic area with fireplaces. *Lake Shore Dr., Rte. 9N, Box 63, Diamond Point 12824, tel. 518/668-5191. 26 rooms. No credit cards. Closed Sept. 15-May 15.*

Split Rail Motel and Cottages. This series of well-kept motel, efficiency, and cottage combinations, some with fireplaces, are stepped down in close proximity from the highway to the water's edge. Accommodations can be adjusted to the size of the party. Games and a playground are available, as well as an outdoor pool, picnic area, and full range of activity on the

waterfront. This Split Rail appeals to families. *Lake Shore Dr.,
Rte. 9N, Box 63, Diamond Point 12824, tel. 518/668–5191. 26
rooms. No credit cards. Closed Sept. 15–May 15.*

Victorian Village Resort. A handsome brick and stone mansion
set back from the highway behind a circular drive lined by huge
pines and spruces serves as this resort's main lodge. The motel
units slope toward the lake. Swimming, waterskiing, boats, canoes, and dockage are available. The grounds of this former
private estate include a tennis court and space for organized
ball games. Breakfast is served in a dining room overlooking
the lake. *Lake Shore Dr., Box 12, Bolton Landing 12814, tel.
518/644–9401. 30 rooms. No credit cards. Closed Nov.–Apr.*

Inexpensive   **Briar Dell Motel.** This is one of the smaller resorts on the steep
shoreline along Lake George. Pleasant motel rooms and cabins
are located on the lakefront. It is rare to find private beach facilities, boats, and dockage at such modest prices so close to
Lake George village. A picnic area with fireplaces is also available. *Shore Dr., Box 123, Lake George 12845, tel. 518/668–4819.
22 rooms. No credit cards. Closed mid-Oct.–Memorial Day.*

King George Motor Inn. The front units of this inn have one of
the area's premier views—north down the length of Lake
George. Rear units view the outdoor pool, playground, picnic
area, and Prospect Mountain. Lawn games and an indoor arcade supplement the activities for youngsters. Breakfast is
served in the coffee shop, which also has a view. *Rte. 9, Lake
George 12845, tel. 518/668–2507 or 800/342–9504. 54 rooms.
AE, DC, V. Closed mid-Oct.–mid-Apr.*

Olympic Region

Very Expensive   **The Point.** One-time home of William Avery Rockefeller, this
elegantly rustic inn is the most exclusive retreat in the
Adirondacks. It is operated in the manner of a sophisticated
private home with no commercial overtones. It has only 11
rooms, but each has its own bath and most have stone fireplaces. Guests are required to dress for dinner. Member of
Relais et Châteaux. *Star Rte., Upper Saranac Lake 12983, tel.
518/891–5674. 11 rooms. Facilities: restaurant, lounge, open
bar, game room, swimming, sailing, and cross-country skiing
on premises. AE.*

Expensive   **Adirondack Inn.** Located eight miles from Whiteface ski area,
this motor inn has 50 well-appointed rooms and suites overlooking Mirror Lake. All rooms feature two double beds, bath,
cable TV, phone, and air-conditioning; some also have refrigerators. *217 Main St., Lake Placid 12946, tel. 518/523–2424. 50
rooms, including 2 suites. Facilities: heated indoor and outdoor pools, saunas, whirlpool, game room, beach, 4 tennis
courts. Ski packages available. AE, DC, MC, V.*

Lake Placid Manor. A turn-of-the-century frame house, directly on Lake Placid, that has been turned into a charming
European-style inn. It has 34 rooms in several cottages and
lodges, all with views of Lake Placid and Whiteface Mountain.
The restaurant is excellent and the inn is adjacent to the Whiteface Resort 18-hole golf course. *Whiteface Inn Rd., Lake
Placid 12946, tel. 518/523–2573. Facilities: private beach with
motorboats, rowboats, and paddleboats; restaurant, cocktail
lounge. AE, MC, V. Closed Nov.*

Lake Placid Hilton. One of the biggest hotels in the area, this
low-rise resort has 178 rooms, all with cable TV, phones, and

balconies with lake or mountain views. There's a restaurant, a lounge with nightly entertainment, and two pools, one in and one out. *1 Mirror Lake Dr., Lake Placid 12946, tel. 518/523–4411. 178 rooms. Facilities: skiing and sailing available, adjacent to a shopping plaza. AE, DC, MC, V.*

Moderate **The Bark Eater.** This small, quiet country inn has eight rooms with shared baths and is a perfect place for those who want to hike with a guide for a week or ski from inn to inn. Fresh-baked goods highlight the breakfast table. *Alstead Hill Rd., Keene 12942, tel. 518/576–2221. AE, V.*

Hotel Saranac of Paul Smith's College. Built in the late 1920s, this property is operated by students at the nearby college. Its restaurant is highly regarded (*see* Dining) and it features a gift shop, and cable TV in all its 92 rooms. *101 Main St., Saranac Lake 12983, tel. 518/891–2200. AE, V.*

Interlaken Lodge. An even dozen rooms comprise the accommodation at this Victorian lodge. The dining room features both Continental and American cuisine, and there are packages for golf, skiing, bicycling, and canoeing. *15 Interlaken Ave., Lake Placid 12946, tel. 518/523–3180. Closed Apr. and Nov.*

Stagecoach Inn. This gabled, two-story, wood-and-stone house (1833) was once owned by Melvil Dewey, a Lake Placid founding father and creator of the Dewey Decimal System. A stay in one of the six rooms, only two of which have a private bath, comes with a full breakfast. *Old Military Rd., Lake Placid 12946, tel. 518/523–9474. No credit cards.*

Inexpensive **Deer's Head Inn.** This is the oldest hotel in the Adirondacks, having been in operation since 1818. It features six rooms, four with private bath in an Early American decor, and three dining rooms. *Court St., Rte. 9, Elizabethtown 12932, tel. 518/873–9903. No credit cards.*

Shulte's. This property features 30 rooms—15 of which are cabins with kitchenettes—a restaurant, and an outdoor pool. *Cascade Rd., Lake Placid 12946, tel. 518/523–3532. V.*

Saratoga Area

Very Expensive **Gideon Putnam Hotel and Conference Center.** A sumptuous, high ceiling graces the interior of this Victorian grande dame located on the grounds of Saratoga State Park. It is in walking distance of the Saratoga Performing Arts Center (SPAC) and mineral baths, and is the site of much social activity when SPAC is in session. *Saratoga State Park, Saratoga Springs 12866, tel. 518/587–4688. 132 rooms, including 22 suites. Facilities: dining room, 3 pools, health club, golf and tennis nearby, cross-country skiing and skating in winter. AE, DC, MC, V.*

Expensive **Adelphi Hotel.** This refurbished Victorian property dates to 1877 and is one block from Congress Park in downtown Saratoga Springs. The sloping floors and Victorian furnishings in the lobby give it a true 19th-century feel. Many of its 28 rooms have been restored. *365 Broadway, Saratoga Springs 12866, tel. 518/587–4688. 28 rooms, all with shower/bath, air-conditioning, phone, and TV. Facilities: Continental breakfast, restaurant (open July and Aug.), bar, cafe. AE, MC, V. Open Apr.–Nov.*

★ **Ramada Renaissance.** Adjacent to the Civic Center, this elegantly furnished brick-and-mahogany hotel, inside an office-building exterior, is for those who love to be pampered. All rooms feature color cable TV and there's fine dining (Sandalwood Restaurant) and entertainment on the premises. *534 Broadway, Saratoga Springs 12866, tel. 518/584–4000. 190 rooms and suites. Facilities: indoor pool, gift shop, newsstand, valet service. AE, DC, MC, V.*

Moderate **Carriage House.** A comfortable place on Saratoga's main street set up to welcome families and seniors. It features 10 air-conditioned kitchen units with refrigerators, cable TV, and free cribs. *178 Broadway, Saratoga Springs 12866, tel. 518/584– 4220. Family, weekly, senior citizen, and ski packages available. AE, M.*

Inn at Ash Grove Farm. On Church Street near downtown Saratoga Springs, this small, country-style place has several bedrooms with fireplaces and offers a full American breakfast. *Rte. 9N on Church St., Saratoga Springs 12866, tel. 518/584– 1445. AE, V.*

Inexpensive **Empress Motel.** All 12 of these neat units have air-conditioning and cable TV. There's a coffee shop on the premises. *Rtes. 4 and 29, 177 Broadway, Schuylerville 12871, tel. 518/695–3231. No credit cards.*

The Arts

Arts Centers The **Adirondack Lakes Center for the Arts** in Blue Mountain Lake (tel. 518/352–7715) features concerts, dramatic presentations, films, and demonstrations of arts and crafts throughout the summer.

The **Lake Placid Center for the Arts** (tel. 518/523–2512) is another hub of cultural activity in the Adirondacks, with films, concerts, and theater presentations during the summer. Jazz and classical-music concerts are part of the winter schedule.

The **Saratoga Performing Arts Center** (tel. 518/584–7100) makes Saratoga the performing arts capital of the North Country. The New York City Opera comes to SPAC in June, the New York City Ballet performs here in July, and the Philadelphia Orchestra is in residence in August. In addition, well-known pop performers are featured attractions in the summer, and dance and theater performances are staged in the Little Theater, next to the main open-air amphitheater. The amphitheater is closed from fall through spring, but drama presentations keep the Little Theater going throughout the year.

Music The **Lake George Opera Festival** (tel. 518/793–6642), highlighted by evening lake-cruise performances, also is held in July and August.

Some of the Philadelphia Orchestra members performing at Saratoga moonlight at the **Lake Luzerne Chamber Music Festival** (tel. 518/696–2771) just up the road in July and August.

Theater Theater performances go on throughout the year at the **Sagamore** (tel. 518/644–9400) at Bolton Landing on Lake George.

9 The Finger Lakes Region

Introduction

Cayuga, Canandaigua, Keuka, Hemlock, Honeoye, Otisco, Owasco, Canadice, Coneses, Skaneateles, and Seneca sound like a roll call for the Indians of the Iroquois Confederacy who dominated this area for more than two centuries. But they are also the names of the Finger Lakes in central New York State.

Iroquois legend has it that the Finger Lakes region was formed when the Great Spirit placed his hand in blessing on this favored land. Geologists have a more prosaic explanation: The lakes were created when Ice Age glaciers retreated about a million years ago. The intense pressure of those ice masses created the long narrow lakes lying side by side, the deep gorges with rushing falls, and the wide fertile valleys that extend south for miles. These features are found nowhere else in the world.

The area is bounded on the west by Rochester and on the east by Syracuse. The glacial lakes run north and south, bordered by Lake Ontario and the Erie Canal to the north, the Chemung and Susquehanna rivers to the south.

The mercurial landscape is notched with gorges and more than 1,000 waterfalls. The highest is Taughannock, at 215 feet—higher than Niagara Falls. It is also one of 20 state parks in the region. Letchworth State Park, with a deep gorge and three waterfalls, has been aptly dubbed the "Grand Canyon of the East." At Watkins Glen State Park you can walk under a waterfall and sit spellbound while being whisked 4.5 billion years into the past with lasers and special sound effects in "Timespell," a twice-nightly sound-and-light show explaining the birth and life of the famous glen.

The Finger Lakes is the land of dreamers—dreamers who founded a religion, began the women's rights movement, invented the camera, were early pioneers in motion pictures, and created great schools and universities. Diversity is the keynote of the region, not only in the variety of natural landscapes but also in the plethora of recreational, educational, and cultural facilities. The area's numerous museums are devoted to such varied subjects as agriculture, auto racing, aviation, dolls, electronics, the Erie Canal, glass, Indians, the 19th century, photography, salt, soaring (or airplane gliding), and wine-making. The region has played a significant role in American social, economic, and political history as the home of statesmen, inventors, industrialists, and writers.

Mark Twain wrote most of his classics, including *The Adventures of Huckleberry Finn*, from his summer home in Elmira. Glenn H. Curtiss put Hammondsport on the aviation map. In 1908 his *June Bug* flew just under a mile—the longest distance of a preannounced flight. Harris Hill is considered the birthplace of soaring, and its National Soaring Museum has the country's largest display of classic and contemporary sailplanes.

Seneca Falls is the home of the women's rights movement, and the National Women's Hall of Fame is on the site of the first Women's Rights Convention, held in 1848. Palmyra was the early home of Joseph Smith, whose vision led to the founding in 1830 of the Church of Jesus Christ of Latter-Day Saints, the Mormons. Every summer in late July this event is commemorated with the Hill Cumorah Pageant, the oldest and largest religious pageant in the United States. Residents of Waterloo dreamed up the idea of Memorial Day in honor of the dead of the Civil War, and the country's first Memorial Day was celebrated May 5, 1866.

Rochester is the birthplace of the Kodak camera and film and the Xerox copy machine. Corning is famous for the Corning Glass Works and its Steuben Glass division, which produces fine works of art. Steuben masterpieces have been presented as gifts to foreign heads of state and are in museums around the world.

Viniculture is another of the Finger Lakes' many offerings. Not only did the retreating glaciers create the Finger Lakes, they also created ideal conditions for grape growing by depositing a shallow layer of topsoil on sloping shale beds above the lakes. The deep lakes also provide protection from the climate by moderating temperatures along their shores.

It all began in 1829 when the Reverend William Bostwick transplanted a few grapevines from the Hudson Valley to the shore of Keuka Lake in Hammondsport to make sacramental wine for his parishioners at St. James Episcopal Church. The grapes grew well, and within a few years grapevines could be found around Keuka, Canandaigua, and Seneca lakes. In 1860, 13 Hammondsport businessmen resolved to form a company "for the production and manufacture of native wine," and created the Hammondsport and Pleasant Valley Wine Company, the first commercial winery to open in the region. It became known as Great Western and later merged with the giant Taylor Wine Company.

The success of the vineyards and wines created new jobs. Young carpenter Walter Taylor arrived in the late 1870s to make barrels for the wineries and began planting grapevines and making wines himself; in time, his winery became the region's largest. Since 1976, when the state legislature eased regulations on the establishment of wineries producing 50,000 gallons a year or less, some 20 small farm wineries have opened in the region, and new techniques and grapes are earning medals for the area's wines at international and national competitions. The federal government has designated the area the official "Finger Lakes Wine District."

Getting Around

By Plane   **American, United, USAir, Continental,** and **TWA** all serve the Rochester and Syracuse airports. **USAir** serves airports at Ithaca and Elmira/Corning.

By Train   **Amtrak** (tel. 800/USA–RAIL) serves both Rochester and Syracuse.

By Bus   **Greyhound** (tel. 716/454–3450 in Rochester; 315/471–7171 in Syracuse) provides service to cities and towns in the region. The Rochester-Genesee Regional Transportation Authority and Syracuse & Oswego Motor Lines (tel. 315/422–9087) provide service within their regions.

By Car Most visitors tour the Finger Lakes area by car. From east to west use Route 17, the Southern Tier Expressway; I–90, the New York State Thruway; or the northern Trail of Route 104. Major north–south highways are I–81, and Route 15, and I–390. All major car rental agencies operate in Rochester and Syracuse.

Scenic Drives Just about every road in the Finger Lakes area provides views of blue lakes, rolling hills, vineyards, and farmhouses. The following are a few drives of particular interest:

Route 14 from Geneva to Watkins Glen. Route 14 borders the western side of Seneca Lake, affording vistas of the lake vineyards, stately 19th-century mansions, and farmhouses.

Route 89 along the western shore of Cayuga Lake. Start the drive in Ithaca, home of Cornell University and Ithaca College, and head north to Taughannock Falls. This route is especially splendid in autumn when the multicolored foliage reflect in the blue lake.

Route 54 and 54A around Keuka Lake. This route around the lake is studded with vineyards, and the trip can be broken up a half-dozen times for winery tours and tastings.

Guided Tours

Bus Tours Escorted bus tours of the region are provided by **Regional Transit Service** (1372 E. Main St., Rochester 14609, tel. 716/288–6050, operates weekdays 8:15–5) and **K-Venures Minicoach** (Box 522, Penn Yan, tel. 315/536–7559). City tours of Rochester and surrounding area are offered by **Rochester Sightseeing Tours** (585 Winona Blvd., Rochester 14617, tel. 716/342–8346); **Personal Tours of Rochester** (Box 18055, Rochester 14618, tel. 716/442–9365); and **Hylan Flying Services** (1295 Scottsville Rd., Rochester 14624, tel. 716/235–0928).

Boat Tours **Capt. Bill's Lake Ride** (Seneca Lake, Rte. 14, Watkins Glen, tel. 607/535–4541) offers 10-mile cruises leaving every hour. Luxury dinner cruises. Individual and group rates. **Capt. Gray's Lake Tours** operates one-hour lecture tours of Canandaigua Lake leaving from the Canandaigua Sheraton at 770 S. Main Street. Contact C. Gray Hoffman, 92 Park Avenue, tel. 716/394–5270 or 394–0429. **Mid Lake Navigation Company** (Box 61, Skaneateles, tel. 315/685–8500) offers morning mail delivery, luncheon and dinner, and cruises on Skaneateles Lake and on the Erie Canal.

Important Addresses and Numbers

Tourist Information **The Finger Lakes Association** (309 Lake St., Penn Yan, 14527, tel. 315/536–7488 or in NYS 800/727–3333 or outside the state, 800/KIT–4–FUN) has free brochures, booklets, and maps. **Rochester Convention & Visitors Bureau** (126 Andrews St., Rochester 14604, tel. 716/546–3070) and **Syracuse Convention & Visitors Bureau** (100 E. Onondaga St., Syracuse 13202, tel. 315/470–1343) also have information, brochures, and maps of their areas. In Rochester, call 716/546–6810 for a listing of daily events. In addition, Canandaigua, Elmira, Geneva, Waterloo, Watkins Glen, and Camillus operate information centers year-round, and 25 smaller communities staff centers during the summer.

Emergencies Police and ambulance, tel. 911.

Exploring the Finger Lakes

The Finger Lakes Region encompasses counties in the center of New York State. Midway between New York City and Niagara Falls, it is anchored on the west by the state's third-largest city—Rochester—and on the east by the fourth-largest city—Syracuse.

The area attracts more than seven million visitors a year, but because it is so vast it rarely seems crowded. And though it has special appeal for outdoors lovers—anglers, hunters, boaters, sailors, campers, and hikers—it also boasts elegant castles and inns, fine wining and dining, first-rate museums, concerts, and art galleries.

The crop that put the Finger Lakes on the tourist as well as the economic map is the grape, and the most popular time to visit is May–October, when the wineries are open for tours, generally on a daily basis. The 11 lakes, from Conesus Lake due south of Rochester to Otisco Lake near Syracuse, offer lush, scenic vistas from every turn in the road. They cover 9,000 square miles, and that collective shoreline covers nearly 600 miles.

Rochester

Numbers in the margin correspond with points of interest on the Rochester map.

The largest city in, and a good starting point to tour, the Finger Lakes is **Rochester.** Although not nearly as large or dramatic as Niagara Falls, there are two 100-foot waterfalls in the middle of the city, which is well situated on the Genesee River. Lake Ontario serves as the city's northern boundary. In the early 19th century Rochester was considered the flour capital of the nation. But as the sources of grain moved westward, Rochester became a nursery and seed capital and acquired the nickname "Flower City," which has stuck to this day.

1 **Highland Park,** between S. Goodman Street and Mt. Hope Avenue, a few blocks from the river, is the site of the annual 10-day Lilac Festival in late May, which draws thousands to see and smell the 22 fragrant lilac varieties. There are also gardens filled with magnolias, azaleas, crab apples, hawthorns, peonies, and other blossoms. A spectacular pansy bed holds more than 5,000 plants. The park's **Lamberton Conservatory** hosts five major displays throughout the year.

2 **The Stone-Tolan House** is believed to be the oldest surviving building in the county, with one wing dating to 1792. Its four-acre site has vegetable and herb gardens and orchards. *2370 East Ave., tel. 716/442-4606. Admission: $1.50 adults, 75¢ seniors, 50¢ students, 10¢ children under 14. Open Mar.–Dec., Fri.–Sun. noon–4 PM.*

Rochester is often called The Picture City, and with good reason. It is the birthplace and home of the Kodak Company. Head north on Goodman Street and turn right on East Avenue to **3** reach the **International Museum of Photography** at the **George**

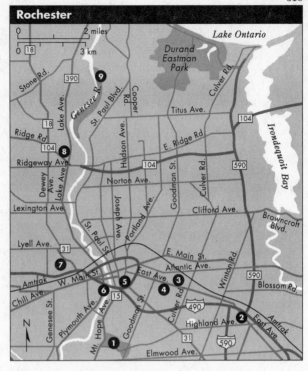

Eastman House, which houses the world's largest collection of photographic art and technology.

Eastman's house was once the largest private home in the city, and the gardens are especially beautiful in May and June. The archives are housed in a library of more than 35,000 books and hundreds of thousands of photographs. The photo galleries, containing some of the world's best photography, are primarily on the second floor. The main floor is furnished much as it was when Eastman lived and worked here. It was in his bedroom at age 78 that he committed suicide, writing in a note: "My work is done—why wait?" In his lifetime he gave away about $100 million. *900 East Ave., tel. 716/271-3361. Admission: $2 adults, $1 students, 75¢ children under 17. Open Tues.–Sat. 10–4:30, Sun. 1–5.*

4 **The Rochester Museum & Science Center** presents exhibits on regional history as well as natural science, anthropology, and human biology, and has Iroquois artifacts and period rooms that depict 19th-century life in the city. The Strasenburgh Planetarium has daily star shows under a 60-foot dome. *657 East Ave., tel. 716/271-1880 (museum), tel. 716/442-7171 (planetarium). Admission: $3 adults; $2.50 seniors and students; 75¢ children under 17, under 4 free. Planetarium fee varies with show. Museum open Mon.–Sat. 9–5, Sun. 1–5. Planetarium shows nightly; weekend and summer matinees.*

Margaret Woodbury Strong, who was the largest single Kodak shareholder when she died in 1969, contributed her considerable fortune and her lifetime collections to a museum named in her honor. She wanted the museum to be called the Museum of Fascinations, and although it was named instead for her, it is

5 truly a house of fascinations. Opened in 1982, the **Strong Museum** houses the country's foremost collection of Victorian furniture; vast collections of 19th-century glassware, ceramics, and silver; an extensive collection of nearly 20,000 dolls; and an array of miniatures, antique toys, and dollhouses. *1 Manhattan Sq., tel. 716/263–2700. Admission: $2 adults; $1.50 seniors; 75¢ children 4–16. Open Mon.–Sat. 10–5, Sun. 1–5.*

6 **The Campbell-Whittlesey House** in the city's historic Third Ward is one of America's finest examples of Greek-Revival architecture. Today it is operated by the Landmark Society of Western New York. *123 S. Fitzhugh St., tel. 716/546–7028. Admission: $1.50 adults, 75¢ seniors, 50¢ students, 10¢ children under 17. Open Feb.–Dec., Fri.–Sun. noon–4.*

7 **Susan B. Anthony House** was home to the 19th-century advocate of women's rights, and it was here that Anthony wrote *The History of Woman Suffrage*. The home is furnished in the style of the mid-1800s. *17 Madison St., tel. 716/235–6124. Admission: $1 adults, 50¢ children under 12. Open Wed.–Sat. 1–4.*

8 Film manufacturing tours of **Eastman Kodak,** the company that George Eastman founded, are available from mid-May through August. (Kodak, by the way, is a nonsense word conceived by Eastman because he wanted a name that could not be translated into another language.) A multimedia orientation to the 2,000-acre facility, where products such as film, photographic paper, and chemicals are manufactured, is followed by a bus tour and a look at the packaging operations where film and those little yellow boxes come together. *200 Ridge Rd. W (Rte. 104), off I–390, tel. 716/722–2465. Tours weekdays at 9 and 1. No children under 5. No charge for groups of 10 and under.*

9 Rochester's **Seneca Park** has hiking trails along the east side of the Genesee River; its zoo features an aviary with uncaged birds, a polar bear enclosure, and an elephant exhibit. *2222 St. Paul St., tel. 716/266–6846. Admission: $1 adults, 50¢ children 10–15, children under 10 and seniors over 62 free. Open daily 10–5, summer weekends and holidays until 7 PM.*

Fairport, Mumford, and Castile

Numbers in the margin correspond with points of interest on the Finger Lakes Area map.

1 For an introduction to the area's wines, visit **Fairport** and the **Casa Larga Vineyards,** just 12 miles east of Rochester. This is a small farm winery, opened in 1978, that bottles primarily varietal wines made from vinifera grapes. *2287 Turk Hill Rd., off Rte. 31 or Rte. 96, Fairport, tel. 716/223–4210. Open Tues.–Sat. 10–5, Sun. noon–5.*

Twenty miles southwest of Rochester via routes 383 and 36 in

2 the town of **Mumford** is the **Genesee Country Village and Museum,** where you can step back into the 19th century. This is a village of 55 buildings gathered from throughout the region and reconstructed here. Highlights include an elegant 1870 octagonal house and a two-story log house, circa 1814. You can watch guides cook, work in gardens, spin yarn, weave, and make baskets, and the country's largest collection of wildlife art can be seen in the **Gallery of Sporting Art.** *Flint Hill Rd., Mumford,*

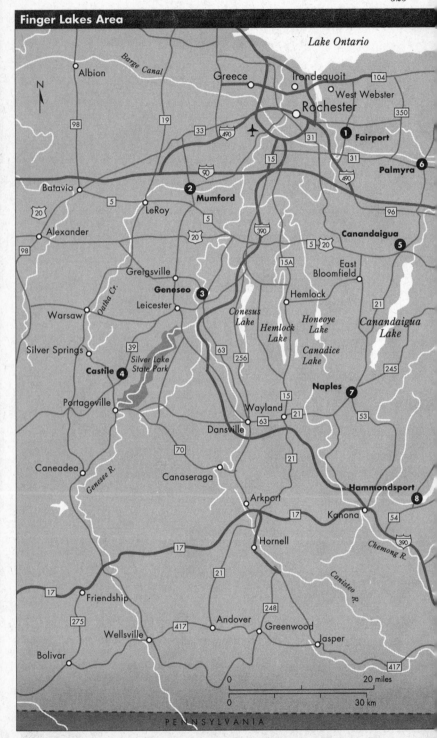

Finger Lakes Area

Lake Ontario

Albion

Barge Canal

Greece

Irondequoit

104

West Webster

Rochester

350

N

98

19

33

490

31

① Fairport

31

490

6

Palmyra

90

② Mumford

96

Batavia

5

20

LeRoy

5

Canandaigua

Alexander

20

5 20

5

Warsaw

Gretgsville

15A

East
Bloomfield

Geneseo ③

21

98

Oatka Cr.

Leicester

Hemlock

Canandaigua
Lake

Conesus
Lake

Hemlock
Lake

Honeoye
Lake

Silver Springs

39

Silver Lake
State Park

63

256

Canadice
Lake

245

Castile ④

Naples ⑦

Portageville

Wayland

15

Dansville

21

63

53

Caneadea

70

Genesee R.

Canaseraga

21

Hammondsport

Arkport

8

Kanona

54

Hornell

17

Chemong R.

390

17

21

Canisteo R.

17

Friendship

275

248

Andover

Greenwood

Jasper

Wellsville

417

Bolivar

417

0   20 miles

0   30 km

PENNSYLVANIA

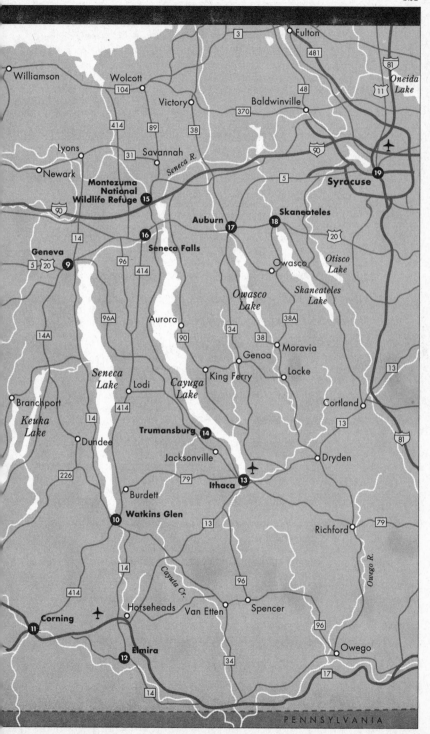

tel. 716/538–2887. Admission: $8 adults, $3.50 children 6–14, children under 6 free, $7 seniors on weekdays. Open Sat. before Mother's Day–3rd Sun. in Oct., daily 10–4.

❸ Aviation buffs will want to go to **Geneseo,** a bit farther south in the heart of the hunt country, to see the **National Warplane Museum.** It is home to one of the nine B-17s still flying in the country as well as such aircraft as the Curtis P-40 Warhawk, the PT-17, the Fairchild PT-19 and PT-26, the Vultee BT-13, and Boeing B-17G used by generals Eisenhower and MacArthur. *Big Tree La., off Rte. 63, Geneseo, tel. 716/243–0690. Open weekdays 9–5, weekends 10–5. Admission: $3 adults, $1 children under 12. Call first as planes may be away for air shows.*

❹ About five miles farther south in **Castile** is **Letchworth State Park,** dubbed the "Grand Canyon of the East." It comprises 14,350 acres along the Genesee River and has few rivals in the east for spectacular beauty. It includes dramatic cliffs, some nearly 600 feet high; three waterfalls, one of which is 107 feet high; lush woods; and the **Glen Iris Inn,** once the country home of the park's donor, William Pryor Letchworth, and now a popular hotel and restaurant (*see* Dining and Lodging). Fall weekends are usually booked years in advance at Glen Iris because of the special seasonal beauty of the park and gorge. The park has extensive camping facilities, fishing, hunting, swimming, and cross-country skiing. The park's **William Prior Letchworth Museum** tells the story of the early days of the area with artifacts, books, and displays. There is also an original **Iroquois Council House,** which was moved here from a nearby location. *For information and reservations on camping facilities, contact Letchworth State Park, Castile 14427, tel. 716/493–2611, and for the Glen Iris Inn, tel. 716/493–2622, or write to the inn at the park address.*

Canandaigua Lake Area

Heading south from Rochester the first of the Finger Lakes is ❺ **Canandaigua,** which can be reached by following I–390 north to U.S. 20 west to the town of Canandaigua, a bustling tourist city especially popular in the summer; its Seneca name means "the chosen place." One of the city's prime attractions is the **Sonnenberg Gardens and Mansion,** a 50-acre estate recognized by the Smithsonian Institution as having "one of the most magnificent late-Victorian gardens in America." Nine gardens, including rose, Japanese, Italian, rock, and Colonial, surround the mansion, which has restored period rooms with some original furnishings. The **Canandaigua Wine Company Tasting Room** located here offers wine tastings. *151 Charlotte St., tel. 716/394–4922. Admission: $5 adults, $2 children 6–16, $4 seniors. Open mid-May–mid-Oct., daily 9:30–5:30.*

Another area attraction is the **Granger Homestead and Carriage Museum.** It includes the restored 1816 Federal mansion of Gideon Granger, U.S. Postmaster General under Presidents Jefferson and Madison and a collection of 40 horse-drawn vehicles dating from 1820–1930. *295 N. Main St., tel. 716/394–1472. Admission: $2.50 adults; $1 children 12–16, under 12 free. Open May–Oct., Tues.–Sat. 10–5; Sun. 1–5.*

❻ About 15 miles north of Canandaigua is **Palmyra,** birthplace of the Mormon religion. Here you can visit the Mormon Historic

Sites, including the repository of historic records translated by Joseph Smith into the *Book of Mormon* and a monument to the Angel Moroni, Smith's spiritual guide. *Visitor Center, movies, guided tours. Rte. 21, north of NYS Thruway Exit 43, tel. 315/597–5851. Free. Open daily 8–6.*

The Joseph Smith House is the restored farmstead of the Mormon church founder Joseph Smith. *Stafford Rd., tel. 315/597–5851. Free. Open 8–6, in summer 8–9.*

❼ The next stop is the village of **Naples** at the southern end of Canandaigua Lake. Many buildings on Main Street date back to the early 1800s. Naples is home to the century-old **Widmer's Wine Cellars,** which has daily tours and tastings during the season. Widmer's is the only winery in the region that ages sherry and port in barrels on the roof. *Rte. 21, Naples 14512; tel. 716/374–6311. Tours and tastings June–Oct. 1–4. Other times, call ahead.*

Keuka Lake Area

The next lake—one of the loveliest in the area—is the 22-mile-long **Keuka Lake,** southeast of Canandaigua via routes 247 and **❽** 364. The village of **Hammondsport** at the southern end of the lake is the birthplace of the Finger Lakes wine industry and is a good base for a concentrated wine tour. The streets are lined with Victorian homes, and a park with an old-fashioned bandstand is in the center of the village.

To relive the early history of aviation, stop in at the **Glenn H. Curtiss Museum of Local History.** It displays the accomplishments of native son Curtiss, a pioneer in aviation and other fields. The famous *June Bug* and *Curtiss Jenny* planes, and other local memorabilia are on display in this jumbled but fascinating museum. *Lake and Main Sts., tel. 607/569–2160. Admission: $3 adults, $2 students, $1.50 children 13–18, $1 children 7–12, $6 family. Open April 15–June, Mon.–Sat. 9–5; July–Oct. daily.*

The area's largest winery is two miles outside of Hammondsport. **Taylor Wine Co.** is operated by **Vintner's International.** Anyone who stops at the Taylor Wine Visitors Center can see a film on the winery and its history—the theater was built in a former wine tank—and take the hour-long tour that is one of the most comprehensive in the area, in which tastings are offered. *Lake St., Hammondsport, tel. 607/569–2111. Free. May–Oct., daily 10–4; Nov.–Apr., Mon.–Sat. 11–3.*

Just a mile north of town is **Bully Hill,** the most talked-about winery in the region. It is presided over by Walter S. Taylor, a grandson of the founder of the Taylor Wine Co. and the closest thing the wine world has to a folk hero. The protracted court fight over the use of the Taylor name (he lost) helped put his winery on the map. **Greyton H. Taylor Museum,** adjacent to the vineyards, is housed in a 100-year-old wood and stone building and displays antique equipment used in tending the vineyards and making wines. *Greyton H. Taylor Memorial Dr., Hammondsport, tel. 607/868–3610. Tours and tastings free. Open Mon.–Sat. 10–4:30, Sun. noon–4:30.*

Time Out The **Champagne Country Cafe** is next door and serves fresh pasta dishes and other light fare along with wine.

Other Keuka Lake wineries include **Chateau De Rheimes** (Pleasant Valley Rd., Box 72-A, Hammondsport, tel. 607/569–2040); **Hunt Country Vineyards** (4021 Italy Hill Rd., Branchport, tel. 315/595–2812); **Heron Hill** (Middle Rd., Hammondsport, tel. 607/868–4241); and **McGregor Vineyard Winery** (5503 Dutch St., Dundee, tel. 607/292–3999).

Seneca Lake Area

East of Keuka Lake is **Seneca Lake,** the deepest (650 feet) of the Finger Lakes and home to the National Lake Trout Derby. The stately city of **Geneva** is at the northern end of the lake. South Main Street has been acclaimed as "the most beautiful street in America." It is lined with 19th-century homes and century-old trees. The scenic campus of **Hobart** and **William Smith colleges** is here, too.

Three miles east of Geneva, overlooking the lake, is **Rose Hill Mansion.** Built in 1839, it is a handsome Greek Revival restoration and National Historic Landmark. Decorated in elegant Empire style, it has 21 rooms open to the public, a carriage house, slide show, and boxwood gardens. *Rte. 96A, tel. 315/789–3848. Admission: $2 adults; $1 children 10–18, under 10 free. Guided tours only. Open May 1–Oct. 31, Mon.–Sat. 10–4, Sun. 1–5.*

Nine wineries surround the southern half of the 36-mile-long lake. The following are open for tours and tastings: **Glenora Wine Cellars** (RD 4 Route 14. Dundee, tel. 607/243–5511); **Hazlitt 1852 Vineyards** (Rte. 414, Hector, tel. 607/546–5812); **Four Chimneys Vineyards** (RD 1, Hall Rd., Himrod, tel. 607/243–6421); **Poplar Ridge** (RD 1, Valois, tel. 607/582–6421); **Rolling Vineyards** (Rte. 414, Hector, tel. 607/546–9302); **Wagner Vineyards** and **Ginney Lee Cafe** (Rte. 414, Lodi, tel. 607/546–9302); **Wickham Vineyards** (1 Wine Pl., Hector, tel. 607/546–8415); and **Hermann J. Wiemer** (Rte. 14, Dundee, tel. 607/243–7971).

The village of **Watkins Glen** is at the southern end of Seneca Lake adjoining the 669-acre **Watkins Glen State Park** (Rte. 14, tel. 607/535–4511). The glen drops about 700 feet in two miles and is highlighted by rock formations and 18 waterfalls. Cliffs rise 200 feet above the stream; a 165-foot-high bridge spans the glen, which is lit at night. **Timespell,** a 45-minute dramatic sound and laser-light show, traces the natural and human history in the gorge. The stirring voice of the narrator says, "We are about to leave human time altogether and go far, far back into the geologic past . . . to a time when the earth was young— over 4½ billion years ago." *The show is presented twice nightly in season and once nightly off-season, beginning at dusk, May 15–Oct. 15. Admission: $4.25. Tel. 607/535–4960.*

Corning and Elmira

Watkins Glen is a good place to break from lake touring. Travel south along Route 414 to **Corning,** famous as the home of Corning Glass Works and its Steuben Glass division.

The Corning Glass Center houses the **Corning Museum of Glass,** which contains the world's foremost glass collection. The present building, designed by architect Gunnar Birkerts, opened in 1980. The center also includes the Hall of Science and

Industry with push-button exhibits, live demonstrations, and films. The exhibits show how glass is made and used in science, industry, and the home. Steuben Glass Factory allows visitors to watch craftsmen create works of art. There are gift shops, including the Steuben shop and a separate shop for Corning products with a large selection of discount items. *Off Rte. 17, tel. 607/974-8271. Admission: $4 adults, $2 children 6–17, children under 6 free, $3 senior citizens, $10 family. Open daily 9–5.*

The **Rockwell Museum** has more glass art, including Carder Steuben glass and the largest collection of western American art in the East. The exhibits are housed in the restored 1893 Old City Hall. *Denison Pkwy. and Cedar St., tel. 607/937–5386. Admission: $3 adults, $2.50 senior citizens. Open Mon.–Sat. 9–5, Sun. noon–5.*

Corning's downtown Market Street has been restored to its 19th-century glory and is listed on the National Register of Historic Places. Free English-style double-decker buses provide transportation to the glass center and down Market Street.

The 1796 **Benjamin Patterson "Inn" Museum** consists of a restored furnished inn and former stagecoach stop, a 1784 log cabin, a 1878 one-room schoolhouse, and a restored barn with an early agricultural exhibit dating from 1850–1860. The museum is filled with furnishings, crafts, and costumes of the area dating to 1784. *59 W. Pulteney St., tel. 607/937–5281. Admission: $2 adults, $1 children 6–18. Open weekdays 10–4.*

The **Wine Center & Market** provides an introduction to winemaking history and lore. Tastings are held in what was once the Baron Steuben Hotel ballroom. *Baron Steuben Pl., tel. 607/962–6072.*

⑫ Traveling southeast along scenic Route 17, the next stop is **Elmira,** site of an important Revolutionary War battle. The **Newtown Battlefield Reservation** marks the location of the battle won by Major General John Sullivan over a large force of Indians and Tories.

Elmira is also where Samuel Clemens, better known as Mark Twain, spent more than 20 summers and wrote many of his classics, including *The Adventures of Huckleberry Finn.* His wife, Olivia Langdon, grew up here, and Clemens loved the Chemung Valley area, which he called "the garden of Eden." Clemens and his family are buried here in a grave marked by a 12-foot granite monument. Clemens's study, with a typewriter like his (he was one of the first to submit a typed manuscript to a publisher) and some original furniture, was moved from Quarry Farm, just outside town, to the campus of **Elmira College** in 1955. *Mark Twain Study, Elmira College, tel. 607/734–3911. Free. Open daily in summer, rest of year by appointment.*

The Elmira area is known as the "Soaring Capital of America," and the area's hills and valleys present ideal airplane soaring and gliding conditions. The **National Soaring Museum** displays more than a dozen fully assembled historic gliders and sailplanes as well as artifacts pertaining to motorless flight. You can sit in a flight simulator to experience the soaring sensation. For the real thing, take a sailplane ride at the adjacent glider field or just watch the sailplanes perform (*see* Participant Sports). *Harris Hill, tel. 607/734–3129. Admission: $1.50 adults, 75¢ seniors and students, children under 12 free. Open daily 10–5.*

Cayuga Lake Area

⑬ Ithaca, best known as the home of **Cornell University,** is north of Elmira at the southern tip of Cayuga Lake, the longest of the Finger Lakes at 66.5 miles. The town is more spectacular than most in the Finger Lakes because of the deep gorges and more than 100 waterfalls that run throughout it, and it was a favorite location for movies during the silent era. Ithaca is also the birthplace of the ice cream sundae.

Cornell University, founded by Ezra Cornell in 1865, is situated on a hill overlooking Cayuake and Ithaca. The sprawling 13,000-acre campus encompasses farms and expirimental crop lands. Triphammer Bridge offers a splendid view of Fall Creek Gorge, Triphammer Falls, and Beebe Lake.

Cornell Plantations lie along the gorges bordering the campus. The 2,800 acres include beds of azaleas, lilacs, peonies, wildflowers, rhododendrons, and viburnums. There are lakes, ponds, streams, bogs, swampland, wooded areas, and an arboretum, as well as a magnificent collection of Japanese tree peonies. Of special interest is the **Walter C. Muenscher Poisonous Plants Garden.** The **Robison York State Herb Garden** has more than 800 herbs. There's a gift shop, and guided tours are available by prior arrangement. *1 Plantation Rd. near Rte. 366, tel. 607/255–3020.*

⑭ Just northwest of Ithaca is **Trumansburg** and the **Taughannock Falls State Park** (Rte. 96, tel. 607/387–7041). The 215-foothigh falls in a rock amphitheater with 400-foot walls is the highest straight-drop falls east of the Rocky Mountains. The 737-acre park has complete camping facilities and offers swimming, fishing, boat launching, hiking trails, and cross-country skiing.

Ithaca is also the starting point for the **Cayuga Wine Trail.** The lake's wineries offering tours and tastings include: **Americana Vineyards** (4367 E. Covert Rd., Interlaken, tel. 607/387–6801), **Knapp Vineyards** (Ernsberger Rd., Romulus, tel. 315/549–8865), **Lakeshore Winery** (5132 Rte. 89, Romulus, tel. 315/549–8461), **Lucas Winery** (RD 2, County Road 150, Interlaken, tel. 607/ 532–4825), and **Plane's Cayuga Vineyard** (6800 Rte. 89 at Elm Beach, Ovid, tel. 607/869–5158).

⑮ The **Montezuma National Wildlife Refuge,** at the north end of Cayuga Lake, gives migrating birds a protected rest and feeding area and serves as a nesting ground for numerous others. There are more than 6,300 acres of cattail-covered marshland, swampwoods, and fields with easy access from Exits 40 and 41 of the Thruway.

⑯ About five miles west of the north end of Cayuga Lake is **Seneca Falls,** birthplace of the women's rights movement in America. On July 18, 1848, the first women's rights convention brought 300 people to the Wesleyan Methodist Chapel at 126 Falls Street. Famous former residents include Amelia Bloomer, who popularized the undergarment bearing her name, and Elizabeth Cady Stanton, organizer of the first women's rights convention.

The **Women's Rights National Historical Park** includes a visitor center and the restored **Elizabeth Cady Stanton Home** at 32 Washington Street. The center chronicles the development of the women's movement through changing exhibits, slide programs, and interpretive talks. *116 Falls St., Seneca Falls, tel. 315/568-2991. Free. Stanton Home, daily 9-5. Park open Apr.-Nov., daily 9-5; Dec.-Mar. weekdays 9-5.*

Just down the stairs is home of the **National Women's Hall of Fame.** The hall honors famous American women, past and present, such as humanists Jane Addams and Eleanor Roosevelt, painter Mary Cassatt, and sportswoman "Babe" Didrickson Saharais. The stories of these famous American women are told through portraits, photographs, biographies, memorabilia, and audiovisuals. *76 Falls St., Seneca Falls, tel. 315/568-8060. Donation. Open Apr.-Nov., Mon.-Sat. 10-4, Sun. 1-5; Dec.-Mar. Mon.-Sat. 10-4.*

17 Heading east on Route 20, we come to **Auburn** at the northern end of Owasco Lake. South of Auburn on Route 38A is the reconstructed **Owasco Stockaded Indian Village,** with an early longhouse as well as a round hogan. There are crafts programs and demonstrations of what Native-American life here was like more than 1,000 years ago. *Emerson Park, Rte. 38A. Admission free. Open daily 10-5.*

Auburn was the home of William Henry Seward, New York governor, U.S. senator, and secretary of state for presidents Lincoln and Johnson. He was a leading figure in the founding of the Republican party and in the Alaska purchase. Alaska's banks and schools are closed every year on the last Monday in May in his honor. The **Seward House** has original furnishings, and most of the 15 rooms open to the public are filled with Seward's personal possessions. The second-floor gallery contains Seward's collection of 132 prints and photographs of world leaders he met on diplomatic missions around the globe. *33 South St., tel. 315/252-1283. Admission: $2.50 adults, $1 children 7-18, children under 7 free, $2 seniors. Open Apr.-Dec., 1-5.*

Auburn was also the home of Harriet Tubman, who used it as an "underground railroad" station for the more than 300 slaves she led to freedom. During the Civil War she served as a Union Army spy and scout. Special tours of the **Harriet Tubman Home** are available by appointment. *180 South St., tel. 315/253-2621.*

Skaneateles Lake Area

Though it is one of the smallest of the Finger Lakes, **Skaneateles Lake,** seven miles east of Auburn on U.S. 20, is one of the loveliest. (Skaneateles is Indian for "beautiful squaw.") Today tasteful storefronts housed in 19th-century brick build-
18 ings line the main streets of **Skaneateles.** The Sherwood Inn *(see* Dining and Lodging), overlooking the lake, has been welcoming travelers since 1809. This is a town of wealth and elegance. Sunday afternoons are reserved for polo games during the summer. You can tour the lake while the mail is being delivered on a unique morning mail ride operated by Mid-Lakes

Navigation Sailboat Co.; there are also luncheon and dinner cruises *(see* Guided Tours).

Syracuse

19 The final stop on our Finger Lakes tour is **Syracuse,** known as "Salt City." The Indian chief Hiawatha chose this location as the capital of the Iroquois Confederacy in the 16th century. The **Onondaga Indian Reservation** at Nedrow is now the seat of the Indian Confederacy. Salt brought the Indians, the French, and subsequent settlers to Syracuse and, for many years, Syracuse was the source of most American salt.

The **Salt Museum** has exhibits and a reconstructed 1856 salt factory where salt processing is demonstrated. The museum, built during the Depression as a work relief project, is housed in a replica of an early salt block, and focuses primarily on the salt industry during the Industrial Revolution. *Onondaga Lake Park, Liverpool, tel. 315/451–7275. Admission: free. Open May–Oct., 10–5.*

The state's fourth-largest city, Syracuse has played host to the New York State Fair since 1841 and is also home to one of the country's largest private educational institutions—Syracuse University.

The Erie Canal no longer runs through Syracuse, but the era is recalled at the **Erie Canal Museum,** the last of seven weighlock buildings in the state through which canal boats passed. It is a National Register Landmark building with indoor and outdoor exhibits that explore the construction and operation of the canal. Visitors board a 65-foot reconstructed canal boat to view the exhibits. *318 Erie Blvd. at Montgomery St., tel. 315/471–0593. Open Tues.–Sat. 10–5. Tuesday free. Wed.–Sun. adults $1, children 5–12 50¢.*

The **Discovery Center of Science & Technology** offers hands-on displays dealing with gravity, perception, chemistry, light, sound, electricity, optics, magnetism, mechanics, space, and the human body. There is also a planetarium and a museum shop. *321 South Clinton St., tel. 315/425–9068. Admission: $2 adults, $1 children under 12. Planetary show 50¢. Open Tues.–Sat. 10–5, Sun. noon–5.*

The county's **Burnet Park Zoo** has recently undergone a $10-million renovation. There are more than 1,000 animals and birds in nine separate complexes that re-create natural habitats—from arctic tundra and arid desert to tropical rain forest. A wildly decorated zoo bus provides free transportation from downtown on the weekends. *S. Wilbur Ave., tel. 315/425–3774. Admission: $2.50 adults, $1.25 children 5–14, children under 5 free, $1.25 senior citizens, $8 family. Open daily 10–4:30; Memorial Day–Labor Day until 7.*

Sainte Marie de Gannentaha or **French Fort** is a re-creation of a French Jesuit Colonial settlement established on the shore of Onondaga Lake in 1656. Authentically costumed interpreters perform traditional craft demonstrations. *Onondaga Lake Pkwy., Liverpool, tel. 315/451–7275. Free. Open daily, May–Oct.*

What to See and Do with Children

Children usually enjoy the **wine tours,** and all of the wineries that offer tours and tastings provide grape juice for children and nondrinkers. Some even provide hayrides during the fall harvest season (*see* Exploring).

Genesee Country Museum (*see* Exploring).

Margaret Woodbury Strong Museum (*see* Exploring).

The **Victorian Doll Museum** has more than 2,000 identified collector dolls, a toy circus, a puppet show, a doll hospital, and a gift shop. *4332 Buffalo Rd., North Chili, 10 miles west of Rochester, tel. 716/247–0130. Admission: $1.50 adults, 75¢ children. Open Tues.–Sat. 10–4:30, Sun. 1–4:30; closed holidays and Jan.*

Wild Winds Farms and Village has gardens, a log fort, a petting zoo, a nature center, a maple-sugar house, and a restaurant.

Discovery Center of Science & Technology (*see* Exploring).

Off the Beaten Track

Visitors to **Gates-Rockwell Department Store** in Corning who expect a typical small-town department store will be surprised to find a wealth of art treasures, Carder-Steuben glass, antique guns, toys hanging on the walls, and displays amid the regular items for sale (display items are not for sale). This store houses some of the overflow from the Rockwell Museum. *23 W. Market St., Corning, tel. 607/962–2441. Open Mon.–Wed. and Sat. 9–5:30, Thurs. and Fri. 9–9.*

The town of **Waterloo** calls itself the birthplace of Memorial Day, and the **Memorial Day Museum** is a 20-room mansion full of items about that holiday, the Civil War, the two world wars, and the Korean conflict. The museum contains photographs and displays of newspapers, clothes, and knickknacks of the time when Waterloo first established the day to honor its fallen soldiers. *35 E. Main St., Waterloo, 315/539–2474. Admission free. Open Memorial Day–Labor Day, Tues.–Fri. 1:30–4.*

Misty Meadow Hog Farm is the place for anyone who has ever wanted to pet a pig. This is a working family farm with piglets and full cycle of production. There are haywagon rides, crafts, and a farm kitchen restaurant. The farm sells its own frozen meat. *Vineyard Rd., off Rte. 89, Romulus, tel. 607/869–9243. Tours July and Aug., Tues.–Sat. 11 AM, 1 and 2 PM.*

Millions of fish eggs are hatched and cared for at the **New York State Fish Hatchery,** which started in 1865 and is the oldest fish hatchery in North America. It raises rainbow trout, and chinook and coho salmon. *Rte. 36, 16 North St., Caledonia, tel. 716/538–6300. Admission free. Open daily 8–4.*

The **Norton Chapel of Keuka College** near Penn Yan is on a lovely spot at the edge of Keuka Lake. It was modeled after a Latin cross. Artist-craftsman Gabriel Loire of Chartres, France, designed the mosaic glass windows.

Participant Sports

Boating

In addition to the Finger Lakes, there are boating opportunities on Lake Ontario and the Barge Canal. There are numerous boat launching sites throughout the area. The two longest lakes, Seneca and Cayuga, are connected by a canal that, in turn, is connected to the Erie Canal, thereby linking them all to the waterways of the world.

Fishing

The area has long attracted fishing enthusiasts, who are drawn here by the record-breaking brown trout, rainbow trout, bass, pike, pickerel, salmon, and panfish. The area is also known for its large lake trout. Opportunities include deep trolling in lakes, off-shore spincasting, stream fishing, smelting, and ice fishing in winter. Lake Ontario has been successful with a restocking program for chinook and coho salmon. Be sure to check the latest Health Department advisory on eating fish from Lake Ontario; there are restrictions because of chemical contamination. Call Lake Ontario Hotline, tel. 716/ 473–1824 or 716/589–9211, for latest fishing update. *For information on licenses, seasons, and limits contact the Department of Environmental Conservation, 6274 E. Avon-Lima Rd., Avon 14414, tel. 716/226–2466.*

Golf

Nearly 30 golf courses in the region welcome visitors. In Elmira, there's the 18-hole Chemung Valley and 18-hole Mark Twain. In Ithaca, Cornell University has an 18-hole golf club and there's the 9-hole Newman Course. In Rochester, there is a new 18-hole Genesee Valley course and an old 18-hole course. In Syracuse, there's the 18-hole Tanner Valley, and there are 9-hole courses in Geneva, Cayuga, and Watkins Glen.

Hunting

Some of the state's best hunting takes place in the Finger Lakes. Steuben County, where Corning is located, has one of the largest deer harvests in the state. The ruffed grouse is considered "king of the game birds" in the southern Finger Lakes. Wild turkey, which has made a fantastic comeback in the region, is also a much sought-after game bird. To the north there is excellent goose hunting adjacent to federal and state game refuges. The area is part of the Eastern Flyway for migratory birds. *For information on licenses, seasons, and bag limits, contact the Department of Environmental Conservation, 6274 E. Avon-Lima Rd., Avon 14414, tel. 716/226–2466.*

Skiing

Cross-country skiing is available in the state and local parks, as well as in the Green Mountain National Forest. The largest downhill ski centers are Bristol Mountain (Rte. 64, Canadaigua, tel. 716/374–6331) and Greek Peak (Rte. 90, Cortland, tel. 607/835–6111). Both offer lessons and rentals.

Soaring

The Elmira area's hills and valleys present ideal soaring and gliding conditions. For rides and instruction, contact Harris Hill Gliderport (RD 3, Elmira 14903, tel. 607/734–3128) or Schweizer Soaring School (Chemung County Airport, Rte. 17 between Elmira and Corning, tel. 607/739–3821). In Syracuse, contact Thermal Ridge Soaring (115 Kittell Rd., Fayetteville 13066, tel. 315/446–4545).

Spectator Sports

Auto Racing

Watkins Glen International has major professional road racing June–September. Events include Camel Continental, Trans-Am Nationals, Supervee, Vintage Cup, and 24-hour Firestone Firehawk. *For schedules, contact Watkins Glen International, Box 500, Watkins Glen 14891, tel. 607/535–2481.*

Baseball

The Rochester Red Wings—an International League farm club of the Baltimore Orioles—plays at Silver Stadium from April through October. The Syracuse Chefs AAA baseball team plays from April to September at MacArthur Stadium.

Basketball

The highly rated Syracuse University baseketball team plays at the university's Carrier Dome November–March.

Horseracing

Thoroughbreds run at the Finger Lakes Race Track, Thruway Exit 44 and Rte. 96, April–November, tel. 716/924–3232. Harness racing takes place at Batavia Downs in Batavia and the Syracuse Mile in Syracuse.

Dining and Lodging

Dining Restaurants in the Finger Lakes are as varied as the lakes and communities. Rochester and Syracuse boast some fine dining rooms, as do several smaller cities and towns. Ithaca on Cayuga Lake has a surprisingly large assortment of top restaurants, in part due to the large university community and the university's hotel-management school.

Highly recommended restaurants are indicated by a star ★.

Category	Cost*
Very Expensive	over $25
Expensive	$18–$25

Moderate	$10–$17
Inexpensive	under $10

*per person, not including beverage, tax, or tip

Lodging The region's hotels, motels, and inns cater to a wide range of tastes and pocketbooks. Country inns have been a tradition in the area since the early 19th century, but lately they have been "rediscovered." Many lakeside motels have lower rates off-season; some close after November 1 and do not reopen until May. The peak season is summer.

Bed-and-breakfast inns have been growing in this region recently. Most are in historic homes and farmhouses. Some accept major credit cards, but many do not; be sure to inquire in advance when making reservations. Rates range from budget to expensive. **Cherry Valley Ventures,** tel. 315/677–9723, handles reservations for a number of bed-and-breakfast establishments.

Category	Cost*
Very Expensive	over $90
Expensive	$70–$90
Moderate	$50–$70
Inexpensive	under $50

*Sales tax throughout the region is 7%. In Monroe County (Rochester) there is an additional 2% occupancy tax on room charges, while Onondaga County adds a 3% occupancy tax. Rates are based on double occupancy.

Canandaigua Lake Area

Dining **Crickett's of Canandaigua.** Rochester residents consider it worth the drive to experience this gourmet French restaurant in a century-old building in downtown Canandaigua. Crickett's has a well-stocked wine cellar featuring many local vintages. *169 Main St., Canandaigua, 716/394–7990. Jackets required. Reservations advised. DC, MC, V. Expensive.*

Gay 90s Tap Room. A local favorite since 1895, the Gay 90s Tap Room in the Naples Hotel serves traditional American fare with an emphasis on steak, prime ribs, and seafood. *Main St., Naples, tel. 716/374–5630. Dress: informal. Reservations advised in summer. AE, MC, V. Expensive.*

Bob's and Ruth's. Reminiscent of an old-fashioned diner, Bob's and Ruth's features chicken hot off the spit and homemade soup and pies. One entire wall is stocked with wine bottles, many of them from the area. *Rtes. 21 and 245, Naples, tel. 716/374–5122. Dress: informal. MC, V. Moderate.*

★ **Wild Winds Farms & Village.** This working farm features all natural foods: fresh-baked breads, pastries, crepes, quiches, and vegetables grown on the grounds. The flowers on your plate are edible. There is a country store, sugarhouse, nature trail, greenhouses, and gardens. *Clark St., 3 mi west of Naples, tel. 716/374–5523. Dress: informal. Open Memorial Day–Oct., lunch daily and dinner, Fri. and Sat. AE, MC, V. Moderate.*

Lodging **Sheraton Canandaigua Inn.** This is a large and busy resort, the most complete one in the area. It occupies a prime lakefront site. The rooms were recently renovated and some have balconies and private patios. It's popular with families because of the family plan and facilities. *770 S. Main St., Canandaigua 14424, tel. 716/394–7800. 147 rooms with bath. Facilities: pool, dining room, cocktail lounge, conference facilities for 300, sauna, playground, laundry, game room, recreation room, docks. AE, CB, DC, MC, V. Expensive.*

Maxfield Inn. This historic mansion dates from 1841. The front part of the inn dates from the 1860s. The first bottled wine and sherry in the area came from the inn. Many of the old bottles are still in the cellar. High tea is served daily. *105 N. Main St., Naples 14512, tel. 716/374–2510. 6 rooms. Facilities: 3,200-bottle wine cellar; includes breakfast with fresh sticky buns and fruit salad. No credit cards. Moderate.*

The Vagabond. This inn is located high on a secluded hill. The rooms are elegantly furnished; there is one suite with a Jacuzzi. *330 Slitor Rd., Naples 14512, tel. 716/554–6271. 10 rooms with bath. Facilities: pool, full breakfast included. MC, V. Moderate.*

Kellogg's Pan-Tree Inn. This is an economical but comfortable motel on the lake, opposite the park, a swimming beach, and the marina. The rooms are simply furnished. *130 Lake Shore Dr., Canandaigua 14424, tel. 716/394–3909. 15 rooms with bath. Facilities: restaurant, private patios. Open late Apr.–Oct. MC, V. Inexpensive.*

Cayuga Lake Area

Dining **L'Auberge Du Cochon Rouge Restaurant.** This award-winning
★ restaurant in a restored 1840 farmhouse is presided over with the utmost attention to detail and imagination by owner-chef Etienne Merle. The dining rooms have fireplaces and planked floors, and there is even a private dining room for two. Friday nights mean lobster festivals. The wine list is extensive. Specialties include rack of lamb, soufflé Etienne, magret of duck, sweetbreads, and salmon prepared with caviar. The dessert trolley consists of specialties made by the pastry chef and is hard to resist. *1152 Danby Rd., Ithaca, tel. 607/273–3464. Reservations recommended. AE, DC, MC, V. Dinner only. Very Expensive.*

Aurora Inn. Nineteen eighty-eight marked the 155th year of this landmark inn overlooking Cayuga Lake. The menu features fresh seafood, duckling, chicken, steaks, and pork chops. *Main St., Aurora, tel. 315/364–8842. Dress: informal. Closed Jan. and Feb. AE, MC, V. Expensive.*

Oldport Harbour. Ask for one of the dockside tables and dine by the water on seafood flown in daily from Boston. Lunch and dinner cruise boat leaves from dock from spring to early fall. *702 W. Buffalo St., Ithaca, tel. 607/272–4868. Dress: informal. Reservations recommended. AE, DC, MC, V. Expensive.*

The Station Restaurant. This restaurant is a National Historic Landmark. Dine in the reconstructed Lehigh Valley Railroad Passenger Station or on board a real train car. Specialties include prime ribs, fresh seafood, and veal. *806 W. Buffalo St., Ithaca, tel. 607/272–2609. Jackets required. Reservations recommended. Closed Mon. AE, MC, V. Dinner only. Expensive.*

Taughannock Farms Inn. There are four dining rooms in this 1873 Victorian mansion, which overlooks the park and Cayuga

Lake. Multicourse dinners include orange-date bread, minted grapefruit, apricot frappe, a choice of 15 entrees—such all-American fare as roast turkey, duckling, lamb, prime ribs, shrimp, and fresh fish—and a tempting dessert selection. The inn has five guest rooms and serves breakfast to its guests. *State Rd. 89/Gorge Rd., Taughannock Falls State Park, Trumansburg, tel. 607/387–7711. Reservations required. Closed Dec.–Mar. No credit cards. Dinner only. Expensive.*

Turback's. This long-established restaurant—a converted 19th-century mansion filled with Tiffany lamps—is considered the "grande dame of Ithaca." It features regional New York State food. There is a wine shop on the premises. *Rte. 13, Ithaca, tel. 607/272–6484. Reservations recommended. AE, D, MC, V. Dinner only. Expensive.*

Abby's Restaurant. No other restaurant in central New York exemplifies the movement to nouvelle American cuisine better than Abby's. This modest-looking restaurant will appeal to those with sophisticated tastes. Specialties include cape blackfish with multicolored peppers, mako shark teriyaki, and Norwegian salmon prepared on a mesquite grill. *309 Third St., Ithaca, tel. 607/273–1999. Reservations recommended. AE, DC, V. Closed Sun. Moderate.*

Lodging **Rose Inn.** This country inn set amidst 20 acres of apple, spruce, and maple trees, provides guests with such amenities as velour robes. Flowered quilts and antiques brighten the rooms. The mahogany circular staircase is the focal point; it took two years for a master craftsman to complete it. Gourmet dinners are served with prior arrangement. *Auburn Rd., Ithaca 14850, tel. 607/533–4202. 16 rooms with bath. Facilities: Continental breakfast, telephone and TV in living room. AE. Expensive.*

The Statler Hotel. This hotel, a landmark on the Cornell campus, serves as a training ground for students in the School of Hotel Administration. It reopened in March 1989 after extensive renovation. *Cornell University Campus, Ithaca 14853, tel. 800/541–2501 or 607/257–2500. 150 rooms with bath. Facilities: conference center, 3 restaurants, cocktail lounge. AE, MC, V. Expensive.*

Aurora Inn. This 156-year-old landmark on the lake is just down the road from Wells College; guests may use the college's golf course and tennis courts. Some rooms have four-poster beds and antique furnishings. There is a large porch, and the ground-floor sitting rooms feature portraits of early innkeepers and the early days of Wells College. *Main St., Aurora 13026, tel. 315/364–8842. 17 rooms with bath. Facilities: dining room, Continental breakfast included. Closed Jan.–mid-March. AE, MC, V. Moderate–Expensive.*

Ramada Inn and Divi Executive Tower. A large, bustling hotel in the heart of town, this property is packed on football weekends. The rooms are comfortable and newly renovated. *222 S. Cayuga St., Ithaca, tel. 607/272–1000. 177 rooms with bath. Facilities: indoor pool, sauna, cafe, bar, airport transportation. AE, CB, DC, MC, V. Moderate–Expensive.*

Corning–Elmira Area

Dining **Pierce's 1894 Restaurant.** This award-winning family-owned
★ restaurant is located in a big, rambling brick building with Victorian parlors. Fresh flowers grace every table, enhanced by linens, fine silver, and china. The wine list features wines of the

region. Specialties include seafood such as blackened Norwegian salmon and Dover sole, and veal steak with asparagus. *228 Oakwood Ave., Elmira Heights 14903, tel. 607/734–2022. Reservations recommended. AE, D, MC, V. Closed Mon. Dinner only. Expensive.*

Rojo's & The Greenhouse. Rojo's offers casual fare such as quiche, burgers, and onion soup. The dining room is decorated with antiques, and there's an outdoor cafe. The adjacent Greenhouse is a real greenhouse and serves up American fare including veal, seafood, and beef. It's just two blocks from the Glass Center and Market Street. *36 Bridge St., Corning 14830, tel. 607/936–9683 or 607/962–6243. Dress: informal. AE, MC, V. Closed Sun. Moderate–Expensive.*

Sorge's Restaurant. This old-fashioned Italian restaurant, complete with red-and-white-checkered tablecloths, dark-wood paneling, and comfortable atmosphere, serves ample portions of good food. There are daily specials, Friday fish fries, and a pasta buffet. The prices are quite economical. *66-68 Market St., Corning, tel. 607/937–5422. Dress: informal. Reservations recommended. No credit cards. Moderate.*

Taste of China. This popular Corning restaurant is well-known in the Southern Tier. There is an extensive Cantonese/Szechuan menu, and the walls are decorated with Chinese lanterns and murals. *84 E. Market St., Corning, tel. 607/962–6176. Dress: informal. AE, DC, MC, V. Moderate.*

Turf Club. This restaurant, outfitted with a horse-racing Specialties include chateaubriand, steak Diane, and prime ribs. Desserts are baked on the premises. *131 E. Corning Rd., Corning, tel. 607/936–3900. Dress: informal. Reservations recommended. AE, DC, MC, V. Closed. Sun. Dinner only. Moderate.*

Lodging   **Corning Hilton Inn.** Within a short walk of historic Market Street attractions, the Hilton is a focal point of renovated Corning. The rooms are large and comfortable with subdued decor; some are quite elegant. *Denison Pkwy. E, Corning 14830, tel. 607/962–5000. 180 rooms with bath. Facilities: indoor pool, cafe, bar, entertainment. AE, CB, DC, MC, V. Expensive.*

Best Western Lodge on the Green. This is an attractive motor inn about three miles outside of Corning. It's popular with families. There are studio rooms. *Rte. 417 W, Painted Post 14870, tel. 607/962–2456. 135 rooms with bath. Facilities: pool, cafe, bar, meeting rooms. AE, CB, DC, MC, V. Moderate.*

Holiday Inn. About three miles outside of Corning in Painted Post, this property caters largely to families during the summer and school breaks. *304 S. Hamilton St., Painted Post 14870, tel. 607/962–5021. 105 rooms with bath. Facilities: pool, wading pool, cafe, bar, laundry, shop, barber, beauty shop. AE, CB, DC, MC, V. Moderate.*

Rosewood Inn. Each of the six antique-filled rooms in this 1860 three-story Tudor inn is named after a famous Corning area resident, such as Frederick Carder, the genius who founded the Steuben Glass Co., and Benjamin Patterson, Corning's first innkeeper in 1796. The inn is just two blocks from Market Street. *134 E. First St., Corning 14830, tel. 607/962–3253. 6 rooms, 4 with bath. Facilities: TV in common room, full breakfast. DC, MC, V. Moderate.*

Huck Finn Motel. Despite its name, this is a basic modern motel, which started operating long after the tales of Huck Finn were written in the region. The rooms were recently renovated. *Rtes. 14 and 17, Horseheads 14845, tel. 607/739–3807. 40 rooms with bath. Facilities; pool, coffee shop. AE, MC, V. Inexpensive.*

Keuka Lake Area

Dining **Pleasant Valley Inn.** The formal dining rooms in this 19th-century Victorian inn are surrounded by vineyards and the imaginative menu makes full use of local produce and wines. Fresh flowers decorate every table and many corners of the inn. Lunch and dinner are served. *Rte. 54, Bath-Hammondsport Rd., Hammondsport, tel. 607/ 569–2282. Jackets required. Reservations advised. AE, CB, MC, V. Dinner only. Expensive.*

The Vintage. The large picture windows here provide a panorama of the bluff and Keuka Lake; specialties are beef and fresh seafood. There are private docks for diners arriving by boat. This is a particularly popular spot during the summer season. *Rte. 54A between Hammondsport and Branchport 14840, tel. 607/868–3455. Dress: informal. AE, DC, MC, V. Open May–Oct. Expensive.*

Lakeside. Located in an 1881 homestead overlooking Keuka Lake, this is a popular spot with area residents and cottagers, with many a diner arriving by boat. Specialties include seafood, prime rib, and chicken dishes. *Rte. 54A, 7 miles north of Hammondsport, tel. 607/868– 3636. Dress: informal. No reservations. AE, CB, DC, MC, V. Moderate.*

Snug Harbor. This restaurant has a Victorian look both indoors and outdoors. In the summer you can dine outdoors with a view of the lake. Specialties include seafood and prime rib. *Rte. 54A, 1½ mi north of Hammondsport, tel. 607/868–3488. Dress: informal. Reservations for parites of more than 8. MC, V. Moderate.*

Lodging **Pleasant Valley Inn.** This large, rambling Victorian inn with a vineyard just outside the front door has antique-filled rooms and a large elegant dining room. A bottle of wine awaits every guest. *Rte. 54, Bath-Hammondsport Rd., Hammondsport 14840, tel. 607/569–2282. 2 rooms with shared bath. Facilities: full breakfast included. AE, MC, V. Moderate.*

Viking Resort Apartment Motel. The range of accommodations makes this resort appealing to families: apartments, housekeeping cottages, and studio units with kitchens. Many rooms have wood paneling and a rustic feeling. A large yacht gives cruises on the lake for a small fee. There are also free rowboats and a large expanse of lake frontage. *680 E. Lake Rd., Penn Yan 14527, tel. 315/536–7061. 38 units with bath, including apartments and cottages. Facilities: pool, sauna, hot tub. No credit cards. Open Apr.–Oct. Moderate.*

Colonial Motel. This quiet motel, just down the road from Keuka College, has boat rentals and is near swimming facilities. The rooms have kitchenettes. *175 Lower Lake Rd., Penn Yan 14527, tel. 315/536–3056. 16 rooms with bath. Facilities: boat rentals, kitchens. AE, MC, V. Weekly rates available. Inexpensive.*

Vinehurst Motel. An otherwise basic motel, the Vinehurst has a distinguishing feature—it's surrounded by vineyards. The effect can be quite heady in the fall when the grapes hang heavy on the vines. *Rte. 54, Hammondsport 14840, tel. 607/569–2300. 32 rooms with bath. MC, V. Inexpensive.*

Letchworth State Park Area

Dining and **Genesee Falls Inn.** This 110-year-old inn a half-mile from the
Lodging south entrance of Letchworth State Park was recently renovated. The guest rooms are done up in old-fashioned flowered
wallpaper and antiques. There are also five modern rooms in an
adjoining motel unit. The public areas and bar are filled with
19th-century memorabilia. The fare in the Victorian-style dining room is all-American: roast duckling, steak, chicken, and
ham. There's also an informal coffee shop for breakfast and
lunch. Bread and desserts are made on the premises. *Rte. 436,
Portageville 14536, tel. 716/493–2484. 10 rooms with bath, 2
with shared bath. 5 in inn and 5 in motel. Facilities: bar, coffee
shop, dining room. Restaurant: dress informal. Reservations
advised. No credit cards. Closed Jan. Moderate.*

★ **Glen Iris Inn.** This inn was home of Buffalo industrialist and
philanthropist William Pryor Letchworth, who donated the
lands that became Letchworth State Park in 1910. The rooms,
each named for one of the species of trees that abound in the
park, are simply furnished. The telephone is available in the
private lounge on the second floor, which contains some of
Letchworth's furniture. Rooms here are often fully booked several years in advance during the fall foliage season. The dining
room features specialties such as chicken Chesapeake (breast
filled with crab and spinach), prime rib, scallops *anaspassia*,
and veal. Finger Lakes wines are featured. *Letchworth State
Park, Castile 14427, tel. 716/493–2622. 22 rooms with bath, 15
in inn and 7 in nearby motel. Facilities: dining room, gift shop,
organized park activities including nature hikes, pools, fishing, hunting in season. Jacket for dinner. Reservations
advised, especially in fall. AE, MC, V. Moderate.*

Rochester Area

Dining **Chapels.** The former criminal detention pen in the Rochester
★ City Hall has been transformed into an ultrasophisticated restaurant where diners are greeted by liveried waiters and a
wine steward. There are three rooms with vaulted brick ceilings and walls. A small sign is a tipoff to the dining experience:
It reads "Cuisine Du Marché," or food of the market. The menu
is based on whatever is fresh at the market that day and
changes with the seasons. Among the specialties: Veal sweet-
bread pasta with white truffles, sea bass fillets with escargot
and peppers, and rosettes of beef with mustard, green beans,
and lyonnaise potatoes. The extensive wine list includes area
wines. *30 W. Broad St., Rochester, tel. 716/232–2300. Jackets
required. Reservations recommended. Closed Sun. Dinner
only Sat. AE, CB, DC, MC, V. Very Expensive.*
Edwards Restaurant. There are leaded-glass windows from a
synagogue, tapestries from a Presbyterian church, oak paneling from a Catholic seminary, and George Eastman's hunting
trophies in this Victorian-style edifice, which was built in 1873
as the Rochester Free Academy. Dining areas include the Hunt
Room, Pontchartrain Room, Tapestry Room, English Library
Room and the crimson and black Oriental Room. The menu includes such imaginative dishes as scallops Parisienne, shrimp
Emanuel, sautéed venison, stuffed quail, mako shark, chicken
veronique, and beef Wellington with mushroom pâté. *13 S.
Fitzhugh St., Rochester, tel. 716/423–0140. Jackets required.*

Reservations recommended. Dinner only Sat. Closed Sun. AE, CB, DC, MC, V. Expensive.

Richardson's Canal House. This restored original Erie Canal tavern (on the national register), has a patio where you can dine outdoors for lunch in warm weather. Fixed-price selections include duckling, seafood, and beef tenderloin. There's folk music on Friday nights. *1474 Marsh Rd., Pittsford, tel. 716/248–5000. Jackets required. Reservations recommended. Closed Sun. Dinner only Sat. AE, CB, DC, MC, V. Expensive.* The Canal House also runs **Oliver Loud's Inn,** an old restored stagecoach inn on the canal with 8 rooms, each with a private bath and telephone. Full cable television is available upon request. *1474 March Rd., Pittsford, tel. 716/248–5200.*

Spring House. This four-story brick house in Southern Colonial style was once an Erie Canal inn and has been serving food to hungry travelers since 1822. The house specials include prime ribs, steaks, and seafood, and all pastries and breads are baked on the premises. *3001 Monroe Ave., Rochester, tel. 716/586–2300. Jackets requested. Reservations recommended. Closed Mon. Lunch Tues.–Fri., dinner Tues.–Sun., brunch Sun. AE, MC, V. Expensive.*

Victor Milling Company. Housed in an old mill, this restaurant is a favorite dining spot for people in the Rochester area. The cozy atmosphere is accentuated by an open hearth. Specialties include lamb chops, seafood bisque, chicken dishes, and salads. *75 Coville St., Victor, tel. 716/924–4049. Reservations recommended. Closed Sun. MC, V. Moderate.*

Crescent Beach Hotel. This replica of a Victorian hotel boasts a lovely garden and a patio overlooking the lake. Specialties include seafood and prime ribs. There's dancing here on Friday and Saturday. *1372 Edgemere Dr., Rochester, tel. 716/227–3600. Dress: informal. Reservations recommended. Closed Jan. and Feb. AE, MC, V. Moderate.*

Daisy Flour Mill. A restored mill, dating from 1848, alongside a stream, this restaurant is filled with old mill artifacts and antiques. It specializes in veal, game, and fresh seafood. *1880 Blossom Rd., Rochester, tel. 716/381–1880. Jackets required. Reservations recommended. Dinner only. AE, CB, DC, MC, V. Moderate.*

Lodging **Holiday Inn-Genesee Plaza.** This large, luxurious Holiday Inn is connected to the new Convention Center. The top floors have a good view of the Genesse River and the falls. *120 Main St., Rochester, 14604, tel. 716/546–6400. 467 rooms with bath. Facilities: pool, airport transportation, restaurant, bar, entertainment, laundry. AE, CB, DC, MC, V. Very Expensive.*

Stouffer Rochester Plaza. This is a large luxury hotel and is centrally located on a city park along the Genesee River. The rooms are also large and well designed. *70 State St., Rochester 14616, tel. 716/546–3450. 364 rooms with bath. Facilities: pool, restaurant, bars, meeting rooms, airport transportation, luxury level with private lounge, complimentary breakfast. AE, CB, DC, MC, V. Very Expensive.*

Strathallan. Located in a quiet, residential neighborhood, this hotel started life as an apartment house; there are one- and two-bedroom suites as well as one room that converts to a three-bedroom suite. The rooms are large and nicely furnished, many have balconies. *550 East Ave., Rochester 14607, tel. 716/461–5010. 155 rooms with bath. Facilities: bar, restaurant,*

meeting rooms, entertainment, airport transportation, sauna, activities room, solarium. *AE, CB, DC, MC, V. Very
Expensive.*

Genesee Country Inn. Once a mill, dating from 1830, with two-
foot-thick walls, this inn is about a 20-minute drive from Rochester and about a half-mile from the Genesee Country Village
and Museum (*see* Exploring). It's located on six acres of woods,
waterfalls, and ponds with resident ducks and trout. Antiques
and period reproductions give guest rooms an authentic touch,
and many of the rooms also feature hand stencils. A guest book
in each room invites comments, and they are uniformly enthusiastic. Afternoon teas are served. *948 George St., Mumford,
14511, tel. 716/538–2500. 10 rooms with bath. Facilities: small
meeting rooms, full breakfast included. AE, DC, MC, V. Moderate.*

Rose Mansion and Gardens. A country inn in the middle of the
city. This property is set behind a stone wall on five acres of
gardens and orchards. In 1867, the horticulturist George
Ellwanger enlarged what originally was a simple farmstead
and gave it its present-day Tudor style. There are five fireplaces, a grand piano, oak paneling, book-filled cases, and a
most imposing, working Hooks & Hasting pipe organ (circa
1883) on the staircase landing. Each room is named after a rose
and has Victorian-era antiques; three have working fireplaces.
Most of the bathrooms, though modernized, contain original
fixtures. *625 Mt. Hope Ave., Rochester 14616, tel. 716/546–
5426. 10 rooms with bath. Facilities: Continental breakfast included. AE, MC, V. Expensive.*

Seneca Lake Area

Dining
★
Belhurst Castle. This elegant 100-year-old Romanesque mansion is located on the shores of Seneca Lake. Some of the dining
rooms have fireplaces, and all are trimmed with intricately
carved woodwork. During the summer months the terrace is
open for dining. The chef is an avid hunter who prepares such
game dishes as venison and pheasant in season. Other specialties include veal Oscar, rack of lamb, and veal piccata. *Box 609,
Geneva, tel. 315/781–0201. Jackets required. Reservations recommended. AE, CB, DC, MC, V. Expensive.*

The Dresden. Located near the lake in the heart of fishing country, this local favorite has a wood-paneled dining room and
large picture windows. Specialties include king crab and prime
rib. *Rtes. 14 and 54, Dresden, tel. 315/536–9023. Dress: informal. Closed Mon. No credit cards. Moderate.*

Wing Tai Oriental Restaurant. The dining rooms are decorated
with Chinese murals. The extensive menu features Cantonese,
Hunan, and Szechuan dishes and there's a large selection of
Finger Lakes wines. *Castle and Main Sts., Geneva, tel. 315/
789–8892. Dress: informal. Closed Sun. AE, MC, V. Moderate.*

Pumpernickel. This friendly, casual dining spot features
homestyle cooking: fried chicken, fried fish, homemade breads
and desserts. The food's good and a bargain, too. *825
Canandaigua Rd., Geneva, tel. 315/789–9655. Dress: informal. Closed Wed. No credit cards. Inexpensive.*

Lodging
★
Belhurst Castle. This unique inn where the guests are trans-
ported back into a luxurious, gilded age was built by noted
architect Albert W. Fuller—it took 50 workmen, laboring six

days a week, four years (1885 to 1889) to complete this fantasy for the original owner, Carrie Harron Collins. Its current owners have renovated the rooms with care and style: A spigot on the second floor dispenses local wines—free to guests. One suite, a former Victorian dancing room, has an 18-foot-high ceiling, a sauna with a window overlooking the lake, a porch, a spiral staircase leading to a turret, a large living room, and equally enormous bedrooms. All the rooms have modern bathrooms, TV, and telephones; many have working fireplaces. Throughout, there is intricately carved oak, cherry, and mahogany, and more stained glass than in many churches. *Box 609, Geneva 14456, tel. 315/781–0201. 12 rooms with bath. Facilities: dining room, swimming and boating in lake, 25 acres landscaped grounds. AE, CB, DC, MC, V. Very Expensive.*

Historic James Russell Webster Inn. Hosts Leonard and Barbara Cohen welcome the discriminating traveler to their home. The inn, an 1845 Georgian mansion full of antiques, has two suites, one in the Palladian, and one in the Italianate style. Dinners are special occasions. The prix fixe menus often feature duck, lobster, veal, and salmon. Those coming to dinner are requested to make reservations several days in advance, since every meal is personally planned and designed. *115 East Main St., Waterloo 13165, tel. 315/539–3032. Reservations required. MC, V. Very Expensive.*

★ **Geneva-on-the-Lake.** This three-story lakeside mansion, listed on the National Registry of Historic Places, was built in 1911 by malt tycoon Byron Nester after a 16th-century villa in Frascati, near Rome. Since then it has been a Capuchin monastery, an apartment complex, and now an elegant, all-suite resort. Each suite is decorated distinctively and stocked with local wine, coffee, and fresh fruit. Several suites have working fireplaces. There are 10 acres of formal gardens and a large pool lined with classic statuary, pillars, and urns. The elegant Lancellotti dining room serves up fine Continental dinners while violinists and singers provide background musical entertainment. A variety of weekend specials are offered throughout the year. Friday night wine-and-cheese parties and Sunday night buffets are included in the weekend plans. *1001 Lochland Rd., Geneva 14456, tel. 315/789–7190. 29 suites with bath and kitchens. Facilities: Continental breakfast included, pool, dock with marina nearby, dining room. AE, MC, V. Very Expensive.*

Rainbow Cove Motel. This attractive motel's chief asset is its lakeside location. Though the rooms are standard, there's a gently sloping bathing beach, docks, and marina. There's even a diving school. The restaurant serves home-style cooking and has large picture windows with views of the lake. *Rte. 14, Himrod, tel. 607/243-7535. 24 rooms with bath. Facilities: game room, recreation and meeting hall, pool, docks, marina, scuba school, dining room. AE, MC, V. Open May–Oct. Inexpensive.*

Skaneateles Lake Area

Dining **Krebs.** This 1899 landmark is operated by the third generation of the founding family. The seven-course dinners are what made Krebs famous, but there are lighter meals for those with smaller appetites. Specialties include prime ribs, lobster Newburg, and broiled chicken. Bread and desserts are baked on the premises. There's a formal English garden and Early

American decor with antiques throughout. *53 W. Genesee St., Skaneateles, tel. 315/685–5714. Jackets required. Reservations required. AE, CB, DC, MC, V. Open May–Oct. Dinner daily, brunch Sun. Expensive.*

Mandana Inn. Serving travelers since 1835, this inn is decorated with Colonial-era antiques. Boston scrod, fresh lobster, and home-baked cheesecake are featured on the menu. *Rte. 41A, 6 miles south of Skaneateles, tel. 315/685–7798. Jackets required. Reservations recommended. AE, CB, DC, MC, V. Closed Jan.–Mar., also closed Tues. Dinner only. Expensive.*

★ **Sherwood Inn.** Originally a stagecoach stop (in 1807) this inn overlooks the lake, and the tables on the porch are a must on hot summer nights, since the inn has no air-conditioning. The decor in each of the several dining rooms is Early American, and there are plants, fresh flowers, white linens, and candles all about. Specialties include veal *rollatini*, prime ribs, and duckling bathed in a orange liqueur sauce. *26 W. Genesee St., Skaneateles, tel. 315/685–3405. Jackets required. Reservations recommended. AE, CB, DC, MC, V. Expensive.*

Doug's Fish Fry. People come here from miles around for fresh seafood—trucked in daily from Boston. The fish fries are a real bargain, and the chowder legendary. *8 Jordan St., Skaneateles, tel. 315/685–3288. Dress: informal. No credit cards. Moderate.*

Syracuse Area

Dining　**Pascale Wine Bar & Restaurant.** This historic Victorian town house, dating from 1875, is graced with period decor and antiques. There's an extensive wine list which includes Finger Lakes wines, available by the glass. The equally imaginative menu features saddle of venison, duckling, fingerling trout, and crab sautée à la Provencale. Everything baked on the premises. *304 Hawley Ave., Syracuse, tel. 315/471–3040. Jackets required. Reservations recommended. Closed Sun. AE, CB, DC, MC, V. Dinner only. Very Expensive.*

Glen Loch Mill. A converted feed mill (1870) set in a glen next to a waterwheel provides the setting for this special restaurant. There's entertainment on Friday and Saturday nights, and outdoor dining during the warm weather. Specialties include Norwegian *caulviac* and prime ribs. All baking is done on the premises. *4626 North St., Jamesville, 10 miles south of Syracuse, tel. 315/469–6969. Jackets required. Reservations recommended. AE, DC, MC, V. Expensive.*

Poseidon. This restaurant has the atmosphere and decor of a Mediterranean island cafe. Dishes are prepared at tableside and include souvlaki, red snapper, and veal. All baking is done on the premises. There's also a pianist. *770 St. James St., Syracuse, tel. 315/472–4474. Jackets required. Reservations recommended. Closed Sun. AE, CB, DC, MC, V. Expensive.*

Coleman's Authentic Irish Pub & Restaurant. Situated in the heart of a firmly entrenched Irish neighborhood, this pub is like a bit of the Old Sod: Menu items are written in both English and Gaelic, and green is the regulation color. Menu items include Irish soda bread, soups, and seafood. *100 S. Lowell Ave., Syracuse, tel. 315/476–1933. Dress: informal. AE, DC, MC, V. Moderate.*

Ichiban. Dinner at the Ichiban is both a meal and entertainment. Every dish is prepared tableside by a master chef on a hibachi. There is a traditional sushi bar. *602 Old Liverpool Rd., Liverpool, tel. 315/457–0000. Reservations recommended. MC, V. Dinner only. Moderate.*

Sterio's Landmark. Housed in the historic Gridley Building, dating from 1869, this restaurant features fin-de-siècle decor; there's also an outdoor dining area. Specialties include rack of lamb, chateaubriand, and fresh seafood. Open for dinner and breakfast. *103 E. Water St., Syracuse, tel. 315/472–8883. Jackets required. Reservations recommended. Closed Sun. AE, CB, DC, MC, V. Moderate.*

Lodging   **Sheraton University Inn & Conference Center.** If you want to be in the center of university life, this is the place to stay. Rates often go up during special university events. There are conference facilities here, so it's a popular meeting spot, particularly the lobby. Rooms are large and attractive. *801 University Ave., Syracuse 13210, tel. 315/475–3000. 232 rooms with bath. Facilities: indoor pool, bar, dining room, entertainment, gift shop, health club, tennis and golf privileges. AE, CB, DC, MC, V. Very Expensive.*

Hilton at Syracuse Square. This large, modern property in the center of the city attracts a meetings-and-conventions crowd. It is connected to, and shares facilities with, the older Hotel Syracuse. The plant-filled lobby is bright and bustling. Rooms are spacious. *500 S. Warren St., Syracuse 13202, tel. 315/422–5121. 201 rooms with bath. Facilities: dining room, garage, bar, nightclub, shopping arcade, barber, beauty shop, game room, indoor tennis, and health club privileges. AE, CB, DC, MC, V. Expensive.*

Holiday Inn-University Area. Downtown and close to Syracuse University, this hotel is popular for conferences and for those attending sports events at the university's Carrier Dome. *701 E. Genesee St., Syracuse 13210, tel. 315/474–7251. 290 rooms with bath. Facilities: indoor pool, sauna, restaurant, bar. AE, DC, MC, V. Moderate.*

Hotel Syracuse at Syracuse Square. This is an older, traditional center-city hotel that connects to the adjacent Hilton. Together, they serve as a focal point in downtown Syracuse. All public areas have been renovated and outfitted with comfortable chairs, plants, and a restaurant that spills out into the lobby. The simply furnished rooms are on the smallish side. *500 S. Warren St., Syracuse 13202, tel. 315/422–5121. 525 rooms with bath. Facilities: dining room, nightclub, entertainment, garage, 5 two-bedroom units. AE, DC, MC, V. Moderate.*

★ **Sherwood Inn.** An inn has stood on this spot overlooking the lake since 1807, and the present property, named after the first innkeeper, dates back 100 years. The rooms, many of which have lake views, have been renovated and are decorated with antiques. There are no TVs or telephones in the rooms, but all the baths are modern. The bridal suite has a large canopy bed and a sitting room. Several rooms are doubles with a connecting bathroom. *26 W. Genesee St., Skaneateles 13152, 315/685–3405. 16 rooms with bath. Facilities: dining room, bar, Continental breakfast included, public beach opposite, boat rentals. AE, CB, DC, MC, V. Moderate.*

Bird's Nest. This economical motel near the lake is popular with families. There are outdoor picnic tables and grills, and some rooms have refrigerators. The rooms are decorated simply. There are some honeymoon suites. *E. Genesee Rd., Skanteales 13152, tel. 315/685–5641. 28 rooms with bath, 3 with kitchens.*

Facilities: pool, playground, duck pond. Open year-round. AE, CB, DC, MC, V. Inexpensive.

Red Roof Inn. This motel delivers just what it promises: a clean, economical place to spend the night. *6614 N. Thompson Rd., Syracuse 13206, (Thruway Exit 35 at Carrier Circle), tel. 315/437-3309. 115 rooms with bath. Facilities: adjacent restaurant. AE, DC, D, MC, V. Inexpensive.*

Campgrounds Because of the traditionally cold winters, camping facilities generally are open only from April or May until October. However, several are open year-round. A number of state and county parks have camping facilities, and there are also some private campgrounds. The selected campgrounds listed below offer full hookup, laundry, and sanitary facilities:

Canandaigua KOA, 5374 Farmington Rd., Canandaigua, tel. 716/398-3582. 120 sites. Facilities: swimming, fishing, children's area, recreation building, restaurant, store. Open Apr.–Nov.

Cayuga Lake State Park, 2664 Lower Lake Rd., Seneca Falls, tel. 315/568-5163. 286 sites. Facilities: swimming, fishing, launching ramp, recreation building, children's area. Open May–Oct.

Hamlin Beach State Park, 2 miles west of Rte. 19, Hamlin, tel. 716/964-2121. 264 sites. Facilities: swimming, fishing, boat launching ramp, camp store, recreation building, children's area. $10. Open Apr.–Oct.

Keuka Lake State Park, Rte. 54A, Bluffpoint, tel. 315/536-3666. 150 sites. Facilities: swimming, fishing, boat launching area, children's area. $9. Open May–Sept.

Letchworth State Park, Rte. 19A, Castile, tel. 716/493-2611. 270 sites. Facilities: swimming, fishing, children's area, recreation building. $10. Open May–Oct.

Watkins Glen State Park, Rte. 14, Watkins Glen, tel. 607/535-4511. 303 sites. Facilities: swimming, fishing, children's area. $10. Open Jun.–Sept.

The Arts

Except for the colleges and universities with on-campus music and theater programs, the arts scene is largely centered in Rochester and Syracuse during the winter season.

Music

Rochester Philharmonic Orchestra (100 East Ave., tel. 716/222-5000) is one of the country's major orchestras and plays at the Eastman Theatre. During the summer the orchestra's home is Finger Lakes Performing Arts Center in Canandaigua (tel. 716/454-7091).

Eastman School of Music (Gibbs and E. Main Sts., Rochester, tel. 716/275-3111) also performs at the Eastman Theatre (above). Part of the University of Rochester, it is one of the nation's most prestigious schools of music and presents concerts and recitals.

Syracuse Symphony Orchestra (Civic Center of Onondaga County, tel. 315/424-8222) is a major symphony orchestra that performs in the Civic Center of Onondaga County, an unusual building complex combining a performing arts center with government offices.

Theater

Several theaters in the area present entertainment from plays to concerts, some of which are geared for the tourist season.

GeVa Theatre (Woodbury Blvd. & Clinton Ave., Rochester, tel. 716/232–1363) is Rochester's only resident professional theater. It stages eight productions a year in a renovated historic building that also houses a cabaret. Sunday brunch is served.
Masonic Temple & Auditorium Theater (875 E. Main St., Rochester, tel. 716/454–7743) offers touring Broadway productions, concerts, and solo artists.
Downstairs Cabaret (151 St. Paul St., Rochester, tel. 716/262–2300) is Rochester's only professional Equity musical theater.
Salt City for the Performing Arts (601 S. Crouse Ave., Syracuse, tel. 315/474–1122) presents drama, comedy, and musicals.
The **Syracuse Area Landmark Theater** (362 S. Salina St., Syracuse, tel. 315/475–7979) provides facilities for concerts, plays, dances, and classic movies in a National Historic Landmark building (circa 1928) filled with carvings, gold leaf, and ornate decorations.
Syracuse Stage (820 E. Genesee St., Regent Theater Complex, Syracuse, tel. 315/443–3275) is Syracuse's professional theater company.
Samuel L. Clemens Performing Arts Center (Clemens Center Pkwy. and Gray St., Elmira, tel. 607/734–8191) presents theater, dance, jazz, and classical artists year-round.
Smith Opera House for the Performing Arts (82 Seneca St., Geneva, tel. 315/789–2221) presents year-round professional and amateur productions and films in a historic 1,500-seat theater.
Corning Summer Theater (Glass Center, Corning, tel. 607/974–8271) presents professional companies during July and August in the Center's auditorium.

10 Niagara Falls, Buffalo, and Chautauqua

Introduction

Cynics have had a field day with Niagara Falls, calling it everything from "water on the rocks" to "the second major disappointment of American married life" (Oscar Wilde).

Others have been more positive. Missionary and explorer Louis Hennepin, whose books were widely read across Europe, first described the falls in 1678 as "an incredible Cataract or Waterfall which has no equal." Nearly two centuries later, novelist Charles Dickens wrote, "I seemed to be lifted from the earth and to be looking into Heaven. Niagara was at once stamped upon my heart, an image of beauty, to remain there changeless and indelible."

Writer Henry James recorded in 1883 how one stands there "gazing your fill at the most beautiful object in the world." And a half-century later, British author Vita Sackville-West wrote to Sir Harold Nicolson, "Niagara is really some waterfall! It falls over like a great noisy beard made of cotton-wool, veiled by spray and spanned by rainbows. The rainbows are the most unexpected part of it. They stand across like bridges between American and Canada, and are reproduced in sections along the boiling foam. The spray rises to the height of a sky-scraper, shot by sudden iridescence high up in the air."

Understandably, all these rave reviews began to bring out the professional daredevils, as well as the self-destructive amateurs. In 1859 the great French tightrope walker Blondin walked across the Niagara Gorge, from the American to the Canadian side, on a three-inch-thick rope. On his shoulders was his reluctant, terrified manager; on both shores stood some 100,000 spectators. "Thank God it is over!" exclaimed the future King Edward VII of England, after the completion of the walk. "Please never attempt it again."

But sadly, others did. From the early 18th century, dozens went over in boats, rubber balls, and those famous barrels. Not a single one survived, until schoolteacher Annie Taylor did in 1901. Emerging from her barrel, she asked the touching question, "Did I go over the falls yet?" The endless stunts were finally outlawed in 1912, but nothing stops the determined: In 1985 two stuntmen survived a plunge, and two years later, someone who had conquered the falls mastered the rapids below the falls.

Besides daredevils, the other things that spring to mind at the mention of Niagara are honeymoons and suicides. The first honeymooners arrived in 1803: Jerome Bonaparte (brother of Emperor Napoleon) and his bride, the daughter of a prosperous Baltimore merchant. On a grand tour of the Northeast, the newlyweds stayed a week, inaugurating a tradition. And although Bonaparte himself was an unsavory sort, he had the aura of royalty, prompting thousands of American couples to imitate him. Oscar Wilde's vituperations notwithstanding, by the mid-1800s honeymoons at Niagara had become quite the rage. They were a definite status symbol for young couples. There was even a popular mid-19th-century song:

"Oh the lovers come a thousand miles
They leave their home and mother
Yet when they reach Niagara Falls
They only see each other."

The dark side to the Niagara picture is that it attracts those bent on suicide. Telephones manned by trained counselors are situated at strategic spots near the brink, and some would-be suicides have been saved by a call.

Part of the longest unfortified border in the world, the falls are actually three cataracts: the American and Bridal Veil Falls, in New York State, and the Horseshoe Falls in Ontario. The falls are responsible for the invention of alternating electric current, and they drive one of the world's largest hydroelectric developments. And it really is all that water (more than 700,000 gallons per second in the summer) on its way from four of the Great Lakes—Superior, Michigan, Huron, and Erie—to the fifth, Ontario, that makes Niagara what it is: the most accessible and famous waterfall in the world. There may be taller cataracts in Africa, South America, and even elsewhere in New York State, but the sheer size and tremendous volume of Niagara are unsurpassed.

As with many other geographic features, Niagara's origins are glacial. More than 10,000 years before the first inscription, "My Parents Visited Niagara Falls and All They Got Me Was This Lousy T-Shirt," the glaciers receded, diverting the waters of Lake Erie northward into Lake Ontario. (Before that, they had drained south; such are the fickle ways of nature.)

There has been considerable erosion since, more than seven miles in all, as the soft shale and sandstone of the escarpment have been washed away. Wisely, there have been major water diversions for a generating station (1954) and other machinations (1954–1963), which have spread the flow more evenly over the entire crestline of Horseshoe Falls. The erosion is now down to as little as one foot every decade. At that rate it will be some 130,000 years before the majestic cascade is reduced to an impressive rapids somewhere near present-day Buffalo, 20 miles to the south.

For many Americans, Buffalo has an unjust reputation as the Blizzard Capital of the United States. At least once a year it seems to crop up on television news spots about winter whiteouts and wicked windchill factors. Despite the fact that the heaviest snowfall is where the people want it—in ski country south of Buffalo—and that recent winters have been remarkably mild (snow had to be imported for the city's winter festival in 1987 and 1988), Buffalo's snowy image persists. The snows are caused in part by the city's location on Lake Erie, but the lake also acts as a giant air conditioner in the summer. Days are warm, but seldom excessively so. Once a depressed, industrial city, it is now undergoing a major regeneration. Buffalo is home to the nation's only inland naval park and has a splendid new baseball stadium in the heart of a rebuilding downtown. The waterfront has been undergoing a renewal, and the acres of undeveloped lake frontage hold the promise of a transformation on a grand scale.

Buffalo is a city of Victorian and turn-of-the-century elegance, a city of taverns and churches, a place with a strong ethnic tradition. It has the largest St. Patrick's Day Parade west of New

York City and the biggest Pulaski Day Parade, a celebration of Polish heritage, east of Chicago.

Though Buffalo is the state's second-largest city, it is definitely "small town" when compared to its glamorous downstate sister. Friendliness and affordability are its selling points. Distances aren't great and it's easy to get around. The city has a distinct style, a product of its rich ethnic, cultural, and architectural heritage.

The focal point for most visitors to Chautauqua County, which follows the shores of Lake Erie south of Buffalo to the border of Pennsylvania, is the Chautauqua Institution. The center for arts, education, religion, and recreation, founded in 1874, today has a full complement of schools and day camps, a lecture series, and performances in its 6,000-seat amphitheater. At nearby Cassadaga Lake is the Lily Dale Assembly, a spiritualist center begun in 1879, which still attracts mediums and the psychically curious. Other highlights of a visit to the region include the Amish community in the Conewango Valley; the ski resorts of Ellicottville; tours and tastings at area wineries; Fredonia, one-time Seed Capital of the United States; and Westfield, the self-proclaimed Grape Juice Capital of the world and home to Welch's Foods.

The county takes its name from its largest lake, which is 22 miles long and was called "Jad-dah-gwah" by the Indians. French explorers landed on the Lake Erie shores of the Chautauqua area in 1679. Their quest was for a southward passage to the Ohio and Mississippi rivers, and the route connecting Lake Erie with Chautauqua Lake, known as the Portage Trail, offered an answer. Indeed, the dispute between France and England over possession of this trail led to the French and Indian War.

In 1874 John Heyl Vincent, a Methodist minister, and Lewis Miller, an industrialist, established a training center for Sunday-school teachers on the shores of Chautauqua Lake. The Chautauqua Institution rapidly grew into a summer-long cultural encampment, and tent-show proprietors crisscrossed the country with their own versions of Chautauqua's lectures, drama, and music. The Chautauqua circuit faded into history, but the institution is now well into its second century.

The institution offers an unusual mix of arts, education, religion, and recreation during the nine-week summer season. Nine U.S. presidents, from Ulysses S. Grant to Gerald Ford, have delivered addresses here. Other notables have included Leo Tolstoy, William Jennings Bryan, and Amelia Earhart. In 1985 the institution hosted the first in a series of conferences on U.S.–Soviet relations. Two years later, more than 200 Soviet citizens came to Chautauqua and lived with American families for a week.

Chautauqua County is the largest American grape-growing area outside of California; its vineyards produce more Concord grapes than any other area in the country. The 50-mile drive from Silver Creek to Ripley, along the shores of Lake Erie, is known as the Chautauqua Wine Trail. Along the route are five wineries, roadside fruit and produce stands, and antiques shops.

Arriving and Departing

By Plane   Greater Buffalo International Airport is the primary point of entry by air for the Buffalo–Niagara Falls area. The Niagara Falls Airport, which failed to make a go of regularly scheduled service, currently handles military and charter planes. Buffalo's airport is served by USAir, American, United, Northwest, Continental, Pan Am Express, Enterprise, Mall, and Delta. In the Chautauqua area, USAir serves the Jamestown airport, which is 16 miles from Chautauqua. USAir, American, United, Northwest, Continental, Pan Am Express, and Enterprise serve the Buffalo Airport. With advance reservations, limousines meet planes in Buffalo for the $50 round-trip ride to the Chautauqua Institution. Contact **Chautauqua Limousine** (tel. 716/753–7010) or **Care-Van** (tel. 716/665–6535 or 716/688–1162).

Between the Airport and Niagara Falls and Buffalo   Shuttle buses between the Buffalo airport and major hotels in Niagara Falls are operated by **Niagara Scenic Bus Lines, Inc.** (tel. 716/648–1500 or 716/282–7755). The one-hour shuttle runs from 8:30 AM to 8:30 PM; fare $8 each way. Taxi service to Niagara Falls is also available; fare, $30. It is about 10 miles from the airport to downtown Buffalo, and average taxi fares are $15. Many hotels have their own shuttle buses, with free phones by the baggage area in both the airport's terminals. The **Niagara Frontier Transportation Authority** (NFTA) MetroBus also provides bus service with a fare of $1.20.

By Train   **Amtrak** has two connecting stations in Buffalo: 75 Exchange St., downtown (tel. 716/856–2075) and 55 Dick Rd., Cheektowaga, south of the airport (tel. 716/683–8440). The Amtrak station in Niagara Falls is at Hyde Park Boulevard and Lockport Road (tel. 716/285–4224 or 800/877–7245).

By Bus   **Greyhound** (181 Ellicott St., tel. 716/855–7511) operates from the Ellicott Street Bus Terminal in Buffalo and the Niagara Falls Transportation Center, 4th and Niagara Streets in Niagara Falls.

In the Chautauqua area, Jamestown and Fredonia are served by **Greyhound** (tel. 716/485–7541), **Blue Bird Coach Lines** (tel. 716/484–1900), and **D&F Transit** (tel. 716/485–7541). Limousine and taxi service is available to the Chautauqua Institution via **City Air Bus Ltd.** (tel. 716/489–3470).

Chautauqua Area Regional Transit System (CARTS) operates two round-trip buses daily between Jamestown and Westfield. The system may be used for shopping trips or to make travel connections. Call collect, tel. 716/665–6466. The Institution provides free shuttle-bus service from 9 AM to 9 PM. **Jamestown Area Regional Transit System** (JARTS) (tel. 716/664–2805) buses leave Jamestown hourly, starting at 9 AM. Buses circle the lake, stopping at various points, including the institution.

By Car   Access from the east, west, and south is primarily via I–90, the New York State Thruway. The expressway spur, I–190, leads from I–90 at Buffalo, across Grand Island to the Robert Moses Parkway into Niagara Falls. Approaches from the west and north are via a number of highways in Canada, including the Queen Elizabeth Way with three bridges funneling traffic stateside. Highways leading to Buffalo from the south are U.S. 219 from Ellicottville and Route 400 from South Wales, both of which connect with I–90.

Getting Around

The major sights in Niagara Falls can be easily reached on foot. Although most people arrive by car, it is best to park the car and just walk.

By Subway NFTA MetroRail provides light rail rapid transit service in Buffalo. The system is above and below ground. The above-ground portion is free; the fare to go underground is 80¢, and tickets must be purchased at the stations. Bus-to-train or train-to-bus transfers are free. Each station is decorated with original paintings, photography, or sculpture. For information, tel. 716/855–7211.

By Bus NFTA provides bus service within the Buffalo area, including Niagara Falls. The fare is $1 within both cities; $1.35 between cities; 40¢ children 5–12, under 5 free. Bus-to-bus transfers are 5¢; exact fare is required. Buses generally operate 5AM–12:30 AM. For information, tel. 716/855–7211.

By Taxi Taxi rates in Buffalo are $2.25 to start and $1 for each additional mile. Taxi rates in Niagara Falls are $1 for the first tenth of a mile and 10¢ for each tenth of a mile thereafter.

Scenic Drives

Niagara Parkway Thirty-five miles of perfectly maintained parkland, this highway follows the Niagara River from Ft. Erie, Ontario (across from Buffalo) to Niagara Falls and on to Niagara-on-the-Lake. The stretch from Queenston to Niagara-on-the-Lake is particularly agreeable, with lovely homes and farms, vineyards, and orchards along the riverbank.

Robert Moses Parkway This is the most scenic route to Niagara Falls from Grand Island. Continue on the parkway to Lewiston and Youngstown along the Niagara River.

Route 20A from East Aurora Heading east through rolling hills and charming dairy farms, this drive is especially worthwhile in the fall.

Routes 430 and 394 The drive around Chautauqua Lake is particularly beautiful during the early fall, but spring and summer also offer splendid views of the lake, hills, and boats across the water.

Route 62 Drivers who follow this route through the Conewango Valley near Jamestown are likely to be slowed down by the numerous horse-drawn carriages, the mode of transportation for the Amish people who live in the valley; but this will afford you more opportunity to relish the scenery.

Important Addresses and Numbers

Tourist Information The **Niagara Falls Tourism Information Center** (4th and Niagara Sts., tel. 716/284–2000) is open daily 9 AM–7 PM; during the Festival of Lights, 4–10 PM.

The **Niagara Falls Convention & Visitors Bureau** (345 Third St., Niagara Falls, tel. 716/278–8010) has guides, maps, and brochures. Its 24-hour recorded message (tel. 716/278–8112) summarizes the day's events and gives suggestions on sights and activities. The **Greater Buffalo Chamber of Commerce** (107 Delaware Ave., tel. 716/852–7100) is open weekdays 9–5.

The **Chautauqua County Vacationlands Association** (2 N. Erie St., Mayville 14757, tel. 716/753–4304) is open weekdays 9–5. The association also operates an information center on the New York Thruway at Ripley. Open daily. Brochures and information also are available at **Northern Chautauqua Chamber of Commerce** (212 Lake Shore Dr. W, Dunkirk 14048, tel. 716/366–6200); **Lakewood Area Chamber of Commerce** (Box 51, Lakewood 14750, tel. 716/763–8557); and **Southwestern Gateway Tourist & Visitors Bureau** (101 W. 5th St., Jamestown 14701, tel. 716/484–1101). **Chautauqua Institution** (Chautauqua 14722, tel. 716/357–6200) provides brochures on its events, concerts, the summer school, and accommodations.

Emergencies Dial 911 for police and ambulance. Hospitals in Buffalo closest to downtown hotels are **Buffalo General Hospital** (100 High St., tel. 716/845–5600) and **Millard Fillmore Hospital** (50 Gates Circle, tel. 716/887–4600); in Niagara Falls, the **Niagara Falls Medical Center** (621 10th St., tel. 716/278–4000) is just a five-minute drive from the falls; and in the Chautauqua area is **WCA Hospital** (207 Foote Ave., Jamestown, tel. 716/487–0141). Hospital emergency rooms are open all night.

Guided Tours

Orientation Tours **Boat 'n Bus Tours** (tel. 716/285–2211) offers a 3½- to 4-hour comprehensive tour of the U.S. and Canadian sides of the falls plus a trip across the Rainbow Bridge and a ride up the Skylon Tower for a high-elevation view of Niagara Falls. **Bridal Veil Tours** (tel. 716/297–0329) gives a four-hour tour of the falls with pickup at area hotels, motels, and campgrounds. It also runs custom and special-events tours.

Gray Line of Niagara Falls (tel. 716/694–3600) has daily sightseeing tours of both Niagaras.

Special-Interest Tours **Buffalo Guide Service** (tel. 716/852–5201) has personalized tours in small vans of the Buffalo area. **Silent Partners** (tel. 716/854–4434) custom-designs tours of Buffalo and Niagara daily year-round.

Exploring

The Niagara Falls Area

Numbers in the margin correspond with points of interest on the Niagara Falls map.

There are two cities called Niagara Falls—one in the United States and the other in Canada. Beyond the famous waterfall, viewable from both sides of the border, from the water in the Maid of the Mist boat, from above in towers, helicopters, or planes, the main attractions are easily reached on foot from the cataract.

The Niagara River forms the Canadian–U.S. border. The area north of the falls on both sides of the river is primarily orchards and vineyards. Stateside, the historic community of Lewiston is the site of Artpark, the only state park in the nation devoted to the arts. Farther north, where the river opens into Lake Ontario, are the scenic villages of Youngstown on the U.S. side and Niagara-on-the-Lake on the Canadian side, about a 20-

minute drive from the falls. The latter is replete with many inns, restaurants, and shops, and is the site of the famous Shaw Festival every summer.

A 20-minute drive in the other direction is Buffalo, another waterfront community. Attractions are more diverse and spread out, and a car can be really helpful especially if you are interested in water sports, skiing, hunting, or some of the area's spectator sports.

Any tour of Niagara Falls begins at the falls themselves. For a good orientation of the falls, stop at the visitor center in the **Niagara Reservation State Park,** the oldest state park in the nation. The center has an information booth, displays, a snack bar, and daily screenings of *Niagara Wonders,* which captures the falls from every possible vantage point and provides a brief look at the area before the modern-day tourist invasion. *Admission for film: $2 adults, $1 children 3–12, $1.50 senior citizens. Open daily 10–9.*

❶ **Goat Island**—part of the state park—offers the closest possible views of the American Falls and the upper rapids. Niagara Viewmobiles sightseeing trains can be boarded at several locations on Goat Island and at Prospect Point near the **Observation Tower.** The 40-minute tour includes a close-up view of the falls; stopovers are permitted at Goat Island Heliport, Cave of the Winds, Terrapin Point, Schoellkopf Museum, Aquarium, and Three Sisters Islands. *Goat Island, tel. 716/282–0028. Admission: $2 adults, $1 children 5–11. Open daily 9 AM–10 PM, June 24–Sept. 1; daily 10 AM–6 PM, May 15–June 23 and Sept. 2–Oct. 15.*

Queen Victoria Park (tel. 416/356–4699), on the Canadian side, is the best place for viewing **Horseshoe Falls.** To fully appreciate the power of the falls, many visitors take a ride on the *Maid of the Mist,* which can be boarded on either the American or Canadian side. In operation more or less continually since 1846, this trip has become as much a symbol of Niagara as the falls themselves. Just about every celebrity and head of state who has ever visited the falls has taken a ride on the boat. Theodore Roosevelt called it "the only way to fully realize the Grandeur of the Great Falls of Niagara."

Everyone is provided with heavy black or blue rubber slickers with hoods. On warm summer days some riders enjoy the feeling of the heavy spray without the slickers, but even with them, you will definitely get wet. The captain expertly guides **❷** the boat past the base of the **American** and **Bridal Veil Falls** and almost into the thunderous deluge of the Horseshoe Falls. Spray stings the face and hands and blurs vision. Of course, it is all perfectly safe, and only once has one of the *Maid of the Mist*'s cork life preservers been used. Back in the summer of 1960, seven-year-old Roger Woodward was swept over the falls after a boat he was in stalled and broke up on rocks near the brink. He was wearing an orange life jacket, so passengers spotted the child quickly and threw him the preserver. Plucked from the turbulent waters, he became the only person in history to survive a plunge over the falls without a protective device. He returned 20 years later on his honeymoon. *Niagara River at base of falls, tel. 716/284–8897. Admission: $5.25 adults, $2.50 children 6–12; plus 70¢ on Canadian side for incline railway or*

Niagara Falls

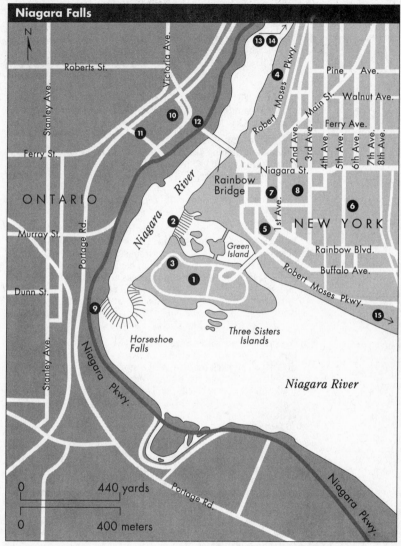

N

Roberts St.

Stanley Ave.

Victoria Ave.

Ferry St.

ONTARIO

Murray St.

Portage Rd.

Dunn St.

Stanley Ave.

Niagara Pkwy.

Portage Rd.

Pine   Ave.

Robert Moses Pkwy.

2nd Ave.
3rd Ave.
Main St.
Walnut Ave.

Ferry Ave.

4th Ave.
5th Ave.
6th Ave.
7th Ave.
8th Ave.

Niagara St.

Rainbow Bridge

NEW YORK

1st Ave.

Rainbow Blvd.

Buffalo Ave.

Robert Moses Pkwy.

Niagara River

Niagara River

Green Island

Horseshoe Falls

Three Sisters Islands

0   440 yards
0   400 meters

American and Bridal
Veil Falls, **2**

Cave of the Winds
Trip, **3**

Clifton Hill, **11**

Falls Street Station, **8**

Goat Island, **1**

Grand Island, **15**

Lewiston, **13**

Maple Leaf Village, **10**

Native American
Center for the Living
Arts, **5**

Niagara Falls
Museum, **12**

Niagara Splash Water
Park, **6**

Schoellkopf Geological
Museum, **4**

Table Rock Scenic
Tunnels, **9**

Wintergarden, **7**

Youngstown, **14**

50¢ on American side for Observation Tower. Open daily 9–7, mid-May–late Oct.

❸ The **Cave of the Winds** trip is one way to almost touch the falls by following wooden walkways to within 25 feet of the base. In 1984 a Korean visitor was hit by a 15-pound chinook salmon trying to swim up the great cataract. He wasn't hurt, but definitely surprised. *Rain slickers and foot coverings are provided. Trip starts on Goat Island, tel. 716/282–8979. Admission: $3 adults, $2.50 children 5–11. Open daily 9–7, mid-May–mid-Oct.*

For insight into the geological history of the falls, visit the
❹ **Schoellkopf Geological Museum** in Niagara Reservation State Park. A geological garden and nature trail are on the grounds; tours of the park area are scheduled regularly. *Main St. near Rainbow Bridge, tel. 716/278–1780. Admission: 50¢ adults. Open daily 9:30–7, Memorial Day–Labor Day; daily 10–5, Labor Day–Nov. 1; Wed.–Sun. 10–5 the rest of the year.*

❺ Just a few steps from the Niagara Reservation Park is the **Native American Center for the Living Arts,** or "The Turtle," because of its turtlelike look. It houses a museum and art gallery focusing on American Indian heritage, culture, symbols, and art. Iroquois dance performances are held during the summer season, and it has a gift shop and restaurant. *25 Rainbow Mall, tel. 716/284–2427. Admission: $3 adults, $1.50 children 6–12, $2 senior citizens. Open May 1–Sept. 30, daily 9–6; Oct. 1–Apr. 30, weekdays 9–5, weekends noon–5.*

❻ **Niagara Splash Water Park,** behind the convention center, offers waterlovers a variety of ways to experience water directly. The park features a five-story water flume, six-story speed slides, a lazy river ride, year-round wave pool, activity pool, remote control boats, cruiser, and a sand beach. *700 Rainbow Blvd., tel. 716/284–3555. Admission: $10.50 adults, $9.50 children 4–12; after 5 PM, $6.95 for everyone. Open daily 10–10, May 31–Labor Day.*

On the other side of the Convention Center and connected to
❼ the Radisson Inn is **Wintergarden.** This seven-story, indoor tropical garden is free and open daily. (In the spring and summer it is a popular site for weddings, especially on Saturdays.) During the Festival of Lights—late November to mid-January—the garden is decorated with thousands of multicolored lights.

Between the Convention Center and Wintergarden is the new
❽ **Falls Street Station,** a complex of shops and restaurants with the theme of turn-of-the-century Niagara Falls. Adjacent to the station is the **Falls Street Faire,** an indoor entertainment center featuring amusement rides and fast-food restaurants.

To sample the falls from another country, cross the Rainbow Bridge into Canada. **Niagara Falls, Ontario** is a real contrast in atmosphere and style, from the perfectly manicured gardens along the Niagara Parkway and Queen Victoria Park to the garish and somewhat tacky souvenir shops and mélange of museums along Clifton Hill.

Parking can be quite difficult, especially on summer weekends, so hop aboard the **Niagara Parks People Mover,** a loop bus system that allows you to get off and on as many times as you wish for one price: $1 adults, 50¢ children. It operates daily 9–11, mid-May–mid-Oct.

⑨ At **Table Rock Scenic Tunnels,** you don a weatherproof coat and boots, and an elevator takes you down to a fish-eye view of the Canadian Horseshoe Falls and the Niagara River and a walk through three tunnels cut into the rock. *Open mid-June–Labor Day 9 AM–11 PM; 9–5 the rest of the year. Tours begin at Table Rock House, in Queen Victoria Park. Tel. 416/358–3268. Cost: $3.75 adults, $1.90 children 6–12. Closed Christmas and New Year's Day.*

If you want to see the falls from on high, you can take a helicopter ride over the falls or an elevator up the three towers on the Canadian side. **Niagara Helicopters** (Victoria Ave. at River, tel. 416/357–5672) let you see the falls at an unforgettable angle. Yes, they do accept major credit cards, so you won't feel the cost for weeks. *Departures Mar.–Nov., 9 AM–sunset.* The **Skylon Tower** and the **Minolta Tower** have restaurants and observation **⑩** areas. The **Kodak Tower** is in the **Maple Leaf Village,** a complex of shops, museums, and rides, including the world's second-largest Ferris wheel.

The **Elvis Presley Museum,** in Maple Leaf Village, has the King's cars, jewelry, clothing, and furnishings from his Graceland and Hollywood homes. *5705 Falls Ave., tel. 416/357–0008. Admission: $3.95 adults, $2.50 children 6–12. Open year-round 9 AM–10 PM, Jan.–Mar. weekends only.*

⑪ A variety of museums are located on the walk up **Clifton Hill.** They also offer some good rainy day diversions and are usually open in the evening. **Circus World Display** has an array of circus-related shops, an arcade, and an old-fashioned fun house. *4848 Clifton Hill, tel. 416/356–5588. Admission: $2 adults, $1.50 children 6–12. Open daily 9 AM–midnight.*

Louis Tussaud's Waxworks features life-size reproductions of the most famous and infamous people in historically accurate costumes and settings. *4915 Clifton Hill, tel. 416/354–7521. Admission: $4.95 adults, $2.75 children 6–12, $4 senior citizens. Open daily 9 AM–midnight.*

For views of the record breakers of history, visit the **Guinness Museum of World Records,** containing hundreds of exhibits that made it into the Guinness record book. *4943 Clifton Hill, tel. 416/356–2299. Admission: $4.95 adults, $4.50 students, $3.50 children 6–12. Open daily 9 AM–10 PM.*

For another perspective on the strange and wonderful, visit **Ripley's Believe It or Not Museum,** with its 500-odd exhibits of strange, surprising, but true happenings and facts. *4960 Clifton Hill, tel. 416/356–2238. Admission: $4.95 adults, $2.75 children 6–12, $4 senior citizens. Open daily 9 AM–11 PM.*

If you enjoy a good scare, stop at the **House of Frankenstein.** The museum warns foolish mortals to beware, because once you walk up the 13 stairs you are on your own. Exhibits abound in blood and gore. *4967 Clifton Hill, tel. 416/356–8522. Admission: $3.95 adults, $2 children 6–12. Open daily 10–10.*

⑫ **Niagara Falls Museum,** at the Rainbow Bridge, includes everything from shlock to quality. Here you'll find the Daredevil Hall of Fame, dinosaurs, and a very solid collection of Egyptian mummies dating from before the Exodus from Egypt. There are also Indian artifacts and zoological and geological exhibits. *5651 River Rd., tel. 416/356–2151. Admission: $5 adults, $4*

*students and senior citizens, $2 children 6–12. Open June–
early Oct., 9 AM–midnight; Nov.–May, weekdays 10–5, weekends 11–5.*

Flower lovers should not miss the **Niagara Falls School of Horticulture,** six miles north of the Horseshoe Falls. Students in the
school maintain all the gardens along the 35-mile Niagara Parkway, which runs from Fort Erie to Niagara-on-the-Lake. The
school contains 100 acres of gardens, including a magnificent
rose garden that is at its most glorious in June.

The **Floral Clock** is less than six miles north of the falls, along
River Road. Nearly 20,000 plants that bloom from earliest
spring to late autumn make up one of the world's biggest,
bloomin' clocks. Chimes ring every quarter-hour, and it actually keeps the right time. Adjacent to the clock are the Cen-
tennial Lilac Gardens, with 256 varieties of lilacs and more
than 1,500 bushes which bloom during May.

Just north of the clock is the village of Queenston. From here
you can take the Lewiston–Queenston Bridge across the river
13 to the United States and the historic village of **Lewiston,** seven
miles north of the falls. It's best known as the home of **Artpark.**
The only state park in the nation devoted to the visual and performing arts, Artpark encompasses 200 acres along the
Niagara River. You can sit at the feet of a storyteller in the
woods, don a mask and join a company of actors, watch your
child create a puppet, or try your hand at Oriental brush painting. Nightly concerts and plays are staged by the Buffalo
Philharmonic Orchestra, touring companies, and big-name entertainers. *Artpark, Lewiston, 14092, tel. 716/694–8191. Park
is free but concerts and plays run from $4 to $24. Parking
$2.50. Open daily June 28–Sept. 11.*

14 Continue north to **Youngstown,** home of **Old Fort Niagara,**
about 15 minutes from Artpark. Occupied by the French, British, and Americans, the fort's original stone buildings have
been preserved in their pre-Revolutionary state. French Castle, the oldest building in the Great Lakes area, was built in
1726. Military reenactments, battles, grand reviews, tent
camps, fifes and drums, crafts, and archaeological digs are
scheduled throughout the year. *Youngstown 14174, tel. 716/745–
7611. Admission $4 adults, $2 children 6–12. Open daily 9 AM–
7:30 PM July 1–Labor Day; closing hours vary at other times.*

South of Niagara Falls, there are 19 islands in the Niagara Riv-
15 er. By far the largest is **Grand Island,** which is about five square
miles larger than Manhattan. If you have kids, take in its **Fantasy Island Park,** with more than 100 rides, shows, and
attractions. Diving, musical, and stunt shows are held daily.
There are five theme areas; picnic areas; and rides, including a
log flume, waterslide, and dragon coaster. *2400 Grand Island
Blvd., tel. 716/773–7591. Admission: $12.95 adults, $9.50 children 3–11, $8.50 senior citizens. Open daily 11:30 AM–8:30 PM,
mid-June–Labor Day.*

On the southern tip of Grand Island is **Beaver Island State Park,**
which has a fine beach, marina, and golf course. Back in 1825,
Major Mordecai Manuel Noah, a lawyer and judge, founded Ar-
arat on Grand Island as a refuge city for Jews who were being
persecuted in Europe. The plan failed for lack of support, but
the cornerstone is on display in the Grand Island Town Hall.

Buffalo

Numbers in the margin correspond with points of interest on the Buffalo map.

❶ The best place to begin touring Buffalo is at its **City Hall,** considered one of the finest examples of Art Deco. The 28th-floor observation deck offers views of Lake Erie and the surrounding city, its radiating street plan modeled after Washington, DC. Louis Sullivan's 1895 Guaranty Building is acknowledged to be one of the most influential skyscrapers ever built and a prime example of Sullivan's ideas of functional design and terra-cotta ornament.

The nearby **Hyatt Regency Buffalo** is an elegant hotel with an atrium spanning an entire city block. The hotel started life as an office building designed by architect E. B. Green, who masterminded a number of the city's most stately mansions; its transformation into a hotel won several awards. The walls throughout the hotel's public areas are covered with original artwork by area artists. On a clear day, the 38th-floor restaurant in the **Marine Midland Center** (open for lunch only on weekdays) offers impressive views of the area, including the spray from the falls.

❷ Just beyond the Marine Center is the **Naval and Servicemen's Park,** the country's only inland naval park. It is home to the destroyer USS *Sullivan* and the cruiser *Little Rock*, both of which are permanently berthed in the Buffalo River and are open for exploration. There is also a PT boat, aircraft, guided missiles, and Servicemen's Museum. *1 Naval Park Cove, tel. 716/847–1773. Admission: $3.50 adults, $2.50 children 5–16 and senior citizens, $10 family. Open daily 10–5 Apr. 1–Nov. 30.*

Hop on the city's Light Rapid Rail System, partially underground, whose stations are decorated with original art and sculptures commissioned for the project. Stop on Allen St. in
❸ the heart of **Allentown,** one of the nation's largest historic preservation districts. It is filled with 19th-century Victorian homes, boutiques, restaurants, and art galleries. The Allentown Art Festival, the second weekend in June, is one of the largest outdoor art shows in the country.

North on Delaware Avenue, within a block of Allen Street, is
❹ the **Theodore Roosevelt Inaugural National Historic Site,** a Greek-Revival structure dating from 1838, when it served as headquarters for military officers. The library where Theodore Roosevelt was sworn in as the 26th president has been restored. Displays cover Roosevelt's inauguration and the assassination of President McKinley in Buffalo in 1901. An art gallery on the second floor has changing exhibits. *641 Delaware Ave., tel. 716/884–0095. Donation: $1. Open daily 10–5.*

Head north on Delaware, which turns into Chapin then Lincoln Parkway, for a total of two miles; at the entrance to the
❺ Scajaquada Expressway you'll find the **Albright-Knox Art Gallery,** which has brought worldwide acclaim to Buffalo, largely through the efforts of industrialist Seymour Knox. It houses a superb collection of contemporary art, as well as a comprehensive general collection, and was the first U.S. museum to buy works by Picasso and Matisse. Alternatively, parallel Delaware by taking Elmwood Avenue, one block west,

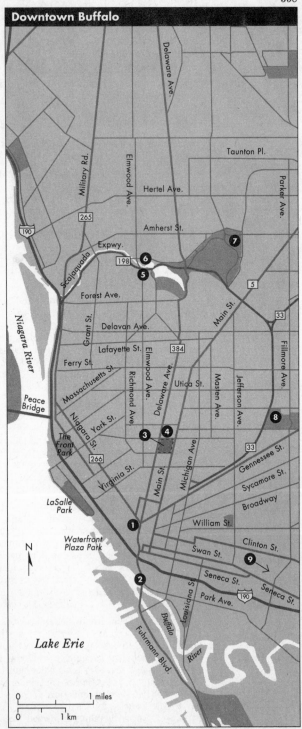

Downtown Buffalo

Albright-Knox Art
Gallery, **5**
Allentown, **3**
Buffalo and Erie
County Historical
Society, **6**
Buffalo Museum of
Science, **8**
Buffalo Zoo, **7**
City Hall, **1**
East Aurora, **9**
Naval and
Servicemen's Park, **2**
Theodore Roosevelt
Inaugural Site, **4**

Delaware Ave.

Taunton Pl.

Parker Ave.

Hertel Ave.

Military Rd.

Elmwood Ave.

265

190

Amherst St.

7

Scajaquada Expwy.

198 **6**

5

5

Forest Ave.

Main St.

33

Grant St.

Delavan Ave.

Lafayette St.

384

Ferry St.

Elmwood Ave.

Fillmore Ave.

Massachusetts St.

Richmond Ave.

Delaware Ave.

Utica St.

Masten Ave.

Jefferson Ave.

8

Niagara River

York St.

3 **4**

Michigan Ave.

33

Gennessee St.

Peace
Bridge

Niagara St.

266

Sycamore St.

The
Front
Park

Virginia St.

Main St.

Broadway

1

LaSalle
Park

William St.

Clinton St.

9

Waterfront
Plaza Park

Swan St.

N

Seneca St.

2

Seneca St.

Park Ave.

190

Louisiana St.

Lake Erie

Buffalo River

Fuhrmann Blvd.

0   1 miles

0   1 km

to the Albright-Knox. Elmwood is a cheery, bustling street of shops, bars, and eateries. *Museum shop and restaurant. 1285 Elmwood Ave., tel. 716/882–8700. Donation. Open Tues.–Sun. 10–5.*

⑥ Just across Scajaquada Creek is **Buffalo and Erie County Historical Society,** the only remaining building from the Pan American Exposition of 1901. The emphasis is on area history and Indian culture with a variety of imaginative, changing exhibits. *25 Nottingham Ct., tel. 716/873–9644. Admission: $2.50 adults, $1 children under 12, 90¢ senior citizens, $5 family. Open Tues.–Sun. 10–5.*

Head east on Nottingham Road along the northern edge of Delaware Park for a mile, turn left on Amherst Street to the **⑦** **Buffalo Zoo,** one of the country's oldest. Highlights include a tropical rain forest, a gorilla habitat, and a simulated Asian forest. There's a new $2-million habitat for tigers and lions. The children's petting zoo is popular and includes camel and elephant rides. *Delaware Park, tel. 716/837–3900. Admission: $3 adults, $1 children 11–16, 50¢ children 4–10, $7 family; admission free several days a month. Open daily 10–5.*

Leave the zoo in the opposite direction, continuing less than a block on Amherst, turning right (south) on Parkside Drive to the Scajaquada Parkway (Rte. 198). Go east for two miles to **⑧** Martin Luther King Jr. Park where you'll find the **Buffalo Museum of Science.** It features exhibits on anthropology, archaeology, astronomy, botany, geology, and zoology, including gigantic insect models and a children's discovery room. *Humboldt Pkwy. at Northampton St., tel. 716/896–5200. Admission $2.50 adults, $1 children 3–17, students, and seniors. Open daily 10–5. Kellogg Observatory open Sept. 1–May 31, Fri. 5–10 PM, weather permitting.*

⑨ Twenty miles southeast of Buffalo, via Route 400, is the picturesque village of **East Aurora,** home of the Roycroft Movement. Elbert Hubbard, "the sage of East Aurora" and a successful soap company executive turned philosopher and writer, founded the movement in 1895. At its height, more than 500 Roycrofters were working as printers, coppersmiths, furniture makers, silversmiths, potters, artists, and innkeepers. The historic **Roycroft Inn,** filled with Roycroft furniture, is under renovation. The 14 buildings in the Roycroft Campus are designated a National Landmark, and have been transformed into shops, art galleries, a museum, town offices, and the County Extension Service.

In the third quarter of the 19th century East Aurora was known as "the world's trotting nursery." Racehorses were raised and trained here on large farms and the "world's only one-mile covered racetrack" was nationally known. The village's racing history is celebrated during the last weekend in July, when horse-drawn carriages parade down Main Street Stop in to see the 17 stained-glass Tiffany windows in Baker Memorial Church, four of which were signed by Louis Tiffany.

Millard Fillmore practiced law in East Aurora before moving on to Buffalo and later to the White House as the nation's 13th president. The **Millard Fillmore House** (24 Shearer St., tel. 716/652–5362) is open to the public.

The Chautauqua Area

Numbers in the margin correspond with points of interest on the Chautauqua Area map.

The Chautauqua Institution, about 70 miles southwest of Buffalo, is the magnet that draws visitors to the shores of the 22-mile-long Chautauqua Lake. The institution is a walking town (no cars are allowed except to load or unload), a perfect Victorian village with contemporary amenities. It is a self-contained community with a full range of summer sports and endless opportunities to exercise the mind.

For exploring outside the institution, a car is recommended. The region can truly be said to appeal to myriad tastes and interests, from boating to hunting and fishing, from antiquing to wine-tasting, and from the arts to world affairs.

❶ A tour of the Chautauqua area begins at **Silver Creek,** southwest of Buffalo on the shores of Lake Erie. From there you can follow the so-called Chautauqua Wine Trail, via the New York State Thruway, Route 20, which is preferred, or Route 5, along Erie's vineyard-dotted south shore. Several of the wineries along this route offer free tours and tastings: **Woodbury Vineyards Winery,** *S. Roberts Rd., off Rte. 20, 3 miles south of Dunkirk, tel. 716/679–WINE. Mon.–Sat. 10–5, Sun. 1–5.* **Chadwick Bay Wine Co.,** *10001 Rte. 60, 1½ mi south of Exit 59, off the NYS Thruway, tel. 716/672–5000. Mon.–Sat. 10–5, Sun. noon–5.* **Merritt Estate Winery,** *King Rd., off Rte. 20, tel. 716/965–4800. Mon.–Sat. 10–5, Sun. 1–5.*

❷ **Dunkirk,** the largest community on the south shore of Lake Erie, was so-named because of its resemblance to the harbor at Dunkerque, France. This is a typical lakeshore community, where boating and water sports are essential elements of the lifestyle. **The Historic Dunkirk Lighthouse and Veteran's Park** at Point Gratiot is the chief tourist attraction. Visitors may climb the 95-foot lighthouse for a bird's-eye view of the ar a or visit the museum dedicated to the armed forces; there is a separate room for each branch of the service. *Off Rte. 15, tel. 716/ 366–5050. Apr.–June, daily 9–4; July and Aug., daily 9–9; Sept.–Nov., weekdays 9–2.*

❸ **Fredonia,** three miles south of Dunkirk on Central Avenue, was the site of America's first gas well (1821); the streets were lit with gas lamps when Lafayette stopped here on his American tour. Ironically, given the number of vineyards in the area, this is also the place where the Women's Christian Temperance Union was founded in 1873. Today Fredonia is a charming college town of attractive 19th-century buildings, a number of which have been restored in recent years. A prime example of successful renovation is **The White Inn;** stop for lunch or stay the night (*see* Dining and Lodging).

Those interested in spiritualism may want to take Route 60
❹ south to **Cassadaga,** home of the **Lily Dale Assembly.** This spiritualist center, established on the shores of Lake Cassadaga in 1879, attracts mediums from throughout the United States and Canada. In summer, there are daily lectures, workshops, and sessions with clairvoyants. Private spiritual readings can be arranged. *1 mi off Rte. 60 at Cassadaga, tel. 716/595–8721. Open June 27–Sept. 1.*

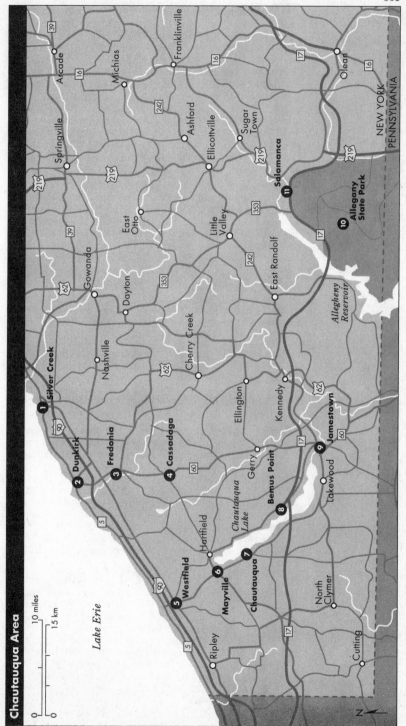

Chautauqua Area

Lake Erie

10 miles

15 km

NEW YORK
PENNSYLVANIA

Arcade

Michias

Springville

Franklinville

Ashford

Ellicottville

Sugar Town

Salamanca

Olean

East Otto

Little Valley

Allegany State Park

Gowanda

Dayton

Cherry Creek

East Randolf

Allegheny Reservoir

Silver Creek

Nashville

Ellington

Kennedy

Jamestown

Dunkirk

Fredonia

Cassadaga

Gerry

Benus Point

Lakewood

Hartfield

Chautauqua Lake

Westfield

Mayville

Chautauqua

Ripley

North Clymer

Cutting

N

If you continue southwest along Route 20 from Fredonia, you'll
⑤ reach **Westfield,** home of Welch's Foods and the self-proclaimed
Grape Juice Capital of the world. Westfield is also an antiques
center; some 20 dealers display their finds in 19th-century
homes (*see* Shopping). The 1928 lighthouse at nearby Barcelona
Harbor was the first in the world to be lit by natural gas.
Charles Edgar Welch, who founded the town and the grape-
juice business, always asserted that "God did not mean for the
grape to be fermented." Those who prefer to decide for themselves may want to stop at the **Johnson Estate Wines,** to sample
some that has been. Tastings are available year-round, but are
even more frequent in July and August. *W. Main Rd., 3 mi
southwest of Westfield, off Rte. 20, tel. 716/326-2191. Daily
10-6.*

Head inland off Route 20, on Route 394 to the north end of
⑥ Chautauqua Lake and the town of **Mayville.** This is the home of
the 90-ton *Sea Lion,* a hand-built replica of a 16th-century English merchant vessel. In the summer tours of the ship are
available, and a 90-minute cruise on the lake is offered on Saturdays; reservations are essential. *Chautauqua Lake Historic
Vessels Co., 15 Water St., Mayville 14757, tel. 716/753-7823.
Cruise cost: $25. Tours available June 1-Sept. 30.*

Mayville is also the home port for the *Chautauqua Belle,* a Mississippi River–style steamboat that does regular lake cruises
as well as brunch and dinner cruises. In summer, the *Belle* sails
Tues.–Sun. at 1, 2:30, and 4 PM. *Chautauqua Lake Historic
Vessels Co. (see above).*

⑦ In **Chautauqua,** the 856-acre **Chautauqua Institution** is just a
few miles farther south along the lake on Route 394. Here a visitor can fish for record-breaking muskellunge in the morning,
attend a lecture by an internationally known speaker before
lunch, play golf in the afternoon, study music or a foreign language before dinner, and attend an opera or concert at night.

Admission to the institution grounds and the wide range of accommodations and restaurants is by gate ticket, which can be
purchased for periods of a day, a weekend, a week, or the eight-
week summer season. The ticket admits you to the amphitheater and most events on the grounds except operas and plays, for
which separate tickets are sold. A gate ticket is required for
anyone 13 years and older. In keeping with the institution's religious origins admission is free on Sunday. *Chautauqua
Institution, Chautauqua 14722, tel. 716/357-6200. Gate admission ranges from $13 for Mon.–Wed. after 5 PM to $885 for
the 8-week season. Weekend rates: $34 adults, $14 children
13-17.*

⑧ **Bemus Point,** a good spot for fishing enthusiasts, can be
reached by taking Route 394 south to Stow, then following U.S.
17 across the lake via a bridge. There are several boat liveries
in the town, and fishing guides can be arranged here. The Casino at the ferry landing has a small steamboat museum and
refreshments. Next to the casino is a small beach and good
swimming. During the summer you can ride the Bemus Point–
Stow Ferry (tel. 716/753-2403) across the narrows of the lake.
The cable-drawn ferry, in operation for more than 170 years,
carries cars ($2.50 each way) as well as individual passengers
($1) and livestock (50¢).

⑨ **Jamestown,** with a large population of Swedish derivation, is at the southern tip of Chautauqua Lake. In 1988 the city celebrated 350 years of Swedish settlement in America. It has two areas of architectural interest where buildings span the 75 years from Gothic-Revival to Art Deco styles. The **Old Northside and Southside Walking Tours** (tel. 716/483–7521) start at the **Penton Historical Center,** a museum housed in a Civil War-era mansion built for New York Governor Reuben E. Penton. The building is on the National Register of Historic Places. The museum has Italian and Swedish heritage rooms and is a good resource for genealogical material. *67 Washington St., tel. 716/ 483–7521. Open Mon.–Sat. 10–4.*

⑩ Outdoors lovers and anyone interested in Indian culture should head east on Route 17 to the 65,000-acre **Allegany State Park** (tel. 716/354–2535) and Salamanca, the only city on an American Indian reservation. The park, the largest in the state parks, has 75 miles of hiking trails and offers fishing, swimming, and hunting for deer, small game, and turkey in season, and camping year-round. The Seneca Iroquois National Museum on the Allegany Indian Reservation, adjacent to the state park, has exhibits on the history and contemporary culture of the Seneca Nation of Indians. *Rte. 17, tel. 716/945–1738. Open May 1–Oct. 1, Mon.–Sat. 10–5, Sun. noon–5.*

⑪ In the town of **Salamanca, the Salamanca Rail Museum,** housed in a restored 1912 passenger depot, has exhibits and operates rail excursions during the summer and fall. *170 Main St., tel. 716/945–3133. Open Mon.–Sat. 10–5, Sun. 12–5.*

What to See and Do with Children

Niagara Falls Exploring the falls can be exciting for children and adults alike, whether viewed from the deck of the *Maid of the Mist,* the Niagara Viewmobile, the Cave of the Winds trip, or from a tower or railing.

Aquarium of Niagara Falls. The performing dolphins, sea lions, and electric eels are only a few of the aquatic creatures from around the world on display here. *Whirlpool St. at Pine Ave., tel. 716/285–3575. Admission: $4.95 adults, $2.95 children, $3 senior citizens. Open Memorial Day–Labor Day, daily 9–7; the rest of year 9–5.*

Marineland. Killer whales, dolphins, and sea lions are big attractions here. On the grounds are an aquarium and a game farm with bear, deer, elk, and buffalo. The Hot Air Fantasy Show has 20 animated singing characters. There are a few rides for adults and children. Plan on spending at least half a day here if you want to see everything. *7657 Portage Rd. on the Canadian side, tel. 416/356–8250. Admission varies with season: summer, $14.50 adults, $9.95 over 59 and children 4–9; spring and fall, $12.95 adults, $6.95 over 59 and children 4–9; winter, $5.95 adults, $4.25 over 59 and children 4–9.*

Mahoney Silver Jubilee Dolls' House Gallery. The 140 dollhouses here, decorated and furnished in the style of houses built between 1780 and 1985, are worth more than $1 million. This large collection is in Ft. Erie, Ontario, just across the Peace Bridge from Buffalo. Ft. Erie marks the beginning of the Niagara Parkway, which ends in Niagara-on-the-Lake. *657 Niagara Blvd., Fort Erie, Ont., tel. 416/871–5833. Admission: $2 adults, $1.50 children 5–15. Open daily 10 AM–4 PM.*

Maple Leaf Village. This amusement complex sports a 350-foot observation tower, one of the largest Ferris wheels on the continent, and a huge IMAX theatre. There are also rides, musical shows, shops, boutiques, and restaurants. *5685 Falls Ave., Niagara Falls, Ont., tel. 416/374-4444. Admission to the village is free. Outdoor rides are open June 15-Sept. 15. Visiting the observation tower costs 99¢. Combination price of $9.95 includes unlimited use of rides and a number of attractions.*

Buffalo　　**Buffalo Museum of Science** has a hands-on exhibit room for children 6-12. Children and their parents may handle prehistoric stone tools, touch a stuffed alligator, learn about snakes, play musical instruments, and try on African clothing. *Humboldt Pkwy. at Northampton St., tel. 716/896-5200. Admission: $2.50 adults, $1 students, senior citizens, and children 3-17, and $5 per family. Open daily 10-5.*

The **Children's Zoo,** part of the Buffalo Zoo, has animals for petting and riding. *Delaware Park, tel. 716/837-3900. Admission: $3 adults, $1 children 11-16, 50¢ children 4-10, $7 per family. Open daily 10-5:30.*

Theater of Youth (TOY) Company (Center Theater, 691 Main St., Buffalo), stages several major children's shows each year. Tel. 716/856-4410 for schedules and ticket information.

Chautauqua　　**Chautauqua Institution** has a complete program of activities for young people from 2½ years to college age. There is a children's school for those up to six years old, and a summer day camp for children 6-15. Both programs run weekdays during the season. The Youth Activities Center (tel. 716/357-6200) plans and coordinates activities for high school and college-age youth.

Gadfly III, a cruise boat, sails from the institution's bell tower daily except Monday during the season (tel. 716/753-3528).

Sea Lion Project Ltd. (RD 1, Sea Lion Dr., Mayville, tel. 716/753-2403) has boat rides on three craft that are popular with children—the Bemus Point-Stow Ferry, the steamer *Chautauqua Belle,* and the *Sea Lion,* a replica of a 16th-century English ship.

Off the Beaten Track

Back of the Beyond. This is a bed-and-breakfast establishment with self-guided tours through organic herb, flower, and vegetable gardens with samples included. It is about 20 miles southeast of Buffalo. *7233 Lower E. Hill Rd., Colden, tel. 716/652-0427. Open daily.*

Broadway Market. Head to this store at 999 Broadway, in the heart of Buffalo's Polish neighborhood, to sample Polish kielbasa and other ethnic specialties.

Forest Lawn Cemetery. The resting place of President Millard Fillmore and Seneca Indian Chief Red Jacket is at 1411 Delaware Ave., in the middle of Buffalo.

Griffis Sculpture Park in Ashford Hollow is the creation of Buffalo artist Larry Griffis, who turned 400 acres of meadow and woods into a sculpture garden. His metal figures—"Dancing Lady," "Round Man," and "Poet" add an artistic aura for hiking or cross-country skiing. *Rte. 219. Open daily.*

Kazoo Museum. Visit the world's only metal kazoo manufacturer. *8703 S. Main St., Eden, tel. 716/992-3960. Admission free. Open Tues.-Sat. 10-5, Sun. noon-5.*

Panama Rocks, just off Route 474 and eight miles southwest of Chautauqua Lake, is a private park with self-guided walking tours of caves, cliffs, crevices, and passages formed more than 300 million years ago. The Indians used these rocks and caves for shelter long before the arrival of French explorers in the mid-1600s. For a time in the early 1800s, outlaws used the rocks to hide their loot, and local legend has it that a cache of gold is buried here. *Panama, tel. 716/728-2845. Admission: $5 adults, $2 children under 12. Open May 1-Oct. 26, 9 AM-sunset.*

QRS Music Rolls, along the river in Buffalo, is the world's oldest and largest player-piano roll manufacturer. *1026 Niagara St., tel. 716/885-4600. Admission free. Tours weekdays only at 10 AM and 2 PM.*

Vidler's (690-694 Main St., East Aurora) is one of the last of a vanishing breed: a real five-and-dime. It has fresh popped popcorn for 5¢, slanted wooden floors, aisle after aisle of items including some for 5¢ or 10¢, and a large collection of Fisher-Price toys (East Aurora, the home of the giant toy company, is about 20 minutes southeast of Buffalo).

Shopping

Most Buffalo and Niagara Falls area stores are open weekdays 9-5:30 and Sat. 9-5:30 except in the suburbs, where stores are open until 9. Downtown stores are closed Sunday but usually open noon-5 on Sundays in the suburbs. The sales tax is 7% in Niagara County (Niagara Falls) and 8% in Erie County (Buffalo). The **Factory Outlet Mall** at 1900 Military Road in Niagara Falls (tel. 716/773-1797) has more than 70 manufacturer outlets offering savings of 20%-70%. The **Factory Outlet Mall** at 1881 Ridge Road in West Seneca (tel. 716/674-8920) has more than 30 manufacturer outlets. Both are open Mon.-Sat. 10-9 , Sun. 10-5.

Antiques

The village of Westfield in Chautauqua County has 20 antiques dealers. **Stockton Sales Antiques & Collectibles** (6 Mill St., Stockton, tel. 716/595-3516) has 30,000 square feet of barn space packed with antiques, collectibles, furniture, and reproductions. The **Lock Stock & Barrel Country Store** (Rte. 62, Ellington, tel. 716/287-3675) is a country grocery and antiques store. **Good Morning Farm** (Rte. 394, Stow, tel. 716/763-1507) is a 19th-century farm with seven shops featuring local arts and crafts, as well as a restaurant and bar.

Participant Sports

Boating

With the region's ample supply of lakes and rivers, waterborne recreation is a definite diversion. **Seven Seas Sailing School** (Erie Basin Marina, Buffalo, tel. 716/856-4109) and **Serendipity Sailing Services** (2493 Garrison Rd., Ridgeway, Ont., tel. 416/894-0696) provide sailboat rental and instruction. **Bouquard's Boat Livery** (1581 Fuhrmann Blvd., Buffalo, tel.

716/826–6189) and **Wolf's Boat House** (327 S. Ellicott Creek Rd., Tonawanda, tel. 716/691–8740) rents motor boats.

Fishing

After years of negative publicity regarding pollution in the area, conditions have improved and lake trout and other fresh-water fish have returned to Lake Erie, Niagara River, and Lake Ontario. **John M. Sander's Fishing Guide** is a detailed guide to area fishing, available in sporting-goods stores and bookstores. There is still a health advisory against eating fish from Lake Ontario and the Niagara River below the falls. Consult the New York State Department of Environmental Conservation (DEC) (tel. 716/847–4600) for health and license information. Write or call DEC (50 Wolf Rd., Albany 12233, tel. 518/457–5400) for booklets on Great Lakes fishing and state boat launching sites. Bass, trout, muskie, salmon, and north-ern pike are being caught in large numbers. There are a number of charter fishing operators in the Buffalo, Lake Erie, and Niagara River area, and at Lake Ontario in Niagara County. They include **Great Lakes Fishing Charters** (8255 West Point Dr., Amherst, tel. 716/741–3453), **Olcott Charter Service** (6460 Hope La., Lockport tel. 716/434–9902), and **Downrigger Charters** (2683 Grace Ave., Newfane, tel. 716/778–7518).

Chautauqua Lake attracts serious anglers who come to challenge the native muskellunge, or "muskie," that is famous for its fight and size. Minnie Methuselah III has haunted Chautau-qua since 1974. A "tiger" muskellunge, she weighed 44 pounds and stretched 52 inches that year when she was tagged with the number 2C-2963. Whoever catches her will have boated a record catch—and a $1,000 reward. Muskies often live to the age of 30.

Good-size walleyed pike, bass, and panfish are also caught in Chautauqua Lake. Lake Erie and Cassadaga and Findley lakes also provide good fishing. Ice fishing is popular during the winter. Some selected charter sportfishing outfits are:

Chautauqua Lake Charters, Box 1187, Chautauqua 14722, tel. 716/753–5255.
The Frenchman Boat, Box 231, Ashville 14710, tel. 716/763–8296.
J&C Charters, 4976 Webster Rd., Fredonia 14063, tel. 716/672–5674.
Pequod II Charters, 33 Newton St., Fredonia 14063, tel. 716/673–1117.
Salmon Tracker Charters, 6 Pennington Pl., Cassadaga 14752, tel. 716/595–3917.

Horseback Riding

Chautauqua area stables give lessons, rent horses, and provide well-marked trails for riding at about $10 an hour. They include **Crackerjack Farms** (Bemus-Ellery Center Rd., Bemus Point, tel. 716/386–5054), **Danero Riding Stable** (Hewes Rd., Mayville, tel. 716/789–4600), and **Double D.A.B. Riding Stable** (Welch Hill Rd., Ripley, tel. 716/736–4418).

Hunting

Excellent hunting opportunities for whitetail deer, wild turkey, upland birds, waterfowl, and small game abound within an hour's drive of Buffalo. For information on licenses, seasons, bag limits, permissible weapons, public hunting grounds, and private preserves, write Department of Environmental Conservation (DEC) (50 Wolf Rd., Albany 12233 or tel. 716/457–5400).

Skiing

Kissing Bridge (Rte. 240, Glenwood, tel. 716/592–4963), the closest ski center to Buffalo and also one of the largest in the area, is only a 45-minute drive from downtown. **Holiday Valley** (Rte. 219, Ellicottville, tel. 716/699–2644) is the most extensive ski center in the area. Cross-country skiing is allowed in the city's parks. For ski conditions, tel. 800/CALL–NYS.

The Chautauqua area's other ski resorts for both downhill and cross-country skiing are **Cockaigne,** Cherry Creek (tel. 716/287–3223) and **Peek 'n Peak,** Clymer (tel. 716/355–4141).

Tennis and Golf

There are more than 100 public tennis courts and a number of public golf courses in Niagara–Buffalo. Contact the Buffalo Parks Department (tel. 716/855–4200) or Erie County Department of Parks and Recreation (tel. 716/846–8352).

Windsurfing

For equipment rentals and lessons in windsurfing, parasailing, and waterskiing contact **Windsurfing Chautauqua** (Chautauqua 14722, tel. 716/789–2675).

Spectator Sports

Baseball The **Buffalo Bisons** AAA baseball team plays at gleaming new Pilot Field in the heart of downtown (tel. 716/878–8055).

Football The National Football League **Buffalo Bills** play at Rich Stadium (Orchard Park, tel. 716/649–0015).

Hockey The **Buffalo Sabres** professional hockey team plays at War Memorial Auditorium (tel. 716/856–3111).

Horse Racing **Buffalo Raceway** (Erie County Fairgrounds, Hamburg, tel. 716/649–1280) has harness racing. **Ft. Erie Raceway** (Bertie St., off Hwy. 3 just one-half mile from the Peace Bridge in Ft. Erie, tel. 416/871–3200) has thoroughbred racing.

Dining

Buffalo has given the world two classics—Buffalo chicken wings and beef on weck. The former is served mild, medium, or spicy hot, alongside blue cheese dressing and celery; the latter consists of roast beef—carved on the spot—and heaped on a fresh, flaky kimmelweck roll that has been sprinkled with coarse salt. Buffalo, however, abounds in casual, rather inexpensive restaurants, many of which reveal surprising flourishes.

The emphasis in the Chautauqua area is on seafood and American-style menus. Reservations are necessary in the summer, especially if you plan a pretheater meal at the institution.

Highly recommended restaurants are indicated by a star ★.

Category	Cost*
Very Expensive	over $25
Expensive	$18–$25
Moderate	$10–$18
Inexpensive	under $10

per person without sales tax, service, or drinks

Buffalo

Very Expensive
★
Rue Franklin West. This French restaurant is housed in a 100-year-old Victorian brick house. Every dish is extra-fresh and prepared from scratch. The menu changes seasonally but is imaginative year-round. Special chocolate desserts. Extensive wine cellar. *341 Franklin St., Buffalo, tel. 716/852–4416. Jackets required. Reservations advised. AE, MC, V. Dinner. Closed Sun., Mon.*

Expensive
Asa Ransom House. This dining establishment-cum-inn (four rooms) is in a picture-perfect country setting. It is a historic house, parts of which date back to the 18th century, and is appropriately crammed with antiques. The friendly waitresses are dressed in Early American costumes. Two of the house dishes are corned beef with apple raisin sauce and salmon pond pie (salmon in a deep dish with tomatoes, topped with a cheese pastry). *10529 Main St., Clarence, tel. 716/759–2315. Jackets required. Reservations advised. MC, V. Dinner; lunch only on Wed. Closed Fri. and Sat.*

Lord Chumley's. A venerable, dependable restaurant in a rather elegant brownstone in Buffalo's trendy Allentown District. The menu is extensive, offering both American standards and a few Continental dishes. Order the Caesar salad. *481 Delaware Ave., tel. 716/886–9159. Jackets required. Reservations advised. AE, CB, DC, MC, V.*

★ **Old Orchard Inn.** This charming restaurant originated as a farmhouse in the 1860s and was later a hunting lodge and tearoom. Large stone fireplaces burn warmly in the winter. The expansive grounds feature a duck pond and sweeping views of the countryside. Specialties include chicken fricassee with biscuits, chicken pot pie, and fresh fish. Old-fashioned dinners on Sundays feature turkey, ham, roast pork, and prime rib. Crustless-lemon angel pie is also a specialty. *2095 Blakely Rd., East Aurora (about 20 miles southeast of Buffalo), tel. 716/652–4664. Jacket required. Reservations advised. AE, MC, V. Dinner.*

Parkside Sweet Shoppe. A beguiling little spot that, except for its menu, is unchanged from its origins as a 1920s neighborhood soda bar. Now, however, it is justly known for its thorough commitment to thoughtfully prepared and served food. The menu is comprehensive in its own small way, supplemented with evening specials. *2304 Main St., tel. 716/834–4222. Dress: informal. Reservations advised. AE, DC, MC, V. Lunch and dinner.*

Salvatore's Italian Gardens. Salvatore's would be at home on the Las Vegas strip. It's an extravaganza with life-size statuary, fountains, and colored lights. The dining rooms are equally ornate; new ones appear constantly at the owner's whim. There is a wide selection of Italian dishes, but the house specialty is steak à la Russell, tenderloin prepared at tableside. *6461 Transit Rd., Cheektowaga, tel. 716/683–7990. Jacket required. Reservations advised. AE, CB, DC, MC, V.*

Moderate **Anchor Bar.** Buffalo chicken wings were invented here in 1964 by the late owner, Dominic Bellissimo, and tons are served up every week, accompanied by celery and blue cheese dressing. Anchor wings have been flown all over the country by former residents homesick for this delicacy. Other traditional Italian dishes are also in demand. *1047 Main St., Buffalo, tel. 716/886–8920. Dress: informal. No credit cards. Lunch and dinner.*

Brick Alley Bistro. A small and charming place with a diverse menu, running from standard lunch fare to rather ambitious dinner undertakings, served with casual elegance. As the name suggests, both the dining room and the alley-entrance bar are brick-walled. In the summer the sidewalk cafe opens. *1375 Delaware Ave., tel. 716/881–1151. Dress: informal. Reservations advised. AE, MC, V. Lunch and dinner.*

★ **Chef's Restaurant.** This spot has long been praised by politicians, media folk, and just about everyone who works or visits downtown. It is especially busy on hockey and baseball nights. Owner Louis Billittier personally oversees the kitchen, which serves traditional southern Italian dishes. *291 Seneca St., Buffalo, tel. 716/856–9187. Dress: informal. Reservations advised. AE, MC, V. Lunch and dinner. Closed Sun.*

Eckl's Beef & Weck Restaurant. This dining establishment serves beef on weck supreme. It is housed in a renovated 100-year-old house not far from Rich Stadium, where the Buffalo Bills play. Owner Dale Eckl personally carves the beef to order, dipping the weck roll deftly into the roast beef juices to retain the roll's flaky texture. Fish fries are also popular. *4936 Ellicott Rd., Orchard Park, tel. 716/662–2262. Dress: informal. No credit cards. Lunch and dinner.*

Harbour Marine. A favorite restaurant especially in the summer, primarily because of its location at a busy marina on the Niagara River. It offers a fine view of the Canadian shore. White fish Oscar and fish fries are specialties. *2191 Niagara St., Buffalo, tel. 716/877–9349. Dress: informal. Reservations advised, especially during the summer. AE, MC, V. Lunch and dinner.*

Pettibones Grille. This is a new and quite elegant restaurant in the Pilot Field baseball stadium in downtown Buffalo. A game ticket is required for buffets at game time, but the restaurant is open year-round. The decor matches that of the baseball park outside—red chairs, green walls, and a deep green carpet. But the menu is a far cry from peanuts and Crackerjacks, favoring such items as grilled steaks and chops; grilled, broiled, or baked red snapper; swordfish or shrimp en brochette; and Manicotti Antoinetta (with lamb and artichokes). The desserts include a selection of Rich products (the Rich family owns the Buffalo Bisons baseball team as well as the restaurant and made some of its millions with Coffee Rich creamer). *Pilot Field. Enter on Washington St. and take the elevator to the mezzanine level, tel. 716/846–2000. Dress: informal. No reservations accepted. AE, CB, DC, MC, V. Lunch and dinner.*

Shooters. The newest place on Buffalo's rapidly developing waterfront and the one that seems most to capture the recreational spirit of things. In addition to its wide-ranging casual menu, it offers 700 boat slips with valet service, sun decks, patio eating and drinking, a swimming pool, and pervasive festivity. *325 Fuhrmann Blvd., tel. 716/854–0416. Dress: informal. AE, MC. Lunch and dinner.*

Inexpensive   **Towne Restaurant.** In the heart of Allentown, this restaurant was once just a hot dog stand specializing in dogs with spicy hot sauce. It just grew and grew and now resembles a Greek taverna, complete with stucco walls covered with scenes of Greece. The owner hails from Rhodes and knows the meaning of Greek hospitality. Lemon chicken and moussaka are specialties, as is rice pudding. *186 Allen St., tel. 716/884–5128. Dress: informal. AE, MC, V. Breakfast, lunch and dinner.*

Chautauqua Area

Expensive   **Athenaeum Hotel.** The large dining room in this Victorian hotel
★   is the most venerable dining establishment at the institution. There is a prix-fixe menu. The food is simple but good and makes use of the fresh local produce. The two-dessert dinner is an Athenaeum tradition, designed, perhaps, to make up for the firm policy of no alcohol. Ask to see Thomas A. Edison's table by the window that overlooks the huge front porch. A shy man, Edison used to enter and leave the dining room by the window. The porch, with its rows of wicker rockers, is the spot for predinner socializing. *Chautauqua Institution, tel. 716/357–4444. Jacket required for dinner. Reservations required. No credit cards. Open only during 8-week summer season. Breakfast, lunch, and dinner.*

Galley. This popular restaurant and tavern has a nautical decor and overlooks Dunkirk harbor. There is outdoor dining as well as a private dock for those who arrive by boat. Specialties include quiche and seafood spinach soufflé. *2 Mullet St., Dunkirk, tel. 716/366–3775. Dress: informal. Reservations advised in summer. MC, V. Lunch and dinner.*

Inn at the Peak. The elegant Tudor-style restaurant at this ski and golf resort specializes in roast beef and has an extensive wine list. During the winter, the fireplaces burn brightly and warmly. *Ye Olde Rd., Clymer, tel. 716/355–4141. Jacket required. AE, DC, MC, V. Lunch and dinner.*

★   **The White Inn.** A charter member of the elite Duncan Hines Family of Fine Restaurants, the White Inn now has new owners who are striving to reestablish its national reputation. The large dining room has a garden decor: linen cloths and fresh flowers on the tables. Winning entries from the Culinary Olympics on the menu include Lamb Wyoming, seafood sausage, and seafood symphony—fresh clams, shrimp, crabmeat, oysters, scallops, and garden vegetables served in an open pastry shell. Local wines are featured. For dessert the chocolate mousse cake is a chocolate lover's dream. *52 E. Main St., Fredonia, tel. 716/672–2103. Jackets required. Reservations advised. AE, MC, V. Lunch and dinner.*

Moderate **Good Morning Farm.** This 150-year-old farmhouse, embellished with antiques, baskets, and large wood beams, serves country-style meals; everything is made from scratch. Specialties include stuffed chicken, a seafood sampler called Anchor's Away, and homemade breads, muffins, and desserts. The chef, an artist, has her works on display. *Rte. 394, tel. 716/763–1507. Dress: informal. AE, MC, V. Open Memorial Day–Labor Day.*

The Tally-Ho. Another favorite at the institution is this restaurant that has been operated by the Streeter Family for more than 50 seasons. There are two dining rooms, one specializing in charcoal-broiled steaks and the other a family-style dining room. The decor is Victorian. *Chautauqua Institution, tel. 716/357–3325. Jacket required for dinner. Reservations required. No credit cards. Open summer season only. Breakfast, lunch, and dinner.*

★ **Ye Hare'N'Hounds Inn.** This charming old English-style inn on the lake is noted for fresh seafood, beef, and veal. There is a private dock for guests arriving by boat. On fine days ask for a table outside. *Rte. 430, Bemus Point, tel. 716/386–2181. Dress: informal. AE, MC, V. Open year-round. Lunch and dinner.*

Niagara Falls

Expensive **Clarkson House.** An 1818 landmark, this place is especially popular during the Artpark summer theater season. Lobster is flown in daily from Maine, and steaks are a favorite. *810 Center St., Lewiston, tel. 716/754–4544. Dress: informal. Reservations advised in summer. AE, DC, MC, V. Lunch and dinner.*

★ **John's Flaming Hearth.** Although the menu was recently expanded, this Niagara Falls standby is still justifiably famous for its charcoal-broiled steak. Beef cattle are raised on a ranch in Colorado and must pass a tenderizer test. Seafood, chicken, and veal are also on the menu. Pumpkin ice cream pie is a dessert specialty. *1965 Military Rd., Niagara Falls (across from Factory Outlet Mall), tel. 716/297–1414. Jackets required. Reservations advised. AE, CB, MC, V. Lunch and dinner.*

The Red Coach Inn. With a spectacular view of the upper rapids of the falls, this 1923 inn has an old English atmosphere with wood-burning fireplaces and an outdoor patio that is terrific for summer dining. Prime ribs are one specialty. Others include Boston scrod and seafood sausage mornay. *2 Buffalo Ave., Niagara Falls, tel. 716/282–1459. Dress: informal. Reservations advised in summer and on weekends. AE, DC, MC, V. Lunch and dinner.*

Skylon Tower. Ride the outside elevator high up the tower for some of the best views of the falls, then dine in the revolving dining room on lobster, fresh fish, beef, and veal. *5200 Robinson Rd., Niagara Falls, Canada, tel. 416/856–5788. Jackets required. Reservations advised. AE, MC, V. Lunch and dinner.*

Wintergarden Restaurant. The restaurant, part of the Radisson Inn, sits within the towering tropical gardens of the Wintergarden and has a distinctly tropical feeling, particularly striking in winter. It is just a three-minute walk from the brink of the falls. Special dishes include pasta primavera, Cornish hen, and chicken florentine. *240 Rainbow Blvd., Niagara Falls, tel. 716/282–1212. Dress: informal. Reservations advised. AE, MC, V. Lunch and dinner.*

Moderate
★

Fortuna's. Since 1945 this place has attracted area residents. The Italian home cooking includes such favorites as lasagna and ravioli. *827 19th St., Niagara Falls, tel. 716/282–2252. AE, MC, V. Closed Mon. and Tues. Dinner.*

Pete's Market House. All the restaurant basics—steak, lobster, veal—are here in a warm, bustling environment. The lines are long, the portions are huge, and the prices are low. *1701 Pine Ave., tel. 716/282–7225. Dress: informal. No reservations. No credit cards. Lunch and dinner.*

Top of the Falls. This is the place for lunch at the falls if you like the feeling of being on top of them. The restaurant serves the usual luncheon fare, such as hamburgers, chicken, and hot roast beef. *Goat Island, Niagara Falls, tel. 716/285–3316. Dress: informal. AE, MC, V. Lunch only, except for groups of 50 or more.*

Lodging

Hotels and motels in the Niagara Falls–Buffalo area fall primarily into two categories: major chains and lower priced budget properties. In Niagara Falls, high-season rates apply from Memorial Day through Labor Day. Prices are highest in the immediate vicinity of the falls; elsewhere they remain the same year-round. Most of the area's hotels and motels tend to be moderately priced.

On the Chautauqua Institution grounds you can stay in stately Victorian hotels, guest houses, apartments, modern condominiums, or rooms in denominational houses operated by various religious groups. Some condos are available on a weekly basis, although most apartments are available only during the eight-week season. Since many people return year after year, reservations are essential. **Chautauqua Accommodations Referral** (Chautauqua 14722, tel. 716/357–6204) can help in locating lodgings at the institution.

Bed-and-Breakfast Reservations for the Niagara Falls–Buffalo area can be made with **Rainbow Hospitality** (9348 Hennepin Ave., Niagara Falls, tel. 716/283–4784). The accommodations vary from historic homes near the falls and an elegant Victorian mansion on the banks of the lower Niagara River to a working farm about 10 miles outside the city. Prices average $40–$45 for a double. Some B&Bs welcome children, but others do not; inquire in advance. The **Bed and Breakfast Association of Western New York** (Box 1059, Sinclairville 14782) handles information and reservations for the Chautauqua area.

Highly recommended hotels are indicated by a star ★.

Category	Cost*
Very Expensive	over $90
Expensive	$70–$90
Moderate	$50–$70
Inexpensive	under $50

per double without sales tax, service, or drinks

Buffalo

Very Expensive   **Hyatt Regency Buffalo.** This converted office building has a three-story glass atrium overlooking Main Street, and combines the best of the new and the old. The rooms are individually decorated with original works of art. Because many rooms were once offices, they have interesting, irregular shapes. *2 Fountain Plaza, Buffalo 14202, tel. 716/856–1234. 400 rooms with bath. Facilities: in-room movies, indoor pool, hot tub, 2 restaurants, bar, entertainment, drugstore, beauty shop, concierge, free airport transportation, tennis, golf, racquetball privileges, health club. Regency Club with private lounge. AE, CB, DC, MC, V.*

Expensive   **Asa Ransom House.** Parts of this exquisite country inn date to the early 19th century. In 1799, the Holland Land Company offered lots here to "any proper man who would build and operate a tavern upon it." The first to accept was Ransom, a young silversmith. There are four bedrooms in the new section of the building, each furnished with antiques and period reproductions. The Green Room has two double beds and a view of the herb garden. No smoking allowed in the bedrooms. *10529 Main St., Clarence 14031, tel. 716/759–2315. Breakfast included. MC, V. Closed Fri. and Sat.*

Buffalo Hilton at the Waterfront. The best rooms at this luxury property overlook both the Niagara River and Lake Erie. It features an expansive health club with a pool, tennis courts, and indoor jogging track. The waterfall in the lobby restaurant creates a tropical feeling. *Church and Terrace Sts., Buffalo 14202, tel. 716/845–5100. 475 rooms with bath, including suites and studio rooms. Facilities: in-room movies, indoor pool, 3 restaurants, 3 bars, entertainment, gift shop, drugstore, free garage, free airport transportation, 6 indoor tennis courts, 4 racquetball courts, handball, squash, health club, game room, sauna in some suites, refrigerators available. Executive Level with private lounge. Children free. AE, CB, DC, MC, V.*

Moderate   **Lenox.** In the historic Allentown District, this hotel is venerable but still comfortable. Many suites have permanent guests and most of them are senior citizens. *140 North St., Buffalo 14201, tel. 716/ 884–1700. 50 rooms with bath. Facilities: restaurant, bar, free airport transportation. AE, CB, DC, MC, V.*

Inexpensive   **Best Western Inn Downtown.** This is an economical hotel located along stately Delaware Avenue in downtown Buffalo. The rooms are standard motel fare. *510 Delaware Ave., Buffalo 14202, tel. 716/886–8333. Facilities: wet bar in suites, children free, health club privileges. AE, CB, DC, MC, V.*

Chautauqua

Very Expensive   **Hotel Athenaeum.** This "grande dame" of Chautauqua hotels ★ was built in 1881 and at one time was reputedly the largest wooden hotel in the country. Many visitors have been returning for generations. It is a National Historic Site that has hosted all manner of presidents and celebrities over the years. The hotel recently underwent a two-year, $2-million restoration. The restoration was painstaking and precise—paints were matched exactly to conform to the original. The result is a spruced up and most comfortable Victorian hotel. All guest rooms have new paint, bedspreads, and carpeting, but no TV. *Chautauqua*

Institution 14722, tel. 800/862-1881, in NYS 800/821-1881. 160 rooms with bath. Facilities: dining room and all the facilities of the Institution. Summer only. American plan only with breakfast, lunch, and dinner included. No credit cards.

St. Elmo Hotel. This hotel-and-condo complex opened June 1988 on the site of a razed hotel of the same name. It was built in traditional Victorian style to blend in with the surrounding hotels, homes, and cottages. All standard rooms and the one- and two-bedroom condos have furnished kitchen, telephone, cable TV; most have private porches. *1 Pratt Ave. 14722, tel. 716/357-ELMO. 64 rooms with kitchen and bath; Facilities: dining room, health club, shop, laundry room. American plan on request. Open year-round. AE, MC, V.*

Moderate **Cary Hotel.** This Victorian hotel has an excellent location—one block from the amphitheater. Although the rooms were recently remodeled, they are all furnished in Victorian style—some even have the original flowered wallpaper. There are no phones or TVs in the rooms; the only ones are in the lobby. There are two large porches filled with rocking chairs. The atmosphere is friendly and homey. *9 Bowman Ave. 14722, tel. 716/357-2245. 28 rooms with bath; 2 also have kitchens. Facilities: dining room. No credit cards.*

Hotel Lenhart. This old-fashioned hotel on the lake has been operating since 1881, and under one family's management for three generations: formal family portraits line the stairway. Rooms are simply furnished and have neither telephones nor TV. Brightly painted blue, red, green, and yellow rocking chairs beckon from the front porch. There is a beach, park, and marina next door. MAP (breakfast and dinner) is mandatory in the summer. The dining room is rather formal with starched linen tablecloths, fresh flowers, and home-style meals (choice of three entrees.) *Rte. 17, Bemus Point 14712, tel. 716/386-2715. 53 rooms, 43 with bath. Facilities: dining room. No credit cards. Open Memorial Day–Sept. 15. Off-season rates June and Sept.*

★ **Webb's Resort and Marina.** This Chautauqua Lake resort strives to offer something for just about every interest, from a marina and bowling alleys to a goat-milk fudge factory with tours and tastings. The average motel-type rooms have recently been refurbished. *Rte. 394, Mayville 14757, tel. 716/753-2161. 26 rooms with bath. Facilities: 5 dining rooms, marina, cable TV, game room, restaurant, pool, gift shop, bowling alleys, fudge factory. AE, MC, V. Open all year.*

★ **The White Inn.** Chautauqua County's oldest continuously operating hotel was named for Dr. Squire White, the "father of Fredonia," who first built a small house on this site in 1811. His son's home, built on the same site, was turned into an inn in 1919. Currently owned by two philosophy professors who renovated all the rooms and public areas, the inn is furnished with antiques and fine furniture reproductions from nearby Jamestown. (Some of the antiques are for sale.) The rooms are large and comfortable, individually decorated, and all have new plumbing. *52 E. Main St., Fredonia 14063, tel. 716/672-2103. 20 rooms with bath. Facilities: dining room, bar, Continental breakfast included daily except Sun. AE, MC, V.*

The William Seward Inn. This inn, overlooking Lake Erie, was built in 1821 as the home of Secretary of State William Seward who served under President Lincoln and was responsible for the purchase of Alaska. Totally renovated and filled with antiques, it has a homey, comfortable feeling. *S. Portage Rd., Westfield 14787, tel. 716/326–4151. 10 rooms with bath. Facilities: gourmet breakfast included, skiing nearby. MC, V.*

Niagara Falls

Expensive **Holiday Inn Resort & Conference Center.** Located about a 15-minute drive from the falls, this is a true resort with just about every type of facility—golf, ice skating, indoor and outdoor pools, fishing, boat dock, bikes, exercise rooms, and saunas. *100 Whitehaven Dr., Grand Island 14072, tel. 716/773–1111. 265 rooms with bath. Facilities: dining room, cocktail lounge, coffee shop, rental bikes, and 2 pools. AE, CB, MC, V.*

Days Inn Falls View. A longtime landmark at the falls, this property has recently undergone a much-needed renovation. Ask for one of the renovated rooms. The top floors with a view of the Upper Rapids are best. The rooms are compact but attractive. The hotel has the same owner as John's Flaming Hearth Restaurant; the dining room is a real asset. *201 Rainbow Blvd., Niagara 14301, tel. 716/285–9321. 200 rooms with bath. Facilities: dining room, cocktail lounge. AE, CB, MC, V.*

Inexpensive **Bit-O-Paris Motel.** This is not quite Paris, but it is a comfortable and economical motel along motel row. There are several two-bedroom units, which are handy for families. *9890 Niagara Falls Blvd. 14304, tel. 716/297–1710. 25 rooms with bath. Facilities: pool, refrigerators, whirlpool bath. AE, MC, V.*

«**Coachman Motel.** This motel represents one of the best values near the falls. It is just three blocks from the Convention Center and the falls. *523 Third St. 14301, tel. 716/285–2295. 19 rooms with bath. Facilities: Refrigerators. AE, MC, V.*

Campgrounds

Campgrounds are open from May to October. Exact opening and closing dates vary. Following are some area camping facilities:

Niagara–Buffalo **Darien Lakes State Park** (10289 Harlow Rd., Darien Center, tel. 716/547–9242). *158 sites. Facilities: fireplace, flush toilets, swimming, fishing, children's area, recreation building. $9. Open June–Sept.*

Niagara Falls KOA (2570 Grand Island Blvd., Grand Island, tel. 716/773–7583). *350 sites. Facilities: fireplaces, flush toilets, hot showers, swimming, fishing, boat rentals, store, laundry facility, children's area. $15. Open May–Oct.*

Niagara Falls North KOA (1250 Pletcher Rd., Lewiston, tel. 716/754–8013). *100 sites. Facilities: fireplaces, flush toilets, hot showers, swimming, children's area, store, laundry. $15. Open Apr.–Oct.*

Niagara's Lazy Lakes Campground (4312 Church Rd., Cambria, tel. 716/433–2479). *140 sites. Facilities: fireplace, flush toilets, hot showers, swimming, fishing, boat rentals, children's area, recreation building, store, laundry. $12. Open May–Oct.*

Chautauqua Camping facilities in the area include state and private campgrounds ranging from rustic woodland sites for tents to those with all utilities and programs of entertainment and recreation. **Lake Erie State Park,** a 318-acre woodland park along Lake Erie, has campsites, some with electrical hookup, as well as cabins. Reservations may be made through Ticketron telephone outlets by writing Ticketron, Dept. C.G., Avenue of the Americas, New York, NY 10019; or by contacting Red House Rental Office, Allegany State Park, Allegany. Commercial campgrounds listed below offer full hookup, laundry, and sanitary facilities:

Camp Chautauqua (Rte. 394, Stow, tel. 716/789-3435). *450 sites. Facilities: on lake, swimming, fishing, boat rentals, children's area, store, recreation building. $18. Open year-round.*
Chautauqua Family (Dinsbier Rd., Mayville, tel. 716/753-2212). *35 sites. Facilities: swimming, fishing, children's area, store. $10. Open May–Sept.*
Forest Haven Campground (Page Rd., Kennedy, tel. 716/267-5902). *106 sites. Facilities: pool, store, recreation building, children's area. $10. Open May–Oct.*
KOA Lake Erie/Westfield Kampground (1 E. Lake Rd., Barcalona, tel. 716/326-3573). *116 sites. Facilities: 2 pools, fishing, children's area, recreation building, store. Open Apr.–Oct.*
Safari Camp Chautauqua Lake (Rte. 17 and Thumb Rd., Dewittville, tel. 716/386-3804). *100 sites. Facilities: pool, children's area, recreation building, store. Open year-round.*

The Arts

The Buffalo–Niagara Falls area is surprisingly rich in the arts, from Artpark—the country's only state park devoted to the performing arts—to a renowned art museum and the Buffalo Philharmonic Orchestra, which enjoyed a triumphant European tour in 1988. Opera, theater, dance, and film are all on the program at the Chautauqua Institution during its eight-week summer season. *For tickets and information, contact Chautauqua Institution, Chautauqua, 14722, tel. 716/357-5635.*

Theater

Buffalo has long been respected for its theater. Actress Katherine Cornell was born and played here. The theater district on Main Street between Virginia and Chippewa streets has undergone a renaissance. A lane in the district is named after native son Michael Bennett of *Chorus Line* fame.

The **Alleyway Theatre** is an intimate theater in the heart of the Theater District. *One Curtain Up Alley, Buffalo, tel. 716/852-2600.*
Kavinoky Theatre is a professional theater on the D'Youville College campus. *320 Porter Ave., Buffalo, tel. 716/881-7668.*
Lancaster Opera House is an elegantly restored 19th-century opera house now used for plays and operettas. *21 Central Ave., Lancaster, tel. 716/683-1776.*
Pfeifer Theatre is home to the State University of New York at Buffalo's Department of Theater and Dance. Performances Oct.–Dec. and Feb.–May. *681 Main St., Buffalo, tel. 716/831-3742.*
Shaw Festival in nearby Niagara-on-the-Lake, Ontario, is a world-renowned theater festival featuring the works of Shaw and his contemporaries in three theaters. *Open May–Oct., tel. 416/468-2172 for ticket and accommodations information.*

Shea's Buffalo Theater is the showplace of the district. It is an ornate crystal palace which has been restored to its original grandeur. It boasts one of the largest Wurlitzer organs ever built. Theater, dance, opera and music, national touring companies. *646 Main St., Buffalo, tel. 716/847–0050.*

Studio Arena Theater is the city's resident theater with live performances September to May. World premieres and pre-Broadway productions are staged here. *710 Main St., Buffalo, tel. 716/856–5650.*

Concerts

Buffalo has had a long tradition as an important music town, both classical and jazz. Although he doesn't play often in Buffalo, funk star Rick James was born in Buffalo and lives in nearby East Aurora. The Arts Council of Buffalo and Erie County (700 Main St., tel. 716/856–7520) provides information about all area arts and music events on **ARTSline,** a 24-hour hotline (716/847–1444). The renowned 87-member **Buffalo Philharmonic Orchestra** (tel. 716/885–5000) celebrated its 50th anniversary season during 1985–86. The orchestra performs in Kleinhans Music Hall, Symphony Circle, acclaimed as being acoustically perfect.

Michael D. Rockefeller Arts Center, State University of New York College at Fredonia (tel. 716/673–3217). Concerts are given during the school year by Fredonia Chamber Players, student orchestras, and such professional orchestras as the Buffalo Philharmonic Orchestra. In addition, nationally known musicians perform here.

Film

A new theater complex in the heart of the Buffalo Theater District—decorated with huge photos of Buffalo theaters from an earlier age—has been attracting crowds. Art films and repertory films are shown regularly at area colleges and universities and the Albright-Knox Art Gallery (tel. ARTSline 716/847–1444).

Nightlife

Cabaret

Canterbury, *2250 Niagara Falls Blvd., Tonawanda, tel. 716/695–3557.*

Forks Hotel. Magicians perform here every weekend. *Broadway and Union Rd., Cheektowaga, tel. 716/683–6545.*

Red Jacket Inn, *7001 Buffalo Ave., Niagara Falls, tel. 716/283–7612.*

Daffodil's is a lush restaurant with weekend entertainment. *930 Maple Rd., Williamsville, tel. 716/688–5413.*

Jazz

Anchor Bar, birthplace of Buffalo chicken wings, with jazz on the weekends. *1047 Main St., Buffalo, tel. 716/886–8920.*

Blue Note features regular jazz combos nightly. *1677 Main St., Buffalo, tel. 716/883–5826.*

Colored Musicians Club. The name refers to the club's origins in the '30s as the union local for black musicians. *145 Broadway, Buffalo, tel. 716/855-9383.*

Marshall's. Nothing but the blues. *1678 Main St. Buffalo, tel. 716/881-4185.*

Tralfamadore Cafe. The largest and best-known jazz club in the area. *Theater Pl. off Pearl St., tel. 716/854-1415.*

Rock

Alibi Lounge. A popular swinging rock club on the falls. *7121 Niagara Falls Blvd., Niagara Falls, tel. 716/283-9896.*

Bachmann's Surfside. Especially popular with the young crowd during the summer. *4471 Lake Shore Rd., Hamburg, tel. 716/627-7960.*

Nietzsche's. An affably bohemian place, as likely to feature reggae or blues as folk or slam. In the heart of Allentown. *248 Allen St., Buffalo, tel. 716/886-8539.*

Surf Club. Chautauqua's premier party bar. *Bemus Point, tel. 716/386-5088.*

Country-Western

Al-E-Oops. *5389 Genesee St., Lancaster, tel. 716/681-0200.*

Country Club. *2186 Seneca St., Buffalo, tel. 716/824-8448.*

Golden Nugget. *2464 Seneca St., West Seneca, tel. 716/825-9013.*

Hello Dolly's Lounge. *481 Niagara Falls Blvd., Tonawanda, tel. 716/836-9357.*

Wagon Wheel. *7201 Niagara Falls Blvd., Niagara Falls, tel. 716/283-9861.*

Comedy

The Comedy Line. National artists and open mike. Fridays. *Holiday Inn, Fredonia, tel. 716/673-1351.*

The Comedy Trap. National acts and open mike. *1180 Hertel Ave., Buffalo, tel. 716/874-LAFF.*

Stuffed Mushroom. National acts and open mike. *2580 Main St., Buffalo, tel. 716/835-7971.*

Folk

Belle Watling's Eating and Drinking Establishment. Folk groups on weekends. *1449 Abbott Rd., Lackawanna, tel. 716/826-8838.*

Buffalo Irish Center. Mostly Irish music, of course. *245 Abbott Rd., tel. 716/825-9535.*

Paddy O's Restaurant. Again, lots of Irish music and singers, especially on weekends. *4000 Bailey Ave., Amherst, tel. 716/835-4000.*

Network of Light. Coffeehouse series on weekends. *224 Lexington Ave., Buffalo, tel. 716/882-1205.*

Index

Personal Itinerary

Departure   *Date*   9/24   MONDAY

         Time   2:00

Transportation

Arrival   *Date* 9/24   *Time*   3:30

Departure   *Date* 9/25   *Time*

Transportation

Accommodations   BECKMAN ARMS
           Rhinebeck

Arrival   *Date* 9/25   *Time*   8 PM.

Departure   *Date* 9/26   *Time*

Transportation

Accommodations   JACOB KIP B&B
           Rhinebeck

Arrival   *Date* 9/26   *Time* 3:30

Departure   *Date* 9/27   *Time* 10:A.M.

Transportation

Accommodations   Alberto Allegra
           WINDHAM

Personal Itinerary

Arrival *Date*   *Time*

Departure *Date*   *Time*

Transportation

Accommodations

Arrival *Date*   *Time*

Departure *Date*   *Time*

Transportation

Accommodations

Arrival *Date*   *Time*

Departure *Date*   *Time*

Transportation

Accommodations

Arrival *Date*   *Time*

Departure *Date*   *Time*

Transportation

Accommodations

Addresses

Name	*Name*
Address	*Address*
Telephone	*Telephone*
Name	*Name*
Address	*Address*
Telephone	*Telephone*
Name	*Name*
Address	*Address*
Telephone	*Telephone*
Name	*Name*
Address	*Address*
Telephone	*Telephone*
Name	*Name*
Address	*Address*
Telephone	*Telephone*
Name	*Name*
Address	*Address*
Telephone	*Telephone*
Name	*Name*
Address	*Address*
Telephone	*Telephone*
Name	*Name*
Address	*Address*
Telephone	*Telephone*

Fodor's Travel Guides

U.S. Guides

Alaska
Arizona
Atlantic City & the
  New Jersey Shore
Boston
California
Cape Cod
Carolinas & the
  Georgia Coast
The Chesapeake Region
Chicago
Colorado
Disney World & the
  Orlando Area

Florida
Hawaii
Las Vegas
Los Angeles, Orange
  County, Palm Springs
Maui
Miami,
  Fort Lauderdale,
  Palm Beach
Michigan, Wisconsin,
  Minnesota
New England
New Mexico
New Orleans

New Orleans (Pocket
  Guide)
New York City
New York City (Pocket
  Guide)
New York State
Pacific North Coast
Philadelphia
The Rockies
San Diego
San Francisco
San Francisco (Pocket
  Guide)
The South

Texas
USA
Virgin Islands
Virginia
Waikiki
Washington, DC

Foreign Guides

Acapulco
Amsterdam
Australia, New Zealand,
  The South Pacific
Austria
Bahamas
Bahamas (Pocket
  Guide)
Baja & the Pacific
  Coast Resorts
Barbados
Beijing, Guangzhou &
  Shanghai
Belgium &
  Luxembourg
Bermuda
Brazil
Britain (Great Travel
  Values)
Budget Europe
Canada
Canada (Great Travel
  Values)
Canada's Atlantic
  Provinces
Cancun, Cozumel,
  Yucatan Peninsula

Caribbean
Caribbean (Great
  Travel Values)
Central America
Eastern Europe
Egypt
Europe
Europe's Great
  Cities
France
France (Great Travel
  Values)
Germany
Germany (Great Travel
  Values)
Great Britain
Greece
The Himalayan
  Countries
Holland
Hong Kong
Hungary
India,
  including Nepal
Ireland
Israel
Italy

Italy (Great Travel
  Values)
Jamaica
Japan
Japan (Great Travel
  Values)
Kenya, Tanzania,
  the Seychelles
Korea
Lisbon
Loire Valley
London
London (Great
  Travel Values)
London (Pocket Guide)
Madrid & Barcelona
Mexico
Mexico City
Montreal &
  Quebec City
Munich
New Zealand
North Africa
Paris
Paris (Pocket Guide)
People's Republic of
  China

Portugal
Rio de Janeiro
The Riviera (Fun on)
Rome
Saint Martin &
  Sint Maarten
Scandinavia
Scandinavian Cities
Scotland
Singapore
South America
South Pacific
Southeast Asia
Soviet Union
Spain
Spain (Great Travel
  Values)
Sweden
Switzerland
Sydney
Tokyo
Toronto
Turkey
Vienna
Yugoslavia

Special-Interest Guides

Health & Fitness
  Vacations
Royalty Watching

Selected Hotels of
  Europe

Selected Resorts and
  Hotels of the U.S.
Shopping in Europe

Skiing in North America
Sunday in New York

Help us evaluate hotels and restaurants for the next edition of this guide, and we will send you a free issue of Fodor's newsletter, TravelSense.

Title of this guide:

1 Hotel ❑   Restaurant ❑   *(check one)*

Name

Number/Street

City/State/Country

Comments

2 Hotel ❑   Restaurant ❑   *(check one)*

Name

Number/Street

City/State/Country

Comments

3 Hotel ❑   Restaurant ❑   *(check one)*

Name

Number/Street

City/State/Country

Comments

General Comments

Please complete for a free copy of TravelSense

Name

Number/Street

City/State/Zip

Business Reply Mail

First Class   Permit № 7775   New York, NY

Postage will be paid by addressee

Fodor's Travel Publications

201 East 50th Street
New York, NY 10022